The History of the
United States Army

George Washington

The History of the United States Army

By

WILLIAM ADDLEMAN GANOE
Colonel of Infantry, United States Army

Revised Edition

ERIC LUNDBERG
Ashton   Maryland
1964

Reprinted by Eric Lundberg, Ashton, Maryland 1964

PRINTED IN THE UNITED STATES OF AMERICA

"THESE ARE THEY——"

GEORGE WASHINGTON
FREDERICK VON STEUBEN
SYLVANUS THAYER
WINFIELD SCOTT
EMORY UPTON
ARTHUR WAGNER
DOUGLAS MACARTHUR

FOREWORD

WHAT follows is meant to be neither a study of campaigns and battles nor a treatment of military policy. Those subjects have been covered thoroughly under their own titles. The coming chapters strive to tell a plain, straightforward story of those of our people who have answered our country's voice in its many cries for help and protection. The tale records the homely and the heroic service of the soldier in the sweat of peace as well as in the ruck of war. And there results a life history of that institution which has been the greatest single factor in the building of our nation—the United States Army.

Other countries have long ago told with care and affection the histories of their armies. For us, up until 1924, there had been no collected sketches and few authoritative accounts. No chronological record of the soldier's existence from 1775 to 1942 has ever been set down in any one place.

When the publishers of this book first approached the author with the suggestion of such a work, the prospect, frankly, did not look inviting. But, as the five years of research went along, so much unexplored matter and so many amazing episodes came to light that interest increased in spite of obstacles. As a consequence, there are statements in this volume which have heretofore found little publication; some which have been purposely withheld from general knowledge, and others which have never been published at all. In releasing this material the author has not scrupled to tell the truth, both pleasant and unpleasant, wherever the telling might be constructive.

Naturally, in the limited size of this narrative, many interesting details had to be discarded in order to preserve balance and perspective.

Page references to authorities consulted have not been used because of the fretting interruption to the reader. Instead, the bibliography and dates are carefully given. Most of the bibliography contains secondary sources, the primary sources being found principally in the Old Files and Old Records Sections of the Adjutant General's Office, Congressional Library, and repositories of the Army War College, Washington, D. C. Other original sources were found in the New York, West Point, Boston, Boston Corps of Cadets, Service School libraries and in miscellaneous documents and letters found in the original thirteen states. The most helpful and accurate secondary source was Dr. Justin Harvey Smith's monumental two-volume history, *The War with Mexico*.

I thank the public for the chance it has given me to revise this story about the Army and bring it up to date, for two reasons: first, I was not satisfied with the latter part of the history as it was; and second, I have the opportunity to place the seventh vital and immortal builder of our Army and defense in his true light before our country, my original source in this case being himself and his confidences and inspiration to me personally.

W. A. G.

CONTENTS

ix

ILLUSTRATIONS

The History of
The United States Army

CHAPTER I

DRAB BEGINNINGS

(1775–1776)

WHEN Washington, accompanied by the uncertain *July 2 1775* Charles Lee and Horatio Gates, entered the American lines besieging Boston, he unconsciously marked the start of the United States Army. Although the groups of armed countrymen, scattered in a semi-circle from Charlestown Neck to Boston Neck, were not then known by such a name, they were nevertheless by his coming transformed from separate New England militia into a single force fighting for the rights of all the colonies. The thirteen little governments by this move abandoned their previous rôles of independent pioneers and for the first time united for defense under one properly constituted leader. His arrival, then, is bound up with our first national military establishment, whose growth for the next eight years is a part of him and to a great extent a result of him.

It had taken eleven days for him to make the journey on horseback from Philadelphia, whence he had set out four days after the battle of Bunker Hill and five days after the Continental Congress had selected him as commander in chief.

His election had been a queer one, where violent prejudices had swept aside sound judgment. John Hancock, a wholesale merchant of no military experience, desired the command of the forces. Artemas Ward, a former officer of the French and Indian wars, was, since he was already in charge of the Massa-

1

chusetts troops, a rival for the office. Hancock, President of
Congress and an ardent patriot, appealed to the people of New
England. Ward was pushed by Paine, who had been a fellow
student at Harvard, and by another member who volunteered
the pleasant argument that the soldiers seemed satisfied with
Ward. But the southern delegates objected, not because Hancock was a flabby merchant nor because Ward was too fat to
mount a horse, but because they would have none of a New
Englander. Besides, Hancock was a bit too anxious for the
position in the presence of John Adams, whose natural antagonism to the wishes of others was acutely aroused. It was soon
felt that the new incumbent would have to be a person who
could unite the north and the south, the puritan and cavalier,
the forces engaged and not engaged. Washington, a man of
quiet manners, a resident of the borderland between the two
parties, and the husband of the wealthiest woman in the country, answered the trifling qualifications imposed by the legislators. The more he was mentioned, the more negatively
prominent he became particularly because he did not blight
any one's whims. He was finally unanimously elected without
the slightest question having been raised concerning his fitness
as a soldier or commander. It is doubtful if many of the members knew that he had been an expert scout, the hero of Fort
Necessity, the aide-de-camp to General Braddock, and the head
of the Virginia militia. It is certain they did not care, any
more than they had been interested in the fitness of Ward and
Hancock, who possessed none. So, at the very birth of our
government, feeling supplanted wisdom, pettishness crowded
out calculation, and hot favoritism overruled cold reason. The
ominous sound of such legislative talk is going to echo disas-
trously through the succeeding pages of this story. At this
point it remains for us to be thankful that Washington was a
meritorious accident. In spite of sewing-society methods he,
the preëminent military leader of the country, became commander in chief.

June 21
1775

    He accepted the honor with expressions of his unworthiness,
refused a salary, and set out for Cambridge to meet his command and to attempt to bring order and discipline out of
irregularity and insubordination. One year and one day before

the adoption of the Declaration of Independence, under the elm which afterwards bore his name, he drew his sword in the presence of his heterogeneous army and formally took command.

Was ever a commander presented with a more motley throng? In the same companies were blue coats faced with buff, black coats faced with red, and hunting shirts of brown trimmed with fringes, streamers and scarlet needlework. The townsman, clad in gay hues and covered with coat or blanket, touched elbows with the woodsman wearing his dull homespun. A company of Stockbridge Indians in feathers, paint and nakedness vied in color with the Connecticut dragoons in vivid red coats not unlike the British. There were long trousers, overalls, and breeches with or without gaiters or with fringed leggings of deerskin. Stuck in the triangular hat were gaudy sprigs of various sizes and shapes. Irish, German, Scotch, Puritan, and Quaker contrasted their Caucasian faces with the shiny African in his powdered wig, while graybeard and child stood side by side. Even the officers had no distinctive uniforms.

Nor did this sundry collection of male beings live in a true camp. That term implies to us regimental blocks of company streets in straight, regular rows, with officers' tents at one end and picket-lines at the other. The soldier of the Boston Siege lived in the open or in a kennel of his own making. The higher officers billeted themselves in near-by houses, Washington being accorded a deserted Tory mansion. Save in some companies of Rhode Island regiments where tents had been secured, the rank and file contented itself with rolling up in a blanket under the trees or stars. When the elements compelled some sort of shelter, it was built according to the caprice and choice of site of the occupant. There were structures of linen, sailcloth, boards, stones, brush, and turf, and all possible combinations of these. There were booths and huts of varying shapes and sizes, with or without windows. Such shacks clung in scattered patches about the various earthworks to be defended.

Cooking was an individual or club performance undertaken at such hours as the stomach dictated. So long as duties were attended, it little mattered how or when nourishment might be prepared. Habakkuk Simpkins, being a reclusive puritan, broiled his steak alone meal after meal, and drank his mug of beer in holy thought; whereas Patrick O'Brien messed in company with a dozen Ezras and Ezekiels and with loud oaths smacked his lips over the savory stew concocted by one of the number.

Everything bespoke irregularity, especially the organizations. Previous to Bunker Hill the barest fractions of commands had reported for duty. The shortages were accentuated by casualties in that battle and sickness afterward. Even had the organizations in the beginning been thoroughly complete, the rolls would have differed remarkably in effective strength, for each state added to the chaos by having its units independently constructed. Massachusetts varied from 590 to 649 men per regiment, whereas Connecticut authorized 1,000. Steuben later declared he saw regiments ranging from 3 to 23 companies. A Massachusetts company consisted of a captain, a lieutenant, and 59 men. A Connecticut company added 11 men, 4 corporals, and a second lieutenant. A Massachusetts general was also a colonel of a regiment. Rhode Island field officers were also captains of companies. When a colonel was absent from his company, it was commanded by a captain lieutenant. The scheme was evidently devised to reduce the number of officers, but it produced discord and placed double responsibility upon officers incapable of handling one organization.

Added to the discouragements attendant upon this conglomerate mass of men, which resembled in discipline, uniform and organization more nearly a Greek ekklesia than an army, was the low type of commissioned officer. The pernicious system by which he was obtained explains his inefficiency. Any popular member of a community who could enlist the necessary quota for a company became a captain; likewise for a regiment, a colonel. The remainder of the company officers were generally elected by the privates; and the field officers, by the company officers. However, in Maryland all the officers were elected by popular vote just as municipal officials at a town meeting. Everywhere rum and bribery played important parts in recruiting and electioneering. By these methods the commander was beholden to the commanded, and the qualifications of an officer were confined to popularity, zeal in raising men, ability to pay the tavern bills and, perchance, some questionable inducements. Just how little military knowledge or training influenced selection can be seen from the account of a New Jersey private:

"After this we chose our officers. When on parade our 1st Lieutenant came and told us he would be glad if we would excuse him from going, which we refused; but on consideration we concluded it was better to consent, after which he said he would go, but we said: 'you shall not command us, for he whose mind can change in an hour is not fit to command in the field where liberty is contended for.' In the evening we chose a private in his place."

This prudish picture of democratic punishment for vacillation is no less that of the private controlling the officer. Stock-jobbing, insubordination, desertion, and mutiny flowed naturally from such a source. It was difficult for Obadiah Perkins to take orders from Israel Hampton on parade in the evening, after Israel with jollified flow of spirits had lured Obadiah with blunted senses into signing the enlistment blank in the morning. It was easy to slip from under Israel's authority and to go home when the hay was to be put under cover. Who was Israel to instruct him? A creature of his own contrivance. No wonder Obadiah, when on sentry duty, allowed the British to purloin his rifle, or failed to show any courtesy toward his superiors. Scarcely able to read or write, he easily confused the new national freedom with personal liberty, and resented any inroads upon the abandon that had been his with his own dog and gun, in his own woods. Nor was his officer prone to reprimand or punish him when there was a vote to be lost or popularity to be curtailed.

Not stopping in the regiment, this method of election crossed the threshold of Congress and controlled the choice of general officers. Already Washington's election has suggested the personal whims and petty jealousies prevalent in the proceedings of that body. The attributes of the major generals first chosen will reveal somewhat the success of its methods.

They were in order of rank: Artemas Ward, already partially described, but in addition accused of cowardice at Bunker Hill; Charles Lee,[1] former British officer with service in many European campaigns, who turned out to be more despicable in treachery than Benedict Arnold; Philip Schuyler, politician, delegate to Congress, with former service in the French and Indian wars, a loyal officer but possessed of a demeanor which operated against him; Israel Putnam, a farmer, a former private in the French and Indian wars, of great energy but meager military ability. Not a very promising collection of right-hand men. But Congress afterward, more on account of the inefficacy of its system than any inherent malevolence, accustomed itself to supplanting the worthy with the unworthy, withholding praise from the meritorious and bestowing it upon the inglorious, and even plotting against Washington himself. Little doubt is left that he would have been removed before 1777 had it not been for the universal regard in which the army held him.

So absorbed was he in his huge task, however, that he had little time for self-consciousness or sensitiveness to criticism. The quality and quantity of his supplies, as well as of his men, gave a determined check to any immediate offensive and turned his efforts into channels of desperate reconstruction.

Powder was short. It is estimated that at the beginning of hostilities there were on sale not a hundred pounds in all the colonies. Thirty rounds per man in the American camp is a high estimate. Washington himself mentions the exploit of maintaining around Boston, within gunshot of the British, a thirteen-mile chain of sentries who had not an ounce of powder. Even salutes with the cannon were forbidden on account of the waste.

Lead would have been as rare as powder had not the statue of George III, on Bowling Green, New York, been handily melted down, cooled, dissected, and dealt out in small quantities to the soldiers. They, in turn, during dull afternoons in camp, remelted their weighty allotments in melting pans, poured the contents into bullet molds, and saved the product for individual use. The bullet thus fashioned by hand was suited to the par-

---

[1] Not of the Robert E. Lee family of Virginia.

ticular caliber of firearm by means of different-sized holes in the bullet mold.

These missiles at close range were possibly as deadly as any small projectile ever contrived. In their construction the junction of two hemispheres of molten metal left a ridged seam which operated much as does the soft-nosed or "dum-dum" bullet of to-day. It tore out whole muscles, smashed bones and rent the flesh, leaving large ragged wounds from which where were comparatively few recoveries. Aside from the tearing effect, the impact of the bullet was enough to stop a man in motion more effectively than the modern high-velocity projectiles.

During the hot July afternoon, when the soldier had completed molding the bullets for his or his mate's use, he had to turn his attention toward the personal manufacture of cartridges. It was found quite early in the war that there resulted greater speed and safety in loading with a previously prepared casing for the ammunition than with the loose powder and ball. Accordingly, the private rolled, as the cigarette maker does his tobacco, each one of his bullets and an inch or so of powder into paper cylinders about the diameter of the bore of his piece. These he stowed carefully in a leather pouch or box which usually contained places for twenty-three cartridges.

The remainder of the equipment of the individual was mostly what the recruit could bring with him. An enlistment blank enjoined the soldier to "furnish a good firearm, cartouch box, blanket, and knapsack." In lieu of the firearm he was directed to bring a good cutting sword, cutlass, or tomahawk, and later a shovel, spade, pickax, or scythe straightened and made fast to a pole. The powderhorn was included without the saying, for its delicate legend usually revealed the strong personal attachment of the owner. His "cartouch box" slung on one hip, and his powder horn or flask on the other, both suspended by broad straps of leather or web, gave to the Revolutionary volunteer his well-known, cross-belted appearance. Some were fortunate enough to own a wooden canteen resembling a small truncated barrel, or a bayonet fashioned by the nearest smith into a long bulging knife and attached to the individual rifle in the simplest way. During this stationary warfare very few of these awkward drinking vessels or sheathed short swords dangled from the persons of the Americans. Later on, marching and fighting brought about a natural increase.

The main weapon of the Revolution, however, was the fire-lock or flintlock as it was indifferently called. Its mechanism and peculiarities account largely for the parts played by both sides in subsequent fighting. The fact that Washington lacked from three to four thousand, in order to arm his force com-pletely, reduced his effectiveness to the equivalent of less than twelve thousand.[2]

The question naturally arises as to why there should exist this lack among people dependent in a great measure upon a firearm for protection and sustenance. The answer resolves itself into that of expense. A townsman looked askance in those days upon a luxury that cost from two to five pounds and represented to him what the purchase of a piano or an auto-mobile means to the average citizen of to-day.

Those who were the proud owners of a musket or rifle appear to us as scarcely to have possessed a defensive weapon. Its firing device consisted of a three-and-a-half to four-foot barrel along the under side of which ran a steel ramrod; a hammer into which a piece of flint was inserted; a "battery" or upright piece of steel against which the spark was struck; and a flashpan containing loose powder which, upon receiving the spark from the battery, ignited through a small hole the charge in the chamber. Such were the clumsy means of pro-

---

[2] "In 1744 a Philadelphian wrote to a member of Parliament that there were sufficient gun makers in the colonies to make 100,000 stand of muskets per year at 28 shillings each, and powder was already made. Yet, although the Revolution was imminent, and the need of a store of firearms apparent, the home consumption was such that the outbreak of hostilities found the colonists poorly provided. This negligence on the part of the colonists seems inexcusable.

"For more than a year the outbreak of hostilities was expected daily. Committees of correspondence had been active, and a union of the thirteen colonies against the mother country was assured; there was no national government, no executive, yet each colony for self-protection should have established armories—and did not. In New England small stores of am-munition and old guns were collected from the people and from old town supplies stored since the French wars or before, but the main reliance seems to have been upon the personal property, arms which existed in almost every household throughout the land."—CHARLES WINTHROP SAWYER, Firearms in American History.

jecting an ounce ball through a short and highly curved trajectory.

Yet the undisciplined woodsman with his seven-foot, fourteen-pound mass of wood and steel would deliver a bulls'-eye hit in the face of a smashing kick. The farmer was not so accurate at long range, and the townsman very little better than the present generation as a whole. But as a rule the Revolutionary Army shot well.

Shortly after he took command Washington arranged a spectacular review for the purpose of showing the New England militia the effect of accurate shooting on the part of the woodsmen. A pole was set up and a marksman stepped off 250 paces. The farmer or townsman would scarcely have wasted powder at such a range. But the riflemen from the forest, firing singly, rarely missed the pole.

In one early battle the farmers with their muskets (usually the Brown Bess) finding themselves without bullets, loaded their weapons with scrap iron, nails, or jagged odds and ends of metal, waited until the enemy was within easy range, aimed at the foot or knee, and let the jump of the piece disembowel the victim. Many a Revolutionary soldier was certain to hit a small target at 60 yards. There is one instance of a soldier who at that range, while his brother held a board 5 by 7 inches between his knees, fired, without a rest and from the standing position, 8 balls through the target without touching his kinsman. A British officer at Bunker Hill noticed such a person to have brought down 20 epauleted redcoats before the expert rifleman himself fell. But at the same battle it took the American so long to reload that the British rushed in with the bayonet and forced a retreat.

The disadvantage was due to the impossibility of reloading quickly and the lack of bayonets. After his piece was discharged, the soldier, instead of merely pulling his bolt, had to execute tedious motions. He reached in his box for a cartridge, bit from the end enough paper to let out the powder, a small portion of which he shook into the pan, and poured the remainder into the barrel through the muzzle. He then rammed home the bullet and paper sheath. Replacing the ramrod he was again ready to fire.

The proceeding was all the more delayed in the early days of the Revolution when the powderhorn was used instead of the handmade cartridge. If the wind was blowing, it was almost impossible to place any powder in the pan, and if the uneven mixture of sulphur, carbon and saltpeter was damp, there was little reason for putting it into the rifle at all. The barrel, even after a few discharges, became so hot that the weapon was most uncomfortable to hold. The flint, too, was good for an average of only sixty firings.

Added to these handicaps, there were in use in the beginning of the war, no less than thirteen different kinds of muskets, three kinds of musketoons and as many kinds of rifles as there were gunsmiths to make them. The calibers varied from thirteen-gage to thirty-gage (gage meaning the number of spherical balls to the pound). There were master armorers and private factories at Westfield, Massachusetts, at Rappahannock Forge, Virginia, and at Philadelphia, but no manufacturing arsenals in the present sense of the word. Soldiers side by side in ranks could scarcely use one another's weapons and could not load with one another's bullets.

Necessity naturally led to some sort of precision and uniformity in handling the weapon, if for no other reason than the prevention of accidents.

One soldier forgetful of the proximity of his uncorked powderhorn started a conflagration that burned for several hours and caused him discomfort for several weeks. Another having snapped his piece on a "delayed" charge was, upon recocking and firing, promptly kicked to death. John M'Murtry, not realizing that there was a load in his rifle, sent a bullet through a double partition of inch boards, a single board of a berth, the breast of a man named Penn, and left a mark against a stone chimney. Nowadays, we are prone to forget the force of black powder close at hand, and the fact that the Continental developed as great respect for his own rifle as for the enemy.

The drill of the time attempted to systematize loading and to familiarize the enlisted man with the proper use of his savage weapon. But there were as many regulations as there were methods of putting the same regulations into effect. No two companies drilled alike, and all drilled badly. A Marylander in 1776 watching the home contingent on parade remarked that it was the finest body of men he had ever seen out of step. The "Sixty-fourth" edition of the *British Manual,* the *Norfolk Discipline,* Timothy Pickering's *Easy Plan* and Colonel Bland's treatise were all used indiscriminately. They differed to a great extent from each other and were taken up at the whim of the locality. The commands for firing and loading in one set consisted of 19 separate motions as follows:

1. Half-cock your firelocks! (1 motion)
2. Handle your cartridges! (1 motion)
3. Prime! (1 motion)
4. Shut your pans! (2 motions)
5. Charge with cartridge! (2 motions)
6. Draw your rammers! (2 motions)
7. Ram down your cartridge! (1 motion)
8. Return your rammers! (1 motion)
9. Shoulder your firelock! (2 motions)
10. Poise your firelocks! (2 motions)
11. Cock your firelocks! (2 motions)
12. Present! (1 motion)
13. Fire! (1 motion)

It is hardly remarkable that the British routed the dependable Revolutionary marksman while all this was happening. With our overwrought sense of fire effect from magazine rifles, automatics and machine guns capable of deluging the enemy in an instant with mortal sleet, the enforced slowness of the soldier of 1775 is hard to conceive. If we are apt at times to criticize the vigor of Washington in not overwhelming his opponents with a ponderous volume of fire, let us remember the heavy technic through which he had to labor.

The larger weapons of artillery were fewer and less effective than the small arms. At the time of Washington's arrival there had not been much effort to obtain an adequate supply of big guns. Brass and iron cannons were so uncomfortably absent that he, until the few days preceding the British evacuation, was unable to contend with the fire of the enemy. Congress made a mild legal attempt to manufacture a uniform type of these weapons, but the records fail to show any enforcement of the law. Colonel Richard Gridley, left in command of the artillery of Massachusetts, was on account of his senility disinclined to exertion in obtaining cannons and balls elsewhere. The hard service of the "gun pointers," "bombardiers," and "mattrosses," as the enlisted artillerymen were styled, made the work as distasteful as that of a stevedore. In fact the besieging force had to sit calmly exposed to the fire of the besieged. So common did the sprinkle of heavy projectiles become that an order had to be issued to keep the American soldier from attempting to stop the rolling balls with his feet. It appears that more casualties occurred from this characteristic performance than from the accuracy of the enemy.

Beyond the material lack of firelocks, ammunition, equipment, and cannon, that which essentially distressed the commander in chief was the immeasurable deficiency in trained and disciplined manhood.

Peculation and stockjobbery were rife among the officers. Little conception of the dignity and honor necessary to inculcate discipline was found in them. When captain, lieutenant, and ensign placed their salaries in a common fund with the enlisted men, drawing at the end of the month each the same share, the official intent was doubtless generous and democratic, but such officers commonized themselves and made it easy for Lieutenant Jones to filch Private Smith's blanket.

Mediocrity and cowardice were more common than theft and embezzlement even among officers who had never before been intrusted with funds. It can safely be said that a distinction, especially in the New England regiments, between officer and men did not exist. Lieutenant Whitney was tried and convicted later for "infamous conduct in degrading himself by voluntarily doing the duty of an orderly sergeant." A cavalry staff officer was found unconcernedly shaving one of his men while visitors were present in camp. Others were tried for undue brutality in beating their men into insensibility. The attempt at discipline manifested itself either in extreme familiarity or brutality and often both. Cowardice also had been especially manifested at Bunker Hill. One officer before the battle informed his company that he would overtake them directly. He did—the next day. On the authority of General Lee and Captain Chester it is known that during the action many companies had not so much as a corporal to command them. The captain goes so far as to say that "the most of the companies of this Province are commanded by a most despicable set of officers." No doubt he was right but he was scarcely allowing for the fact that much of courage comes with discipline, the self-confidence accompanying the skill, as was demonstrated many times later.

With such a set of officers it is not astonishing that the enlisted men were expressions of a misconstrued liberty or freedom. Men departed to their homes at will after Bunker Hill, often having obtained a substitute from home, more often having omitted that courtesy. Washington stated of them that "they regarded their officers no more than broomsticks." Any direction or interference emanating from above was a violation of their personal liberty for which they were fighting. They had come out of their own accord to drive the British from Boston. That work had better be accomplished before December, for then their enlistment would run out and they would depart willy-nilly.

In the face of Washington's earnest entreaty, his appeal to their manhood and patriotism to stay with him only one month longer in order to save the Revolutionary Army from extinction, the Connecticut militiamen callously walked home in a body when their enlistments expired. A large part of the other militia did likewise.

It was not because they were in need that they forsook the cause. The privates of Massachusetts militia were receiving $36 every lunar month as pay, an equivalent of at least $150 in modern purchasing power, and, in addition, the following ration authorized by the Third Provincial Congress:

"One pound of bread, half a pound of beef, and a half pound of pork, and if pork canot be had, one pound and a quarter of beef; and one day in seven they shall have one pound and a quarter of salt fish instead of one day's allowance of meat. One pint of milk, or, if milk cannot be had, one gill of rice; one quart of good spruce or malt beer; one gill of peas or beans, or other sauce equivalent, six ounces of good butter per week; one pound of good common soap for six men per week; half a pint of vinegar per week per man, if it can be had."

Conceding what he provided for himself, we learn that the private at the outset of the Revolution was receiving more from the states than in 1918 before Château-Thierry. It is a curious fact that these very patriots who resented so thoroughly the mercenary troops sent against them from England were themselves but highly paid hirelings of their own government. Indeed, where a private citizen had been drafted by his own municipality it was common for him to be excused by paying a stipulated sum. Either in shirking or enlisting, the soldier was a commodity. In the average case he appears to have been actuated less by zeal in defense of his country than by greed for reward. His pusillanimous conduct became so common later that Congress could enlist very few recruits in competition with the states which generally paid higher wages and bounty. In an address to the soldiers in November of '75 the General said:

"Never were soldiers whose pay and provision have been so abundant and ample. . . . There is some reason to dread that the enemies to New England's reputation may hereafter say it was not principle that saved them, but that they were bribed into the preservation of their liberties."

Something is to be said on the other side. The Middle States and Virginia responded nobly to a call for volunteers by sending 12 companies of riflemen who enlisted for one year and marched in some cases 800 miles to the siege. These first troops raised by continental authority became the backbone of the force which finally achieved independence. Massachusetts itself furnished more men than any other state during the war. If there was reluctance, much of it can be attributed to the lack of system in these dim beginnings and to the small assets of a people who had not yet become rich by manufacture. Back on the farm there was very little laid by for Mollie and the children. And many of the higher officers who had means and an old-world intolerance of the lower caste were inconsiderate of a private's position.

The discouragements which beset Washington were of greater magnitude than those General Schuyler, in the North at this time, described as being such that if Job had had to bear them his "name had not been so famous for patience." Ill-disciplined and cowardly officers, deserting soldiers, and lack of every supply necessary for campaign, placed the commander in chief in the position of a hunter with an empty rifle confronting a grizzly. But to heighten his difficulty telling troubles arose in other quarters.

Sickness was breaking out in camp. Already smallpox was scourging the troops in Boston, and it was a question as to how soon it would enter the American camp. Sanitation was foreign to the militiamen. Dirt and filth were kept down at home through the natural instinct of womanhood, but away from that environment the soldier took little care of his person and personal surroundings. The medical department mainly consisted of a number of jealous, bickering doctors with no chief. Hospitals were but pesthouses where the stricken victim was dropped upon the floor or straw to die or recover at the pleasure of Providence and with the annoyance of quackery. It had not yet become fashionable for women to nurse the soldier. No comforting attentions of feminine care reached his cold, bleak shelter where he groaned through torturous days and nights, awaiting death as a restful deliverance. The effective strength of Washington's army kept dwindling and the attractiveness of the soldier's life before Boston kept diminishing.

In the meantime, Quebec added another loss to the army. *Sept. 1775* Washington, shrewdly estimating Arnold's brilliant ability, gave him 1,050 men for the surprise of the Canadian stronghold. Arnold had pleaded his power to duplicate the surprise of Ticonderoga. The little force started out with great hopes, *Sept. 11 1775* crossed Massachusetts and New Hampshire and struck through the Maine wilderness. The unbroken country, inconceivably thick, impeded their march. Supplies gave out, bateaux of provisions were lost, and hunger became so frightful that three dogs, entrails and all, were eaten in one afternoon. Swampy ground, limited shelter, and frozen clothing brought sickness and death. The progress for 83 miles up Dead River is one ghastly tale of misery. The band of about 700 which emerged

two months later on the St. Lawrence had undergone frightful-
ness only to meet defeat.   Arnold's message, which should have
apprised Montgomery of his presence, fell into the hands of the
British commander at Quebec.   In the attack the noble Montgomery was killed, Arnold was wounded, and the American
force repulsed.   Although Arnold showed masterly skill in
drawing off his men and escaping to safety, the expedition was
none the less a disaster numerically and morally to the incipient
Revolution.

Washington felt this defeat acutely, especially since the undertaking had met with his sanction.   But long before the news
of its result had reached him he had been met with misunderstandings from a more hectoring source.

Congress, two hundred miles from the seat of activities, at
a time when mails were slow and telegrams unknown, ques-
tioned the wisdom of a commander who lay with a superior
force inactive for months before the enemy.   They could not
realize that the largest part of his numbers existed only on
paper.   Neither could they visualize the hampering effect of his
disorganization and needs.   The populace was crying "On to
Boston!"   So this little body of delegates, who made laws that
could not be executed and raised money that could not be collected, undertook to tell him not only what to do but how to do
it.   One member suggested, when there was scarcely enough
powder all told to fire a full-fledged salute, that he bombard the
British ships in the harbor.

Above the calumnies of people and lawmakers Washington
kept his temper serene and his energy unflagging.   All his
efforts bent toward the correction of evils for the sole purpose
of taking the offensive.   He raised the standards of discipline
throughout the command by the establishment of courts and the
trial of offenders.   In general orders he announced that bravery
would meet with reward and cowardice with certain justice, no
connections, interest, or intercessions, availing to prevent the
strict execution of punishment.   He dismissed colonels and captains alike, and brought to time enlisted men as well.   The
simple process of the martial law of the period possibly gave
quicker returns than modern technical methods.

Although the punishments of drumming out of camp, the

wooden horse, the pillory and flogging by rawhide on the naked back seem to us now to be severe, they were in vogue at that period of the world and seemed proper to the men of that time. Unusual punishments, such as branding on the hand and pouring salt and water on the lacerated back of the victim who had a few hours before received fifty lashes, were other delicate attentions of the law. Washington seems, however, to have discouraged the wooden horse, a peaked device on which the culprit in a sitting posture was strapped so that the end of his spine supported rigidly the weight of his body against the sharp edge. After a very few minutes he fainted and in most cases was injured permanently. Reprimands, extra hours of labor, riding on a rail, and apologies were used for lesser offenses. Sometimes a culprit was made to walk slowly at the point of a bayonet between the lines of his comrades while they smote him with belts, switches or any handy implement on the naked back. Naturally, the stricter enforcement of discipline on Washington's part induced among men, whose previous lives had been expressive of personal liberty, more desertions than before. On the other hand, those who remained were receiving the schooling necessary for the soldier and the future of the Revolution.

Of bringing the besieging force up to adequate strength, *Oct. 1775* Washington finally showed Congress the necessity. A Congressional Committee visited him with the avowed intention of giving him enough men. With representatives from the northeastern states it came to the conclusion that 20,370 were required to man the lines adequately. Accordingly, 26 regiments. were requisitioned: 16 from Massachusetts, 5 from Connecticut, 2 from Rhode Island, and 3 from New Hampshire, with the hope that most of the necessary levies might be obtained by reënlistment of the troops then around Boston. One month *Nov.–Dec. 1775* later the new force totaled 966 men; two months later, 5,917; and three months later only 10,500 of the required 20,370. In *Jan. 14 1776* the meantime, 50 men of each regiment had to be granted furloughs in order to induce them to reënlist. Thus, Washington *Dec. 1 1775* lost immediately the use of a large proportion of the 10,000. Besides, nearly the whole of the former army around Boston would vanish because of the completion of enlistment at the end of the year. After all this effort to get men, Washington was

compelled to call out 5,000 militia and minute men from the
adjacent colonies.   Many of these refused to come and those
who responded would do so only on condition that their service

Jan. 15
1776

would expire early the next year, or after less than one month's
service.   Thus at the beginning of the year Washington had
practically no army.

Nov. 11
1775

In collecting what he had, his task of selection seemed impossible.   He told the President of Congress early in the fall
that

> "they (the privates) will not enlist until they know their
> colonel, lieutenant colonel, major, and captain, so it is necessary
> to fix the officers the first thing."

Here Washington had to turn aside from organizing his rank
and file in order to determine what officers should be chosen.
Congress had sent him blank commissions to be filled out and
returned.   Before he could make up a single unit he must
attempt to sort out a few possibilities from the mass of the unfit.
Evidently he called upon his general and field officers for this
purpose, as regimental rosters afterwards showed.   As a matter
of fact these men were scarcely superior to their juniors in character and ability.   Some of their remarks foreshadow the
"Efficiency Reports" and "Qualification Cards" of the present
day, and reveal largely that partiality and animus were not
eliminated from the recommendations.   First Lieutenant
Joseph Youngs is described as "a very low-lived fellow"; Captain David Hobby, "a bad officer and at present under an arrest
and will, in all probability, be cashiered"; Second Lieutenant
Elihu Marshall, "a good officer, will make a good adjutant";
Captain Ames Hutchins, "of a low-turn and had better be dismissed the service."   Washington in this way, although possibly
by imperfect means, gained some idea of who should be commissioned.

To improve the artillery he succeeded in having appointed
Colonel Henry Knox as its chief.   That aggressive officer transported, on sleds and trucks over the hills of Vermont and Massachusetts, more than fifty cannons, including mortars and howitzers, captured at Crown Point and Ticonderoga.   Shells were
obtained from the plundered King's store in New York.

The powder shortage was more distressing and less easily remedied. Washington's reluctance in acknowledging the scarcity is shown in his correspondence where, lest the communication fall into the hands of the enemy, he omits the name of the coveted article in describing its absence. No powder plants turning out tons of ammunition, nor laden trucks of shot and shell to be kept sedulously from the prying eyes of spies, existed then in the colonies. Explosives came from abroad or were crudely mixed together in the private home. One countryman brought to the hall of Congress a whole barrel of powder he had himself manufactured. The Committee of Safety in Philadelphia published a description of the process of making saltpeter and sent trained men from town to town to instruct others in the art. Washington called upon the adjacent states for as much as they could furnish and kept beseeching Congress incessantly. One Governor, in answer to his request, complained that he had not enough powder to repel even a short attack upon his town. But the uninterrupted pleas began after a time to meet with more response.

The increase of firelocks was not so rapid. This coveted treasure would be carried away by the deserting men and left at home as an asset to the family store along with the spinning wheel and harpsichord. If the soldier by chance felt inclined to reënlist he would do so in another regiment, thereby acquiring a new weapon. Some are said to have accumulated as high as eight rifles in this thrifty way. Washington in the autumn of '75 issued an order for the prevention of this practice by seizing the firelock of the departing soldier and purchasing it if it was fit for use. In spite of his efforts to retain these weapons, two thousand men in the following February lacked arms.

The health of the army was keenly desired by Washington even at that early stage of medical science. He repeatedly issued orders for the cleanliness of the camp and men, and forbade the unlicensed sale of liquor to the soldiers. He requested Congress to regulate the hospitals. The legislators responded by providing him with a medical staff under a director general.

Even the matter of uniform as an aid to military respect

was of moment to the Revolutionary leader. Since funds were lacking for the adherence to any widespread order in this regard, he contented himself with the announcement that the commander in chief, generals, aides, field officers, captains and subalterns would wear ribbons and cockades of an appropriate color for each grade.

Congress had actually placed on Washington the burden of making an army as well as manipulating it. He was compelled to build when he longed to fight—to settle the issue. He was forced to be a collector of supplies when he hoped to be a leader of men. He was urged to wage hot war against a well-trained army, while his means were transient bodies of irregulars who went more than they came. The months of '75 passed away in dismissing and commissioning officers, begging for powder, arms, and men, and disciplining those who stayed long enough to be organized.

Jan. 1
1776

At the very beginning of the next year Congress made a move which, though not immediately fruitful, was to have a decided effect upon the final outcome of the Revolution. It decided to govern apart from the militia and minute men the little handful of soldiers it had directly raised. Because it made the term of enlistment longer for these continental troops than that which the colonies prescribed for their men, Washington was to have a small, stable nucleus about which he could congregate the constantly changing recruits sent by the governors. In the dark hours to come, it was this constant little band that was to make possible the continuance of the Revolution.

It is interesting to note that on the very day Congress determined upon such a course, there was raised over Boston camp the single flag of the colonies. It consisted of the crosses of St. George and St. Andrew and thirteen alternate white and red stripes. This fluttering hint of unity and autonomy supplanted the various banners of the different localities such as the "Pine Tree" emblem and the British banner on which was written "Liberty and Union."

Such a bright omen of the first day of the year of Independence was touchingly in contrast to the real state of affairs. While the country was face to face with a stout invader, one

American army had casually disappeared from the front, while barely half of the other had reluctantly assembled there. It was fortunate that the enemy remained astonishingly inactive of its own apparent volition. It was also a blessing for the Revolutionists that Howe was so charged with Whig sentiment that he would not attack the untrained, ill-supplied fragments of provincials whom he could easily have defeated. The 5,000 New England militia called in December would be gone on the 15th of January. The 10,500 of the new force were decimated by furloughs. The man-power was at a lower ebb than at any period since Washington had assumed command. To add to the tension it was understood that spring would bring reënforcements from England into Boston harbor. The commander in chief beheld six months' anguish and appeals to patriotism consummated in a product of impotence.

Notwithstanding his discouraging outlay, he called a coun- *Jan. 16 1776*
cil of war with the hope of some aggressive action. The generals agreed that an attack should be made, but could not conjure up any visions of success. It was finally decided to ask the New England colonies to raise 13 regiments for three months. In response to Washington's call only 10 of those organizations arrived about a month later, 3 being dispatched to lessen the imminent danger of Schuyler in the north.

Slight activity began to express itself along the lines in the *Early February 1776*
shape of sharp skirmishes. But Washington was waiting for powder and ice. With the support of the latter he would cross the harbor and with enough of the former he would deal a hard and unexpected blow. Again he called a council of war, but his project for attack was vetoed because it was thought to be too hazardous. Instead it was decided that Dorchester Heights, which the vacillation of Howe had left unoccupied and whose possession would render Boston untenable, should be seized and fortified.

At once Washington notified the near-by towns that they should have their militia ready to march at a moment's notice for three days' service. He collected fascines, gabions, hay, barrels, bateaux, floating batteries, bandages, carts, and intrenching tools. In spite of deserting soldiers and quarreling *March 2 1776*
officers he felt several weeks later that he had enough powder

and men to warrant operations. To disguise his scheme he
March 2, 3, 4
1776
kept up for several hours on three successive nights a heavy
artillery bombardment. So furious did the cannonading appear to one excited spectator that he declared he had seen as many as seven cannon balls in the air at one time!

March 4
1776
Late in the evening of the third day General Thomas with 2,000 men went forward to occupy the heights. Working with approximately 800 men in the darkness, he succeeded by silence and exertion in completing two redoubts before dawn. For the expected assault he prepared barrels filled with earth and stones to be rolled from the fortress down the hill upon the enemy. But this device of the days of Xenophon was not to be used.

The British awoke on the morning of the fifth to see a phantom fort in the place of the pastoral hill of the night before. Howe, in speaking of the occurrence later, stated: "It must
March 4, 5
1776
have been the employment of at least 12,000 men." He realized that this mirage or reality spelled attack or evacuation for his idle troops. Storms for several days prevented his crossing the harbor in boats to the assault. The delay let the American force so strengthen its works that the British commander assured himself of their impregnability, whereupon he, in turn, called a council of war which came to the conclusion that the evacuation of Boston was the only alternative. A fortnight afterward that decision was converted into action by Washington's fortifying Nook's Hill.

Curious things have happened to troops in their rounds of striking diversities of campaign, but it is safe to say no spectacle in a similar situation ever presented itself to a commander quite like the one Washington viewed from his threatening hill
March 17
1776
on St. Patrick's Day, 1776. After having impersonated for eight months the part of a bold and harmless menace, like a child with outstretched arms barring the sidewalk to a man, he witnessed 11,000 hostile troops in neat red uniforms, with bulging knapsacks and polished cartridge boxes crammed with good ammunition, marching peacefully towards their commanding ships lying off shore. No gun disturbed the quiet; nor confusion, the repose. A few silent cannons pointed from a fortified eminence were literally pushing Howe into the sea.

So it came about that after the British had sailed ostensibly *March 20 1776* for Halifax, the American commander found in the city large stores of wheat and ammunition together with 250 pieces of artillery. He discovered also that during the whole siege extending over two thirds of a year he had actually lost by death in action less than twenty men. In spite of the desertions, dishonesty, strolling and ill-disciplined troops, losses by sickness and disaster, the veritable quicksand of disappearing soldiery and lack of the commonest essentials for decent defense, this first venture of the Revolution was such a miraculous success that the Congress voted a medal to the commander in chief. It also gave thanks to God.

CHAPTER II

THE ARMY LEARNS TO WALK AND RUN

(1776–1777)

March 17
1776
AFTER Howe had put to sea, leaving Boston to Washington and his curious following, the American commander turned his attention to the central avenue of the country, the Hudson. He felt that the next place of attack by the enemy would be New York City. Having provided a holding force of about 5,000 against a possible return of the British to Massachusetts, he hastened south and west with the remainder. Except for the numerous armed journeymen who had oscillated at will between the siege and their firesides, the Revolutionary army for the first time became a mobile force. The hardships of march, bivouac and temporary camp—the true rigors of war—began to settle their dampness upon the ardor of the patriot soldier.

Over the primitive roads, narrow trails and grassy lanes of New England, the long line in Indian file threaded its straggling way to New London. Behind each company of musketeers followed the fifer and drummer giving vent to such enlivening strains as "The Pioneer's March" or "Roslin Castle." Banners of red, brown and yellow bearing homemade legends preceded the battalions. Gaps of varying sizes opened and closed within and between companies. Cannons mounted on rickety carriages rumbled along on awkward and noisy cart wheels. Farmer Stout going into the fields in the early morning beheld the epauleted generals in the van of the column; returning to his dinner he watched the progress of the multiform companies; and walking between the furrows in the dusk of the evening he heard the loud cries of the cart drivers and tinkling bells of the cattle bringing up the rear.

Impressed by this big display of a small force, the gawking

24

yokel and adventurous townsman took down their fowlingpieces
from over their fireplaces, and fell in behind their kinsmen or
friends in the hope that they too might take part in the general
excitement of bagging a few redcoats.

Where the eager came by ones, the disheartened left by twos.
The Massachusetts militiamen grew timid at the sight of the
strange wilderness of Connecticut far from home. He was
physically uncomfortable, too. His feet, bound in low, ill-
fitting shoes and unused to the long stretches and rapid, even
gait of the march, were hot and blistered. Added to the twenty
pounds of lead, steel, wood and leather on his person, he had
accumulated at some recently visited farmhouse a frying pan,
salt pork, dried venison or a coffeepot with which he had carefully bulged his homely hunting shirt. Had he not done so he
would have lacked nourishment at the end of the day's march,
for under General Mifflin's service of supply the wagons either
dumped their contents far from the hungry or did not arrive
at all.

In consequence of such discomfort, the near-by thicket, the
wayside tavern, or the smiling face of a maid was an attraction
too strong to be withstood by the young soldier, especially when
his officers and noncommissioned officers had neither force nor
semblance of disciplinary power to call back the truant. After
the long line had passed from sight over the next hill, he slowly
drifted homeward and was gathered unto his people. At his
own threshold he was met by the saintly mother, the good wife
and the village smith who agreed they could not exactly see why
a Massachusetts Bay man should fight under a New Jersey
officer for the sake of New York settlers.

Washington finally arrived in New York, where he found *April 13*
that Lee, who had been sent ahead from Boston and was then in *1776*
the south, had well begun the work of defense. Kingsbridge
at the northern end of Manhattan, redoubts around the southern
end, and earthworks at Brooklyn Heights on Long Island were
under way. At once the American commander set to work to
complete these widely separated fortifications, in which task he
found his soldiers most skillful. Sapping, like shooting, was
an art in which the American was expert. The frontiersman
and Maine woodsman proved to be ready with the ax and dex-

trous in matting revetments out of the tangle of wildwood infesting the Bronx and the Battery.

To gain recruits Washington marched and countermarched his ragamuffin collection up and down the Island. But the wavering loyalist, instead of being enraptured, was inclined to be disgusted at the sight of the ill-clothed soldiers and coarse officers. With his mediocre official family Washington was hampered by sporadic drills, puerile instructions and lamentable ignorance of discipline. Colonels were repeatedly instructed in orders that unless they broke sentries of the practice of sitting down on post, the delinquents could not justly be shot for sleeping thereon. Captains had to be directed to see that every man when he came into action had twenty-four cartridges in his pouch and a good flint in his piece. Subalterns were desired to salute at ceremonies by doffing their caps until they could master the intricate operation of presenting their fusees.

Such was the summer's work of the dwindling force. Its play was that of Tory-baiting, a mild pastime which consisted in catching a luckless loyalist, stripping, tarring, feathering and riding him on a rail or in a cart as an object of ridicule and missiles. In many cases the victim was permanently injured. Another expression of this sport was that of collecting about the house of some British sympathizer in the dead of night and of raising a sudden cry of "Fire"! In that period of the world when no snorting engines or convenient hydrants played their prompt parts in the quenching of flames, such a sinister sound meant to those within the wooden dwellings suffocation or cremation. Naturally, the occupants came pouring forth in scant attire only to find themselves objects of indignity on the part of a heterogeneous soldiery, some of whom immediately began looting the house.

Washington found himself powerless to check these misdemeanors or to enforce discipline in general on account of lax officers and floating recruits. He was so distraught by the weak character of his personnel that he recommended to the Committee of Safety that Congress provide a proportion of two to one against the British in order to make up in numbers for the American deficiency in quality.

On account of the limited powers of the delegates, Congress *June 3*
1776
was then busy making laws it could not enforce, voting money
it could not raise, and making armies it could not assemble. It
called out 13,000 militia from Connecticut, New Jersey, New
York, and Massachusetts, and provided for a "flying camp" of
10,000 in New Jersey to be enrolled from Pennsylvania, Maryland and Delaware. As to the militia they were slow in coming and the "flying camp" really never materialized. Though
the name of the latter has a brisk, American sound, it should
more appropriately have been termed evanescent or fleeting
camp. The idea was to collect the armed inhabitants into a
large reserve without having regular enlistments. But when
the majority of those who were regularly enrolled would not
stay, it is easy to see why those who had to take no obligations
would not come at all. In gaining troops, Congress was truly
in the position of calling "spirits from the vasty deep."

The fact that the recruit was hard to get should have convinced the members that once he was obtained his term of
service should be for a relatively lengthy time, if for no other
reason than the training derived from experience in the field.
It does not seem possible that reasonable men should repeat the
mistakes of the previous year by limiting enlistment periods
to six months and less, in the face of Washington's entreaty to
the contrary. But that was exactly what the delegates did.

On the other hand, they framed a resolution for a per- *June 12*
1776
manent committee of five to form a Board of War and Ordnance. This body, to which all military questions were to be
referred, was the first suggestion of a War Department. But
such organization was unimportant in comparison to the
Declaration of Independence. The formal separation from the
parent country should have shown the civilians and the army *July 4*
1776
that they were officially alone and self-reliant. Whether the
soldiers realized the added burden placed upon them is difficult
to infer from Washington's description of the reception of this
daring document which he ordered to be read at the head of *July 8*
1776
each brigade. "The measure" he wrote, "seemed to have their
most hearty assent."

Following the Declaration, however, Congress found it
necessary to increase the "flying camp" because of the quick

efflux and slow influx of recruits. As one would raise his bank account by merely adding figures in his check book, so the lawmakers created four battalions of militia from Pennsylvania, three from New Jersey, and two of continentals from Virginia. The colonies made it continually more difficult for the central government to obtain soldiers. Connecticut and Massachusetts began offering to their recruits $33.33 over the bounty allowed to the continentals or regulars enlisted by Congress for the duration of the war. New Jersey bid $53.33, whereupon Massachusetts and New Hampshire raised their offers to $86.66. No wonder the soldier went to the highest bidder, especially when that bidder, the commonwealth, required only a "few months' walk" in return for this enormous gift. It was too much to ask of human nature that a man serve ten times longer for far less bounty. And to add to the temptation for militia service, the states were paying in sound money while the Congress, if it remitted at all, was dealing out depreciating notes. Miraculously the Amos Farnsworths stayed with the continental colors despite the poor profit and lengthy discomfort, but they were of the handful who believed independence to be a vision of God and the fight for it beyond the vanities of this world.

July 19 1776

Aug. 9 1776

Congress indulged itself also in making four new major generals: Heath, Spencer, Sullivan and Greene. It passed over Pomeroy, Wooster and Thomas, for apparently no reason other than that described by Chase of Maryland when he stated that the delegates were persisting in the error of recommending "persons from personal friendships who were not suitable." John Adams, who, as Belcher asserts, was "unhappily incapable of seeing conspicuous merit in any one but himself," stated there would be "less danger in vesting the power (of appointment) in any assembly than in giving it to a general." On the other hand, Duane of New York declared he would "rather take the opinion of Washington than of any convention." It afterwards transpired when the commander in chief took over the appointing power that subordinates were selected because of their familiarity with the business of arms.

Howe, whose army had landed on Staten Island the day following the adoption of the Declaration of Independence, finally determined to venture over to Long Island. He took with him at least 20,000 effectives from his total force of 35,000.

The American army was in the incubation period of its chronic complaint—torpid enlistment. Congress had legislated over 50,000 men into the service, yet Washington in order to oppose the British general could collect barely 8,000 fit for duty. *Aug. 22 1776*

It is not remarkable that Howe by an admirable turning movement overwhelmed the little outpost of 2,500 near Flatbush, as one would pinch a piece of pulp between the thumb and forefinger. According to one captured American, who confessed after the battle that his duties had been to "flank a little and carry tidings," it would appear that the service of security and information had been carried along very well. As a matter of fact the Americans had no cavalry, nor had they much idea of the use of patrols. The five officers who had been employed for that purpose over the Jamaica road, the forefinger of the British attack, were easily captured as the enemy's column came along. Putnam, in his usual zealous blundering, sent more troops into the trap after he was made cognizant of the force on the flank. Another American leader ingenuously stated that the Jamaica road was a "route we never dreamed of." Stirling and Sullivan were captured, the latter while hiding in a cornfield. One brilliant colonel, outstripping the others in the general retreat, destroyed without authority a very necessary bridge, thus aiding the British in scooping more successfully the flying Americans. About 2,100 were killed or captured, some few making their way back to Brooklyn Heights. *Aug. 27 1776*

How little the private realized the results of the battle is to be gleaned from one diarist who set down this effective epitome:

"Our Army on Long Island Have ben Engaged in battle with the Enimy and Killd And taken a good many on Both sides."

That afternoon six hours of daylight remained for Howe to exterminate not over 5,500 disheartened Americans and so end the Revolution. Being immersed in Whiggish thought, he did not move. The next morning rain rendered the American *Aug. 28 1776* powder useless. Again the British opportunity for easy victory with cold steel must have impressed Howe. And again he ignored the invitation. Certainly the scattering fire encouraged by Washington among those who could keep their powder dry did not deceive a tried soldier like the British commander.

Taking advantage of Howe's hesitancy, Washington ordered Mifflin, his quartermaster general, to "collect every flat-bottomed boat and other craft . . . fit for transporting troops." The little army had at its back a deep channel and in its front an overwhelming number of the best trained soldiers of Europe. A large percentage of the colonial troops had left their blankets and equipment on the battlefield several miles away. Their powder was wet with rain and their spirits dampened by defeat.

Aug. 29 1776

Under cover of a fog Washington completed the transportation of this entire force to the Manhattan shore. Thanks to its sagacious leader, London weather and a British general, the American army lived to fight another day.

Sept. 15 1776

But that day, as will be seen when Howe arrived in pursuit several weeks later, adds no brilliant luster to American arms.

In the meantime, Congress received from Washington the description of the effect upon the troops of the disaster of Long Island:

Letter Sept. 2 1776

"The check our detachment sustained on the 27th ultimo has dispirited too great a proportion of our troops and filled their minds with apprehension and despair. The militia instead of calling forth their utmost effort to a brave and manly opposition in order to repair our losses, are dismayed, intractable, and impatient to return. Great numbers of them have gone off—in some instances almost by whole regiments, by half-ones, and by companies at a time."

John White, writing from Rhinebeck after these parties had time to arrive home, confirms Washington's statement by saying:

"I suppose there are not less in this and the Northeast Precinct than thirty (deserters) who keep in the woods and are supported by their friends."

When Howe landed at what is now East 34th Street, the *Sept. 15 1776* effect upon the untrained colonial levies was what might have been expected.   Washington again records, in characteristically conservative style, this pitiful event:

"As soon as I heard the firing, I rode with all possible des-patch toward the place of landing, when, to my great surprise and mortification, I found the troops that had been posted in the lines retreating with the utmost precipitation, and those ordered to support them (Parson's and Fellow's brigades) fly-ing in every direction and in the greatest confusion, notwith-standing the exertions of their Generals to form them.   I used every means in my power to rally and get them into some order, but my attempts were fruitless and ineffectual, and on the appearance of a small party of the enemy, not more than 60 or 70, their disorder increased, and they ran away in the great-est confusion without firing a shot."

"Every means in my power" consisted in riding in among the fugitives and beating officer and man unavailingly with the flat of the saber until the scourger himself was barely rescued from the enemy.   The one defect that aroused the anger of the Father of his Country was cowardice.

The letter quoted had no more than reached Congress be- *Sept. 16 1776* fore that body made two enactments affecting the army.   One was the completion of the "The Articles of War" with the injunction that they be read every two months at the head of each company, troop and regiment.   Two hours were required in mouthing this legal recital of offenses and penalties, four-teen of which prescribed death.   The unlettered soldier, know-ing how few of the punishments were actually executed, was far from being impressed.   The other act promulgated after great reluctance on the part of the delegates was fully as fruit-less.   It called for the creation of 88 battalions of continentals or regulars to be taken proportionally from all thirteen colonies. If the soldier engaged for the entire war he was offered $20 in money and from 500 acres of land for a colonel to 100 for a private.   The weak central government now raised its induce-ment and began to bid against the powerful colonies.   But it gave to the states the right of naming the officers of this force, Congress perfunctorily issuing commissions.

The 88-battalion measure showed advancement in the attempt to establish a regular continental army for which Washington had contended through so many months, but the bounty system was the inauguration of wasteful legislation. Further, in delegating to the states the appointment of officers, Washington's plans of organization were frustrated. He could not advance or appoint a single subordinate without first consulting the governors who were in many cases several months' journey away. Invariably it turned out that state preference lay with the influential novice rather than with the able veteran.

The day Howe, by the very appearance of landing, put so many Americans to flight, he could easily have entrapped Putnam at the southern end of the Island by merely moving onward. Although he was conversant with this fact, he chose to accept an invitation to dine at the Murray House on Murray Hill with some charming ladies. Putnam being unopposed was extremely successful in making his escape.

The next morning, Washington, finding Howe still inert, determined to develop his whereabouts. Selecting a body of 120 rough and ready mounted men known as Knowlton's Rangers, he sent them forward to gain contact. In a skirmish known as Harlem Heights they acquitted themselves nobly by pursuing the foe and giving more blows than they took. Although from a military point of view the engagement was indecisive, it did much to restore the failing courage of the Americans.

Yet it did not check desertions enough to show any effect upon the dwindling force. Signs of absenteeism were particularly noticeable in the service of supply where great quantities of beef were left to putrefy on the ground. Congress acknowledged the general disintegration by adding to its bid for continental troops an annual gift of two linen hunting shirts, two pairs of overalls, one leather or woolen waistcoat with sleeves, one pair of breeches, a hat or leather cap, two shirts, two pairs of hose and two pairs of shoes. Nevertheless, Washington's backing fell off so materially that he was forced to retreat to White Plains or be cut off.

Oct. 8
1776

Oct. 12
1776

The British, in following him, were met by Glover's brigade *Oct. 18* at Pell's Point, where the red-coated ranks in the open were *1776* mowed down by the Americans behind stone walls. The untrained woodsmen again demonstrated their ability to hit the target as long as there was a sufficient barrier between the enemy's bullet and their bowels. In this uneven action the Americans had 16 casualties against some 800 of the British, so that the morale of the retreating army received another slight pulsation.

When the actual battle of White Plains occurred, however, *Oct. 22* nothing but a rainstorm which wet the ammunition and stopped *1776* temporarily all hostilities, saved Washington's puny force from decisive defeat. In his disadvantageous position he was compelled to withdraw to the heights of Newcastle for safety.

Then came the disaster of Fort Washington, which gave *Nov. 16* Long Island, Manhattan and New Jersey to the enemy. Over *1776* a month previous Washington had sent word to Greene, the commander of the fortress, that the place was untenable and should be abandoned. Here Congress intervened by directing Greene not to relinquish it except under dire necessity. In consequence, Howe surrounded and captured it with an overwhelming force and by a well-planned maneuver, taking 2,600 prisoners with many stores and provisions. Not only was it a serious loss in itself, but its fall necessitated the precipitate evacuation of Fort Lee across the river. In all, Congress by its interference in a business to which it was an absolute stranger and from which it was far removed, contributed to the British 146 pieces of artillery, 12,000 shot, 2,800 small arms, and 400,000 musket cartridges.

A regimental adjutant before the assault, becoming an "old countryman" (deserting to the enemy), with all the plans of the fort, furthered congressional effort. In taking over the prisoners the British were highly amused at the "butcher and baker" who made up the commissioned personnel, and especially at one captain who insisted upon styling himself "keppun."

The campaign of New York was ended with Washington *Nov. 20* fleeing south. As he crossed the Hudson, the New York and *1776* the New England militia of four states left him almost in a body. He was pushed so rapidly across the Hackensack that

Nov. 28
1776
he had to abandon much of his commissary stores, baggage, and over thirty cannons. As he moved out of Newark, Cornwallis on his heels entered the other end of the town. Indeed, if the British had not been retarded by Howe, the patriot remnants could easily have been swallowed up or put to flight.

Nov. 29
1776
The colonial troops were only too anxious to depart. The New Jersey and Maryland militia, finding that their terms had expired, left the colors forthwith in the face of Washington's most earnest entreaties. Only the sturdy continentals remained. Winter was coming on. Clothing was ragged and scant. Many a man was marching in his bare feet so that lameness and sickness resulted.

The soldier blamed the colonial assemblies for neglect. The assemblies blamed the people at large, where the onus seems justly to lie. For it is proved by several authorities, among whom is Dr. Benjamin Rush, that the townsmen were not pinched but rather were living in a prosperous and well-fed condition. In their complaisant and ignominious apathy they heeded neither the Revolution nor the suffering soldier. So

Dec. 2
1776
low did the hungry, footsore, cold tatterdemalions sink in numbers that it was seriously projected, when they had crossed the Delaware into Pennsylvania, that they retire to Augusta County, Virginia, in order to conduct a lawless, predatory warfare wherever and whenever they could harass the British. Such a course would nominally have ended the Revolution.

To add to the losses by desertion Washington had to suffer from those of defection. Lee who had been left behind in the north did not move after repeated orders from his commander in chief to join the main body. Already he had begun his insidious plotting. Being second in command he felt that, with a little success on his part, say, cutting the British line of retreat in New Jersey, he could supplant Washington. After inexcusable delay he moved out at the speedy rate of 40 miles in 8 days! While at a farmhouse, three miles outside his own

Dec. 13
1776
lines, where he had been engaged in writing disloyal notes to Gates, he was surprised and captured by a few British. The enemy felt that it had spirited away the brains of the Revolution. Nothing could have better promoted coöperation with the commander in chief than the removal of this despicable

conspirator, unless, perhaps, Gates had also been taken.   As it turned out Stirling,[1] next in command, immediately marched to Washington's aid with all dispatch.

Panicked by the British advance through New Jersey, Congress packed its portmanteaus, hoisted its printing press aboard a wagon and fled to Baltimore.   There, before any news of Washington's coming successes could reach it, it breathlessly "vested him with full, ample, and complete powers to raise and collect sixteen battalions of infantry . . . to appoint all officers below the rank of brigadier general . . . to take, wherever he may be, whatever he may want for the use of the army."   In addition to this plenipotentiary arrangement it allowed him to raise 3,000 light horse, 3 regiments of artillery, and a corps of engineers, and to establish their pay.   Congress was not averse in times of great extremity to unloading responsibility on the already weighted shoulders of Washington.

To his lot little beyond the blackest cowardice, desertion and defeat had fallen since the Declaration of Independence. After having been despoiled of means, he was rudely saddled with complete authority.   The force at his immediate disposal was not more than 3,300, half of whom were volatile militia. At the existing rate of dissolution ten days more would end the army and make freedom a byword.   Under this yoke the heart of a man and the soul of leadership alone changed the course of events.   Singly and without show, while shattered and all but forsaken, Washington determined upon an offensive. Since he had collected all the Delaware River boats, he was unassailable until the enemy could construct rafts.   His information from patriots in New Jersey showed that the British were scattered throughout the state in small garrisons.   Rall was at Trenton with 1,500 men, and Dunlop at Bordentown with a similar number.   The Hessians had thrown up no intrenchments and Christmas day would be an occasion of feasting and drunkenness.   Besides Sullivan and Gates had joined Washington with their northern reënforcements.

The plan was simple and audacious.   Christmas night Gates was to cross the river against Dunlop.   Ewing was to cross just

Dec. 25
1776

---

[1] Sullivan and Stirling had both been exchanged.

below Trenton in order to cut off Rall's retreat, while Washington was to cross nine miles above the town. Three parallel columns were simultaneously to sally into the enemy's country.

Just one third of the plan was executed. Gates complained of being ill, but was not so indisposed as to be prevented from hastening away in order to intrigue with Congress. Ewing found the river very full of ice and was certain that Washington must have failed in his attempt. The desperate northern column was left to make its way between the floating cakes unassisted. All night long in sleet and darkness Washington and Knox toiled and urged the miniature transports. Not until three o'clock was the force safely landed and not until eight did they come in sight of their objective. Drunkenness and overconfidence let the town lie in unpreparedness until the Americans were within musket shot. Otherwise, bereft of a part of his army and delayed by the slow crossing, Washington's shivering soldiers could easily have been scattered, while the Trenton Hessians escaped to Dunlop. As it turned out·the Americans took nearly 1,000 prisoners, 6 field pieces, 4 flags and 12 drums with the loss of 2 officers and 1 private wounded. A private described the engagement as follows:

"This morning at 4 a clock we set off with our field pieces, marched 8 miles to Trenton whare we ware atacked by a number of Hushing & we toock 1000 of them besides killed some. Then we marchd back And got to the River at Night and got over all the Hushing."

Nevertheless, this apparently elated diarist refused to be tempted by the $10 extra bounty which Washington, pledging his own private fortune, was compelled to offer the militia as an inducement to stay with the colors for a few days more. Neither was it particularly significant to this patriot that the Americans had taken so many "Hushing" and that there had occurred the first offensive action and real victory of the war. Like many others he drew his wages and bounty money and departed.

Before the remainder could do likewise, Washington recrossed the river into the land of the enemy, and occupied

Dec. 29
1776

Trenton with not more than 5,000. In the meantime Cornwallis had collected 8,000 trained men at Princeton. Leaving
3 regiments in the town the British commander set out for the
American army, arriving within striking distance by nightfall.

Washington was not only compelled to shift his position
to the south of the town but was in the same plight in which
he found himself at Long Island—deep water in his rear and
an overwhelming force in front. This time, however, due to the
determined skill of the American leader the little army did not
retreat. At one o'clock A.M., it moved out over the roundabout *Jan. 3
1777*
Quaker Road, leaving 700 men behind to keep the fires burning and to imitate camp noises. It arrived in Cornwallis'
rear near Princeton at sunrise when the British brigade of the
rear guard was crossing Stony Brook to join the main force
near Trenton. Perceiving a small party of Americans (Mer-
cer's men), Colonel Mawhood (English) faced about in order
to capture what he estimated to be a few colonial companies.
For some time he was successful on account of the superiority
of the British bayonet. But suddenly he found himself confronted with Washington and the whole American army which
was supposedly twelve miles away at Trenton. Washington
pursued the British regiments as far as Kingston. He made
prisoners of 200 cooped in old Nassau, and inflicted a loss of
about 400 on other troops. Since his men were too fatigued
to carry out the original intention of seizing the stores at
Brunswick, and had vastly exceeded their resources in their
daring, he camped that night at Somerset Court House. The
next day he went into winter quarters on the heights of Morris- *Jan. 4
1777*
town.

Washington's daring and skill had caused his little force to
outnumber that part of the enemy he had attacked. Had he
failed in any part of his plan he would have been annihilated
and gone down in history as a fool. As it was, when Cornwallis wheeled about, Washington knew that his own superiority had fallen to inferiority. The astute American commander quickly took the defensive.

To this movement he was forced as much on account of
the condition of his men as their numbers. Marching in the
frigid cold without proper nourishment and uniform. the sol-

dier's sufferings were possibly greater than those at Valley Forge.[2] It was estimated by eyewitnesses that the ill-fed, ill-clothed, ill-supplied and exhausted American army could then have been put to flight at Morristown by one well-equipped and drilled battalion.

Obscured by the brilliant skirmishes of Trenton and Princeton, the true situation between the contending forces should not be overlooked. The British in their victorious battles around New York had taken almost as many prisoners as Washington had soldiers in his camp. The untrained, come-and-go patriot had been an easy prey to the seasoned veterans from abroad. The American had not yet learned to march in the open, under fire and against breastworks. Through lack of discipline and training he was bound to be an easier victim than the soldier who knew what to do instinctively and made offensive action possible.

Jan. 13
1777
The treatment of the American prisoners certainly did not stimulate the patriot to try conclusions with the British. Ethan Allen during his incarceration wrote that he had suffered everything short of death. Many others were sharing a like fate. To prevent ill treatment to Lee, Washington informed Howe that every cruel act would meet with retaliation. The mockery of this thoughtfulness is expressed in the fact that Lee at that very hour was concocting plans for the complete overthrow of Washington's army and the American cause.

It is certain, though, that Howe was attempting to make captivity for the "rebels" more distressing than death. The prison ships, *Jersey, Hunter, Whitby, Scorpion, Stromboli* and *Good Hope,* were floating "black holes." The hatches and other openings of the crowded traps were so sparse and barred as to make air and light real luxuries. The stacking up of the dead was as regular as sunrise. The highest privilege a prisoner could receive was to go ashore with a burial party. The emaciated bodies were flung into shallow holes in the sand only to be washed by the next storm about the vessel where they floated before the occasional view of the next victims. During the war 10,000 are said to have perished on the *Jersey* alone.

---

[2] To be described in the next chapter.

In the sugar houses and churches of New York, the land prisons of the British, conditions were even worse. Unprincipled overseers are said to have fed the dead and starved the living. The deceased captives, mortifying in their own filth, were often found to have placed in their mouths pieces of stone or plaster, their last hope of nourishment. Very few of the released survived, some dying in their tracks before reaching home.

It is possible that Howe's prison system was one of the principal deterrents to recruiting. It may in part explain the reluctance of the American soldier to reënlist even after being stirred by Tom Paine's *Crisis* read at the head of each regiment:

"These are the times that try men's souls. The summer soldier and the sunshine patriot will in this crisis shrink from the service of his country, but he that stands now deserves the love and thanks of man and woman."

At Morristown those parts of the militia which had with effort been induced to stay on after Trenton were leaving in shoals, taking with them what Government property suited their fancy. After two years of war Washington's whole energy had to be expended in pleading with Congress and the country for an army. He was left with nothing whatever with which to undertake operations. Consequently, the hostilities of the remainder of the winter manifested themselves only in ineffective partisan warfare among New Jersey farmers.

Congress did not increase its prestige by appointing Stirling, *Feb. 19 1777* Mifflin, Saint Clair, Stephen and Lincoln as major generals, passing over Arnold, the senior brigadier, who had demonstrated more soldierly qualities and leadership than any other general save Washington and perhaps Greene. Dissatisfaction arose among the troops in that their natural leader should be so treated. The unjust situation is explained by the fact that Arnold was a friend of Schuyler, and Schuyler, due to Gates' plotting, was *persona non grata* to Congress.

By March, thanks to the indifference of a well-fed and erroneously revered population, the force at Morristown had dwindled to less than 3,000, over 2,000 of whom were worthless militia who would depart the next month. Within two-days' march was a British army of 10,000 trained soldiers which could have taken the Americans with less loss than it was experiencing from the rebel community.

To add to Washington's misfortunes, General Tryon, the royal governor, had landed near Fairfield, Connecticut, and marched to Danbury where he captured more than 1,600 tents and other stores. Generals Silliman and Wooster pursued the British, harassing them at Lexington until Wooster was killed. Arnold, who had been on a visit in the neighborhood, voluntarily led in his impulsive way several hundred militia to the fray. Although he had two horses shot under him he succeeded in inflicting much loss on the escaping British. Congress, forced to recognize him for this exploit, reluctantly made him a major general but did not restore him to his former relative rank.

Finally after four months, the army at Morristown under the act creating 88 battalions came up to a total of about 7,500. Although Washington was able to move out of camp he was not strong enough to undertake an offensive. Selecting a strong position near Brunswick he placed himself between Howe and Philadelphia. Then ensued a series of adroit maneuvers on the part of Howe to entice Washington into giving battle. After three attempts to lure the Americans toward unfavorable ground, during each of which Washington returned to his

strong position, the British took to their boats on Staten Island and sailed Washington knew not where. For two months Howe at sea and Washington on land played at hide and seek. The Americans first moved north as far as Haverstraw on the Hudson, then returned as far south as Philadelphia and had partly retraced their steps northward, when verification of the news

that the British were in the Chesapeake turned them again south.

Although the army had been harassed by marching and countermarching and knew with a vengeance the meaning of locomotion, it did not, while Howe was in obscurity, lose in numbers. Congress had again resorted to the fickle militia, calling out approximately 11,000 from the surrounding states.

When Washington finally marched through Philadelphia with drums beating, the flag of the Union (13 stars and stripes) flying, the generals and their aides all gold and lace riding on frisky mounts, and the "ragged, lousy, naked regiments" carrying burnished arms, the whole force came up to the magnificent total of 11,000 fit for duty. *Aug. 24 1777*

Before the army travels further, it is necessary to speak of a curious malady—"foreignitis"—which affected it most strangely. The American agents in France had been besieged and besought by European adventurers for commissions in our service. Most of the applicants were without merit or interest in the cause. That Franklin in his Parisian apartments was not deceived by them is evidenced by the closing sentence of one of his replies:

"If, therefore, you have the least remaining kindness for me, if you would not help to drive me out of France, for God's sake, my dear friend, let this your twenty-third application be your last."

Silas Deane was less discerning. He made great promises to trained and untrained alike. In consequence, little foreign migrations waited upon Congress and importuned Washington when he had just been given plenary powers and was in the thick of his troubles after Trenton. In one instance Deane had given Du Courdray a commission as major general of artillery. Knox, as brigadier, and chief of that arm had served successfully for over a year. Greene and Sullivan shook hands with Knox that they would all resign their commissions provided the displacement occurred. Washington, besides, protested against the appointment because he would be saddled with a man whose qualities he did not know and about whom he should have been consulted. Congress was forced to repudiate Du Courdray's commission. But others came who could not be warded off so easily. Upon their advent the junior American officers protested that they themselves were native born, had served from the beginning and were now unfairly "jumped" by a foreigner. The enlisted men detested being ordered about by a titled fellow with a broken accent. This antipathy caused even Canadian officers to be tried and retried on the flimsiest pretexts until many were forced to resign their commissions.

Just as the convalescent can sometimes attribute good effects to certain diseases, so to a few exceptions among the foreigners, without whose aid it is doubtful if America had won the war, the country owes deep gratitude: Steuben, Lafayette, Pulaski, Kosciusko and Du Portail. Of these Steuben by his ability and Lafayette by his affluence, influence and noble attitude were preëminent.

Congress, in bestowing the rank of major general on Lafayette, gave forth these democratic sentiments:

"That in consideration of his zeal, illustrious family and connections he have the rank of major general in the army of the United States."

Nowhere in the history of the Revolution did our lawmakers intimate by the slightest token that there existed such a thing as military technic or efficiency. Family, caste, friendship, favor and politics seemed to be the determining factors in awarding splendid commissions. Arnold, the most brilliant divisional commander of the war, was passed over time after time by incompetents until he finally responded to ill treatment with treason.

Two days after Lafayette's arrival Washington received the news that Howe was in the Chesapeake. The American commander marched south to meet the British, having obtained reliable information by the service of scouts; but finding the opposing force superior, he withdrew to a defensive position north of Chad's Ford across the Brandywine.

Sept. 11
1777

Howe tried the same pinching movement he had used at Long Island. This time, however, he changed the relative positions of the thumb and forefinger. Knyphausen moved out over the eastern thumb in order to keep Washington occupied and make him believe he was opposed by the entire force. Howe with Cornwallis made a detour over the long forefinger in order to cross the western forks of the Brandywine and surprise the American flank.

Washington, perceiving the plan, sent Sullivan across the
upper reaches of the river in order to keep Howe engaged,
while he, Washington, could cross and overwhelm the inferior
force of Knyphausen's before help could arrive. Sullivan,
without making sufficient reconnaissance, reported that there
was no enemy across the river so that he was consequently
withdrawn. Shortly afterward the news came to Washington
that the whole British army had crossed near the point where
Sullivan should have kept the enemy engaged. It was too late
for the American army to carry out the original plan. It could
not defeat the weak fraction on the thumb while the larger
force on the tip of the forefinger was absent. Howe was already hitting Washington on two sides. Sullivan's militia on
the right flank gave way like sheep and the rout began. Although Greene came to the rescue and covered the retreat,
Washington was forced to withdraw to Chester with losses about
equal to those of the British.

Next day he moved north to Germantown, where, upon *Sept. 12 1777*
finding that Howe was still inactive, he prepared to force the
issue again. Crossing the Schuylkill he hastened south. The
two armies met at Warwick Tavern where the rain began to *Sept. 16 1777*
fall in torrents. The Americans without rainproof clothing
of any kind, in their tight-fitting, uncomfortable, unsuitable
garments, were drenched to the skin. Their "cartouch" boxes
were soaked through so that all idea of any engagement, other
than with bayonet or bow and arrow, vanished. Washington
removed his saturated musketeers behind the Schuylkill near *Sept. 17 1777*
Perkiomen.

Convinced that Philadelphia would soon be in British hands
Congress[3] again precipitately packed off westward, this time
to York. Finding the burdens of war excessive and quite out
of hand, it magnanimously passed them over to Washington
who was virtually given dictatorial powers within seventy miles
of his headquarters for sixty days. His hands were free to
meet the enemy in any way he chose.

Finding that Howe was moving westward along the south
bank of the Schuylkill, he attempted along the north bank to
keep pace with him. But the disaffection of the Germans and

---

[3] It had returned from Baltimore.

Quakers in that vicinity withheld valuable information, so that, when Howe suddenly wheeled eastward, Washington was not apprised of the fact. The British were across the river and well on their way to Philadelphia before Washington was aware of the countermarch.

At Germantown Howe retained 6,000 men while he scattered the remainder, with the exception of 3,000 in Philadelphia, throughout New Jersey. As soon as Washington was satisfied of this faulty disposition, he at once decided to fall upon the inferior force at Germantown and overwhelm it. By setting out at night he would march with four columns along parallel roads, converge and attack simultaneously at dawn. The militia was to close in around the British flanks and cut off its retreat while the continental troops made the main attack in the center. All arrived near their separate destinations, and the plan would have been carried out admirably had not any one of the following occurrences taken place. A dense fog settled over the troops so that forty feet was the visual limit. The militia on one flank never appeared; on the other, they fired a few random shots over the creek which they were to cross and dispersed. The Chew House in rear of the American objective had been barricaded by five companies of British so that no amount of cannonade, torch flame or rifle fire could dislodge the occupants. General Stephens in a drunken condition led his column off the trail and fired into Wayne's troops. Greene, thinking the firing at the Chew House and in his rear was that of the main body of the enemy, withdrew. A general panic and retreat ensued. Washington was glad to collect all his forces at Skippack Creek by nightfall without the loss of his cannons.

The troops of Washington's army so far had begun and ended their open fighting by running. They had scarcely been present long enough as a whole to be trained to do otherwise. The men had no chance to exhibit their natural courage so long as many of their leaders were ill-disciplined. General Conway, for instance, was found, during the action at Germantown, resting in a farmhouse. When asked by two field officers why he was not with his brigade, he mumbled a feeble excuse about the indisposition of his horse.

Oct. 4
1777

While Washington was impotently beating himself away against Howe in the south, Burgoyne's army in the north was streaming down from Canada in an endeavor to join Clinton so as to separate New England from the remainder of the colonies.   Ticonderoga had fallen because Saint Clair had omitted the obvious precaution of seizing a commanding hill. The Americans then retired, leaving no usable article in their wake, so that Burgoyne's army, cutting its way through a denuded wilderness, made slow and difficult progress.

If the British force had been hampered by hardship and disease, the American force had grown thin in addition by desertion.   In August 2 Massachusetts regiments had left the northern camp while Washington was gaining recruits in the south.   Schuyler's force was decreasing to such an extent that only 4,000 troops remained to him, one third of whom were negroes, boys and old men too aged for field service.

Smallpox, too, as well as "inoculation frolics" had wrought fearful havoc.   At that time vaccination was a novel immunity, administered by transmitting the infection from the stricken to the well.   In civil life, where people were healthy and comfortably surrounded, this method of transmission of the disease induced no great amount of mortality.   The doctor's argument, that more died from the epidemic taken in a natural way than from inoculation given while in a healthy condition, seemed to prove itself with the civil population.   But when the malady was transported out of its time to the army, consideration was not given to the wasted, exposed, and emaciated condition of the subject.   With the soldier, shoes, whole breeches, and overcoats were absent quantities, and hunger ever present.   More died from wounds by bacilli than from lead.   The doctors in the field became violent spreaders of contagion rather than skillful guardians of health.   The remedies of quackery of that age, snakeroot, rum and gentian, distilled earthworms, and lukewarm snail-water added not over much to recovery.   In spite of the general's specific orders to the contrary, surgeons so persisted in their pernicious scratchings that they had to be tried by court-martial.

A change in the moral tone of the troops came with the battle at Bennington, Vermont, where in their advance the British had attempted to round up some supplies and had been met and defeated by an overwhelming number of farmers. The victory gave to Schuyler many new recruits. To add to the general revival, Arnold was returning from meeting Saint Leger who had advanced from Oswego to join Burgoyne. By a clever ruse the American commander and his reënforcements had scattered the Canadians, English, and Indians, leaving the valley of the Mohawk cleared of the enemy. His successful 600 would soon lend personal aid to the main body.

Just when Schuyler had successfully built up optimism from depression and was gaining adequate numbers, Congress decided on the brilliant scheme of sending the subtle Gates to take over the northern command. Schuyler received the blow without comment, increased his energies in building up his positions and prepared to meet the enemy descending upon him.

When Gates arrived, although the fruits of victory were ready to be plucked, the new general did his utmost to let them rot on the limb. The American army far outnumbered the British and Kosciusko had skillfully planned the fortifications on Bemis Heights. Nevertheless the British approached the flank of the strong position in such a way as to threaten to enfilade the lines. Gates refused to move, more interested in showing the teamsters an easy way of retreat than in forging ahead into battle. Arnold, realizing the danger of passive resistance, forced his new commander by moral suasion to order the left wing forward. With the expectation of aid to follow, Arnold fell upon the enemy at Freeman's Farm, but was unable to dislodge them. Seeing himself in a disadvantageous position and with no reënforcements, he whirled about and attacked the British center. Even with the odds against him he would have held his own had not British reënforcements arrived. All this time Gates withholding aid from his subordinate had sat behind entrenchments when he could not have helped knowing that his overpowering forces would have routed the British. Even as it was, night fell upon the two armies with more losses to Burgoyne than to Arnold.

Of this engagement Gates sent a report to Congress in which he made no mention of Arnold and his heroic deeds. Schuyler's staff officers having attached themselves to Arnold felt the slight so much that a feud arose which was heightened in bitterness by Gates' inexplicable delay throughout the next eighteen days. Arnold's natural ardor and bravery chafed under such unwarrantable inaction. After one heated argument with his chief he applied for permission to leave the army. When his application was immediately granted, he found himself besought by his officers and men to remain. Gates, however, refused to receive him back so that he occupied a singularly unofficial status without command.

In the meantime Lincoln, after retaking Mount Independence, joined Gates, raising the latter's force to more than twice that of the British. Still Gates sat looking into the distance. *Oct. 8 1777* Burgoyne, who had already set October 12 as his limit of time for holding out, determined to force a passage to Clinton farther down the Hudson. Again he attacked the American left. Unable to bear the sight of the American inaction in the face of such an offensive, Arnold, with fury and without authority, rode at the head of his men, who followed him amid cheers. He drove Burgoyne into his camp, repulsed Balcarras and took a strong redoubt, where he ended a day of heroism and victory by being carried from the field wounded. While all this was happening, Gates in his own tent held ethical discourse with a captured British aide as to the merits of the Revolution.

Following much wrangling, during which Gates had learned of the fall of Fort Montgomery and of the contemplated advance of Clinton and during which Burgoyne was in ignorance of these events, the British surrendered at Saratoga. The *Oct. 17 1777* victory was credited to a hero who was in reality a dilatory weakling. It belonged to an intrepid, skillful leader who afterwards succumbed to treason.

One soldier in his diary wrote his estimate as follows:

"Arnold was a smart man; they didn't serve him quite straight."

Another characterized him thus:

"A bloody fellow he was. He didn't care for nothing; he'd ride right in. It was 'Come on, boys!' twasn't 'Go boys!'—

there wasn't any waste timber in him. He was a stern-looking man but kind to his soldiers. They didn't treat him right—but he ought to have been true."

On the other hand, this remark seems to epitomize another soldier's opinion:

"Gates was an old granny-looking fellow."

This summary seems to be the only surviving camp description of this reclusive warrior.

The country went into hysterics over this first decisive victory. Gates was at once a national hero paramount to all others. Many acclaimed him and denied Washington.

The news of the capture of Burgoyne came as a boon to the ragged, defeated main army at Skippack Creek. The hopes of Washington's command were to a degree revived. But they were also alloyed with the significant knowledge that Howe had *Oct. 19 1777* moved into Philadelphia and, with his 20,000 trained troops, was spending his third winter in another large and luxurious American city, this time the capital of the country. As the cold weather came on, desertions in the Revolutionary ranks grew to large proportions. Washington moved to Whitemarsh, *Dec. 19 1777* where he remained three weeks. Then he sought winter quarters at Valley Forge.

These first lessons in mobility for the army had been hard and discouraging. Trenton, Princeton and Saratoga were the only visible returns of over a year's effort. Though the first two were brilliant, bold strokes, they were candidly but skirmishes having little bearing on the outcome of the war. Saratoga, then, was the single prize of all this grueling. The British effort to cut the country into two parts had been paralyzed, and a large force had been captured.

On the other hand, the troops from overseas had won Long Island, New York, White Plains, Forts Washington and Lee, the Brandywine and Germantown. As a consequence Howe had moved practically when and where his fancy took him.

In the meantime a prosperous people had begrudged its suffering army a miserly support. Its Congress had fussily

pecked at Washington and his following without returning anything palpably constructive.   As a body it had rebuked Stark,
displaced Schuyler, ignored Arnold, cast aspersions on Greene
and Knox, court-martialed Sullivan, Saint Clair, Wayne, and
Matthews because they had lost engagements, and ousted Trumbull, the commissary general, so that shoes and clothing lay
rotting in hogsheads by the roadside undelivered to the needy
troops.   But greatest of all, many of the delegates had plotted
with the coward Conway against Washington himself.   The
majority held Charles Lee and Horatio Gates in the highest
repute and left the main army to work out its own deliverance
at Valley Forge.

CHAPTER III

THE ARMY FINDS DISCIPLINE AND SUCCESS

(1778–1781)

Dec. 19 1777, to June 18 1778

VALLEY FORGE stands as the Gethsemane of American history. It has come to be the national equivalent of vicarious sacrifice. It commonly suggests no other claim for greatness. What hardships our soldiers at other times have endured, and what Valley Forge really accomplished for the United States, are totally eclipsed by records of frozen feet and hungry stomachs close to a comfortable city.

When the British took up winter quarters in Philadelphia, Washington put the hills and the Schuylkill between himself and Howe. His army found itself in an undeveloped, wooded country which was so dense that every effort had to be bent on making it fit for existence. The soldiers at once were set to work to cut fuel and such logs as would do for building. Huts were reared, chinked with mud or clay and thatched with straw. Window openings, usually two in number, were closed with oiled paper. The construction of these rude shelters was arranged so that each regiment reaped the result of its own labor and laid out its own street. The brigades, each having two such streets, stretched beween Trout Creek and Valley Creek in the shape of a wide V whose point was away from the river.

Dec. 20 1777

So scarce was straw, because the farmers refused to haul it, that many roofs were incomplete and many a soldier had to sleep on brush or bare ground. Washington was compelled to issue a proclamation which made it plain to the surrounding population that the grain would be immediately threshed and the straw sold, or the whole would be taken and paid for as straw. Even then it was almost impossible to carry out the

50

threat because of the lack of transportation. Had not soldiers harnessed themselves to carts of their own making, very little provender of any sort would have been brought into the camp.

To the mismanagement and neglect of the lawmakers and to the apathy and defection of a large part of the civilian population can be justly attributed this unnecessary suffering. General Mifflin had resigned as quartermaster general. Congress had waited a month before it acted upon his resignation, and then three months before it appointed a successor. In the meantime horses starved to death by the hundreds, and provisions and clothing lay rotting in many places by the roadside. In Valley Forge there was at one time not a "single hoof of any kind to slaughter, and not more than twenty-five barrels of flour." At another, the army went a week without any kind of flesh to eat. When there was any, it was so poor that one wag among the soldiers declared, when he saw a butcher carrying a hindquarter, that it was so thin he could see the latter's breeches buttons through it. Though Washington issued a proclamation ordering the people to have the cattle fattened, it did little good. The soldier was glad to get meat of any quality. His diet was often fire-cake and water for days at a time. The commander in chief in an appeal for aid stated that the soldiers had scarcely tasted vegetables of any kind, had but little salt or vinegar and no proper drink. Along the line of huts in the evening could be heard the cry, "No meat, no meat!" James Thacher, while speaking with Washington in the camp, heard through the chinks in the logs voices exclaiming, "No pay, no clothes, no provisions, no rum!" The following poem addressed to Washington may or may not in its facetiousness have some underlying truth in it:

Oct. 10 1777

Dec. 22 1777

Feb. 1778

> And for the beef—there needs no puff about it;
> In short, they must content themselves without it,
> Not that we mean to have them starved—why, marry,
> The live stock in abundance, which they carry
> Upon their backs, prevents all fear of that!

Even clothing sufficient to cover officers and men was lacking. Lafayette in his memoirs stated that "the unfortunate soldiers were in want of everything; they had neither coats, nor hats, nor shirts, nor shoes; their feet and legs froze until they grew black, and it was often necessary to amputate them." One old soldier, having received a furlough, had to spend two days in cutting up a blanket from which he made a coat and moccasins so that he might undertake the journey home. On December 23 there were 2,898 men unfit for duty on account of lack of shoes and clothing; on February 5 the number had risen to 3,989.

Officers were no better off than the men. One general [1] stated that he saw officers at a grand parade "mounting guard in a sort of dressing gown made of an old blanket or woolen bed cover." This same general's aides gave a dinner to which only officers who did not possess a whole pair of breeches were invited. Guests were abundant.

Jan.
1778

It was probably due to these conditions that Washington recognized the impractical type of clothing of the time and suggested to Governor Trumbull a woolen double-breasted jacket and overalls or trousers. But any clothing would have been satisfactory to the commander in chief, for he said disgustedly, "Perhaps by midsummer, he (the soldier) may receive thick stockings, shoes, and blankets, which he will contrive to get rid of in the most expeditious manner. In this way, by an eternal round of most stupid management, the public treasure is expended to no kind of purpose, while the men have been left to perish by inches with cold and nakedness."

Camp sanitation, under conditions that were insanitary and with soldiers who were ignorant, was almost unknown. Washington reiterated his orders on cleanliness so often that they appear to have grown customary rather than useful. He showed

March 13
1778

how carcasses of dead horses lay in and near camp, how offal lay unburied near the commissary stalls and how much "filth and nastiness" lay among the huts. To show his appreciation of contrary conditions, he states that "nothing does or can contribute more to the health of soldiers than a clean camp, clean clothes and victuals well-dressed." However, in huts unprovided with chimneys, poorly ventilated and crowded beyond capacity, where the smarting smoke from the cooking mingled

---

[1] Steuben.

with the stench of the unbathed bodies and where the mass of
occupants was suffering with itch and scurvy, it is not surprising that virulent diseases abounded.

Such hardships among undisciplined men were natural
forerunners of every sort of absenteeism. The knowledge that
warm houses contained sleek men with paunches, who spoke
loftily of "the cause" but casually forgot the colonies' defenders,
did not spread a feeling of patient endurance. To a considerable distance from the camp the countryside was filled with *March 3 1778*
straggling soldiery. The death penalty for desertion was rarely
inflicted; and the next heavier, 100 lashes, was in no wise a
deterrent. A Tory stated that 1,134 deserters had come into *March 26 1778*
Philadelphia and given themselves to the enemy.

Passes into the city had to be forbidden. Officers granted *March 15 1778*
leaves and furloughs so promiscuously that Washington was
compelled to arrogate those powers to himself. Through the
loose detached service methods a company's rolls were no indication of who was in camp. In one case where 12 men were
marked "present," they were truthfully accounted for as follows: one, as valet to a commissary, had been 200 miles away
from the army for 18 months; another as valet to a quartermaster, had been absent in the north for 12 months; and the
remainder as drivers of carriages, bakers, blacksmiths, car-
penters and coal porters had been gone for years. Officers
themselves left their organizations on flimsy pretexts and many
were captured through their own folly or carelessness. So, for
one reason or another, Washington's army by March was reduced to 4,000 fit for duty against an enemy of 20,000.

Congress, at a safe distance from possible activities, could
not understand why Washington did not drive the British from
Philadelphia. He was met with everything from mild lack of
confidence to downright abuse. John Adams, who never strayed
far from the comforts of civilization, gave it out that he was
"sick of Fabian systems . . . and weary with so much insipidity."
Such sentiments soon grew to be those of the civilians in general. Few of those in power visited the camp to see for themselves the suffering and dwindling of the little army, and few
others were directly interested in the deplorable conditions
forced on these defenders of liberty. Yet the urge of the "stay-

at-homes" grew apace and by no means increased the morale
of the officer and soldier.

Into this unhappy situation there suddenly came a fortune
as great as it was unforeseen. There was bestowed upon our
ragged troops the greatest gift that they could have received—
the gift of discipline. That automatic obedience to authority,
which transforms crowds into units, had previously been notice-
ably lacking. Its absence had often caused brave men to exhibit themselves as cowards. But now in this dark hour it
fell providentially from the hands of a foreigner so that the
troops began to function as an army, and Valley Forge became
a Pentecost instead of a Gethsemane.

Curious fact! this new stamina was imparted by a Prussian; and more curious still, by a Prussian who, because he
lived before the days of Prussianism, suited the genius of the
American soldier exactly. Lafayette had brought zeal, soldiers
and money, but von Steuben brought efficiency, an efficiency he
tempered with energy, tact and kindness.

We must remember that von Steuben had come from the
court of the great Frederick, the Frederick who despised the
German tongue and persisted in employing French customs and
language exclusively. Von Steuben had been an aide on that
versatile leader's staff. He combined the thoroughness of German drill and training with French adroitness and imagination.

Dec.
1777

He told Congress that he had come to serve "a nation engaged in the noble enterprise of defending its rights and liberties." He asked only to have his necessary expenses de-
frayed while in the service and to be reimbursed for the loss
of his own income only in case the cause was successful.

Feb. 23
1778

On arrival at Valley Forge he was shocked to see the distress of the forces. He was surprised to find no uniform drill,
no similarity of organization and no team work of any kind.
He observed afterwards that he had found more quartermasters
and commissaries in the camp than in all the armies of Europe
together.

In spite of the fact that his French cook took French leave
the minute the kitchen facilities—one camp kettle under a tree
—were pointed out, and that the Baron was compelled from
then on to lead a life of Spartan frugality and discomfort, he

set in motion at once the business of organization, discipline and training. For Washington, having recognized Steuben's particular merits, had not waited for Congress to act but had immediately appointed him as inspector.

Rising at three in the morning, smoking his pipe and drinking his cup of coffee, Steuben proceeded to the parade ground, where he personally taught drill movements. He would illustrate the manual of arms by using the musket in his own hands. Such a democratic demonstration shocked the higher officers who were still imbued with the British idea of aristocratic aloofness. But Steuben's tact and his sensible dealings made even the cavalier see the fruitlessness of trusting everything to the noncommissioned men. Steuben forced the discovery that in a country where caste is obnoxious an officer must gain results by more direct means. Accordingly there was established that dignified contact between officer and soldier wherein respect is engendered by fairness and ability.

At first the new inspector was particularly struck with the attitude of the officers. He said "the captains and colonels did not consider their companies and regiments as corps confided to them by the United States for the care of the men as well as the preservation of order and discipline. The idea they had of their duty was that the officers had only to mount guard and put themselves at the head of their regiment or company when they were going into action." He forthwith organized the officers into squads, sections and companies for drill under his personal direction. In this way he raised up an excellent corps of instructors. Some time after this plan had been in operation he beheld a colonel instructing a recruit, whereupon he exclaimed, "I thank God for that!"

He was instrumental in having a guard of honor for the commander in chief augmented. The order is significant.

"Headquarters, Valley Forge,
"March 17, 1778.

"One hundred chosen men are to be annexed to the guard of the commander in chief, for the purpose of forming a corps, to be instructed in the maneuvers necessary to be introduced into the army, and to serve as a model for the execution of them.   As the general's guard is composed of Virginians, the hundred draughts will be taken from the troops of the other states.

"Description of the men.

"Height, from 5 feet 8 to 5 feet 10 inches; age, from twenty to thirty years; robust constitution, well limbed, formed for activity, and men of established character for sobriety and fidelity.   They must be Americans born."

Taking particular pains with these, Steuben succeeded in presenting to the whole army a concrete example of the proper evolutions.   Since drill then was the largest part of the training, the service performed shed its helpful influence on many later military events.

His drill regulations show his good sense and humanity. On them are based all subsequent ones in our service, and by them long-needed exercises were put in vogue for the first time. He reduced the number of motions for loading to fifteen.   He prescribed a uniformity of arms and accouterments throughout the army.   He formed the "company in two ranks at one pace distance, with the tallest men in rear" . . . and "the shortest men in the center."   He divided the company into two sections or platoons and the regiment into eight companies.   He split regiments of more than 160 privates into two battalions.   He assigned to the flank companies the most experienced officers actually present with these units.[2]   He established such a sensible "position of the soldier without arms" that for hygienic reasons alone many of its features might with advantage be used to-day.   "He (the soldier) is to stand straight and firm

---

[2] The order from right to left was: first captain, colonel, fourth captain, major, third captain, lieutenant colonel, fifth captain, second captain.

The establishment of 1778 allowed to each battalion of infantry 477 privates with pay at $6.66 per month; artillery, 336 matrosses at $8.33 per month; cavalry, 324 dragoons, $8.33 per month; provost, 43 provosts or privates, $8.33 per month; three companies in the engineering department, each to have sixty privates at $8.33 per month.   A regiment of infantry had 1 colonel (who was also a captain), 1 lieutenant colonel (also captain), 1 major (also captain), 6 captains, paymaster, adjutant, quartermaster, 1 surgeon, 1 surgeon's mate, 8 lieutenants, 9 ensigns, 1 sergeant major, 1 quartermaster sergeant, 27 sergeants, 1 captain lieutenant (over the colonel's company), 1 drum major, 1 fife major, 18 drums and fifes, 27 corporals, 477 privates: in all 585.

upon his legs, with his head turned to the right so far as to bring the left eye over the waistcoat buttons; the heels two inches apart; the toes turned out; the belly drawn in a little, but without constraint; the breast a little projected; the shoulders square to the front and kept back, the hands hanging down to the sides, with the palms close to the thighs." He introduced a "common" step of 24 inches and a cadence of 75 to the minute, which seemed to suit the rugged country, the heavy accouterments, the dense lines and slow firing with which the soldier then struggled.

The march in general had been limited to crude formations in line and column of files. Steuben not only made these movements uniform, but added the column of platoons, thus lessening the unnecessary length of road space for tactical movement and the opportunity for straggling.[3] He caused the platoon to wheel much as it does now in "platoon right" and to execute the "oblique step" in order to break from, and form, company. The latter was a curious sidling movement in which the soldier stepped off to the right or left oblique while he kept his "shoulders square to the front." But the evolutions themselves were quite simple. For instance, at the preparatory command, "Take care to display column to the left," all understood that the column of platoons was to form line to the left front. At the second command, "To the left—face!" all except the leading platoon faced to the left. At the third command, "March!" all the rear platoons obliqued to their places where their commanders halted them and dressed them to the right. The sagacity with which he made every man in ranks an integral part of the drill is illustrated by the way he discarded sole dependence upon music or the beat of the drum, and made each individual soldier responsible that he regulated his march by watching the gait of the officer or element in front of the platoon. Whenever there was no such officer or element, a sergeant was to be placed six paces to the front. Such were some of the sensible drill movements (which in those days were battle movements also) that Steuben found useful.

Knowing, however, that drill was valueless without the

---

3 Marching and wheeling by fours or squads did not come into vogue until many years later, after the Civil War.

discipline of daily routine, he went minutely into field and company administration. He prescribed that troops should camp by battalions. He allowed sinks to be dug no nearer to occupied tents than 300 feet. He charged field officers with seeing that their camps were pitched regularly and properly, especially that kitchens and sinks were put in sanitary places. He outlined methods of getting wood and water by means of an organized system of signals and formations. He established roll calls of "troop" and "retreat" under arms and the "reveille" and "noon" without arms. He charged the noncommissioned officers with the making of an accurate check of their squads at tattoo to see that the men were in bed. At the "troop beating" he required company officers to "inspect into the dress of their men," to "see that the clothes are whole and put on properly, their (the soldiers') hands and faces washed clean, their hair combed, their accouterments properly fixed and every article about them in the greatest order." He inaugurated the Saturday-morning inspection which the captains were to conduct for their individual companies in order to "examine into the state of the men's necessaries."

If his technic was simple and fitting, his application of it was just and human.

Let us quote from his regulations, in use at Valley Forge, and afterwards published in 1779 under the authority of Congress, the first standard set of regulations for our army:

INSTRUCTIONS FOR THE CAPTAIN

A Captain cannot be too careful of the company the state has committed to his charge. He must pay the greatest attention to the health of his men, their discipline, arms, accouterments, ammunition, clothes and necessaries.

His first object should be to gain the love of his men by treating them with every possible kindness and humanity, inquiring into their complaints, and when well founded, seeing them redressed. He should know every man of his company by name and character. He should often visit those who are sick, speak tenderly to them, see that the public provision, whether of medicine or diet, is duly administered, and procure them besides such comforts and conveniences as are in his power. The attachment that arises from this kind of attention to the sick and wounded is almost inconceivable; it will, moreover, be the means of preserving the lives of many valuable men.

INSTRUCTIONS FOR THE LIEUTENANT

He should endeavor to gain the love of his men, by his attention to everything which may contribute to their health and convenience. He should often visit them at different hours; inspect into their manner of living; see that their provisions are good and well cooked, and as far as possible oblige them to take their meals at regulated hours. He should pay attention to their complaints, and when well founded, endeavor to get them redressed; but discourage them from complaining on every frivolous occasion.

INSTRUCTIONS FOR THE ENSIGN

The ensign is in a particular manner charged with the cleanliness of the men, to which he must pay the greatest attention.

When the company parades, and whilst the captain and lieutenant are examining the arms and accouterments, the ensign must inspect the dress of the soldiers, observing whether they are clean, and everything about them in the best order possible, and duly noticing any who in these respects are deficient.

He must be very attentive to the conduct of the noncommissioned officers, observing that they do their duty with the greatest exactness; that they support a proper authority, and at the same time do not ill treat the men through any pique or resentment.

Here is the golden text of all leadership—his *"first object should be to gain the love* of his men by treating them with *every possible kindness and humanity."* Such consideration

Steuben immediately couples with the duty of infinite care of the company that the state has committed to the charge of the captain.   Then the vital advice of individual treatment—of knowing every man by *name and character*—is all too well understood by any one who has ever attempted to handle manhood in the mass.   And finally the special visitation of the sick rounds out the thoughtful attitude a company officer should school himself to employ.   When analyzed, this simple paragraph spells self-control, high sense of duty, fidelity of performance and loyalty to the inferior as well as to the superior.

Knowing full well that the captain could not, without specific help, bring his company up to standard, Steuben assigned the subalterns particular tasks.   The lieutenant was to be zealous in regard to the "health and convenience" of the soldier, and the ensign in regard to "neatness and cleanliness." Steuben here discreetly laid emphasis on the development of self-respect and pride, qualities which are the leading strings of success.   Then he capped the whole by setting a check upon ill treatment which arises through "pique or resentment."   Understanding how partiality and prejudice may be the ruin of discipline, he closed his instructions by putting a special guard on that sort of injustice.

Steuben spent much time in developing a keen sense of responsibility in the company officer in comparison to that of the field and general officer.   He knew that if the individual soldier had affection and regard for his immediate leaders, the higher commands would take care of themselves.   He realized that the pride and bearing of the rank and file were the keynotes to achievements in the field, as was demonstrated many times in the World War.

Could any set of instructions more grippingly embrace the essentials of discipline?   Have so few words ever more perfectly tempered kindness with justice and balanced rule and appeal?   By following these simple principles, could not any body of men, whether soldier or civilian, be directed without friction?   Why, then, were these doctrines omitted from later regulations?   Why did they have to be ferreted out from a dusty volume whose leaves were yellowed with age and whose print was in old script with its "s's" that looked like "f's"?

Painted from life by Ralph Earl.
Courtesy of William M. Austin, New York City.

Frederick von Steuben

Mainly because training, as we shall see, was discarded for a long time after the Revolution, did the true picture of Steuben grow indistinct. Naturally only the rigors of necessary discipline were remembered in connection with him. He has thus been tabled in later years as a hard taskmaster. Legislators have held his work up to contempt in that he early molded our army into Prussian inflexibility. The substance of such an attitude seems to rest on the fact that he hailed from Prussia. By the same argument objection was once made to Christ on the ground that he came from Nazareth. Writers and speakers have been erroneously thankful that the army has survived Steuben's hard lines whereas, in truth, he brought us up out of unsuitable aristocracy, unspeakable chaos and, above all, the misuse of authority. He knew that leading was better than driving and he proved that his human methods were practical and successful.

That he followed his own advice is shown by many instances. For example, once after Arnold's treason, when Steuben was standing by listening to the roll call of a company, he heard a man answer to the name of Arnold. Promptly inviting the soldier to his tent, the baron told the private that he was too good a man to bear a traitor's name, whereupon he gave him permission to be known as Steuben.

Due to such painstaking care and labor, the festering camp began to take on the semblance of order and organization in spite of the lack of supplies. Disease was lessened. Arms remained with the colors.[4] Soldiers on detached service as servants were returned to the fighting force. Officers began to father their organizations. The human touch, zeal and dignity that have since characterized the best American leaders became noticeable. Troops began to be complimented in orders on their drill. By taking the attitude that the "indifferent *April 14* quality of clothing instead of excusing slovenliness and unsol- *1778* dierly conduct, ought rather" to excite each man to compensate for those deficiencies by redoubled attention to his personal appearance, Steuben was successful in building morale upon less than nothing.

----

[4] During the next year, 1779, only twenty firelocks disappeared in contrast to the thousands missing before Steuben came.

So a foreigner with such a thick brogue that he was largely unintelligible, against odds of national and provincial jealousy and notwithstanding the powerful calumny that was usually heaped upon the efficient friends of Washington, earned a substantial reputation. His work could not be ignored. Congress was morally forced to recognize him. Accordingly Washington's orders one day announced to the camp that von Steuben had been made a major general and inspector general of the army.

May 9
1778

We are soon to see some of the direct effects of his efforts.

The spirits of the little army that strove with its emaciated self in pitiful efforts at training were unexpectedly raised by the news of the French Alliance. Washington proclaimed a holiday. The ragged, but clean, soldiers had a chance to show on parade their new and well-acquired maneuvers. The commander in chief dined in public with his officers; cannons were discharged, fusees were fired, toasts were drunk and huzzas were given by the officers and men with great ceremony. The form and precision here displayed heightened the pride of corps throughout the rank and file.

May 6
1778

May 18
1778

Out of this alliance came the necessity of giving Lafayette a command, for which he had been constantly begging. Washington assigned him 2,500 picked men ostensibly for the purpose of conducting a reconnaissance toward Philadelphia. At Barren Hill this small but vital American force found itself completely surrounded by an overwhelming number of British. The only means of possible escape was the apparently impassable Schuylkill in the patriots' rear. A ford, however, was accidentally discovered over which the troops would have to pass rapidly while pressed by the enemy. This highly difficult crossing was to be a test of discipline in the American soldiers. As a matter of fact, they were formed by their officers without hesitation or confusion, were marched across the stream without crowding and were well on the way before the British discovered the escape. The drill and training acquired under Steuben were chiefly accountable for the survival of Lafayette and his command.

With the coming of spring and the prospect of help there came internal relief for the army. Food and clothing grew better, almost sufficient. Greene, at the solicitation of a com· mittee from Congress, had been appointed quartermaster-general to succeed Mifflin.[5] Jeremiah Wadsworth had, in addition, been made commissary general. Their services were efficient, though Congress and the country accused them of extravagance. The troops fared for over a year following their appointment better than at any time previous, and there were fewer recorded complaints. As Washington had predicted, summer saw the soldier at last provided with heavy clothing.

When Howe decided to sail back to England without hurting the American army in the field and Clinton relinquished Philadelphia, Washington, leaving Arnold in that city, pursued the British through New Jersey. Having now the usual increase of "sunshine patriots" he outnumbered the enemy by 1,000. At Monmouth Court House the advance guard of the *June 28 1778* Americans came upon the rear guard of the British. Washington ordered Lee to attack with the hope of getting the enemy's wagon train. Evidently through jealousy or defection Lee not only failed to carry out his commander's intentions, but was actively responsible for the breaking up of the troops and their retirement to the rear. Although they were pursued by the British and, through lack of proper leadership, retreated in more or less disorder, nevertheless they were capable of being reformed quickly into a proper battle line, after what would formerly have been a demoralizing retreat. Again the work of Steuben became the deciding factor. The Americans having rallied, drove off the British. But the defeat of Clinton's forces was impossible, because the day had been cleverly wasted by Lee. The enemy slipped away under cover of darkness to New, York. The temperature throughout the action had been very high, reaching, some say, ninety-six, so that there were more casualties from the heat than from firearms. Soldiers were found dead without a mark on them. In the north this was the last general engagement of the war, because the British were too strong for Washington to take the offensive again. But the action showed that the American troops with a fair amount of discipline and training and against nearly an equal force, could give a good account of themselves.

---

5 Greene was allowed to retain his line commission.

The next attempted offensive in New England was conspicuously impotent. General Sullivan had collected 10,000 New England militia and untrained troops for the purpose of taking Newport. Washington, besides, had sent him Lafayette with 2,000 men and allowed him 4,000 French troops. With a force between 13,000 and 15,000 he was to overwhelm the British garrison of 6,000. When he moved over to Butts' hill a storm tore down the tents, killed some horses, wet the powder and discomfited the men. Many of the militia forthwith went home. Finally Sullivan began the investment of the city. But the French fleet refused to coöperate, whereupon the militia deserted so fast that Sullivan and Greene [6] felt they would soon have no force at all. Sullivan retreated to Butts' hill where the British attacked. The remaining Americans, among whom was a black regiment under Colonel Christopher Greene, fought well from behind earthworks; but they finally had to withdraw from the island.

In the "far west" near Pittsburgh another part of the army, though small, was preparing to do a great service for the country. Lieutenant Colonel George Rogers Clark, with 150 men, set out to take what are now Kentucky, Illinois and parts of Michigan, Indiana and Ohio away from the British, hostile Indians and the French. After hardships, similar to those of Arnold in his march to Quebec and far worse than those of Valley Forge, Clark succeeded in capturing Kastaskia without bloodshed. When 80 men left him because of the expiration of their enlistments, he simply recruited young Frenchmen of the neighborhood and hung on. By a combination of apt arrogance and soft words that prevented a struggle, he won over the whole of the Illinois country, including Vincennes. Although that town was shortly retaken by a superior force of British, he made an unexpected winter march, and by a well-planned attack with exhausted troops recaptured the place. After reading Roosevelt's *Winning of the West* one is convinced that this little campaign ranks as a combination of suffering and daring ahead of anything of the kind in history. For these men moved to their goal so fast that huts were impossible. The harsh winter

Aug. 15 1778

Aug. 20 1778

Aug. 29 1778

July 4 1778

Feb. 25 1779

---

[6] General Nathaniel Greene.

found them digging fresh holes in the snow each night, caught them often advancing waist-high in mud and ice water for hours at a time, and saw them ever alive to the terror of the lurking tomahawk.   Clark finally won the "Old Northwest" for the United States, and was promoted to the grade of brigadier general.

The Indian massacres in northern Pennsylvania and south- *July 3–Nov. 11 1778* ern New York drew other expeditions.   General Sullivan with 2,500 men moved up from Easton, Pennsylvania, along the Susquehanna to Elmira, New York.   At the same time he sent *July 1779* Colonel Brodhead with 600 men up the Allegheny from Pittsburg and General James Clinton with 1,500 men along the Mohawk Valley and the upper reaches of the Susquehanna. The purpose was that of terrorizing the Indians and destroying their crops, villages and warriors.   It was felt that the protection of the settlers had to be gained at any cost, so that women and children among the redskins sometimes suffered the fate of the men.   Such a mission was distasteful to the officers and baneful to the soldiers.   The callous coating left upon the patriot's mind is revealed by an incident quoted from a lieutenant's diary:

"At the request of Major P——, sent out a small detachment to look for some dead Indians—returned without finding them.   Toward morning they found them and skinned two of them from their hips down for boot-legs, one pair for the Major, the other for myself."

The object was achieved with great thoroughness.   Sullivan's army returned to New Jersey after a difficult march of *Oct. 1779* over 700 miles.

After Monmouth the main army took up winter quarters at White Plains.   Later Washington placed 7 brigades at Middle- *Nov. 1778* brook and Elizabethtown and 6 at West Point.   This winter, due to its mildness and to Greene and Wadsworth, seems to have found the army in better condition with regard to clothing, food and shelter than ever before.   But the soldiers were ragged, and officers in general were in a destitute condition. Congress did not gain many recruits by allowing Washington to offer secretly $10 extra bounty. Those who left the army, even after the bounty of $80 and half pay for seven years (that Congress had previously offered and that the soldier rarely got) did not give glowing accounts of their military life. The militia went home to find that the civilian did not feel the war at all. It was this splendid heedlessness on the part of the public rather than the hardship of camp that disgusted the soldier. Washington said in a letter to Harrison:

"If I were to be called upon to draw a picture of the times and of the men, from what I have seen, heard, and in part know, I should in one word say that idleness, dissipation and extravagance seem to have laid fast hold of most of them; that speculation, peculation and an insatiable thirst for riches seem to have got the better of every other consideration, and almost every order of men."

Naturally the patriot said, "Why should I suffer and die for such people?" Had the states actually given good food and clothing, recruiting would have been successful without any bounty. As it was, the country profiteered, bankrupted itself and gave Washington no proper force.

In the south, the taking of Savannah by the British did not raise the spirits of the army. After that occupation, Lincoln took command in Charleston. With about 3,600 ill-disciplined men the new southern commander tried to advance to the Savannah River. But his force, made up principally of raw recruits, fled whenever hardship or the enemy were to be encountered and in those dense regions became disorganized raiding parties. In minor engagements Colonel Moultrie drove off the British from Port Royal Island and Colonel Pickens scat-

tered some loyalist guerrillas. When Lincoln moved on Augusta, his 1,500 troops under General Ashe were surrounded by the British and practically annihilated. Reënforced by fresh

militia, Lincoln continued his advance. But the English crossed the Savannah and drove Moultrie back to Charleston, who seems to have had a difficult time in keeping the enemy from getting the city. The following extract from one of his

letters throws light on some of his experiences:

"As the enemy was so near, I was desiring one of my aides to go and bring off our rear guard from Coosohatchie to join us immediately; but Colonel John Laurens (who joined me two days before) being present, he requested me to permit him to go on that service; which I readily consented to, thinking him to be a brave and experienced officer; I told him at the same time that I would send 150 good riflemen to cover his flanks, lest the enemy should be too close upon him; I accordingly sent Capt. James with one hundred and fifty picked men, and 100 men of the out piquet to join him; these altogether made a body of 350 men, which was one-fourth of my little army; but instead of Colonel Laurens' bringing off the guard, as he was desired, he very imprudently crossed the river to the east side; and drew them up on the opposite bank of the river, taking those 150 who were sent to cover his flanks, and the 100 men of the out piquet and joined them to the guard; while he left the houses on the hill for the British to occupy; in this situation did he expose his men to the fire, without the least chance of doing them any injury; after remaining some time he got a number of men killed and wounded; and was wounded himself; he desired Capt. Shubrick, who commanded after he left the field, to stay a little longer and then to bring off the men; had not Capt. Shubrick moved off at the very instant that he did, his party would have been cut off from their retreat and every man of them would either have been killed or taken prisoner; we heard the firing very distinctly at Tullifiny, and supposed it was our retreating guard coming in; but presently Col. Laurens came up to me, wounded in the arm; I said to him: 'Well, Colonel, what do you think of it?' 'Why, sir,' said he, 'your men won't stand.' Upon which I said; 'If that be the case I will retreat.' "

Between official ignorance and troop inconstancy General Moultrie had his troubles. His resolution and thrift, however, saved the city. Then the southern army went into summer quarters at Sheldon.

In the north, Washington, on account of the dearth of everything needful for campaign, could undertake but desultory offensives. Wayne with a small force and rare bravery cap- *July 16 1779*

Aug. 19
1779

tured Stony Point with the bayonet. But Clinton with a superior force later took it back. Then "Light Horse Harry Lee" [7] captured 200 of the enemy at Paulus Hook where Jersey City now stands, and the military work in the north was ended.

Sept. 23
1779

In the south D'Estaing suddenly appeared off Savannah and began a siege of that city. Lincoln joined him in these operations. When the French commander found that he had to put to sea, a premature assault was decided upon. But the British, having been apprised by a deserter of the plans of the allies, drove them off with great loss. What was left of the little southern army made its way safely across the river, but the whole of the country south of Charleston passed into the hands of the British.

Oct. 8
1779

Oct. 19
1779

Sept. 18
1779

The main army in the north was again ill-supplied with clothing. Congress recommended to the states that they provide clothes for their own soldiers, and voted to the officers one "suit" consisting of one hat, one watch coat, one body coat, four vests, four pairs of breeches, four shirts, four stocks, six pairs of stockings and four pairs of shoes. But this pretentious outfit was not provided. Later, clothing arrived from France but there was not enough. General Glover wrote:

Nov. 25
1779

"The whole army has gone into winter cantonments excepting General Nixon's and my brigades, who are now in the field (eight hundred of my men without shoe or stocking) enjoying the sweets of a winter campaign while the worthy and virtuous citizens of America are enduring the hardships, toils and fatigues incident to parlors with good fires and sleeping on beds of down."

Nov. 18
1779

Although Congress had offered $200 to a recruit to enlist for the period of the war, and one of the states had reached $750, a suit of clothes once a year and 100 acres of land, Washington's force scarcely totaled 26,000 effectives. He himself says:

"That of this number, comprehending four hundred and ten invalids, fourteen thousand nine hundred and ninety-eight

---

[7] The father of Robert E. Lee.

are stated as engaged for the war; that the remainder by the expiration of enlistments, will be decreased by the 31st of December, two thousand and fifty-one; by the last of March, six thousand four hundred and twenty-six; by the last of April, eight thousand one hundred and eighty-one; by the last of June, ten thousand one hundred and fifty-eight—and shortly after twelve thousand one hundred and fifty-seven."

This winter was spent by the main army at Morristown, *1779–1780* New Jersey. For suffering it was worse than Valley Forge. The pay was far in arrears. A large proportion of soldiers had no suitable covering at night and often the whole army went for five or six days without even bread. The cold was so severe that for forty days at the other camp near West Point no water dripped from the roofs.

While the northern troops were suffering at Morristown and West Point the southern troops were being pressed in campaign. *Feb. 11* Sir Henry Clinton with Cornwallis and 10,000 men landed *1780* from New York below Charleston. The little force of American regulars and volunteers in that city should have tried to escape and save itself. But Lincoln, not realizing his power- *April 11* lessness, as one more skilled in the art of war might have done, *1780* let himself be surrounded. When Fort Moultrie fell, he saw *May 12* that it was useless to hold out and surrendered the city with *1780* 5,000 men. The entire south now belonged to the enemy.

There the colonists confined themselves to partisan strife. Sumter on the Catawba and Broad rivers, Marion among the Peedee swamps and Pickens and Clark along the Saluda made a predatory warfare on all Tories. The actions were bloody and useless.

In the meantime Knyphausen in the north, having been left in command of New York by Clinton when the latter went south, misinterpreted the attitude of mind of the impoverished American soldier. He crossed into New Jersey in the hope of *June 6* winning over some of the army at Morristown by promises of *1780* comfort. But the Whig patriot was not so easily influenced. Although he might grumble at a greedy and neglectful populace that would cheerily let him starve, he despised the Tory with an ingrained hatred. Accordingly the militia all along Knyphausen's march made it very uncomfortable for the British so that he was forced to return to New York.

June 23
1780

When Clinton arrived back from Charleston and heard of the fate of Knyphausen's expedition, he himself determined to attack Morristown. Greene, however, blocked the roads so successfully when the British approached the town, that he stemmed the advance. Although he was finally forced to retire, the American troops acted with such precision that Clinton had to content himself with the burning of Springfield and to return to New York. Here again was a recovery due mainly to the teaching of Steuben.

A new commander in the south was necessary since the fall of Charleston. Washington desired Greene to have the post, but Congress appointed Gates, "the hero of Saratoga." The

July 25
1780

new commander took over a force of about 2,300 men at Hillsboro that had been operating under De Kalb. Of these, 900 had never been in action and were ignorant of the use of bayonets.

Aug. 13
1780

Gates sat still for a couple of days until Cornwallis had time to reënforce Rawdon and then set out to meet the enemy. The forces engaged near Camden. Gates seems to have made no reconnaissance, no estimate and no definite plan. He allowed the poorest militia to be placed opposite the best trained veterans of the British. It was natural that the former fled at the first onset and thereby left the American regulars to be cut to pieces in their tracks. Gates disappeared so fast that he reached Charlotte sixty miles away that night. The smaller British force had killed, wounded and captured about 2,000 Americans, whereas it had lost barely 300. This battle or rout was the most disgraceful defeat of the war. The Revolutionary southern army had vanished.

The northern army in the vicinity of Tappan, N. Y. (near the New Jersey state line), had practically evaporated also. Not only had the expiration of enlistments taken place, as Washington had foretold, but the men had deserted by the hundreds, many to the British. In addition to the few regulars

Oct.
1780

trained under Steuben, only that militia which came out solely to protect its own fireside remained. This small band had so little to eat that it practically had to live off the country.

The following order issued in another northern camp reveals

the pathetic attempt of the remnants to preserve order and discipline in the face of the last act of the tragedy of this dark year.

"Headquarters,
"Orange Town, Sept. 26, 1780.

"The truly martial appearance of the Troops yesterday, the order and regularity with which they made the different marches, and the facility with which they perform'd the several manoeuvers, do them the greatest credit, and open the most flattering prospect of substantial service to the country, and military glory to the Army.

"Nothing can be more pleasing to the Officers who feel for the honor of the Army, and the Independence of America, than to see the rapid progress which has been made by the Troops in military discipline. The good conduct of all the officers yesterday, gave the Gen'l the highest satisfaction and the particular service of the Inspector-General,[8] and those in that line, deserve his especial thanks.

"Treason of the Blackest Dye was yesterday discovered. General Arnold, who commands at West Point, lost to every sentiment of honor, of private and public obligation, was about to deliver up that important Post into the hands of the enemy. Such an event must have given the American cause a deadly wound.—Happily the Treason was discover'd in time to prevent this fatal mischief. The providential train of circumstances which led to it, affords the most convincing proof that the Liberties of America are the object of Divine Protection. Our enemies, despairing of carrying their point by force, are practising every base art to effect, by bribery and corruption, what they cannot accomplish in a manly way.

"Great honor is due to the American Army that this is the first instance of Treason of the kind, where many were to have been expected from the nature of the dispute; and nothing more brightly ornaments its character, than the firm resistance with which it has constantly met the seductions of an insidious enemy. Arnold has made his escape to the enemy; but Mr.

---

[8] Von Steuben.

Andre, the Adjutant-General of the British Army, who came out as a spy to negotiate the business, is our Prisoner!

"His Excellency the Commander in Chief has arriv'd at West Point from Hartford, and is no doubt taking the proper measures to unravel fully so Hellish a plot."

Oct. 7 1780

The letters of Washington and the French officers show that they despaired at this time of the independence of the states. The only redeeming feature of the year was the partisan battle of King's Mountain in the south. Campbell, McDowell, Shelby and Sevier surrounded Ferguson and killed, wounded and captured about 900 with little Whig loss. But this small affair was little compensation for the fall of Charleston, the defeat of Camden, the plunder of the country, the treason of Arnold and the lack of an army.

Sept. 30 1780

Dec. 2 1780

Nevertheless the war had to be pressed in the south or the southern states would be lost. Greene, who had resigned as quartermaster-general,[9] on account of new organization which permitted corruption, was sent to succeed Gates. He took command of 2,300 men at Charlotte, 1,100 of whom were regulars. All the wagons had been lost, there was not a dollar in gold in the whole force and the naked soldiers were living after the manner of animals. But if his army was worn down and he was confronted by Cornwallis, Rawdon, and Tarleton, he yet had Steuben, Morgan and Kosciusko to depend upon.

Jan. 1 1781

While Greene was trying to bring the southern military patient to life, the remnants of the northern army were trying to reconcile the inequality of the bounty, the complete absence of pay and the utter contempt for the soldiers' agonies. Some states were offering as high as $1,000 per man over the sum provided by Congress. Such lavishness gave to the unstable militiaman, who served only for a short time, almost a fortune in contrast to the pittance allowed but seldom given to the Continental who stayed on year after year and suffered all manner of tortures. Accordingly, six regiments of the Pennsylvania line reached the limit of their endurance. Instead of deserting as the militia had done, they rose to press their long series of grievances.

---

[9] Timothy Pickering, President of the Board of War, succeeded him.

After an officer had been killed in the attempt to restore order, the rioters marched toward Princeton with an "astonishing regularity and discipline." Wayne, who was in command at Morristown, was allowed to accompany them. Congressional representatives finally pacified them by promising to make up the arrears in pay, and to give each soldier a pair of shoes, overalls and a shirt. That the legislators felt themselves properly on the defensive is shown by the fact that they readily agreed to bring no one to trial for the outbreak.

The mutineers refused to accept bribes from General Clinton who offered them every consideration if they would come into the British service, but rather gave his representatives up to be shot as spies.

At this time the reduction of the Continental army and its *Jan. 1* reorganization went into effect. Just when soldiers of this *1781* character were most pressingly needed, Congress through lack of funds was forced to cut down their number. Officers were to choose among themselves who should be retired. The establishment was to consist of "4 regiments of mounted and dismounted dragoons, or legionary corps; 4 regiments of artillery; 49 regiments of infantry;—and 1 regiment of artificers." An infantry regiment was to consist of 612 files, exclusive of officers, sergeants and musicians. The officers displaced as well as those who remained were to have half pay [10] for life.

The New Jersey line, hearing of the apparent success of the *Jan. 20* Pennsylvanians, decided to mutiny also. One night at Pomp- *1781* ton Colonel Shreve, suspecting their feelings, ordered his men to fall in, but only a few obeyed him. They then marched toward Chatham and after having much debate with the state commissioners, returned to Pompton. In the meantime, the American General Howe with his brigade had arrived by Wash- *Jan. 27* ington's order from West Point. At daybreak the mutineers *1781* found themselves surrounded. Howe ordered them into ranks without arms, executed two of the leaders on the spot, rebuked the rest and the mutiny was over.

While the northern army was in the throes of organization and disorganization, some of Greene's troops were having

---

[10] This they never received. But Greene was successful in having some of the ousted ones placed in command of militia organizations.

activity in the south. Cornwallis sent Tarleton to capture Morgan's inferior force which at this time was separated from Greene. Morgan took up a position near Hannah's Cowpens with an unfordable river in his rear. This curious selection he explained as follows:

"I would not have a swamp in the view of my militia on any consideration; they would have made for it and nothing could have detained them from it.—As to retreat, it is the very thing I wished to cut off all hope of. I would have thanked Tarleton had he surrounded me with his cavalry. It would have been better than placing my own men in the rear to shoot down those who broke from the ranks. When men are forced to fight they will sell themselves dearly."

This true hero of Saratoga had learned to know the militia. He placed the really raw ones very far in front and told them that all he expected of them was to fire two volleys. Then they could run as usual and as they would do anyway, but they must run in a certain direction around the flanks. He showed them the path they should follow and warned them not to disturb the good regulars in rear. Then he apprised the remaining troops of the outlined flight so that there would be no misunderstanding as to its meaning. The militia did not quite get through with their volleys but they did go where they were told and formed again in time to help complete the discomfiture of Tarleton.

Jan. 17
1781

This ingenious adaptation of tactics to human weaknesses caught the superior British force between two fires and completely routed it. Out of its total of 1,150 men, 784 were killed, wounded or captured against 11 Americans killed and 61 wounded. Tarleton himself barely escaped with his life.

Congress was forced to recognize Morgan [11] with a medal.

March 16
1781

Greene at this time was following Cornwallis whom he met later at Guilford Court House (Greensboro, N. C.). The southern army of 4,400 men was composed of raw militia and

---

[11] At Saratoga, Morgan had been as brave and successful as Arnold. But Congress had treated him almost as badly as the latter.

of regulars who had never been in action. Greene's dispositions were similar to those of Morgan just described, but Cornwallis fought more carefully than Tarleton and Greene's troops were physically and mentally poor. The battle lasted five hours with much slaughter on both sides. During the long strain many Americans dropped exhausted from lack of food. Greene himself fainted when the action was all over.

Although it was an apparent victory for the British, Greene pursued the victor until the Virginia militia refused to go any further because their time had expired.

In the meantime Lafayette, whom Congress had assigned *Feb.* *1781* the task of capturing Arnold, had been marching his 1,200 American veterans up the Delaware and down again in the hope of seizing his prey. In one of his marches north, Washington gave him command of the army of Virginia which had lately been made and put under Steuben. Before going south to take over that force, Lafayette put shoes and clothing on his men by *April 29* *1781* issuing drafts on the French treasury. When he arrived in Richmond, he found the Virginia army in a good state of discipline under Steuben who placed himself under his youthful commander's orders without hesitation and with the utmost loyalty. But Lafayette's command, although good in quality, was so small that it had to spend its time during the summer in dodging the strong British forces.

Greene, farther south, fought an indecisive action with *April 18* *1781* Rawdon at Hobkirk's Hill. Marion, "Harry" Lee and Sumter managed to drive the British out of the up-country of the Carolinas with the exception of Ninety-six, which Greene besieged. *April 23* *1781* When Rawdon brought British reënforcements, Greene had to raise the siege and take his men into summer quarters on the High Hills of the Santee. The heat now was too intense for either army.

Because Lafayette's force was "not strong enough even to be *Aug.* *1781* beaten," he could be well pleased at his success in merely keeping out of the way of Cornwallis. But when that British commander retired to Williamsburg and later to Yorktown with 7,000 men, Lafayette sent Wayne to keep Rawdon from reënforcing Cornwallis. His idea of keeping the British separated was, as we shall see, most appropriate.

Greene simultaneously decided to carry the war into the enemy's country and forthwith marched toward Eutaw Springs. When the British retired from that place, he vigorously attacked and drove them from the field with great loss. But the undisciplined American militia in pillaging the British camp drank so much rum that they were useless on the counter-attack of the enemy. Eutaw Springs was retaken. In extenuation it may be said that many of Greene's soldiers were so naked that they had to tie pieces of moss on their shoulders and sides to keep the firelocks and cartridge boxes from chafing the skin.

Three things happened now which gave Washington a plan and a hope. The administration of the army became more sound under a civilian superintendent of finance instead of a Board of Treasury; a clothier general operating under the superintendent, Robert Morris, began to get clothing to the troops; and De Grasse wrote that he was sailing for the Chesapeake with 25 ships. Washington secretly decided to bottle up Cornwallis. He collected in that country between the Bronx and Dobb's Ferry, the French from southern New England and the Americans from the Highlands, as if to lay siege to New York. Then he marched to Sandy Hook, having written to the various governors of his contemplated attack on New York. He was well on his way to Philadelphia before his intentions were suspected.

At that place Rochambeau gave the troops $20,000 in gold which bought them many necessaries and raised their spirits. At the Head of Elk in Maryland they were joined by the French who were surprised at the large number of ragged soldiers among the Americans. From there and from Annapolis the rest of the journey was made by boats. The allies with 8,800 Americans, 7,800 French and a French fleet of 20,000 sailors and 2,000 guns invested Yorktown, while Cornwallis, who could have escaped, calmly watched the process.

In the meantime Clinton in New York sent Arnold to harass New England in order to call some of Washington's troops away from the south. But Washington was not so easily turned aside. Arnold, however, pressed the New Londoners. How they responded can be inferred from the following extract from Colonel Hemstead's diary:

"Soon after our arrival, the enemy [12] appeared in force in *Sept.*
1781 some woods about half a mile S. E. of the Fort, from whence they sent a flag of truce, which was met by Capt. Shapley, demanding an unconditional surrender, threatening, at the same time, to storm the Fort instantly, if the terms were not accepted. A council of war was held, and it was the unanimous voice, that the garrison was unable to defend themselves against so superior a force. But a militia Colonel who was then in the fort, and had a body of men in the immediate vicinity, said he would reënforce them with two or three hundred men in fifteen minutes, if they would hold out; Col. Ledyard agreed to send back a defiance, upon the most solemn assurance of immediate succor. For this purpose Col. —— started, his men being then in sight; but he was no more seen, nor did he even attempt a diversion in our favor."

The taking of New London, however, was quite useless to the British as long as Clinton did not directly reënforce Cornwallis. Yorktown was bound to fall with the French odds alone so great against the town. But Lieutenant Feltman in his journal was not altogether pleased with the conduct of American troops:

"Page 20. 15th Oct'r. '81. . . . The enemy threw a num- *Oct. 15*
1781 ber of shells this day and wounded a great number of men, especially the militia; several were wounded this day in their sleep, such is the carelessness of those stupid wretches who are not acquainted with the life of a soldier."

Yorktown capitulated without more glory to our army than *Oct. 17*
1781 that the siege was conceived by Washington and aided by American troops. Had not the French outfitted them with clothing and shoes, it is doubtful if they could have been present at the capture, except in the nude. Had not the French had an overwhelming amount of men and materials, it is certain Yorktown could not have been captured before Clinton could have aided Cornwallis.

---

[12] The British under Arnold.

But those American soldiers who had been through the training at Valley Forge gave good accounts of themselves at the siege. Many a life was saved by Steuben's discipline and training and many lost for lack of them.

When it was all over "Light Horse Harry" Lee made this tragic lament:

"Convinced as I am that a government is the murderer of its citizens which sends them to the field uninformed and untaught, where they are to meet men of the same age and strength, mechanized by education and discipline for battle, I cannot withhold my denunciation of its wickedness and folly."

How pathetic, in this story of men willing to brave death for those at home that those at home responded by killing through neglect more of them than did the enemy!

This ghastly truth apparently failed at this time to make any impression upon the public, for training and discipline in the intervals between calamities are going to be thrust down. Preventive medicine, applied to war, is about to be a thought foreign to the public mind. Unready youths are going to be fed by the government into the flaming breach as helpless babes before the burning mouth of Moloch.

CHAPTER IV

THE ARMY FLUNG ASIDE

(1781–1811)

YORKTOWN did not end the war. Only a small division had been taken. Our army had at no time been able to force the British from the Continent. Still luxuriating in New York, Charleston, and Savannah, were almost three times as many of the enemy as those lost by Cornwallis.

Washington had to husband his strength. Of the French, only Rochambeau with a small army remained. Lafayette and De Grasse had sailed for France and the West Indies. The American army was going through the usual stages of depletion. The commander in chief sent Lincoln north to prepare winter quarters for the main army in New Jersey and along the Hudson, and Saint Clair and Wayne south to reënforce Greene.

With these additions Greene came out of summer quarters *Nov. 19* to start active operations. But the nudity and hunger of his *1781* men drove him to negative measures. Now that a great victory had been won the people gave less than ever any thought to the troops. Supplies failed for long periods. The soldiers, forced to live off the near-by farmer or townsman, simply heightened their unpopularity. Being much of the time without food and *Oct. 25* clothing, they besides grew loathsome. Greene wrote that *1781* "numbers of brave fellows who had bled in the cause of their country had been eat up with maggots." In a position he took up near Charlestown his savage-looking men fared better. But the relief was temporary, for soon one third of his force was reported so naked that the men could not leave their tents and were reduced to such nourishment as they could find or filch.

Dec. 6
1781

Although the northern troops had more clothing, they also had more cold. The scarcity of food was about the same. Mr. Comfort Sands, most unsuitably christened, undertook to supply the army. But he supplied it so much according to his own profit that the soldier's appetite was quite overlooked. He would arrange to have the cattle driven into camp just when hunger had reached the limit of endurance. He would make the officers draw rations when it suited his convenience rather than their needs. So the northern camps lived alternately well and poorly according as Sands' caprice satisfied or intensified natural cravings.

April 22
1782

In the spring Congress made a scale of rations and pay for officers.[1] The major general received the grand sum of $31.60 a month and five rations. The lieutenant received $3.15 a month and one ration. It is interesting to compare these sums with the $1,000 bounty already offered the private for enlisting. In this instance, the money and provisions were to be treated as separate items. If the officer could not draw his rations monthly they were forfeited, for they could not be commuted

[1] Rank	Rations Per Day	Pay Per Month
A Major general	5	$31.60
Brigadier general	4	25.30
Colonel	2	12.60
Lieutenant colonel commandant	2	12.60
Lieutenant colonel	1½	11.00
Major	1½	8.00
Chaplain	1½	8.00
Captain	1	6.30
Subaltern	1	3.15
Surgeon	1½	4.60
Surgeon's mate	1	3.15
Quartermaster-general	4	25.30
Deputy quartermaster, with the southern army	1½	12.60
Deputy paymaster, with the southern army	1½	11.00
Deputy clothier with the army	1	3.15
Deputy paymaster with the army	1	....
Commissary forage	1½	11.00
Field commissary	1	6.30
Field commissary with southern army	1	6.30
Director-general hospitals	2	....
Chief physician	2	....
Hospital surgeon	1	....
Mates	1	....
Stewards	1	....
Wardmasters	1	....

into money. However, these figures are merely studies in black and white, because the soldier seldom received his pay in any shape.

Parades and reviews, the military exercises of that day, were the constant work of Washington's officers in spite of their penury. The little army of about 6,000 was kept up to as high a state of morale as living conditions would permit because of the expected resumption of activities. The commander in chief's orders abound in appreciation here and condemnation there for some well or badly executed maneuver.

On one occasion he instructs the commandant of artillery, *May 31* who seems to have been a sort of ordnance officer, to issue ten *1782* rounds of blank ammunition per man. Shortly afterward appears, "A Plan for Conducting the Rejoicing on Thursday," the birthday of the Dauphin of France. For this ceremony a great colonnade was built upon the parade ground at West Point. Washington dined at four o'clock in the afternoon with his officers and ladies. All the surrounding garrisons on both banks of the Hudson turned out their troops so that they could "display [2] in full view of West Point." A running fire of artillery and musketry was delivered at prearranged signals. After dinner thirteen separate toasts were drunk "and each toast announced by the discharge of artillery." As soon as the thirteenth was quaffed, the officers rose from the table and joined their respective commands. After more musketry and cannonading, "the officers commanding corps with an audible voice" prayed "to God to bless the Dauphin of France." Though such a ceremony seems to be as much a test of capacity as religion, it lent spirit to the troops in their hard life.

That target practice was one of the functions of drill is *June 16* apparent from one of Washington's observations. Although *1782* the light infantry had "performed with great precision," he was "sorry to find . . . that they did not take so good aim as he expected."

The following order will disclose both the pains then taken and the officer responsible for the training.

_____

[2] Be in regimental front.

"Head-Quarters,
"Newburgh, June 18, 1782.

"The review of this army by brigades being now completed, the Commander-in-chief is happy in this opportunity to present his thanks to major general the Baron Steuben, for the indefatigable assiduity and singular attention exhibited in the late inspections and reviews, and for his eminent services in promoting the discipline of the army on all occasions; and at the same time to express his approbation of the present laudable disposition and pride of corps which seem to be diffused throughout the army. From this spirit of emulation, and a consideration of the amazing contrast between the past and present appearance of the troops, the General anticipates the happiest consequences; but, being persuaded that appearance alone is not sufficient to establish the reputation and ensure the success of our arms, and that frequent and repeated exercise is absolutely necessary to constitute the perfection of discipline, he requests in the most pointed terms, that the commanding officers of divisions and brigades will punctually exercise the troops alternately every other day, in brigade and by detail.

"In the course of these exercises the officers are permitted to vary the maneuvers as time, circumstances and inclination may prompt, provided they do not deviate from the established principles. But, in all cases, the General entreats the officers to pay the most minute attention to the soldier's method of priming and loading, as well as of leveling and taking aim. This is a matter of great consequence; he hopes, therefore, that the utmost pains may be taken to instruct every individual in this essential part of his profession."

Aug. 7, 11
1782

Many means were invented by the higher commanders for the purpose of offsetting the low spirits induced by hunger and raggedness. It was at this time that the "service stripe" or war chevron seems to have had its origin. Any soldier who had served more than three years with "bravery, fidelity and good conduct" was to wear on his left sleeve a stripe "of angular form." If he had served more than six years he was to wear two stripes. All stripes were to be of the color of the "facings" of the corps to which the man belonged.

The hat seemed to be the most difficult article to obtain and the one dearest to the soldier's pride. Those who could get it, cut it, cocked it and decorated it according to the regimental design. Those who were without it were in a sorry plight. They had no chance to cut a military figure. Washington placed this deficiency on the part of a certain regiment side by side with the "want of exactness in performing . . . maneuvers" due to "the badness of their position in the mountains."

As to insignia of rank, worsted shoulder knots were pre- *May 14* scribed for noncommissioned officers. The sergeant was to have *1782* two, one on each shoulder, whereas the corporal was to have only one on the right shoulder. For officers, Washington had recommended to the army two years previously that major generals wear two epaulets with two stars upon each, that brigadiers wear two but have only one star on each, that field officers all alike wear two plain gold epaulets and that captains wear only one on the right shoulder and subalterns one on the left.[3] It is likely that before this time officers or men had had little opportunity to comply generally with this order. At this date a nicety and self-respect in dress seem to have accompanied the state of developed discipline, so far as the officer's purse could permit.

But throughout the rank and file it was most difficult to obtain a uniform mode of wearing the hair. In those times of dyed wigs and long locks it was a knotty problem to have the hair trimmed and tied in the same manner or the wigs of the same color in any organization. The tonsorial allowance of two pounds of flour and one-half pound of rendered tallow may or may not have succeeded in giving a sleek appearance.

A more suitable organization seems to have been one of the *Aug. 21* greatest concerns of this year. The artillery, cavalry, sappers *1782* and miners were placed upon a more sound basis. The light infantry companies—one in each regiment—were formed into separate battalions. The personnel of these foot troops had been picked with a view to obtaining men of good physique and marching ability who could act as pioneers. Since Steuben had

---

[3] The generals, in addition, wore feathers in their hats and different clothing from the soldier. The other officers wore the clothing of the corps to which they belonged.

prescribed advance and flank guards for the march, it is likely that these companies performed a great part of reconnoissance duty. Yet other troops helped out in this work because he had been careful to show that men so engaged should be frequently relieved.

Shortly after the separation of the light infantry, Washington ordered a general removal of all troops down the river to Verplanck's Point. The journey was attended with extreme orderliness. The little force disembarked and prepared a clean and well-decorated camp. On the new site were entertained Rochambeau's soldiers who were returning overland from the south and were on their way to New England where they were going to embark for France. Levees and festivities were conducted on a grand scale for over a month. French officers expressed surprise at the good appearance and efficiency of the American soldier whose reputation gained in his undisciplined years was hard now to overcome.

After the national courtesies, the American troops returned to the hills back of Newburgh for another winter. They had become expert in building rude temporary structures. They now made cabins sufficient to hold eight soldiers comfortably and larger ones for noncommissioned officers. They went so far as to have a great assembly hall, called the chapel, where services, courts-martial and public entertainments were held. It is said on good authority that the timbers of these buildings were joined so skillfully that they neither had nor required a nail or other piece of metal.

This, the eighth winter of the war, saw the soldiers as much as ever derided and neglected by the country. Economy was made to bear hardest upon those who had shouldered the burdens of the conflict. The half pay promised to the officers had never been produced. They were humiliated on social occasions. They had received not over one sixth of their pay during the whole Revolution. Their private resources were at an end and their friends were wearied out and disgusted with their repeated applications. They could not invite foreign officers or associates to a meal, so scant was the ration and so wanting any funds. Since nothing had been given them for clothing after 1777 they were constantly chilled by the zero weather and often in the unspeakable hospital. They had waited in the vain hope of relief by Congress. The "deranged officers," who had been squeezed out of the service by the union of smaller regiments and who had been provided for in no way, oftentimes had to sell their clothing for support or to beg. They were treated by the public as idlers living on the public bounty and were derided by their neighbors as "half-pay officers." These very leaders who had risked their lives to quell mutinies, who had stood before death and torture in order to make the country safe and independent, were ridiculed and neglected. So great was the public stigma on these men that the word "soldiering" came into use as a synonym of idleness.

If the country had given the continental soldier public honor and had made him independent for the rest of his life it could not have begun to repay him for his services. But when it failed in its promises and even scorned him in public the name of ingrate is scarcely a strong term. As shall later be seen, this attitude is not going to be confined to Revolutionary days.

Under such punishment for having committed the crime of bearing untold misery for one's country, it would not have been criticizable had there been a continuous round of mutiny or even an overthrow of the weak central government. On the contrary, these officers, now disciplined under Steuben's humane régime, decided merely to address those in power with their pleas. The shame lay in their having to beg for that which was their just due.

The Massachusetts officers agreed first to approach their own legislature. Accordingly a committee went to Boston where it was well received and was promised everything by Hancock and Adams. But upon a weak excuse of a private letter from a congressional delegate who discouraged the half pay, the matter was postponed indefinitely. Although this action caused more discontent, the officers, following Washington's advice, refrained from resigning. Instead they began to prepare a petition to Congress. Officers of other states were invited by the Massachusetts line to join in the request. Accordingly a joint memorial was drawn up. The facts set forth in their conservativeness, simplicity and pathos should have drawn

Sept. 1782

Dec. 1782

Jan. 6
1783

humiliation from an ogre. When the paper was presented to the central legislative body, the members were inclined to be

Feb. 13
1783

incensed at the apparent irregularity of such a procedure, but they conceded the point under pressure and reluctantly referred the matter to a committee. While the decision was still pending, a copy of the King's speech in parliament seemed to indicate peace. Congress then went into a committee of the whole on funds. The army's condition was considered as of no more importance than other questions. So it was attempted to refer the claims of the officers to the states, but the motion failed.

March 10
1783

The committee then brought in a report to give five years' full pay, but the proposition was rejected.

March 12
1783

At this juncture the famous Newburgh addresses were mailed to Congress by Washington.

These two anonymous tracts had been distributed throughout the camp.[4] Their fiery style had the double effect of admiration and conviction. The first one called for a meeting of all the officers on a certain date and implied that plans would be made to resort to force. Washington, who had had his ear to the ground all this time, realized the peril. He issued an order which condemned the anonymous call and postponed the meeting four days. By such action he properly compromised the effect of the document and gained time for reflection. But the author of the first publication embarrassed the commander in chief still further by issuing a second address and stating that Washington's recognition in orders was equivalent to his sympathy.

In the "Chapel" or "Temple" the officers met on the date set by Washington. He himself unexpectedly appearing among them was naturally the first to speak. In that calm dignity so peculiarly his own, he explained how the substance of the addresses appealed to their passion rather than their reason, how his past life would show that he was not indifferent to the interest of the army, and how foolish it would be to sully by one rash act the glory they had already attained. He then called upon them to give "one more distinguished proof of unexampled patriotism and patient virtue" so that posterity could say, "Had

---

[4] Later found out to be the work of Major John Armstrong, aid-de-camp of General Gates.

this day been wanting, the world had never seen the last stage of perfection, to which human nature is capable of attaining." Few eyes were dry when he had finished. This magnificent man capped his physical and mental triumphs with the greatest moral victory attainable—the victory "over jealousy, just discontent and great opportunities."

Washington wrote the President of Congress again. This *March 18 1783* time he enclosed new resolutions of moderation and wisdom made at his advice after the meeting just described. The delegates voted in consequence a commutation of five years' full pay in cash or in six-per-cent securities at the option of Congress, mainly because they feared to do otherwise. Although this amount was less than satisfaction, the officers were in such need of relief that they had to accept the measure.

The rank and file were in a worse plight. In addition to the sufferings the officers had borne, they had had to build all the quarters and perform other menial tasks without exterior aid. In other words, they had been compelled to carry their own comfort into the wilderness and in return to jeopardize their lives for the saving of the nation.

When Congress announced the cessation of hostilities, the *April 11 1783* discharge of the men enlisted for the war became a new puzzle. In the publication of this event to the soldiers Washington was *April 19 1783* rightly fearful that they could not distinguish between cessation of hostilities and actual declaration of peace. He felt it would be hard to hold them in the service, especially in view of the fact that the Connecticut noncommissioned officers were *May 1783* already claiming half pay. To solve the dilemma, Congress promptly put the responsibility on Washington of granting either furloughs or discharges as he chose. And then, as an achievement of great generosity, it permitted the soldiers to keep their arms and accouterments.

Hostilities ceased unexpectedly because of the situation abroad rather than our power. As a consequence neither officer nor soldier foresaw the predicament of either waiting in the service until some future payment should be made or of going home penniless in the hope that he might at some time receive something. When the order for granting furloughs was issued, all appealed to Washington in pathetic frenzy. But the most he could do was to send a message to Philadelphia urging the immediate issue of the contemplated six-month certificates of three months' pay. A faint prospect of three months' pay after the half pay promised by Congress and wrung through such misery and self-restraint! But the furlough was too strong a temptation to both soldier and officer so that they left without any pay. Only about a thousand three-year men were retained to watch New York, the only place of British occupancy remaining. In the south the enemy's troops had been withdrawn principally for European political reasons. So the army went home without even a ceremonious "thank you" from the nation. To this day most of them are unpaid—and will be.

June 13
1783

It was the recruits only who mutinied; 280 of them from Lancaster and Philadelphia bloodlessly drove Congress to seek safety at Princeton. Washington sent General Howe, who had suppressed the New Jersey malcontents, to do the same in Pennsylvania. But the affair had already subsided when the regulars reached the scene of difficulty. On account of the uprising 4 men received corporal punishment.

Without further ado the army kept dwindling until Congress ordered its disbandment. Washington's last general order issued to the troops at Princeton, sent them out into the new democracy with sagacious words of construction. So from their leader within the army they received encouragement but from no one without.

Nov. 2
1783

With the one regiment of infantry and two battalions of artillery that remained, the commander in chief later marched into one end of New York while the British under Sir Guy Carleton marched out at the other.

Nov. 25
1783

Not long afterward Washington's officers assembled at Fraunces' Tavern to bid him farewell. Gathered in the high-ceilinged room were the infantry officers with their blue cut-away coats faced with white, their white buttons, silver epaulets, black gaiters, and white-braided cocked hats with black plumes; the artillery officers with their scarlet facings, yellow buttons, gold epaulets and yellow-braided cocked hats with black and red plumes; and here and there a general officer in his blue and buff and with stars upon his gold epaulets.

Dec. 4
1783

Under these picturesque uniforms beat the hearts of true men who loved their commander. For the last time they stood before him who had always been wise and kind. For eight years he had suffered with them all manner of ills. Having formed the habit of trust in such unfailing control, they were about to scatter into a country of doubtful management and cold attitude. Their depression was keen. When in the silence it was necessary for the great man to speak, he tried to advise them; but his voice broke. Filling a wine glass, he gave a simple toast to their happiness, and requested them to take him by the hand. Stifled by emotions they accompanied him to Whitehall Ferry, where they watched his boat until it slowly passed from sight.

At Annapolis he formally resigned his commission to Congress and quietly retired into private life. *Dec. 22 1783*

Though Mr. H. G. Wells [5] is content with disposing of Washington with the single colorful statement that "he was a conspicuously indolent man," Mr. Green, the great English historian, speaks of him thus:

"No nobler figure ever stood in the forefront of a nation's life. Washington was grave and courteous in address, his manners were simple and unpretending; his silence and the serene calmness of his temper spoke of a perfect self-mastery; but there was little in his outer bearing to reveal the grandeur of a soul which lifts his figure, with all the simple majesty of an ancient statue, out of the smaller passions, the meaner impulses of the world around him. . . . It was only as the weary fight went on that the colonists discovered, however slowly and imperfectly the greatness of their leader: his clear judgment, his heroic endurance, his silence under difficulties, his calmness in the hour of danger or defeat, the patience with which he waited, the quickness and hardness with which he struck, the lofty and serene sense of duty which never swerved from its task through resentment or jealousy, that never through war or peace felt the touch of a meaner ambition, that knew no aim save that of guarding the freedom of his fellow countrymen,

---

[5] *Outline of History.*

and no personal longing save that of returning to his own fireside when their freedom was secured. It was almost unconsciously that men learned to cling to Washington with a trust and faith such as few other men have won, and to regard him with a reverence which still hushes us in the presence of his memory."

After the peace, the discharged soldier or officer went about the country hunting to adjust himself. His occupation was gone, his means were used up, his body was ailing, hurt or emaciated, and his unkempt, ragged appearance brought only gibes from the people. Ex-soldiers, who had suffered most, died quickly. The remainder went often from town to town in order to find work. Many of the officers in following the example of Greene and Washington had used their private means to finance the war, and were bankrupt. General Clarke, who almost single-handed had presented the states with an empire, was deprived of his commission and died in misery and poverty.

Jan. 3 1784

Knox, who succeeded Washington, had to continue to disband the remainder of the army until it numbered less than 700 men. Finally Congress passed this astounding legislation:

June 2 1784

"And whereas, standing armies in time of peace are inconsistent with the principles of republican governments, dangerous to the liberties of a free people, and generally converted into destructive engines for establishing despotism;

"It is therefore resolved, That recommendations in lieu of requisitions shall be sent to the several States for raising the troops which may be immediately necessary for garrisoning the Western posts and guarding the magazines of the United States, unless, Congress should think it expedient to employ the Continental troops now at West Point in the service aforesaid;

"Resolved, that the commanding officer be and he is hereby directed to discharge the troops now in the service of the United States, except twenty-five privates to guard the stores at Fort Pitt and fifty-five to guard the stores at West Point and other magazines, with a proportionable number of officers, no officers to remain in service above the rank of captain."

How sane men could come to a result so far at variance with the incidents of their own time seems to us inexplicable. Had it not been the "standing" part of the army that had been responsible for the few successes of the Revolution? Had it not been the need of stability that led Washington to say:

"Regular troops alone are equal to the exigencies of modern war as well for defense as offense, and whenever a substitute is attempted it must prove illusory and ruinous. No militia will ever acquire the habits necessary to resist a regular force. The firmness requisite for the real business of fighting is only to be attained by a constant course of discipline and service. I have never yet been a witness to a single instance that can justify a different opinion, and it is most earnestly to be wished that the liberties of America may no longer be trusted, in any material degree, to so precarious a dependence."

Eighty men—the army! Even they, it was specified, were "to guard the stores." Picture them at West Point, all that remained of Alexander Hamilton's battery,[6] oiling the trunnions of three and six pounders, mowing grass on the magazines and doing their turn at guard. The army—a few watchmen not even glorified. All the training, all the safeguard that Washington and Steuben had built up with such great care was wantonly tossed aside. But even this sacrifice would not have been so terrible were not hundreds of lives to be lost by the discard.

Congress had, however, indulged in a vague legislation which called out from the different states for twelve months 700 *June 3* enlisted men and a proper proportion of officers. An officer *1784* from one state, under this law, might command men from another. The purpose of the enactment was to garrison the frontier posts to be evacuated by the British according to the treaty. But this tepid measure was to prove useless.

Hardly a year had elapsed when it was demonstrated that

---

[6] Afterwards Battery F, Fourth Artillery.

this force could not be raised so as to be effective in the face of so short an enlistment. The Indian depredations were coming on so fast that it was impossible to recruit a new levy every year. And in the meantime frontier settlers were being massacred.

April 1, 7, 12 1785

Accordingly the term of service was extended to three years. The organization was a mixed regiment of 8 companies of infantry and 2 of artillery. The officers were: 1 lieutenant colonel commandant, 2 majors, 8 captains, 10 lieutenants (1 as adjutant, 1 as quartermaster and 1 as paymaster), 10 ensigns, 1 surgeon and 4 surgeon's mates. The highest ranking officer received $82 per month and the private $4.[7]

Sept. 1785

General Knox as Secretary of War and Lieutenant Colonel Harmer as commandant were in charge of this regimental army. Although it was the first organization to have the functions of regular troops, it was not so styled. Congress had said that "standing armies were dangerous to a republic" and it was going to stick to its original story in spite of the facts.

Other happenings proved that such a force was insufficient. The British, Spanish, French and Indians on the frontiers,

---

[7] COMPENSATION PER MONTH

Rank	Salary Cash
Lieutenant colonel commandant	$50.00
Major	45.00
Captain	35.00
Lieutenant	26.00
Ensign	20.00
Surgeon	45.00
Mate	30.00
Sergeants	6.00
Corporals	5.00
Musicians	5.00
Privates	4.00
	Subsistence
Lieutenant colonel commandant	20.00
Major	20.00
Captain	12.00
Lieutenant	8.00
Ensign	8.00
Surgeon	16.00
Mate	8.00
	Forage
Field Officers	12.00
Surgeon	6.00
Regimental Staff	6.00

where the foreign trappers had little faith in the new government, made such numerous incursions that the army had to be
increased; 1,340 additional noncommissioned officers and privates were authorized, who were to be on the same footing as
the previous 700. The whole was to be called a "legionary
corps." Of the new men only 2 companies of artillery were
ever enrolled. Consequently the entire resistance of the country—less than 1,000 men—was tied to the chain of forts in
the northwest and south, and along the coast.

Lonely garrisons dotted the border from Fort Pitt to Vincennes. Great tracts of dense woods full of bear, panther and
deer cut the little parties of from 25 to 100 soldiers away from
civilization. So wild was the life, so certain the attack of the
savage that the officers or men dared not take with them wives
or families.

The fort was usually built in stockade form. Its rectangu-
lar fence of logs, pointed at the tops and loopholed for the
flintlocks and iron and brass cannon, was reënforced at the
four corners by blockhouses. The enclosure was usually divided
into two parts by a high stockade fence similar to the outer
one. In case a blockhouse or other wooden part was burnt or
a breach made in the outer fence, the occupants could retreat
to one side or the other. The two enclosures contained, on the
one hand, the guardhouse and parade—and, on the other, the
quarters of the officers and men and the magazines. The supplies were usually placed in the blockhouses.

The officers' quarters were log shacks consisting of two
rooms, each one occupied by an officer. Although the commanding officer might have two and a hall, such an assignment was
a luxury. The enlisted men huddled together in small barracks for the sake of warmth. With only open fireplaces to
heat the buildings, with supplies coming by boat or caravan
very occasionally and with the chill of winter and monotony,
it is no wonder that rum was popular.

Yet these men with their smart cocked hats, their tight
gaiters, their polished cartridge boxes, their clean white belts,
their shaven faces and their powdered hair turned out daily
for drill, guard mounting and parade as if the eyes of the
world were upon them. Every few nights each soldier, muf-

fled in bear and coon skin, watched as a sentry in the unheated blockhouses or at a desolate post outside. The lurking red-skin was ubiquitous. A wink of sleep, a tomahawked sentinel and one pine torch well applied meant death to the garrison.

These soldiers had built the fort with their own hands. It was really theirs more than the government's. But not for a moment did they forget their duty to their nation and to each other. Each day there were quantities of fuel to cut, sinks to fill and the policing of every cranny of the inclosure for health's sake. There were drills and parades. But what recreation? Hunting was so dangerous on account of the Indian that often it had to be forbidden. There were no movies, no libraries, no illustrated magazines. Even a book was a rarity. Although few of the men could read and write, a Bible or a letter was soon frayed from excessive fingering. Eating with the same men, seeing the same faces, doing the same chores—imprisoned on the outskirts of one's own country!

Thus the little garrisons carried on in order to keep murder and rape from the contiguous settlers. Every single soldier who could be enlisted and many more were needed on the frontier. There was consequently no foot-loose command with a chance for proper training or for use in defense in the entire country.

Dec.
1786

Accordingly, in Massachusetts, when dispute over debt arose, Daniel Shays collected some old soldiers of the Revolution, easily dispersed the militia and forced the court to adjourn. With no ready troops to oppose the movement Shays led 2,000 men to the arsenal at Springfield where he was held at bay. It took General Lincoln with 4,000 soldiers raised by the state to disperse Shays' force, after bloodshed and much tumult.

The obsession of universal peace had played its usual part after eight years of unstable equilibrium. Civilization had been torn by what then appeared to be a world war. The wish being father to the belief, it was decided by the public there would be no more resort to arms. Shays' rebellion awakened the states to the realization that the smallest apparent causes can sometimes, presto, be the largest ructions. Because of the current feeling John Adams was actuated to say:

"National defense is one of the cardinal duties of a statesman. . . . The subject has always been near to my heart. The delightful imaginations of universal peace have often amused, but have never been credited by me."

Accordingly the Congress went to the magnificent extreme of allowing the original 700 enlisted men to reënlist for another three years, thus attempting to save transportation by retaining the former troops. The infantry was arranged in a regiment by itself and the artillery was separated into four companies of the same size each as those of the infantry. This small force was the invitation of over three million people for more bloodshed. *Oct. 3 1787*

Such was the futile provision when the country created its Constitution which made the President commander in chief of the army, and also made Congress responsible for the nation's defense. The actual number of men then in the service was 595. Under the new government the Department of War was established with its secretary whose duties covered military commissions, land grants and naval and Indian, as well as army affairs. Knox and Harmer were continued in office. Every person enlisted or commissioned was required to take an oath of allegiance. The commissioned officers were appointed by the President and all persons in the army were referred to as "in the service of the United States." *1788*   *Sept. 29 1789*

The reaction from the Constitution was first materially felt in the military establishment when the new strength of the army was placed at 1,216 enlisted men. This law which repealed the provisions of the year before was extensively detailed. It made the length of service three years for officers as well as for the rank and file. It allowed 2 inspectors with "pay and subsistence of captain." It provided that subalterns as adjutants should receive $10 and "Quarter and Pay masters" $5 extra pay per month. It raised the forage for majors and surgeons from $6 to $10, and gave to the enlisted man the following clothing and rations: *April 30 1790*

"One hat, or helmet, one coat, one vest, two pair of woolen and linen overalls, four pair of shoes, four shirts, two pair of socks, one blanket, one stock and clasp, and one pair of buckles (annually).

"One pound of beef or three quarters of a pound of pork, one pound of bread or flour and half a gill of rum, brandy or whiskey (daily.)

"Two quarts of vinegar, two pounds of soap and one pound of candles (every hundred days)."

It then tore down the whole structure by cutting the pay of the private to $3 per month, and deducting besides $1 for hospital stores and clothing, so that he really received only $2 in cash; then it added a little salve by giving officers wounded or disabled in line of duty a pension of $9 per month, and enlisted men $5.

The entire force was to be organized into 1 infantry regiment of 3 battalions, and 1 artillery battalion. Each battalion was to have 4 companies, 1 major, 1 adjutant, 1 quartermaster and 1 surgeon or surgeon's mate. The infantry company was to consist of 1 captain, 1 lieutenant, 1 ensign, 4 sergeants, 4 corporals, 2 musicians and 61 privates. The artillery company was provided with 2 lieutenants instead of a lieutenant and ensign.

Shortly after this law was passed the western settlers were marauded by the Indians aided and abetted by the British. Since the Revolution over one thousand souls in the vicinity of Kentucky alone had perished by arrow and tomahawk. Congress was besieged for aid. But there was yet no army outside of the little garrisons scattered on the frontier, and President Washington was powerless to call out a single additional regular soldier.

July 15
1790
Therefore, Governor (General) Saint Clair of the Northwest Territory raised about 1,100 militia which under the system of the time consisted of "old men, boys and untrustworthy substitutes," untrained and undisciplined. The leader chosen by Saint Clair proved to be incompetent and was often drunk. However, General Harmer added 320 regulars to this force, superseded in command Saint Clair's choice and led the whole force into the Maumee country. It was not long until one of his detachments was ambushed and 400 of the remainder

at the Maumee River had half of its number killed or wounded.
What was left of the main force escaped, but the Indians were
filled with new courage for murder and rapine so that hundreds of settlers were killed and plundered as a result of the
disadvantage.   General Harmer was exonerated from blame
on acount of the poor quality of his troops.

From this affair came the creation of a second regular regi- *March 3*
ment of infantry. The pay schedule and organization was to be *1791*
the same as that of the previous regiment, but the strength was
to be 50 men less. To this toy army there was added a major
general, brigadier general, brigade major, quartermaster and
chaplain.[8] In addition, levies for six months were allowed to
be raised by the President.

Instead of paying the soldier a sum sufficient to get a good
type of man, Congress again resorted to the pernicious bounty
system, which allowed to each recruit of the regulars $6 and
of the levies $3. More pernicious still was the allowance to each
recruiting officer of $2 for each new man enlisted by him. Not
only was a low type of soldier obtained but desertion and waste
were the results as in the Revolution.

In the meantime the ravages of the Miami Indians became
so hurtful that General Saint Clair was sent against them.
His force was made up of men "purchased from prisons, wheel-
barrows and brothels at $2 per month." On his way he built
Fort Hamilton (north of Cincinnati) and Fort Jefferson (near
Greenville). The levies under this system turned out to be
more disgraceful in desertion and disorder than the militia *Nov. 3*
had been. When the Indians charged at a branch of the *1791*

8 "Sec. 6.   That in case a major general, brigadier general, quartermaster, aid-de-camp, brigade major, and chaplain, should be appointed,
their pay and allowances shall be respectively, as herein mentioned: the
major general shall be entitled to $125, monthly pay, $20 allowance for
forage, monthly, and for daily subsistence fifteen rations, or money in lieu
thereof, at the contract price.   The brigadier general shall be entitled to
$94, monthly pay, with $16 allowance for forage, monthly, and for daily
subsistence twelve rations, or money in lieu thereof, at the contract price.
That the quartermaster shall be entitled to the same pay, rations, and forage, as the lieutenant colonel commandant of a regiment.   That the aid-
de-camp be entitled, including all allowances, to the same pay, rations
and forage, as a major of a regiment.   That the brigade major be entitled,
including all allowances, to the same pay, rations, and forage, as a major
of a regiment.   That the captain be entitled to $50 per month, including
pay, rations and forage."

Wabash, these untrained men fled through the regulars, whose regimental officers were all killed in trying to stem the tide. General Saint Clair had eight bullet holes in his clothing. An equal force of Indians routed these poor troops, killing 632 and wounding 264 out of about 1,400.

In addition to the above losses another calamity visited the army. The Indians had become bold and arrogant by their successes over our impotent troops. As a consequence Lieutenant Colonel Hardin and Major Trueman, sent on a pacific mission to the hostile towns of the Indians, were treacherously murdered.

These disasters again threw Congress into a whirlpool of army legislation, but, as always, too late to prevent disaster.

March 5 1792

The lawmakers authorized the recruiting of the existing 2 regiments of infantry up to 960 men apiece. It created 4 more regiments of the same strength, one of which was to consist of 2 infantry battalions and a squadron of 4 troops of light dragoons. Each troop was to be officered by 1 captain, 1 lieutenant and 1 cornet; and each infantry company by 1 captain, 1 lieutenant and 1 ensign. The dragoons were to serve dismounted when so ordered. The pay was made free of all deductions. The monthly cash ranged from $166 for a major general to $3 for a private.

A curious feature was an additional indefinite cavalry force for the frontiers, raised for such periods, with such organization and with such strength as the President might decide. The 3 additional infantry regiments were to be raised or discharged at the discretion of the President.

March 28 1792

A little later Congress authorized a maximum of four brigadier generals for the army.

May 8 1792

Then came the universal militia law which made every male citizen between 18 and 45 years a constructive soldier. The captain or company commander was to be responsible for the enrollment of every eligible man in his district. Each soldier notified was to equip himself, within six months,

"with a good musket or firelock, a sufficient bayonet and belt, two spare flints, and a knapsack, a pouch, with a box therein to contain not less than twenty-four cartridges, suited to the bore of his musket or firelock, each cartridge to contain a proper quantity of powder and ball; or, with a good rifle, knapsack, shot pouch and powder horn, twenty balls, suited to the bore of his rifle, and a quarter of a pound of powder; and shall appear, so armed, accoutered, and provided, when called out to exercise, or into service; except, that when called out on company days exercise only, he may appear without a knapsack. That the commissioned officers, shall, severally, be armed with a sword and hanger, and espontoon; and that, from and after five years from the passing of this act, all muskets for arming the militia, as herein required, shall be of bores sufficient for balls of the eighteenth part of a pound. And every citizen so enrolled, and providing himself with the arms, ammunition, and accouterments, required as aforesaid, shall hold the same exempted from all suits, distresses, executions, or sales, for debt, or for the payment of taxes."

Here was a distinct attempt to standardize the calibers of the flintlocks throughout the country. The whole force was to be organized into divisions and brigades. The lower units were to be organized as those of the regular army. One company of "grenadiers, light infantry or riflemen" was to be created for each battalion; and 1 company of artillery and 1 troop of horse, for each division. The commissioned officers were to furnish themselves with good horses of at least fourteen and a half hands high and were to be "armed with a sword, and a pair of pistols, the holsters of which to be covered with bearskin caps." The state adjutant general was to distribute all orders from the commander in chief of each commonwealth.

Then followed the legionary organization promoted by General Knox, secretary of war. The militia comprising the able-bodied men of the entire country were to be divided into 3 corps. The advanced corps was to consist of those between the ages of 18 to 20; the main corps, between 21 to 45; and the reserved corps, between 46 to 60. Of the advanced corps the men under 20 were to receive instruction for thirty days at "annual camps of discipline."

All the regular troops were to become a legion. The author- *Dec. 27 1792* ized 5,120 were to have 4 sublegions. The regiment as an organization was discarded. There was to be no rank intervening between a brigadier general and a major. Each sublegion was to consist of 1,280 men commanded by a brigadier general, and was to be made up of 12 battalions of infantry, 1 battalion of riflemen, 1 company of artillery and 1 troop of dragoons. The whole legion was to be commanded by a major general. The intention was apparently to cut down the number of officers and to avoid the horrid term, "regular army."

The legion for the regulars was to have a short life, but the law and legionary organization for the militia became dead letters almost as soon as enunciated. The states were not penalized for failure to raise troops nor was the soldier for omitting to provide himself with so much equipment. The federal government took no steps to raise or organize this force. But the law is interesting in that it recognized at this early date the principle that every able-bodied citizen should be an active defender of his country. It remained inactive and was often noticed as a pretty statute on the books for over a century, during which time it was to be our only militia law.

The regular army of the borders was now extremely pressed by the Indians who were bold and confident from their previous victories. The lives of innocent settlers were being lost while all these sentiments were being written into enactments.

June 1792

Things came to such a pass that Washington chose Anthony Wayne to organize a force and suppress the rapacious tribes in the west. Wayne arrived at Pittsburg and began a work of discipline and training that was to last almost a year. It was necessary for him to stop and prepare while savage depredations were continuing. Although the caliber of recruits was the same as before, he claimed in the next spring to have 2,500 "worthy of being trusted in campaign." Moving the legion to what is now Cincinnati he there awaited orders which arrived in time in the fall to let him march to Greenville which he named in honor of General Nathaniel Greene. Here he gave his soldiers intensive drill so that later he was able to send a strong detachment to the scene of Saint Clair's defeat where he built Fort Recovery and repulsed 2,000 Indians with heavy loss. After having been joined by some mounted Kentuckians, he started toward the Maumee towns. His army numbered

May 1793

Oct. 1793

Dec. 1793

June 30 1794

2,643, all that he could obtain from the 5,120 authorized. With *July 27 1794*
this comparatively small band he was to combat a greatly superior force of redskins.   At the junction of the Maumee and
the Anglaise rivers he built Fort Defiance.   When the Indians *Aug. 1794*
refused peace, he went to meet them in the vicinity of Presque
Isle.

He disposed his troops with the injunction that they fire *Aug. 20 1794*
once and then drive the Indian from cover with cold steel.   The
battleground, "Fallen Timber," was a wide path in the woods
made by a previous tornado.   The twisted trunks and branches
embedded in artificial and natural entanglements of brush made
an ideal cover for the savages.   Even their brilliantly painted
faces were hidden.   But the hunting shirt and cap of the United
States soldier were in evidence.   The white, red, yellow and
green plumes [9] of the sublegions made four separate bands of
color in the surrounding foliage.   The dragoon with the white
horsehair crest of his brass helmet flying in the wind charged
the fierce fire without wavering.   The men with their bayonets,
the company officers with their short sabers, the field officers
with their longer ones and the trooper with his still longer
horseman's sword hunted the Indian out of his hiding place
and ran him through or simply ran him.   For these officers in
their half-boots and these men of the odd numbered sublegions
in black wigs and even numbered sublegions in white, were
drilled and disciplined troops.   The savage afterwards stated
that he "could not stand up against the sharp ends of the guns."
Neither could he face soldiers who by time and practice had
assimilated precision and obedience.   The victory was complete,
the Indians losing at least twice as many as the Americans.
As a consequence, the frontier settler lived in peace for a long
time.

The other regular troops at this period were scattered as
follows:

398 at posts on the upper Ohio.
73 in the Southwest Territory.

---

9 The officers and men when not in the field wore cocked and round hats
respectively.   The officer wore the plume of his sublegion, and the soldier
wore on his round hat, which had a brim 3 inches wide, a strip of bearskin
7 inches high and 7 inches wide.

146 in Georgia.

369 at seacoast fortifications and recruiting rendezvous.

April 2
1794

May 9
1794

During the spring of this year Congress had made several feeble laws affecting the army. It authorized one or two more arsenals in addition to the ones at Carlisle and Springfield. Harper's Ferry was chosen. To the legion of the United States it added 764 enlisted men, with a proper proportion of officers, to be known as the corps of artillerists and engineers. After absorbing the 4 companies of artillery already in the service, the corps was to consist of 4 battalions of 4 companies each, to be commanded by a "lieutenant colonel, commandant." The company was to be officered by 1 captain, 2 lieutenants and 2 cadets. A cadet was to have the pay, clothing and rations of a sergeant. An extra ration of "four ounces of beef, two ounces of flour, a half a gill of rum or whisky" was to be tendered to the frontier soldier.

June 7
1794

Aug.
1794

While Wayne was pursuing the Indians, universal peace at home was disturbed by the whisky insurrection. After riots, not without bloodshed, 7,000 men in Pennsylvania refused to disperse at the order of the President. It was necessary, because there was no regular force, to call upon the governors of Pennsylvania and the surrounding states for militia. Although the troops of the Keystone State could not be collected on account of sympathy with the rioters and were therefore useless, the militia of some other states succeeded finally in dispersing the malcontents and saved the nation further embarrassment. No one has ever answered the question, "What would the President have done had all the states refused?"

Jan. 5
1795

The insurrection led to another series of acts featuring the army. A premium was placed on the reënlistment of the trained soldier by raising the monthly bounty, clothing and pay allowance to $9 for a sergeant major down to $6.66 for a private, gunner or bombardier. When the cavalry officer or private furnished his horse, arms and accouterments he was to receive 40 cents a day in addition to his pay, and when the enlisted man furnished his own rations and forage he was to receive 25 cents a day. The militia who had gone with Wayne were to be included in this scale. The pay in cash for all grades of enlisted men was to be raised $1 per month, in addition to an initial bounty of $16 for those who reënlisted, and $14 for recruits. Congress was beginning to realize it must pay decently for decent men, but it continued the wasteful bounty system.

The legion was to be completed to 4,800 enlisted men,[10] all *March 3* *1795* enlistments to be terminated at the whim of the government, although three years was specified. The pay allowances and rations were to continue at practically the same rate. In addition to their pay all persons in the service were to receive a definite number of rations: a major general 15, a brigadier 12, a major 4, and so on down to a private, who received 1.

Scarcely had this legislation been carefully enacted before *A Law* *May 30* the legion was abolished. The army from then on was to *1796* consist of 4 regiments of infantry, 2 companies of light dra- *Effective* goons and the corps of artillerists and engineers as already *Oct. 31* organized. Instead of the previous 5 legionary generals, there *1796* were to be but 2, a major general with two aides and a brigadier general. Three legionary generals had to be either "deranged" or demoted two grades.[11] The pay, rations and forage remained about the same.

This act also provided that the President must confirm court-martial sentences which in time of peace included the death penalty or the "dismissal" of an officer.

The next year a Judge Advocate, to be taken from the line *March 3* *1797* and to have extra pay and rations, was for the first time provided. The office of major general was abolished. A quartermaster-general and a paymaster-general were also created, who with the Judge Advocate and brigadier general were to form a "General Staff." [12] The pay of lieutenants and ensigns was raised and officers commanding separate posts were to have their rations doubled. Officers "deranged" by the previous act were to be given six months' pay and subsistence.

Hoyt's *Treatise on Military Art,* published "according to act of Congress," presented a set of drill regulations for the *1798*

---

[10] Exclusive of the corps of artillerists and engineers.
[11] The grade of colonel had not existed since the Revolution.
[12] Although a general staff in name, it had none of the great functions of such a body, such as wisely foreseeing weaknesses in case of war.

cavalry. The author frankly stated that the manual was an adaptation to mounted troops of the principles of Baron von Steuben. The regiment was divided into 2 squadrons of 4 troops each. But Hoyt improved on Steuben by having the cadence in the manual the same as the intervals between parts of the command rather than a "second of time." Throughout the treatise the dragoon is armed with sword and pistol.

April 27
1798

The imminent trouble with France caused the legislators to increase the corps of artillerists and engineers by 3 regiments, to be enlisted for five years. A company was to be officered by 1 captain, 2 lieutenants and 2 cadets, and otherwise to be made up of 4 sergeants, 4 corporals, 42 privates, sappers and miners, 10 artificers, and 2 musicians.

The harbors were to be thoroughly defended. The sum of $1,150,000 was voted to erect and improve fortifications, to purchase cannon, small arms, and military stores; and for the hire, purchase and employ of foundries and armories virtually as the President saw fit. This provision was an early intimation of the lavishness of the country with regard to war material. Quite in contrast was the attitude toward discipline and training. The comprehension of their value has always been awkward for the American mind.

May 28
1798

In the event of war the President was authorized to call out 10,000 enlisted men for three years at a bounty of $10, to organize and officer this force about as he chose and to appoint a lieutenant general at $250 per month, who was allowed 4 aides and 2 secretaries. The Executive was empowered to appoint an inspector general with rank of major general and an adjutant general with rank of brigadier. Soldiers were exempted from all "personal arrests for any debt or contract" during their service. This army was never called out.

July 6
1798

The next law voted 30,000 stands of arms to be sold to the governments of the respective states.

July 16
1798

Since war was apparently at hand, a frenzy of legislation took place. The regular infantry regiment was increased by 3 extra staff officers, an adjutant, a quartermaster and a paymaster who had heretofore been selected from the existing lieutenants. A surgeon and 2 mates were added to the regiment. Its companies were increased by 2, each one consisting of 1 captain, 1 lieutenant, 1 ensign, 4 sergeants, 4 corporals, 1 musician and 60 privates. The regimental staff was made up of 1 sergeant major, 1 quartermaster sergeant and 2 senior musicians. Three brigadier generals having been subtracted when the legion was abolished were now again authorized.

Twelve additional regiments of infantry and 6 troops of dragoons were to be enlisted for, and during, "the existing differences between the United States and the French Republic." A regiment of light dragoons—the first regiment of horse provided for by the new government—was to be formed from the 2 old troops and 6 new ones. The bounty was $12 for these men. The volunteers were never called out, because it had already become customary in the United States to be engaged in war before training could begin.

The first indication of a medical establishment was given *March 2 1799* in Congress the following year. A physician general, an apothecary general, a purveyor and "a competent number of hospital surgeons" were authorized.[13]

The war scare still being prevalent, a contemporary law provided, in case of imminent war "between the United States and a foreign European power," to raise additionally 24 regiments of infantry, a regiment and battalion of artillerists and engineers and 3 regiments of cavalry. The complete nullification of this grand paper force was that it was not required to serve outside its particular state for more than three months.

The organization of the regular infantry and cavalry regiments was changed again by adding a cadet to each company *March 3 1799* and by making a regiment consist of 2 battalions of 5 companies

---

[13] "Sec. 6. That the compensations of the said several officers shall be as follows: of the physician general, $100 pay per month, and $50 per month, which shall be in full compensation for forage, rations, and traveling expenses; of the purveyor, $100 pay per month, in full compensation for his services, and all expenses; of the apothecary general, $80 pay per month, and $30 per month in full compensation for forage, rations and all expenses; of each of his deputies, $50 pay per month, and $16 per month, in full compensation for forage, rations, and all expenses; of each hospital surgeon, $80 pay per month, and $40 per month, in full compensation for forage, rations, and all expenses; of each mate, $30 pay per month, and $20 per month, in full compensation for forage, rations, and all expenses; for each steward, $25 pay per month, and $8 per month in full compensation for forage, rations, and all expenses; *Provided*, That none of the officers aforesaid shall be entitled to any part of the pay or emoluments aforesaid, until they shall, respectively, be called into actual service."

each. The artillery was changed to 4 battalions of 4 companies each with 2 cadets per company. The titles of ensign and cornet were abolished and replaced by second lieutenant. The office of colonel did not yet exist. The pay for a private was raised to $5 and one ration; for a cadet to $10 and two rations; for a major of cavalry to $55 and four rations; for a major of infantry to $40 and three rations; and for a lieutenant colonel $75 and six rations. An allowance for forage was given all mounted officers. Two regiments were to constitute a brigade and 2 brigades a division. It was apparent that the soldiers had heretofore been clothed entirely from standard sizes, for the law now allowed 25 cents a garment for alterations to "coats, vests, overall and breeches" so as to fit the wearer.

The uniform at this time was changed to suit the new organization of the army. The commander in chief had three silver stars on his gold epaulets. The general officers wore blue coats with lining, cape and cuffs of buff, with no lapels, and with caps, cuffs and pockets embroidered. The general officers (except the staff) wore white plumes, and line officers red plumes.

The shoulder strap made its first appearance. A lieutenant colonel still wore two silver epaulets, but a major one epaulet on the right shoulder and a strap on the left. A captain wore an epaulet on his right shoulder, a lieutenant one on the left shoulder (there being no apparent distinction between first and second lieutenants), and a cadet only a strap on his left shoulder. The noncommissioned officers wore red worsted epaulets; staff sergeants, one on each shoulder; line sergeants, one on the right shoulder; and corporals, one on the left shoulder. The artillery and infantry wore blue coats with red facings whereas the cavalry wore green coats with white facings. All wore cocked hats with a black cockade having an eagle in the center. The enlisted man's cockade was of leather and his eagle of tin. The regiments were distinguished by the numbers on their white buttons.

How all this new organization and these numerous regulations could have been put into effect in the face of an approaching French army can be answered when we look at the

turmoil and powerlessness in which the country found itself
thirteen years later. We can only be thankful that the well-
trained French army never appeared.

The disturbances of these times call attention to the undisciplined condition of the country. One John Fries led a *March 7*
rebellion in Pennsylvania. He had collected a large body of *1799*
men who were opposed to the war tax. Although a presidential
proclamation ordered the rioters to disperse, an armed force
was necessary to put down the insurrection.

In the midst of all this furor, an event occurred which *March 14*
should have made the populace stop and think. Washington *1799*
died suddenly at Mt. Vernon. The nation had not yet learned to
appreciate the greatness of this man. But the Revolutionary
soldiers knew him, missed him, and mourned him. They had
been close beside him when the fire tested him and them together. They knew that he was the Revolution—he was the
new country. Iron-hearted and soft-handed he had been their
friend and leader. He had met the blackest of men and times
and turned both to account. The members of the army told
the nation these things about the fireside, near the forge, over
the counter and in the churches. And the country listened,
but not till many years later did it quite comprehend.

No sooner had Washington died and the trouble with *May 14*
France apparently passed over, than Congress tore down the *1800*
greater part of the military structure it had raised. It violently
threw into the discard his soundest counsel. All regular forces
except the first 4 regiments of infantry, 2 regiments of artillerists and engineers, 2 troops of light dragoons and "the general and other staff" were ordered to be discharged; 3,399 men
were cast out of the service.

That some few who remained evidently had an interest in
their profession, is shown from the attention to details. For
the 2 remaining troops of dragoons there appeared from the
press of E. A. Jenks "an exact set of cavalry exercises, an
approved work." The volume explained the manual of the
pistol and sword, and exact movements for the horsemen.

Effort at Harper's Ferry was made to standardize the rifle
by the manufacture of the model 1800. By it a single caliber
of .62 was devised for the whole army. In rifle regiments

officers carried it instead of a sword. The weapon for them was slightly lighter and more ornamented than the enlisted man's. A rampart rifle weighing 20 pounds or more was also made at the arsenal. It was used solely to fire over parapets.

Dec. 19
1801

In spite of the fact that the actual strength of the army, notwithstanding the organization provided, numbered only 248 officers, 9 cadets and 3,794 enlisted men, Congress was not satisfied with this reduction.

March 16
1802

There being every indication of peace, that body further scorned Washington's sentiments and contracted the fighting

Effective
June 1
1802

force of the country to 2 regiments of infantry, 1 regiment of artillerists of 4 battalions (of 5 companies each), and 1 corps of engineers consisting of 1 major, 2 captains, 2 first lieutenants, 2 second lieutenants and 10 cadets. Three military agents [14] were also provided for, and the grade of colonel for the first time since the Revolution came into being in the artillery. Of the general officers, a brigadier was the only one allowed. The pay, subsistence and forage remained about the same, except that the brigadier received $225 per month and nothing else.

The great redeeming feature of this legislation was the actual establishment, under the guise of a corps of engineers,

---

[14] "Sec. 17. That it shall be the duty of the military agents, designated by this act, to purchase, receive, and forward to their proper destination all military stores, and other articles for the troops in their respective departments, and all goods and annuities for the Indians, which they may be directed to purchase, or which shall be ordered into their care by the department of war. They shall account with the department of war, annually, for all the public property which may pass through their hands, and all the moneys which they may expend in discharge of the duties of their offices, respectively; previous to their entering on the duties of their offices, they shall give bonds with sufficient sureties, in such sums as the President of the United States shall direct, for the faithful discharge of the trust reposed in them; and shall take an oath faithfully to perform the duties of their respective offices. . . .

"Sec. 27. That the said corps, when so organized, shall be stationed at West Point, in the state of New York, and shall constitute a military academy; and the engineers, assistant engineers, and cadets of the said corps, shall be subject, at all times, to do duty in such places, and on such service, as the President of the United States shall direct.

"Sec. 28. That the principal engineer, and in his absence the next in rank, shall have the superintendence of the said military academy, under the direction of the President of the United States; and the secretary of war is hereby authorized, at the public expense, under such regulations as shall be directed by the President of the United States to procure the necessary books, implements, and apparatus for the use and benefit of the said institution."

THE ARMY FLUNG ASIDE

of the educational institution that was to have such a decided influence upon the future of the country. The United States Military Academy at West Point was born.

Washington, as early as 1793, had indicated the desirability of a Military Academy in his message to Congress. Timothy Pickering had earlier suggested West Point as the place. Although Washington was opposed in his views by Jefferson, the first President showed in 1796 that his original desire had been intensified. But when Jefferson, after he had studied the question, became a most zealous advocate of the plan, the idea of a Military Academy seemed to be right from every point of view.

George Barron, a civilian, had established, previous to the above act, a mathematical school at West Point for the few cadets then in the service. But the government of young military men appeared to be incompatible with the systems in vogue in ordinary schools, for the "institution ran into disorder and the teacher into contempt."

Even after the act of 1802 only a few of the officers authorized were appointed. Major Jonathan Williams became the first superintendent. To his lot fell such instruction as reading lectures on fortifications, teaching the use of instruments and conducting practical exercises in the field. The two captains, W. A. Barron and Jared Mansfield, taught algebra and geometry. The limited curriculum of this nebulous school was also hindered by the intermittent appearance of the teachers, who were ordered away for such duty as erecting fortifications in various parts of the country.

Cadets were quartered in the old "Long Barrack" of the Revolution. They were instructed in a two-story "academy" building which was also the dwelling of the superintendent.

They were limited by no entrance examinations and no age, physical or mental qualifications. They were not amenable to martial law, had no class rank and demanded the right to select such branch of service as pleased them. But the Corps was begun and the foundation of great possibilities laid.

Much could hardly be expected immediately from such a school. In these times when the most exciting duty for an officer away from the frontier was to sit on a court for the trial of a lieutenant colonel who refused to cut off his cue and trim his whiskers to a prescribed line, of a major for selling milk to his command or of a lieutenant for shooting his captain's ducks, little could be expected in the way of teaching bristling, pregnant, trenchant truths.   These officers, trussed up in their great single-breasted blue coats with high standing collars that hampered relaxation, could scarcely have the speed of olive drab.

March 3
1803

April 18
1806

Feb. 24
1807

While West Point was being established the country was disturbed by the ominous prospect of a war with Spain.   Congress accordingly issued a host of militia calls that were to stretch over several years.   First of all 80,000 were authorized for one year.   Then a similar law made the period of service six months.   Later 30,000 were authorized to be enlisted for one year.   All these enactments were inoperative almost as soon as made.

During this inconsequential agitation, 2 army officers, Captain Meriwether Lewis and Lieutenant William Clark,[15] with 4 sergeants, and 23 privates and Indian interpreters traversed, between midsummer, 1803, and the autmn of 1806, the entire continent from east to west and back again from west to east. The exploit is so famous in general history that little need be said of it here.   Following the Missouri they made their way to the coast.   Taking accurate surveys and constructing maps and creating friendships with the Indians, many of whom were seeing a white man for the first time, they picked their way from prairie to mountain and from mountain to the coast.   To the suffering, hardihood and daring of these soldiers the United States owes the opening of the west.

April 30
1806

While Lewis and Clark were gone, the idea occurred to General Wilkinson, commander of the army and governor of Louisiana Territory, to send out a similar expedition.   Lieutenant Zebulon Montgomery Pike (afterwards General) with 1 sergeant, 2 corporals and 17 privates explored the head waters of the Mississippi.   After enduring much that Lewis and Clark had undergone, he returned less than nine months later to St. Louis, having made peace with the northern Indians and learned much of their country.   Without an educated partner

---

[15] Brother of George Rogers Clark.

he had acted as astronomer, surveyor, commanding officer, clerk, spy and guide for the expedition.

General Wilkinson was so much pleased with the results *July 1807* that he sent Pike with 1 lieutenant, 1 sergeant, 2 corporals and 16 privates south toward the mouth of the Mississippi. The mission of this young officer was to effect an interview and good understanding with the Yanctons, Tetons and Comanches and to return certain captured Osage Indians to their home. Not only was Pike successful in this enterprise, but he explored the region about the peak which bears his name and beguiled the Spaniards into taking his party prisoners to Santa Fe, where he learned much of Spanish intentions, customs and the nature of the country. The exploration furnished unusually valuable information and was given the personal approbation of the President.

To return to the army proper the little force had dwindled *Feb. 4 1805* at one time during this exploration period to 175 officers, 12 cadets and 2,389 enlisted men. Morale in the service was low. The older officers were, as a rule, idle, ignorant and intemperate because appointments were dependent almost entirely on politics. It was not difficult to sidetrack into the service "swaggerers, dependents, decayed gentlemen" and those thought fit for nothing else. The Military Academy had furnished but a very few junior officers. Besides, the soldier had come to be such a plaything of the government that often excellent men hesitated to accept a position that might unexpectedly be no more to-morrow.

Here is an instance of the laxity with which the people handled military matters. Twenty-six years after the virtual *April 10 1806* close of the Revolution, the country woke up to the fact that it had not dealt fairly with those who had fought in that war. With most of the actually deserving ones deceased, it generously provided for the remainder. This anachronism emphasized not only a lack of past justice but the extravagance of spending almost $20,000,000 for widows who survived till almost as late as our war with Spain in '98. But most of the soldiers who really deserved this pension never received it.

In the meantime the war with Great Britain was threat- *April 12 1808* ening. Again the army, which recently had been cut down, was increased; 5 regiments of infantry, 1 regiment of rifle-men, 1 regiment of light artillery and 1 regiment of light dra-goons, to be enlisted for five years were added. Two cadets were to be assigned to each company or troop. The regiment of dragoons was to be composed of 8 troops, whereas the other regiments were to have 10 companies. The pay was to remain about the same.[16] But the failure to increase the staff made the work of raising and organizing these 6,000 additional men almost impossible.

1808   The reason for the "light artillery" in this legislation may be due to the fact that *Maneuvers of Horse Artillery* by General Kosciusko appeared that year. The manual's introduction enunciates this remarkable principle:

"The use of artillery in battle is not against the artillery of an enemy, for that would be a waste of powder, but against the line of the enemy in a diagonal direction when it is destructive in the extreme."

The maneuvers consisted of detaching limbers, making fast prolonge and drag and executing similar evolutions to those in Steuben's regulations for infantry. The book showed the armament of the company to be six pounders and two five-and-a-half-inch howitzers, although four and eight pounders might be used.

1810   In 1810 little of account happened for the army. The uniform was radically changed to single-breasted coats without facings and with silver lace along the buttonholes. There was also prescribed the silk hat (much like the civilian one at present) with a cockade on the side.

West Point's faculty was increased by teachers of "drawing and of the French Language."

Congress was far from negligent of its fortifications and seacoast defenses. It mistakenly had the notion that such construction would keep an enterprising enemy from landing on our shores. Although it had accepted archaic plans of pur-

---

[16] The brigadier was to receive $104 a month, 12 rations and $16 for forage.

ported engineers in political favor and had used them with great loss and against the advice of Major Joseph G. Swift,[17] it still had a mass of fortresses along the coast to show for the several millions it had expended. Just before the second war with Great Britain there existed 24 forts, 32 inclosed batteries *1811* and works of masonry with an armament of 750 guns of various calibers; 12,610 soldiers were needed to man these strongholds.

While Great Britain was about to strike from the east and north, the savages were again breaking out in the west. The hostile Indian tribes under Tecumseh and his prophet brother were collecting in force with manifest intentions of bringing destruction to the white settlers along the Wabash. General William Henry Harrison collected a band of regulars and militia to combat them. His knowledge of the savage caused him to keep his command constantly on the alert. He took up a final position on the west bank of the Tippecanoe River where *Nov. 7* he was later attacked. The struggle was desperate and success *1811* for our troops much of the time doubtful. But the fact that the riflemen were fighting on the defensive and were superior marksmen finally gave Harrison the advantage.

In these post Revolutionary years the army passed through swift periods of rise and fall. It was the thermometer of the nation's fear. At first, under the constitution, it was barely 1 regiment, then 2 in 1789, 3 in 1791, a legion corresponding to 5 in 1792, 6 in 1796, 9 in 1798, 6 in 1800 and 3 again in 1802. In 1808 it suddenly sprang to 11 regiments each having 8, 10 or 20 companies depending upon the law by which the particular organization was born. But the actual number of soldiers recruited, irrespective of laws, seemed to vary little. In 1805, the army consisted of 2,732 officers and men; in 1807, of less than 2,500; and 1809, 2,965; although the authorized strength during these years showed differences of nearly 400 per cent.

How could any organization under such whimsical change be otherwise than far below standard? How could the velocity of such expansion and contraction do else than break the joints of our land defense? There could be no unity or spirit in the

---

[17] The first graduate of the Military Academy.

army under such sudden measures of giving and taking away.

Aside from a very few men who had graduated from the Military Academy and others who, like Winfield Scott, had entered the service with the highest motives, the officers took little interest in their profession. Politics rather than qualifications commissioned them. Steuben's work had been rooted up and nothing had been planted in its place save West Point, which as yet could give few results. The old training had passed out when the army had been flung aside. Too often was the officer at this time an idler or martinet, and often both. When Congress and the people took so little interest in proper national defense, such decadence was to be expected.

A good man, who might under better conditions have enlisted, sensed the instability of the army and shied at the unknown. Either in entering or leaving the service of his country he would be unpopular. His pay would be low and his life hard and dangerous. His treatment, too, was likely to be bad. He hesitated to give up his chances in civil life when he did not know how long the government might keep him. In spite of the small wages, he might have come into the army had there existed an established pride of corps and a distinction in being a defender of his nation. But when both these elements were taken away, the excellent recruit was hard to obtain.

Dec. 24 1811

Congress had to offer to any man who would enlist or reënlist for five years a bonus of $16 bounty, to be paid at once, and 3 months' pay and 160 acres of land upon honorable discharge. As an added inducement his heirs were to receive all this gratuity if the soldier died or was killed in line of duty.

With ordinary attention to the happenings of the Revolution thirty years before and to the first man in peace as well as war, who had just died, Congress could have made an excellent, economical force. But it had forgotten the magic word "training." Because it had not listened to the voice of experience and wisdom, it could not in a twinkling find a substitute for time. Nor could it organize efficiently or economically after the panic was once started.

To Washington, the country accorded mourning for thirty days, the annual observance of his birthday, a high monument, the name of the capital of the nation and the splendid title of "Father of his Country," but it consistently spurned the advice he held most dear:

"To be prepared for war is one of the most effectual means of preserving peace. A free people ought not only be armed but disciplined."

CHAPTER V

THE ARMY IN NAME

(1812–1820)

NO period casts upon the United States a more justifiable shadow than the one which includes the second war against Great Britain. Almost thirty years had passed since the first one, when nearly 400,000 frantically raised soldiers had sought to drive little more than 40,000 of the enemy from our shores. At the end of this illuminating interval, the government found itself with larger resources and a firmer control, but with nothing that might be mistaken for trained forces. Men of the type of Washington, Steuben, Greene and Morgan had passed out. There had meanwhile been no incentive to produce soldiers technically schooled for battle and campaign. Bereft of ordinary means of keeping afloat, the country was about to plunge into war.

The opening of 1812 saw the army almost as heterogeneously organized, or disorganized, as when Steuben appeared at Valley Forge. Congress had established companies ranging from 64 to 100 men; and regiments, from 10 to 20 companies. Although the regular establishment had been raised to 11 regiments, less than one fifth of the added numbers had been recruited and no provisions had been made for a competent staff to handle the increase. Only 71 cadets had so far been graduated from a Military Academy of irregular and infantile curriculum. Even if such men as Thayer, Swift and Totten were beginning to give good accounts of themselves, they were so young and few that they scarcely formed a nucleus.

The several thousand regulars were chained to the frontier forts and the coast line. They could not be withdrawn for combined use without inviting massacres of the frontiersmen and the loss of possessions. The First, Fourth and Fifth regi-

116

ments of infantry were scattered in small groups along the
vast stretch of territory on the edges of the Great Lakes and
on the borders of Ohio and Indiana; the Seventh was spread
through Kentucky; the Sixth was found in the southwest; the
Second in the vicinity of New Orleans; and the Third along
the frontier of Georgia and Florida. The artillery in small
detachments was dotted along the coast from Maine to Georgia
and the regiment of dragoons was broken up and used as foot
troops with the infantry.

Off in their primitive inclosures, the little companies, platoons and sections formed their ranks for morning parade with
white belts immaculate, breast plates polished and "silk" (or
"plug") hats shined to a gloss. The musketeer in his blue
coatee with bullet buttons and herring-bone buttonholes, the
rifleman in the full-dress gray coat of a modern cadet, and the
officer in his high black boots with gilt spurs marched solemnly
and punctiliously before the commanding officer. If from the
blockhouse there came the cry "Indians," the scene suddenly
took on more action. Each man knew his part. The hunting
shirt and nankeen overalls replaced the coatee and the tight-
fitting breeches. The dress quickly changed, but the discipline
remained. Through straining days and nights the meager garrison watched every loophole for the fatal fiebrand or the
crawling redskin. After hours of sleeplessness, hunger and
oftentimes fever, the defenders finally convinced the savage of
the futility of his errand. Then came the burials, the ministra-
tions to the sick and the repairs to the stockade. The few, who
had become fewer, returned to the routine of toil and isolation.

To help in the protection of these frontiers Congress au- *Jan. 2*
thorized the enlistment of 6 companies of "Rangers" for twelve *1812*
months. Then, because of threatening war with England, it *Jan. 11*
added to the regular troops 10 regiments of infantry of 18 *1812*
companies each, 3 regiments of artillery of 20 companies each
and a regiment of light dragoons of 12 companies. After the
increase, the army theoretically consisted of 17 regiments of
infantry, 4 of artillery, 2 of dragoons and 1 of rifles, together
with a corps of engineers composed of 16 officers and 4 cadets.[1]

---

1 "Sec. 3. That to each regiment raised under this act, whether of
infantry, artillery or light dragoons, there shall be appointed 1 colonel,

The new legislation amounted to paper energy. If sufficient recruits could not be had for the former army certainly the acquirement of fresh ones on the same conditions was ridiculous. In this strait, Congress, instead of raising the inducement for men who could be held long enough to be trained, resorted to calling out 30,000 volunteers. This move gave the same reaction as Glendower's "spirits from the vasty deep."

However, from the mist of these legislative acts there did arise a Quartermaster's Department. Although imperfectly created, it was the first legal recognition of an actual supply staff. Military agents were supplanted by a quartermaster-general, with rank of brigadier, four deputy quartermasters and an elastic number of assistants, depending upon the requirements of public service. The act itself looked very well, but it had so many "riders" pertaining to the ordnance and subsistence branches that confusion and delay resulted. Some one said it should truly have been entitled "An act for the speedy enrichment of contractors and the periodical starvation of the troops of the United States." But it was at least a step toward making an organized supply department.

Finding out for certain that it could not raise the army it had voted, Congress now hedged on its original idea by reducing the period of enlistment for 50 per cent of the volunteers to eighteen months. Finally it threw up its hands altogether and passed its responsibility to the States by asking the Governors to have 80,000 officers and men ready to march at a moment's notice. What came of this request will be seen later.

The signal legislation of this period was the improvement that Congress, under the direction of President Madison, made in the Military Academy. The authorized number of cadets was raised to a maximum of 250. The Corps of Engineers was increased by 6 officers. A force of 94 enlisted men was

---

2 lieutenant colonels, 2 majors, 2 adjutants, 1 quartermaster, 1 paymaster, 1 surgeon, 2 surgeon's mates, 2 sergeant majors, 2 quartermaster sergeants, and 2 senior musicians.''

Other sections allowed 2 major generals and 5 brigadiers, and fixed the pay at the prevailing rate for all except the major general who was to receive $200 for pay, $20 for forage, and 15 rations per month.

formed into a "company of bombardiers, sappers and miners," who afterwards gave actual demonstrations to the cadets.

The instructional staff was augmented by a professor of natural and experimental philosophy with rank and pay of lieutenant colonel, a professor of mathematics, and a professor of the art of engineering, the last two with rank and pay of major.[2] Cadets were placed under the established discipline of academy regulations, were to be organized by the superin-tendent into companies, were to be encamped three months out of the year and were to be "trained and taught all the duties of a private, noncommissioned officer and officer." Although this uplift to the Academy was not to bear fruit in this war, it was to be a boon to the next one and to the interval between.

The eve of war saw another development in the staff. The *May 14 1812* Ordnance Department made its appearance. Its head was to be styled commissary-general of ordnance, and to have the rank of colonel, an allowance of $500 a year and 4 rations a day for clerks. He was to have associated with him 1 assis-tant with rank of major, 4 with rank of captain and as many with rank of second lieutenant as the President saw fit to give.

The first activity of the year was instituted in the west before war was declared. Colonel William Hull, a valiant officer during the Revolution and then governor of Michigan, was requested by the Secretary of War to take command of the western forces, to accept a commission as brigadier general and to lead the troops to Detroit. Well knowing the situation and the kind of untrained men upon whom he had to rely, he refused the appointment. But upon being importuned later, he ac-cepted. Late in May he arrived at Dayton, Ohio, and took *June 10 1812* charge of 1,200 militia who were hopelessly ill-supplied. With these he reached Urbana, where he was joined by the Fourth Infantry of regulars, numbering only 300 effectives. From there he started to cut his way through 200 miles of wilder-ness. With a large proportion of undisciplined, hungry men who had to be urged along often at the point of the bayonet by

---

[2] If these professors were selected from the Corps of Engineers instead of the line they were to retain their rank in that corps but to have the same pay and emoluments as those of the rank indicated for the professor-ships.

the regulars, he attempted to work north and at the same time protect his rear. Naturally, the progress was slow when he had to cut roads, build bridges and garrison the blockhouses he constructed.

In the east General Dearborn, who was in command of the army, could not obtain even poor troops. When he called for some of the 80,000 the President had requisitioned, in conformity with the recent law, he was met with a cold rebuff. The governors of Massachusetts and Connecticut would not, on the express order of the Secretary of War, send a single soldier. They stated that since their particular states were in no danger of invasion they could not comply, and then rested their case on constitutional nicety and legal minutiae.

June 1812

General Hull was in almost as awkward a position as General Dearborn. The authorities in Washington, without any realization of his obstacles, were urging him by heavy packets of correspondence to hasten his advance to Detroit. Such governmental heckling was so usual it would not here be commented upon, were it not for a blunder of criminal omission. Of the declaration of war no mention was made in those letters carefully sent by messengers. That vital information was intrusted to the public mails and to such conveyance as chance in a rugged country provided. As a consequence the commander of our army in the field did not know of the existence of a state of war until July 2, several days after the Canadian government had been discreetly apprised of the fact by our Secretary of the Treasury. Such conscientious consideration of the enemy to the exclusion of our own troops did not raise the spirits of General Hull's force.

War declared June 18 1812

Once the struggle had started Congress realized that although an army scattered in little detachments might resist savages successfully with conglomerate regimental organizations, some sort of uniformity was necessary to make them operate as a team. Accordingly the strength was set at 10 companies per regiment, more nearly conforming to Steuben's idea.[3] Why such an obvious detail had been ignored in peace, admits of but one answer.

June 26 1812

---

[3] "Sec. 1. That the infantry of the army of the United States shall consist of twenty-five regiments, and that a regiment shall consist of one

A little later other legislation gave the President authority to appoint two more brigadier generals, to place federal officers over volunteers and to confer honorary brevet rank for over ten years' service in any one grade and for "meritorious conduct." This attempt to better the officer personnel without spending money proved to be more harmful than helpful. The honor was empty and rank became confused. *July 6 1812*

Hull finally arrived at Detroit. When a few hundred Michigan militia had joined him, he crossed into Canada in spite of the fact that 180 of the Ohio volunteers refused to accompany him. *July 12 1812*

In the vicinity of Sandwich he spent about a month supplying himself off the country, trying to win over the inhabitants and seeking to get some howitzers and cannon which he lacked. Finally he decided to attack the British post at Malden. But on the eve of the venture, being apparently impressed with the caliber of his troops and the fall of Michimackinac,[4] the key to the trade routes, he returned to Detroit with his whole force.

After he had placed his troops behind fortifications of the strongest type, about 1,300 British and Indians threatened to attack him. Though well armed and equipped, Hull surrendered without any show of resistance. Detroit fell and the northwest passed into the hands of the British. What the British commander thought of the militia at the capitulation is shown by the ease with which he allowed them to go home, whereas he took the regulars as prisoners to Montreal, where, after many hardships, they were finally exchanged. Much has *Aug. 16 1812*

---

colonel, one lieutenant colonel, one major, one adjutant, one paymaster, one quartermaster sergeant, two principal musicians, and ten companies.

"Sec. 2. That each company shall consist of one captain, one first lieutenant, one second lieutenant, one ensign, four sergeants, six corporals, two musicians, and ninety privates.

"Sec. 4. That each troop of cavalry, or light dragoons, shall consist of one captain, one first lieutenant, one second lieutenant, one cornet, four sergeants, six corporals, two musicians, one master of the sword, one saddler, one farrier, one blacksmith, and sixty-four privates; and the pay and emoluments of a master of the sword shall be the same as those of a riding-master, and the pay and emoluments of a blacksmith shall be the same as those of a farrier.

(June 26, 1812.)

[4] Mackinaw, a regular army frontier post about 270 miles northwest of Detroit. The small garrison completely unaware of the existence of war had been on July 17 surprised and captured by a Canadian force familiar with the state of hostility.

been written of this disgraceful capitulation both in condemnation and defense, but whatever has been said on either side has never been at variance with one fact: the government trusted to senility in command and inexperience in rank and file—about all that it had allowed itself to have.

The operations of other American commands during the remainder of the year were almost as futile. Along the Niagara frontier General Stephen Van Rensselaer had been attempting *Sept. 1 1812* to collect a central army. About this time it numbered altogether 691 men—unpaid, unfed, un-everything as was the custom. It, therefore, had to wait until later for any activity. At Ogdensburg General Jacob Brown of the New York militia had driven off from behind earthworks a superior force of British, but the numbers engaged were so small as to make the effect on the war very little. In the west, General Hopkins with 4,000 Kentucky militia attempted to punish the hostile Indians along *Oct. 10 1812* the Wabash and Illinois rivers. The state volunteers assembled at Fort Harrison with enthusiasm. But on the march the hardships on these undisciplined men brought insubordination and disobedience. In five days they had abandoned their General and dispersed to their homes.

Oct. 11 1812 General Van Rensselaer having later collected at Lewiston about 2,500 New York militia and 450 regulars—mostly recruits—planned to take the heights of Queenstown across the river. His idea was to send over 600 of the best troops first. *Oct. 13 1812* But boats seemed to be lacking at the last minute so that only about 225 made the crossing. This little force gallantly attacked and took the heights. There they withstood charge after charge throughout the day, vainly hoping for reënforcements. Overpowered at last by superior numbers, most of them were either killed or captured. During these terrible hours an overwhelming force of American militia on the New York side looked on calmly at the slaughter. Tomes says:

"They were ordered, threatened and entreated. The militia, nevertheless, were not disposed to move. As one half of the boats had drifted away or been swamped in the confusion, the men pleaded the want of means to carry them over. It was then suggested that they should cross in detachments; and as the general became still more urgent in his entreaties, he so far prevailed, as to induce a militia company handsomely equipped to consent to go. Just as they were entering the boats, however, a firing was heard from the opposite side of the river; and these gallantly arrayed soldiers halted and firmly stood their ground, declaring they would not cross. Moreover, they took occasion to express their scruples about invading foreign territory and affirmed that they, as militia, had constitutional objections which no general could induce them to waive on that occasion."

Corporal Stubbs in his diary seems to corroborate this account from a different standpoint, the standpoint of the gallant fellows on the Canadian shore:

" . . . But we were now in our turn unfortunate, for one half of our army was yet on the other side of the river, nor would the cowardly dogs come over to assist us when they saw the d—d red coats cutting us up like slain venson!—The enemy now doubled their numbers while every shot diminished ours, in truth they got the better of us, and again got possession of their batteries altho we let fly showers of ball and buck shot into their very teeth and eyes! AH! the poor yankee lads, this was a sorry moment for ye! they dropped my brave companions like wild pigeons, while their balls whistled like a northwest wind through a dry can brake!—our Commander ordered a retreat, but nature never formed any of our family you know for runners, so I wadled along as well as I could behind, but the redcoat villians overhaul'd me, and took me prisoner! but not until I had a fare shot at their head commander General Brock, who galloping his horse after my retreating comrads, bellowed out to 'um like a wounded buffalo to surrender, but I levelled my old fatheful bess, which never disappointed me in so fare a mark, and I heard no more of his croaking afterwards—of 1,000 which crossed over but a few escaped biting the dust!— As for porr me, I expected they'd kill and scalp me, but after stareing at me as if I had been born with two heads, and enquiring of what nation I was, and from what part of the world I came, their Colonel ordered me liberated, who said to me, 'old daddy, your age and odd appearance induces me now to set you at liberty, return home to your family and think no more of invading us!'—This I promised him I would do, but I didn't mean so for I was determined I wouldn't give up the chase so, but at 'um again.''

So Queenstown added another humiliation to our arms and revealed the shocking fact that untrained men would not even go to the rescue of their stricken comrades. An effort in the west did not turn out much better. General Harrison tried to lead a column into Canada. His call for recruits brought the quick response that is usual with men who know nothing of the hardships of campaign. About 10,000 militia of Kentucky, Tennessee, Virginia, and Pennsylvania started to plod through the cold swamps of the north. A slight fray with the Indians was the test of their endurance. Some deliberately returned to camp and others to their homes. The remainder stayed only at the earnest entreaties of their officers. At any rate the numbers dwindled to such an extent that the work of the year for these troops stopped.

Oct.–Nov. 1812

General Dearborn, the commander in chief of the northern department, had 6,300 troops along the northern boundary. With 2,200 at Sackett's Harbor, under the immediate command of General Smythe,[5] and 5,000 at Plattsburg he controlled an army over six times as strong in man power as all the Canadian forces. Had they been trained, combined and hurled as a single unit against the enemy, one campaign would have sufficed for the war. But General Dearborn was satisfied with fractions and small ones at that. He reserved for himself the force at Plattsburg. Although the 5,000 there were sufficient in themselves to take Montreal, he was content with using only 1,500 under Colonels Pike and Clarke for an expedition against a small British post on the river La Colle. Subdividing this command still further into two detachments he sent them out in the nighttime. One drove the small force of Indians and Canadians away without capturing them. The other, hearing the firing, mistook the assaulting troops for the enemy. The

Nov. 20 1812

---

[5] General Van Rensselaer had resigned in chagrin after Queenstown. General Smythe was his successor.

resulting picture discloses two American commanders firing into each other effectively while the enemy escaped.

General Dearborn and his troops now being weary went into winter quarters at Plattsburg.

General Smythe remained the one hope of the year. So far he had been content with issuing soul-stirring proclamations to the surrounding inhabitants. "Volunteers!" he had written, "I esteem your generous and patriotic motives... You will show the *eternal infamy* that awaits the man who, having come within sight of the enemy, *basely shrinks* in the moment of trial. Soldiers of every corps! it is in your power to retrieve the honor of your country."

By means of such turgid outflow, he had induced at least 4,500 men to come to him. After the repose of General Dearborn, he burst into fresh torrents of words, plainly admitting the defects of previous commanders and his own eminent fitness to gain the victory.

Having collected at Black Rock seventy rowboats and numbers of bateaux, he announced the exact date of invasion to be November 28. On the eve of the appointed day, he sent over the river under cover of the night a small advance guard which spiked the enemy's cannon and returned in safety.

The next day 2,000 men under General P. B. Porter took to the boats early in the morning preparatory to rowing across the stream. General Smythe with the remaining number (over 3,000) paraded in full view of the enemy's forts. To the hostile cannonade his batteries replied with a fire of shells and red-hot shot. All seemed to be ready for attack. But throughout the morning the troops waited for the order to proceed. In the afternoon General Smythe, without explanation, gave instructions for the vanguard to disembark and for all to return to their quarters.

So openly resentful were some of the men who had been wheedled into leaving their firesides, that the General promised to invade Canada at a later date.

Accordingly three days afterwards the command was drawn *Dec. 1* up as before. Again the boats were entered and again the *1812* troops waited for the order to proceed. This time the General was conducting a council of war. He had forgotten up until that time that an invasion was not to be undertaken without the approval of his principal officers. His real reason was that now that some of his troops had refused to enter the boats he was mistrustful of the stability of his men. At any rate, as afternoon approached, he again ordered the troops to disembark and to be informed that the invasion was given up for the season.

Thompson says:

"The scene of discontent which followed was without a parallel. Four thousand men without order or restraint indignantly discharged their muskets in every direction. The person of the commanding general was threatened. Upward of 1,000 men of all classes of society had suddenly left their homes and families, and had made great sacrifices to obey the call of their country under General Smythe's invitation."

Scorned and hunted, Smythe finally took refuge in his own home in Virginia. Having "come within sight of the enemy" and "basely shrunk" he became the victim of his own words. On the other hand, he possibly had a just fear that the militia would desert him at the last moment.

The closing year saw the militia dispersed, the regulars in winter quarters and Congress again casting about to get soldiers. Legislative efforts resulted in raising the pay on a scale ranging from $12 for a sergeant major to $8 for each "private, driver, bombardier, mattross, sapper and miner." But the act was a little late to do much good.

Dec. 12
1812

At the opening of 1813 a detachment of General Harrison's force, commanded by General Winchester, made its way through a two-foot snow and high drifts on its way to the rapids of the Maumee. The men, having harnessed themselves to sledges in order to transport their own baggage, covered the required distance of forty miles in ten days. One soldier described his difficulties on this march as follows:

Jan.
1813

"Our tents were struck, and in half an hour we were on the road. I will candidly confess that, on that day, I regretted being a soldier. We marched thirty miles under an incessant

rain (on the day before the snow had fallen so deep as to be up
to a man's waist), and I am afraid you will doubt my veracity
when I tell you that in eight miles of the best of the road, it
took us over the knees and often to the middle.   The Black
Swamp would have been considered impassable by all but men
determined to surmount every difficulty to accomplish the object
of their march.   The water was about six inches deep on the ice,
which was very rotten, often breaking through to the depth of
four or five feet.   The same night we encamped on very wet
ground, but the driest that could be found, the rain still continuing.   It was with difficulty we could raise fires; we had no
tents; our clothes were wet; no axes; nothing to cook with, and
very little to eat.   A brigade of pack-horses being near us, we
procured from them some flour; killed a hog; our bread was
baked in the ashes, and our pork we broiled on the coals—a
sweeter meal I never partook of.   When we went to sleep, it was
on two logs laid close to each other, to keep our bodies from the
damp ground."

   While gathering supplies [6] from the surrounding country,
General Winchester was informed that the Americans at *Jan. 18*
Frenchtown thirty miles away were in need of succor.   Aban-   *1813*
doning much of his work of provisioning the northwestern
army, he sent Colonel Lewis with 550 men at once to the town.
This force with reënforcements of 150 men attacked with such
vigor that it drove the British and Indians away.   Nor could
the enemy retake the position after repeated assaults.
   But discipline and training tell more sometimes in sealing
a victory than in gaining it.   After the enemy had apparently
left the field, the inflated officers and soldiers neglected all cau-   *Jan. 20*
tion.   When General Winchester with another detachment of   *1813*
350 had joined them, they became so reckless that they straggled
over the country at will and established no outpost.   In this condition they were surprised in the early morning by about a
thousand British and Indians, who had arrived within gunshot   *Jan. 22*
before they were discovered by the Americans.   *1813*

---

   [6] Had not General Harrison made himself a glorified supply officer in
this campaign the soldiers would have had nothing to eat.

Jan. 23
1813

In the action that followed, half the command was easily captured by the enemy because it had taken up a hasty and untenable position, and the next day the whole of General Winchester's previously successful force was surrendered.[7]

Jan. 20
1813

Legislation during this inconsequential excursion was exerting itself just as effectually; $24 in addition to the existing bounty of $16, three months' pay and 160 acres of land were offered to a recruit, and $4 to the officer who procured him. To each regular regiment there was added 1 major and to each troop or company 1 third lieutenant and 1 extra sergeant. A member of the militia was allowed to enlist in the regular army; heretofore, by existing law, he had been prohibited from so

Jan. 29
1813

doing. Twenty extra regiments were to be raised for one year and 6 major generals and 6 brigadier generals were added to the army.

Feb. 24
1813

The appointees to the higher grade were Harrison, Wilkinson, Hampton, Lewis, Davie and Ogden; to the lower, Izard, Pike, Winder, M'Arthur, Cass and Howard.

The written strength of the regular army was now 44 regiments of infantry, 4 regiments of artillery, 2 regiments of dragoons, 1 regiment of rifles, 1 corps of engineers and the staff. It is doubtful if a sixth of this 58,000 men was ever recruited.

A *New System of Discipline* for infantry being adopted, the drill of that time was returned to the French system. Companies and platoons were formed in 3 ranks at 2 feet distance. A regiment was organized into 1 or 2 battalions, depending on the number of companies. A platoon consisted of 32 men and a section of 8 men. In wheeling, the front rank moved on a circle, the middle rank on a "less circle to the front" and the rear rank on a "circle still less." The maneuvers were, in general, so complicated that they were difficult for the recruit to master.

Smith's *Artillery Tactics* conformed more nearly to Steuben's principles. A company of 1 captain, 2 lieutenants, 4 sergeants, 4 corporals, 6 gunners, 6 bombardiers and 32 mattrosses paraded in 1 rank; a company of double that size, in 2 ranks.

---

[7] Killed, 397; wounded, 27; prisoners, 522.

In wheeling, receiving and manning the piece at the park and in limbering and unlimbering the pieces, the movements were precisely worked out in detail. The batteries were taught to fire while advancing and retreating, to move with either the right or left in front and to "display" pieces either to the left or right. Chisel marks were placed on the "base ring" and "swelling of the muzzle" of the gun in order to get a proper line of sight and elevation for firing at a target. The system for so doing was elaborate. Because the guns were not uniformly made, each piece had to have its own chisel marks, carefully and mathematically worked out by the battery officers, or the shooting with cannons would be ineffective. It is needless to say in this undisciplined fracas that the artillery did not figure greatly.

One of the very few land successes of this war was an expedition led by General Pike [8] against York (Toronto). With *April 27 1813* about 1,700 picked men he attacked a stronghold garrisoned by about 850 Canadians and Indians, mostly militia. Under a trained officer, the Americans advanced bravely and would have taken the fortress without much loss had not a magazine within the works of the enemy accidentally exploded. The havoc and death resulting on both sides were tremendous. General Pike and about 280 of his men were killed. But since the United States troops were the first to rally they charged the place and took it. With greater numbers and more training than the enemy, our forces gave a good account of themselves.

Shortly after this victory the War Office printed the *Mili-* *May 1 1813* *tary Laws and Rules and Regulations for the Armies of the United States.* The initial appearance of such a work was the forerunner of the present *Army Regulations.* At that time it comprised information such as the rank of regiments and officers, duties of the staff departments, rules governing promotion and other instructional matter. The following extract marks an advance in prescribing punishments:

"And be it further enacted, That in lieu of whipping, as provided by several of the rules and articles of war, as now

---

[8] Zebulon Pike, for whom the famous peak was named.

used and practiced, stoppage of pay, confinement, and deprivation of part of the rations, shall be substituted in such manner
as is hereinafter provided."

Just how much this substitution was observed will be seen later.

The *Army Register* appeared also. It contained a complete
list both of regular and volunteer officers and showed a conglomerate mixture of elements making up the army: 1 regiment of artillery; 2 regiments of dragoons; 1st, 2d and 3d regiments of light artillery; 25 regiments of regular infantry; a
rifle regiment; 14 regiments of one-year infantry; 5 regiments
of volunteer infantry for the war; 12 companies of rangers;
4 regiments, 1 battalion and 1 company of "United States volunteers" and 5 companies of "sea fencibles." It also showed
the country to be divided for military administration into nine
districts with a brigadier general in charge of each.

May 1
1813
The uniform regulations were issued in most specific form.
Just how many inches a button should be placed from the bottom of a coat was carefully shown. Blue was prescribed for
infantry and artillery. Any ornament such as red collars and
cuffs or lace was forbidden. Leather caps were substituted for
felt.[9] Generals in dress uniform were to be distinguished by
cocked hats and other officers by the long chapeaux similar to
the one worn in recent years by the naval officer in full dress.
Cotton pompons were substituted for feathers. The standing
collar was to reach the tip of the ear, and the coats themselves
were to be decorated with horizontal tape, buttons and blind
buttonholes.

The firelock was practically the same as the one used during
the Revolution. Most of the powder was obtained from Kentucky where it was greatly needed and largely manufactured.
Although another arsenal was established at Rome, New York,
the making of arms and ammunition for the army was mainly
carried on by private plants.

In the west the British and Indians to the number of over
2,000 were laying siege to Fort Meigs which had been built and
was now defended by Harrison. When he heard that General

---

[9] The tall "tar-bucket" seen at a cadet full-dress parade.

Clay with about 1,200 Kentuckians was coming to his rescue he determined on an offensive. A part of the approaching reënforcements was directed to spike the enemy's guns and *May 5 1813* immediately join the main body under Harrison. But the 800 untrained men, after having wrought the necessary harm to the hostile artillery, disobeyed orders by attacking the enemy. The consequence was that they were surrounded and over 80 per cent of them either killed or captured. General Harrison being left in the lurch, could do no more than carry on a passive defense. The hostile Indians having no liking for siege warfare *May 9 1813* soon caused the abandonment of the investment of Fort Meigs, much to the unexpected relief of the American troops.

In the north General Dearborn, against little resistance, *May 27 1813* occupied Fort George and other smaller strongholds on the Niagara frontier. During these operations Generals Winder and Chandler were taken prisoners, and Colonel Boerstler, thinking on slight cause that he was surrounded, immediately surrendered himself with 542 men.

However, General Brown did repulse a force from Canada *May 29 1813* at Sackett's Harbor. The defensive action of his troops may be judged by this officer's official report of the affair:

"My orders were that the troops were to lie close and reserve their fire until the enemy had approached so near that every shot might hit its object. It is, however, impossible to execute such orders with raw troops, unaccustomed to subordination. My orders were, in this case, disobeyed; the whole line fired, and not without effect; but in the moment while I was contemplating this, to my utter astonishment, they rose from their cover and fled. Colonel Mills fell gallantly in brave, but vain endeavor to stop his men. I was, personally, more fortunate. Gathering together about one hundred militia, under the immediate command of Captain McNitt, we threw ourselves on the rear of the enemy's left flank, and, I trust, did some execution. It was at this last moment that the regulars under command of Lieutenant-Colonel Backus, Light Dragoons, first engaged the enemy, nor was it long before they defeated them. Hurrying to this point of action I found the battle still raging, but with obvious advantage to our side."

July 6
1813

About a month after this General Dearborn on account of illness requested to be relieved. General Wilkinson was chosen to succeed him. Age and infirmity gave place to age and fatuity. The result hereafter treated should not be surprising.

While the larger forces were being collected and demoralized, some smaller units of the regulars were giving good accounts of themselves. For example, in the west a young officer

Aug. 2
1813

by the name of Groghan with 160 regulars was attacked at Fort Stephenson by over twice that number of British. By resolution, foresight and uncommon bravery he and his men drove off the enemy. His only cannon was a six-pounder gun loaded with slugs and grapeshot, which he used very ingeniously. The effect on the surrounding community was a discreet withdrawal of hostile marauders.

In contrast to this action was an affair in another part of the country. The Creek Indians in the south were brandishing their red war clubs. Fort Mims, about 40 miles northeast of Mobile, was garrisoned by about 240 Mississippi militia, who with about 300 women and children occupied the stockade.

Aug. 30
1813

Although many well-founded reports of a coming Indian attack should have warned the inmates, the news made little impression on these untrained men. At 11:00 o'clock in the morning 600 savages came within ten yards of the stronghold without discovery. Swarming through the open gate they succeeded in killing about 400 souls. As a result the whole southeast was in a state of fury and panic.

While the south was in chaos over this unnecessary massacre General Harrison undertook an offensive in the north. Having managed to collect, feed, hold, and transport to the southern

Sept. 25
1813

side of Lake Erie about 7,000 troops of whom about one fifth were regulars, he landed on the Canadian shore only to find the British General Proctor fleeing before his superior force. The

Oct. 5
1813

Americans proceeded to take Malden and Sandwich without a skirmish. At the Thames River they caught up with the enemy, consisting of 800 British and about 1,500 Indians, who were defensively disposed between the banks and the marshes. A cavalry charge by the mounted Kentuckians and the killing of Tecumseh gave the greatly superior force of Americans the victory. However, the fighting was hard and credit should be

given the partially disciplined troops of Harrison, who stood
their ground well.

Since the massacre at Fort Mims in the south, General
Andrew Jackson had been at work collecting militia at Huntsville. In spite of petty interference by the Secretary of War,
Armstrong,[10] Jackson had been successful in rounding up about   *Oct. 11*
2,500 men. With these he started his march through Tennes-   *1813*
see toward the Coosa River.

While General Jackson, with his arm in a sling, was thus
moving at the head of his troops in the south, General Hampton
near Lake Champlain, with about 5,000 freshly recruited men,
and General Wilkinson at the foot of Lake Ontario, with about
8,000, planned a joint invasion of Canada. Added to jealousies
and bickerings between these two officers was the unwelcome   *Oct. 31*
presence of a third party, Armstrong, who had left Washington   *1813*
to meddle at the front. The troops were all recruits, even to
the Fourth Regular Infantry whose trained men had been taken
to Canada after Hull's surrender. Affairs were generally in
disorder. Colonel Swift, the first graduate of the Military
Academy, and then chief engineer of this army, on his arrival
at Sackett's Harbor

"found everything in a most disgraceful and deplorable condition; no plan of campaign studied or definitely fixed; the
enemy's positions unknown, and the St. Lawrence unexplored;
supplies deficient through neglect or incompetency of the War
Department; expense of transportation enormous, that of a
single field-piece costing over a thousand dollars; our troops
mostly recruits, and sick from eating contract provisions."

In this chaos General Hampton marched quickly and
eagerly on Montreal before Wilkinson would be able to gain
honors. It looked as though the great force under Hampton
would be able to consume the paltry 800 Canadian regulars at
that place. But the British Commander took a chance on the
quality of the United States troops. He played the old, simple   *Oct. 26*
trick of Gideon's Band. Distributing his buglers well over   *1813*
separated positions where they independently sounded their

---

[10] Author of the Newburgh addresses and member of the Conway Cabal.

calls, he led the American commander to believe that a large force was assembled. Although the barest common sense should have convinced Hampton that the British had less than 5,000 men, he immediately withdrew and went into full retreat, thankful that the enemy did not pursue. Thus the Americans gave up without firing a shot.

Meanwhile, Jackson in the south had arrived in the vicinity of the Indians' rendezvous. Having learned that the Creeks had posted themselves at the Tallasahatchee, he sent General Coffee with 900 mounted troops to destroy them. The natives were decoyed much as the men of Ai in the Bible. Enticed from their wigwams by a few interpreters, who fled before the savages, the Creeks found themselves suddenly in the midst of an overwhelming force of Americans who promptly exterminated them.

Nov. 3
1813

A few days later while Jackson's force was building Fort Strother, he was notified that another body of hostile Creeks was besieging friendly ones at Talladega. Not waiting for a moment he set out with 2,000 men. When he found the river too deep to ford, he crossed it by setting a foot soldier on a horse behind a mounted one. He thus succeeded in the dark in getting all his floundering soldiers on the other side.

Nov. 7, 8
1813

While he was reconnoitering the enemy's position and was resting his wearied troops who had marched all night, he was suddenly informed that General Cocke had called away General White's column which Jackson was commanding and which was to protect his rear. Such ignorant meddling left Jackson completely cut off in the wilderness. In this predicament he did the only sensible thing. He immediately, in the nighttime prepared for the attack. Again following out the tactics of Joshua against the men of Ai he would have annihilated the savages, had it not been for the fact that some militia of Roberts' brigade gave way and Colonel Bradley, a recent soldier, refused to move forward because he claimed he need not fight until attacked. Even at that, the Indians were driven away with loss. Jackson's training and determination accounted for the flight of the hostile tribe.

Nov. 9
1813

General Wilkinson in the north finally started his movement toward Canada. At Chrystler's farm near Williamsburg his

Nov. 11
1813

advance guard of about 1,600 men met a force of 800 British regulars. After two hours' fight, in which the Americans came off second best, his superior force retired to their boats. A few *Nov. 12 1813* days later, having heard of Hampton's refusal to join him, he gave up the idea of invasion and went into winter quarters. Although 8,000 men were at the disposal of the American commander to meet no more than 2,000 British, he recoiled and sought comfort in blaming Hampton.

Whereas the northeast found neither real leaders nor soldiers, the south found a leader but few trained soldiers. Yet demoralization in both cases was evident. The speed of the march and the hunger of the ill-supplied camp was too much for Jackson's untried troops. When they attempted to leave him, he barred the path of the militia with muskets of the volunteers; and likewise the volunteers, with the militia. He had to resort finally to persuasion and promises. When only 190 men consented to remain, he placed himself at the head of the departing troops and said he would go with them. But he made them promise that if provisions were met on the way they would return. When they did come up with a drove of cattle, nothing but a threat to shoot them down kept them with the colors. They then made the plea that their enlistments were expiring and that they should be allowed to go home. *Dec. 10 1813* Several threats to open fire on the mutineers finally quelled their intention.

After the complete subsidence of any aggressiveness on the part of the northern troops who had quailed before an inferior enemy, the Canadians openly accepted the tacit invitation to pillage the shores of the United States. Our lack of training and discipline was to waste more lives and property. The winter coming on, the armies of Hampton and Wilkinson *Dec. 19 1813* dwindled to several thousand men. General McClure wantonly abandoned Fort George which had been won at so much sacrifice; and then for no legitimate reason burned Niagara, thereby making homeless several thousand innocent inhabitants during a cold winter. In or about the army there was little spirit or system. Small bands of British took Fort Niagara with *Dec. 30 1813* scarcely any opposition, occupied Lewiston, Youngstown and Manchester and burned Black Rock and Buffalo.

Thus the year passed out with very little save disgrace for the undisciplined and ill-managed American soldiery.

Jan. 12
1814

General Cass wrote to the Secretary of War as follows:

"I have passed this day the ruins of Buffalo; it exhibits a scene of distress and destruction such as I have never before witnessed. . . . From the most careful examination, I am satisfied that not more than 650 men, of regulars, militia and Indians landed at Black Rock. To oppose these, we had from 2,500 to 3,000 militia. All, except a very few of them, behaved in the most cowardly manner. They fled without discharging a musket."

In the south General Jackson was no better off for troops than the northern generals. Bereft of all the soldiers of the year before, he was reduced to 900 new raw militia. However,

Jan. 21, 22
1814

he did have some experienced officers. With their aid he was able to lead his troops against the Indians, whose detachments on two occasions he put to flight.

Jan. 27
1814

By this time it was so difficult to get recruits that the $16 and 3 months' pay for enlistment were raised to $124 cash, of which $100 was to be paid immediately upon the soldier's entry into the service. Men did not care to become a part of a disgraceful mob. The term of enlistment for the 14 regiments of one-year men was raised to five years. By way of increase, 3 regiments of riflemen, consisting of 10 companies (each company having 1 captain, 1 first, 1 second and 1 third lieutenant,

Feb. 10
1814

1 ensign, 5 sergeants, 4 corporals, 2 musicians and 90 privates) were also authorized.

General Wilkinson having prolonged the inactivity of his 4,000 men longer than was seemly, determined now to prevent the British from entering Lake Champlain by the river Sorel. Accordingly his force marched to attack 200 of the enemy in a fortified mill called La Colle. Trees had been felled across the

March 30
1814

Americans' path. The mire was so heavy in the woods that the large guns broke down. The lighter artillery could scarcely be dragged. The men when they reached their destination had to stand in snow a foot deep and fire through a forest so dense that the enemy was screened from view. On the other hand, the

British with deadly aim wrought so much havoc that Wilkinson decided to withdraw, going back later to Plattsburg where he failed to renew hostilities; 4,000 Americans withdrew before 200 of the enemy. Although Wilkinson received so much blame for this that he was forced to retire, it should be noted in his favor that he had found it necessary during the engagement to place a sergeant behind each platoon with orders to shoot down any man attempting to flee.

Congress during these flights of soldiery was ever ready to vote splendid organizations. The first, second and third artillery regiments were reorganized into 12 battalions with 6 lieutenant colonels in command. Each company was to have 1 captain, 1 first lieutenant, 1 second lieutenant and 1 third lieutenant, 5 sergeants, 1 quartermaster's sergeant, 8 corporals, 4 musicians and 100 privates. The 2 regiments of dragoons were combined into 1 consisting of 8 troops. Each troop was to have 1 captain, 1 first lieutenant, 1 second lieutenant, 1 cornet, 5 sergeants, 8 corporals, 1 riding master, 1 master of the sword, 2 trumpeters, 1 farrier, 1 blacksmith, 1 saddler and 96 privates. Officers were given allowances for "waiter" or servant hire. A major general was entitled to wages for four and the officer personnel of a company to three. No soldier from the line was permitted to act as a waiter. An attempt was also made to equalize promotions by an adjustment of the relative rank of officers. For the first time major generals in the selection of their aides were confined to captains or subalterns of the line, and brigadiers to subalterns. *March 30 1814*

Theoretically, the army at this time consisted of 44 regiments of infantry, the corps of artillery, 1 regiment of light artillery, 1 regiment of dragoons, 4 regiments of rifles, the corps of engineers, the rangers and the sea fencibles. *April 1 1814*

After an unsuccessful attempt to recapture the post of Mackinaw, when our forces acted as ignorantly as Braddock and were slaughtered by the enemy with as much ease as the "venson" of which Corporal Stubbs spoke, the operations of the north concentrated themselves on the force of General Brown. About 3,500 men had been collected at Buffalo in the early spring and summer under the direct supervision of Brown, Scott and Ripley. After two years of war the training and discipline that had been discarded as lost arts after the Revolution were brought from their hiding places. These young generals personally and studiously taught and trained their men, giving those rudiments whose knowledge would have saved many lives in the preceding years of this war, and incidentally have gained the aim of the United States.

When these troops were sufficiently able to handle themselves they were taken by boat to Fort Erie which surrendered without resistance. They then pushed a detachment of the enemy over fifteen miles to the Chippewa and there engaged a force of 5,000. A bold attack, complete response to trained officers, the use of the bayonet, with which the Americans were now completely armed, drove the superior numbers of the Canadians from the field.

July 4
1814

July 25
1814

Afterward General Scott in pushing across the Chippewa was practically hemmed in by overwhelming odds. His force not only attacked and held its own, but General Brown displayed uncommon teamwork in marching to Scott's aid. When darkness stopped the battle of Lundy's Lane the British had sustained more losses than the Americans. The bravery and skill of this action can be determined from the following:

"All that remained of the brigade after that terrible conflict did not exceed 220 men—the Ninth, Eleventh and Twenty-second regiments consolidated under Major Leavenworth, not altogether 100. Many of the cartridges with which the Americans fired, when attacked on the hill, were taken from the cartridge boxes of the English lying dead around them. Men and officers, after five hours' constant fighting, were completely exhausted, and many almost fainting with thirst. There was no water nearer than the Chippewa."

A small force of trained soldiers had met superior numbers on hostile soil and won victories. Although compelled on account of its size to retire from the Canadian shore after the siege of Fort Erie,[11] it nevertheless had saved depredations in the United States and given a distinct setback to the boldness

---

[11] The 1st Regular Infantry was present at this siege.

of the enemy.   A short continuance of such efficiency on the
part of the army would have ended the struggle.

But it was very hard to get Americans to train, as will be
seen by the coming experiences of men dressed in soldier's
uniform.   The crowning disgrace of the war was yet to take
place.

In the Tenth Military District [12] which had just been *July 4*
formed, little anxiety had been felt over 3,000 British troops *1814*
who had been hovering about in the Chesapeake for over a year.
A large force of trained and hostile British soldiers was within
modern artillery range of the nation's capital.   A dilatory
circular was finally issued by our government calling upon the
Governors for 93,500 men.   A dribbling argument as to the
number of troops to be employed occupied several weeks, the
Secretary of War contending that not over 3,000 should be
called out.   General Winder saw no reason why 4,000 militia
could not do the work.   A state of restless recruiting resulted.
During this time the British were marching uninterruptedly
through the very heart of the country and heading directly for
Washington.   Just outside of that city at the little town of
Bladensburg, 5,400 American militia, 400 regulars and 600 *Aug. 24*
sailors and marines were finally collected.   Indeed, they were *1814*
slung into camp just a few hours before they were called upon
to do battle with the approaching enemy.   Tomes has described
the conditions of the camp as follows:

"While their leaders were stupid with perplexity, the soldiers were wild with disorder.   A veteran officer declared that
the camp resembled a race-field, and that it was as noisy as a
fair.   The militia and the sailors, overflowing with drink, were
boisterous with mirth and quarrel; and the countersign was
given so badly by the unsoldierly sentinels, that it could be
heard at a distance of fifty yards."

As the enemy was nearing this American assemblage, the
President borrowed a pair of dueling pistols from the Secretary

---

[12] It consisted of Maryland, District of Columbia and part of Virginia
now separated from the former 5th District.

of the Treasury, who felt he had better not go, and then accompanied the Secretary of War and General Winder to the proposed battlefield. Aroused to the fact that the British were really coming, these men of state, since they could almost hear the rifles of the enemy, hurried from the Capitol. When the 1,500 trained British soldiers were almost at Bladensburg, these three gentlemen fell to arguing and discussing the situation as if it were something quite new. Three thousand American militia and a few hundred sailors and marines were somehow posted on the heights above the river—badly. Orders were issued by one commander and countermanded by another. Troops moved here and there without plan or regularity. The British regulars came over the bridge steadily in the face of heavy losses. At this and the sight of harmless hostile rockets the American militia scampered like errant schoolboys, spreading the contagion of flight to General Winder's forces who were poorly posted in rear. The artillery could fire only to the front because the pieces had been scattered between the intervals of improperly selected positions. No one seemed to know what to do except disappear. General Winder,[13] who had been a lawyer up until the war, reported the flight by saying, "To my utter astonishment and mortification—when I regained my position, I found the whole of these regiments were flying in the utmost precipitation and disorder." In speaking of the Eighth Maryland he showed that "this corps which had heretofore acted so firmly, evinced the usual incapacity of raw troops to make orderly movements in the face of the enemy and their retreat in a very few moments became a flight of absolute and total disorder." Of the whole of the troops he said that "such of them as could be halted, instead of making efforts to rally, gave themselves up to the uncontrolled feelings which fatigue, exhaustion and privation produced, and pursued their way, either toward home, or in search of refreshments and quarters." In stating

---

[13] "His appointment had been 'based not on the ground of distinguished professional service or knowledge,' but simply on a presumption that, 'being a native of Maryland and a relative of the governor, Brigadier Winder would be useful in mitigating the opposition to the war, and in giving an increased efficiency to national measures within the limits of the State'" (Upton).

his defense of this flight he maintained that "no advantage of position is proof against groundless panic, and a total want of discipline, skill and experience." But such opinions did not prevent General Winder himself from issuing orders for the retreat through Washington and Georgetown. This hodge-podge army actually fled through the capital of the nation and left it open to plunder and rapine. Over twice as many Americans as the enemy left their own homes open to loot, and did so without having made more than a pretense of defense. Picture the newly dressed militiamen zealously slinking homeward or lolling about the streets of the city with a wary eye for the enemy; wagons and carts burdened with snatched household effects; darkey and aristocrat jostling one another in precipitate escape; Mrs. Madison looking vainly through a spyglass for her husband, the President; and secretaries and generals fleeing in carriages this way and that. Behold Brussels during Waterloo! Why the enemy chose to be satisfied with burning the public buildings has never been explained. The "defenders" certainly gave a wider invitation.

How unnecessary was the flight, is shown by the figures. All told there were only 66 casualties out of 5,000 American soldiers. Of this loss the large percentage was borne by sailors, marines and regulars. It is almost certain that no more than 8 militiamen were killed.

Small successes by detachments of trained troops could not compensate for the fall of Washington. Although the Second Infantry at Fort Bowyer in the south and a few hundred under General Macomb at Plattsburg were making gallant defenses against Indians and British, the effects were local. As far as the war was concerned, it was affected very little by such minor actions. *Sept. 1814*

It came to an end with inconsequent attempts at tardy reconstruction. Several proposals for general conscription were given to Congress and rejected. Two new arsenals were established at Watervliet, New York, and Pittsburg, Pennsylvania. The recruiting laws were revised to allow a recruit under twenty-one to have four days' grace before he was sent to his organization, to allow a master to receive part of the bounty money of an enlisting apprentice, to raise the land bounty from *Oct. 1814* *Dec. 10 1814*

160 to 320 acres and to permit a civilian to hire a substitute to go to the front in his place. But nothing was mentioned with reference to training.

Dec. 24 1814

Such futile acts only accentuated the weak military situation and were appropriate concomitants of the sad ending of an inglorious war. For humiliating as it is for the land forces to acknowledge, it is only true and fair to state that hostilities stopped solely on account of political conditions and a successful navy.

Dec. 1 1814

After the peace had been signed, General Jackson at New Orleans, ignorant of the state of international affairs and momentarily expecting an advance by the British against the town, used his great energy and skill in building up the morale of the citizens and collecting more troops. He gave New Orleans a touch of discipline in stating that those who were not for the cause were against it. Accordingly many were compelled to join the ranks. He took over the entire district with dispatch and ruled it with an iron hand.

Jan. 8 1815

When Pakenham, the brother-in-law of the Duke of Wellington, landed with about 8,000 British troops, he found himself in low swampy ground affording no cover nor means of retreat. His position was as unfavorable as could be imagined for a military leader.

On the other hand, Jackson, knowing that he could not trust his 5,000 militia in the open, bent all his energies to making more impregnable, a natural defensive position between the Mississippi and a cypress swamp. The merits of his selection were heightened by a deep canal, a sort of moat which ran along the front of the proposed parapet. He reënforced this natural barrier until it partook of the nature of a redoubt. Behind it, he placed his untrained riflemen so that certain fractions could load while the others were discharging their pieces. By such disposition he could keep up a continuous fire. He so protected and pointed his cannon that they could sweep any attacking columns with cross fire. In addition, he had the gunboats in the river and the fort from the opposite bank prepared to rake the enemy.

Jan. 8 1815

In spite of the Americans' formidable position and his own lack of scaling ladders, Pakenham in utter foolhardiness attacked. Naturally his men suffered over 2,000 casualties in a few minutes.

But Jackson could not trust his troops to pursue the fleeing British. He had an object lesson at this time across the river. A few hundred of the enemy were easily putting to flight an overwhelming number of Louisiana and Kentucky militiamen who had been forced into the open. He was thus prevented from clinching his victory because of the unreliability of his own troops. So he had to allow Pakenham to withdraw the remaining British forces.

After peace was generally known to exist, the army began to fall off in numbers until it totaled 33,424 out of a possible *Feb.* 62,773. Several attempts by Congress and the army were made *1815* to overcome by quality the lack in quantity. The Ordnance *Feb. 8* Department, for example, was placed on a firmer basis by mak- *1815* ing it consist of 1 colonel, 1 lieutenant colonel, 2 majors, 10 captains, 10 first lieutenants, 10 second lieutenants and 10 third lieutenants. But the new urge came too late to be of value in a disgraceful and ignominious war that should have ended in a few months had George Washington been heeded and Steuben's training continued after the Revolution.

A board of officers consisting of Generals Scott and Swift and Colonels Fenwick, Cumming and Drayton, who had been *Feb. 25* ordered "conformable to the House of Representatives" to pre- *1815* pare a set of Infantry Drill Regulations "after the pattern of the *Rules and Regulations for the Field Service and Manoeuvres of the French Infantry*," now submitted the results of their labor. This was the first work of its kind actually prepared by a regularly constituted board of American officers.

William Duane's *Hand Book for Infantry* which had been approved by the Secretary of War in 1812, had been in use. It had since 1809 provided for 3 ranks in a company; had done away with the oblique step, the lock step and the deploy step. In firing, the front-rank man loaded and fired his own piece, the middle-rank man fired both his own and his rear-rank man's piece and the rear-rank man merely loaded the middle-rank man's gun. Thus the middle-rank man fired almost twice as fast as his front-rank man and loaded every other time the piece he fired. Volley firing was discouraged.

In presenting his volume to the public, Lieutenant Colonel William Duane showed the spirit of the times three years before the war of 1812:

"There is no discipline; there is even no system; and there are gross misconceptions on the subject. There appears to have been a disposition to discourage the acquisition of military knowledge."

His work consisted of seven parts, touching on almost every phase of contemporary military education. But it was complicated and the natural result of the state of the times he shows above.

Feb. 25 1815
The newly adopted regulations edited by the Board of Officers simplified Duane's system principally on account of the sad experiences of an ill-conducted war. Battalions were divided into 8 companies each. The first and second companies were formed into one grand division, the third and fourth into another, and so on. There were 4 officers to a company: 1 captain, 1 first lieutenant, 1 third lieutenant and 1 ensign. For the first time the instruction was divided into three schools—the soldier, the company and the battalion. The commandant of each regiment was enjoined to assemble at his quarters all the officers of the command so as to explain to them what these three schools meant. Commands of "caution" were distinguished from those of execution by different kinds of type. The length of the ordinary step was increased to 28 inches and the cadence to 90 per minute. The manual of arms continued the practice of Steuben in having the intervals between motions a second of time. The execution of the motions was practically the same as in the Revolution. However, emphasis was placed upon taking extra time with priming, putting the cartridges into the barrel and ramming home. Officers to-day can be glad that there is such a thing as fixed ammunition when they read the following problems confronting the drill master in 1815:

"The instructor will remark, that the soldiers who, without apparent hurry, load with steadiness and coolness, are those who load best and quickest; because they turn the ramrod with-

out catching against, or interfering with those of the men beside
and before them; because they enter it, without frequent attempts, at once into the muzzle, and in returning it into the
pipe; because they ram home best; because they do not spill the
powder in priming; and because, finally, they do not let fall
cartridges in taking them out of the cartridge-box; all essential
objects, on which the instructor must make the recruits bestow
the utmost attention."

A single method of firing on the part of a company was
enunciated. The right file was to fire first, the next file on the
left was to aim the instant the first had fired, and this process
was to continue toward the left of the company. After each
file had fired once, each man was to load and fire at will. The
fusillade was stopped by a ruffle of the drum.

With the noise of black powder and the long firelocks the
recruit had difficulties that seem absurd to us as we withdraw
the bolt and look in the chamber. His perplexities had to be
definitely guarded against as follows:

"When the firings shall have been executed, it shall be
required of the soldier to be attentive in observing, when he
half-cock, whether smoke proceeds out of the touch-hole, which
if it does, indicates certainly that the piece has gone off. If the
smoke does not appear, the soldier, in lieu of reloading, will
turn off to the rear, in order to prick the touch-hole, and prime
a second time. If the soldier thinks he has fired, and proceeds
to load again, he ought, at any rate, to discover his mistake, if
any exists, in ramming home from the length of ramrod pro-
jecting out of the muzzle; and he would richly merit punishment, were he to load a third time under all these circumstances."

The normal formation of a company consisted of 2 ranks.
However, provision was made for "the occasional order of 3
deep." [14]

---

[14] The manual consisted of the following positions: Present arms,
shoulder arms, advance arms, order arms, pile arms, take arms, support
arms, carry arms, fix and unfix bayonets and secure arms. Priming and
loading was done still by twelve commands.

Target practice was suggested. Each battalion was encouraged to provide several targets, 5 feet 10 inches in height and 22 inches in width. "They must be marked by 3 stripes 4 inches broad, drawn horizontally across the target and of striking color, one stripe across the top, another across the middle and a third across an equal distance from the top and middle." The soldiers were to be practiced at a distance between 60 and 300 yards, "aiming at different heights according to the distances."

There were two main elements of instruction emphasized. The trigger was to be pulled forcibly with the forefinger without stirring the head or altering the direction of the firelock, and the balls fired off were to be carefully gathered in order to be used again. As a reward to the best marksmen in each company, their names were to be "taken down."

March 3
1815

In the war just passed the army had played its part in burlesque and tragedy. It had been more pitiful than in the Revolution. Yet when the affair was over, the country did not absurdly disband its entire force, principally because there was the fresh memory of a sound spanking. Instead, a law was passed limiting the army to 10,000 men and a corps of engineers.[15] The corps of artillery was organized according to the law of March 30, 1814, and the regiment of light artillery, to that of April 12, 1808. A regiment of infantry was newly made up of 1 colonel, 1 lieutenant colonel, 1 major, 1 adjutant, 1 quartermaster, 1 paymaster, 1 surgeon, 2 surgeon's mates, 1 sergeant major, 1 quartermaster sergeant, 2 principal musicians and 10 companies. Each company consisted of 1 captain, 1 first lieutenant, 1 second lieutenant, 4 sergeants, 4 corporals, 2 musicians and 68 privates. There were 6 general officers all told, 2 major generals and 4 brigadiers. The pay went back to the low rates of the acts of March 16, 1802, and of April 12, 1808, except for major generals who received the modern pay of the act of Jan. 11, 1812. Supernumerary officers and men had to be discharged by May 1, the "deranged" officers being accorded three months' pay.

Some sinister effort must have been at work to deprive all

---

[15] The engineers were to remain as already organized.

the old regiments of their traditions and spirit. For no plan could have more shrewdly damned any existing pride and affiliations than the following:

The old 1st Infantry went into the new 3rd Infantry; the old 2nd went into the new 1st; the old 3rd, into the new 1st; the old 4th, into the new 5th; the old 5th, into the new 8th; the old 6th, into the new 2nd; the old 7th, into the new 1st; and the old 8th, into the new 7th. The new 1st was then made up of the old 2nd, 3rd, 7th and 44th; the new 2nd, of the old 6th, 16th, 22nd, 23rd, and 32nd; the new 3rd, of the old 1st, 17th, 19th, and 28th; the new 4th, of the old 12th, 14th, 18th, 20th, 36th, and 38th; the new 5th, of the old 4th, 9th, 13th, 21st, 40th, and 46th; the new 6th, of the old 11th, 25th, 27th, 29th, and 37th; the new 7th, of the old 8th, 24th, and 39th; and the new 8th,[16] of the 5th, 10th, 15th, 31st, 33rd, 34th, 35th, 39th, 41st, 42nd, 43rd, 45th.

Not only were the units of the army diabolically jumbled but its size had to shrink to about one-sixth its former self. Officers and men had to be ejected and the remainder readjusted with a natural wrecking of ambition and spirit. Neither was there any solace to the remnants in being sent in small *May 1815* scattered fractions to lonely frontier posts and seacost fortifications. The First Infantry, for instance, being deprived of all the officers of the old First, Second and Seventh was sent to Pass Christian, Louisiana. The Second in the same way was stationed at Sackett's Harbor and Plattsburg, N. Y. The Third was scattered along the Great Lakes in small forts such as Detroit, Mackinac, Howard, Dearborn, Knox, Harrison, Wayne and Crawford. The Fourth was charged with the small posts on the frontier of Georgia and South Carolina. The Fifth and the Third had their headquarters at Detroit and helped in garrisoning the western forts above mentioned and Fort Armstrong, Atkinson, Brady, Gratiot, Howard, Winnebago. The Sixth went to Governors Island, N. Y. The Seventh went to Fort Gibson, Arkansas, and the stockades in that vicinity.

---

[16] Some of these remnants the Eighth was supposed to take over had never been organized. The list includes rifle regiments, making a theoretical 48 to account for.

The artillery corps garrisoned the seacoast forts from Mobile to Boston and the regiment of light artillery was parceled out with the infantry, as was also the regiment of rifles. The corps of engineers was stationed at West Point, N. Y., its officers being taken for duty in constructing forts and improvements at various places in the United States.

1815

So the year passed out with the various little groups plodding to their posts and building their lonely log cabins and stockades.

The *Register of the Army* having made its first appearance before the end of the year showed the 2 major generals to be Jacob Brown and Andrew Jackson, and the 4 brigadier generals to be Alexander Macomb, E. P. Gaines, Winfield Scott and E. W. Ripley. The ordnance, medical, apothecary, pay and purchasing departments were all tabulated in detail. Although the apothecary department had an apothecary general, the medical department seemed to have no head. There was, in addition to the office of "adjutant and inspector general," that of a plain "adjutant general."

Discussions with reference to supplies of ordnance were prolific at this time. One concerning hand grenades is worth quoting in the light of recent events:

"Ordnance Office,
"Washington, January 23, 1816.

"In former times the hand grenade was used as an arm for a portion of the infantry. It is entirely gone out of use for that purpose. Grenadiers are now armed with the musket, and in some services (as the French) with a sabre also.

"They are picked companies of stout men, usually placed on the flanks of the battalions, and being generally chosen to form the storming party in the attack of fortified places, they retain the name of grenadiers from the former use of those troops, and the weapon with which they were then armed. The superiority of the musket had caused it to supersede the hand grenade as an arm for troops. The grenade may be put in numbers into the ditches and passages where the troops are collected.

"For this purpose proper provision is made in our service. The six-pounder shell is used as the hand grenade, and shells of any caliber as rampart grenades."

This extract, though it gives a glimpse into the historic cycle of the hand grenade, shows more fully the discussions in these times over arms and ammunition. There seemed to be a feeling among the legislators that deficiency in military operations was due to lack of supplies. Few realized yet that training was the all-important step toward efficiency. Armories and seacoast material were voted almost in prodigality. And *Feb.* then the building craze seized our lawmakers. For a time it *1816* was difficult for artillery and ordnance experts to keep the authorities from building a lot of useless structures instead of manufacturing a sufficient quantity of needed materials.

The uniform of the war was to a great measure retained, though some minor changes show a slight departure. A mixture of civilian and military dress was prohibited, except that all military persons, irrespective of the remainder of their dress, were to wear on their hats black cockades with gold eagles. Although collars were to rise to the tip of the ear they were to be only "as high in front as the chin will permit in turning the head." The generals, corps artillery officers and infantry officers wore chapeaux. The light artillery wore round, stiff, black caps, seven inches high, with a visor. A tassel fell from the top of the right side of this heavy headgear. The mounted men wore pantaloons, and the infantry breeches. The light artillery wore coatees whereas the other branches wore long coats with full skirts. The rifleman and cadet wore gray, the rifleman having a short coat and the cadet a coatee. The cadet wore the common round hat with the cockade and eagle, his trousers having black silk lace down the side and an Austrian knot in front. Officers wore sashes when on duty. The Jefferson or high-shoe was prescribed as in 1814.

The Congress added to the "general staff" 1 inspector general, 1 paymaster-general, 3 topographical engineers, 1 quartermaster-general and 1 commissary general of purchases. Official recognition was thus for the first time given to a fairly competent staff. Although citizens and not soldiers were allowed *April 24* *1816* to fill the new appointments, the establishment of the offices themselves was a distinct advance.

April 29
1816
As for material, an annual sum of $250,000 was appropriated for purchase or manufacture of arms and equipment for the militia. Out of 18 projected arsenals 5 were completed during the year: at Watertown, Mass.; Frankford, Pa.; Baltimore, Md.; Greenleaf's Point, D. C., and on the James River near Richmond, Va.

Jan. 23
1817
The artillery armament comprised 24, 18, 12 and 6 pounder cannon, 8 inch and 24 pounder howitzers and 10 and 8 inch mortars. In the manufacture of so many calibers, the ordnance department claimed there was much useless difficulty and expense. Accordingly there was a decided attempt to reduce the number of different types of large guns.

To show the immaturity of our government in handling military matters in these early times, the method of delivery of orders is a good example. It seems that it had been the custom since the early part of the second war with Great Britain, for the President or Secretary of War simply to send an order to any junior army officer without giving responsible superiors any knowledge of the fact. No attempt was made to inform intermediate commanders of the contents of such instructions. In the meantime the commanders of departments, who were charged with the responsibility for the work of a subordinate, found themselves suddenly deprived of his services. Indeed, in many cases the higher commanders were not aware that important labor had ceased because the responsible officer had gone elsewhere. It was due to just such a case that General Harrison had come into dispute with the Secretary in 1814 and had resigned his commission. Although General Andrew Jackson had had similar trouble at the same time, affairs did not grow serious for him until three years later. An officer under his command who had been making at his direction secret surveys for government purposes was suddenly spirited away by the War Department to New York City where the surveys were exposed. Jackson, not knowing of the officer's absence, was going on the assumption that his subordinate was proceeding with the important and delicate work, he, Jackson, had assigned; when one day he was surprised to read in the public print of the officer's presence in the north and of the exposure of the survey. Accordingly the general issued an order in the Division of the South that no officer would obey any order "emanating from the Department of War," unless it came through the proper channels. Soon afterward General Ripley, who was serving under Jackson, received instructions from the War Department which he refused to obey on the ground of General Jackson's order. Before a decision could be reached, Mr. Calhoun became Secretary of War and in his usual far-sighted manner adroitly put a quietus on the unbusinesslike practice. *April 22 1817*

In the wilderness of military chaos of these early years, the voice of a real prophet rose to do signal good for future army officers and scientific men. Since Steuben's arrival at Valley Forge no more valuable asset had been given to the military service than that which was added about the middle of this year. Captain Sylvanus Thayer became the fifth superintendent of the Military Academy. His advent marks a new era not only for the army but for education in general. He organized the corps of cadets into a battalion of 2 companies commanded by a cadet colonel. He created the office of commandant of cadets who was responsible for the tactical instruction and discipline. It was during his superintendency that the cadets were taken on practice marches to Boston, Philadelphia and Princeton in order to widen their scope of training. He introduced the section and section-room method, the weekly standing reports, the scale of daily marks, the dependence of class rank upon scholarship, the blackboard system and the *Annual Register*. A very few students were grouped under a single instructor, who marked their recitations accurately. By such a system a maximum amount of thoroughness and individual effort was required of the cadet. *July 1817*

Captain Thayer had traveled in Europe and studied at its best schools. From abroad he imported among other things analytical mathematics. In short, he gave to America its first scientific school which stood alone for almost half a century in the Western Hemisphere.

But even beyond these improvements, by his wisdom and human dignity he laid the foundation for the development in the youth of that marvelous thing—character. He understood how quibbling, vacillation, or a false statement might be the ruin of a whole campaign. He saw that, whereas in other professions such weaknesses might lead to the loss of property or money, in the business of arms the lives of stalwart men and a nation's standing were at stake. Honor, therefore, was to be the first consideration of the soldier and the guardian of his every act. Character was to be built carefully. So the West Point cadet came to be tenacious above all else of the "honor of the corps" in general and of his own straightforwardness in particular. Later, the motto of the Academy—"Duty, Honor, Country"—grounded itself in lives of sacrifice. The stamp of Thayer and his doctrines is recognized in the names of such graduates as Lee, Grant, Sherman, Longstreet, Jefferson Davis, Sheridan, Stonewall Jackson, Meade, McClellan [17] and a host of others.

Dec. 1
1817

While this great foundation was beginning to be laid at the Military Academy, Mr. Calhoun became Secretary of War as the year closed. He found an army which actually numbered 8,221 men and another arsenal established near Augusta, Ga. He also found the brewing strife with the Seminoles across the border in Florida.

What General Jackson did in that southern conflict is so well known in the country's history that a word about the army here is sufficient. The Seminoles had fallen upon and massacred 47 men and women moving on a peaceable errand. Other smaller depredations had been numerous. When finally General Gaines with 600 men was besieged at Fort Scott by several thousand Indians, General Jackson, without first asking the Governors, quickly called out the Tennessee militia and marched on the enemy. With the Fourth and Seventh Infantry, one battalion of artillery and several thousand militia and friendly Creeks he invaded Florida, defeated the hostile

Jan., Feb.,
March
1818

tribes, captured the Spanish strongholds and executed two British subjects who had abetted the outrages of the Indians. In the first three months of this year General Jackson by cutting

---

[17] Most of these were cadets during Thayer's superintendency or shortly thereafter.

a little red tape put an end to the atrocities in the south with almost no bloodshed.

Shortly after these activities, Congress made some rather constructive laws for the military establishment. It created *April 14 1818* the office of surgeon-general [18] and a chaplain at the Military Academy who should be professor of geography, history and ethics. It improved the quartermaster, subsistence, inspector and adjutant general departments and provided a Judge Advo- *April 16 1818* cate for each territorial division. It gave to those officers holding "brevet" rank, the pay and emoluments of that higher grade, so long as they had a command commensurate with it. Legislation also limited the artillery corps company to 1 captain, 2 first and 2 second lieutenants and the light artillery company to 1 captain, 1 first and 2 second lieutenants.

One of the lieutenants in each case was to act as a "con- *April 20 1818* ductor of artillery or ordnance officer" and to receive $10 per month extra.

Uniform standards of manufacture and collection of war materials seemed to be wanting. The expenses of the arsenal *Sept. 28 1818* at Springfield, Mass., were $162,500 for manufacturing 12,500 stands of arms—about $13 per stand. The figures reveal that about the same number were manufactured at a cost of a little over $15 apiece at Harper's Ferry. A contract with a private concern was made for 180 field-pieces and for 50 tons of shot *Aug. 1818* and shell for the militia. Later 150 tons of heavy cannon and mortars and 50 tons of heavy shot and shell were added to the contract. The specifications called for little more than caliber and weight. At the end of the year Pittsburg Arsenal *Dec. 2 1818* had about 12,000 stands of arms, New Orleans 20,000, Newport, Kentucky, 4,000 and Detroit, 3,000.[19]

---

[18] Salary $2,500 per annum as others of "General Staff."

[19] Mostly muskets. The model "1817, Harper's Ferry" rifle had the following characteristics:

"Total length about 51½ inches. Length of barrel about 36 inches. Calibre of bore without grooves .52. The bore is heptagonal and the seven narrow grooves are at the apices. Of course they are quite necessary. The depth of the grooves is one-hundredth of an inch. The pitch is one turn in 50 inches. Weight of the rifle with its steel ramrod 10 pounds. It was not at first supplied with a bayonet, but later a ten-ounce socket bayonet was issued with it for certain special demands of service. The charge was 90 to 100 grains of fine grained powder and a half ounce spherical bullet loaded bare. Loading became difficult after fouling accumulated. The muzzle velocity was about 2,000 f.s" (Sawyer).

March 19
1819
Early May
1819

June 8
1819

1819

Dec. 6
1819

1819

The movement of the Sixth Infantry from Plattsburg, N. Y., to Saint Louis, Mo., illustrates the distances traversed by the army and the progress of the frontier westward. The regiment marched from Plattsburg through New York and Pennsylvania, and arrived at Pittsburg where it encamped. It then embarked on small transport boats, moved down the Ohio and encamped at Belle Fontaine, Mo. Almost three months were required for the journey.

Captain Long with his company made an exploration into the region of the Colorado. Making surveys and notes, he explored much of the country others had missed, and discovered the mountain which still bears his name. He completed this work in 1820.

During this year two arsenals were established (though apparently not completed) at Baton Rouge, La., and Detroit, Mich. Complaint came from the Ordnance Department, however, that there was a deficiency of cannon, shot and shell, and that it would be provident to get these "not perishable" articles in peace when prices were low. The economy of this measure was urged especially since the government had no arsenals for big guns.

The handling of the larger weapons was given great attention. During the year there appeared a *Treatise upon Artillery* by H. Lallemand, who acknowledged on the title page that he was an "ex-general" of the French Imperial Guard and that the work had been translated by "M. de Russy under the eye of the author." However, the production, whether authorized or not, was comprehensive. Its four volumes [20] covered about

---

[20] "The first volume contains a general description of cannon, projectiles, caisson, gun, and other carriages, with small arms; on the organization, instruction, and position of the personnel (these articles form the basis of a system of artillery), a nomenclature necessary in the field, the EXERCISE of cannon in the field, at sieges, in fortified places, and in sea coast batteries; the school of field guns, in plain and mountain countries; maneuvres of horse and field artillery; the maneuvres of force (or the application of the mechanical powers to artillery), and the construction of batteries.

"The second volume contains a sketch on the composition and division of armies; it treats of the quality and distribution of artillery in an army; its conduct in the field, its position and duty in action, as well as in the attack and defense of field works; the theory and tables for firing, the charges and ranges of cannon; construction of artillery bridges; charging and packing caissons, and other carriages; composition of the equipage, all that any artilleryman should then know. The quick match pouch, the leather thumb piece which the gunner put over his fingers when he "shut close" the touch hole, the bricole to draw the pieces, the locking chains, the sponges and rammers, the copper ladles which served "to load the pieces in case of need," the priming horn containing powder to pour into the vent, the mortar ladle to clean the chambers of mortars and howitzers, the splints which wedged in the bomb in the mortar, the spatula, a shovel-like instrument, which drove in the splints, the stone mortar tapeon upon which the stone basket was laid before it was fired, were some of the various instruments used in discharging cannon. Fuses were placed in bombs before they were fired from howitzers and mortars. The mattrosses sponged, loaded, rammed, pricked, primed, fired and furnished ammunition. The gunners tended the vent and elevated or gave direction to the piece. An artificer or corporal attended the caisson and issued ammunition. Batteries were preferably horse drawn. Positions of the gun detail were established with great nicety. On the carriages were two trunnion plates, one for traveling and the other for action, so that the piece had to be carried a certain way on the march and a different way during combat. The changing of these positions was accomplished with great accuracy and ceremony.

Aside from its employment in furthering military technic, the army was used exntensively in the construction of public

---

ammunition, and supplies for field, siege and garrison artillery; preparing all kinds of fixed ammunition and fire works; instructions for the chief inspectors, and for conductors of artillery and convoys; finally, practical rules founded on experience.

"The third volume treats on field fortifications, comprising the trace, the dimensions, and the secondary means of defense; summary of permanent fortification; on the execution and service of artillery in the attack and defense of places, and on their supplies of provisions; Castramentation; military reconnoitrings; method of solving, by means of a cord and stakes, the most necessary geometrical problems, for field purposes.

"In the fourth volume, I enter into details on the constructions of gun carriages, caissons, etc., etc. I treat upon the cordage, iron, and the wood used in the artillery; on the manner of keeping magazines, arsenals, depots of arms; on the fabrication and receipt of guns and small arms; on projectiles, iron, steel and lastly, on the fabrication of powder. These establishments are not always under the direction of artillery officers; but they should, notwithstanding, possess a sufficient knowledge to enable them, when necessary, if not to direct, at least to inspect them." (Extract from introduction of volume itself.)

works. The government partially realized its economic value in the expression of the following enactment:

March 2
1819

"That, whenever it shall be found expedient to employ the army at work on fortifications, in surveys, in cutting roads, and other constant labor, of not less than ten days, the noncommissioned officers, musicians, and privates so employed shall be allowed fifteen cents, and an extra gill of whisky or spirits, each, per day, while so employed."

But the country had reached that psychological stage after a war where it was recumbent and fat. Peace seemed to be assured, and the returns for army expenditure looked indistinct.

Secretary Calhoun had been met with the usual cry from Congress for the reduction of the army or at least a reduction in costs. In reply he showed conclusively that the armed forces were doing more for the country than any civilian body, that the ordnance, engineer and artillery officers were filling as great a civilian need as military, that the frontier posts were being pushed along the Mississippi, Missouri and Red rivers in order to protect our trade and that a thinner line would be wasteful. In spite of his cool and absolute logic Congress demanded the army's reduction to 6,000. Accordingly Mr.

Dec. 12
1820

Calhoun was forced to suggest palliative measures in order to keep the force from falling below that figure. In doing so he gave utterance to a truth which has been ignored ever since to the nation's sorrow:

"Economy is certainly a very high political virtue, intimately connected with the power and the public virtue of the community. In military operations, which, under the best management, are so expensive, it is of the utmost importance; but by no propriety of language can that arrangement be called economical which, in order that our military establishment in peace should be rather less expensive, would, regardless of the purposes for which it ought to be maintained, render it unfit to meet the dangers incident to a state of war."

During the years after the second war with Great Britain the army tried to bring itself out of the ignorance and decadence into which it had been tossed after the Revolution. What trained forces remained to the country were used almost ceaselessly in defending and developing our wild frontier. But the only civilians who knew the army's work and understood the nation's need were a limited few like Calhoun. Politics did not know, need to heed nor care to consider the necessity for trained fighting men. The farce of 1812 had made little impression upon the general public. We had come out all right—that was enough. Just why or how we had "come out" was a matter of little concern. That with 527,654 so-called soldiers we had been unable to defeat not over 5,000 British Regulars, that for two years and a half so small a hostile force had brought devastation within our borders and had killed and wounded 5,614 Americans and that our nation had uselessly spent for all this discard of training over $50,000,000, had not come to be realized by the voter. He was developing the inside of the country without much thought of its edges. But out there the army, having passed through its nameless period, was growing in quality while the government was looking with skeptical eyes at its size. It was too much to expect over 7,000,000 people to support 10,000 soldiers.

CHAPTER VI

THE ARMY BLAZES THE TRAIL

(1821–1844)

I F the civilization of the bulk of our country were a commodity, it should belong to the army. The thin cordon of hardy soldiers that pushed the foes of peace persistently back across prairie and through jungle, made safe the trader, trapper, and settler inside the circle. It was the troops that cut the trails, built the roads, dug the wells, surveyed the land, braved the savage, suffered in silence and opened the chest of southern and western riches.

With the stigma of Revolutionary days and 1812 still following the military man, it was easy for the civilian to brand the whole army as contemptible, especially when some coxcomb among the officers made a spectacle of himself. Cast adrift from the life of town and farm, the soldier just over the horizon was easily forgotten and seldom considered. That he was hewing the way for delicate feet to follow, pushing through showers of sleet and arrows and possessed of the same passions, hopes, and capacity for pain as the man behind the counter or plow, were thoughts remote from the minds of Boston and Baltimore. Either pacifying or suppressing the Indian, was no more, it is true, than the labor of his profession, no more than the job he had undertaken. But really he *was* risking his life that the nation might be happier and greater.

March 2
1821

Congress, echoing the appreciation of the people, reduced the army. One major general, 2 brigadiers, 44 ordnance officers and 3 regiments of infantry, artillery and riflemen were cast out of the service without any provision for their welfare. The Ordnance Department was abolished after having been built up through years of technical study and research. To

158

replace it an extra captain and 56 enlisted men were allowed
the artillery for ordnance work.[1] The office of Judge Advocate
was also discontinued.

Another general demoralization of regiments took place *May 4 1821*
when by the effect of this law the Sixth Infantry was consolidated with the rifle regiment and boiled down to the strength
of one regiment after wholesale discharges.   The Eighth *June 1 1821*
Infantry was disbanded entirely.   The Light Artillery Regiment, Ordnance Department and Corps of Artillery were
shrunken into 4 regiments of artillery,[2] known as the First,
Second, Third and Fourth.

Most of the artillery naturally occupied the coast line, the
Third being stretched from Annapolis, Md., to Charleston, S.
C. The Infantry was mainly on the frontier of the south and
west.

The Sixth Infantry, for example, having constructed Fort
Atkinson at Council Bluffs, started the first settlement in Nebraska and the first stronghold west of the Missouri River. The
troops built a sawmill and gristmill and had 506 acres of land
under cultivation. Though the walls of barracks and quarters
were made of logs, the roofs were shingled and the floors
planked. If the quarters for the men had eighty-eight rooms
and those of the officers were more commodious than formerly,
it was because the brains and energies of those soldiers converted stark forests into habitations.

The reduction of the army stagnated promotion to an extraordinary degree. Although every officer of worth who could be
retained was absorbed in the reorganization, many had to be
discharged. Those who remained found themselves members
of a minority whose vacancies were filled to the choking point.
In the artillery, especially, during these days of regimental
promotion, it was hard to rise when four lieutenants in a company had to wait for a captain. Each soldier of this reduced
army found more guns and more miles of front on the borders

---

[1] The army, after the law went into effect, consisted of 7 regiments of
infantry, 4 regiments of artillery, the engineer corps, as before established,
1 major general, 2 brigadier generals, 1 adjutant, 2 inspectors general,
1 quartermaster-general, 1 commissary general and 1 paymaster-general.

[2] Each regiment had a light battery, which, however, was so only in
name.

to be cared for than formerly. On the one hand, personal advancement was blocked, and, on the other, more work was required. All these blights on human endeavor were hardly conducive to meeting with a good will the hazards of a soldier. Yet the remaining handful attacked the wilderness with a will.

March 27
1821

Neither was the precision of the little army tarnished by the blows it had received. The uniform order is an instance. For many pages it goes into great detail as to the quality and make of clothing, and as to how it should be worn. Blue was for the first time prescribed as the national color for cloth. The chapeaux de bras was worn without plume or feather by all officers except those of the company. The rank and file and company officers wore the stiff high hat or "tar-bucket" (much like the cadet full-dress hat now). Pompons of different colors adorned this head piece: artillery wore yellow; light artillery, red and white; infantry, white; and rifle companies, green. Gold and silver tassels for company officers and worsted ones for enlisted men hung down on the right side of the cap.

The shoulder strap as an insignia of rank of officers seems to have been discontinued, though the epaulets worn as before were retained. Instead of the straps, captains wore one-stripe chevrons of gold or silver lace on each arm above the elbow and subalterns one on each arm below the elbow. Sergeant majors and quartermaster sergeants wore a worsted chevron on each arm above the elbow, sergeant and senior musicians one on each arm below the elbow, and corporals one on the right arm above the elbow. Wings, or little rolls on the shoulder, were worn both by company officers and enlisted men. Pantaloons were buff, white or blue, blue and buff for wear off duty and white for parade. Gray woolen ones were allowed for winter wear of enlisted men of the artillery and infantry. The coat was about the same as before, the cadet continuing the gray coatee and the rifleman the green jacket. Red silk sashes for all officers on duty came into general use.

The laced bootee or modern type shoe was provided for all enlisted men. A higher boot was required to be worn by company officers; one to reach to the calf of the leg, by engineers; and "high military boots," by mounted officers with troops.

In contrast to this ornate clothing, weapons of greater accuracy and range than heretofore carried were issued to the soldier. The government had on hand something less than 10,000 rifles at the arsenals of Harper's Ferry and Springfield. The smooth-bore was beginning to disappear in the service. Three contractors in Middletown, Connecticut, and Mr. Deringer in Philadelphia, manufactured for the army several thousand rifles in this decade each one costing about $14.50 or an equivalent of about $75 now. Although the breech-loader had been experimented with by the Ordnance Department, the invention of Mr. Hall of Yarmouth, Maine, had not succeeded further than an output of 200. The great defects were the powder leaks and the lack of interchangeability of parts. The small-bore "squirrel rifle," firing balls between 90 to 200 to the pound, were used greatly by militia in its customarily sudden calls into the service.

A private publication called the *Artillerist* appeared this *1821* year, apparently for the militia. It detailed extensively everything from the manual of the sword to six "divisions of movements" for the battery. Cuts, guards, St. Georges, mullinets, and parries for fencing were carefully set forth, as well as drill movements, such as how the "pieces being in battery" should "march in retreat or in advance toward the enemy."

There now being no cavalry in the service, its maneuvers had to be kept alive solely by regulations for the volunteers. *1822* Lieutenant Colonel Pierce Darrow accordingly adapted such a work to Scott's regulations, calling it *Cavalry Tactics.* He confessed at the beginning that the organization of a cavalry regiment was so radically different in most of the states that it was quite impossible to give a standard type. He compromised, however, by laying down "the order of formation" for two regiments of different size. He conformed to the law of 1820 in prescribing that regiments should be called battalions, and that companies should be posted in line according to the dates of the captains' commissions.[6]

---

[3] The following extract will show how he solved two difficulties:

"A regiment of cavalry, in this, and many of the states, comprises but four companies, which are styled a squadron, of which I shall first give a detail of arrangement. The second method of formation embraces eight

Early
1822

While the army was trying to better its efficiency, it was in reality low in spirit. The injustice upon the officers who had been "deranged," "razed" or transferred was so apparent that the matter was taken up by many citizens who forced an investigation by a Committee of Congress. The members came to this remarkable conclusion: "While the committee pay just respect to officers retained in the service, they wish not to detract from merits of the many valuable officers who have been left out of the army or reduced in rank." This magnificent tribute was the sole consequence of the fatiguing labor of the lawmakers. No material provision was made for those "valuable" men suddenly cut off without a farthing.

The army had to continue to perform its own tasks and those of the men taken away by the legislators. Its dispersion had to be so thin that as a defensive force it was ridiculous. The Second Infantry for instance, in trying to keep in advance of its part of the receding frontier, made long journeys which

June
1822

disclose what was taking place throughout the service. In January the regiment had been moved from Plattsburg to Sackett's Harbor, N. Y. A few months later five of its companies and headquarters sailed to Sault Sainte Marie where they built Fort Brady. Less than 800 men tried to cover almost 8,000 miles of front, open to Indian raids and lesser encroachments.

Jan. 29
1822

The 4 puny regiments of artillery scattered their harbor forts through Eastport and Portland, Me.; Portsmouth, N. H.; Marblehead and Boston, Mass.; Newport, R. I.; New London, Conn.; New York City, West Point, Sackett's Harbor, Fort Niagara and Plattsburg, N. Y.; Philadelphia, Pa.; Baltimore, Annapolis and Fort Washington, Md.; Norfolk, Va.; Smithville, N. C.; Charleston, S. C.; Savannah, Ga.; Amelia Island, Fort Gadsden, Fla.; Fort Bowyer and Mobile Bay, Ala.; Fort

---

companies, and two squadrons, first and second; each squadron is divided into two grand divisions, and numbered from right to left, 1, 2, 3, 4; the whole are styled a battalion when in the field.

"The habitual habit of formation is in two ranks, but it is frequently practiced, where the companies are small, to parade the squadron in one rank. This may be allowed on particular occasions, and when there are but four companies to parade together, as it will greatly facilitate the exercise and movements; but this should by no means prevent their acquiring a perfect knowledge of their duty in two ranks.''

Petite Coquille, La.; Fort Saint Philips, Council Bluffs, Saint Peters, Miss.; Mackinaw, and Fort Shelby, Mich. The armaments totaled 28 forty-two pounders, 226 thirty-two pounders, 413 twenty-four pounders, 228 eighteen-pounders, 3 ten-inch seacoast mortars, 32 ten-inch siege mortars, 5 eighteen-inch mortars, 10 eight-inch howitzers and 46 twenty-four-pounder howitzers. Neither could the fortresses be well manned nor the guns be all cared for or operated under such limitations of man power.

The provision for so many large weapons, with their requisite balls and ammunition, illustrates the attitude of the country toward materials for war. Somehow, our citizens have always been ready to spend money for the making and storing of arms to the disregard of the construction of a soldier and the soldierly character. It has been difficult for them to see that it takes longer to make the operator and superintendent than the missile and gun. While satisfied with its meager army, Congress at *March 3 1823* this time provided $5,000 for a national armory on "the western waters" to be selected by a "skillful engineer" or ordnance officer. Galena, Ill., seems to have been the choice because of the mines there and the fact that the War Department was still charged with the management of geological activities later given over to the Interior Department.

As the little army tried to stretch itself over many different activities and along thousands of miles of wild territory, it had its share of combats with the savage, which went along incessantly. These "small affairs" were scarcely noted by the newspaper and too often forgotten by the people. A few soldiers were cut down here, an officer lost his life there and the story of their deeds sank almost at once into oblivion. Even *June 1823* as large an action as that of the Sixth Infantry, when Lieutenant Colonel Leavenworth drove back the Arikara Indians who had put General Ashley's party in jeopardy, has gone unrecounted in our general histories.

While the few trained forces on our frontiers were repelling the Indian by superior knowledge and training, Colonel Thayer back at the Military Academy was raising the standard of military and educational work. In addition to the advancement which he had already brought, he used senior cadets of

Sept. 10
1823

excellent qualifications as assistant professors in order to give larger individual instruction. He succeeded in getting Congress to provide for these men, selected wholly on their merit, $10 a month as extra pay for the "honorable distinction." He then ordered extra buttons to be worn on their dress coats, so as to make the remainder of the Corps of Cadets see the stamp of authority placed upon the new position. By such methods, he was able partially to overcome the shortage of commissioned instructors in a microscopic army, to make scholastic competition among cadets higher and to improve the thoroughness of West Point courses.

It was the scientific instruction at the Military Academy that made possible an engineer corps which constructed many of our public works. In this year Congress appropriated $30,000 for surveys of roads and canals of national importance

April 30
1824

and allowed the use of the corps of engineers and two other "skillful engineers" to carry on the labor. Most of the highways and explorations of this period were made by army officers—then the only home-grown scientific men of our country.

Another event in scientific instruction was the establishment of the "artillery school of instruction" at Fortress Monroe, Virginia, for the purpose of familiarizing the artillerist

1824

with his duties. Although its curriculum and plant were quite unformed, the foundation was laid for the service school that was to have a beneficial influence later on the development of our larger weapons and mines.

The scientific knowledge of army officers spurred others to try their skill in making improvements. A curious inven-

1824–1825

tion came into use at this time in the militia. Simeon North of Middletown, Conn., who had been making rifles for the army, invented a few 4 and 5 shot repeaters. He put a small extra barrel in rear of the regular flintlock bore so as to have the ammunition slide into place in front of the chamber. The magazine did not revolve, was impractical and soon came into disuse. But the device illustrates the attempt at this time to produce a greater volume of fire and more rapid loading.

1825

The drill regulations or "Infantry Tactics," as they were then known, went into great detail in this period. The oblique step required the feet to be planted at 18, 25 and 44 inch dis-

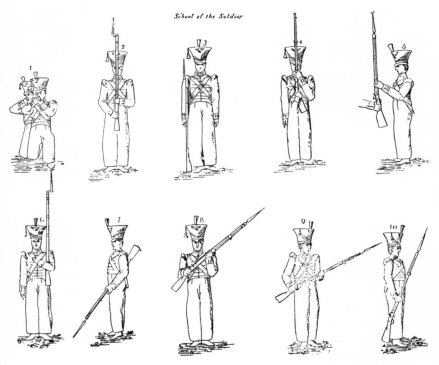

School of the Soldier

1. Represents a soldier of the first and second ranks kneeling and aiming.

2. Represents a soldier after presenting arms.

3. Represents the position of ordered arms.

4. Represents the soldier presenting his firelock, for inspection.

5. Represents the soldier receiving his musket from the instructor, after inspection.

6. Represents the soldier after the third motion of support arms.

7. Shows the soldier, after the second motion of secure arms.

8. Represents the soldier after executing the command, "port—ARMS."

9. Represents the soldier after the second motion of charge—BAYONET.

10. Shows the soldier in the position of trail arms.

tances at various times in the execution of the movement. Eight
plates showed how a company should march precisely through
different parts and kinds of defiles. The utmost nicety was
required of a "battalion of the first line passing through a
battalion of the second line," a "column of attack forming
square against cavalry," "the deployment of the column for
attack," and a line of eight battalions oblique to the enemy in
forming parallel to him by "echelons of brigades." The first
company on the march, being detached as an advance guard,
had its own supports and reserves.

Along with the changes in drill went those of the uniform.
A cloth "foraging cap or chakos" trimmed with lace was now *1825*
permitted company officers and enlisted men "when on duty,
absent from their companies." The new headpiece was light
and in some respects like the modern cap. It was evident that
the bell-crown "tar-bucket" was quite too much for those who
were not allowed to wear the light chapeaux de bras. A frock
coat with a skirt to come to the knee was required of all officers
whenever full dress was not otherwise prescribed. The insignia
of rank was worn upon the collar.

Some changes of station again mark the progress of the
frontier outward. Two of the companies of the Fourth Artil- *April*
lery were sent south from Fortress Monroe. The Third In- *1826*
fantry went west from Fort Howard, where it helped build
Camp Miller, afterwards known as Jefferson Barracks, Mis- *Sept.*
souri. *1826*

A "Cavalry Tactics" by a board, of which Major General
Scott was president and several militia generals were mem- *1826*
bers, appeared this year. It covered the training of young
horses, care and equipment of mounts, nomenclature of pistol
and sword, drill in 1 or 2 ranks, formations of a regiment
of 4 squadrons in order of battle, schools of the trooper and
squadron and elaborate maneuvers corresponding to those of
infantry tactics.

A similarly complete regulation appeared for artillery.
Everything from the "hound-box" to "perch" was completely
explained. The work gave exhaustive schools of the gunner, *1826*
the piece and the battery, and included evolutions of batteries
and a manual of the howitzer. A battery consisted of 6 pieces,

which were numbered from right to left, each piece with its caisson being drawn by four horses. The battery was divided either into 3 sections or 2 half-batteries. Both the cavalry and artillery maneuvers were copied from Scott's infantry movements as, for example, the command, "Break from the right and march to the left."

According to the *Abridged Tactics for Infantry* the soldier in the position of attention put his heels as near together "as the conformation of the man will permit." He executed "eyes right" as he does now. The company fell in and was sized in "two ranks, tallest men on the right," and was then divided into platoons and sections. Loading was done by 12 commands, and "P'sent," "Port" and "Pile" arms were a part of the manual. There was volley firing in addition to firing by file as before.

While the little army was trying to improve itself, legislation was moving like the hen that pecks at particles all day and occasionally lays an egg. Extra pay of $10 a month was given to the officer who actually was in command of a company. The purpose was to alleviate the distress of junior officers who had difficulty in living on their pay. But only the senior subalterns whose captains happened to be absent profited by the measure. Sometimes, naturally, good captains were detached in order to give the increased pay to straitened lieutenants. In any case, only a few could receive the small benefit of the law. Instead of giving a substantial increase to every soldier, Congress thus resorted to a petty compromise which caused discrimination, did not raise the general morale and was on the whole wasteful.

Yet the army went on improving itself and boring into the wilderness. The frontier extending further west, Colonel Leavenworth with four companies of the Third Infantry selected the site of the fort in Kansas which still bears his name. There he established a cantonment. The Sixth, in the meantime, joined forces with the remainder of the Third at Jefferson Barracks, where was started an informal Infantry School of Practice. To this primitive place of instruction, as to the Artillery School of Practice at Fortress Monroe, all the "brevet second lieutenants" were sent upon joining.

1826

March 2 1827

April, May 1827

While the army was thus trying to advance technically so
as to make itself more efficient, it had many besetting trials
with which to contend.

Brevet rank, that great anomalous bugbear which was to
have such a disturbing influence on the spirit of troops, was
given a standing it had not heretofore had.   The adjutant gen-   *June 16*
eral issued an order which deemed officers holding brevet rank   *1827*
to be on duty and to have command according to their brevet
commissions when they were actually commanding enough
troops to warrant such higher grade.   If a brevetted officer was
really commanding double the number of men which ordinary regimental rank entitled him to control, the brevet rank
became actual.   A captain who was also a brevet major, for
example, exercised command as a major when he was on duty
over a detachment composed of not less than 2 companies.
Naturally such an incongruity led to discontent.   Those who
had had no opportunity to be brevetted or those who, although
brevetted, did not command the required number of men were
through chance denied the higher grade.   Men of long service
and experience were often, then, commanded by their actual
juniors.

Neither did disease help the morale of the army.   The
troops on duty in the south were so reduced by fever that Brigadier General Jacob Brown had to transfer large numbers over
considerable distances.   The Fourth Artillery alone had lost
(mostly from yellow fever) during the six years of its stay, 16
officers and 220 enlisted men.   Yet Congress inquired into the
expense of changing the Fourth to the north coast, the Third
to the New England coast and the First and Second to the
south.   It had not been borne in upon the minds of the lawmakers that soldiers in the wilds were dying fast.   When Gen·
eral Brown showed that it was unfair to exterminate regiments
in unhealthful places while others were in a land of comparative
conveniences, his dispositions were approved.

Whereas the artillery had posts in civilization to which it
could be moved, the infantry had to live constantly on the
borders.   It is hard to realize now the terrible scourges of
plague and epidemic that riddled the commands of the frontier.
Resistance was lessened by exposure.   Flies, roaches, mosqui-

toes and rats were so abundant that they were almost ineffaceable. Scientific investigation had not yet shown the fatality lurking among these pests. The soldiers, in crowded buildings and unacquainted with the need of ventilation, disseminated small pox, yellow fever, malaria and typhoid without understanding their sources. Danger from disease for the military man was many times as great as for the citizen who had his own room and dined at home.

1827

If an undeveloped, small medical department had its troubles, the task that fell upon the staff in general was just as great. The Ordnance Department had been taken away from the army by the false economy of costly reductions. Those who kept up a part of the ordnance duties now masqueraded as artillerymen. A lieutenant colonel and 4 captains of artillery, stationed in Washington, attempted to supervise the arms and equipment of the entire service. Such condition was typical of the big burden that fell upon the few who made up the army.

1828

1829

The movement of troops over tremendous distances was but an evidence of the attempt to have soldiers in two places at once. The First Infantry which had occupied Baton Rouge and vicinity was sent to Fort Crawford, Fort Snelling and Fort Winnebago at the other end of the Mississippi. The headquarters of the Fourth Artillery were changed to Philadelphia.

May
1829

Four companies of the Sixth Infantry started as an escort to a party of traders bound from Fort Leavenworth to Santa Fe. The journey there and return was to require two years of fighting, thirst and exhaustion. The endurance and determination of these men broke a path for Kearny and Doniphan later, and blazed this trail for the first time.

1829

While the small army was desperately trying to hold the borders, it was also bringing the drill regulations up to a more practical and efficient standard. Improvement in the quality of maneuver went on, even if the numbers of troops to execute the movements were few. The new *U. S. Infantry Drill Regulations* consisted of three main schools: the soldier, the company, and the battalion. It was the most thorough and progressive work of its kind since Steuben's manual and showed again the energy of Major General Winfield Scott. The book contained a special section for light infantry and riflemen.

Loading while kneeling and lying down, forming single file, advancing by files, diminishing and increasing front, and firing in extended order, seem to point to the development of the service of security. The 2 rifle companies in each battalion were, therefore, posted on the right and left. Executing the manual "by the numbers" was provided for so that the recruit could be the more carefully instructed. Inspection arms was described much as it exists to-day except that the ramrod was sprung in the barrel before the piece was taken by the inspector. Since the bores of the muzzle loaders could not be readily looked through, such precaution was necessary in order to make certain that the piece was unloaded. Target practice made its first modern advance. An eight-inch bull's-eye with an exterior ring was placed in the middle of the upper half of the target and between the horizontal bands, evidently to simulate the vital part of a human being. A soldier was required to begin at 50 yards in order to gain confidence, and then gradually proceed back to 140 yards which was considered point-blank range. Because the sight was fixed, he had to aim below the bull's-eye more and more as he advanced toward the target from 140 yards.

A *System of Exercise and Instruction of Field Artillery* *Under Dept of War, March 2 1829* showed that the proper service was with horses in action, and that the proper calibers for the field were 6-and-12-pounder guns and 24-pounder howitzers. This regulation includes the term field artillery, light and horse artillery. The book is complete and a counterpart of the *Infantry Tactics*.

As the army labored on improvement, Congress seemed to be more interested in destruction than construction of the armed *1829* forces. It tried now to do away with the office of major general or general in chief of the army. When the matter came to an issue, views of the committee on military affairs and of the Secretary of War were called for. Both Mr. Harrison and Mr. Peter B. Porter showed how the army had to have a head who was a soldier, just as much as a ship needed a captain who was a sailor. If the office were taken away, the work would be improperly done by a civilian secretary on the advice of junior staff officers by whom he was surrounded. The result was that Congress retained the office without recognizing its authority in purely military affairs, so that administration by the Secretary for a long time clogged the machinery and gave a precedent for much mismanagement in the Civil War.

Within the army military procedure was likewise shaken by the operation of the orders on brevet rank. Officers by this time had become so confused that in many cases they were at a loss as to who was actually in command. The consequence was that an order from Washington separated command from

Aug. 13 1829

brevet rank. Although an officer sat on a court in accordance with brevetted grade, he was forbidden to exercise command corresponding to such grade unless especially assigned by the War Department for that purpose. So confusion was somewhat allayed but not overcome.

These interruptions could not stem the steady progress of the army in pushing our boundaries outward. The movement of the Third Infantry is an illustration of the advancement of

Nov. 26 1829

the frontier. Two companies left Jefferson Barracks for Black Creek, Choctaw Nation. Four more companies left for the

Dec. 14 1830

southeast corner of what is now Oklahoma on the Red River. These places represented the outlying sections of our western boundary. Wild regions infested by savages were reclaimed by roads, forts and the surveys made by this daring handful of soldiers.

Indian uprisings later becoming threatening along the Mississippi, the Sixth Infantry was concentrated at Jefferson Barracks, with the specific purpose of taking care of the Sac and Fox Indians commanded by Black Hawk. That part of

Sept. 1831

the Fifth Infantry at Fort Winnebago was moved to Fort Armstrong (Rock Island, Ill.). The Third was sent to Cantonment Jesup, La.

In the meantime, administrative changes caused a bettering

1831

of conditions at Washington. The topographical engineers were

March 1832

organized into a regular bureau of the War Department, and after eleven years' absence, an Ordnance Department again made its appearance. Congress established the latter as a branch separate from the artillery so that it could now function with some sort of benefit for the service and advancement along broader and more technical lines.[4]

---

[4] It is interesting to note that in 1830 a change was attempted in the

Then General Scott entered upon the first of the duties   *1832*
which were to make his and the army's name so famous for pacification.   In South Carolina the *Nullification Proclamation* had
angered the people of that state to such an extent that they were
on the point of secession and possibly civil war.   President
Jackson sent General Scott to Charleston to look after the
difficulties.   The General's great tact, forbearance, and humanity bridged over the gulf and kept the government out of war.

In the west the activities of Black Hawk were such that it
was known a large force would be necessary to subdue him.
General Atkinson, with the Sixth Infantry and 900 Illinois   *June*
volunteers concentrated at Dixon's Ferry.   The government   *1832*
acting with exemplary promptness, made provisions for raising
600 mounted rangers, the first intimation of cavalry since   *June 15*
1821.   It also prepared to send General Scott with troops from   *1832*
the east.   To get to the scene of activities, a large part of the
Fourth Artillery covered by rail, boat, and marches 1,800 miles
in 18 days.   Such dispatch at a time when transit was not
modern is almost unparalleled.   But the eastern troops were
never destined to engage with Black Hawk for they lost more
than 30 per cent of their number by Asiatic cholera en route.
The Second Infantry at Detroit was similarly struck down by
the disease.   Though the concentration contemplated 1,300
regular troops from the Lakes and the Atlantic, the whole force
was blocked by the plague.   At Rock Island, Ill., General Scott,
foreseeing the dire effects of drunkenness in connection with
the disease, forestalled intoxication by a characteristic order:

"That every soldier or ranger who shall be found drunk or
sensibly intoxicated, after the publication of this order, be
compelled as soon as his strength will permit, to dig a grave
at a suitable burying place, large enough for his own reception,
as such graves cannot fail to be wanted for the drunken man
himself or some drunken companion.   This order is given as

---

paper cartridge with which the soldier loaded.   Instead of having to bite
the end and discard the wad, the foot soldier could thrust the whole cartridge into the chamber.   The paper envelope, having been made combustible
by a preparation of niter was consumed at discharge.   The improvement
was of doubtful value, especially when the paper became wet, so that the
cartridge did not come into general use.

well to serve as a punishment for drunkenness, as to spare good and temperate men the labor of digging graves for their worthless companions."

Although Scott did not get to the fight the above will intimate that he had a well-disciplined force in hand.

*Aug. 2
1832*

General Atkinson in the meantime had, with parts of the First and Sixth Infantry, come up with Black Hawk at the junction of the Bad Axe and the Mississippi. After a bloody battle of three hours, Atkinson signally defeated the savages.

*July 21
1832*

In the meantime the Illinois volunteers had met the enemy at the Wisconsin River and driven him back. When they had joined General Atkinson the augmented force effectively put a quietus on Black Hawk.

1832

Yet the army did not always treat the savage with the rifle. Captain Bonneville of the army took an indefinite leave of absence in order to study the Indian in his native haunts. Disguised as a fur trader, he made his way with 110 men to the heart of the Rockies, where he lived among the Nez Percés and Flatheads for five years. His daring labor was the wedge for peace with many tribes of Indians for years afterward.

*Nov. 2
1832*

Shortly after Scott's experiences in getting his troops west, "ardent spirits" disappeared from the ration. Liquor was forbidden to be introduced into any fort, camp or garrison by any soldier or sutler, and sugar and coffee were issued in place of whisky. So it came about that the army was the first institution of our government to prescribe prohibition for its personnel.

*Ordered
June 11
1832
Operative
July 4
1833*

Along with such restrictions came changes of uniform which were intended to create a greater appeal to self-respect. Officers wore double-breasted coats coming to the knee, the different branches had the same colored facings on their coats as were prescribed during the Revolution, cocked hats returned, and all officers and noncommissioned officers had epaulets on both shoulders. Rank was distinguished by the materials and sizes of the straps of the epaulet, on which was placed the regimental number. The eagle for the colonel came into vogue for the first time as did the rows of buttons for generals in groups of fours, threes and twos.

Sylvanus Thayer

It then became apparent to Congress that if the Indian was to be pursued, cavalry was necessary.   After eleven years *March 2 1833* of absence a regiment of dragoons made its appearance.   One colonel, 1 lieutenant colonel, 1 major, 10 companies, each with 1 captain, 1 first lieutenant and 1 second lieutenant made up this new mounted contingent of 600 privates.

At the same time, enlistments for the whole army were reduced to three years and the pay of a private increased to $6.[5] Although he received only $5 of this amount for the first two years, he was given the remaining $24 at the expiration of that time, provided his conduct had been good.   A reënlisted soldier received the full $6.   All premiums were henceforth prohibited to recruiting officers and no man who had been convicted of a criminal offense could be enlisted.

How well this last provision was carried out seems to be disputable.   Small pay, little recreation, hard duty and little opportunity for advancement were not appealing to well-bred young men.   Since the Military Academy furnished all and more of the officer personnel, commissions from the ranks were rare.   The down-and-outer, the foreigner, and the adventurer made up to too great a degree the rank and file.

The consequence was that the personnel of a company had to be controlled with an iron hand.   Ignorant men could be restrained from mutiny by fear alone.   Beating, which had been prohibited many years before, was still prevalent in these isolated places.   Desertion in one instance met the following fate:

"The court found him guilty as charged and sentenced him to be tied to a stack of arms and to receive ten lashes for five

---

[5] The allowance for clothing for three years consisted of: *March 20 1833*

1 cap complete	3 cotton jackets
2 coats complete, for artillery and infantry	6 cotton shirts
1 coat complete, for ordnance and dragoons	6 flannel shirts
	9 pairs boots
6 pairs woolen overalls	9 pairs stockings
9 pairs cotton overalls	2 blankets
2 woolen jackets, for artillery and infantry	1 forage cap
	1 great coat
3 woolen jackets for ordnance and dragoons	1 leather stock
	3 pairs of drawers.

successive mornings with a cat o' nine tails on his bare back in the presence of the command, to have his head and eyebrows shaved, to forfeit all pay and traveling expenses and to be drumd out of service."

The rawhide, however, was still used as in the days of the Revolution. One officer forgot himself so far as to be court-martialed and severely punished on the following charge:

CHARGE 1

"Conduct subversive of good order and Military Discipline." Specification: In this: That he, the said Lieutenant Colonel W—— of the 6th Regiment U. S. Infantry, while commanding the regiment in question, did punish with stripes and lashes, private Thomas Powell of Company 'D,' of the regiment aforesaid—the punishment so administered being of such extreme severity as to have disabled the said Thomas Powell from the performance of his duty, for the period of nine days. This at Jefferson Barracks, in the state of Missouri, on or about the 12th of December, 1828."

For sleeping on post in hostile country a soldier was sometimes ordered to be shot. Sometimes, also, the firing squad was given secret directions to aim high over the head of the blindfolded victim kneeling on his coffin before his grave. After the volley, the prostrate convict was pardoned before his fellow soldiers because of previous good conduct.

Cruelty naturally sprang up in a wilderness where one's existence depended upon the obedience of men who could neither read, write nor understand the reasons for discipline. There were instances where officers privately flogged their men. Physical superiority throughout the country was playing a large part in the settlement of affairs, and so it was in the army.

The guardhouse was a log fortress usually outside the walls of the stockade. The ordinary type had two compartments, one for the guard and the other for the prisoners. The open room held those charged with moderate offenses, but cells at one side restrained the deserter, the rioter, and the more heinous criminal. These latter compartments about 8 feet long, 3 feet wide and only 3 feet high made it impossible for the culprit to stand upright during his confinement.

The constant danger to the isolated fort is shown by the diligence with which those approaching it were challenged. The countersign was normally used with great care. The person approaching was called upon to "stand" by the sentry, and then to "advance with the countersign, and give it." If the word was correct, the sentry said "Right, pass"; if not, he called a noncommissioned officer of the guard.

The daily guard, fatigue, and routine of other duties were often interrupted by more exciting occurrences. The arrival of the "express rider" at an unusual hour of the night, the "orderly call," the parading of the garrison with knapsacks packed, the hustle and bustle of the "waiters," the discomfort of weighty accouterments and tight garments, the long, dreary, hungry march, the contact with the first painted warriors, the running fight, the unexpected whoop of a fresh band of savages, the final drive after hours of sweaty, muddy, bloody struggle, the search for the dead and wounded, the return to the fort, the gloomy burials with final volleys over the graves of good companions, were incidents in the monotony of the soldier's life. And the apothecary in Philadelphia went on undisturbed even by a headline of what the nth Infantry had done for the civilization of the nation's territory. The soldier had plenty of one thing—hazard. And this he accepted without complaint.

While the small bodies of troops were pounding away on the frontier, the army as a whole was being bettered. The *June 1834* organization of the First Regiment of Dragoons was soon completed. The service now had mounted troops to use against the Indian. The medical corps, too, was helped by legislation. The quality of its officers was raised, when all new appoint- *June 30 1834* ments of assistant surgeons had to be censored by an army medical board.

Field artillery had its real birth during this year. The *1834* Ordnance Department tested out two different types of carriages, the "stock-trail" and the Gribeauval. It especially went into the merits of brass and iron weapons, with results favoring the former. As to sizes, 6- and 12-pounder guns and 12- and 24-pounder howitzers seemed to survive.

1834

An Abstract of a System of Exercise and Instruction of Field Artillery was written by J. L. Wilson for the South Carolina militia. Two gunners and 2 first, 2 second and 2 third mattrosses served the piece (16- or 24-pounder). Grape shot was loaded by means of bags holding lead bullets. Cartridges of powder were made into cases covered by flannel boiled in oil. Pieces were touched off by a torch, and the powder in the chamber ignited by the use of a quick match and a portfire. The former was a long homemade fuse like a round lamp wick and the latter was a small paper case of powder made more inflammable by the admixture of antimony.

1834

Less than 4,000 regular soldiers now guarded over 10,000 miles of seacoast and frontier for 15,000,000 of people. Five hundred infantrymen and artillerymen in Florida constituted the nation's only safeguard in a country of 52,000 square miles, infested by thousands of Seminole and Creek Indians.

Dec. 28 1835

It was natural that the savage began to feel his power to such a degree that his confidence and cruelty led him to murder parts of the Second and Third Artillery and Fourth Infantry marching peacefully from Fort Brook to Fort King; 107 regular officers and men were killed. At the same time 2 other officers were murdered near Fort King. This affair, commonly known as Dade's massacre, fired the country and especially the army.

Dec. 31 1835

Almost immediately General Clinch with 6 companies of artillery and infantry regulars and about 400 volunteers met approximately 1,000 Indians at the Withlacoochee and drove them back. Of the trained soldiers 57 officers and men were killed. Why only 30 officers and men of the volunteers got into action has never been satisfactorily explained. Had the whole force been used it is likely the Florida war would have ended at once. All the few trained soldiers could do was to repulse the Indians who went further away into their hiding places and became more wary.

It was during this war that the most trying duty that could fall to the lot of troops was performed by nearly all of the regular army constantly for four long years. Moving from swamp to swamp in search of an enemy that never appeared, dying by battalions with fever and exposure, never able to bring on a decisive engagement with the elusive natives, never daring to separate into small groups without being exterminated by savages who sprang from the soil, at night disturbed by decoys and alarms, always on the move fighting shadows, starved for supplies, burned or plundered by the Indian, hindered by thickets, marshes, tropical forests, morasses and jungles of unknown poisons and mysterious extent, balked by the enemy who was never to be trusted in council and resorted to any ulterior means to gain a scalp, the little army of less than 1,000 regulars tried to clean out a vast country occupied by over 3,000 Indians. In spite of the handicaps the soldier built 90 forts and stockades and 480 miles of road. This great wedge of development and safety the army accomplished at the price of misery, disease, and death.

The First Artillery was the first one to reach Florida from *Jan.* the north in order to reënforce the command already there. *1836* General Scott, in charge of the Eastern Department, was also *Jan. 9* sent to the scene of the trouble by the War Department. And *1836* it was wise that the regular troops were appearing, for General Call had reported mutiny among his volunteer troops and Governor Eaton had shown that his had all gone home. Florida was left alone with its handful of trained soldiers, whose companies were now rendered so small by the lack of legislation that scarcely an average of 30 men could be mustered for duty.

General Gaines, in the meantime, in command of the Western Department, having no information from the War *Feb. 3* Department, hastened with about 1,100 men for Tampa to *1836* avenge Dade's massacre. Pushing on to Fort Drane where Scott had a reservoir of supplies for the right wing of his troops, he was there besieged. When the siege was raised not only were Gaines' troops starving and subsisting on horse flesh, but *March 6* the supplies for Scott's troops were all used up. Here we have *1836* the picture of two forces of United States troops acting utterly independently of each other and in opposition. Part of the reason for this mismanagement can be attributed to the absence of the telegraph and rapid transit.

General Gaines then calmly went back to his command, leaving General Clinch to resuscitate the starving soldiers.

In addition to these troubles the Creek Indians now began to show signs of hostility in southern Alabama and Georgia. Although the Second Infantry did some notable work in escorting emigrating tribes, there were so few soldiers, in proportion to the number of savages and settlers to be protected, that the task seemed hopeless.

General Scott was without an adequate force. Although the Sixth Infantry, some artillery and the volunteers were on their
way, the situation in Florida was not then helped. Futile and tardy enactments by Congress gave authority for "10,000 men" and an additional regiment of dragoons, but such action was far from collecting, organizing, training and putting on the ground the numbers voted. Besides, the 10,000 were to be discharged at the end of "six or twelve months" and the extra regiment of dragoons was to be disbanded at the will of the President. Although the dragoons were to be accepted for three years, the volunteers were to go out either in a year or a half year as they chose. What raw troops would decide is not undecipherable after what had already transpired in our history. To add to this fruitlessness, the governors of Georgia and Alabama had ordered thousands of soldiers into the field who were useless because they had no arms.

The Third and Fourth Artillery and Fourth and Sixth Infantry took part in a succession of small actions, such as Macinope, Fort Drane, Wahoo Swamp and Withlacoochee, wherever any Indians could be induced to appear. In the meantime the savage was carrying on raids of extermination on every white man, woman, and child who could be seized in Florida, southern Alabama and Georgia. A massacre would occur in one place while the troops were at another. Seldom was the meager force in that wide country able to catch up with a foe that was capable of rapid disappearance. History little records the deeds of heroism and discomfort of Scott's troops.

One commander wrote:

"There are here 11 companies of artillery; the whole presents a fighting force of 110 men; and while we are entitled to 55 officers, we have here only 6 for company duty."

The country would not allow the officer or enlisted man to do the job right by making or having a sufficiently large trained force. So scarce were subalterns that President Jackson had to order them to the front from detached service. With companies that were squads, needing few officers, and having less, with useless pilgrimages that were able to cover but small fractions of the hostile territory and with the ever-present disease that was more deadly than the bullet, morale in the service was naturally low.

Promotion was so slow that a lieutenant had little hope of ever becoming a captain. For sixty-nine graduates of the Military Academy there were no actual vacancies so that they had to be attached as brevet second lieutenants to their companies. These young men with exceptional education under the régime of Colonel Thayer, seeing futures less lucrative and hopeful than those of uneducated mill hands of their own town, resigned in shoals. One hundred and seventeen officers went out in 1836. During this decade, the service lost and the civilian gained the benefit of such men as Horace Bliss, celebrated engineer; W. C. Young, President Panama Railroad and Hudson River Railroad; R. R. Parrott, inventor of the gun bearing his name; Alexander D. Bache, one of the most famous educators and scientists of his time; Albert Sidney Johnston; N. B. Buford; Leonidas Polk; Jefferson Davis; Joseph E. Johnston; George G. Meade; and Henry Du Pont, proprietor of the Du Pont Powder Mills.[6]

1836

Efforts within the service to produce good results were almost pathetic. *Tactics and Regulations for the Militia* gave to the volunteer a volume containing all that should be known by him of infantry, cavalry and artillery drill. One apparently novel thing emphasized was the deployment of the light infantry and rifle companies and battalions "as skirmishers," and their "rallying and assembling."

1836

The uniform showed marks of evolution toward later changes. Although the epaulets were retained for full dress of officers, shoulder straps of the type worn on the officers' blue dress coat before the World War came into vogue for generals

---

[6] All graduates of West Point.

and colonels in "undress." Majors and company officers wore slashed flaps, buttons and loops on their sleeves. The major wore a slash 6½ inches long, 4 loops and 4 buttons; and the subalterns, a slash 3½ inches long with 2 loops and 2 buttons. The cadet full-dress coat and overcoat were almost as they appear now, although a gray vest was included in the wardrobe. All staff officers wore aigullettes on the undress coat. Chevrons for noncommissioned officers in dress uniform were replaced by the same sort of slashings on the sleeve as for captains and lieutenants, except that the material was worsted cloth instead of gold lace. For undress, the chevrons for sergeants and corporals were approximately of the same design as now, save that they were pointed downward. It was prescribed that the hair should be "cut short or what is generally termed cropped; the whiskers not to extend below the lower tip of the ear, and in a line thence with the curve of the mouth."

Promotion for company officers was within the regiment; for field officers, within the same branch of the service. Added to the inequalities of such procedure throughout the army, brevet rank continued to create much dispute and many unusual situations.

July 7 1836

During the year General Scott was recalled from the scene of hostilities in order that his conduct in not prosecuting the war more quickly might be inquired into. Between General Gaines, the raw troops, and Congress he had not had a chance. Supplies and transportation were wanting and his difficulties approached those of Schuyler or Washington at their worst. It had now grown to be a national habit to take the tools away from a commander and to inquire at the seat of government into his conduct when he failed. Of course, General Scott was fully acquitted, and the enemy was not harmed by his absence.

The army, in small detachments like lost souls in the desert, went about seeking the enemy. It might as well have hunted, like De Soto, for the fountain of youth. At the small councils the chiefs made peace and afterward broke faith. The actions though small caused marching and countermarching that keenly harassed and provoked the troops.

The Third and Fourth Artillery and the Third, Fourth and Sixth Infantry regiments bore the brunt of this unusual hunt in the dark against treachery and disease. The First Infantry *July 31 1837* and some of the newly organized Second Dragoons were on their way south. But trouble was brewing in Canada to such a degree that most of the remaining regulars were needed in the north.

In the south General Jesup was unable to report more than *Oct. 21 1837* 30 Indians killed and 500 captured. Colonel Zachary Taylor, however, having taken a company of the Fourth Artillery, the First and Sixth Infantry, some Missouri volunteers, Morgan's spies, some pioneers and pontooneers, and some Delaware In- *Dec. 19 1837* dians—a force of 870 altogether—set out through the fastnesses of Florida with orders to defeat the Indians wherever found. After much search a body of savages, large enough to be at- tacked, was found hidden in a hummock of thick saw grass five feet high. To approach the position the soldiers had to wade to their knees in mud and water. Although such a quagmire prevented the use of horses and made the advance of foot troops hazardous, Taylor attacked. When Colonel Gentry of the raw troops fell, most of the volunteers fled to their baggage and could not be persuaded to return. Colonel Zachary Taylor describes the remainder of the battle thus:

"The enemy, however, were promptly checked and driven back by the Fourth and Sixth Infantry, which, in truth, might be said to be a moving battery. The weight of the enemy's fire was principally concentrated on five companies of the Sixth Infantry, which not only stood firm, but continued to advance until their gallant commander, Lieutenant-Colonel Thompson, and his adjutant, Lieutenant Centre, were killed, and every officer, with one exception as well as most of the non-commis- sioned officers, including the sergeant-major and four of the orderly sergeants, killed and wounded of those companies; when that portion of the regiment retired a short distance and were again formed, one of the companies having but four men left untouched.

"Lieutenant-Colonel Foster with six companies, amounting in all to 160 men, gained the hummock in good order, where he was joined by Captain Noel, with the two remaining companies of the Sixth Infantry, and Captain Gillam, of Gentry's volun- teers, with a few additional men, and continued to drive the enemy for a considerable time, and by a change of front separated his line, and continued to drive him until he reached the great Lake Okeechobee, which was in rear of the enemy's position, and on which their encampment extended for more than a mile.

"The action was a severe one, and continued from half past twelve until 3:00 P.M., a part of the time very close and severe. We suffered much, having 26 killed and 112 wounded, among whom are some of our most valuable officers. The hostiles probably suffered, all things considered, equally with ourselves, they having left ten dead on the ground, besides doubtless carrying off many more, as is customary with them when practicable."

Dec. 25
1837

Thus was fought the Battle of Okeechobee Swamp on Christmas Day.

After the battle one officer gave an account of the Florida country and situation not overly flattering to either:

Feb. 8
1838

"We (Colonel Taylor's army) have just returned from the Everglades. These Everglades are, at the northwest, termed wet prairies. They are large wet prairies, or grassy lakes, and of which the Indians know but little, and where they cannot live a month without great suffering.

"We saw but few Indians, and they fled rapidly at our approach. We took about sixty horses and ascertained that their cattle were exhausted. Colonel Taylor has taken about 600 head. We found on our last excursion but few cattle tracks, and only two cows were taken. The Indians are suffering for food, in all their camps we find that they have subsisted on palmetto roots and the cabbage tree, which are never eaten by them except when hard run.

"One hundred and thirty Indians and negroes have come in since the Battle of Okeechobee, and they say many more will come in soon, and that they are tired of the war, and destitute of provisions.

"Florida is generally a poor, sandy country. The southern portion is nearly all prairie, wet and dry alternately. Not more than one-tenth, at the utmost, of Florida is fit for cultivation,

and I would not give one good township of land in Illinois or
Michigan for every foot of land in East Florida."

That the army has been as much a peacemaker as a war
wager, has not been a prevalent conception. Yet its recorded
dealings with other nations and with the savages will prove that
it has tried zealously to prevent conflicts. The year 1838 was
particularly one of peacemaking by the army for the benefit
of the country. General Scott had been sent north by the government for the purpose of preventing a third war with Great
Britain. Sympathizers with Canadian rebels or patriots had
led the border states to take up the quarrel of the Canadian
revolutionists. Some citizens of the United States, those elements
untrained, undisciplined and unorganized, had actually taken
part in hostile enterprises. The acuteness of the situation was
all the more aggravated by the necessary absence of our trained
troops in Florida, along the coast and on the western frontier.
Scott was without organized power to hold our violators of
neutrality in check. By a combination of skillful addresses
and personal conferences he averted the catastrophe and pre- *Jan.*
vented a useless waste of lives. His exertions with our citizens *1838*
and the British agents in Canada were the entire reasons for
the prevention of rupture.

After our instability had been so obviously shown by this
lucky outcome and by the slaughter and fruitlessness in Florida,
the stingy size of our army at last became patent. Congress at *July 5*
length gave voice to an increase. It allowed to every artillery *1838*
company 16 extra privates and to every infantry company 38.
It added a company to each regiment of artillery and another
regiment of infantry to the whole establishment. It propor-
tionately increased the officers in the engineer corps, the topographical engineers, medical and other staff departments. It
gave to each person in the service, except general officers, an
extra ration for every five years of service. It raised the enlisted pay to a scale ranging from $17 for a sergeant major
down to $8 for a private. It prescribed that $2 a month was
to be withheld until the expiration of enlistment. It replaced
the bounty by three months' reënlisted pay. It gave to any
enlisted man, serving continuously for ten years, 160 acres of

land. It allowed the council of administration at any post to hire a chaplain at $40 a month and the Military Academy to have a professor of chemistry, mineralogy, and geology. It authorized 1 regiment of infantry to be equipped as light infantry and 2 to be armed with rifles.

Since Scott had made the peace with Great Britain possible it was necessary to see that no fresh causes for war arose. Part of the newly organized Eighth Infantry was accordingly used in small bodies on the lake boats to enforce the neutrality and to arrest any suspicious American sympathizers.

1838 to 1840

While this small contingent of the army was keeping peace in the north, General Scott again was ordered on another delicate mission in which the slightest error of performance meant war and the loss of many lives. The Cherokees, who still inhabited parts of Georgia and North and South Carolina, their native home, had, under questionable inducements on the part of our civil agents, agreed to emigrate west. The real truth was that since gold had been discovered in this region, our people were covetous of that part of the Indian country. This tribe had always been friendly and had largely taken up the education and customs of the states. The whole Cherokee nation realized that it had virtually been robbed of its territory. In spite of this feeling, some had emigrated, but about 15,000 refused to leave their mountain homes.

General Scott was accordingly chosen to bear the brunt of the affair by having to direct the emigration. His masterful appeal to the Cherokees not to compel war, his instructions to his soldiers to be gentle and firm, his square dealing and his quick demonstration of force, by drawing a circle of troops about the Indians, brought the desired result. Parts of the 4 regiments of artillery, the Fourth Infantry, a portion of the Second Dragoons and some Georgia militia were the troops designated for this work. Scott's arrangements were so complete and his promises so fully carried out that the Indians even submitted at his suggestion to vaccination. Nothing for the ordinary comfort of these people had been forgotten by him. One authority states that $2,500,000 was saved the government by this peaceful emigration. How much loss of life was prevented is inestimable. In addition to keeping us out of war,

Scott and his troops retrieved the opprobrious reputation of the government, and washed clean the dirty smudges of our enviousness.

Further south in Florida matters had come to a standstill. Seeing the futility of protecting the inhabitants of that country or of rounding up the Indians with so few trained forces, General Jesup asked to be relieved. Colonel Zachary Taylor took his place. What the new commander did will be seen later. *May 15 1838*

Meanwhile it is scarcely fair to center the attention at this time upon the south and east. While the troops in Florida were fighting fever and hardship, the little stockades in the near west were protecting the settlers and having their brushes with the savage. Although none of these actions was large enough to record separately, they were none the less severe and difficult. The redskin was beaten off only to return later. Something had to be done in the way of permanency. Though surveys were constantly injected into the unknown middle west country by army engineers, aided by other troops, more extensive feelers had to lengthen themselves into the infested plains before the troops could progress gradually and intelligently outward. One of the big moves at this time, which did so much for our country later, was the expedition of a then unknown young man. John C. Fremont was commissioned a second lieutenant of topographical engineers and sent with Mr. Nicholet, the distinguished astronomer, west of the Mississippi and north of the Missouri. This was the beginning of the magnificent explorations (to be described later) that were to make the "Pathfinder" so famous. *June 7 1838*

It may be interesting at this point to digress a moment in order to note certain advances in technique within the army. The Jenks breechloading rifle was tried out by the Ordnance Department. Although the weapon was thought unfit for infantry, a similar carbine was judged to be practicable for cavalry. The Board that pronounced upon the venture felt convinced that breechloading produced no advantage and was slower, especially because of the fouling of the piece. Since the muzzle-loader had to be rammed each time before firing, the bore would naturally, they thought, be kept cleaner than in a breechloader. *1838*

Sept., Nov. 1838

March 1839

The Second and Sixth regiments of Infantry were finally entirely concentrated in Florida. What happened to a part of the Second might be cited as typical of conditions under which all the troops then marched. Captain Russell was taking the men of his company to Fort Dallas. With a part of them he was going by boat down the Miami River when the party was fired on by Indians from the shore. Immediately he ordered his men to row toward the savages and attack. Being the first to land, he had scarcely started the fight when he fell pierced by five bullets. His lieutenant continued the disadvantageous action not without success and brought back in safety the body of the captain. But so overwhelming was the number of Indians that all the few soldiers could do was to make a break for safety.

March 1839

While such tragedies were taking place, General Scott was ordered on his fourth mission to save the peace of the United States. It seems that the state of Maine had got into altercation with the Canadian authorities over its boundaries. The governor had gone so far as to call out 8,000 militia. When General Scott arrived his diplomatic handling of the situation closed the issue. Here again we have the trained soldier using all proper means to avoid war. All through these pages we will find that he who understands hardships and the business of arms not only does not want strife but does everything he can do to prevent it. But when the struggle becomes inevitable he acts as the skilled surgeon who cuts deep in order to gain a quick recovery.

Summer 1839

To be in better shape for the disturbances that were constantly threatening, the army chiefs sought to collect and drill the troops. A "Grand Camp of Instruction" was held at Trenton, New Jersey. All the regulars that could be scraped together in that part of the country went through some maneuvers. Among other things one battery of each artillery regiment took over horses from the dragoons and was formed into a light battery. This concentration was doubtless another forerunner of the modern summer camp.

May 18 1839

The war in Florida being unusually prolonged, General Macomb, general in chief, visited the scene of activities. After consultation with the principal Indian chiefs with whom he made a treaty he announced to the army and the public that the war with the Seminoles was over. This was the third time in three years that peace with these savages had been announced to the fighting forces by some high authority. On the previous occasions the Indians had broken faith with the addition of many Christian graves to the soil of the south. General Macomb's prognosis proved to be no exception.

For scarcely a month passed before events made force again necessary. Colonel Harney was on a march with 40 men toward the Caloosahatchee River. His men had camped with the same feeling of security that Dade had had three years before. The Indians met on the way seemed to be most friendly. But just before dawn one morning the camp was attacked and 18 of Colonel Harney's men massacred, he and the others barely escaping. Hostilities naturally were renewed with all the discomforts, horrors, and fruitlessness of past years. *July 23 1839*

Inside the army, the work of improvement went steadily on notwithstanding the ebb and flow of peace. The field artillery took another stride forward when Captain Robert Anderson translated the *French Regulations* so as to cover both the "horse and foot" artillery in one manual. It dealt with the passage of difficult ground in detail, and covered the maneuver of the battery from the "passage of carriages" to the "countermarch." Every conceivable manner of going "into battery" was explained with great thoroughness. These regulations contributed highly to the efficient part field artillery was going to play in the Mexican War. *1839*

During the ensuing year the regular regiments were moved about the country in a wild endeavor to stamp out the terrors of the frontiers. The newly organized Eighth Infantry, having finished its duty in helping to keep the peace with Great Britain, was started from Sackett's Harbor for the Wisconsin territory. The Winnebago Indians had left their reservation and were committing outrages. Going overland and by boat, the regiment arrived at Camp McKeon whence it proceeded against this tribe. *1840* *May 2 1840* *May 28 1840*

During this period the Seventh Infantry was taking part in actions near Fort King and Fort Drane, Florida. The Sixth was doing similar work. The Fifth was holding the Indians in check in the northwest. The Fourth was helping the Sixth and

Seventh in Florida. The Third was in the southwest, opening roads in the Sabine country in Texas, even to the extent of clearing the river of its undergrowth and jammed logs. The First and Second were scouring Florida. The field artillery was left to prevent further trouble in Maine. The Second and Third were in Florida and the Fourth on the lake frontier helping the Fifth Infantry. The First Dragoons were in the north and the Second in Florida.[7]

May 1
1840

Evidently the means provided for solving the Seminole situation were few. General Taylor having found the task beyond him, asked, as his predecessor had done, to be relieved. General Armistead took his place. The new commander divided the territory into seven military districts for the purpose of making the tasks of the troops specific. His forces were augmented by the arrival of the Eighth Infantry which had just rounded up the Winnebago Indians and had traversed the entire frontier to go south. The Third came from Texas a little later.

Oct.
1840

While the army was contending with the Seminoles, the administration at the Military Academy was signally helped. Congress recognized the office of Commandant of Cadets which Colonel Thayer had provided previously. The commandant, under the superintendent, was made responsible for the military instruction of the corps. Becoming now the chief instructor of infantry, cavalry and artillery tactics as well as of practical military engineering, he was able to unify the teaching of these subjects so vital to young army officers.

July 20
1840

In Florida, responsibility for suppressing the Seminoles again became too heavy. General Armistead at his own request was relieved from command and Colonel Worth took his place. Although the First Infantry left for Forts Snelling, Crawford and Anderson in the northwest and the remaining troops were weary of so much length without strength, the new incumbent hit upon a successful plan. Pursuing the original idea of General Scott, he did not hunt the enemy directly but rather his dwellings and standing crops. General Sprague gives an intimate glimpse into these activities:

May 31
1841

---

[7] The disposition of these regiments is correct only in a general way, because few of them at this time could be serving as a unit in any one place.

"Fever and dysentery were the prevailing diseases. Officers and soldiers were inevitably exposed to the vicissitudes of the climate. Day after day they were wet to the skin, then subjected to a burning sun, causing an atmosphere to arise from the heated sand almost unsupportable.

"The bands of Indians, which for years had lived from season to season, in the enjoyment of abundance, celebrating their corn dances and festivals, harassing the white man as suited their convenience or inclination, were now driven in small parties to remote and unhealthy hiding places. The foundation of the contest was reached, which inspired all with the hope of future success."

One of the curious incidents of this campaign is shown by Colonel R. H. Wilson, in his history of the Eighth Infantry:

"At the end of September, 1841, A, C, E, and G were at Punta Rassa where, owing to the fact that at certain periods during great storms the land was subject to overflow from the waters of the Gulf, platforms were erected sufficiently high it was supposed for protection, on which were pitched the tents of officers and men. On the night of October 10th a terrific storm arose which soon grew to a tornado, and at dawn of the next day all that could be seen of the cheerful, busy camp of the day before were the uprights and roofs of the hospital. In the branches of two large, moss-mantled live-oaks which stood in the center of what was once Camp Caloosahatchee, were clustered, close as spines upon the prickly pear, all the men of the command—some 200—who, true to their teachings, had clung to their arms through all these trying hours, and not one had perished."

Speaking of arms, it is well to note that heretofore no large arms had been made by government arsenals. Only carriages and small arms had been manufactured by the army. However, at this time an advancement was made in having ordnance officers inspect the making of government cannon in private plants. The quality of the output was thus materially raised. The small arms then on hand included 672,542 mus- *1841*

kets, 25,154 rifles, 7,287 carbines and 22,047 pistols.[8] The
large guns in use consisted of the following kinds and sizes:
8-inch Columbiad, 10-inch mortars and howitzers and 42, 32,
24, 18 and 12-pounder guns—smooth bores.

A real improvement in small arms took place when the
model 1841 rifle made its appearance. It had a percussion lock
and used a reduced powder-charge. Besides keeping the
motions of loading a muzzle-loader to the minimum, it modified
the kick. It proved to be the most accurate and dependable
spherical bullet rifle ever made and marked the end of the production of flintlocks. Springfield and Harper's Ferry arsenals
began to turn out several thousand of these every year and to
remodel the flintlocks.

The place of the dragoon was materially helped by the
appearance of the first extensive *Cavalry Tactics* issued "by
order of the War Department." The manual provided for a
drill of 2 ranks, the rear rank taking two feet from head to
croup. A regiment consisted of 5 squadrons and each squadron
of 5 platoons, 2 platoons formed a division. A captain commanded the squadron with a junior captain second in command.
The lieutenants each commanded a platoon. The term "troop"
had not yet come into use.

While the army was improving its training and technic
internally, it was also extending itself externally. The Big
Cypress Expedition and the plundering campaigns of Colonel
Worth were having their effect. That officer made an estimate
that there remained only 300 Indians of both sexes abroad.
The others in a starving condition, having lived on palmetto

*Winter
1841
Feb. 14
1842*

---

[8] The arsenals and depots holding these included:

Allegheny arsenal.	Rome arsenal.
Apalachicola arsenal.	Saint Louis arsenal.
Augusta arsenal.	Washington arsenal.
Baton Rouge arsenal.	Watertown arsenal.
Champlain arsenal.	Watervliet arsenal.
Detroit arsenal.	Charleston depot.
Fort Monroe arsenal.	New York depot.
Frankford arsenal.	Palatka depot.
Kennebec arsenal.	Rock Island depot.
Little Rock arsenal.	Tampa Bay depot.
Mount Vernon arsenal.	Harper's Ferry armory.
North Carolina arsenal.	Springfield armory.
Pikesville arsenal.	

root and cabbage, had surrendered without bloodshed to the
troops. The President after some hesitancy approved Wo rth's *May 10*
suggestion that the war terminate. However, some of the regu- *1842*
lars stayed in the south to make sure of peace and succeeded in *Aug. 14*
capturing the last of the savage chiefs, even after peace was *1842*
declared.

The First, Second, Fourth and Sixth Infantry regiments
were sent north and northwest, the Second to Lakes Ontario and
Erie, and the First, Fourth and Sixth to Jefferson Barracks,
Missouri.

The regular troops had lost throughout the war by death
1,466 officers and men from a maximum strength of 4,191 [9]
souls, or over 41 per cent.

Had there been a sufficiency of trained troops at the beginning when the Indians were willing to try conclusions and
were assembled, this great mortality could have been reduced
nine-tenths. Instead, volunteers were called out time and again
at a cost of several million dollars which netted the United
States nothing. The untrained men as usual could not fight
because they did not know how. At the outset our miserly
attitude with regard to the soldier had robbed us of a speedy
peace and the lives of a great number of good men.

Peace was no sooner announced than the army was reduced
from 12,539 to 8,613 for a population of 17,000,000. At the *Aug. 23*
most, 1 man in every 2,000 persons kept alive the elements of *1842*
discipline and training. The country thus laid itself open to
more murder and bloodshed.

However, the shrinkage was made by simply reducing the
number of men in a company. No commissioned officers were
cast out of the service. Although the staff was cut down, army
organization was not greatly disturbed. A piece of economy
was inaugurated in the replacement by ordnance officers of
civilian superintendents at Springfield and Harper's Ferry
arsenals. But a setback was given the cavalry when a regiment
of dragoons was transformed into one of riflemen.

Now that railroads had been extended and new roads had
been built, especially in the east, communication between the

---

[9] Those actually enlisted and commissioned,

outlying army and the seat of government was quicker than before.   Accordingly the eastern and western divisions of the army, commanded each by a general officer, were done away with and nine separate departments [10] created.   By such distribution each of these smaller commands could deal directly with the general in chief in Washington and avoid the delay of long and winding channels of correspondence.

In the following year the cadet body of the Military Academy was for the first time legally composed of young men from

all parts of the United States.   The students were required to be appointed according to congressional districts.   Each representative was to have one appointment of a youth actually residing within his district.   Ten cadets were to be appointed at large.   Although such a custom had been in practice, never before had it had legislative sanction.

Shortly afterward a school for drill for the brigade was originated at Jefferson Barracks.   Although the scope and kind of work was limited, the attempt showed an effort in the service to train large units.   The Third and Fourth Infantry regiments which were then stationed in Missouri, constituted the person-

---

[10] ''Department No. 1.   West Florida, and the states of Alabama, Mississippi, Louisiana, Tennessee and Kentucky.   Headquarters, from the 1st of November to the 30th of June, in each year, at New Orleans, and for the remainder of the year at the Bay of St. Louis, or Baton Rouge, as the commander may elect.

''Department No. 2.   The country west of the Mississippi, north of Louisiana and Texas, and south of 37th degree of north latitude.   Headquarters, Fort Smith.

''Department No. 3.   The state of Missouri (above the 37th degree of north latitude); the state of Illinois; the Iowa territory; that part of the Wisconsin Territory west of the 13th degree longitude west from Washington; and the Indian country north and west of the lines indicated. Headquarters, Jefferson Barracks.

''Department No. 4.   The states of Indiana, Ohio and Michigan; the part of the Wisconsin Territory, not included in Department No. 3, and the Indian Country north.   Headquarters, Detroit.

''Department No. 5.   The states of Pennsylvania, New York, Vermont, New Jersey, Connecticut and Rhode Island.   Headquarters, Troy, N. Y.

''Department No. 6.   The states of Massachusetts, New Hampshire, and Maine.   Headquarters, Portland.

''Department No. 7.   The states of Delaware, Maryland and Virginia. Headquarters, Fort Monroe.

''Department No. 8. The states of North Carolina, South Carolina and Georgia.   Headquarters, Sullivan's Island, Harbor of Charleston.

''Department No. 9.   (Temporary) east and middle Florida.   Headquarters in the field.''

nel. These organizations by their application gained a reputa- *1843*
tion for smartness and precision, raised their esprit and prepared themselves well for the Mexican War in which they were
to take part.

Already the rumblings of that war could be heard in Texas,
where the struggle for independence was progressing. The
infantry regiments of the brigade school were sent to Camp
Wilkins, Camp Salubrity and Grand Encore, Louisiana. The *Spring 1844*
Second Dragoons were ordered to Fort Jesup. This force constituted the first installment of Taylor's "Army of Occupation."
On this account the act making the Second Dragoons into rifle- *April 4 1844*
men was repealed.

Some years before this Lieutenant John C. Fremont, it will
be remembered, had started out with some troops in order to
make explorations in the region of the Missouri River. Up to
this time he had surveyed the Des Moines River, the Platte
River, and a large part of the country between the Missouri
River and the Rocky Mountains. He had also gone over the
Rocky Mountains to the mouth of the Columbia River and had
explored most of what is now Oregon and Northern California.
He had traversed over ten thousand miles of freezing mountain
and sickly basin. Now a lieutenant colonel, he found himself
in California ready to take up the conquest of that country.

The little army in its garrisons and camps, though interrupted by uprisings here and there, went on with its discipline
and training day by day. The soldier at sunrise found himself
in ranks. Hurrying into his room or tent he made his bed,
swept his quarters and set his belongings in order so as to be
ready for inspection twenty-five minutes after reveille. After
he had eaten his breakfast, he cleaned his musket or his rifle,
polished his breastplate, cartridge box and buttons, brushed his
hat, pompon and clothing, and generally prepared himself for
parade at nine o'clock. At that dress ceremony, he saw the
national colors raised to the top of the flag pole, heard the "Star
Spangled Banner" played, beheld his officers move to the front
and doff their hats to the commanding officer and then he himself, while yet in ranks, marched with his company in review.
After the ceremony was over he changed his dress uniform for
the more comfortable one of fatigue, if he was not detailed for

guard that day. If on guard, he prepared himself more thoroughly in dress uniform for inspection, paying particular heed to his rifle and the cleanliness of his person. At guard mounting which took place immediately after parade the soldier awaited the results of inspection to see whether he would be selected as the neatest and most immaculate man in ranks. If he were so selected he was appointed orderly at headquarters and was not required with the others to walk post and guard prisoners at work. If he was not on the guard detail for the day, he attended drill shortly after guard mount. Throughout the remainder of the day he helped in his fatigue uniform to make the post cleanly and to repair and construct those parts of the garrison that were ever in need of such labor. Since the small fort or stockade was far away from civilian help, the soldier shod the horses, fixed the chimneys, mowed the grass, picked up and carted away the débris, repaired the boots, sawed and planed the wood, fitted and nailed the lumber into buildings and performed all manner of chores for the garrison. Dinner was usually at one o'clock; the roll call of retreat, when the national colors were lowered, was at sunset; and tattoo, another roll call, was at nine o'clock. The soldier was in bed at nine-thirty when taps was sounded by the drum.

Such was the routine of the army in the lonely and desert places of the nation. Too often these rounds of duty were interrupted by the call to arms or the order for a movement over weird distances. The long march, fraught with the same discipline and training as in the post, took the soldier to an unknown region where he was confronted afresh with rounding out his small comfort by the work of his hands, or where his hardships and dangers were excruciating torture.

But these men seldom forgot their duty to the pioneer and those at home. Creeping boldly to the edges of the frontier, which they pushed further and further outward, these little bands of trained and disciplined Americans wove the capillaries of civilization as thickly as they could through the wilderness. They had come from the heart of the country, but in spite of the fact that the heart beat feebly at times for them, they pressed onward dutifully and loyally. They knew hardship and death. They were not itching for war. They wanted peace, but they knew that they could attain it quickly, after the strife was inevitable, only by having sufficient strength and skill.

Scott had saved the nation from great loss of life and serious embarrassment only by the narrowest of margins. By his indefatigable energy and uncommon tact he had persuaded mobs, convinced politicians and made diplomats see that the government was really at heart not anxious to take up arms. One minute he would calm rioters and the next judiciously placate foreign agents. An undisciplined and sometimes disloyal part of the civil population had placed the United States in a compromising position. His was a duty of honorable service to his flag. As an army officer his mission was to wrap his country with protection at any cost to himself. He had to be all things to all men, to the Canadian as well as the Cherokee, to the troublemaker as well as to the soldier.

Though Scott was a man of high merit in such tasks, other army officers tried whenever they could to rid themselves of strife wherever the savage could be mollified. Macomb, Clinch, Taylor and many junior officers treated with the Seminole as long as there was a hope of keeping him in check without bloodshed. But the Florida Indian was faithless. He understood force alone. The great pity was that there were too few of the trained army to end the affair quickly and thereby save the lives of many of its members and of the thousands of settlers, men, women and children, who were cut down by the tomahawk and scalping knife, during the long years of hopeless tracking.

Even with these handicaps, the fortresses and stockades arose as safe retreats for the pioneer settlers and the roads wound their rugged ways through sickly swamps and choking forest, in spite of the lurking bow and arrow. The soldier's jaw was set, his arm was flexed even as he toppled under a burning sun, with a hot fever or a fiery wound. Though his bones were laid in the dismal dust of nowhere, the work went on. When the automobile to-day tours safely from New York to Palm Beach, from Chicago to Kansas City, the anguish and courage of these determined Americans is commonly overlooked. But each mile is none the less a silent witness to their constructiveness.

CHAPTER VII

THE ARMY WINS AND WIDENS THE BOUNDARIES

(1845–1859)

THE army is about to have a taste of real victory, to win a war, to overcome the entire enemy in the field. It is soon to cross into a foreign territory, meet superior numbers, bear gross hardships and stick to its colors. It is going to go continuously forward and not be turned spasmodically backward. It will press the foe through cactus, swamp and mountain passes into the very gates of the hostile capital and then take the city. It will return as a conqueror to safeguard the remaining wilderness of the nation. It will prove to the world that the American soldier, trained, disciplined, and well led is the acme of bravery and hardihood.

1845   In the year before the Mexican War, the army consisted of 8 regiments of infantry, 2 of dragoons and 4 of artillery, 3 general officers, the corps of engineers, the corps of topographical engineers and the following departments: adjutant general; quartermaster, inspector general; commissary; medical; pay; purchasing; and ordnance. The whole represented a paper strength of 8,613 men and an actual strength by the end of the year of 5,300. The army's effective force was less than at any time since·1808, though the population since that time had doubled.

These troops were occupying more than 100 posts. The artillery was largely on the Atlantic coast. The infantry and cavalry together occupied the broad line of the Great Lakes and the western frontier outlined by the Mississippi, Missouri, Arkansas, and Red rivers. The main posts in the west were Fort Snelling, near St. Paul, Jefferson Barracks, near St. Louis, Fort Leavenworth, in western Kansas, and Fort Jesup, in western Louisiana.

Winfield Scott was the major general in chief and the two brigadiers were Gaines and Wool. Taylor was colonel of the Sixth Infantry, Twiggs of the First, and Kearny of the Second Dragoons. One of the colonels, Walbach, was 82 years of age, such senility being due to the lack of provision for proper retirement of officers. The officers of the lower units, however, were the great compensating factor of the coming war. Grant, Thomas, Reynolds, Hancock, Lee, McClellan, McDowell, Meade, Beauregard, Hooker, J. E. Johnston, Longstreet and "Stonewall" Jackson were in the service. And many who had resigned in the period surrounding 1836 were about to come back to the colors as volunteers, notably Jefferson Davis.

The Military Academy furnished nearly the whole quota of these trained young men. Approximately 500 graduates were already with the colors. A similar number were in civil life, many of whom came into the service with the state troops in the course of the war.

In contrast to the excellent results that were going to be obtained from having these skilled officers, were the debates in Congress which tended toward the abolition of West Point. A feeling that there was being raised up a sort of aristocracy by that institution led the unacquainted into the belief that it should be abolished.

Three times this cavil had nearly plucked the hen that laid the golden eggs. Secretary of War Eustis, just before the conflict of 1812, had tried to wreck West Point by open attack. At the close of the same war Colonel Swift had had to borrow $65,000 from a private individual in order to keep the school running, because Congress refused to appropriate the current expenses. And now the Academy lay in the throes of political hatred and ignorant juggling. Luckily the only setback that came of all this controversy was the reduction of pay of each cadet to $24 per month. Twice the Academy had been saved *March 3* *1845* by the prospect of war and once by the intervention of a private individual.

While the cradle of the army was being disturbed, the higher officers were looking after technical betterment. General *March 6* Scott's regulations entitled, *Instructions for Field Artillery,* *1845* *Horse and Foot,* appeared. The Secretary of War in issuing it enunciated a new rule. He bound not only the regulars but the militia also to the use of no other "exercises and maneuvers." This was a great step toward uniformity. The "school of the battery" prescribed completely movements by hand and by horse, and covered every possible contingency with which the battery might find itself confronted in action. For detachments of from 2 to 9 men in serving the piece, the duties were precisely described and each man numbered. The firing [1] was explained with great care. The pieces of the field artillery were the 6-pounder gun and the 24-pounder howitzer, both of bronze.

For regular infantry the muskets and rifles were being rapidly provided with percussion locks for caps, so that two motions of the manual—opening and closing the pan—were eliminated. In the main, however, the army all through the coming war had to be provided with the old flintlock musket,

---

[1] 22. "Firing. No. 4 stands in line with the knob of the cascable, covering No. 2. At the command Load, he steps to his right, takes the portfire stock out of its socket with his right hand, takes hold of the lighted end of the slow match from under the apron of the box, and, blowing it, lights the portfire; he then steps back to his place outside the wheel; holding the portfire stock firmly in the right hand, finger nails to the front, the portfire stock touching the wheel and the portfire inside of it.

"When the piece is not provided with a slow match box, the linstock is used. In this case, as soon as the piece is unlimbered, No. 4 steps in and takes the linstock from its socket, steps back again, and plants it in his rear, facing to his right and stepping off with his right foot for that purpose. He then draws back his foot and faces to the front. He lights the portfire by facing and stepping off in the same way.

"At the command Fire, he raises his hand slowly, clear of the wheel, turning the back of the hand to the front, brings the portfire rather in front of the vent and fires. As soon as the gun is fired he lowers the portfire slowly. When a lock is used he takes the lanyard in his right hand, moves to the rear so far as to keep the lanyard slack, but capable of being stretched without altering his position, which is to be clear of the wheel. Should the tube or cap fail to explode the charge, the gunner immediately commands, 'Don't advance, the tube or cap's failed'; upon which No. 2 steps inside the wheel close to the axletree; No. 3 advances outside the opposite wheel and gives his priming wire to No. 2, who pricks the cartridge; he then gives him a tube or cap which he fixes, and both resume their posts. No. 4 is answerable that the slow match is kept burning.

"At the command Cease Firing, No. 4 shifts the portfire stock into his left hand, cuts off the lighted end of the portfire, and places the stock in its socket; if a linstock is used he puts that up also. When using a lock he coils the lanyard round the neck of the cascable, or unhooks it and carries it in his hand, as the mode of attaching it to the lock may require."

because a lack of appropriation had prevented a sufficiency of rifles. Since 1839, the superintendency of construction of muskets by regular officers, instead of civilians, had reduced the cost per weapon from $17.44 to $11.02 and saved the government over $70,000. By such thrift more rifles could be purchased, but there were yet not enough. Captain J. T. Cairns in a work called the *Recruit,* described the nomenclature of the "Fusil, Musket or Firelock" and gave elementary instructions for their use, including "Right shoulder shift—arms." The *1845* bayonet with a clasp, which permitted the separation of that weapon from the firearm, was largely distributed to regular troops.

Political feeling over the coming conflict had caused the concentration at Fort Jesup, of the Third Infantry, 8 com- *June* panies of the Fourth Infantry and 7 companies of the Second *1845* Dragoons, all under command of Brevet Brigadier General Taylor. This force, then thought to be large, was the actual beginning of the "Army of Occupation."

Texas now being annexed, Taylor was ordered to some port *June 15* where he could readily embark for the Texas frontier. Accord- *1845* ingly he proceeded with his troops to New Orleans. Under later orders he moved by boat to Aransas Bay, Texas. With poor craft he was finally able to land at St. Joseph's Island a *July* force of about 1,200. These men he took by boat through the *1845* mouth of the Rio Grande and thence 25 miles further up the river to Corpus Christi.

Due to the inactivity of the enemy he was left undisturbed. But he did not improve his time by gaining information of the country and possible hostile forces or by training his troops. He seemed to be pleased to wait for the Mexicans and trust to chance.

He was, however, blest with a number of trained junior officers who took a pride in their companies. In spite of the neglect of the higher command, the young captains and lieutenants molded by Thayer's systems, gave care and lent precision to the smaller units. Besides, Taylor, although he little realized the fact, could have well been thankful for his two daughters. Through them he luckily possessed two sons-in-law who afterwards built the career that steered him toward the

White House. Bliss, his adjutant, as brilliant and educated an officer as the service held, headed off much mismanagement and wrote the reports that went back home. Jefferson Davis, the colonel of a Mississippi regiment in the greatest battles in which his father-in-law was engaged or rather disengaged, was the principal factor in turning the brave old gentleman's vacant leadership into victory. So Taylor, who chatted pleasantly with the soldier one minute and ignorantly sacrificed his life the next, was protected in the office and on the battlefield by domestic attachment.

Aug. 31
1845
Finally 7 companies of the Seventh Infantry, the remainder of the Fort Jesup troops, 2 volunteer artillery companies from New Orleans and a small force of Texas Rangers joined him.

Then throughout the fall and most of the winter, while Taylor sat inanimate, other troops were leaving bare the frontiers of the country to assemble at Corpus Christi. The Seventh and Eighth Infantry came from Florida; the Fifth from the northwest; the Fourth from Jefferson Barracks, Missouri; the Third from Fort Jesup; the Second Dragoons from Mississippi and Texas; and 10 companies of the First Artillery and 4 of the Third Artillery from Florida. Most of the artillery acted as infantry but apparently 2 companies were retained as field artillery. Some Texas Rangers and New Orleans field artillery brought his entire strength up to 3,900 men.

Taylor's camp was far short of comfortable. The canvas was little more than mosquito bar. The "norther" would one minute pour frigid water through the sievelike tents and a torrid sun would steam the occupants the next. Wood was collected with the greatest difficulty so that camp fires, except for cooking, were impossible. The drinking water was brackish. There was little or no amusement. Sickness abounded and spirits were low.

Nor was the monotony and discomfort relieved by maneuvers or any expedient to keep the command busy. Taylor did not know much of the art of war, did not believe in teaching it, and did not understand even how to maneuver his regiments. Naturally all the evils that flow from idleness overtook his troops.

The question of brevet rank and his settlement of the affair

did not better the unity of his little army. It seems that the list
of colonels at this time was badly confused. Some officers held
a brevet grade higher than their regular rank, while others held
simply the latter. Twiggs on the list of colonels was senior to
Worth. But Worth was also a brevet brigadier general. Each
claimed that he was the senior and would command in Taylor's
absence. Scott in Washington decided in favor of brevet rank
in conformity to the law. As a consequence Worth was given
command in preference to Twiggs, who had throughout the
lower grades been senior to Worth, and who had never had the
chance to win brevet honors on the battlefield. But Taylor,
after the decision was made, called a review in which he gave
Twiggs the seniority over Worth. When Taylor saw that he
could not carry out this order without trouble, he countermanded
the review. He thus showed himself not only unwilling to comply with orders, but also incapable of causing others to do so.
It logically followed that this little force came to lack confidence
in their chief. Had it not been for the effort of the junior
officers to overcome such demoralization, all traces of discipline
would have vanished.

So Taylor sat and waited for the Mexicans without exploring his surroundings, finding out about the enemy's intentions
or improving the small American command.

When instructions from higher authority told him that he *Feb. 3*
should encamp at some favorable point along the Rio Grande, *1846*
he was unprepared for a march anywhere. But then and then
only did he begin to find out something of the roads and towns
that lay about him, a matter which delayed him three weeks. *Feb. 24*
Then he delayed himself another two weeks before he was *1846*
March 8
finally on the road to Matamoras. *1846*

The march was an excursion welcomed by the troops. Those
who were not too sick to go, had the relief of activity and a
change of scene. The weather was fair. Except for the tarantulas, rattlesnakes, and centipedes, the camps along the way
were novelties of strange objects and animals. Dressed in his
thick, blue-cloth uniform, and carrying a heavy knapsack,
blanket, musket and cartridge box, the soldier underwent unexpected physical torture under the burning sun. Thirst in the
"alkali" dust raised by the tramp of the men, was suffocating

March 28
1846
and difficult to quench with saline water.   Ultimately the column came out through the chaparral on to the Rio Grande, across which lay the towers of Matamoras.

At this camp, as at Corpus Christi, was assembled the largest regular force collected since the Revolution.   The numbers were a little less than 3,000.   Although Taylor issued peaceful letters to the Mexicans, he planted four 18-pounders in command of the city and began the erection of a bastioned
April 7
1846
redoubt, called Fort Brown.[2]   This fortress was poorly placed in a salient of the river so that it could be easily enfiladed by an enemy.   E. Kirby Smith in his diary gives an account of these days:

"This morning we found the enemy had been busy during the night erecting breastworks and planting cannon opposite to us.   What will be the result of all this I can only conjecture. We certainly ought not with so small a force be left here to face the whole Mexican nation.   General Ampudia with more than three thousand veterans will, it is said, in a few days reach Matamoras.

Entries
April 5–9
1846
"We have been as busy as a light infantry company on drill ever since we arrived eleven days ago.   Such a night as last night I have never known in all my soldiering.

"The arms were put in forming order and the men sat or stood about in miserable groups, without any possibility of sleeping, and at reveille this morning our whole brigade was marched to the works, it being our detail on a large fortification, which we are constructing as rapidly as possible. . . . We are here neither in a state of peace nor war. Our pickets and patrols have exchanged some shots, and several deserters have been killed in attempting to cross the river."

The first hostilities occurred with the crossing of the river by the Mexican General Torrejon with about 1,600 cavalry. General Taylor had ignored the advice of Marcy, the Secretary of War, to get some hard-riding Texans for use as scouts.   Indeed he had been content with only that information which

---

[2] Afterwards Brownsville.

came into the limits of the camp. Accidentally hearing of the
Mexican movement, he sent Captain Thornton with about 60
dragoons to reconnoiter. Naturally under such a slipshod view
of the enemy, the captain soon found himself hemmed in by the
Mexican command. Though he tried to cut his way out, he soon *April 25 1846*
saw the hopelessness of his task after several of his men were
killed or wounded, and was compelled to surrender. This was
the incident that caused the declaration of war.

Even after this affair, Taylor took no aggressive action or
precautions. He was not even aware of the Mexican main
column which was coming over the river right under his very
nose. When, through no effort of his own, he finally understood that the enemy was already between him and his base, he *May 1 1846*
at once retreated to Point Isabel, leaving the Seventh Infantry
and Bragg's battery at Fort Brown.

After provisioning his troops, he returned toward Matamoras with about 2,200 men, having obtained 200 at Point
Isabel. Hampering himself by taking the wagon train with
him against the advice of his officers, he moved out slowly.
Oxen hitched to the ammunition wagons did not quicken the
progress.

Neither were the spirits of the men raised by such delay.
The blue-coated soldier at night bivouacked in the dust without
complaint but with an anxiety to meet the enemy. Lying down
in his fatigue uniform with its colored trimmings he arose after
a night of discomfort to face whatever might be in store further
toward the Rio Grande.

At Palo Alto the Americans came in sight of the Mexican *May 8 1846*
Army. Between chaparral and marshes the two lines were
drawn up opposite each other, the enemy being astride the road
to Fort Brown. Taylor's artillery, better handled than the
Mexican heavy pieces, was so effective that it cut great swaths
in the enemy's lines while they were forming. An attempt to
turn the Americans' right by a superior force of Mexican
cavalry was met by a hollow square of the Fifth Infantry.
Then the grass was set on fire by the powder wads from the
shells, so that a dense smoke screen kept the two armies from
seeing each other well. In this haze, the disciplined American
leaders, though getting few. directions from Taylor, promptly

and of their own accord, met the Mexican attempt to encircle
the left. Ringgold's and Duncan's batteries seemed to move
quickly and instinctively to the place where they were most
needed. Though our troops were on the defensive, the fire of
our artillery was deadly in spite of the smoke. But there was
not enough remaining daylight for either side to have a decision.
However, darkness came down with about seven times greater
loss to the Mexicans than to the Americans.

*May 9
1846*

In the morning Taylor's little army, ready to renew the
battle, was surprised to see the enemy's column disappearing
through the chaparral toward Matamoras. But the Americans
could not pursue and follow up their advantage with more than
several hundred men, because most of the troops had to be used
in fortifying the encumbering wagon train before it could be
left behind.

*May 9
1846*

About 8 miles to the north of Matamoras, the Mexicans took
up a position which made it difficult for American artillery to
operate and be effective. Behind an old river channel which
crossed the road at right angles, Arista, the Mexican general,
placed his entire command. The bed, or Resaca de Guerrero,[3]
was full of ponds and mud and in many places impassable.
The Americans, all told about 1,700, came upon the Mexican
artillery planted in the road and almost immediately thereafter
there was collision. The dense growth of mesquite and cactus
made it impossible for one company to see another. Men losing
touch with their comrades had to spend their energies in hacking
through nature in order to find the enemy. The mass gave place
to the individual. A general was little more than a subaltern.
An officer led the troops immediately around him. But discipline and training told as the Americans beat their way forward
through the thick undergrowth and amid the hottest fire of
shrapnel and bullets. Sinking in the mud, floundering through
swamps, the American right, accidentally finding its way around
the Mexican flank, pressed the enemy who fought desperately.
The vigor of the assault, more than the plan of it, dismayed the
enemy who gave way more and more until a panic seized the
whole force. Many were captured, but Taylor's forces could

---

[3] The battle was called Resaca de la Palma.

not pursue because they were scattered and exhausted. At that, only about 4,000 of the Mexicans succeeded in crossing the river, where many were drowned in their flight.

Taylor, instead of reorganizing his army and pressing his advantage, proceeded to Fort Brown, where the beleaguered garrison was relieved of its strain.

While Taylor was thus inert along the Rio Grande, back in *May 13 1846* Washington Congress was declaring war and gorging the military establishment with much that could not give results for many months, and more that was wholly worthless. Now that the clash of arms was upon us, it was ready to organize a sufficient army. General Scott's previous sound advice to have a modest 24,000 men, to train them in camps at home and to put them in the field at Vera Cruz, had been ignored. Though such a method would have saved hundreds of lives and thousands of dollars, Scott's idea was regarded by the legislators as far fetched. Justin Smith says in *The War With Mexico* that "for an elect body our Congress fell below all reasonable expectations."

After the fashion of a foolish virgin it now permitted the *May 13 1846* President to call out 50,000 volunteers [4] "for twelve months" or "for the war." The militia were to serve only 6 months. The short enlistment again was to defeat efficiency and be expensive.

The regular army, on the other hand, was to have its companies raised from 64 to 100 privates during hostilities. Since the period of enlistment was to be for 5 years, recruits for the regular army were hard to obtain in competition with the volunteers and militia, whose short terms were attractive. But in this legislation Congress heeded Scott and authorized, though too late for adequate fulfillment, a very good, economical force. Had such a thing been done 2 years previously, thousands of three-months men who had been called out by Gaines and Taylor from Louisiana, Alabama, Mississippi, Missouri and Texas, would not have had to undergo useless marching and

---

[4] The volunteers had to furnish their own clothes, horses and horse equipment. For such "use and risk" the donor was to receive 40 cents a day, in addition to the pay of a regular soldier.

the ravages of disease in reaching Taylor's rendezvous. There they remained too short a time to be little more than embarrassing.

May 13
1846

Congress also added to the permanent establishment, "a company of sappers, miners and pontoniers" of 100 men who were to be a part of, and stationed with, the corps of engineers at West Point.

May 19
1846

A ten-company regiment of mounted riflemen was created in order to establish military stations on the route to Oregon and to take the place of regular troops called to the front. Though the officers were mostly political appointees, the regiment was the beginning of the Third Cavalry.

While these laws were being made, Taylor, instead of making short work of the demoralized enemy, contented himself with sending to Point Isabel for planks and mortars and in making a trip there himself. For eight days he was inactive, much to the disgust of his skilled subordinates.

May 17
1846

His enemy was finally so much encouraged by his silence that Arista requested a suspension of hostilities. Although Taylor disapproved such action, he gave permission for the Mexican army to retire, provided it gave up its property. Arista did not directly reply to this proposition but shortly afterward left the city at Taylor's approach. The latter marched in amid the friendly greetings of the natives, whom he treated with great consideration. But Arista, nevertheless, had made his escape with his soldiers and all the munitions he could carry.

While Taylor was resting in his oasis in the desert, Matamoras, an expedition was being fitted out farther to the north at Fort Leavenworth, Kansas. Colonel Kearny, the commander and colonel of the First Dragoons, was ordered to take possession peacefully or by force of northwestern Mexico. At the stockade of the Fort, which then consisted of a square of wooden buildings with blockhouses, was collected about 1,600 men: the First Dragoons, the First Missouri Mounted Volunteers (Colonel Doniphan), 1 company and 1 battery of artillery under command of Major Clark, 2 companies of volunteer infantry, the Leclede Rangers and 15 Delaware and Shawnee Indians.

Kearny, without waiting to organize all his troops, sent *June 6 1846* them off by sections. The regular dragoons were the first to go. Then came Doniphan's regiment, and so on. Those in advance had to break their way through the roughest of country. After passing over unwooded areas where cooking was largely impossible, where the water was brackish, the way uphill, the mosquitoes and buffalo gnats scurrilous, the food scarce and scurvy prevalent, the whole command finally found itself on the Arkansas near Bent's Fort. So great were the sufferings that *July 29 1846* some died and many were driven into delirium. And again Valley Forge had a competitor in the way of soldierly grit. The march, however, seasoned the raw troops and Kearny's strictness brought discipline.

While Taylor and Kearny with their meager thousands were trying to conquer Mexico, Congress was slowly realizing that its attention to the army had been superficial. At this late date, it created an additional major general and two more *June 18 1846* brigadiers for the war. It gave to a volunteer company an elastic strength of 64 to 100 privates and another second lieutenant. Seeing that it had asked of the recruit more than could reasonably be expected, it gave to every volunteer soldier $3.50 per month as a clothing allowance, and 75 cents as subsistence and forage allowance for every twenty miles of journey to the place of rendezvous.

Then realizing that the most vital matters had been overlooked, it allowed the President during the war to organize the forces into brigades and divisions and to appoint such general officers as he saw fit. It required a brigade to consist of 3 regiments; and a division, of at least 2 brigades. The irony of this last enactment is apparent when we know that such organization had had to be made by the commanders in the field long before the intelligence of the nice little law reached them.

As an instance of the hurry into which all departments of the army were plunged by the nearsightedness in times of peace, the Ordnance Department had to issue in the first year of the war:

Eighteen- and 24-pounder siege cannon, 8-inch siege howitzers, 8- and 10-inch siege mortars, coehorns, 6- and 12-pounder bronze field cannon, 12- and 24-pounder bronze field howitzers, 12-pounder mountain howitzers, caissons, traveling forges, battery wagons, artillery harness, 20,000 rounds of siege artillery ammunition, 3,000 rounds of field artillery ammunition, 60,000 rounds of 8- and 10-inch mortar shells, 1,000 cannon balls, 400,000 pounds of black powder, 1,300 war rockets, 24,000 muskets, 3,000 rifles, 2,000 carbines, 1,000 pistols, 2,000 sabers, 2,000 noncommissioned officers' and musicians' short swords, 12,000,000 cartridges, 400,000 flints and 1,000,-000 percussion caps.

Horses, too, had to be supplied in greater numbers. Taylor found that the artillery, which had had little chance to practice, needed two more animals to draw each filled caisson.

As for Taylor's army, it was living at Matamoras as best it could. Outside of the slight pursuit of Arista, which netted a few prisoners, and the search through the town for concealed munitions and supplies, there was no military activity save an expedition of a small force under Colonel Wilson, to Reynosa, 60 miles away. Taylor spent most of his effort on keeping supplied from the base at Point Isabel.

The volunteers who had been called by Gaines and Taylor were beginning to pour in, such influx creating a need for more supplies and spreading an infection of lawlessness. The new so-called troops were eager for excitement and resentful of restraint. Stretched in small camps from Point Isabel to Matamoras, they lacked control and supervision. Most of them were three-month men who would not stay for twelve months. They had marched through bad country under generally unskilled officers, many of whom could not drill a squad. Some, indeed, had been absent from their companies on the march, weeks at a time. One brigadier general came in a light buggy in which he proposed to make the campaign. The officers, as a rule, had been elected as in previous wars so that most of them knew not what to do. Some generals like Pillow hindered more than they helped the progress of discipline. As a result there were too often brawls, riots and shooting frays. Five months at least of hard drill was necessary to prepare such troops for action. They would neither stay nor submit, and Taylor did

not insist on their training. Meade said these volunteers were
one costly mass of ignorance, confusion and insubordination.
Trained regular officers in the lower grades found themselves
outranked by former juniors who had been dismissed from the *July 31 1846*
army for incapacity or misconduct. About 20,000 men were
finally collected, a large proportion of whom had to be sent home
almost immediately with great expense and no help to the
government.

Taylor in this situation decided to go west to Camargo.
With the urge in the States for action, he had to do something.
His untutored mind would not admit of skill or prevision. So
he went up the river, not knowing the conditions of the town
he was going to occupy, nor even having any idea of its
strategic importance, because it had none. The troops suffered
intensely with the heat and thirst. The discouraged volunteers,
knowing nothing of care for their health, were sick to the extent
of a third of their number. The First Tennessee, for example,
was reduced from 1,040 to 500 men fit for duty. In addition,
frogs, ants, scorpions, tarantulas, centipedes and mosquitoes
disturbed the soldier's comfort.

When Camargo was occupied it was found to be a small *July 31 1846*
town that had been inundated by the spring freshets. Since
it had no supplies of its own, provisions had to come from
Point Isabel. Now that the troops were over a hundred miles
farther from the coast than they were at Matamoras, the only
result of this movement was an added difficulty of transportation.

While Taylor thus sat in useless and trying Camargo,
Kearny, near Bent's Fort, was reënforced by a regiment and
battalion of Missouri volunteers. Having sent a message to
Santa Fe showing the uselessness of resistance and the pro- *Aug. 2 1846*
tective quality of his mission, he left his camp for the long
march to that place over what is now the route of the Atchison,
Topeka and Santa Fe Railroad. The way was through high
ranges of mountains, over buttes and ridges and along the valleys. The rations were so scarce that flour, water and salt pork
were the main diet. Taking over by tact and force the village
of Las Vegas, on the way, he crept on with his troops to San *Aug. 15 1846*
Miguel. There, when the mayor wavered, Kearny assured him

Aug. 18
1846

Aug. 19
1846

Aug. 22
1846

that he had captured his town. Treating the people and crops with consideration, he pressed on twenty-eight miles toward Santa Fe, knowing that a large force of Mexicans was barring his path. On approaching his goal, after leaving the artillery on a commanding hill, he learned that the Mexican force had fled south. Among the little adobe huts without floors, Kearny raised the Stars and Stripes and pronounced Santa Fe under government of the United States. It was there that the Peublo Indians came in and submitted. Then Kearny issued a proclamation of assurance of a free government and began the erection of Fort Marcy to defend the town. So far a great country had been taken with no bloodshed.

While Kearny was occupying Santa Fe, Taylor was making ready for an advance southwest toward Saltillo. Instead of employing a good secret service as Scott had advised, Taylor as usual went forward trusting to developments. Again his movement was intended to give an answer to the public cry for action rather than to be effective.

Aug. 19
1846

Sept. 5
1846

Aug. 25
1846

Sept. 15
1846

Cerralvo, sixty miles away, was the first objective. Worth, with the Second Division of regulars, moved out first. Persifer F. Smith with the Second Brigade of mixed troops, Twiggs with the First Division of regulars and Butler with the "Field Division" of volunteers, followed. Finally headquarters left, and the whole army of about 15,000 was on the move. The march was over stony ground and through thorny bushes. Heat and thirst wrought such distress that starts in the march were made as early as three o'clock in the morning. At length the advance troops came into the beautiful town of Cerralvo. It had plenty of springs, the houses were of stone and supplies abundant. Finally all of Taylor's command except the Texas volunteers and those who had been sent further west, were concentrated in the town.

A squadron of the Second Dragoons accompanied by Captain McCulloch's Texas Rangers set out in the van for Monterey. The rangers carrying heavy rifles, powderhorns, bowie knives and Colt's revolvers, and dressed in irregular uniforms, were in appearance not much unlike the Revolutionary volunteers. The march now being through fertile fields and high hills, the spirit of the command rose. About a thousand Mexican cavalry hovering in front lent zest to the progress.

When the main body arrived at Marín, Taylor learned that *Sept. 17 1846* at Monterey there would be possibly decided opposition. But the army of 3,080 regulars and 3,150 volunteers went eagerly forward.

As they approached Monterey they were greeted by fire *Sept. 19 1846* from the well-fortified stone city situated on rather high ground. To reduce this stronghold the Americans had only 4 field batteries, a 24-pound howitzer and one 10-inch mortar. Reconnoitering parties set out and discovered that the western end of the city was vulnerable in flank. Mansfield's prisoners confirmed the assumption that night.

The Americans having confidence after Palo Alto and Resaca de la Palma that they could overcome a superior force, were in no mood to be thwarted. Worth with about 2,000 men advanced to the right of the city in order to turn Independence Hill and occupy the Saltillo highway, which was the only avenue of retreat southward for the Mexicans. Advancing about seven miles through thick country and having his rangers stampeded by Mexican cavalry, he was stopped by darkness and a heavy storm.

The next day he moved forward only to meet a charge of *Sept. 21 1846* Mexican cavalry. With the aid of Duncan's battery the enemy was driven back on the town. Then the column spent the rest of the day in charging Federation Ridge and in taking three forts. At nightfall about 500 men, mostly regulars, were sent forward to Independence Hill, the main flank position.

In the meantime at the eastern end of the city, Taylor had not been meeting with as good results. He had evidently looked upon the capture of this stronghold much as he viewed a brush with the Seminoles in Florida. He seemed to have little plan or method. He sent Garland forward with the following directions:

"Colonel lead the head of your column off to the left, keeping well out of reach of the enemy's shot, but if you think (or you find) you can take any of them little Forts down there with the bay'net you better do it—but consult with Major Mansfield, you'll find him down there."

This queer bit of haziness was a sample of Taylor's mental grip of the situation. Though Garland's mission expressed in such an equivocal order was not overly intelligible, he advanced through fields and thickets and crooked streets in the face of a withering fire. The artillery could not do much execution and the units by such misdirection were separated. But before noon, at a crucial moment, when the engagement at the eastern part of the city seemed to be lost, Colonel Jefferson Davis led a charge that took the principal outlying fortress. Even so, the First Ohio farther to the right had to retreat with heavy loss.

On the western side of the town, Worth's troops under Colonel Childs, who had led his men to the foot of Independence Hill, had crouched at the base all night in the rain and cold. In the early morning they quietly crawled toward the summit. At dawn, with a rush and sharp fighting, they took the crest and sent the garrison fleeing.

Sept. 22
1846

Taylor's troops far on the other side of the city saw the tide of Americans rise higher and higher and the Stars and Stripes finally wave over Independence Hill. But during this day Taylor did nothing beyond shifting a few details from the captured redoubt. Neither did he coöperate with Worth or send him any word. Worth realized he must depend on himself. Expecting fire from the commanding positions around him, he disposed his troops (now numbering about 1,000) in the valley, so as to ward off counterattacks. Without coöperation he had taken three redoubts and a commanding fort and had cut the line of communications of the enemy. But he was left alone to work out his own salvation.

Sept. 22
1846

Sept. 23
1846

The next morning Quitman who was occupying the captured works on the east side of the town started an attack from house to house on his own initiative. He heard Worth's cannon, which had been dragged to the top of Independence Hill, firing with effect. Little by little Quitman's scattered men closed in. Worth now feeling from the firing heard from Quitman's troops that a general engagement was taking place, started toward the town. Leaving a force to guard the Saltillo highway, he had his men with pickaxes, crowbars and shells with fuses, work from house to house. At noon both sides, weary of the struggle, rested. Taylor, doing no more than the work of a corporal, walked about under severe fire. Night fell with the Mexicans cooped in the Plaza.

When the morning came, the Ohio volunteers who had taken *Sept. 24 1846* the place of Quitman's troops, prepared to renew hostilities when a bugle in front sounded a parley. Ampudia was proposing an armistice. After much haggling, it was agreed that all public property and the city be turned over to the Americans within a week. The individual arms and ammunition were to be retained by the enemy, who was to retire behind a line through Lenares and Rinconada Pass. So Taylor let the Mexicans, who had suffered little loss, go practically as they had come, apparently little concerned as to whether they might fight the Americans another day. He even went so far as to accede to an armistice.

While Taylor was recuperating from his losses at Monterey, while his Texas troops were being discharged because they wanted to go home and while the Second Infantry was arriving to reënforce him, General Kearny, back in Santa Fe was start- *Sept. 25 1846* ing his journey through an unknown wilderness westward. Cutting roads through country over which there was as yet no trail, his effective dragoons, still in shabby clothing and on short rations, pressed toward the Pacific. When well on their way the troops met Kit Carson who told how Fremont and *Oct. 6 1846* Commodore Stockton had already made an attempt to seize California. Such news gave impetus to the weary, half-fed soldiers. Leaving Major Sumner with a portion of his command to hold New Mexico and sending back Colonel Cooke to get the Mormon battalion at Santa Fe, Kearny pushed on with only two companies.

In the meantime, General Wool at San Antonio was trying to get into shape volunteers raised in Tennessee, Ohio, Indiana, Illinois and Mississippi whom he had brought to that point. From there some 1,400 men, including a small portion of the *Sept. 25 1846* Second Dragoons, set out for the march south. It was a dispirited and unsoldierly force, but insubordination and lawlessness were harshly met by the strict discipline of General

Wool. Due to him the volunteer was made to regard the rights of the Mexican civilian. At length this turbulent command came to the Rio Grande opposite the Presidio.

Oct. 8
1846

While this column was breaking its way through cactus, and picking up what food it could, General Taylor at Monterey did not enjoy the success of a victor. Sickness, desertion, and the short enlistment had reduced his command to less than 12,000 effectives. Bandits, hanging on his long line of communications, caused many men to be detached. And the ill-advised armistice brought criticism upon him.

Oct. 15
1846

Everything was at a standstill. The government at this late date of the war had come to no definite plan of campaign. The three independent commands of Kearny, Wool and Taylor were expending exertion and blood in merely driving the unhurt Mexican armies away from the border settlements. No decision could result from the unstrategic dents hammered at random in the edges of the enemy's great territory. While the troops were being wasted by disease and hardship, the authorities at Washington were closing their ears to the Vera Cruz plan suggested by Scott, which was going to strike at the heart of things and end the war quickly. In contrast, the United States soldiers were scattered in ineffectiveness.

Doniphan's command made a fourth separate force. Having reduced the Eutaws to submission and subdued the Navajoes among the snows in the mountains, this officer was preparing to concentrate his forces south of Santa Fe at Valverde. His 800 men, mounted and armed with rifles, hated restraint and were eager for any excitement.

Nov.
1846

Taylor was now forced to notify the Mexicans that the armistice must terminate. With such a change in the situation, he was in the predicament of casting about for activity. Disregarding the advice of the Secretary of War and placing still further distance between his army and its base, he set out west for Saltillo, the capital of Coahuila. Marching over the high tablelands of temperate verdure, the troops came to their destination. The town was hilly, consisting mostly of adobe huts, and was not inviting from the standpoint of supplies or comfort. Leaving Worth in command, Taylor went back to Monterey.

Nov. 13
1846

Nov. 16
1846

Meanwhile, General Wool, without instructions from Taylor, had continued south with his ragged and poorly fed volunteers. *Nov. 21 1846* Having without opposition taken Monclava, about 60 miles north of Saltillo, Wool had had time during the armistice to drill and discipline his men. He then set out south for Parras, *Nov. 24 1846* where he received orders from Worth to join the Saltillo forces. Within two hours Wool was on his way, so complete was his *Dec. 17 1846* reconnaissance and his state of readiness.

While Worth and Wool were trying to effect a junction in the west against the rumored attack by Santa Anna, Taylor at Monterey was splitting his command so as to send part east toward Tampico. Accordingly Twiggs with the First Division of regulars and Quitman with some Georgia, Mississippi and *Dec. 13, 14 1846* Tennessee volunteers set out for Victoria, 200 miles toward the east coast.

Shortly afterward Patterson at Matamoras started, at the direction of the Secretary of War (who had not taken the pains to notify Taylor), directly south for the same place. Patter- *Dec. 24 1846* son's treatment of some 1,500 Illinois and Tennessee volunteers under him showed his ignorance of the military profession. His men went hungry time and again when there was abundant food about them. Many of them through neglect died of exhaustion. And they, generally, cordially hated him for his lordly severity.

The end of the first year of the war found Quitman at Victoria, Wool at Agua Neuva (near Saltillo), Worth at Saltillo, Patterson en route to Victoria[5] and Butler at Monterey. Doniphan was at El Brazito near El Paso with 500 men. Kearny had reached San Diego, California, and Cooke was marching to Kearny's assistance. The first year of the war closed with these scattered columns spending their vigor and blood in indecisiveness.

What Cooke and Kearny had done can be seen from Cooke's order issued to his battalion after the march:

"The lieutenant colonel commanding congratulates the bat- *Jan. 31 1847* talion on their safe arrival on the shore of the Pacific Ocean,

---

[5] Taylor was personally nearing Victoria to join Quitman.

and the conclusion of their march of over two thousand miles. History may be searched in vain for an equal march of infantry. Half of it has been through a wilderness where nothing but savages and wild beasts are found or deserts where for want of water, there is no living creature. There, with almost hopeless labour, we have dug deep wells, which the future traveler will enjoy. Without a guide who had traversed them we have ventured into trackless tablelands where water was not found for several marches. With crowbar and pick and axe in hand we have worked our way over mountains which seemed to defy aught save the wild goat and hewed a passage through a chasm of living rock more narrow than our wagons. To bring these first wagons to the Pacific we have preserved the strength of our mules by herding them over large tracts, which you have laboriously guarded without loss. The garrison of four presidios of Sonora concentrated within the walls of Tucson gave us no pause. We drove them out with artillery, but our intercourse with the citizens was unmarked by a single act of injustice. Thus, marching, half naked and half fed, living upon wild animals, we have discovered and made a road of great value to our country."

The remainder of the war with the exception of Buena Vista belongs to Scott. After trying to euchre both Scott and Taylor into false positions, the administration, not valuing the science of war and viewing Scott as a "visionary," finally, having nothing better to offer, had to adopt the Vera Cruz plan. Scott knew that there was only one way to gain a speedy peace. It was to strike at the heart and center of the hostile country with the largest force obtainable.

Jan. 3 1847   Having arrived at Camargo, he found he could not get in touch with Taylor. He, therefore, requisitioned from Taylor's force about 4,000 regular infantry under Worth, 4,000 volunteer infantry, 500 regular dragoons, 500 volunteer dragoons and 2 field batteries.

Jan. 8 1847   Returning to Point Isabel, he personally planned with skill, foresight, and dispatch the details for launching his campaign. His masterful mind went thoroughly into the business of providing everything from supplies to boats. Northers, rains and scarcity of sailors hindered him, but he overcame his obstacles with tireless energy. Even the fact that Taylor was apparently avoiding him did not swerve him from his single purpose.

Taylor had indeed defiantly disobeyed the instructions of the President and Scott for a personal interview between the general in chief and himself. He had gone so far west toward Saltillo that touch with Scott was impossible. The answer may be found in the announcement by Taylor to Senator Crittenden that he was a candidate for the Presidency.

While politics were pushing the pawns of war into haphazard gambits, legislation strove all too late to put in the field more good troops. It now increased the regular establishment by 1 regiment of dragoons and 9 regiments of infantry. One of *Feb. 11 1847* the infantry regiments was to be composed of "voltigeurs and foot-riflemen and be provided with a rocket and mountain howitzer battery." Enlistment was to be for the war only. An additional major, on account of the scarcity of field officers for campaign, was to be promoted in each regiment. Each honorably discharged man of all the forces was to receive a bonus of 160 acres, if he had served for twelve months, and 40 acres, if he had served for less time.

At length Scott set sail for Tampico with the First and Second Pennsylvania, a part of the Louisiana regiment, and the South Carolina, New York and Mississippi contingents. *Feb. 20 1847* Twiggs with his regulars followed. For the next days and weeks the scarcity of transports delayed the remainder.

While Scott was busy preparing to drive his fateful wedge into the vitals of Mexico, activity in the west near Saltillo drew Taylor's forces together for conflict. The main camp had been surprised and had retreated to Buena Vista beyond Saltillo. *Feb. 22 1847* Twenty thousand Mexicans were approaching. Had they come on with a charge, nothing could have saved the American army. Wool had selected the position and had been left in command by Taylor, who had gone back to Saltillo to prepare that place for defense. As it was, the Mexicans drove back Marshall's troops from the top of the mountain. Night gave the first phase of the battle to the enemy.

Next morning the Mexican army in force came through the *Feb. 23 1847* pass. Marshall, who had reascended the mountain, was nearly outflanked by Ampudia, when Washington's battery began to have a telling effect. In the center, Colonel Bowles of the Second Indiana and 4 companies of Arkansas mounted riflemen fled before the Mexican onslaught. The Kentucky and Arkansas dragoons on the mountain, being cut off, also withdrew in panic. Although Bragg, Sherman and O'Brien trained their guns on the Mexicans against great odds, the way to the American's rear lay open.

Taylor then appeared on the scene. Though his brave attitude gave confidence, he uttered few directions, which were poor. The initiative of his trained subordinates came into play in spite of the absence of orders. Davis with his Mississippians and Bowles with the remaining Indianians charged and repulsed Ampudia's cavalry. To Davis especially belongs the credit for stemming the tide. At the head of his Mississippians he fought with dash and daring. Although he had to be carried from the field severely wounded, he had been the main factor in turning defeat into possible victory.[6]

Taylor, without knowing the size of a large force of Mexicans in front, ordered Hardin to charge it. Bissell, McKee and Thomas joined in the attack, but the forces were too overwhelming. Hardin, McKee and Henry Clay perished while standing to the last. But Bragg and Sherman galloped from another part of the field with their tired batteries, and some of the Indiana and Mississippi regiments charged the enemy's flank and rear. Finally, the fire of the batteries became so hot for the Mexicans that they retreated.

The queer battle was over, and so was the day. That night Taylor feared for the fate of his army. He had lost 673 officers and men and about 1,600 had skulked in the rear or deserted. But during the darkness Santa Anna drew off south.

What remained of the American army of the north was then spread out to guard the long line of communications from Agua Neuva to the coast. Thus ended the activities of Taylor's command.

---

[6] For his heroic work, Jefferson Davis was offered the office of a regular brigadier general instead of the ordinary brevet. He, however, declined the position in the regular army.

In the east Scott, having collected all his troops by boat at *Feb. 23 1847* Lobos Island, took strenuous measures to keep smallpox from spreading and to drill his command. Studying the situation, he came to the conclusion that the fortified town of Vera Cruz should be invested from the rear, instead of being frontally assaulted, with the resultant heavy loss to his men.

At this late date in the second year of the war when his campaign was already launched, Congress was busy with enactments that could not benefit him for many months. It voted 2 *March 3 1847* more major generals and 3 more brigadiers to the army. It authorized the organization of the forces into divisions and brigades as before. It gave to each artillery regiment 2 more companies and the authority to have 2 light batteries. It increased the pay and ordnance departments. Having made the mistake of the short enlistment, it attempted to rectify that error by offering $12 bounty to every soldier in Mexico who would reënlist for the war. It recognized distinguished services of the noncommissioned officer by the reward of a brevet of the "lowest grade of rank," and those of a private with a certificate of merit, which carried with it the extra pay of $2 per month.

Before this seeming generosity of the lawmakers could be made known to Scott, he had landed 10,000 men without mishap *March 9 1847* at Sacrificios Island. Through the surf and over the dunes his troops went inland and formed Camp Washington in a semi- *March 13 1847* circular line around the rear of Vera Cruz. They built fortifications and brought up artillery from the fleet for the bombardment. Most of the work had to be done at night and in silence.

At last when the positions were satisfactory to Scott he *March 22 1847* summoned the town to surrender. When the refusal came, the guns from the fleet and on land opened fire. Within four days the occupants of the damaged city, hungry and terror stricken, *March 26 1847* capitulated. Scott's army having lost less than twenty killed, marched into Vera Cruz. He had saved his men, in spite of the urgent impatience of some of his juniors, who wanted to assault the place.

But the glory of this victory was lost in the mind of Scott when he realized what was before him. At his back was an adverse administration, that had given him less than the troops he had asked for. Yellow fever would soon be attacking the coast towns. Supplies and vehicles of every kind had to be collected soon for his march up through the 8,000-foot mountains over which there was one road to the city of Mexico. Only 180 out of the 800 wagons had arrived, and the mules and horses were correspondingly short.

April 8
1847

Finally leaving the First Infantry to guard Vera Cruz he sent Twiggs' division (2,600 men) forward toward Jalapa. Patterson next day followed. Although Scott did not believe that a large force was in his front, he wisely acted as though it were and himself set out on the march, followed by Worth's division.

At Cerro Gordo, Twiggs was held up by fire from a strong position across his path. When General Scott arrived he gave a very clear and comprehensive order for the attack, after gaining information through Captain Robert E. Lee and other officers whom he had sent out on reconnaissance. The action was to be a turning movement against the enemy's rear by Twiggs, supported by Shields' and Pillow's divisions. Even the pursuit was provided for in Scott's directions. The troops advanced through the thickest of tropical undergrowth.

April 18
1847

Twiggs' regulars took Independence Hill with difficulty and loss, and Shields and Riley went on to Cerro Gordo. The Mexican batteries in front fell under Pillow's and Tower's troops. With minor mishaps that were to be expected the heights were taken. Though Pillow's actions and some of Shields' volunteers were criticizable, the execution of the plan moved along with force and dispatch, and what Mexicans could get away fled in panic toward Jalapa. Worth's division pursued. Altogether, thousands of prisoners, 40 cannons, and 4,000 stands of arms were taken.

April 20
1847

Scott then moved the troops over the road to Jalapa which had been cleared by Worth.

There dire problems confronted him. Indeed, in many ways his predicament resembled the trying hours of Washington during the darkest part of the Revolution. Money was scarce. The government had not sent any. Seven regiments and 2 companies of volunteers would go home because their enlistments were expiring and nothing in the midst of this campaign could

stir their patriotism to remain. The government in its usual
calm at home paid and provided for the soldier sparingly. The
commander in the field was left to scrabble. Out of 1 contingent of 3,700 men only 1 company remained. Scott was
assured the recruits were soon to come. But even if they did,
they would be worthless until after five months' training. And
then, after a long delay, they did not come. His force was
reduced to 7,000 in the face of 20,000 Mexicans. Here he was,
in a hostile country, poorly provisioned, and without strength.
And to cap all, the President was scheming at home to supersede him by Benton, who was ignorant of the art of war.

But Scott moved his advance troops on towards Puebla in
spite of his difficulties and by overcoming many of them. Not
over 4,000 privates were able to move forward. Worth started *May 6*
the movement. Fortunately that city made only a show of *1847*
opposition as it was approached by Worth and Quitman, who
entered it. Scott, in the meantime, was organizing his rear and
supplies before moving up. When he arrived in the town, he *May 20*
at once started the drilling, the engineer training and the *1847*
preparation of maps for the interior. It was difficult work
with the morale of the men naturally below par. They had
been paid for only two months out of the eight. Since Scott had
little cash and the Mexicans knew his condition, prices rose pro-
hibitively. But by clever and clean methods, he restored financial equilibrium and caused the city to offer him a place for the
upbuilding of his forces.

With six weeks of steady drill and good treatment of the
inhabitants, on whom he was absolutely dependent for most of
his supplies and for the chance to occupy Puebla, he slowly
emerged by his own efforts with a force of fair quality but poor *July 8*
quantity. Cadwalader and McIntosh ultimately arrived with *1847*
1,100 men and $250,000 in coin. The recruits also came.
Major General Pillow,[7] having done his usual delaying and
demoralizing work, arrived with 2,000 men. Finally General *Aug. 6*
Pierce brought 2,500 more. *1847*

Scott now had about 10,900 effective men. Of the regular
troops all the infantry regiments except the First (which had

---

[7] A general by virtue of having been a law partner of the President.

to be at Vera Cruz), the main portions of the three dragoon regiments, the Second, Third, Fourth artillery, a light artillery battalion, and a howitzer and rocket battalion, were present. The new Ninth, Eleventh, Twelfth, Fourteenth, Fifteenth and the Voltigeur regiments of infantry together with the equivalent of about 3½ regiments of volunteers from New York, South Carolina and Pennsylvania swelled the numbers, and 300 marines made the sum total. As can be plainly seen the large proportion was made up of fairly trained and disciplined troops.

Aug. 5 1847

Aug. 7 1847

As soon as it was possible Scott, in spite of his handicaps, ordered the advance. Twiggs, Quitman, Worth, and Pillow, in the order named and one day's march apart, set out for the heart of Mexico. Passing higher up the mountains the little army now of about 10,700 men, trudged onward until it was about that many feet above sea level. It met many hindrances, among which were 13,000 trees felled as barricades, which it pushed aside. At length it came to the valley of Mexico City.

Aug. 19 1847

Here Scott had to decide which of the four roads he would take toward his final objective. Pushing Captain Robert E. Lee, Beauregard and Worth's brigade ahead to reconnoiter, he found out the lay of the country and decided to approach the capital by the western gate. Then he ordered a force of engineers and Pillow's troops to build a road over the pedregal [8] toward Churubusco. Although he did not yet desire a general engagement, Pillow seemed to know better. That political general attacked a powerful force of Mexicans, who routed the Americans. Scott then coming on the scene, saw that San Geronimo was the key to the situation. He sent Shields with his brigade to support Smith, who had already gone in the direction of that place. The troops sat and shivered in a storm all night. In the morning they were awakened early so as to go quietly toward their goal and take it with the bayonet. Lee,

Aug. 20 1847

in the meantime, had by superhuman effort carried to Scott complete information as to the whereabouts of his troops. The commander was then able to assemble more men as a reserve, and the battle of Contreras was begun. In seventeen minutes

[8] Lava-bed.

San Geronimo with all its strength was taken. The Mexicans' loss was about 1,700 against that of 100 Americans.

Although the distance was now short to the city of Mexico, Scott knew he could not leave his baggage and Quitman's brigade exposed in rear. So he ordered Worth to clear San Antonio of the enemy. But when Stevens found that the Mexicans were already retreating, he determined to attack them in flight. In the pursuit, the troops came upon the masked and heavily fortified bridgehead of Churubusco. There they were held up for some time because of the unexpected strength of the position. But Scott's handling of a turning movement in the rear caused the defenders to give way after a hard struggle, and Churubusco fell. The enemy was pursued almost to the city gates. The loss to the Mexicans was about 10,000; to the Americans about 950. It was a stubborn battle, but the courage that comes with competent leaders and superior training had counted.

Scott now did one of the most loyal and self-sacrificing *Aug. 21* things ever done by any man in high position. Although the *1847* way to the city now lay open, he forsook the personal glory of capturing the capital of the enemy's country because he felt wisely that such action would not so quickly "conquer a peace." The political conditions were such that a successful assault would mean only a postponement of a permanent settlement and the unnecessary sacrifice of many soldiers.

That night he caused Worth to occupy Tacubaya; Twiggs, San Angel; Pillow, Mixcoac; and Quitman, San Augustin. During the next few days Scott was waited upon by the Mexicans who proposed a cessation of hostilities. Accordingly an *Aug. 24* armistice was agreed upon with the express purpose of negotiat- *1847* ing a peace. Two weeks were wasted in talk, while Santa Anna was violating the stipulations of the agreement. When his *Sept. 7* duplicity was discovered, hostilities had to be renewed. *1847*

Worth in the early morning was sent against Molino del *Sept. 8* Rey, where the troops encountered a very hot fire from the *1847* forts. Stopped, tossed back, leaders shot down, the gallant men returned again, not to be denied. The King's Mill was the first to fall and then Casa Mata after much loss and sharp fighting. But the victory from a fruitful standpoint was barren. Though the Mexican losses were heavier than those of the United States troops, the captured arsenal contained nothing of value and did not further the entrance into the city.

Sept. 11
1847
At a council in which the engineer officers, Lee and Beauregard, argued the various merits of positions and suggested the next move, Scott decided to attack the western gate—Chapultepec.

Sept. 12
1847
An artillery duel between the large pieces in the enemy's fort and our intrenched batteries opened the fight. All day the cannonade continued, not without effect on both sides, but altogether the garrison of Chapultepec suffered more than our troops.

Sept. 13
1847
Scott took the next day for attack. Pillow was to hit in front, Quitman and Worth on the two flanks and Smith in rear. Artillery again opened the fight. The infantry, advancing at eight o'clock, drove in the outlying troops. The fort, a very well-built stronghold, remained to be captured. On the lines went, but when they came to the ditch the scaling ladders did not arrive. The men lay down under galling fire and merely held their own, because nothing could be done in reply to the enemy's guns. But the waiting moments were terrible. At last the ladders came, and the soldiers, withheld from their prize for so long, climbed up the sides, were knocked down, scrambled up again and finally crowded over the walls. Some rough hand-to-hand work and Chapultepec was taken.

Quitman met resistance from a small redoubt which he overcame. Worth was held up at one entrance to the city proper, but, by ingeniously mounting guns on roofs, he drove the Mexicans before him. The gates of Belew and San Cosme were similarly taken, and the Mexican capital lay limp before the army.

Sept. 14
1847
The next day the victorious troops marched into the city, Santa Anna having fled.

The war was not over, but the fighting had ended. Scott appointed Quitman as governor of the city and proceeded at once to reorganize his forces and his long line of supplies.

He had conducted a brilliant campaign with little or no error. With minimum loss of life and time he had marched through the vital territory of a hostile population. Even so, he had been hindered more by the administration at home than the enemy in front.

The volunteers with scarcely any training had been of little help. Most historians have been very hard on them. R. M. Johnston says:

"With officers not competent to maintain discipline, let alone handling their men in action, they made of the Stars and Stripes an emblem of pillage, destruction and outrage. They were 'dreaded like death in every village in Mexico.' They 'fled in every action in which they have been engaged.' At Monterey, volunteer regiments bolted. At Buena Vista, it was only the Mexican turning movement that swept many of them back to their stations. General Pillow begged for a single company of regulars at Cerro Gordo, to prevent a whole brigade from stampeding."

Their lack of training is attested to by many statistics. For example their rate of sickness was three times as great as that of the old regiments. But they themselves were not to blame. Whether patriotism or adventure had been their main motive, they nevertheless underwent hardship voluntarily for their country. They had been jockeyed into a false position by an obtuse and wily control of military affairs. There were not enough trained men on hand, so that the volunteer had to be used, abused and sacrificed.

Training was the thing that the government had ignored. By force of circumstances, rather than by foresight, the army in Mexico consisted largely of trained junior officers with regulars, and trained senior officers with volunteers. Few of the regulars in high command were scientifically skillful in gaining a victory with the least loss, because they were the outcome of stagnant handling in the previous thirty years. Scott stood preëminent and alone. He had pulled himself up by his own boot straps. His clear vision at home and his brilliant work in the field, rank him, in quality, second to no leader of our history. He realized fully conditions and situations and sacrificed his own personal ambition for the peace of the nation. Wherever tribute was due, he gave it without a tinge of meaner feelings. Though not himself a graduate of the Military Academy, he bore no resentment to the West Pointer. He unhesitatingly said at the close of the war:

"I give it as my fixed opinion that but for our graduated cadets the war between the United States and Mexico might, and probably would have lasted some four or five years, with, in its first half, more defeats than victories falling to our share; whereas in less than two campaigns we conquered a great country and a peace without the loss of a single battle or skirmish."

In other fields of this war it must not be forgotten that Stockton,[9] Kearny and Fremont took California, Wool marched with difficult troops south from San Antonio to Taylor and was now in command of that long line which held northern Mexico. Doniphan, too, had beaten with his 800 men 1,000 Mexicans at Brazito, routed 1,200 at Sacramento, taken and held the capital of Chihuahua for two months, crushed a fierce band of Comanches at Paso, coupled up with General Wool and embarked for the United States in the summer of 1847, thus completing a victorious march of 3,500 miles in fifteen months.

If training had shone during hostilities, it was to count more than ever in the occupation of a conquered country. Each of the main cities along Taylor's and Scott's routes had to be ruled justly by a military governor. The rowdy soldier had to be severely punished side by side with the Mexican robber.

In Mexico City Scott's troops, due to necessary distribution and losses, numbered less than 6,000. For three months after the capture, not a single reënforcement provided for by the late laws of Congress had arrived. It was not until the end

Dec. 17 1847

of the year that any reënforcements set foot in the capital. The numbers were finally swelled to 11,000 on paper and 8,000 fit for duty. It was then possible to have sufficient men to occupy the mining towns, and to repel attacks in the outlying districts, such as Jalapa. The efforts of Scott and Wool both tended toward the establishment of firm discipline and peaceful relations with the Mexicans.

---

9 Naval Officer.

It was, however, an uphill task. Physically and mentally the soldiers were in a sorry state. When the government sent the volunteers into a foreign country to wage war, with the injunction that they furnish their own clothing, it had asked a very impossible favor. Poorly paid and much tattered, the state troops had a hard time to be decent in appearance. It was not until very late as usual that Congress passed a law to furnish clothing to volunteers in the same manner as to regulars. *Jan. 27 1848*

Altogether, this stay in a foreign country was naturally distasteful to the troops. The excitement of action had simmered down to the most trying routine. During virtual peace these men were undergoing the discomforts of campaign. What was the hitch, the technicality, that was keeping them from their homes in the states? They had finished what they came out to do. They had done their part. What was the matter with the slow wheels of state? The treaty of Guadalupe Hidalgo had ended hostilities. Why was this occupation among a people, who spoke a different language and did not understand our ways, dragging on so long? Fighting, disease, driving off bandits from supply trains, obeying and enforcing a stringent martial law, and constant drills and parades did not offer much recreation. *Feb. 2 1848*

It is not surprising that desertion, gambling, drunkenness, theft and worse crimes abounded. A host of bootleggers, blacklegs and thimbleriggers offered ready inducements on all sides. Scott stated in one of his reports:

"The same intolerable work at general head-quarters is to be perpetually renewed, or all the credit of this army for moral conduct, as well as gallantry and prowess in the field, will be utterly lost by new arrivals, and there is no hope of bringing up to the proper standard distant posts and detachments."

The only activities of this time were confined to northern Mexico. Colonel Price, who was military governor of New Mexico, got wind of an uprising in Chihuahua. Marching with great speed from El Paso he arrived at Santa Cruz. Having blockaded the town, and having received reënforcements, he forthwith attacked the place. After fighting his way through *March 1 1848* *March 9 1848*

March 16
1848
barricaded streets and executing some rather quick and rough work he was successful. This episode completely ended all armed controversy until peace was actually declared.

However, there arose in the main army near Mexico City an internal strife that lowered morale distinctly. Scott placed in arrest, and preferred charges against, Pillow, Worth and Duncan, one of whom at least was a political spy of the President. The Chief Executive had been averse to Scott's success, because Scott, being a Whig, ought not to become too popular. The actions of the three accused officers were insubordinate. But the President, believing their versions, ignoring his general in chief, and making up his mind at a great distance from the scene of ruction, peremptorily relieved Scott and restored the three officers to command with their highest brevet rank. After having been the prime factor of victory over Mexico, Scott was called home in disgrace.

Robert E. Lee said that now that he had performed his task he was "turned out as an old horse to die." So Scott took his
April 22
1848
leave of an army who trusted in him and loved him as a whole, and Major General Butler, a Democrat, was left in command.

Soon thereafter began the general preparation of the army
June 12
1848
for leaving Mexico. General Worth's Division was the last to quit the capital. In the main plaza the troops were drawn up, each country's colors were saluted and the United States flag gave place to that of the Mexican. Then began the long descent to Vera Cruz. It was a glad body of weary men who finally entered the lowlands of the coast, where they did not wait long
July 22
1848
in that fever district. Five companies of the First Artillery were the last to go just eighteen days after peace had been
July 4
1848
formally declared by the President of the United States.

The newly created regiments had already left for the States. They were to be mustered out at the following places: the Third Dragoons at Jefferson Barracks, the Ninth Infantry at Fort Adams, the Tenth and Eleventh at Fort Hamilton, the Twelfth and Fourteenth at New Orleans, the Thirteenth at Mobile, the Fifteenth at Cincinnati, the Sixteenth at Newport Barracks and the Voltigeurs at Fort McHenry.

The remaining regular army, after the reduction due to legislation, was scattered in reduced numbers over a wide field.

Winfield Scott

Winfield Scott

The First and Second Artillery were rendezvoused at Governor's Island and the Third and Fourth at Fortress Monroe. The First, Second, Third and Fourth Infantry under Twiggs were concentrated at Pass Christian, Louisiana. The Fifth Infantry went to Arkansas and Indian territories, occuping and building Forts Gibson, Smith, Washita and Towson. The Mounted Rifles, Sixth, Seventh and Eighth Infantry went to Jefferson Barracks, Missouri, under command of General Kearny. Eight companies of artillery and 3 companies of the First, and 7 of the Second Dragoons, were stationed on the United States side of the Rio Grande.

Congress now acted wisely in allowing officers of the regular establishment to hold the rank they had attained in the war, by being carried as additional numbers in their grades and by being assigned to their old units. The major who had been added to each regiment was retained, as were many of the staff, together with the 2 companies in each of the artillery regiments. The number of privates in each organization was fixed at 50 for the dragoons, 64 for the mounted rifles and 42 for artillery and infantry. The relatives of each enlisted man who died in the service were voted three months' pay. *July 19 1848*

Long marches by some of the regular regiments were immediately entailed, because of the acquisition from the war of 960,000 square miles of territory, including the present states of New Mexico, Arizona, Colorado, Nevada, Utah and California. Now that this vast country had been gained by the army's successes, it was to be made safe by the army's efforts. A long overland march by 2 companies each of the First and Second Dragoons was made along the Rio Grande, through El Paso, over the Gila and finally into California. The Mounted Rifles likewise, on account of the disturbances in Oregon, where some volunteers had murdered Indians in return for a massacre of missionaries, made its march over rugged country to that territory. A company of the Third Artillery set sail for California around Cape Horn. *Oct. 1848*

The year 1848 passed out with troops scattered over the old and new territory of the United States. The army had to strive for restoration under the handicap of demoralizing reduction. Many of the light batteries had to be dismounted and most of the organizations were reduced.   The actual strength of the army was little over 8;000.

Winter 1848–49

When gold was discovered in California, soldiers deserted for the El Dorado by the wholesale.   Captains in the west found themselves in some cases without a single soldier in their companies.   The small army became still smaller every day. But the remainder and those that could be recruited, as they began to be stationed in the new western territory, helped as they could the "prairie schooner" and the "forty-niner" across wild tracts of unexplored country.

The Mounted Rifles or Third Dragoons made a long march of 2,500 miles from Fort Leavenworth toward Oregon.   But for Fort Laramie and Fort Kearny, there was not a house between Fort Leavenworth and the Columbia River.   The column plodded through trackless wastes, oftentimes without wood, water or grass.

May 1849

The Fifth Infantry lost in one month 46 men by the scourge of cholera that was so prevalent with the emigrant trains.   In addition to sickness and hardship, units were split and sent over long distances.   For instance, 4 companies of the Fifth marched from Fort Leavenworth to Santa Fe and 6 companies from northern Texas to El Paso.   From these places they then made successful expeditions against the Navajo and Apache Indians. Likewise the Fourth Artillery and 2 companies of the First were sent from Fortress Monroe to Fort Pickens and Pensacola, Florida, where they were kept busy constructing roads and keeping the Seminoles in leash.   Other regiments were similarly distributed.

May to Sept. 1849

Several internal changes at this time affected the army.   The office of Judge-Advocate was created.   Heretofore his duties had been performed by the detail of an officer of the line.   The position now became the life work of an officer who could devote himself to legal study.   A captain of the army could be selected and given the brevet rank and pay of a major of cavalry.

March 2 1849

As for drill and training, Cooper's *Regulations for the Militia* brought new developments in drill.   Soldiers were formed into squads for recruit drill and mounted troops for the first time marched and wheeled by "fours."

1849

At this time the army went seriously to work in garrisoning

the new territory in order to make it habitable.   Little by little
nearly all of the troops were occupying tiny posts over the
prairies so as to be ready to push back the Indian before the
civilian occupant.   The small parties of "forty-niners," singularly vulnerable to pillage and outrage, had given the savage
confidence and lust for further attacks.   To offset such incursions wherever they might appear, it was necessary to have
many strongholds.   The First Infantry, for instance, garrisoned *Jan.*
1850
in the southwest, Forts Merrill, McIntosh, Duncan and Ringgold Barracks.   Other regiments built and garrisoned more.
In one engagement with the Indians the First alone lost 8 men *April 12*
1850
killed and wounded.

The pitiful attempt to have a small force everywhere at
once caused long journeys of immense hardship and waste of
time in movement.   The Seventh Infantry, for example, was *June*
1850
sent from Florida to Jefferson Barracks, Missouri, thence to
the Little Arkansas River, back to Fort Leavenworth and then *Oct.*
1850
distributed over the Arkansas frontier, all in less than six
months.

Congress, seeing finally that it was difficult for the army to *June 17*
1850
be in two places at once and that atrocities could not be checked
with the number of troops on hand, gave voice to an excellent
piece of legislation.   It made the enlistment period five years
and allowed the President to recruit each company up to 74
men.   Thus, without the addition of a single officer, the army
could be increased in cases of necessity by 4,488 men.

Congress had been made to have a change of heart in another direction.   The war had proved the merits of the Military
Academy.   Several minor acts showed the confidence of the *Sept. 16*
1850
legislative body in that institution.   The professors of engineering, philosophy, mathematics, ethics and chemistry were given
a flat rate of pay of $2,000 and the professors of drawing and
French each $1,500.   The Superintendent was to receive no less
than the highest-paid professor.

For the army in general, Congress for the first time recognized foreign service in its pay provisions.   Those officers serv- *Sept. 28*
1850
ing in the far countries of Oregon and California were to
receive $2 a day extra and the enlisted men were to have their
pay doubled.

While Congress was busy making these unusually constructive military laws, the Yuma Indian was particularly zealous in molesting emigrants. The country in the vicinity of the Gila was wild and unexplored and the Yumas were exceptionally treacherous. After some difficulty the site of Fort Yuma was established, which gave opportunity for General Smith, commanding the Pacific Division, to send a boat to the head of the Gulf of California. Lieutenant George H. Derby [10] of the topographical engineers was designated to make a reconnaissance of the country from the Gulf to the Fort, in order to establish a route from San Francisco. For 150 miles this officer penetrated this region and mapped the way to the fort.

Winter 1850–51

In a similar manner, Captain Litgreaves, with 50 men, went from Zuni westward until he reached the Colorado, whose course he followed to Fort Yuma. Encountering the hostile Mojaves and Yumas, he made overtures of friendship and kept on his way. Though the journey was rugged and full of hardship, especially from the intense heat, he learned much of the customs of these tribes in addition to making a survey.

1851

To offer havens for the traveler and settler and to have safe places in case of attack in force, many forts had to be erected. Major Heintzelman's troops built Fort Yuma. Other units of the army established Fort Kearny at Grand Island on the Platte River, Fort Laramie in Wyoming, Fort Bridger in Utah, and Fort Hall in Idaho, constituting the main chain of forts which protected the western routes of travel. Besides these garrisons, approximately seventy smaller ones dotted the plains. To construct a fort the soldiers were halted at a likely spot and given tools and the open country. With incredible swiftness and ingenuity they built barracks, officers' quarters, storehouses, guardhouses, headquarters and even the stockade barrier with its blockhouses. So in addition to being required to face the savage, these pioneer soldiers had to build their own shelter or be without any.

1851

Away in these remote places, driving off Indians and constructing strongholds, the troops never lost their punctilious-

---

[10] Nom de plume, John Phoenix, author of *"Phoenixiana"* and other sketches, the first American humorist.

ness. The adherence to a prescribed uniform intimates this quality of self-respect and discipline. The difference in grades was indicated by the buttons on the coat. The major-general's buttons were placed in double rows and in groups of threes, the brigadiers' in twos, and the field officers' without grouping. The company officers had but a single row. The coat was lengthened for enlisted men to halfway between the hip and the knee. The shoulder strap was worn by officers whenever the epaulet was omitted. The shape of the strap and the insignia upon it were the same as persisted down to the beginning of the World War. The present-day chevrons were similarly adopted for the noncommissioned officer. The "cloak" overcoat with frogs of black silk came into vogue.

The French bell tent was prescribed for use of enlisted men in the field. Just why mustaches were allowed to be worn only by cavalry regiments is not quite clear.

As an outgrowth of economy, changes of station and equipment were quite demoralizing. All the light batteries, except *March 1851* Bragg's of the Third and Taylor's of the First, were dismounted. The Third Dragoons returned from the Mexican frontier to the States, all the horses and most of the men being transferred to the First Dragoons. The Fifth Infantry relieved the Seventh in Texas and built Fort Belknap on the Red Fork of the Brazos River. A detachment of the Third Dragoons in *June 1851* taking horses overland to California met the Rogue River Indians whom they repulsed at the cost of the loss of an officer *June 18 1851* and several men. Some of the regiments had traversed the entire country during the year. The Third Dragoons, after having gone from one ocean to the other, had to recruit at *July 16 1851* Jefferson Barracks and reorganize for the third time in five years, on account of casualties.

Great attention was given at this time to heavy and mountain artillery as one of the reactions of the war. Drill regulations issued at War Department direction, covered the service of such pieces as the 8- and 10-inch and 24-pounder howitzers, 8- and 10-inch siege mortars, the coehorn mortar, the 10- and 13-inch seacoast mortars, the stone mortar, the 8-inch columbiad and guns of various calibers. Of the carriages there were the siege, barbette, casemate, flank casemate and columbiad. All cannoneers were required to be instructed in the *School of the Piece, Field Artillery,* before undertaking heavy artillery. As to purpose and use, heavy artillery was classified into siege, garrison and seacoast. The mountain artillery consisted of a 12-pounder howitzer which, with its carriage and ammunition, was packed upon three mules.

Feb. 6 1852

June 6 1852

At no time during this period did surveys and expeditions against marauding Indians cease. Company K of the Third Infantry overcame a band of Apaches with the loss of three men killed, and made a successful expedition against the tribes along the Gila River. Brevet Lieutenant Colonel Craig was shot and killed by two deserters while in command of a survey of the international boundary line of Mexico. Captain Marcy of the Fifth Infantry, with his company, and Captain G. B. McClellan, corps of engineers, explored the Red River from the mouth of Cache Creek to the river's source. They made peace with the Mojaves and found many valuable mineral specimens such as copper and gypsum.

May 1852

July 5 1852

Some of the journeys of the troops were very costly. Eight companies of the Fourth Infantry left New York Harbor for a change of station on the Pacific Coast. The travel was by water, except across Panama. The railroad over the isthmus being at this time incomplete, the regiment had to march a great part of the way. Cholera and fever overtook them. Before they reached San Francisco 107 had died of disease.

Aug. 6 1852

Sept. 1 1852

In the east, confidence in the Military Academy was again expressed by the Congress. The pay of professors and assistant professors was raised as an evidence of the appreciation of instruction imparted at that institution. And the Secretary of War did not lower its standard by appointing as superintendent, Brevet Colonel Robert E. Lee.

1853

In the west, Captain Wright of the Oregon volunteers almost overturned the work of such expeditions as Marcy's by inviting some of the marauding Rogue River Indians in Oregon to have a feast and make a treaty. When they had gathered under his supposed protection, he and his troops opened fire on the defenseless savages and killed all but ten of them.

Such a proceeding naturally caused an uprising among these Indians who made war on the isolated settlers by burning the crops and murdering the innocent whites. The army in that vicinity finally succeeded in subduing the tribe.

The troops in the service were distributed over a wide terri- *1853* tory. The Fourth Artillery was represented at Fort Independence in Maine and on the Rio Grande; the Second Infantry was spread from Goose Lake, Oregon, to Yuma, Arizona; the Fourth Infantry was at Vancouver Barracks, Washington; and most of the First Artillery was in Florida. The remainder of the army was scattered widely between these extremes.

While the meager army was trying to cover so much terri- tory, the Military Academy was thrown into confusion by the *Oct. 11* abrupt change of the course of study from five to four years. *1853* The Secretary of War, against the advice of the faculty of that institution, made this decision and caused the reconstruction of the curriculum after the term had begun. This action disturbed temporarily the Academy's efficiency.

In the journeys of the army in this period, disasters in travel were more common than in later times when the railroad was better developed, hygiene more understood and the ocean steamer more trustworthy. The greater part of the Third Artillery embarked at New York to go to California by way of Cape Horn. Off Cape Hatteras the vessel became unmanageable in a storm, her machinery was disabled, her sails were blown away, her deck was stripped and she sprang a leak. For days she was tossed about without any aid reaching her. Finally a Boston bark, *Kilby,* succeeded in getting off 108 passengers, but the hawser that held the boats together parted *Dec. 29* in the operation. The vessels were so separated that the troop *1853* ship could not again be found. Finally it was sighted by the *Dec. 31* British ship, *Three Bells.* The survivors were taken to New *1853* York and Liverpool. From exposure and drowning over 200 of the 600 aboard perished.

The next year, some of the survivors of this regiment went overland to California straight across the continent, while the other part sailed successfully in the course it had undertaken before.

Notable among the explorations of this year was one which Lieutenant Whipple, topographical engineer, conducted along *Spring* the 35th parallel in search of a railroad route west. His ascent *1854* of the Colorado River in connecting with Litgreaves' previous survey was one of peril and hardship. The result of his efforts proved to be highly beneficial to later transit.

Patrolling the west was a constant duty of the army during these years. The Third Infantry made three expeditions against the Apaches in Arizona where it lost several officers and men. The Third Dragoons were similarly engaged in addition to being constantly on the move between Leavenworth and *June, July 1854* Laramie. The Second Infantry went from Carlisle Barracks overland and down the Ohio by boat to Leavenworth, where it was spread out along the Missouri.

Realizing the value of the soldier and what he was doing for the country Congress raised the pay of the enlisted man by $4 *Aug. 4 1854* a month. In addition, it gave its first recognition to pay for length of service. The soldier's second enlistment gave him an increase of $2 a month over his regular pay and each successive enlistment for five years $1.

1854 The need of a rifle in the hazards of the western service, which not only developed the Indian fighter but made the hunter indispensable, caused more conversions of old weapons by the Ordnance Department than ever before. Besides making the Revolutionary musket capable of using a cap instead of the flint, the arsenals changed the barrel by brazing a lining in the tube so that the bore could be rifled. The department also standardized the caliber at .58.

1855 The model 1855 rifle based upon the above gun was made to use the "hollow base conical bullet" developed by Captain Minie. Besides, a lug was placed near the muzzle of the piece so as to hold the saber or the socket rapier bayonet. This rifle was about four feet two inches in length and weighed about ten pounds.

1855 *Cooper's and Macomb's Tactics* gave instructions as to the care of the rifle, in addition to giving evolutions for infantry, artillery and cavalry. The manual showed minutely how the soldier could make his own ammunition by melting down lead, molding the balls, smoothing the bullets off by rolling them in a barrel and wrapping the cartridges. In addition to having merely ball cartridges, the soldier could use buckshot or ball with buckshot.

Hardee's Rifle and Light Infantry Tactics, although ap- *1855* parently not conflicting with Cooper's and Macomb's, showed at this date striking similarities to Steuben's and yet marked differences. In "the position of the soldier" the heels were "on the same line and as near each other as the conformation of the man" would permit and the eyes were fixed straight to the front, "striking the ground about the distance of fifteen paces." There were four kinds of cadence and step: common time, quick time, double quick time and the run. The first was 90 steps to the minute and 28 inches in length; the second, 110 steps to the minute and 28 inches in length; the third, 165 steps to the minute and 33 inches in length; and the last, a fast run. The manual of loading was accomplished in "nine times" and fifteen motions as follows:

1. Load. One time and one motion.
2. Handle Cartridge. One time and one motion.
3. Tear Cartridge. One time and one motion.
4. Charge Cartridge. One time and one motion.
5. Draw rammer. One time and three motions.
6. Ram cartridge. One time and one motion.
7. Return rammer. One time and three motions.
8. Prime.[11] One time and two motions.
9. Shoulder arms. One time and two motions.

The actual firing was executed in three times and five motions.

Ready. One time and three motions.
Aim. One time and one motion.
Fire One time and one motion.

When the recruit became expert in this long exercise, he could be made to load in "four times" and fire as fast as three rounds in a minute.

Realizing the work the army was doing technically and its impossible task of dealing with the Indians successfully in so vast a territory as the United States now occupied, Congress *March 3* *1855*

---

[11] If Maynard's primer was used, loading could be done in "eight times:"

added 2 infantry and 2 cavalry regiments to the service, thus making 10 all told of the former and 5 of the latter. The officers of the newly created regiments were to be selected so that the field officers and one-half of the company officers of the old regiments would fill the new vacancies. The remainder were to come from civil life. The paper strength of the army now rose to 12,698 men, and the Ninth and Tenth Infantry and Fourth and Fifth Cavalry came into being.

It is interesting to note among the changes of uniform that the cap which had been in vogue in one form or another for almost fifty years, now gave place to the hat of black felt, *Aug. 15 1855* especially for the new regiments. The new headgear was looped up on the right side and fastened with an eagle. Black feathers ornamented the left side, three for field officers, two for company officers and one for enlisted men.

The far west continued to call portions of the army into play in quelling Indian uprisings. The Fourth Infantry in eastern Washington and Oregon had trouble in subduing many tribes under the leadership of the Chieftain Kamiarkin. In Oregon the regular troops were embarrassed by a massacre of Indians on the part of some volunteers who shot down nineteen unarmed savages in cold blood. The effect of such an affair was to cause the reactionary murder of many innocent settlers. *Sept. 3 1855* Portions of the First Cavalry and Fourth Artillery had a hard encounter with the Brule Indians at the battle of the Blue Water. The Third Artillery had many engagements with the Klamath, Puget Sound, and Rogue River Indians, which actions entailed marches over long distances and the loss of many soldiers.

In addition to the Indian troubles the newly created terri- *1855–56* tory of Kansas was torn with factions and outraged over the question of slavery. So acute and so partisan was the strife that the volunteers, who invariably took sides, could do little or nothing. Finally Governor Geary had to call for federal troops to restore some sort of order. Accordingly Colonel Cooke led the Fourth Artillery, acting as cavalry, from Leavenworth. This show of force caused the warring militias to disperse without bloodshed and Kansas was quickly brought to a state of quiescence, many lives being saved by the army's movement.

The newly organized Ninth Infantry arrived on the Pacific coast, having gone by way of Panama, and shortly afterward got into action in an expedition to Fort Walla Walla, Washington. There it met the Indians near the Cascades, dispersed them, and made the ringleaders prisoners. Later it captured 500 of the hostiles near the Wenache River. *Jan. 1856* *March 1856*

The work of the army this year consisted in reorganization, training and fighting. The First Artillery had successful actions in Florida and Texas. One company each from the 4 artillery regiments was dismounted and together garrisoned Fortress Monroe to reëstablish the Artillery School of Practice. The Third Infantry, marching in one month over 500 miles, was busy in the southwest with the Gila and Mogollan Apaches. The Second Cavalry was drilling at Fort Riley, Kansas. The Third Artillery finally routed the Rogue River Indians in Oregon, burned their village and decisively defeated them so that they sued for peace. The Sixth Infantry was at Jefferson Barracks, Mo., and Fort Leavenworth, Kansas. Most of the Fourth Artillery found itself at Fort Brooke, Florida, where the Seminoles again were beginning to give trouble. *1856* *March 1856* *March, April 1856* *Dec. 1856*

So much action in the field caused the uniform to be made more suitable to the needs of the soldier in the wilds. The long baggy trousers, the lower collar, the loose coat and comfortable hat gave more freedom of movement than was possible in 1812. The leather belt worn with the sash was more practicable in holding the sword. The shoulder strap was beginning to usurp the place of the epaulet. And simple knots and braid designated rank on the overcoat. A general had five braids and a double knot, a colonel five braids and a single knot, a lieutenant colonel four braids and a single knot and so on down through the grades. *Jan., Feb. 1857*

Confidence in the army's efforts was again expressed when legislation raised the pay of cadets from $24 to $30 per month. Besides, civilian dependence on the army's explorations was asserting itself in many ways. Lieutenant J. C. Ives, for instance, at the direction of the War Department organized an expedition to find the navigability of the Colorado River and the practicability of routes for supplies. The work was carried *March 3 1857* *1857* on in the presence of hostile Indian tribes and covered several hundred miles. Its value was to manifest itself later in opening up roads and railroads.

March 13 1857

Indian troubles again took the army into many untenanted regions. The Fourth Artillery, after having serious trouble with the Seminoles, especially at Big Cypress, was sent west and distributed through Utah and Nebraska. The Third Infantry was involved in the southwest with the Apaches in the Mogollan Mountains and along the Gila River. The Second Dragoons was so busy between Utah and Texas with its insufficient force that it was kept on the move most of the time. The newly created Tenth Infantry after clashing with the Sioux in Minnesota moved to Fort Kearny, Nebraska. The Sixth Infantry and First Cavalry went from Fort Leavenworth to Fort Kearny, meeting and defeating a large body of Cheyennes on the way. The first of the new cavalry regiments [12] had a severe engagement with the Cheyennes near the north fork of the Solomon River. In these engagements many of the men were wounded and killed with arrows; and with pistol, Allen's revolver and rifle balls. Many small surveying and exploring parties, notably those accompanied by troops furnished by General Clarke in command of the Department of the Pacific, kept up their valuable and trying labors through Arizona, Colorado, New Mexico and Nevada.

1857

It was in this year that the Sharp's breechloading rifle, using a cap, was invented. Although it did not come into use with the troops until several years later, it was the beginning of modern improvement in firearms, was to be the most efficient small weapon of the Civil War, and was to give rise to the name, "Sharpshooter." On the other hand, the Colt revolving rifle which was about the same time issued from that factory, was not destined to play so great a part. The soldiers did not like it because of the large powder escape at the breech and the tremendous kick when several charges exploded at once. But the production of the weapon shows the attempt at this early time to have a rifle that would shoot without the necessity for reloading at every shot.

---

[12] Known now as the Fourth Cavalry.

The largest expedition of this year was the one against the
Mormons. This sect isolated near Salt Lake City refused to
obey the laws of the United States. Accordingly the Fifth and *June 1857*
Tenth Infantry and two batteries of artillery marched from
Fort Leavenworth, Kansas, to subdue them. The Second
Dragoons was to follow. As soon as the Utah country was
approached, bands of harassing Mormons burned and captured
supply trains and drove off the cattle. All forage in front of
the advancing force was destroyed. The men and animals grew
hungry, and the cold became insufferable. When Colonel Albert
Sydney Johnston took command and was reënforced by the *Nov. 3 1857*
Second Dragoons, he did all a leader could do, but he could not
get supplies. His force was a ship at sea with no port for
coaling and provisioning. Over the desolated region the progress had to be very slow, sometimes only three miles a day.
The hostile Mormons would sell nothing, nor was there a chance
to find anything in this remote region in winter. Since the
troops were in such straits Colonel Johnston ordered Captain
Marcy to make his way overland with 40 enlisted men to Fort
Massachusetts, New Mexico, the nearest place where supplies
could be had. The march of this small detachment through
deep snows, near hostile savages and in terrible storms was
fraught with frightful hardships. Horses, mules, oxen and men
died of cold and disease. Finally a remnant of tattered and
emaciated soldiers who had largely subsisted on the carcasses of
dead horses and mules, came to Fort Massachusetts with such
odd appearance and such ailing bodies that they were with
difficulty recognized by the troops at that place. Fifty-one days
had been occupied in the march. In the meantime, the troops
in Utah had been reënforced by parts of the Sixth and Second
Infantry and Mounted Rifles, and had reached Fort Bridger
which they found burned by the Mormons. The plight of
Colonel Johnston's command was scarcely less severe than that
which had confronted Marcy. In tents during zero weather and
far removed from Philadelphia, the command in Utah had to
do for itself. But it was a disciplined lot that went to work
building and hauling wood, water and its few supplies by hand
in the frigid climate. There was no civilization which the soldier could reach or from which he could gain help. And

civilization paid small attention to these hardships which were endured almost without complaint. After Captain Marcy returned, the Mormon city was entered without bloodshed.

June 10 1858

During this movement of Johnston's troops, two minor laws made changes in the military establishment. The Texas border being still in an unsettled state, a new regiment of Texas mounted volunteers was allowed to be enlisted for 18 months. Because they were to furnish their own horses and horse equipments, all below the rank of major were allowed 40 cents a day extra pay. Legislation also gave the Superintendent of the Military Academy the local rank and pay of a colonel of engineers and the commandant of cadets that of lieutenant colonel. The course of instruction of the institution was changed, by order of the Secretary of War, back to five years.

April 7 1858

June 12 1858

April 5 1859

Not only with the Mormon expedition was the army occupied. Other regiments in isolated places were having their troubles. The Navajoes had 6 engagements with the Third Infantry. The Pacific Slope Indians were signally defeated in 3 battles near Spokane River by the Third Artillery. When an outlaw band of Cortinas attacked and blockaded Brownsville, Texas, the Third Artillery with other troops drove them off. The Sixth Infantry made a march overland from Fort Leavenworth, Kansas, to the Pacific coast.

Sept. 1858

The wide dispersion of the regiments during this decade is evidenced by the posts which the Fourth Infantry had garrisoned and in the main built. Forts Vancouver, Reading, Humboldt, Dalles, Steilacoom, Jones, Boise, Lane, Yamhill, Orford, Townshend, Hoskins, Walla Walla, Crook, Terwaw, Cascade, Simcoe, Gaston, Chehalis, Yuma and Mohave—extending from British Columbia to Mexico, are forgotten names of the past. But they were in these times active and necessary havens for the settler.

In occupying so wide a space activities sometimes had to go beyond national protection and become international. War was in sight with Great Britain for the fifth time in the army's history, when the Hudson Bay Company attempted to enforce its law on American citizens occupying Vancouver Island. Captain George E. Pickett was ordered with his company and one gun to occupy San Juan Island and resist the force brought

to bear upon that point. When it took months to get word of
the trouble to Washington and months to get back instructions,
General Harney had to act on his own initiative. Accordingly *July 27*
he had the small contingent under Captain Pickett take up a *1859*
defensive position on San Juan. Several British ships with
overpowering troops and armament tried to convince Pickett of
his error, but the American officer with his one gun stood his
ground and stated to the ships' commander plainly that he was
prepared to resist all encroachments. For some time this
audacious little force of regulars held the British at bay.
Finally General Scott was enabled to settle the differences by
engineering a joint occupation.

So closed the scene of action just before the maelstrom of
the Civil War. A trained army had wrested a peace in a short
time, and prevented the loss of men and money entailed by a
long war. It had made possible the acquisition of a third of
the present United States. It had gone further. It had made
the territories capable of occupancy. It had piloted the traveler
in safety, built roads, protected the mails, opened river routes,
kept the savages in leash and surveyed the routes of our present
railroads east and west. It had held the trail through hunger,
thirst, disease, wounds, disaster, and the untold suffering that
cannot be explained to one who has never experienced such
things, in such places, with such scant conveniences. The
march left its wolf-cleaned skeletons, the fight left its gaping
arrow wounds, the suffering left its shortened lives and civilization pressed in on all sides to gloat over a rich and beautiful
country.

CHAPTER VIII

THE ARMY DIVIDES AND MULTIPLIES

(1860–1865)

WAR, springing sternly from the hearts of the people, is about to rack the nation. The great uprising is first going to split the army and then swell it to puffiness. The Mexican struggle in an unknown country was quickly ended by a single chieftain, trained juniors and disciplined rank and file. The Civil War on our own soil will be dragged along by changing leaders, untrained juniors and undisciplined rank and file. The brilliant captains and lieutenants of Monterey and Cerro Gordo will be the generals of Fredericksburg and Shiloh. And they will look down helplessly over their hordes of irregulars for two years before the bullet all too sadly will have whipped those masses into shape.

1860 The long arguments over the rights of slave and free states had by the beginning of the year settled into fixed convictions. As the citizen was certain of his position, so the soldier in Fort Yuma, Arizona, knew how he stood. The slow mail from Maine or Louisiana determined his sentiments. Although he eagerly awaited the news of the bickerings that were certain to lead to strife, he went on just the same with the work in hand.

Out of 198 companies in the service 183 were strewn over 79 posts of the wild frontier. The other 15 manned the Atlantic coast, 23 arsenals, and the Canadian border. Seldom was so much as a battalion collected in any one place and often a small company was separated into detachments. Less than 13,000 men attempted to hold in security 3,000,000 square miles of territory.

In these ominous hours only one great hand was raised to increase our resistance. Scott proposed the establishment of a sufficient force of regulars against possible trouble. But among

244

the politicians in Washington, his was a voice crying in the wilderness. With Buchanan and Floyd there was not a chance of conviction that widespread training and discipline would save lives. Besides their apparent sympathies with the South, they looked upon Scott as too old to lead troops and therefore too old to give advice.

All this time the two sides to the issue were sedulously hurling burning brands at each other when there was no fire department to quench the flames. A hose in Oregon, a nozzle in Florida, horses in Texas and an engine nowhere! The army was fighting Indians while the factions were wrangling. Fighting Indians! Hunting wolves while the mother country lay in convulsions!

The First Infantry was in Texas, the Second along the *Jan.* Mississippi River as far west as For Kearny, the Third in *1860* New Mexico, the Fourth on the Pacific coast from Puget Sound to the Gulf of California, the Fifth in the Mormon country of Utah, the Sixth in Southern California, Nevada and Arizona, the Seventh in Utah, the Eighth in Texas, the Ninth in Oregon and the Tenth in Utah and New Mexico. The First Artillery was in the Gulf States, the Second along the Atlantic coast, the Third in the vicinity of Vancouver Barracks, Washington Territory, and the Fourth in Utah. The First and Second Dragoons were scattered over the west; the Third was mainly concentrated in New Mexico and the Fourth at Fort Riley, Kansas.

Small disturbances were continually prevalent throughout most of the vast territory the army attempted to cover. For example, in New Mexico near Fort Defiance where the Navahos and Apaches were actively hostile, the soldier's life was far from peaceful. Nestled in the mountains at the foot of Cañon Bonita, scarcely 200 men occupied the loneliest corner of the United States and the key to the Rio Grande. It was called a fort but it was not a fortress. The parade ground, quarters, barracks, prison, storehouses and adobe shacks lay out in the open, protected only by the alertness and man power of the few occupants. Early in the year 5 companies of the Third Infan- *Jan. 17* try had driven off a band of savages whom they had chased to *1860* Sixteen Mile Pond and beaten. And later a small company was *Feb. 8* *1860* successful in putting to flight other harassing Indians. For over a month thereafter the little garrison had lived in comparative comfort. But one night Lieutenant Whipple, who was officer of the day, had suspicions, from those intangible reckonings that come to men experienced in Indian treachery, that there was going to be an attack. Visiting each sentry he saw that the guard was properly instructed and vigilant. Sure enough, at one in the morning just after the moon had set, the war whoop sounded from the opposite hills and 3,000 Navahos and Apaches swooped down upon the 150, most of whom were asleep. But the guard was awake and watchful. Giving the alarm it placed itself where it would be the greatest hindrance. The delay was enough to allow the rudely awakened officers and soldiers to grab enough clothing to cover them, to assemble in orderly formation as if they were on parade and to sally forth. Forming a skirmish line they fired by file at any moving object they could see. Stumbling in the darkness they even charged some savages who were strongly posted in natural stone battlements. When dawn came, the Indians moved off with many of their numbers dead and wounded. The superior discipline and marksmanship of the trained soldier had told. One man killed and a few wounded was the tally of the little post of Fort Defiance. And affairs there went on peacefully for some time, but the size of the post was always an invitation to the painted warriors.

April 30 1860

Troops in other wild sections were playing their part with equal grit and endurance. When some prospectors were massacred in Nevada, parts of the Sixth Infantry and Third Artillery sought out the plundering tribes. At Truckee River, these troops routed the Indians after a severe fight. Some of the Tenth Infantry in New Mexico, of the Sixth at Mad River, California, and of the Third Artillery at Harney Lake and in the Klamath country of Washington Territory had sharp encounters with the savages of those localities, while the Fourth Artillery, operating as cavalry, kept the roads and mail routes open and escorted emigrants over hundreds of miles of barren country in Utah.

June 2 1860

The only legislation for the army this year was an act which among other similar things increased the sugar and coffee

June 21 1860

rations for enlisted men, and created a commission consisting of Senators Jefferson Davis, Solomon Foot, Representative John Cochrane, Major Robert Anderson and Captain A. A. Humphreys to inquire into "the organization, system of discipline and course of instruction at the United States Military Academy." Thirty-two million people were satisfied, so far as their power of resistance was concerned, to fritter their time over coffee and the curriculum of a school while a catastrophe of blood and flame was in sight, while their only real combatant strength was parceled out over so vast a region that months of the speediest journeys could not collect it.

In technic there were a few minor developments. A rifle that was to have some influence on the coming conflict was this year invented by Christopher Spencer. This breechloading weapon was the first of the successful repeaters. It was afterwards thought to be the most finished and ready weapon of the Civil War. It was a seven-shot rifle, loading brass shells through a magazine in the butt. Although the loading was slow, the mechanism was a distinct advance in rapidity over the muzzle-loader. So few of them could be furnished in comparison to the great number of flint and cap lock muzzle-loaders for the myriads of soldiers during the war, that their effect on operations was slight.

Within the army, efforts to improve the tactics for both the *1860* regulars and militia were evidenced by the appearance of *Rifle and Infantry Tactics* and by a translation from the French by Major Robert Anderson, First Artillery, of exercises for artillery. The latter was called *Evolution of Field Batteries of Artillery* arranged for the use of the "army and militia of the United States." The work was sanctioned by the Secretary of War for the exclusive use of the troops mentioned.

Such preparation sums up all our country made for the clash that was at least probable. When South Carolina seceded, *Dec. 20* there were few regular officers who had commanded as much as *1860* an assembled battalion. The militia were only so in name. Although an organization here and there might know how to shoulder arms, the state troops had no field-service training whatever. There was no accessible power in the country to prevent armed citizens in any quantity from doing about as they pleased. John Brown's raid was an illustration. The people were waiting to see what was going to happen. Sanguine hopes were fathers to delusions of no war or a short one. The North, especially, lay curious, concerned and idle while the terror was approaching.

Jan 7 to Feb. 1 1861

Florida, Mississippi, Alabama, Georgia, Louisiana and Texas quickly followed the example of South Carolina. These states sent representatives to a "Congress of Sovereign States,"

Feb. 9 1861

adopted a constitution, and elected a president who was a graduate of West Point and a former United States senator. The South was quick, keen and farseeing in its movements. It

Feb. 28 1861

empowered its new president to take control of operations in its states and authorized him to accept for twelve months as many

March 6 1861

volunteers as he might require. Accordingly he called out 100,000 volunteers as a start.

The North could have inferred that the South was preparing for war and meant business. Yet the central government sat supinely by waiting for the outbreak. In the east a few paltry companies which had had about 600 recruits added to them were given the task of holding all the forts and arsenals, and the nation's capital. The President of the Union, the commander in chief of all the armed forces, with his Secretary of War, instead of making some attempt to establish a capable force for meeting the well-organized South, continued to try compromises when the time for such futility had plainly passed. Naturally, since the weakly guarded arsenals and forts in the southern states were mockeries of strength, the Confederacy

Feb. 1861

seized them. Besides, General Twiggs, in command of the Department of Texas, had surrendered nearly one fourth of the entire army and all the public property intrusted to him. And yet the central government let the army fight Apaches and waited for Sumter. To Buchanan and Floyd, men with muskets were soldiers.

A few days before the President of the Confederacy had called out his 100,000, the President of the Union was making

March 4 1861

his way in disguise to take his oath of office at the capital of the nation. So little strength had the North that it had to let its chief executive sneak into a threatened White House. There he had to begin to formulate plans against an enemy already well organized and powerful in the speed and efficiency it had exhibited.

Having no regular army in sight, he had to fall back on the old law of 1795 and to turn in desperation to the militia of the states. In the meantime, Fort Sumter was fired upon and seized, and 35,000 well-equipped and half-disciplined Confederates were in the act of taking the southern forts and arsenals. At this juncture, Mr. Lincoln called out 75,000 militia for three months, a force only three-fourths as large and an enlistment only one-fourth as long as for the Confederate army already called into the field. He was thus powerless to suppress a single expression of rebellion. *April 12 1861*

To his call for volunteers the governors of those southern states that had not already seceded sent curt replies of refusal. The northern states responded with alacrity and pandemonium. A medley of citizens hastened to adorn themselves as soldiers. With the truly patriotic man there were too often recruited the idler and the adventurer. The contingents—not organizations —were commanded ordinarily by men ignorant of the art of war and frequently without the character necessary for an officer. The soldier chose his commander as he did in the Revolution and all the evils of organization that overflowed Washington's cup poured out on Mr. Lincoln. In an advertisement for recruits one regiment's poster is significant of the view of the untrained volunteer toward the coming three months' excursion:

"As this regiment is to be constantly garrisoned in the forts around Washington, those anxious to enter the military service will find in it the inestimable advantage of exemption from the hardships and privations incidental to camp-life."

Zouaves were paraded through the streets in showy uniforms. A Massachusetts regiment was mobbed while attempting to go through Baltimore; a Pennsylvania one had to turn back on the same occasion because it did not have arms. And this hasty, irregular, undisciplined lot, called an army, was to evaporate in three months, whereas the Confederates' force would still be in the service nine months longer. *April 19 1861*

Furthermore, the small regular army itself felt disintegration. During these months after Sumter, 269 officers out of a total of about 900 resigned their commissions to join the South and 26 were dismissed for the same reason. Sixty-five West Point cadets from the southern states resigned, were discharged or dismissed. But about half of the alumni whose homes were in the South stayed with the North. As to the rank and file those in the service remained with the North with the exception of about 26.

There seemed to be no personal rancor between officers and cadets over the opposite stands they took on secession. Men freely shook hands with each other at parting and expressed feelings of mutual respect. Officers who had resigned left their old regiments on the plains and made long harassing journeys back home to join the Confederacy. It was not without reluctance and tears that they left their old associates and the ties of tradition, friendship, hardship and buffeting bound up with the old flag. Home, friends and the strong organization of the South, which the North in its weakness had permitted, all fixed in them a belief in which they were sincere.

April 20 1861

While the Union was losing the services of these trained officers, the handful that was left attempted to do its bit. Although General Wool, in command of the few trained troops in the East, had not been called upon or consulted by higher authority, he sent to Washington all the organizations he could release. Since he took the precaution to send them around Baltimore, they arrived at the capital without molestation.

In the meantime Washington had been physically severed from the North. The Maryland secessionists had cut all wires and blocked the traffic. The President and Mr. Cameron could not get in touch with the forces that had been called out. Each of these gentlemen suddenly found himself in the throes of managing military affairs of which he was technically ignorant. Mr. Cameron, for instance, rejected offers of regiments of cavalry, because he was doubtful of the value of that arm in our wooded country. Also, cavalry was very expensive. He was perfectly at home, however, in busying himself with dealing out sutlerships to Pennsylvania politicians.

The neglect, throughout the previous decade, of military

affairs was reflected in the housing of the War Department. While other bureaus were occupying palatial stone buildings, the activities of this important function of our government were concentrated in a miserable tenement. There Mr. Cameron, after years of legal and political training, pathetically read regulations and treatises on the art of war in order to give to himself at least the appearance of a head of this gigantic military project.

How different in the South! Mr. Davis, an educated soldier, a brave and trained leader, a hero of several battlefields, and a statesman who had served in the Senate and on the Cabinet, combined statecraft with military efficiency. He was the sole executive. The Confederate States had so organized as to allot to him the quick control of affairs and the man power he requested. Such organization and knowledge were to give to a comparatively small force a touch of unity that was to baffle the heterogeneous masses of the Union for four distracting years.

For a great emergency, the constitution of the United States had made little or no provision. Mr. Lincoln now had to break the law and override the powers of Congress in order to build his foundation. By this time all hope of holding the arsenals and forts in the South was gone. That opportunity had inanely passed. Already the militia of the District of Columbia at the President's call had either refused to be sworn in or to serve outside the District. Sinking sand everywhere. Lincoln was beginning to understand that provision can never make up for prevision. Accordingly he was compelled, in violation of the Constitution, to increase the regular army by 22,714 men and to call out 42,834 additional volunteers for three years.[1] The *May 3 1861* manner of organizing these men was turned over to the Secretary of the Treasury, the Secretary of War having too much to do. In turn, the Secretary of the Treasury was too much occupied to be disturbed by such items, so that he pushed the matter off on 3 regular army officers: Colonel Thomas, Major McDowell and Captain Franklin.

These soldiers, acting on sound lines, recommended a three-

---

[1] He thus added 9 regiments of infantry, 1 regiment of artillery and 1 regiment of cavalry to the regular army.

battalion organization for all regiments, a three-year enlistment and a call for 300,000 volunteers. Although the three-year enlistment was approved, and Congress later had to make a call for a greater number of volunteers, the Secretary of the Treasury disapproved the three-battalion organization for the volunteers because the militia were not "familiar" with it. So the process of making a homogeneous army languished. As usual, the regulars could not be recruited in competition with the inducements offered volunteers. Altogether, the organization of the northern armies was no more developed than Washington's force in 1776.

No provision was made to utilize the experience of regular and other trained officers with the volunteers. The men of the local regiments still elected their officers. If a civilian, who had been a regular officer, happened to be known in a community he was sometimes selected. But more often he was ignored. Grant, who was in business, wrote to the War Department offering his services, but was not even honored with a reply. No attempt was made to transfer regular officers to the new organizations. Indeed many of them in the service served in modest capacities during the entire war while grocers and bankers led regiments indifferently. The governors accepted whole regiments of about 850 men practically as they had been organized at home. The man who raised, equipped and supplied a regiment or brigade really owned it, and no mere governor or president could dictate to it as to who its officers should be or what rank should be given. If the South believed in states' rights, so did the North in the collection of its uniformed recruits. Generals commanding in the field had to apply to the proper governor before an officer of that state could be promoted. In this way the experienced officer was crowded out and some regulars who had accepted state commissions at high rank came to prefer, after they had come in contact with the politics, chicanery and disorderliness of the volunteers, to return to inferior rank with the regulars. What the North lost by such a procedure is shown by the record of those trained officers who did have a chance: 51 major generals, 91 brigadier generals and 106 colonels came from those officers of the old army who either by having been in civil life or by having accepted transfers during hostilities, had the opportunity of advancement. The other 308 the government to its chagrin submerged. It thus tossed at least two thousand years of training into the discard.

On the other hand, the South acted in no such foolish way. It early made a provision to accept the services of officers of the United States army and to let them have their original relative rank. Note the difference in the figures. Of the 250 who espoused the Confederate cause, 182 rose to the rank of general officer, including such men as Lee, Jackson, Longstreet and the two Johnstons. In addition, the Confederacy made gradations of general officers to suit the units they commanded, as was later found best in the World War. On the southern side there was a general for an army, a lieutenant general for a corps, a major general for a division, and a brigadier general for a brigade, whereas on the northern side there were merely major generals and brigadiers for all four units.

The few regulars on the northern side who could be brought from their stations were engulfed in the great vortex of irregular volunteers. Washington was crowded with regiments. A regular battalion of infantry and a scattering few companies of artillery and squadrons of cavalry were scarcely traceable in the crowds of volunteers who were pouring into the city. The quartering of all these uniformed citizens was such a problem that public buildings had to be used as barracks. Even the Capitol itself was given over for that purpose. A German regiment occupied the floor of the House. Beds were in the corridors, a sergeant sat in the speaker's chair, murals were defaced, members' desks broken up and the congressional hall of the nation given over to pillage and abuse. Uncontrolled drunkenness made the denizen of Washington more fearful of friend than enemy. The farmer colonel and apothecary major in many cases walked about the streets in showy uniforms, drew their pay and did not go near their regiments for weeks. It is possible they earned their salary better by their absence. Again, it was true that it costs a nation more to arm its fears than to awe its foes. Already the country had used in these few months money enough to have supported a sufficient and trained force for the ten years preceding.

In other places, too, there were scenes of waste. The first levies were on their way to aid McClellan in West Virginia, Patterson in Maryland and McDowell in Washington. Around the cities of the North they had been assembled with the over-sanguine conception that the "secesh" would soon "give up." An excursion into the South and the whole thing would be over. The recruits, for they were mostly such, not knowing whether their regiments would be accepted spent their time sight-seeing, spending their money in saloons and generally adding to their demoralization. In their restlessness to be off and their igno-rance of what was going to happen to them, they after a time became surly, depressed and often unruly. Since the govern-ment had not made up its mind as to what was going to become of the three-month men, rumors would come into camp one day that they were to be discharged, another day that they were going to be accepted for three years, another that it was optional as to whether individuals would reënlist for three years. Or-ders would arrive only to be quickly countermanded. In this state of anxiety they became disobedient and even mutinous. Many captains, for the first time saddled with authority, pil-fered the rations of the companies. One soldier in writing home shows the reaction of such confusion on raw troops.

"Such a feeling pervades the minds of the soldiers that discipline is played out. Company K refused to turn out to roll call the other morning, and day before yesterday, not a man of them appeared on dress parade. Company F would not come out on parade yesterday.

"Night before last a row broke out in a beer saloon near the depot and some of the Pittsburg boys cleaned out the whole thing, broke in the doors and windows, smashed up the glass and furniture. A crowd collected and Colonel Grant was obliged to call out Companies B, G, and I, with their guns to disperse them. Company G charged down the road and across the railroad track through the thickest of them. They made quite a determined stand on the track, and some six or eight were wounded before they would leave."

With such a state of discipline it is not remarkable that

columns here and there undertook to win battles at will. Butler *June 10 1861* at Big Bethel, near Fortress Monroe, was repulsed; Lyon at *June 18 1861* Boonville, Missouri, dispersed the Confederates; Patterson after occupying Harper's Ferry was compelled to withdraw and *June 18 1861* send most of his troops for the protection of Washington; and McClellan prepared for his campaign in the mountains of West *June 23 1861* Virginia. The Union troops seemed to be dispersed with local purposes of their own, whereas the Confederates had been concentrating in northern Virginia.

In these movements many instances of lack of training demonstrated the unfitness of the forces to do anything decisive. Lack of reconnaissance caused 2 regiments under Butler to fire into each other with loss. When they did get into action, the first volley of the Confederates drove them into the woods from which it took their officers over two hours to induce them to return to the charge. Nearly all of Patterson's troops were three-month men who were clamoring to be gone. They were already largely without shoes and entirely without pay. Colonel Biddle testified afterward as to their conduct:

"The General then went to the other regiments, but found that it was not feasible at all; from one-half to two-thirds refused to go. He finally got to an Irish regiment and made a very powerful appeal to them, knowing the Irish character very well. He carried them with a sort of shout, and they all said they would remain. They all lifted up their muskets. But he had hardly turned his back when they hallooed out "Shoes and Pants!" "Shoes and Pants!"

McClellan in an eight-day campaign in West Virginia gave *June 6–14 1861* a touch of morale to the North, even if the results he obtained did not have much effect on the outcome of the war. With 5 ill-disciplined brigades he operated among the Rich and Cheat mountains against an inferior force of Confederates under Pegram and Magruder. Although McClellan's flank attack under Rosecrans was delayed for a day by the weariness of his unseasoned troops, Pegram's men were demoralized from the threat and thrown into disorder in the retreat. Altogether the well-planned skirmishes gave to the side of superior numbers the possession of West Virginia by the Union. Finally the northern forces were able to disperse the inferior force under Morris at Carricksford merely by their appearance on the scene.

Up until this time nothing decisive had been attempted by either side because of the inexperience of the troops. At Washington scattering musketry was often heard along the Potomac. But the 30,000 troops that had been assembled under McDowell were by no means ready to move. They had to have staffs for their larger units. The Quartermaster, Commissary and Ordnance departments had neither means of supply nor subordinate officers who knew their duties. The few trained higher officers could not impart their knowledge to a multitude in a short time. Soldiers who had come out for a lark could scarcely be made to see the seriousness of obedience or the necessity of orderliness. They knew nothing of the march or how to take care of themselves. They knew less about how to eat or look after their feet. Sickness reduced their numbers and efficiency.

This was the kind of force on which General McDowell had to rely and which he had had no chance to maneuver. But the heads of the government reflecting the cry of the North, "On to Richmond," decided that he should move this haphazard collection of men somewhere. They felt it was better to have defeat than no action at all. Of the 300,000 scattered throughout the North there were approximately 50,000 in Washington, where breastworks had been constructed. Of the latter only about 30,000 were allotted for McDowell's use, and only 800 of these were trained troops.[2] His testimony before the Senate Committee afterwards was plaintive in its logic:

"I had no opportunity to test my machinery, to move it around and see whether it would work smoothly or not. In fact, such was the feeling, that when I had one body of eight regiments of troops reviewed together, the general censured me for it, as if I was trying to make some show. I did not think so. There was not a man there who had ever maneuvered troops in large bodies. There was not one in the Army. I did not

---

[2] A battalion of 8 companies of the Second, Third and Eighth Infantry, a battalion of marines, a small detachment of the First and Second Dragoons and 6 batteries of artillery.

believe there was one in the whole country.   At least I knew
there was no one there who had ever handled 30,000 troops.   I
had seen them handled abroad in reviews and marches, but I
had never handled that number, and no one here had."

So McDowell became the scapegoat of a nation that had
negligently drifted along.

His plans, however, were laid with the same zeal and intelligence as if he expected victory.   His force was to attack
Beauregard before Johnston, who was supposed to be kept occupied in the Shenandoah Valley by Patterson, could join the
main Confederate Army at Manassas.   McDowell was given
eight days in which to prepare for this offensive.   Although he
exerted himself to the utmost in the interim, there was practi- *July 9
cally no transportation ready for him when the time came for *1861*
the movement.   Nevertheless, he had to go, knowing full well
that Confederate videttes were in sight of Washington and that
the prop upon which he leaned was weak and rickety.

Leaving Washington, the troops carried three days' rations *July 16
in their canvas knapsacks and everything else that a recruit *1861*
could stow away.   The heat and weariness of the march soon
told on them.   Throwing away blankets, blouses and even
rations, which the camp followers soon picked up, they marked
their journey with waste.   Feet became blistered.   Men left the
ranks at will, got water and fruit as they chose, and meandered
for miles along the way.   Some did not reach camp until midnight of the first day's short march.   Units were confused, and
amongst this mob of men, congressmen in carriages, women in
barouches who wanted to see the battle, the curious on horses
and sutlers with their wagons mixed themselves.   By such
process McDowell was enabled to march most of his troops the
enormous distance of fifteen miles in two days.

In this sort of excursion without method by the junior
officers, it was not surprising that Tyler attacked at Blackburn's
Ford prematurely and without orders.   Naturally he was repulsed with loss and with a bad effect upon the troops in general.   Nor was it strange that a whole regiment and a battery
of artillery among the militia shamefully went home in the
midst of these operations because their enlistment had expired;

that McDowell had to halt two days in order to reorganize his command and study the country in the absence of maps and reliable guides; and that this delay gave Johnston time to hurry to Beauregard because Patterson, being bereft of decent troops, could not keep Johnston employed.

July 19
1861

McDowell, with less than 28,000 men at this time was to attack a strongly fortified position held by at least equal numbers. But his decision and orders were such that even then had they been properly executed he might have had some chance of success, for the Confederates instead of clinging to their fortifications determined to take the offensive.

July 21
1861

When the main attack did take place, Tyler was slow in getting into position, and Hunter's brigade, which was a part of the command that was to take the Confederates in flank, rested for refreshments a bit too long by the waters of Bull Run. Yet during the morning the bare thousand of the left wing of the Confederates were pushed back across Bull Run to their strong position. Then the southern masked batteries began to do their deadly work. The unreliable troops on both sides were excited. They formed their lines slowly and badly under fire. The rear ranks and hindmost men of the staggered lines were almost as deadly to friend as enemy. The superior officers had a hard time to get their juniors and rank and file forward. So exposed were the higher commanders in trying to urge their troops to the front that a disproportionate number of leaders were killed or wounded. Late in the afternoon McDowell, in spite of his handicaps, had turned the flank of the Confederate position. Then Johnston came upon the scene. These fresh troops were just enough to turn the tide. A regiment of Confederates, mistaken by the Federals for friends, delivered a murderous fire especially upon the artillery. Then the rout began. One regiment fled and then another. The new volunteers were tired and hungry, but they succeeded in jamming the road in their hurry to get away. Newspaper men climbed down quickly from their vantage trees. Carriages, barouches, carts and horses clogged the highway. Soldiers in their excitement, firing in the air or at each other, stampeded across the fields toward Washington. McDowell's so-called army after having sustained a loss of only 5 per cent had disintegrated. Some did not stop until they reached New York City and most of them made their way that night back to Washington. The single battalion of regulars was conspicuous in its orderliness and energetic daring in protecting the fleeing masses from the enemy. Thus was achieved a battle, the loss of many lives, the waste and destruction of much property by unready forces who were incapable of a decisive stroke. Victory did as much harm to the South as defeat did for the North. Again the country, according to Light Horse Harry Lee, had murdered some of its citizens.

At this juncture the first military bill of the war became a law. While disgruntled volunteers who had been present at the exercises of Bull Run groped about the city without direction, with hats, coats and even rifles gone, while these men without order or cohesion blamed their defeat upon their officers, the battlefield, upon anything but themselves and the false position in which their country had placed them, Mr. Lincoln signed the *July 22 1861* enactment which authorized him to accept 500,000 volunteers for not more than three years or less than six months. In requisitioning the regiments bodily from the states he was not to exceed the proportion of 1 cavalry and 1 artillery regiment to 10 of infantry.[3] A division was to consist of 3 or more brigades and each brigade of 4 or more regiments. To command these higher units the President was allowed to appoint not more than 6 major generals and 18 brigadier generals, who could be selected from the line or staff of the regular army in which organization they were not to lose their grade. The governor had the exclusive right to appoint all the officers below general rank. Only in case of the failure of a governor to do so, had the President authority to furnish officers. To every enlisted man who furnished his own uniform and clothing $3.50 was allowed, and 40 cents a day to every member of a company who furnished his own horse and horse equipment. For each regiment

---

[3] "Each regiment of infantry shall have 1 colonel, 1 lieutenant colonel, 1 major, 1 adjutant (a lieutenant), 1 quartermaster (a lieutenant), 1 surgeon and 1 assistant surgeon, 1 sergeant major, 1 regimental quarter- master sergeant, 1 regimental commissary sergeant, 1 hospital steward, 2 principal musicians, and 24 musicians for a band, and shall be composed of 10 companies, each company to consist of 1 captain, 1 first lieutenant, 1 second lieutenant, 1 first sergeant, 4 sergeants, 8 corporals, 2 musicians, 1 wagoner, and from 64 to 82 privates."

a chaplain, who had to be an ordained minister of a Christian denomination, was allowed to be appointed by its commander according to the vote of the field officers and company commanders actually on duty. A general commanding a separate department or detached army had the power to convene a board of from 3 to 5 officers who were to examine into "the capacity, qualifications, propriety of conduct and efficiency" of any volunteer officers.[4] The law particularly prescribed that vacancies among volunteer officers should be filled by vote. All members of companies were to elect the captain and lieutenants and all regimental officers were to select the remaining commissioned personnel of the regiment. Governors were required to commission such selections. The last part of the law allowed soldiers to send their mail without prepayment, those at home having to pay postage therefor. It also prescribed that the Secretary of War should devise a system of "allotment tickets" whereby the soldier might have some of his pay drawn by his family.

July 25 1861

Three days after this piece of legislation, the President signed another bill which allowed him to call out 500,000 more. Although Congress may not have meant to do so, that body had now given Mr. Lincoln power to summon over 1,000,000 men.[5] The latter half million were to be enlisted for the duration of the war. In addition, the evident absurdity of the few general officers prescribed by the previous law must have caused the lawmakers to add the provision which gave power to appoint as many general officers as were required.

Now that war in all its fury was upon the country, it acted as if such a catastrophe were quite unexpected, as if it had not been brewing for at least ten years. Now that blood was being

July 29 1861

spilled, Congress ran to generous extremes. Not satisfied with the unprecedented force it had already voted for, a third bill became a law within four days of the last one. The regular army was theoretically increased by 9 regiments of infantry, 1 of cavalry and 1 of artillery. An infantry regiment was to contain 2 or 3 battalions, a cavalry regiment not more than 3

---

[4] Within eight months 310 officers had to be got rid of by such a board.
[5] Congress had already sanctioned his previous calls of April 15 and May 3.

battalions of 2 squadrons[6] each; and an artillery regiment not more than 12 batteries, each battery to be officered by a maximum of 1 captain, 2 first lieutenants and 2 second lieutenants. In this reorganization of the regulars a wise provision was made for a major with his staff of 1 adjutant and 1 quartermaster for each battalion, and a major for each 4 batteries of artillery. There was as yet only 1 major for a volunteer regiment. An addition of 4 major generals and 6 brigadier generals was also made for the regulars. Thus the North had to remake its army in the face of the enemy.

Enlistments during 1861 and 1862 were to be for three years and thereafter for five years. The recruitment of this additional regular force was to be intrusted to officers appointed from civil life. This same legislation allowed regular officers to be switched from volunteer to regular units or *vice versa* as the commanding general felt would be conducive to the greatest efficiency.

Then Congress, aghast at the war structure it had raised, became panicked at such a possibility for peace times. Without any means of knowing what the future might hold, it now uttered a statute which provided for the reduction of the army at the end of the war to 25,000 men.

On the same day another act made the militia subject to the same rules as the regular army and their retention possible by the President until sixty days after the next "regular session of Congress." *July 29 1861*

Five days afterward, the President signed another bill "for the better organization of the military establishment." Now that an army had been built up on paper it was found that administration and supply were wanting. Accordingly an assistant secretary of war, 5 assistant inspector generals with rank and pay of majors of cavalry, 10 surgeons and 20 assistant surgeons, an adjutant general with rank of brigadier general and 19 assistants,[7] 8 "commissaries of subsistence," 6 topographical engineers, 19 quartermasters, a chief of ordnance with the same rank and pay as the quartermaster-general with *Aug. 3 1861*

---

[6] Each squadron was to contain 2 companies.

[7] Having respectively rank and pay of 1 colonel of cavalry, 2 lieutenant colonels, 4 majors and 12 captains.

8 assistants [8] were created. To the medical staff was added a corps of medical cadets, not to exceed 50, who were to have the same rank and pay as the cadets at West Point and who were required to have had a "liberal education," to have read medicine for at least two years and to have attended at least one course of lectures in a medical school. "Female nurses" were allowed to be employed by the surgeon-general at 40 cents a day. Any cadet recommended to be discharged from the Military Academy either for deficiency in conduct or studies was not allowed to be reappointed as a cadet or to be appointed to any place in the army before the class of which he was a member had graduated. The oath of the entering cadet was changed so that it might be binding in any question of states' rights.[9] To insure good conduct among soldiers, $2 of the monthly pay was to be retained until his enlistment expired. The ration was increased for the war, but thereafter was to be the same as before. For the first time retirement for officers of long and faithful service or from wounds or disability was made possible by means of a retiring board. The officer could be retired with his pay, or his rations, but not both; or in case his services were not satisfactory, "wholly retired" with one year's pay and allowances.

Aug. 5 1861

Another law, two days later, appropriated $100,000 for fortifications, made it a crime of desertion for any officer who quitted his post after resignation and abolished flogging in the army.

Aug. 6 1861

The next day two bills became a law. One increased the engineers and topographical engineers, each, by 2 lieutenant colonels and 4 majors, gave an extra company to the latter and put promotions of volunteer officers entirely in the hands of the governors. The other increased the pay of the private soldier from $11 to $13 a month.

Such was the mass of legislation enacted in a month. Naturally it could be good only in spots and weak and ex-

---

[8] One colonel, 1 lieutenant colonel and 6 second lieutenants.

[9] "I, A.B., do solemnly swear that I will support the Constitution of the United States, and bear true allegiance to the national government; that I will maintain and defend the sovereignty of the United States paramount to any and all allegiances, sovereignty, or fealty I may owe to any state, county, or country, whatsoever."

travagant in the main. The fact that at first the Congress gave
the President 500,000 men with only 24 generals to command
them, and was compelled later on to give him no limit in this
regard, demonstrates the utter ignorance at the capital of military needs. Of course the election of officers and their appointment by the governors was subversive of discipline and
detrimental to success. Hundreds of the original appointees
drew their pay without rendering the country anything but
harm. Then more money had to be spent in getting rid of
these worthless officers. But nothing could repay humanity
for the lives such so-called leaders had lost at Bull Run. Congress seeing its error made the matter worse by prohibiting
election and by giving the appointment of officers entirely to
the governor. Even so, the pernicious system of voting for
officers, once inaugurated in the separate states, continued.
The hurry of the legislators is again evidenced in the term of
service for the rank and file. With the first 500,000 they made
the mistakes of our previous wars in giving the option of a
six-month enlistment or a three-year enlistment as the recruit
chose. With the second 500,000 they tried to rectify their
error by making the period for the war. It is easy to see that
the recruit chose the six-month period, when three years was
long and the duration of the war uncertain. It is easy to see
also that when a man could enlist under the laxity of the volunteers he would not undertake the severity of the regular service,
so that the increase of the latter establishment languished for
some time. Neither did the separate types of organization for
volunteer and regular forces add to the facility with which an
army should be handled. And then the awful fear of an adequately trained force after the war led the lawmakers, even at
this frenzied time, into making it certain that there would be
no more than 25,000, no matter what the conditions might be
then. It took a war to increase the pay and rations for the
volunteer over that which the regular had had to subsist upon
under as bad if not worse conditions than civil war sufferings.
It took a war to pay just dues to the aged officer of long and
faithful service. But in all these enactments there was little or
no attempt at unity of control or organization. The heterogeneous character of an army composed of regulars, volunteers

and militia with dissimilar units, uniform and equipment was greatly emphasized by these hasty and voluminous laws.

The Confederate States had anticipated the North in its legislation by over two months. Although most of their laws had the same defects as those of the Federals, there were several decided improvements. Mr. Davis was not limited as to the number of volunteers he might accept and he was vested with the exclusive right to commission all officers above the grade of captain. So the Confederacy had not only a single chief for its war activities and a unity of organization, but an earlier start than the Union in training its forces.

At this point the North came to sense the idea that it could not simply hurl animated uniforms at opposing forces with any hope of success. The national murder at Bull Run had caused it to be borne in upon the American mind that possibly there was something in this talk about discipline, training and the soldierly character, that military fitness could not be gained in an hour, and that a lumberman cannot become a captain overnight.

July 27 1861 It was at this time that McClellan was launched on his organization of the Army of the Potomac. Called to Washington after Bull Run he was given command of mixed northern levies for the purpose of drilling, training and disciplining them so that they might work as a single machine. The incoming regiments went into camp in the vicinity of Washington and slowly settled down to the tedious business of learning self-reliance and precision.

The handicaps were colossal. Hordes of soldiers and officers roamed about their tented cities with zeal and inefficiency. They knew little of maneuver, nothing of guard and outpost duty and worse than nothing of discipline and camp sanitation. Everything had to be taught from the ground up. The trained officer was overtaxed and the untrained overworked. All the industrious ones burned the midnight candle and the others fired the flames of discord and demoralization. The soldier in loose blouses, baggy trousers, ill-fitting shoes or boots had a hard time to have a soldierly respect for himself and a harder time to be comfortable and efficient.

His musket was old and too often useless. The Springfield

arsenal was the only service manufactory of small arms in the United States, and its output only 2,500 a month.[10] The Confederates had scooped from the arsenals of the South, thanks to Mr. Floyd, 235,000 muskets, so that they were well armed at the outset. But the Federals were so ill-provided that even flintlocks were issued. Few rifles found their way into the hands of the volunteer. The markets of Europe were scoured by Federal agents for any kind of weapon. The result was that they purchased *any kind* at a high price, and the volunteer suffered accordingly. The calibers under such improvidence were as varied as in the Revolution. Few soldiers could use each other's ammunition. Old English Enfields, German and Belgian smoothbores and American arms of many makes and sizes were distributed to the commands. Some companies had only enough good weapons for the performance of guard duty.

As for rifled cannon, none had been adopted until this time. Although Parrott and Rodman had produced the best and most acceptable types, smoothbore guns of iron and brass and of all calibers were to be found in abundance. Since the government had no foundries of its own, these larger weapons were hurriedly constructed and poorly tested. The consequence was that many burst when they were first fired. One regular field battery had three different types of arms, two 13-pounders, two 12-pounders and two 6-pounders. Throughout the service there were smoothbores varying from 6 to 48 pounders, old mortars, howitzers, and columbiads of brass, cast-iron and wrought-iron. There were Parrott rifled guns throwing 100- and 200-pound projectiles and Rodman guns up to 20 inches in diameter. In a subsequent battle 36 different kinds of balls were picked up from the ground.

There were as many kinds of uniform as arms. The impractical zouave type seemed to be the most usual. But gaudy epaulets and feathers soon gave way to the simple buttoned coat and blunted forage cap of blue. In the Confederate service, the uniform was much the same in style as for the Union, but the gray blouse was almost universally worn.

---

[10] The cost of manufacturing a rifle was $13.93 and there was but a small proportion on hand.

The soft gray felt hat and the folding collar were much in evidence.

Although the Federal militia had in many cases its own state drill, Scott's drill regulations were reprinted in three parts for immediate use. Apparently there were no changes over the regulations issued in 1835. The company drilled in 2 ranks and loaded "in twelve times." With the comparatively few weapons having percussion caps and with the breech-loaders, the motions for loading were reduced to nine and less. After the recruit had passed through the "school of the soldier" he was required to be instructed in "target firing." The records of the corporals and privates, who fired from 3 to 5 rounds per day, were kept for the purpose of dividing the soldiers into three classes: "The most excellent marksmen, the next in accuracy and the most indifferent." The largest part of the ammunition was required to be expended on the last class.

A work entitled *The United States Infantry Tactics for the Instruction of Infantry of the Line and Light Infantry, together with Bayonet Exercises,* elaborated on Scott's Regulations and gave to the infantry needed instruction in the knife and triangular bayonet.

A manual on "Heavy Artillery," as intricate as it was elaborate, showed the juvenile state of our readiness. Guns of every type, irrespective of their peculiarities, were treated of because they had to be used. There were 8-inch howitzers on 24-pounder siege carriages; 10-inch siege mortars, coehorn mortars, 10-inch seacoast mortars, 13-inch seacoast mortars, stone mortars, 8-inch seacoast howitzers on barbette carriages; 10-inch seacoast howitzers on barbette carriages; 8-inch columbiads on casemate carriages; 24-pounder howitzers on flank casemate carriages; 8-inch columbiads on columbiad carriages; and 10-inch columbiads on columbiad carriages. Nor were these all the types that were brought into play. All heavy weapons that could be scraped together had to be called into service whether or not they were appropriate. No wonder the cannoneer was required to understand the service of the piece in field artillery before taking up the heavy.

General McClellan's [11] work on *Regulations and Instructions for the Field Service of the U. S. Cavalry in Time of War* dealt with the conduct of marches and the duties of commanders of "the advanced guard, rear guard, flank guard and rear detachments." It treated at great length the subjects of outposts, patrols, videttes, pickets and main guards. Columns and wheelings of twos and fours in open order came into being with this work and added to the facility of movement of cavalry. The terms dragoon and mounted rifles now disappeared. All such mounted troops were called cavalry.

Drill regulations of the several states had individual treatments. The *Manual for Light Infantry,* by Colonel Ellsworth of the New York Zouaves, is an example. This book adapted the requirements of Hardee's *Manual* to the minie rifle. It was really an enlargement and modification of both Hardee's and Scott's regulations. Loading was done "in eight times," and practice in firing while kneeling and lying was prescribed. The sword manual was explained in minute detail.

Hardee's *Rifle and Infantry Tactics* became the regulations for the Confederates. The author prescribed loading to be done "in nine times" and gave methods for the deployment of the battalion as skirmishers. With the Maynard primer, loading was done "in eight times" and for greater rapidity "in four times." Both Hardee's and Scott's regulations caused the company to change direction by marching in file and by wheeling. Turning on a fixed pivot by fours had not yet been inaugurated for infantry.

So McClellan with mixtures of men, clothing, small arms, ammunition, cannon, sizes of regiments, equipage and regulations tried to weld the incoming irregulars into a unit. Staffs had to be trained and organized, and the whole conglomerate force to be disciplined and made capable of maneuvering in the face of the enemy. His task reminds one of Washington's situation at the opening of the Revolution. In magnitude it surpassed even the undertaking of the Father of his Country, for about 300,000 troops were now collected in the East. One regiment refused to obey McClellan's orders, but upon being

---

[11] McClellan was the originator of the McClellan saddle which is still in use.

surrounded by a force of regulars it succumbed and fell into line. On the whole, though, the army liked McClellan in spite of the severity he had to use as an organizer and disciplinarian. He had only 5,000 regulars present to help in the instruction of the raw volunteer. Besides many of their officers had been taken away to fill higher commands and perform staff duties in volunteer brigades and divisions elsewhere. A large number of the junior officers were as green as those in the volunteer regiments because the lieutenants could not be supplied by a Military Academy of less than 220 cadets. However, McClellan parceled out regular batteries to artillery regiments of volunteers and likewise distributed regular infantry and cavalry regiments among the volunteer brigades. But his trained contingent was too small to speed the instruction. Recruiting in regular regiments was so slow that by the end of the year this basic element numbered only 20,334. Further the newly created regiments such as the Sixth Cavalry and Fifth Artillery, because they were numerically larger and had one more battalion than the volunteers, were unlike the volunteer organizations. Thus McClellan had a more or less disintegrated regular personnel whose members had to adjust themselves to new arrangements for themselves while they were trying to instruct a mass of unskilled levies.

At any rate, both the main armies of the Federals and Confederates had to stop and train, while the civilian population for a year languished with the burden of war and while not one decisive stroke could be struck. The army in Virginia, though better armed and organized than the Army of the Potomac, was suffering from the victory of Bull Run. The South now feeling that the North was in full flight, fell into such lassitude that recruits could be had with the greatest difficulty. So the armies watched each other by balloons and scouts for many months until they might be prepared for something effective.

In the camps about Washington and Alexandria, the first hundred thousand were drilling, reviewing, parading, maneuvering, doing guard and picket duty, having target practice and learning to adjust and wear their clothing and accouterments. Some slept on the ground and some had cots, but as a whole they were comfortable. As the winter came on, the soldiers built wooden frames around their tents, collected stoves and learned to take care of themselves in the open. Messes in each company were gradually formed so that all soon learned how to prepare their meager fare. But they were almost to a man restless to do something, unable to understand the meaning of all this training and delay. Of course there was much sickness. Dysentery and typhoid malaria resulted from the recruit's ignorance of the proper care of himself in the field. Measles and other contagious diseases ran their rounds. Yet in this apparently passive state the northern army was actually preparing to make successes possible for later generals.

The remaining actions of the year occurred in the West, where the forces of Lyon and Sigel combated those of McCulloch and Sterling Price. On both sides the character of troops and methods of guerrilla warfare prevented effective measures at this stage of the conflict. The fact that the commander of the Federals was Fremont, who was a better explorer than general, was a preventive of good teamwork. Besides, the three-month men left General Lyon in the moment when success might have been possible. A company of regular infantry, a part of the Fourth Cavalry and two pieces of artillery were all the ballast the northern commanders in Missouri could count upon. Poorly fed, trained, and paid, the remainder fought about as they pleased.

The only action of any account was that of Wilson's Creek where General Lyon was killed after carrying out a plan that *Aug. 10 1861* should have had better results, had his troops been inclined to discipline. After surprising the Confederates in their camp, General Sigel's men fell into laxity and disorder to such an extent that they were routed. The whole southern force then turned on General Lyon. The disaster which made little or no impression upon the war, was due entirely to raw troops as at Bull Run. Four hundred and eighty-eight lives were squandered in this hotly contested battle.

The unfortunate selection of Fremont [12] as a major general by Lincoln was nowhere more evident than in his neglect of Colonel Mulligan at Lexington, Missouri. In addition to the

---

[12] Fremont had never had the basic training of a soldier.

great blunders Fremont had already committed, he failed to call together his widely scattered troops for the protection of that city. In vain did Mulligan with his 2,700 men call for reenforcements when he saw the city being encompassed by over 20,000 Confederates under Price. For eight days the little

Sept. 12–20
1861

Union force was besieged, the most lackadaisical interest or effort on the part of Fremont being displayed. Finally heat, hunger, thirst and a hot bombardment told the tale of hopelessness. Even though some of the raw men were armed solely with pistols, Mulligan fought on desperately until a portion of the "home guards" hoisted a white flag without orders and fled. The whole garrison fell into the hands of the Confederates. And another inconsequential action had taken place.

In West Virginia Floyd was operating against the Union

Aug. 26
1861

forces under Tyler. At Cross Lanes the Federals went into camp without taking any precautions by patrols or scouts, much as if they were in a peaceful country. The consequence was that Floyd fell upon them, killed a few, captured more and

Sept. 10
1861

dispersed the remainder. Then Rosecrans met Floyd at Gauley Mountain. Late in the day the Union commander undertook to attack the position, but the troops did not respond well. The columns were mishandled and repulsed. Although Floyd retired next day, no particular advantage had been gained by either side. In the retreat during the darkness of the evening, Rosecrans' new troops by shooting at each other added 30 casualties to the list.

Lee, now, being numerically stronger than the Federals in

Sept. 11
1861

West Virginia, took the offensive with his 9,000 men. His plans were well laid but too elaborate for his green command. He and Reynolds played a bold game with each other in the mountains near Elk Water as far as movement was concerned. But when it came to actual attacks Lee, on the one hand, was made timid by his knowledge of the poor quality of his troops. On the other hand, Reynolds after attacking Buffalo Hill found out from the weakness exhibited by his untrained men that it would have been better had timidity been a cautionary measure with him. The leading regiment of the Federals fled in such a decided manner at the first discharge of musketry that they disorganized and panicked the regiments in rear.

While these instructive and costly encounters were in process, McClellan was constructing defensive works, fortified lines and intrenched positions about Washington. With utmost attention to detail, he planned and built breastworks which the most unskilled recruits might hold. He organized 4 regiments into a brigade and 3 brigades into a division. The division thus consisted roughly of 10,000 infantry, a regiment of cavalry, 3 batteries of volunteer artillery and 1 battery of regular artillery. Wagons, mules, ordnance and engineer trains, signal supplies, food, clothing, tentage and a dozen other necessaries had to be assigned to the different units. The staff officers who were to control this outlay of men and material had to be selected in great quantity and be instructed in their duties. The officers as well as the privates had to be taught the rudiments of movement, fire, supply and administration. The signal corps had to be built up from nothing, because the soldiers of the Civil War were the first in this hemisphere to feel the military value of Morse's invention.

McClellan constantly inspected his ever-growing command. He complimented, encouraged, rebuked and classified his men. He placed the new regiments where they would find comrades and learn more quickly. He slowly built a sure foundation of knowledge and morale.

The Confederates at Manassas and Centreville under Beauregard were similarly training. Mr. Davis took an active part in organizing the industries of the South so as to get to the commander of the Army of Northern Virginia, men, arms, ammunition, horses, and provisions. Everything at the southern seat of government seemed to bend toward aiding the commander in the field. Although the strength of this army was inferior to that of the northern one, the Confederates were skillful in keeping their inadequacy a secret.

End of Sept. 1861

When McClellan had about completed his fortifications in the vicinity of Washington, he was embarrassed by an occurrence which did much to destroy the self-reliant spirit he had so successfully built up by his intelligence and personality. He had 7 divisions or the right bank and 4 on the left bank of the Potomac, a total force all told of about 152,000 men and 228 field pieces. Trying to find out about the position of the

Confederates, he ordered General Stone to watch them at Leesburg and to make a demonstration in order to induce them to
retreat. Making a cursory reconnaissance, Stone was led into
the false assumption that there were no Confederates in the
town. He therefore ordered Deven's brigade to cross the river
and take the enemy's camp. Accordingly that commander with

Oct. 21
1861

only 500 landed on the south side of the Potomac and marched
on Leesburg. The Confederates, however, with about 3,000
men under Evans, had warily concealed themselves in the town
until the Federals should commit themselves. Then they sallied forth and drove Deven's back to Ball's Bluff on the river
bank. There the Federals were reënforced by the regiment of
Colonel Baker,[13] a brave but inexperienced officer; 1,900
Federals, huddled in a narrow space and unprovided with
means of retreat, were caught in a trap. The untrained soldiers became demoralized. The well-handled Confederates
mowed down the cannoneers, until there were few to fire the
pieces. A final charge by the Eighth Virginia threw the already retreating Northerners into a wild panic to get across the
river. Baker and many more officers were shot down and a
number were drowned in attempting to swim the river; 223
were actually killed. Out of the 1,900, only 800 recrossed.
And another useless waste of life had thrown the Army of the
Potomac into a state of bewilderment over its leaders.

The affair caused McClellan to withdraw his divisions to the
north side of the Potomac and to make an overestimate of the
Confederate strength—again to protract the strife, the expense,
and the mortality.

McClellan by this time had been drawn in close conference
with Mr. Lincoln, to the exclusion of Scott, who was still general
in chief. Scott's sound advice was no more sought. Accordingly

Nov. 1
1861

he resigned his office and went into retirement. In his letter he
expressed the highest praises of McClellan, who became the
general in chief.

Right here should be drawn a distinction between the presidents of the two sides. Lincoln was the greatest of statesmen

---

13 A former senator and orator.

and men, but was a novice in the science of arms.[14]   Davis was
a trained soldier both in theory and practice, and had no little
experience in statecraft.   This difference between the two
heads, without aspersions on either one, may explain some of
the early catastrophes that befell the North.

The year passed out with training and organizing in the
North and South and small encounters from Missouri to Maryland.   The only action of any importance was a meeting   *Dec. 20*
engagement near Drainesville.   General McCall sent Ord's   *1861*
brigade to seize the supplies of that town.   Stuart with his
brigade in the meantime started from a point near Centreville
to get some provisions between the lines.   The two columns met
unexpectedly.   The Confederates becoming entangled in the
woods fired upon each other; and Ord, by his masterly handling
of his batteries, put them to flight with a loss to the southerners
of 43 killed.

By the beginning of the next year 200,000 Federals in win-   *Jan. 1*
ter quarters lay along the Potomac.   Halleck had about 40,000   *1862*
in Missouri and Buell about the same number in Kentucky.
Buell had replaced Sherman, because the latter had told an
inspector from Washington that it would take 60,000 men to
subdue Kentucky and 200,000 to subdue the West.   At the seat
of government Sherman was thought to be crazy.   As it turned
out, Buell was gradually given the reënforcements that Sherman had asked for, because of necessity.

When Mr. Stanton became Secretary of War, Mr. Lincoln
decided that there should be a movement of the forces.   Ac-   *Jan. 13*
cordingly there was issued the first of the series of pernicious   *1862*
"War Orders."   This one fixed a "general movement of the
land and naval forces" for February 22.   Such a conception
was full of color but absurd to any one of military experience.
McClellan realized that battle movements are dependent upon
tactical and strategical factors rather than sentimental dates.
When he proposed transferring the Army of the Potomac by
water so as to attack Richmond, the President vetoed the plan,

---

[14] It is interesting to note that Abraham Lincoln was a captain of
volunteers who turned out for the Black Hawk War in 1835 and that
Lieutenant Jefferson Davis of the regular army administered to him his
first oath of allegiance.

Jan. 31
1862
and ordered an advance on Manassas Junction. It took a whole month of argument to get any accession to McClellan's idea. In the meantime the great opportunity had passed. According to the Constitution the President was commander in chief, but the Constitution could not in a twinkling make him a trained soldier. Had he been one, he would have upheld the military maxim that it is wise for the commander who is away from the battlefield and troops to give only a general mission to the leader charged with the execution of a plan and thereafter not to heckle him.

But though McClellan was heckled, the fault was not Lincoln's. Both he and his Secretary of War were forced into a position they had not the technical knowledge to fill. Every previous Congress that had sat during peace was to blame. Those bodies had made no distinction between the duties of a political commander in chief and a trained general in chief. They had even refused to give the latter a standing. Nor had they provided training in the nation sufficient to overcome the wildest disorder. There was no chief of staff in the modern understanding of the term and the general in chief functioned with more fear of Washington than of Richmond. A lawyer was by law the chief of captains and a great and good statesman was by act of man suddenly metamorphosed into a general. The Constitution had made it the duty of the lawmakers to raise and support armies, nor did it even hint that those servants of the public weal were to begin to act only after war was long upon us. Those Congresses had failed in the interspaces of peace to give the country physical stamina and direction. The blood of the first two years of the Civil War lies upon them as much as if they had ordered the execution of brave men.

Where the trained officers were far from the seat of the government and therefore less open to its interference, campaigns ran more quickly and smoothly. Grant under the orders of Halleck in the west advanced from Cairo on the center of the Confederate western line of operation. His movement was audacious and unhampered by his own higher command, so that
Feb. 8, 16
1862
he was enabled to capture Forts Henry and Donelson, the key to the Confederate center. As a consequence the Confederates had to withdraw from Missouri, Kentucky and a large part of

Tennessee. This was really the first consequential action since
Fort Sumter had been fired on a year before, and the first real
victory for the Federals.

On the other hand, back along the Potomac "Little Mac,"
as he was affectionately called by his soldiers, was having a
hard time to get started on his peninsular campaign. Another *March 8 1862*
war order stipulated that a force from the Army of the
Potomac, sufficient to make Washington secure, should be left
there and that the Potomac from Washington to the Chesapeake should be freed from the enemy's batteries before McClellan's main force should be transferred to its new base. Without
consulting McClellan, Lincoln also directed that his army
should be organized into four corps and named the commanders.
Before the batteries along the Potomac could be silenced,
McClellan had to occupy Centreville and Manassas, which the *March 10 1862*
Confederates had abandoned. Then Mr. Lincoln, listening to
advice which shook his confidence in McClellan, relieved him *March 11 1862*
as general in chief, but did not appoint a successor. Although
McClellan was retained as commander of the Army of the
Potomac and the Eastern Department, his prestige was de-
stroyed at the beginning of an offensive.

At the same time, Mr. Lincoln united the commands of
Halleck, Hunter and Buell in the west as the Department of
Mississippi, and designated the troops intervening between the
Potomac and the Mississippi as the Mountain Department
under General Fremont. All these army commanders were to
report directly to the Secretary of War. It now turned out that
a President and Secretary of War without military background,
not only virtually, but actually, commanded three large armies.

If the year 1861 is that of unpreparedness, the year 1862
is that of mismanagement.

Not so in the South. While the Union was organizing as a
loose Confederacy, the Confederacy was organizing as a close
Union. The southern government wisely abandoned states'
rights for their army shortly after they had begun to fight for
states' rights as a general policy. Doing away with war regiments, voluntary enlistments and the appointing power of governors for commissioned officers, they vested the control in Mr.
Davis. They made it a duty for every able-bodied man between

18 and 35 to serve his country. They were the first to enunciate in this country a proper draft law, a thing which afterwards proved to be the greatest single stroke of America in the World War. Virginia had anticipated the Confederacy in this action, so that 30,000 from that state were early infiltrated into their main southern army against McClellan. Such enactments gave Mr. Davis the chance to appoint skilled leaders to higher command, to raise his force disproportionately over that of the North and to have a system of replacements whereby recruits would quickly gain the stamina of the older regiments.

March 1862

On the other hand, the North persisted in the volunteer system, in taking bodily regiments and brigades politically made and in having an old regiment diminished by disease, death and desertion beside a fresh regiment of double the number. Under the state system the governors and local politicians were jealous of their localities to such an extent that men from one state, county or town could not be used in organizations from another. The consequence was that some regiments at the end of the war were as low as 100 men while others had many times that number. The incoming units required a relatively longer time to train, because of the absence of any mixture of veterans. And to cap all, the higher commanders might have a brigade of 1,000 or 2,400 men. The name of a unit meant nothing.

While the South was forging ahead on concentration and unity, McClellan's command was being plucked and dispersed. Mr. Lincoln ordered Blenker's Division to the Mountain Department, thus detaching 10,000 men from the Army of the Potomac. Then, after promising to take no more, he ordered McDowell's Division at the solicitation of General Wadsworth to stay in front of Washington, and finally forbade McClellan to use General Wool's force of 10,000 at Fortress Monroe, an action which prevented the use of that post as a base.

March 31 1862

The Secretary of War then issued a general order which further scattered the forces under General McClellan's control. The portion of Virginia and Maryland, lying between the Mountain Department and the Blue Ridge, constituted the Department of the Shenandoah under General Banks; and that part of Virginia. between the Blue Ridge and the Fredericks-

April 3 1862

burg and Richmond Railroad, constituted the Department of
the Rappahannock under General McDowell. The territory of
Virginia and Maryland was now separated into five independent departments, to the detriment of unity, control and
strength of the main army that was already launched on an
offensive against the enemy's principal force.

The Army of the Potomac, now committed to a campaign,
had been so hampered by the central government that it was
necessary for its leader to spend more anxiety on convincing the
powers at home than on engaging the enemy. In spite of all
his discouragements McClellan transported in twenty days his *March 17 to April 6 1862*
entire force to the shores of the Peninsula; 58,000 out of a
possible 109,000 were all he could collect and put in motion
when he promptly advanced on Yorktown through the mud and *April 4 1862*
swamps. Then came the well-known actions which pushed back
the Confederates: the siege of Yorktown (April 5–May 4),
Williamsburg (May 5), West Point (May 7), Hanover Court
House (May 27), and Seven Pines (May 31, June 1).

During this time other Federal troops to almost 300,000
were scattered as follows: Department of the Rappahannock,
41,000; Department of the Shenandoah, 6,000; Mountain Department, 15,000; Fortress Monroe, 10,000; General Thomas
Sherman in South Carolina, 13,000; Army of the Ohio,
95,000; Department of the Missouri, 80,000; and at the
National Capitol, 30,000. Such a distribution was not only a
deprivation of force sadly needed by McClellan, who was fighting the principal battles, but was an invitation for defeat in
detail.

Meanwhile in the west Albert Sidney Johnston was marching with his army, which had been increased by the draft,
toward Grant at Pittsburg Landing in the hope of meeting him *April 6 1862*
before Buell could join him. Surprising the Federals at
Shiloh, Johnston threw them back from their own camps. But
the struggle was so hot that at the end of the day neither side
could advance. Johnston, the general so successful against the
Mormons, was at this stage killed. Beauregard, who succeeded
him, ordered the fight to cease. The delay was sufficient for
Buell's troops to arrive and help drive the Confederates back *April 7 1862*
the next day. Thus, while the troops in the West, far away

from Washington, were being concentrated for a decisive struggle, McClellan's forces were dispersed.

April 16
1862
Wounds and sickness by this time had shown Congress, among other things, that there had to be more organized care of the disabled. Legislation made sound provisions for a medical department that was to have signal benefit during the war. A surgeon-general with rank of brigadier general was to be in charge of the department. Associated with him were an assistant surgeon-general and a medical inspector general who were each to have the rank, pay and emoluments of a colonel of cavalry. Also 10 surgeons, 10 assistant surgeons, 20 medical cadets and as many hospital stewards as deemed necessary by the surgeon-general were added to the service.

Jackson shortly thereafter began his valley campaign along the Shenandoah. The forces of the Federals separated by over 250 miles, and hampered by voluminous orders and suggestions from chiefs distant from the troops were an easy prey to Jackson working on interior lines. He first defeated Schenck and
May 8
1862
Milroy at McDowell, West Virginia. Then he speedily marched toward Luray where he found that Ewell had been ordered away from his command by Lee. But as soon as he
May 25
1862
could make known to Lee that he needed Ewell, the order was immediately countermanded. Jackson was thus quickly enabled to attack Banks at Winchester and drive him across the
May 29
1862
Potomac. Appearing before Harper's Ferry he brought fear and excitement to the powers at Washington. Moving between the forces of Shields and Fremont, who were not in communication with each other, he retraced his steps and repulsed the
June 7
1862
superior forces of Fremont at Cross Keys. Then he turned on Shields and drove him from Port Republic back toward Swift
June 9
1862
Run Gap. Thus having rid the Shenandoah of peril to the South he was at liberty to join Lee at Richmond and swell the Confederate army opposed to McClellan. With a force never above 20,000, Jackson had paralyzed Banks and Fremont, had caused fright in the Union Capitol and had been enabled to reënforce Lee, while 200,000 misapplied Federal troops lay in a semicircle about him. During this time he had received but one order—one mission from Lee: that he should attack Banks and drive him across the Potomac. On the other hand, the

orders, letters and telegrams, first counseling one thing and then another, from Mr. Stanton and Mr. Lincoln, pursued Banks so fast that he, like other commanders along this disjointed line, was in a maze of conjecture.

One result of this campaign was to see the Federal Mountain and Shenandoah Departments united into the Army of *June 26 1862* Virginia under Pope. The other was the reënforcement of the Confederates under Lee not only by Jackson but by 37,000 other troops from the Carolinas and Georgia. Lee, therefore, took the offensive in the Seven Days' Battles of Mechanicsville, Gaines Mills, Savage Station, White Oaks Swamp and Malvern Hill. Though he was severely repulsed at Malvern Hill and lost more than McClellan, he had released himself from the siege and was enabled to compel the Federals to retreat to the James River. Had McClellan not been deprived of troops for the main issue, there is no telling but that the war might have ended here, and several hundred thousand lives have been saved.

As it was, the separated units of the Union were powerless to do otherwise than reorganize and try again. The forces were scattered under eight independent commanders over a distance of about 700 miles. While Lee was moving north on a straight line, Burnside was withdrawing his forces from South Carolina to Fortress Monroe, McClellan was preparing to retire from the Peninsula, Grant was reorganizing in West Tennessee, and Buell was rebuilding the Memphis and Charleston Railroad. Halleck was then ordered to Washington where he was made general in chief. No successor being named for *July 11 1862* his vacancy in the Department of the Tennessee, Grant, Sherman and Rosecrans operated independently.

While Lee was advancing northward as the aggressor against greatly superior numbers and the distributed Federals were trying to collect themselves under the fidgeting of Halleck, legislation buried itself in bounty laws and other matters. One hundred dollars bounty, one fourth of which was to be paid *July 22 1862* upon enlistment, was given to every recruit. The President was authorized to appoint as many as 40 major generals and 200 brigadier generals. Three arsenals were to be built at *July 11 1862* Columbus, Ohio; Indianapolis, Indiana; and Rock Island,

July 17
1862

Illinois. Persons of African descent were allowed to be enlisted to any number the President saw fit. And officers, after they had been borne upon the rolls of the *Army Register* for 45 years or after they became 62 years of age, might retire from active service. However, the President could give them such active duty as they could perform, in which case they were to receive full pay.

Thus while the Confederacy was economically enforcing the draft, we find the Federal government spending $7,500,000 for recruits. Although the Union felt it necessary to take over the telegraph lines, it balked on commandeering the manhood.

Aug. 9
1862

Jackson, in the van of Lee's column, struck Banks at Cedar Mountain. After a good stand by the Federals, the Confed-

Aug. 29, 30
1862

erate force was compelled to retire across the Rapidan. Then Pope's army met Lee's at Bull Run, where the Federal troops were again beaten and again compelled to retire to Washington. The flight of the Union forces was almost as disgraceful and rapid as at the first Bull Run the year before. The road was filled with fleeing men. Straggling reached its climax; 7,000 skulkers were arrested by the Sixth Corps in half an hour. There were with Pope's army no more than 500 cavalrymen fit for duty all told, and 1 corps was without its artillery. Although the Union force was superior in numbers, the acts of its various generals lacked that simplicity and cohesion which comes of experience in working together. Pope, Porter, Hooker, and McDowell, with forces suddenly brought from everywhere, had had no chance to work harmoniously as a team, whereas Lee, Jackson, Longstreet, Hill and Early had become an understanding unity of parts.

Sept. 8
1862

Nothing now stood in the way of Lee, so that he crossed the Potomac and advanced to Frederick, Maryland.

In the West, Bragg's army had been recruited to 50,000 by the draft. Taking the offensive against the Federals who were losing their one-year draft men and whose commands were not

Aug. 24
1862

in a high state of morale, he crossed the Tennessee River above Chattanooga, marched around Buell, captured 2,100 men at Mumfordsville and returned to Frankfort, Kentucky. There he was joined by Kirby Smith's corps, which had defeated Nelson at Richmond, Kentucky. By this move Bragg had gained many recruits in Kentucky and Tennessee and many supplies and prisoners.

Such action was especially made possible because the Federal army of the Mississippi, which had been collected with great pains, had been split. The reason for such division was the desire on the part of the "advisers" in Washington to take Chattanooga. An army of 100,000 men had been so broken up that neither of its parts could reënforce the other. By such faulty disposition the smaller southern force was not fearful of meeting either fraction.

In the east, the fallacy and ineffectiveness found in thus scattering commands brought the army returned from the Peninsula and Pope's army together. They were both ordered to fall back on Washington. McClellan had to begin to reclaim his united Army of the Potomac from the setbacks of fatal dispersions. The teamwork that had been so skillfully wrought in a united army the year before had been set at naught by the absence of divisions and brigades in separate fields. McClellan's work had in great measure to be done over again. Cheers *Sept. 2 1862* throughout the army greeted his appearance to the assembled command. Spirits rose and again the army of the Potomac freshened its hopes.

But the President urged immediate action while General Halleck counseled caution. It was a pity Mr. Lincoln's good judgment had to be tarnished by his advisers. The bugbear of leaving many troops at the capital caught McClellan again between two fires. On the one hand, he was to divide his force and, on the other, attack. In this state he was to beat an enemy whose force and whereabouts were undetermined. His demoralized army had to be reorganized and rejuvenated on the eve of a vital contest. When the captured order, telling of Lee's advance, revealed 5 Confederate divisions on one side of the Potomac and 4 on the other, McClellan's opportunity was blocked by dismal orders from Washington, which made him *Sept. 16 1862* keep one foot of his command near the capital. Then Harper's Ferry ignominiously capitulated because of raw troops and their inglorious commander. Lee could now unite his forces. Nevertheless, McClellan, moving onward, defeated him *Sept. 16, 17* at Antietam and caused him to retire south across the Potomac. *1862*

This victory McClellan accomplished in spite of the fact that many of his troops had been only two weeks in the service, that 71,000 men fit for duty had to be chained to Washington and that he was at first able to attack Lee with only 2 divisions. With the slowness of some of his commanders, particularly Burnside, with the limited knowledge of Lee's strength, with the losses of nearly 20,000 men, with the poor discipline of junior officers and soldiers who were not yet over their demoralization from the defeats of the two Bull Runs, he was scarcely in a position to follow up his victory. Whether it required a month to make certain that this command would not do as the previous ones had done—spend itself in barrenness, chagrin and death—is at least conjectural.

While McClellan was then trying to reorganize his army which was in almost as sad need of discipline and supplies as at the beginning, the army in the west was again active. Buell [15] *Oct. 8 1862* pushed the Confederates back at Perryville, Kentucky, after a bloody battle. *Oct. 30 1862* Grant, who had been assigned the command of the Department of the Tennessee, began the Vicksburg campaign. *Nov. 24 1862* Several weeks afterward the Army of the Tennessee gained the important victory of Corinth.

Oct. 26 1862 McClellan, meanwhile, as soon as he could make a pontoon bridge at Berlin, and had put his army again in some sort of *Nov. 2 1862* shape, started the crossing into Virginia. When he had his main corps safely across, he made plans for striking Culpepper Court House and defeating Longstreet before Jackson could come to the rescue.

At this time McClellan was progressing as rapidly as any *Nov. 7 1862* one could expect. But one night while Burnside and he were discussing the situation in McClellan's tent, a messenger from the President arrived bearing a brief order. When McClellan had read it he simply remarked to Burnside, "You command the army." Political influences had been at work. Here at the outset of a campaign which had received approval, the Army of the Potomac had to swap horses in midstream. Burnside was as much shocked as McClellan, who was ordered to repair to Trenton, New Jersey, and await further orders. Thus

---

[15] Buell had been relieved by Rosecrans and the name of the Army of the Ohio had been changed to that of the Cumberland (October 3, 4, 1862).

McClellan passed out of the Civil War. It is a curious fact that Lee, who had suffered defeat at Antietam, was backed, aided and encouraged without heckling by Mr. Davis, whereas McClellan, who had won a victory, was practically discarded entirely by the administration. The resentment within the northern army was keen, and its spirits accordingly went down.

Burnside, in getting hold of the new reins, found it no light task to move. Changing McClellan's plans of organization, learning the new situation and carrying on the dampening correspondence with Washington, delayed the Army of the Potomac several weeks. Thus a fine opportunity for ending the war was lost through interference by those who were far from the scene of activities.

Finally, after reorganizing his army into 3 grand divisions of 2 corps each, and after waiting for some time for pontoons, the commander of the Army of the Potomac found himself in the vicinity of Falmouth across the Rappahannock from Fredericksburg. While Burnside was trying to stretch a bridge across the river, Lee was collecting all his forces on the other side and growing stronger each day. It was a long time before the pontoons were set in order. Finally, in the face of strong defenses thrown up by Lee's entire army, Burnside sent his army across and attacked. But, though the troops were brave to the utmost, and the slaughter was tremendous, the heights of Fredericksburg could not be carried. Under the pressure from the Federal capital, Burnside felt it necessary to keep up the offensive at any cost. Though the daring Hooker implored him not to make a fresh attack, Burnside was obdurate. Only more slaughter, defeat and the retreat back across the river resulted. *Nov. 19 1862* *Dec. 13 1862*

The night after this awful repulse was as bitter for the Army of the Potomac as any force has ever experienced. The frigid cold, the useless loss, the rightful resentment over their mishandling had sunk the soldiers into the utmost gloom. Desertions and absenteeism sprang up almost as in the Revolution. Confidence in Burnside was lost. The men had not been paid for six months. Food and clothing in the midst of winter were lacking. Many at home soon sent packages containing civilian clothing to the men, and the winter sun of the *Dec. 13, 14 1862* second year of the war went down on fruitless, haphazard endeavors of the Union and on a disintegrating, dispirited army.

Dec. 31
1862
Only the passive victory of Murfreesborough lent any alleviation to the situation. Rosecrans on being attacked at that town had repulsed the Confederates, who finally withdrew.

Congress did not at once do much more for this situation than did the Continental Congress during the dark hours of the Revolution. The central government continued to be the play-
Jan. 6
1863
thing of the war governors. An act allowing 2 assistant surgeons to a cavalry regiment and regulating the size of a troop or company, was followed by an authorization for the Governor
Feb. 7
1863
of Kentucky to raise a force of 20,000 for twelve months. A
Feb. 9
1863
commissary general of subsistence was created. Another measure secured the pay, bounty and pensions for the men of
Feb. 16
1863
the Department of Missouri. Then came an addition of 30 major generals and 70 brigadier generals to the service in
March 2
1863
which it was wisely stipulated that they be taken from "those who have been conspicuous for gallant or meritorious conduct
March 3
1863
in line of duty." The topographical engineers were abolished as a separate corps and consolidated with the corps of engineers, and 19 officers were added to the ordnance. An officer below field rank had to pass, under a board of three seniors, an examination of proficiency before he could be promoted. The bounty had been so extravagantly abused that a provision of law had to prescribe that a soldier on leaving the service in advance of his termination of enlistment must have a discharge certificate for disability before he could receive the bonus. Then for the first time in our history a signal corps was recognized by law, although its parts had been necessarily organized before. It had grown up under the exigencies of war in three phases of work: the aerial telegraph, the field telegraph and the permanent electric telegraph, the last of which the government had taken over in 1861. Now these three were consolidated into a separate bureau. Then came the best and greatest military legislation of the war on the part of the Union. A draft law made every able-bodied citizen between 20 and 45 years of age liable for military service at the call of the President. But the good effect of this act was lessened by the provision for substitution. A man could be permanently exempt

from the draft by the payment of $300 or by furnishing a sub-
stitute.   The law also held a contradiction when it offered
bounties to men who were so plainly told that it was their duty
to serve the nation.

At this late date of the war it was found that the tactics   *1863*
were not uniform or adequate.   Accordingly, *Casey's Infantry
Tactics* was ordered by the Secretary of War to be followed by
regulars, volunteers and militia alike.   Its three volumes
brought a combination of the best of Scott's and Hardee's works
up to date and made certain advances in accordance with the
best usage in Europe.   It was especially thought necessary in
this work

"to fix the formation to that in two ranks; to increase the
rapidity of the gait; to increase the intervals between the
battalions and brigades; to make, in the evolutions, the brigade
the tactical unit; to hold the troops, when in maneuver in
presence of the enemy, in closer order and well in hand; and,
as a general rule, to insist upon deployment upon the heads of
columns, as the safest and most rapid means of forming line of
battle."

The direct step, 28 inches in length, was made at the rate
of 90 to a minute; the double quick step, 33 inches in length,
was made at the rate of 165 to the minute.   Loading was done
in "eight or nine times" according to the primer used.   In
firing at will, loading was done in "four times."   Loading
while standing or lying down was prescribed.   For a company
to march by the flank, each man faced in the proper direction
and formed fours in column by means of the rear rank stepping
over and obliquing into the intervals between the front rank
files.   The method of deploying and marching skirmishers was
delineated at length.   Although there was no school for the
regiment, there was an extensive one for the battalion.   The
evolutions of the brigade were covered in the third volume.

Although the volunteer uniform had by this time come to
consist generally of the short blue coat with lay-down collar,
the blunted forage cap and lighter blue trousers, the regular
had his long coat and campaign hat turned up on each side.

Both wore waist belts for their cartridge boxes, but in addition the regular soldier had a strap over the left shoulder in much the same manner as the Sam Browne belt is now worn.

In the army of the Potomac Burnside's position had become embarrassing. Some of his higher officers had let Mr. Lincoln know of the dissatisfaction in all ranks and of the danger of the new offensive on which Burnside was launched. But Mr. Lincoln, instead of relieving the army's commander or of silencing his critics, took a middle course—a compromise political course. He sent word to Burnside, as the general was setting his machinery in motion, that he should not renew the campaign without consulting the President. Burnside immediately tendered his resignation, which was not accepted.

While these difficulties were besetting the Union, the absence of politics in the Richmond government had made Lee's army superior to anything in the United States for discipline and cohesion.

Middle of Jan., 1863

Burnside, having made a new plan of campaign, asked the President to approve it or to accept his resignation. Authorized

Jan. 21, 22 1863

to carry out his plan, he set to work with avidity, but a heavy rainy season coming on blocked his efforts at crossing the Rappahannock. Then Burnside, unable to bear the criticism against him, asked the President to dismiss Hooker, Brooks, Cochrane and Newton and to take away the commands of Generals Franklin, Smith, Sturgis, Ferrero and Colonel Taylor.

Jan. 25 1863

The President then relieved him of the command of the Army of the Potomac and put Hooker in his place.

The army sorely needed reorganization and morale; 2,922 officers and 81,964 men were absent from it either with or without leave. The political connivings of the states to get men home to vote or to be taken care of in the state hospitals, had robbed the forces at the front of a great number. In addition, nearly 23,000 men, whose nine-month and two-year enlistments would expire in May, had to be used before that time or there would be merely a shadow of an army to oppose the Confederate solidarity. Hooker, therefore, doing away with the grand divisions created by Burnside, began to speed his preparations for the spring.

In the West, at the same time, Grant was preparing in spite

of the high water in the Mississippi, to cross over toward Vicksburg. Assembling and preparing his army he had begun to exhibit the skill of fighting things out on his own line. But it must be remembered he was far from Washington.

Almost simultaneously the two northern armies struck. Hooker crossed two small rivers while Grant crossed one large one. Hooker having marched 45 miles in three days, estab- *April 30* lished himself before Chancellorsville, while Grant with 20,000 men cut loose from his base and placed himself in the enemy's country on the eastern bank of the Mississippi.

Hooker, having sent away his cavalry on a raid and having his forces divided and his flank in the air was attacked by Lee at Chancellorsville. Though "Stonewall" Jackson was killed, this bloody battle was a victory for the South. Hooker had to retire northward.

While the Union army was recovering from this setback, Grant, along the Mississippi, was forging ahead toward Vicksburg. After having taken Port Gibson and Grand Gulf, he was joined by Sherman with 13,000 men. Driving back a Confeder- *May 7 1863* ate force from Raymond, Grant then caused Johnston to evacu- *May 14 1863* ate Jackson. Beating Pemberton at Champion's Hill and Black River Ridge, he began the offensive against Vicksburg. When *May 18 1863* two assaults proved that the town could not be taken by storm, he settled down to a regular siege.

Meanwhile Lee, having made up his mind to invade Pennsylvania, tried to maneuver Hooker out of position behind the Rappahannock. Masked by Stuart's cavalry, Lee started up the Shenandoah valley. When Hooker tried to place himself so as to defeat Lee's forces in detail, he was stopped by the Secretary of War and Halleck, who were disposed to keep Hooker from commanding in another battle. But strangely they let him still keep command of the forces. Thereafter Hooker almost kept pace with Lee by paralleling the southern leader on his eastern flank. Not long after Lee crossed the Potomac at Shepherdstown and Williamsport, Hooker crossed it toward Frederick. Lee then proceeded toward Cashtown, Pennsylvania, eight miles west of Gettysburg.

Meantime Hooker sought permission to cross the Blue Ridge in Lee's rear. When his request was refused, he resigned

June 27
1863
his command. The resignation was accepted. Meade, who wanted Reynolds to have the command of the Army of the Potomac, was given that post. Again the councilors in Washington changed leaders at the beginning of an offensive.

Meade pushed on to meet Lee in Pennsylvania. Although the commanders of each side did not desire then to bring on a *July 1*
1863 battle, Longstreet and Reynolds became so entangled at Gettysburg that they induced a general engagement. The three days' fighting, so well known in American history, resulted after *July 4*
1863 Pickett's charge in the defeat of the southern army. On the same day Vicksburg capitulated and Grant marched into the city. These simultaneous blows sounded the death knell of the Confederacy.

Most of the soldiers on both sides could now be said to be trained. There were fewer such on the Federal side, because not so many men had remained continuously with the colors. The following statement of conditions after Gettysburg would scarcely reveal an over amount of discipline:

"Among twenty-four thousand loaded muskets picked up at random on the field of battle, one-fourth only were properly loaded; twelve thousand contained each a double charge, and the other fourth from three to ten charges; in some there were six balls to a single charge of powder; others contained six cartridges, one on the top of the other without having been opened; a few more, twenty-three complete charges regularly inserted; and finally, in the barrel of a single musket there were found confusedly jumbled together twenty-two balls, sixty-two buck-shot, with a proportionate quantity of powder."

But the fury of this battle was unprecedented. Even if the men were frenzied it must be said that both attacker and defender generally kept their faces toward the enemy under fire.

However, depletion in the ranks from many causes required the utmost effort at recruiting in the North. The draft law, with its loopholes, was not proving successful. The call for 100,000 militia for three months, which Mr. Lincoln had made in the middle of June, produced 16,361 men. The draft brought only 35,782, of whom at least 26,000 were substitutes.

The opposition to conscription took hold of the copperhead and the Unionist alike. All sorts of means of evasion were resorted to. In New York City, when the drafting was begun, the antagonism was unconcealed. Two days later a great riot broke out which threw the metropolis in terror. Negroes were hanged and at least a thousand casualties occurred. Finally, 10,000 troops had to be used in putting a quietus on the outbreak. In other cities, such as Boston, lesser outrages were committed. Finally when the people saw that they had to submit, the hatred of conscription was not openly displayed. Among other ills, the bounty jumper sprang into being. Having enlisted and obtained his bonus, the recruit would desert, reënlist and obtain more money. Had the North used a draft act when patriotism was on the high tide at the beginning of the war, it is quite probable that some of these evils might have been avoided. But one good result of conscription was the spur it gave to volunteering. *July 11 1863* *July 13 1863*

Lee, who was not pursued by the main northern army, moved back to the Potomac. There he was followed by Meade. For the remainder of the year the two eastern antagonists maneuvered in Virginia but produced nothing decisive.

Grant, the victor of Vicksburg, asked to carry on a campaign to Mobile, which would then possibly have accomplished what Sherman later had to do with so much pains. Halleck not only vetoed his plans, but took away from him most of his troops in order to relieve Rosecrans at Chattanooga. But before this reënforcement could be given, Rosecrans was defeated by Bragg at Chickamauga and practically placed in a state of siege at Chattanooga. *Last half of Aug. and early Sept. 1863* *Sept. 19, 20 1863*

Grant, having been called from Mobile to take command of the newly created Military Division of the Mississippi, went north to Cairo. Thence he proceeded toward Chattanooga. *Oct. 10 1863* *Oct. 16 1863*

In the meantime, Mr. Lincoln called for 300,000 volunteers for three years. Though he issued the call, he knew that the draft for these troops would have to be deferred until the Enrollment Act could be revised. Consequently the actual collection of these forces had to be put off until Congress could meet. Thus the North was more than two years behind the South in the efficiency of gaining reënforcements. *Oct. 17 1863*

Oct. 23
1863
When Grant arrived at Chattanooga he began to concentrate his armies; Sherman, Thomas and Hooker brought their
Nov. 24, 25
1863
troops to join him. At Lookout Mountain, Chattanooga and Missionary Ridge, Grant assaulted Bragg's fortified positions and drove the enemy out. Then Sheridan completed the success by pursuing and capturing many prisoners. Grant immediately started for Knoxville, where Burnside was being held
Dec. 4
1863
in check. His coming forced Longstreet to raise the siege. All the main armies of both sides were now in winter quarters.

When the Federal Congress met, instead of setting to work at once to modify the draft law so as to make it effective, an
Dec. 23
1863
appropriation of $23,000,000 was made for the payment of bounties and advance pay. Still at this late date in the war, the Federal government was persisting in wasting its resources because of state influences rather than exerting its authority in the equable enforcement of military service. It was necessary to get reliable men as recruiting agents. Measures to prevent fraud by these enrolling officers and by bounty brokers, were looked upon by the states as "vexatious obstacles." By such an attitude the nothern states, mainly to avoid having their men drafted, resorted to the payment of bounties many times in excess of those paid by the Federal government. Millions
Feb. 24
1864
were wasted in this way. Finally Congress amended the Enrollment Act by giving the President power to call for such number of men as the "public exigencies may require," to proportion his call on any locality to the number of males liable to military duty and to exempt only those who were physically and mentally unfit in addition to those who had served two years honorably in the war. A fine of $5,000 or five years' imprisonment was imposed for resistance to the draft.

The six-month and three-year men were now about to depart
Feb.
1864
from the service. Mr. Lincoln had to make a call for 200,000 in addition to his 300,000 in October, 1863. Of this 500,000, only a little over 300,000 responded.

While the Union was slowly swinging into line on the draft, a marked advance was made in the control of the army. Grant
March 12
1864
was called to Washington, given a commission as lieutenant general and placed in supreme command of the armies of the United States. The political mismanagement of the forces was

ended. A trained soldier took the control of military operations. Three years of war had taught the Union that skilled military men should run armies just as much as educated doctors should manage hospitals. Three years of war had created on both sides veteran soldiers who were the equals of any army of any time. The sad feature, to those who know that armies can be well trained during peace, is that nothing can ever make up for the tens of thousands of lives cast away in diseased camps and on gory battlefields. From now on in this war, the veteran is going to make every engagement decisive, and the Civil War might be said to begin in 1863.

Since the government of the Republic had forced the actual responsibility for the running of its armies on an untrained leader, it was a fortune for the North that the office was filled by so large a soul and so keen a mind as Lincoln's. In a comparatively short time he had sensed his own incapacity, the futility of changing his commanders and the instability of the notions of his advisers, especially the "Aulic Council." For some time he had divined in that sharp, straight reason, so peculiarly his own, that he must fasten on a single man and leave him to his simple purpose. It is almost unbelievable that through the barbed wire of a dozen daily contradictory hints, advices, warnings, propositions and meddlesome propaganda propelled by politicians and mushroom soldiers alike, his vision cut surely forward over a well-surveyed line. He solved his problem long before he could find the man who would put the solution into action. His supreme honesty had declared that he himself was not the man to lead armies. His exceptional judgment had no waste motion. His head was steady and uncluttered and his heart was true and clean. When he found Grant, he acted quickly in the rebound of a great conception. And by this move the North came out of the shadow.

Grant immediately made plans to assemble all the scattered forces into two main armies. Sherman, who was given the command of the Military Division of the Mississippi, was to move from Chattanooga upon Johnston's army, while Meade with the Army of the Potomac was to advance on Lee and Richmond. Grant accompanied the eastern forces. In addition, he made Sheridan the cavalry leader and placed under him most

of the assembled cavalry, which up to this time had been unable
to cope with Stuart on account of its disjointed organization.

March 14
April 23
1864
Mr. Lincoln, meanwhile, called out 200,000 more men for
three years and 85,000 militia for one hundred days.

While Meade crossed the Rapidan, Sherman started from
May 4
1864
Chattanooga. Meade met Ewell at Wilderness Tavern in a
hard-fought contest and finally forced Lee to fall back within
May 7
1864
his entrenchments. While the Army of the Potomac was
May 13–16
1864
maneuvering and fighting for position near Spottsylvania
Court House, Sherman was driving Johnson back at Resaca
south of Chattanooga. Then, the drawn battle of Spottsylvania
May 21
1864
caused Grant to transfer the eastern army to the North Anna
River.

May 25, 26
1864
There Meade's army fought furiously while Sherman's
forces defeated Johnston again at New Hope Church. While
May 27
1864
Grant was maneuvering toward Hanover Court House to turn
Lee's flank, Sherman was repulsed at Kenesaw Mountain. But
the superior numbers and resources of the Union now collected
en masse were slowly telling. Since both sides to the contest
were veteran soldiers, it remained for the one with the larger
man power and resources to wear down the smaller one.

June 1
1864
While Johnston was retreating across the Chattahoochee
before Sherman, Grant began the battle of Cold Harbor. Two
June 3
1864
days later the battle was renewed with fierce fighting but no
progress. Then Grant, finding that his attempts to oust the
July 15
1864
Confederates from their fortified lines were not worth the losses
he was sustaining, moved to Petersburg, where he attacked.
July 17, 18
1864
His continued heavy assaults only drove the Confederates further into their fortified lines. After this contraction Grant sat
July 19
1864
down to a regular siege so as to coop up Lee and his army
within Richmond and Petersburg.

During these movements, legislation, though tardy, came
May 20
1864
forward with some very wise provisions. A regiment of volunteer engineers for the Army of the Cumberland were author-
June 15
1864
ized to be enlisted for three years or during the war, and to be
officered by appointees of the President. All colored men were
allowed the same emoluments upon enlistment as others in the
service. Enlistments for the regular army might be made for
July 4
1864
three years during the Rebellion. An amendment to the En-

rollment Act allowed the President to call out any number of volunteers for one, two or three years with bounties of $100, $200, and $300 respectively.

A call for 500,000 volunteers made by the President *July 18* *1864* brought out 384,882 more men.

While Grant had been drawing his lines closely about Lee, Early along the Shenandoah had attempted to draw Grant off by threatening Washington. Crossing the Potomac at Shep- *July 5, 6* *1864* herdstown, he moved against Washington. At Monocacy he defeated General Lew Wallace. But after having given the *July 22* *1864* capital "a terrible fright" he retired toward Strasburg.

Hood, having been replaced by Johnston in the vicinity of *July 20, 22* *28, 1864* Atlanta, attacked Sherman several times but was finally repulsed, so that he had to withdraw inside his entrenchments.

Early in Virginia attacked and defeated Crook at Kernstown, crossed the Potomac again into Maryland, burned the town of Chambersburg, Pennsylvania, and levied contributions upon other towns. Then Sheridan was placed in command of *Aug. 7* *1864* the Middle Military Division. Near Harper's Ferry he began collecting and organizing his forces to the number of 43,000. *Aug. 10* *1864*

Sherman, in the meantime, being unable to dislodge Hood from Atlanta by direct methods made a diversion towards Jonesboro about 26 miles south of the city. Hood then gave up *Sept. 2* *1864* the capital of Georgia, which was promptly occupied by Sherman.

Sheridan, after some maneuvering against Early, finally *Sept. 19* *1864* won a victory at Winchester. Then following the Confederates, who were inferior numerically, he inflicted a second defeat at Fisher's Hill.

Hood, after having left Atlanta, commenced to threaten *Oct. 1* *1864* Sherman's line of communications by moving back up the route toward Chattanooga. Crossing the Chattahoochee, Hood advanced toward Dallas and then to Resaca, where Sherman had had his first victory over Johnston.

Sheridan in the meantime was putting a quietus on Early, who had started to rout the Federals at Cedar Creek. Sheridan, coming upon the scene from Winchester, turned the morale of the troops and gained such an overwhelming victory that *Oct. 19* *1864* Early could not afterwards take the offensive. The Shenandoah Valley was now cleared of Confederates. They could not use it as a base nor as an avenue for raids against the Federals. Sheridan went into winter quarters at Kernstown and Early at Staunton.

Sherman by the threat of Hood, who had destroyed some railway near Dalton, was compelled to detach Thomas to Nashville and Schofield to Knoxville, Tennessee, in order to protect his long line of supplies. Hood's march had been so swift that Sherman could not catch up with him. But when Hood marched across the mountains toward the Tennessee River, Sherman perceived his design. The Federal leader then caused Schofield to take 2 corps to Nashville so as to have the largest possible force collected under Thomas.

*Nov. 4
1864*

Sherman then assembled 60,000 men in Atlanta. Feeling that Thomas could take care of Hood and knowing that he himself must get a new base if he was to join Grant, he selected Savannah. Then began his famous march to the sea for 300 miles. When he arrived before Savannah, he invested the city.

*Nov. 15
1864*

*Dec. 10
1864*

*Nov. 30
1864*

In the meantime Hood, although he had received a check when he met Schofield, pushed on toward Nashville. There he invested the city. But Thomas, who had coolly awaited him, sallied forth from his intrenchments, attacked him and destroyed his army in the sleet and ice of a very cold battle.

*Dec. 2
1864*

*Dec. 15
1864*

*Dec. 22
1864*

Finally Sherman was able to overcome the resistance of Savannah, which city he entered.

Mr. Lincoln had meanwhile issued a call for 300,000 more men whose services were desired for from one to three years. Only a little over 200,000 responded, because the quotas of some localities were already full. However, the necessity for more troops seemed to have passed. In slightly more than a year the President had called out over a million and a half with the result of obtaining 1,249,709.

The winter for the troops around Richmond was exceedingly severe. Although Grant's forces suffered, Lee's tattered and hungry regiments were in a state of torture because of the siege and the dwindling resources of the Southern States. Desertion among the Confederates was thus materially increased.

*Feb. 1
1865*

Sherman, after completing his preparations at his new base

in Savannah, started his march northward in order to effect his junction with Grant. Johnston, who had been restored to the command of the remnants of the Confederate army in the Carolinas, could not join Lee because he had not the means of transportation. He could only await Sherman, who proceeded *March 7 1865* to cross into North Carolina near Fayetteville.

While these events were in progress, Congress indulged in very minor legislation for the army. The main four acts gave *March 3 1865* a chief of staff to the lieutenant general, allowed the payment of bounties to relatives of deceased soldiers, as in the previous extravagant wars, and caused the President to issue a proclamation that deserters returning within sixty days would be pardoned on condition that they would serve out with their organizations their original enlistments. In case a deserter failed to take advantage of this provision he was debarred from citizenship.

Many northern regiments, without means of replacements, were now so reduced that they were mere skeletons of their former selves. Instead of making a provision for the assignment of new recruits, the lawmakers still further lessened these organizations by taking away those officers who were in excess.

Lee, by this time, felt that something desperate had to be done. He attacked Fort Stedman on the Union right only to *March 25 1865* have his assault fail. Then Sheridan, who had destroyed or captured most of Early's force at Waynesboro, made the Virginia Central Railroad and the James River Canal useless. Meanwhile, Grant had to suspend his counterattack on Lee on *March 29 1865* account of rains. Lee took advantage of the delay by turning like a tiger upon Warren and Sheridan. But when Sheridan was promptly reënforced, he won the battle of Five Forks. *April 1 1865* Grant at the same time bombarded Lee's whole line and assaulted the Richmond entrenchments with success. It was then *April 2 1865* that Lee withdrew from both Richmond and Petersburg. Grant, occupying both cities, started in pursuit. Guns, wagons, *Night April 2, 3 1865* and prisoners were taken. Sheridan cut off Ewell and captured his command. But even in this hopeless retreat Lee held off Humphreys at Farmville. The Confederates having left Rich- *April 7 1865* mond with only one ration were now in a state of physical weakness. Supplies failed them. Hundreds of men dropped and died of exhaustion. Thousands let their muskets fall because they could not carry them further. The anguish of these men can scarcely be appreciated to-day except by those who actually experienced those sufferings or similar ones in the World War. When Grant sent a flag of truce to Lee suggesting the "hopelessness of further resistance," the indomitable Confederate leader who had "put out of action more than three" Federals for every man of his own army, replied by asking for *April 8 1865* terms. Then while Lee's troops continued their retreat unmolested except for rear guard actions, the two leaders continued to communicate with one another. Finally, just as Sheridan was driving Lee's advance guard from Appomattox Station and Gordon's remnants were being detained by Ord *April 9 1865* and Griffin, Lee was sending his flag of truce asking for suspension of hostilities. That very day a conference between the two commanders at the McLean house put an end to the struggle in Virginia and Lee capitulated with the honors of war.

It remained then only for Johnston to surrender to Sherman *April 26 April 20 May 26 1865* near Raleigh, for Cobb to surrender to Wilson near Macon and for Kirby Smith to surrender to Canby across the Mississippi and we can close our eyes upon the war of the Confederacy.

The South had organized early. It had taken the utmost advantage of every trained soldier among its adherents. It had quickly concentrated in main armies. It had made the soldier feel at the outset that he was part of a big unit with many other soldiers to help him. It had placed recruits beside old soldiers and had given confidence to the men in ranks. Its government had clung to its leaders in the face of defeat and had not worried them. It had built up morale at every turn.

The North, on the other hand, had displayed the haste and overconfidence of ignorance. Its primary organization was demoralization. It did not seem to know enough to make use of all the skilled soldiers it had. It allowed the uniformed citizen to gain the idea in his first actions that he was alone and that every Confederate weapon was leveled at him. Its administration had pushed excellent leaders into untenable positions and promptly relieved them when they failed. It had by its ignorance of military conduct and by fatal dispersions

robbed an army of brave souls of the power it deserved.   The
result was an inordinate loss of life and public treasure.

The war was dragged out for four years, because training in
sufficient force and direction had not been kept alive in the
fifties.   Dribblings of untrained levies came to the front as
late as '64.   Bounties as high as $400 per man depleted the
treasury.   The expiration of short enlistments in the midst of
campaign left commanders in the field without an instrument
or pushed them hurriedly into actions where life was wasted.
Disease and desertion under these conditions were beyond reason.   The recruit on arrival in the field ate, marched, slept, and
accoutered himself improperly.   His ignorance of hygiene
made a loss by sickness of 4.7 per thousand in the first year of
the war.   Where 25 men would be wounded 100 more would
be sick.   Such loss could largely have been prevented by knowledge and practice during peace.   Desertion, too, was easy,
where discipline was lax and the confidence in leaders had been
vitiated; 199,105 men deserted on the Union side alone.

It is a curious thing that we Americans, who are noted for
our foresight in business and economics, are almost stupid in
applying prevention to possible national perils.

CHAPTER IX

THE ARMY'S DARK AGES

(1865–1880)

AFTER the curtain falls on the Civil War our view is likely to be riveted on crowds of worn soldiers longingly hurrying homeward, hastily flinging aside muskets, fervidly grasping pruning hooks and feverishly pursuing reconstruction. The tragedy of blood gives place to the social drama. The fighting man plows his fields at the very base of the volcano that has been spouting fire with so much fury. The soldier becomes the civilian, the country becomes complacent and the need for arms is no more.

Such a retrospect would be beautiful, if true. It seems too bad to spoil the illusion by calling attention to conflicts that were snapping their jaws at the very stability of our nation. The Fenians were disrupting Canada and ready to spread their strife across the border. The Indians, more confident than ever because of the withdrawal of the army for the war, were banded together in large bodies and bringing murder and destruction to over half the area of the present United States. The southern states had to be put under military protection until they could resuscitate their control under the coming difficult elections. And Mexico was held by Napoleon, who had made the Archduke Maximilian emperor during the preoccupation of the United States in civil strife. Across the Rio Grande the new government, insecure against the attacks of its republican opponents, was inimical to the interests of the United States and ready to receive with open arms the irreconcilables of the Confederacy.

The situation in Mexico was then thought to be so perilous, and the new empire so much in league with the Confederacy

that General Grant ordered General Sheridan, the new com- *May 17 1865*
mander of the Department of the Mississippi, westward. The
degree of alarm felt at this time is shown by the fact that
Sheridan was not allowed to remain for the grand review in
Washington, where naturally he wished to march with his *May 23, 24 1865*
troops and take his leave of them.

Arriving in Texas, Sheridan caused one column of cavalry
under Custer to go to Houston and another under Merritt to *May, June 1865*
go to San Antonio. Not satisfied with this display of force, he
had one division of the Thirteenth Corps occupy Galveston and
another Brazos Santiago. Then he ordered the Fourth Corps
to Victoria and San Antonio and most of the Twenty-fifth
Corps to Brownsville. Such a large army gave pause to the
Mexican Empire, principally because Sheridan's divisions were
made up of tried veteran soldiers. There was nothing in
quality or quantity across the Rio Grande that could stop these
disciplined men, and Maximilian knew as much. Sheridan,
giving aid to the Republican element both by his moral in.
fluence and by furnishing arms, did not make the emperor's
position more tenable.

Though this threatening empire was set up at our very
doors, it was not the greatest menace to our peace. By the end
of 1862 all of the regulars had been recalled from the west in
order to lend their weight to the absorbing struggle of the
Union. The Indians, unchecked, had organized their smaller
tribes into large forces and made the country west of the Mississippi a scene of massacre and rapine. The work of the army
between 1848 and 1861 had been practically undone, so far as
safety in the great west was concerned. Though the settlers
banded together and protected themselves as best they could,
the strong and subtle savage would conserve his strength and
surprise too often small settlements. He grew so bold that he
penetrated Minnesota by the end of 1862. By that time he had
killed no less than 644 unoffending whites. General Sibley
undertook to punish the tribes of the Great Sioux Nation that
had been the author of these depredations. After taking 500
of them prisoners, he was compelled to cease operations by the
coming of winter. The following spring General Pope organized two columns, one under Sibley and the other under Sully.

Sibley went west from St. Paul while Sully set out from the state of Missouri. The former was to drive the Indians back, while the latter should cut off their retreat. Sibley with his 2,000 men drove the Indians before him, but they were a stubborn enemy. Twice they surprised him and were finally enabled to cross the Missouri River near Apple Creek with the loss of only a few warriors, their tents and provisions. Sully, in the meantime, had been delayed. Though the Indians had crossed the river, he still determined to attack them. By careful work he finally surprised them at White Stone Hill where he dispersed them.

Although these and similar actions of the volunteers were momentarily successful, they were indecisive and the west was in no wise safe. It is true that 2 companies of Kansas volunteers repulsed an attack of the Ute Indians at Fort Halleck in Idaho and that Kit Carson a year later (1864) dispersed with 400 men the Navahos in New Mexico. But the Civil War was of so much import by comparison that the savage could only be slapped at now and then, while he, with growing confidence, reddened his tomahawk and glutted his lust in the quivering flesh of the white.

After the Civil War was over, it was difficult to get the volunteers to act against the Indians. They felt they should go home, because the time and purpose for which they had been called out had passed. Already the mustering out of 1,034,064 volunteers and militia had begun and the regular army was way below strength. General Connor struck a blow along the Powder River when his small force conducted four pitched battles against the Cheyennes, Sioux and Arapahoes and killed several hundred Indians. But the expedition became mutinous. Supplies did not arrive and about 300 of his volunteers deserted him.

Active campaigns against the western tribes could scarcely be conducted with success under such circumstances. The Indian had become powerful and confident. He believed the withdrawal of troops was an indication of the white man's cowardice and inferiority. It was small wonder that the Blackfeet ran wild in Montana, especially through the Gallatin Valley, that the Cheyennes in force were operating along the

Summer 1863

May 20 1865

Sept. 1865

Platte and the Arkansas, the Mescalores were leaving their
reservation and going on the warpath, and the Apaches in New Mexico were showing signs of activity. The white men at their little settlements were ambushed, killed, mutilated and scalped, the women ravished and the children and supplies carried into the tepees of the savages. And so went on the outrages in the west while the government was swiftly dispersing its masses of trained volunteers and slowly organizing its few and scattered regulars.

Equally distressing was the situation in the former Confederate States. About 19,000 Union soldiers were distributed through 134 posts in the erstwhile Confederacy. They were sent there to support the "carpetbagger" and to uphold the stringent laws of a severe Congress. They had to give aid in enforcing, oftentimes, measures in which they did not believe or with which they had no sympathy.

"The terrible oppression of the Southern people embodied in those acts of Congress," writes General Schofield, "has hardly been appreciated by even the most enlightened and conservative people of the North. Only those who actually suffered the baneful effects of the unrestrained working of those laws can ever realize their full enormity."

Although generals in command of the military districts of the South [1] did their best to carry out the laws with kindness, sympathy and justice, they could do little when they were forced to exclude from office all who had given "aid or comfort" to the secession movement; when those who whipped negroes had to be punished; when the black man had to be used as a witness in court and was allowed to vote; and when judges, juries or district attorneys had to be prodded and have their cases at times taken to military tribunals. Riots, too, had to be suppressed, but usually only a show of force caused the prevention of any great amount of bloodshed.

In the North, many Fenians had emigrated after the War

---

[1] The military organization comprehended 19 military departments, controlled by 5 military divisions. Division commanders were Major Generals Meade, Sherman, Sheridan, Thomas, and Halleck.

to Ireland in the hope of gaining freedom from England. The movement was similar in some respects to that made by the Irish after the World War. Many prominent individuals in America were sympathetic to the extent of giving large amounts

1865

of money and many arms to further the rebellion. Such acts were embarrassing to the United States government in its diplomatic relations with England. John O'Neill even prepared an expedition within our borders for the purpose of invading Canada. And the Federal government was powerless, with the dissolution of its war army and its meager regular units, to prevent the threatening activity of the American agitators.

If we take into account the Alabama Claims against England, we find the United States, at the end of the Civil War, completely surrounded with hostility.

The trained veterans of a long war were rapidly disappear-

*Oct. 1
1865*

ing. By fall 800,963 had been mustered out. The regular army was far below strength, because its recruitment had been unable to compete with the large bounty and the short enlistment of the volunteers. Out of the 448 [2] companies, authorized by law, only 295 stood organized at the cessation of hostilities. This weakness was slightly offset, however, by the fact that throughout the year some valuable veteran soldiers, who were discharged from the volunteers, joined the regular army.

Even so, there was a great dearth of rank and file for the permanent forces. How could it be otherwise when the pay of a private for fighting Indians under awful hardship and in lonely places was the enormous sum of $14.87½ per month? [3] The difference between the pay of a private and corporal was $2, scarcely enough to pay the wash bill. When ambition and even decency were taken away by the government from the recruit, it is not to be marveled at that too great a proportion

---

[2] The existing organization of the regular army consisted of 6 regiments of cavalry, 12 companies each (large enough for cavalry); 5 regiments of artillery, 12 companies; 10 regiments of infantry (old), 10 companies; and 9 regiments of infantry (new), of 24 companies each—divided into battalions of 8 companies—giving 1 colonel, 1 lieutenant colonel and 3 majors to a regiment. The only difference in field officers between old and new regiments was that the new had one more major.

[3] Nominal pay was $16 per month, but $1 was deducted till end of enlistment and 12½ cents for Soldiers' Home.

of the offscourings of the community went west to make up the companies' quotas. The untrustworthy material had to be transformed by the officers into capable and faithful soldiers, or life and property might easily slip away.

The work of distributing over the precarious fronts, the regular army and volunteers, when the former were being reorganized and the latter dissolved, was not any simple matter. General Grant cut the Gordian knot by having the regulars spread out over the country as soon as their units could be sufficiently assembled. The Third Artillery was scattered among the coast forts of the northeast from Fort Sullivan, Eastport, Maine, to Fort Adams, Newport, Rhode Island; the First Artillery from Fort Trumbull, New London, Conn., to Sandy Hook, N. J.; the Fourth Artillery from Fort Delaware, Delaware, to the city of Washington; the Fifth Artillery from Fortress Monroe, Virginia, to Dry Tortugas, Florida; and the Second Artillery from Canada to Mexico on the Pacific coast. The Second Cavalry joined General Sherman in the Division of the Mississippi and the Sixth Cavalry General Sheridan on the Mexican border. The 12 companies of the Fifth Cavalry were equally split between the Middle Department, Department of Washington and the Division of the Tennessee. The Fourth Infantry was scattered among the northern forts of Brady, Wayne, Niagara, Ontario, Madison Barracks and Rouses Point as a protection against the Fenians. The Third, Tenth and Eighteenth Infantry joined General Sherman at St. Louis for distribution over the west. The Second Infantry went to Newport Barracks, Kentucky. The Seventeenth and part of the Fourteenth were at Hart's Island, held in readiness *Oct. 18 1865* for emergencies. Other regular regiments were in process of reorganization near Washington, with Sheridan in Texas or scattered through the southern states.

Altogether, our land forces in the latter part of this year were in a most jumbled state. The volunteers in the south and *Fall 1865* west were restless and unruly, now that the big fight was over. One northern regiment had been disarmed at San Antonio, Texas, for mutiny. Brevet major generals and brigadier generals in the volunteers had to a great extent been discharged, and those regulars who had been attached to the state troops were back with their regiments and were serving in minor capacities as field and company officers, or sometimes in the mediocrity of a lieutenancy. Regiments and battalions of United States troops were more scattered than ever, because the army was too small to take care of all the nation's troubles, especially since the volunteers were going out so rapidly. By the end of the year about 900,000 of the war troops had been discharged. More work was thus saddled on the regular and less pay given him in return.[4]

1865

However, by the end of the year, the army had accomplished much in spite of its handicaps. General Sheridan, though forbidden by the State Department to take an active part against Maximilian, had marched his troops, reviewed them and obtained large supplies and much ammunition. The emperor's party was so convinced that this excellent United States army was going to swoop down on Mexico that it withdrew its forces far to the interior from the northern boundaries. The republican side could then gain many adherents and have scope in which to work.

Much had been done to conciliate the red man who had been mistreated by the Indian agents. In too many cases theft and broken promises on their part had made the work of the army difficult. There was a well-ordered attempt on the part of the officers in command in the west to understand the Indian's viewpoint, and to make peace with as many of them as would abide by law and order in return for good treatment and food. When, however, the civilian representatives of our government made profit by delivering poor food and carelessly overturned previous agreements, the Indian lost faith in all white men and looked suspiciously upon treaties. In spite of these conditions, Colonel Leavenworth and Brevet Brigadier General Sanborn

Latter part Aug., 1865

made peace with many of the Apaches, Kiowas and Comanches south of the Arkansas. The agreement was characteristically signed by such gentlemen as Little Mountain, Lone Wolf, Heap of Bears, Bear-Runs-Over-a-Man and Raw Hide Blanket.

Although the volunteers were going out as fast as it was possible to let them go with safety to the country, they held a

---

[4] The pay of a colonel was $211 per month; of a lieutenant colonel, $187; of a major, $163.

grievance against the government. They claimed that the United States had violated its contract with them in keeping them longer than their enlistment called for. Such attitude dispatched their departure into civil life. By the middle of the year, 1,001,670 had been discharged. *June 30 1866*

Restlessness in the regular service was manifested by desertion of enlisted men, mainly because the proper type could not be obtained under the pay and subsistence offered. Officers, too, who suddenly found themselves acting as captains, after they had been general officers through four years of supreme test, could hardly be at the height of their zeal and energy. The sop of brevet rank, which amounted only to a matter of title and uniform, did not help much.[5]

In spite of these handicaps the army went forward in bettering social and technical conditions. In the South situations of the gravest tension were overcome. In the West, peace with many Indian tribes was made, and on the Texas border the demonstrations by Sheridan were making the Mexican throne tremble. When O'Neill led some American forces into Canada in the furtherance of the Fenian movement, General Meade, in command of the Military District of the Atlantic, stationed soldiers of his forces so as to prevent further trouble. Although the wires were cut into Canada no further outbreaks were allowed. *June 1 1866*

Within the army, the Freedman's Bureau, which operated to give succor to the destitute, was governed wisely by Brigadier General O. O. Howard. In one year alone over 15,000 freedmen and their children attended schools established by the Bureau. *1866*

That the army was not asleep along technical lines is testified to by the improvements adopted. One of the two authorized mounted batteries in each artillery regiment was armed with four Napoleon and four 3-inch rifled Rodman guns. Boards of officers were preparing to adopt a standard breechloading weapon for the service. Another arsenal was allowed by Congress at Rock Island, Illinois. A manual for *June 27 1866*

---

[5] Grant was made a full general by Congress and Sherman a lieutenant general. Besides, the latter was given $30,000 for a residence by the people of St. Louis.

military gymnastics appeared, which showed the soldier certain direct methods of keeping fit.

Against the tides of discord that were rising around the nation, the army was striving to be a barrier. But again its attempts were pulverized by the splitting of its units throughout the vast territory of the United States.[6] Since the opening of the year, Congress could not help but see that a larger regular force was necessary if peace was to be assured. But the members haggled from that time until summer. The Senate had seen fit to give a substantial strength to the army and had passed such a measure as early as March, but the House, as always, demurred. Finally, late in July, over a year after Appomattox, the law, which prescribed a certain amount of protection against the country's many enemies, went into effect.

July 13 1866

The legislation started off with a provision in the appropriation act for detailing as Superintendent of the Military Academy an officer of any arm of the service. Heretofore that position had been confined to officers of the engineer corps. This change heralded the transition of West Point from a purely scientific school to one of general education and basic training for all branches of the service.

July 28 1866

Fifteen days later the President signed an act making the army consist of 10 regiments of cavalry, 5 of artillery and 45 of infantry. The companies of cavalry and artillery numbered 12 to a regiment and those of infantry, 10. The authorized strength of the line branches totaled 630 companies. Though the cavalry was increased by 4 regiments, the infantry was not actually brought up from 20 to 45 regiments as the face of the bill would infer. It must be remembered that there were in the service 10 infantry regiments of 10 companies each and 9 of 24 companies each. Congress, instead of making the smaller units into larger ones, did exactly the reverse. It robbed the larger ones in order to make the whole 45 into smaller ones of 10 companies each. In this way it added only 134 companies, a number only half as great as 25 regiments of 24 companies each would require. By such process the standard size of the regiment which had been found most efficient and economical in

---

[6] Six regiments of cavalry, 5 of artillery, 19 of infantry.

the Civil War was decadently abandoned. When it is considered, also, that 4 of the 45 regiments were to be composed of men who had been wounded in the service—the Veteran Reserve Corps—the activity of these units was further diminished, since this new corps could be held only for garrison duty. Besides, 2 of the cavalry and 4 of infantry regiments were to be composed of colored men.[7]

The company strength was made elastic. The President could have a minimum of 50 privates or a maximum of 100 for infantry and cavalry, and a maximum of 122 for artillery. As a start, the commander in chief made a standard of 64 privates for all companies except 10 batteries[8] of light artillery which were to have 122 each. Thus the paper strength of the army after the act amounted to 54,302 rank and file.[9]

Lieutenants had to be selected from volunteers. Grades above lieutenancies had to be filled in equal numbers from the volunteers and the regular army and by men who had had at least two years' service during the war and who had in that service been "distinguished for capacity and good conduct in the field." Regular officers who had held volunteer commissions were not to be considered volunteers but regulars under the above selection. Commissions had to be distributed over the states and territories in proportion to the number of troops furnished by them. With all these strings to selection, it was difficult to cull proper officers.

Several miscellaneous items might be noted in this legislation. A force of 1,000 Indian scouts could be enlisted in the west for aid in operations. The enlistment period for regular cavalry was for five years and for artillery and infantry, three. The general officers consisted of 1 general, 1 lieutenant general,

---

[7] The beginning of the Ninth and Tenth Cavalry and later the Twenty-fourth and Twenty-fifth Infantry.

[8] Two for each artillery regiment.

[9] "Each regiment of infantry provided for by this act shall have 1 colonel, 1 lieutenant colonel, 1 major, 1 adjutant, 1 regimental quartermaster, 1 sergeant major, 1 quartermaster sergeant, 1 commissary sergeant, 1 hospital steward, 2 principal musicians, and 10 companies; and the adjutant, quartermaster and commissary shall hereafter be extra lieutenants selected from the first and second lieutenants of the regiment. Each company shall have 1 captain, 1 first lieutenant and 1 second lieutenant, 1 first sergeant, 1 quartermaster sergeant, 4 sergeants, 8 corporals, 2 artificers, 2 musicians, 1 wagoner." (Extract from Act.)

5 major generals and 10 brigadier generals. Staff departments had in addition an adjutant general, judge-advocate general, quartermaster-general, commissary general, surgeon-general, paymaster-general, chief of engineers,[10] and chief of ordnance, all with pay and emoluments of a brigadier general. The inspector-general's department and the signal corps were apparently left out of this calculation, because 4 colonels with rank and pay of colonels of cavalry headed the former bureau and 1 colonel the latter.

All officers, before being commissioned, were required to pass an examination before a board of five officers from the arm of the service in which the applicant was to serve.

Sutlers at military posts were abolished and the subsistence department was to furnish officers and enlisted men with "such articles" at cost as the inspector generals designated.

Twenty officers from the army could be detailed to act as president, superintendent or professors at colleges and schools in order to further the knowledge of military science. Schools at posts for the basic education of enlisted men were also authorized.

Any officer who had served in the Confederacy in any capacity was debarred from being commissioned in the regular army. Federal officers could be retired with their full rank held at the time they received their wounds or disability. Brevet rank entitled an officer to wear the insignia and bear the title of his highest brevet grade, but debarred him from the corresponding "command, pay and emolument."

Such was the act which was to provide for the common defense. Although it was framed in weighty words, its limiting

---

[10] "SEC. 19. *And be it further enacted*, That the Corps of Engineers shall consist of one chief of engineers, with the rank, pay and emoluments of a brigadier-general; six colonels, twelve lieutenant colonels, twenty-four majors, thirty captains, and twenty-six first and ten second lieutenants, who shall have the pay and emoluments now provided by law for officers of the Engineer Corps.

"SEC. 20. *And be it further enacted*, That the five companies of engineer soldiers and the sergeant major and quartermaster sergeant heretofore prescribed by law shall constitute a battalion of engineers, to be officered by officers of a suitable rank detailed from the Corps of Engineers; and the officers of engineers, acting respectively as adjutant and quartermaster of this battalion, shall be entitled to the pay and emoluments of adjutants and quartermasters of cavalry."

provisions restrained even the force authorized from stretching
out in size great enough to awe the warring tribes and factions
so as to prevent bloodshed. By this time most of the volunteers
had left the service. Since about 1,015,000 had been mustered *Aug. 1*
out, the regular force above prescribed was practically the sole *1866*
defender of the nation.

The boards for commissioning officers and the slow recruitment of proper enlisted personnel caused the actual strength *Sept. 30*
of the regular army to be only 38,540. At the end of the year *1866*
not more than 10,000 volunteers were left in the service, a great
part of them being colored.

When the staff, heavy artillery and the outgoing volunteers
are deducted, it can be seen that not more than 25,000 soldiers
fit for duty constituted the entire bulwark to be held in readiness for Mexico, to enforce law in the south, to ward off Fenian
uprisings in the north, and to hold in check the great masses
of Sioux, northern and southern Cheyennes, Assiniboines,
Piegans, Arapahoes, Kiowas, Pawnees, Miamis, Comanches,
Nez Percés, Flatheads, and many lesser tribes, which swarmed
over the country from Canada to the Rio Grande and from the
Mississippi to the Pacific.

In addition, marauders in Missouri were repeatedly com- *1866*
mitting outrages upon innocent persons, especially negroes.
The communities in that region were in a state of terror. It
was with great difficulty that troops at the direction of General Sherman were able to drive these desperadoes out of the
state.

But the great west with its constant forays of hosts of redmen was the frightful problem for the reduced army. New
strongholds had to be built and telegraph wires installed, with
death lurking behind the trees, in the sagebrush or down in the
cañon. The Indians were legion and the American defenders
corporals' guards. With hammer in one hand and gun in the
other, the soldier alternately built and fought.

Even the main forts such as Reno and Phil Kearny, in
process of construction, held but a few hundred men. At the
latter Colonel Carrington was attempting to complete the buildings and stockade, which he had begun. The small outpost of
civilization measured only 800 by 600 feet. The occupants had

several times been attacked by Indians when the wood parties would go into the forest, but almost miraculously had succeeded in beating off the savages. The soldier-builder was armed mostly with the old Springfield single loader and was quite at a disadvantage against the Indian who had been furnished by the Indian agents with modern repeaters. Once, in meeting a party of the red men, the soldiers were afraid to shoot, because their enemies were armed with revolvers and would slay them before they had time to fire again.

Dec. 21
1866

While the few at the fort were busily completing the head-quarters building and a one-company barracks, 90 men, who had started for the pine woods for more lumber, were surprised by a large body of Indians. Under Brevet Lieutenant Colonel Fetterman, 84 officers and men started out in relief. The rescue party tried to cut off the retreat of what was afterwards learned to be about 2,000 warriors. At first the fort could plainly hear the firing and by noon the rattle of musketry was quite brisk. But soon it ominously decreased in volume. Captain Ten Eyck with the remaining 76 men, all that could be collected, including teamsters and civilians, started out as a second relief about one o'clock. By the time he got to the ridge overlooking the battle ground the firing had altogether ceased and below him in the valley the only thing to be seen was a large band of whooping savages who shortly began to draw off. Not a man of the Fetterman party was left to tell the tale. To this day the manner of death of that gallant detachment remains a mystery. The bodies were found so shockingly mutilated that many could scarcely be recognized, and the details of their appearance could not be printed. Some of the dead could not be located. The body of Lieutenant Grummund, whose wife was in delicate health at the fort, was after long search found next morning. Here lay a half-completed stockade, a handful of protectors and a stricken community in the wildest part of Nebraska. That the Indians did not return to scoop the survivors was no fault of our government.

While such outrages were being committed, the populace at large was quite skeptical of making any systematic effort with sufficient troops for the police of the west. J. P. Dunn, a scholar intimately conversant with conditions then existing beyond the Mississippi, says:

"It was the era of peace—in Washington. The Indians, in the annual reports, were doing nothing but defending themselves from the encroachments of lawless whites. They were ready and willing to do anything, if they could only secure schools and churches. Mr. Bogy, the Commissioner of Indian Affairs, sat back and smiled sarcastically at reports of hostilities. The peace people were busy, working themselves into a white heat over the wrongs to the Cheyennes. The entire country looked contemptuously on the strength of the red men. What! we, who had just put down the greatest rebellion the world ever knew, to be terrified by a few half-starved Indians? Oh, no! The army was cut down to its lowest possible figure, and much of it was employed in the late insurrectionary states. Its arms were chiefly old-fashioned muzzle-loaders, notwithstanding the wonderful improvements that had been made in weapons during the war. The Indians were better armed."

However, the loss at Phil Kearny made the public at least take notice. It was shocked—quite shocked. But its efforts were spent in investigations of the officers in command rather than in an attempt at adequate protection.

But the army itself sent relief. The other troops of the Eighteenth Infantry, who marched to the beleaguered fort, had the first touch of winter campaigning. Advancing through blizzards, with the thermometer ranging from 10 to 30 degrees below zero, these men suffered from frostbite and were sometimes frozen to death. The torture that these soldiers endured without any alleviation through the endless ice and snow was indescribable, but they trudged on. Awakened from their little dog tents when it was too dark to see, reveille was a farce and breakfast in a foot of snow not much better. Often it was not possible to see more than twenty feet ahead of the little column of twos. So strained were their nerves by the constant tension that in several cases a touch or a word would result in the same reaction as shell-shock during the World War.

While the Indian was thus in full cry on the plains, and our troops there were fitfully trying to check him, the situation in Mexico was reaching its climax. The Republic there, by the backing it had received from a large veteran army of Americans, was by now in the ascendency. Early in the year the French troops were withdrawn by Napoleon's order. The monarchy was doomed, and European control of the country of the Montezumas was at an end. How had such a radical overthrow come about without a war involving the United States? When Sheridan first appeared near the Rio Grande frontier, the republican forces were worn and weak. They could see no hope of ultimate power. Now after less than two years, they came into possession of the government. The reason is contained briefly in the great trained force Sheridan displayed in Texas. All Mexico knew its potential ability. So again history records the axiom that a mere show of actual strength often makes unnecessary the sacrifice of human life.

After Napoleon's forces were gone, many of the regiments that served in this enterprise could be released for use elsewhere, especially the cavalry. The army could be organized for work primarily in the south and west. With Grant as full general, Sherman as lieutenant general, and Meade, Sheridan, Thomas, Sickles, Steele, Hancock, Hooker, Canby, Schofield, McDowell, Ord, Cooke, Pope, Howard and Terry as major and brigadier generals the troops were distributed in thirteen departments over the country.[11] All the new regiments were at least skeletonized by recruitment or by transfer from other units. Yet the posts were small and the line was thin.

The soldier's life held no great comfort. That sort of thing he rarely expected. Yet he did wish to live decently and be free from debt. It was difficult enough to have to exist in tents and shacks in isolated places, to wage an uphill fight against Indians and to suppress riots, but when the pay was inadequate, he felt himself to be unjustly treated by a government for which he was constantly ready to risk his life.[12]

At the opening of the Civil War a captain, for instance, received the equivalent of $150 per month. When the volun-

---

[11] Hooker, Canby, Schofield, Ord, Cooke, Terry, Pope, Howard, and McDowell had been reduced one grade because of shrinkage of the Army.

[12] Oddly, pay of general and lieutenant general accorded with grade.

teers came into the service, Congress, feeling that such amount was not enough for a nominal captain, raised the pay by the equivalent of $83 a month. But as soon as the volunteer went out, Congress immediately took away the $83 from the experienced captain. In the meantime prices had soared almost 100 per cent since 1861. The captain was left with his same $150 minus $5 for war tax. The reduction was relatively the same throughout all grades of the army. The consequence was that the regular could barely exist. He naturally asked himself why the volunteer needed so much more for his nourishment and comfort in the marches and battles of the Civil War than did the fighting man in the constant jeopardy and remoteness of the west.

After much urging and great arguing, the Congress, which had increased its own salaries 100 per cent since the war, *March 2* *1867* finally passed a pay bill which partially relieved the beggary of the man who bore the brunt of the nation's perils. All officers below the rank of major general received a flat increase of 33⅓ per cent; "field and other mounted officers," the same emoluments as cavalry officers of like grade; and the enlisted man for three succeeding years, only, the same pay as the volunteer at the close of the Civil War.

How little the lawmakers were interested in having an economic and adequate second line is seen in their action on a possible militia law. After having been shown by plea and example that such a thing was necessary, they went to the radical extreme of striking the word "white" out of the old law of 1792, so as to include colored soldiers. That was all. The government persisted in using a fruitless provision that was seventy-five years old, although the states in many cases had established their own National Guards.

It was during this year especially that the ex-Confederate *1867* leaders of the South did their best to establish peace, law and order in the southern states. The great generals came out openly with earnest requests for the people to abide by the law. So insistent were they in this matter that they were criticized and sometimes lampooned for their stand. One southern writer claimed that Beauregard, Longstreet and Hampton were little more than "burglars because they counseled submission to

military acts." Of course, the aim of the northern leaders was
the same as that of their former antagonists—and sometimes
classmates. It was another instance where the trained soldier
of both sides worked in his community toward cementing the
bonds of peace, while those with lesser experience in war wished
to prolong the strife.

On the plains, too, the soldier was trying to make lasting
settlements with the Indians. He encouraged friendly relations and tried to overcome all controversies by a square word
rather than a round bullet. His record will show that he preferred reason to rifles. Nevertheless, he tried to keep himself
prepared and ready for his foe, so as to show his superiority
speedily when the crisis came, to give the marauder a whole-
some respect for the American soldier, and to make the redskin
think twice before he started on the warpath. When in the
peace conferences, the Indian claimed dishonesty on the part
of the Great Father in Washington, it was sometimes embarrassing. An extract from a contemporary newspaper may
allow one to read between the lines:

*May
1867*

"For the rest, General Hancock's campaign is now ended.
His object was to make peace with tribes which would accept it,
and to make war with the rest. In the hostile part of the
expedition, little has been accomplished; but the pacific conferences with the Comanches, Arapahoes and Kiowas promise
good results. The great 'talk' with the Kiowas at Fort
Larned, Kansas, was the last, and in many respects the most
important, of the Indian conferences. The great chief of the
Kiowas, Satanta, made a fine defense of himself and his tribe
in his oration, disclaimed the desire for war, and fastened upon
the Indian agents the charge of embezzling the annuity goods.
To the latter accusation, General Hancock essayed no reply,
but referred it to Washington."

In these conferences it was hard for the officer to justify to
the Indian the wrongs he felt were taking place. At that point
he had to keep silent. It was difficult, too, to get action in
Washington, when he reported the misdeeds of other government agencies. Politics usually intervened.

While the generals were having their "peace talks," the Indian was carrying on just the same his war of extermination on the whites, whether soldier or settler. Communication between the widely separated outposts of the army was usually dangerous and fatiguing. One officer at a lonely post wrote back east the following sketch:

"We have finally succeeded in opening communication with Fort C. S. Smith, ninety miles above here on the Big Horn River. Up to three days ago we had heard nothing from them for two months, and were very anxious about them; but after repeated trials by mountaineers and miners near here to go through, we at length succeeded in sending two messengers, Sergeant Grant, of my company, and Sergeant Graham, of Company G. They started from here on foot, with snowshoes, and took to the mountains, with only ordinary clothing and six days' rations of hard bread and lard. Each night they *cached* one day's rations, and left a memorandum of what had happened to them. They finally, after much suffering and hunger, reached Fort Smith with our dispatches. They stayed two days, and were sent back with a half-breed named Boyer, each mounted, and with two pack mules. When they came to the Little Horn River, they saw where a buffalo had been killed, and moccasin tracks around it, and immediately left the road and made for the hills. When they had gone about five miles and crossed a hill they stopped, looked back and saw about fifteen Indians after them. Their horses were blown, and Sergeant Grant had to shoot his. The other two men, getting frightened, ran away from him and left him afoot. He ran toward a clump of pines, about five hundred yards distant, and while so doing, he fell into a hole in the snow, and found that he had been running on the edge of a precipice of a sheer two hundred feet fall, and had fallen on a little ledge of rocks, the entrance of which was through a hole that was covered with snow. He sat down under the cliff and waited. He had a Spencer carbine, breech-loading, and eighty rounds of ammunition, and he says he felt perfectly safe. He heard the Indians yelling about him, and soon they commenced to throw stones down the hole, which was about ninety feet deep, and just sheltered him. Then one

Indian jumped down into the hole, armed with a Henry repeating rifle. When he (the Indian) saw Sergeant Grant he dropped his gun and gave a yell, and starting back fell over the ledge, which was narrow. In a few minutes another Indian let himself down, and Grant shot him, and threw his body over the bank. This was about nine o'clock in the morning. The Indians stayed near the hole until nearly dark, when a thick fog came up and they went away. He cautiously followed them, keeping in their trail for about three miles, till they again struck the river, when he tore up his overcoat and made wrappings of it for his feet to hide the shoe nails, and went up the river on the ice. He traveled four days and on the evening of the fourth day got into the post.

"When Grant made his appearance, covered with ice, and with the Henry rifle he had captured, Graham thought it was his ghost. He is very sick in the hospital now, with pleurisy and exhaustion, resulting from his suffering and exposure."

Space prevents recording the many acts of daring and times of suffering daily connected with the life of the little forts. Glimpses, here and there, into the thickest of the fights, the wayside heroism of individuals, the straining alertness of small detachments, and the general spirit of troops anxious to make peace, but ready to fight to the last ditch, can but sparingly reveal the never-ending self-sacrifice of the soldier. What he gave to his country, he tossed off without a whimper.

Although it is natural to dwell on this phase, it must not be forgotten that the staffs back east were working toward the technical and practical advancement of military work.

The Ordnance Department was adapting and standardizing weapons from knowledge gleaned in the Civil War. All sorts of breechloading repeating rifles were tried out with the hope of getting the best arm for the service. Rodman's, Remington's, Spencer's and Roper's patents underwent test. But the hitch came when money was asked for to equip the army. Large rifled cannon had nevertheless come to stay, as well as metal carriages. The Gatling gun, firing from 80 to 100 cartridges in a minute, gave the service a rapid-fire weapon.

It was in this year that *Upton's Infantry Tactics* for *Aug. 1 1867* drill in double or single rank was adopted by the War Department. This system was the greatest single advance in exercises and maneuvers since the regulations of Steuben. Heretofore we had borrowed principally from the French when we wished to improve our systems. Brevet Major General Upton ingeniously devised, principally from his understanding of the Civil War, a set of regulations, peculiarly suitable to the American soldier. His results were obtained mainly from experience with troops. At West Point he tried out his methods with cadets and was able, in an exhibition drill given there, to take a company with no previous knowledge of his new regulations, and in an hour and a half make it go through the entire school of the company without a break.

The manual was far simpler of execution than in any previous work of the kind. The marchings were made notably more facile and precise. The secret of the new movements depended upon the wheeling by fours, which was then for the first time enunciated in our country. This practical arrangement allowed the front rank to keep its place under any conditions and obviated the facings, inversions and cumbersome turnings previously thought necessary to cause a unit to change direction. Although we now call Upton's marching unit a squad, in reality it is nothing more than his set of fours. "Fours right about," "Right forward, fours right," and similar movements for the first time came into vogue. The fixed right and left was done away with, so that commanders had liberty of action on the march and for formation in battle. The skirmishers had supports which infiltrated into the line when needed. When two ranks were not necessary, a single rank could be formed so as to lessen the growing casualties due to the range and effectiveness of advanced weapons. The main features of Upton's tactics are still in use.

While the army was thus striving to better its efficiency, it was still kept busy with the Indians over a wide region. The extent of operations was widened by the purchase of the new country of Alaska. A garrison of 250 men, consisting of a *Dec. 1867* company of artillery and a company of infantry, under General Jefferson C. Davis,[13] who had his headquarters at Sitka, attempted to police that new territory. One night a sentry on duty near the powder magazine saw a moving light in his vicinity. After challenging and receiving no answer, he fired and wounded an Indian. The chief of the tribe the next day asked General Davis for compensation for the injury. When the request was denied, the chief raised the British flag over the village. Davis then sent word that if the colors were not replaced by the United States emblem, he would open fire. The Stars and Stripes were raised the next day, but the Indians became surly and threatening for some time.

June 1868

With such a small force in the midst of so many hostilities, the army's situation was precarious. Accordingly the Second Artillery was stationed on the island of Kadiak and several companies of the Twenty-third Infantry established a post at Cook Inlet. The difficulties of transit in this remote country

July 16 1868

were unbounded. One vessel on the uncharted coast was broken up, and everything was lost but the lives of the troops. After one month of great hardship, the survivors were rescued. Nevertheless, in spite of handicaps General Davis succeeded in holding the natives in check.

While all this was going on in the extreme north, the position of the army in the southern states was changed by Congress. The former commonwealths were restored to the position

June 25 1868

they occupied before the war. The various military departments stationed there no more exercised enforcement or military control, unless called upon to do so by the civil government. The obnoxious duties of the soldier were somewhat lessened. But there were still to arise many occasions where the state governments called for force. Whenever such action was taken, destruction of life and property was prevented.

Although the soldiers were dispersed over a vast country and had diverse tasks to perform, Indian troubles were the main consideration of the army, for it was never for a minute allowed to forget them. Hardly a week passed, during those seasons of the year when Indians could operate, that the War Department did not receive some report of raiding, outraging,

---

[13] Not to be confused with Jefferson Davis, President of the Confederacy.

or murdering the ranchmen and their families. When the soldier husband left the fort to punish the redman for his misdeeds, the soldier wife fed and ministered to the homeless survivors who had taken refuge in the army's stronghold built by the army's own hands. By succor and punishment the little companies pressed civilization into the remote nooks of our great land.

But it was a little disappointing sometimes to see the fruits of gruelling labor destroyed. Often after the army had spent years in building up a fort out of the wilderness, the stronghold had to be carted away or demolished. Back in Washington it would be decided that the site of the stockade would make a good reservation for the Indians or that the government needed it for other uses. Thus was Fort Defiance, New Mexico, abandoned and moved seventy miles. Fort Reno was *Aug. 15 1868* demolished. Fort Phil Kearny, which had been built, as we have seen, through almost daily bloodshed, was similarly discarded.

During these three years succeeding the Civil War the Indian had in no wise been intimidated. The tiny forts, far from each other, could do little more than drive back the red warriors after the outrages had been committed. The Indian respected one thing only—force—and when that was not forthcoming he grew bolder and more cruel. The victory at Fort Kearny had whetted his appetite. His increasing strength allowed him to molest parts of the country the meager army could not reach. By now the whole savage west was infected with lust for the destruction of the whites. Conspicuously, the Cheyennes under Roman Nose, a physical giant, had in one month killed or captured 84 settlers in Kansas. In that sparsely settled country they practically swept that state bare and even attacked the builders of the Kansas Pacific Railroad.

Major Forsyth, of Sheridan's Staff, collected some 50 scouts in order to trail this band and locate its whereabouts. Each man's equipment consisted of a horse, saddle, bridle, haversack, canteen, blanket, knife, tin cup, Spencer repeating rifle and a heavy Colt's revolver. Four mules bore the small extra supplies and ammunition. No tents were carried.

For six days they scoured the country (they had only seven

days' rations), finally coming up with the Indians at the Arikaree River. While the little detachment was encamped there, it was awakened early one morning by the cry from the sentry, "Indians." Forsyth barely managed to keep most of the horses from being stampeded and to draw off his party to a little island in the partially dry river bed. Hundreds of savages surrounded him on all sides, firing from both banks and hemming him in. His scouts dug in and the fallen horses formed a sort of breastwork. Roman Nose charged down the river bed with several hundred warriors. Half a dozen times he came on, only to be repulsed at each assault. Once a few braves gained the island, but could not retain it. When Roman Nose splendidly leading his last charge, was killed, the attacks became weaker. But the Indians, although they did not rally any more to the offensive, hovered about. Possibly 80 warriors had been killed, while Forsyth's 51 had suffered 23 casualties, nearly 50 per cent. Forsyth himself was wounded in three places and his second in command, Beecher,[14] was dead. The little force, with such a hindrance of wounded, could not make a break for it. After harrowing trials a messenger finally made his way through to Fort Wallace. For nine days the unscathed, wounded and dead were huddled together for protection, and subsisted on putrid horseflesh and a few plums. Then the wretched and delirious survivors were rescued by troops from the fort. Such were the acts and the fate of a small party of soldiers who sallied forth into the wilds.

Aside from engagements of that character, battles and skirmishes which could have been avoided, were by mismanagement often forced on the army. The Indians were at this time managed by the Peace Commission and the Indian Department. These two independent controls seldom jibed and rarely settled a difficulty without ruction. The army had to be called in as a last resort, usually after affairs were so snarled that a fight was the only recourse. It did not help the spirit of the military man to be left to catch all the kicks and cuffs after he had been ignored in council. Many times he had a reasonable notion that his advice, if heeded, might have prevented hostilities.

---

[14] Nephew of Henry Ward Beecher.

Some 300,000 Indians now roamed the plains. To overcome the main force of these, General Sheridan had all told 1,200 cavalry and about 1,400 infantry. While the savages were moving in such quantity, he had too few troops to do the double duty of scouting and winning decisive victories. Accordingly he determined to wait until winter, when the failure of grass and the blight of cold weather would collect the redmen *Fall* in large enough bands to make it worth while assembling his *1868* troops for attack. At that time 107 people had been killed, 57 wounded, 14 women outraged and murdered, one man, four women and 24 children taken into captivity, 1,627 horses, mules and cattle stolen, 24 ranches and settlements destroyed, 111 stagecoaches attacked and 4 wagon trains annihilated. This enumeration does not include the soldiers who had fallen in many actions. In committing these atrocities, the Indians had lost only 11 killed and 1 wounded. Sheridan felt that something decisive, no matter how desperate, would have to be undertaken, if further depredations were to be hindered.

From Camp Supply in what is now Oklahoma, he started his campaign. One column, the Seventh Cavalry under Custer, *Nov. 23* was to go south while the remainder was to go northward later. *1868* Custer set out at four o'clock in the morning amidst a blinding snowstorm which sunk the thermometer to its depths. To Wolf Creek, fifteen miles distant, he had to make his way entirely by compass. Camping there in the snow with the temperature 7 degrees below zero, his little command fought the sleep that foretells death by freezing. Along the banks of this stream he continued his march until he came to the Canadian River. The *Thanksgiving* water there was not frozen enough to bear the troops so that *Day, Nov. 26* they had to break the ice and ford through the icy current. *1868* Not long afterward, one of Major Elliott's scouts reported the fresh trail of Indians. Custer left his wagons under guard and had his troopers take one day's rations of coffee and hard bread. Many of the soldiers and some of the officers were by now suffering with frostbite and snow blindness. That terrible Thanksgiving night the dinner consisted of hardtack and coffee. Here were men staving off death from cold in order to fight a hard battle with savages who showed no mercy. In the moonlight the troops continued their march by following the Indian

trail. When within a mile of one of the outlying Indian fires,
an Osage scout said he smelled smoke. Shortly afterward, by
stealthy movement through the snowdrifts, the officers could
make out a patch of black under the dim rays of the moon. It
turned out later to be the camp of Black Kettle's band of
Cheyennes formerly led by Roman Nose.

Custer gave orders to his officers, who worked quietly without their sabers, to lead their various squadrons into designated
positions surrounding the village, which could be plainly seen
to be on the banks of the Washita. When the troops had taken
their assigned positions in utmost quiet, the pain and discomfort grew more bitter than ever. Four hours until dawn had
to be spent in the intense cold of the night without so much as
a beating of the hands to ward off the cold. After the suspense
Nov. 27
1868
and suffering of a lifetime, a bugle broke the stillness just as
the dawn was beginning to show. It was the signal for the
charge. Though almost numb the horsemen grasped their
reins, mounted and were nearly upon the camp before their
presence was suspicioned by the savages. In an hour, Black
Kettle's band of 103 was no more. The squaws and children,
though some of them had used rifles with success, were taken
prisoners.

But just as Custer was about to complete the destruction of
the tepees, the valley below seemed to be alive with warriors.
It was then realized that the principal bands of Kiowas,
Arapahoes, Cheyennes, Comanches and Dog soldiers had had
their camp of about 2,000 red skins close by. The situation for
Custer was grave, almost as much so as in a more fateful battle
later. His ammunition was running low, the men were suffering extremely without their overcoats and the Indians were
coming on with a rush. Dismounting his men and forming
them in a semicircle about the camp he had taken, he awaited
the onslaught. The issue of the battle swayed back and forth
and it looked doubtful for the little handful of soldiers at this
juncture. But Major Bell, the quartermaster, having heard
the firing, drove a wagon of ammunition right through the
midst of the savages and on into his own lines. The day was
saved. Although the fighting continued during the remaining
daylight, the Indians finally withdrew.

An unknown number of Indians were killed in the fight subsequent to the taking of the village. Altogether, 53 squaws and children were captured, together with 875 ponies, 1,123 buffalo robes and skins, much powder, lead, arrows, tobacco, rifles, pistols, beef and other supplies. The Black Kettle village was burned. But Major Elliott and Captain Hamilton [15] and 19 soldiers had been killed and many were wounded.

Custer had struck a blow at the depredations of these tribes. With the loss of so much material and warriors their future activities were curtailed. But he and his command were in a delicate position as to their own safety. With all possible dispatch he made his way back to Camp Supply with such harrowing sufferings to men and animals as few commands have ever experienced.

The main tribute that Custer and his troops received for their work was a series of articles in the public press branding him as a slaughterer of the innocent.

Another detachment under Major Evans, consisting of 7 companies of the Third Cavalry, 1 company of the Thirty-seventh Infantry and a battery of mountain howitzers, left Fort *Nov. 18 1868* Bascom, New Mexico, for the punishment of the Comanche and Kiowa Indians. The troops marched the distance of 185 miles *Dec. 7 1868* down the Canadian River, where they constructed a redoubt for defense. Pushing out from there without tents, they spent *Dec. 18 1868* their Christmas eve at a dry camp near the Washita Mountains. That was a satirical holiday never to be forgotten by those soldiers. Hunger, cold and thirst conspired to rob their comfort. Indeed they were glad to exist through the night. At a cañon in these mountains, a band of Comanches was finally met who tried to defend the pass. But when one of the howitzer shells burst in their midst, they scattered over the country in every direction. Sixty lodges, containing buffalo meat, corn, meal, flour, tobacco, coffee, sugar, salt, axes, hammers, hatchets, knives, powder, lead, bullet molds, saddles, lariats, bow and arrows and some very fine rifles were taken by the troops. As a result, many of the Cheyennes, Arapahoes and Comanches came in and surrendered unconditionally and without blood-

---

[15] Grandson of Alexander Hamilton.

shed. Major Evans, when he returned to his depot, had covered in the dead of winter 400 miles in 29 days.

General Grant was now the President-elect. Though he showed conclusively in his reports that the existing forces were insufficient to cope even with the Indians, there was a general cry in the east for the reduction of the army. Grant knew that the best way to have peace in our territories was to have a force of sufficient size to establish it. Yet the public clamored for chopping expenses irrespective of results. There was a war party who strove for a quick peace by means of adequate protection and a peace party who brought on indecisive engagements by the establishment of weakness. The so-called peace party won. The army, in its already weakened state, was sliced and large fragments cast away.

The very day before Grant took the oath of office, a clause of the appropriation bill decreased the 45 regiments of infantry to 25. No new commissions, promotions or enlistments could be made until the contraction was complete. The enlistment for all troops was to be for five years.

The incoming President was saddled with a law which he knew would cost the country the lives of valuable men. In his appointment of General Schofield as Secretary of War and General Cox as Secretary of the Interior, he did as much as he could to overcome the woes that had been forced on him.

General Schofield was in a sad state of embarrassment over the army. If he waited to contract the infantry until casualties would take off the proper number of officers, the men enlisted in '66 and '67 for three years would all be gone. Many forts would have to be abandoned, to the great waste of life and property. He therefore, had to produce the shrinkage at once in order to reorganize for the immediate future. Accordingly, field officers who were to be retained were chosen in Washington; and the junior officers, in the departments. The senior in each grade was kept in the service in so far as such disposition was thought to be in the interest of efficiency. Many officers, who happened to be absent from their commands, were peremptorily cut off from the service. Excellent men of heroic record in the war and on the plains, who had a few years before been practically promised a life vocation by the government, were cast back into their communities with lost years and a sorry face before their friends. They had borne their share of suffering and hardship for their country only to have the sieve of politics hold them as dross.[16] The "Benzine Board" had the unwholesome task of sending out over 750 officers with one year's pay. The effect of this discard was to stagnate promotion for years and to make the retained soldier of gallant service feel unsafe in his position against the whims of party leaders.

Under these recurrent blows that kept striking the army during these years, officers and men may at times have grumbled, but they at no time became slack in their work. The newly organized units were sent in larger measure than before across the Mississippi.

While the regiments were plodding toward waste places across the continent, let us note for a moment a massive project of civilization for whose success the military man was responsible. The Union Pacific Railroad was completed this year, *May 10* connecting the two oceans and binding the country together. *1869* General Dodge, an army officer of Civil War fame, had been the Chief Engineer. General Sherman had aided the work in every way by personal help and by ordering troops for its protection. At vulnerable points, soldiers had constantly driven off the Indians who were especially hostile to this inroad of the white man. Their buffalo hunting ground was cut in two and their country was about to be overrun with the palefaces. As a consequence, the railroad builder had to work and fight. The gangs were mostly discharged veteran soldiers who were organized into companies and battalions and who could drop their picks and grasp their rifles in a twinkling. General Dodge, who had served under Sherman, writes:

"The organization for the construction of the Union Pacific Railway was upon a military basis, nearly every man upon it had been in the Civil War; the heads of most of the engineering parties and all chiefs of the construction forces were officers in the Civil War; the chief of the track-laying force, General

---

[16] Repeated after the World War.

Casement, had been a distinguished division commander in the Civil War, and at any moment I could call into the field a thousand men, well officered, ready to meet any crisis or any emergency."

Sheridan and Crook also more than satisfied the heavy demands of the railroad chiefs. So great was the dependence on the army itself that Oakes Ames said, "What makes me hang on is the faith of you soldiers." It is fair to state that this great bridge of progress and unification could never have been built had it not been for the army and army training.

The regimental band and 4 companies of the Twenty-first Infantry were present at the driving of the golden spike, a few miles west of Ogden, when east and west were made into one. It is said that the soldier musicians piped lustily at the exercise.

Since the army was pared down to almost laughable size, the Indian tribes underwent no setback, as the troubles of the railroad alone will show. Hundreds of settlers were being killed, and not a day passed that some company "somewhere in the west" was not called upon for rescue or control work.

Summer 1869

Because the Piegans were especially active, a battalion of 4 companies of the Second Cavalry under Major Baker was sent to Fort Ellis in Montana. Many crimes had been committed there by some of the tribes of the Blackfeet, Bloods and Piegans. Since most of the Blackfeet were in British territory, the only Indians that could be reached by the army were

Jan. 6 1870

the Bloods and Piegans. Major Baker left his post with his 4 companies and proceeded to Fort Shaw where he picked up

Jan. 19 1870

2 companies of mounted infantry. The weather was intensely cold and, to make matters worse, the marching from Fort Shaw had to be done at night on account of the necessary secrecy. For five days the troops camped in ravines in the snow, only

Jan. 23 1870

to march again through the cold night. Near the Big Bend of the Marias, they came upon the camps of Bear Chief and Red Horn consisting of 37 lodges. The attack was a complete surprise, especially since smallpox had broken out among these tribes, so that even the few precautions taken by them in winter had been overlooked. In all, 173 Indians were killed, including Red Horn. Many squaws and children were captured and 300 ponies were taken. Hastening on to Mountain Chief's camp the troops found only a deserted village, which they burned. Pressing forward into the country of the chiefs of the Bloods, Baker called upon the warriors to give up the stolen horses in their possession or receive the treatment of the Piegans. The horses were discreetly turned over and the little force made its way back to the forts. Whatever else may be said of this spirited expedition, it quieted the Piegans and the Bloods who forever thereafter ceased their pillaging of the unprotected whites. The very people in the east who made outcry against this mode of warfare, were the ones who were responsible in many cases for starving these Piegans later, because of insufficient appropriation and care.

It was at this time that the Apaches, the most subtle savages we have ever dealt with, broke out from their reservations. *1870* From their fastnesses in New Mexico and Arizona, they would sally in small groups, never in large bodies, and pounce upon their prey much as did the mountain lions, their neighbors. To stalk these human animals was impossible for a white man. General George Crook was sent to command the Department of Arizona in the hope that he could solve the problem. Never did the War Department choose a more suitable commander. How closely he followed Steuben's plan of discipline is shown by Bourke's estimate of him:

"This was the point in Crook's character which made the strongest impression upon every one coming in contact with him—his ability to learn all that his informant had to supply, without yielding in return the slightest suggestion of his own plans and purposes. He refused himself to no one, no matter how humble, but was possessed of a certain dignity which repressed any approach to undue familiarity. He was singularly averse to the least semblance of notoriety, and was as retiring as a girl. He never consulted with any one; made his own plans after the most studious deliberation, and kept them to himself with a taciturnity which at times must have been exasperating to his subordinates. Although taciturn, reticent, and secretive, moroseness formed no part of his nature, which was genial and sunny. He took great delight in conversation, especially in that wherein he did not have to join if indisposed.

"He was always interested in the career and progress of the young officers under him, and glad to listen to their plans and learn their aspirations. No man can say that in him the subaltern did not have the brightest of exemplars, since Crook was a man who never indulged in stimulant of any kind—not so much as tea or coffee—never used tobacco, was never heard to employ a profane or obscene word, and was ever and always an officer to do, and do without pomp and ceremony, all that was required of him, and much more.

"No officer could claim that he was ever ordered to do a duty when the Department commander was present, which the latter would not in person lead. No officer of the same rank, at least in our service, issued so few orders. According to his creed, officers did not need to be deviled with orders and in-structions and memoranda; all that they required was to obtain an insight into what was desired of them, and there was no better way to inculcate this than by personal example."

General Crook at once undertook to put a quietus on the lawless in his most characteristic way. Bourke again says:

"A campaign against the Apaches in their eyrie fastnesses among the rugged Sierra Madres could but be a series of de-tached fights. In fact, for many years and until the various bands of the whole tribe were finally rounded up, that was all there was to it, but it involved nearly twenty years' heartbreak-ing work, exhausting privation, bitter disappointment and the loss of many a gallant soldier, and was eventually accomplished only when our own troops, by persistent endeavor and repeated scouts, had mastered the general trend of valley, stream, and cañon, learned the location of the few water holes in the beds of the dry water courses, the rare springs in the hills, and the isolated passes through the unexplored mountain ranges, to-gether with the stern fact that a trail once discovered must never be abandoned, but doggedly hung to and searched out, hour by hour, day by day, or on very rare occasions cornered and obliged to fight to a surrender or annihilation.

"General George Crook, who was, without doubt, one of the very best and ablest Indian campaigners our Government has ever had, and at the same time one of the most absolutely just and true friends the Indian has ever known, when he was assigned to the command of the Department of Arizona adopted and put in practice a new course toward this people. First, he personally went over the country and obtained all possible knowledge of it and of the Apaches. Then, by guaranteeing their safety, he finally, after much trouble, succeeded in getting some of the leading Apache warriors to come in for a talk. His reputation as an honest and true man had reached even this people in the fastnesses of the Sierras, and finally, after much hesitation, a few of them came. He told them that their stay on the war path meant eventual extermination. That things were changing in their section of country and civilization was advancing, and would continue to do so, and set forth the advantages of peace, offered them immunity for the past, and protection for the future if they would surrender and settle down to a peaceful life. Otherwise, he must and would fight them to extermination. Furthermore, if all the bands would not accept the offer of the United States Government and come in, he would gladly offer immunity to those who would accept it, and wished them, in case the bad Indians would not give up the war path, to assist him in their capture; that there were both good and bad white men and good and bad Indians, but the good white men forced the bad ones to obey the law, and he expected that the good Indians would assist him, just as the good white men assisted the officers of the law in keeping peace and maintaining order. Runners were sent out to the various bands, and in a few months all the well-disposed Indians came in and surrendered. After a suitable length of time he put his troops in motion against the defiant bands.

"But when our troops moved against them it was with this tremendous difference: Each small command moved with eight or ten friendly Apaches, duly enrolled, clothed, equipped, and paid as United States scouts.

"In pursuit of the Indians all the soldiers divested themselves of every superfluous garment, and did not load themselves down with even a single ounce of impedimenta that they could possibly do without. In summer they were almost as naked as the savages themselves, and were sunburned to the color of mulattoes, while in place of boots and shoes they wore buckskin moccasins or rawhide sandals tied to their feet with thongs of the same material, which enabled them to follow their foes on the rocky trail at night silently, and with such sleuth-like movements that on several occasions, all undiscovered, they traced them to their very lair."

General Crook, as Sheridan had done, decided upon a winter campaign, because he believed the Apache would have to come down from his high mountains on account of the cold.

Fall 1870

The Fifth and some of the Third and First Cavalry, and Twenty-first Infantry set out late in the fall.

Against only those Indians who refused peace on any terms did Crook proceed. The progress of the troops, especially in

Winter 1870–1871

the Tonto Basin, was tedious and difficult. Through deep cañons and over alkaline deserts they marched and counter-marched as the Apache would double on his trail. In five years, one of these regiments had 97 engagements and another marched over 6,400 miles.

A happy climax of General Crook's efforts was to be ex-pected. The Apache saw the fruitlessness of trying to escape the cunning scouts of his own tribe, backed up by the power of the trained, hardy soldiers. After five years most of these Indians came into the reservations and submitted. No fewer battles and actions under such wild conditions and against such a resolute enemy have ever been recorded.

July 1 1871

While the soldier in Arizona and over the west was thus straining himself to make the wilderness safe for democracy, the Congress pleasantly set another mark against the army by re-ducing the number of major generals to 3 and brigadiers to 6.

The incongruity of such a measure is further shown by the fact that troops had still to be in the south as well as the west.

Aug. 9 1871

The New Orleans riots shortly afterward broke out. The main one occurred near the customhouse. It seems that the two fac-tions of the state were bitterly divided over the election of Governor Warmouth. Some 4,000 whites and blacks collected near that public building and became so threatening that

3 companies of infantry were sent by General Emory to the scene of the demonstration. With 2 Gatling guns this little group of 150 soldiers pushed through the infuriated mob and dispersed the throng without bloodshed. Such instances of trained troops acting as preventive medicine are so replete in our history that elaboration is unnecessary.

By the beginning of the next year the shrunken army had *1872* been completely reorganized. But it had to stretch itself far in order to cover the entire United States and Alaska. The heavy artillery naturally had to cling to the Atlantic. Only 2 light companies of each artillery regiment could be used for service elsewhere. Rarely were as many as 2 companies of any branch assembled at any one post.[17] General Sherman supervised the army from Washington. Lieutenant General Sheridan com- *Sept.* manded the Division of the Missouri. Under him were Major *1872* General Hancock, commanding the Department of Dakota, Brigadier General Pope, commanding the Department of the Missouri, Brigadier General Ord, commanding the Department of the Platte, and Brigadier General Augur, commanding the Department of Texas. Major General Meade commanded the Division of the Atlantic. Under him were Brigadier General McDowell, commanding the Department of the East, and Brigadier General Cooke, commanding the Department of the Lakes. Major General Schofield commanded the Division of the Pacific. Under him were Brigadier General Canby, commanding the Department of the Columbia and Lieutenant Colonel George Crook, commanding the Department of Arizona.

It was in this year that the full-dress helmet with its plumes *1872* and the coat with its aiguillettes were made a part of the uniform. The forage cap was of a little higher crown than the one in the Civil War. The campaign felt hat without trimmings persisted. The fatigue uniform of blue was worn in the field except where commanding officers had to make such appropriate changes as did General Crook. Brevet uniforms, while officers were on duty, had been prohibited. (July, 1870.) Only actual rank was permitted to be referred to in orders. However brevet insignia could be placed on the collar of the coat.

---

17 The Engineers consisted of one battalion distributed between Wellett's Point, New York Harbor and West Point, N. Y. (five companies).

Target practice was emphasized to a greater extent than ever before. Estimating distant drill and the construction of butts and pits were required much as they are to-day. The sliding target had not yet come into use. Wingate's *Manual of Rifle Practice* covered a course of 90 rounds for each man.

In upper California and lower Oregon a tribe of Indians called the Modocs broke into prominence mainly because of the unfair treatment by the government of these heretofore peaceable redmen. They had always been tractable and in one case had gone so far as to help voluntarily in saving a white settlement, the town of Yreka, from the flames. It seems that the government in Washington had made a treaty with these Modocs which it failed to put into force for four years. At the end of that time it refused to carry out all the provisions. Nevertheless, the Modocs continued to dwell peaceably on their reservation in upper California until the Klamaths of lower Oregon (their ancient enemies) began hectoring and bullying them, saying that they had stolen part of their reservation. The Modocs complained of their situation and asked to be moved to a small strip of land bordering on Lost River and unoccupied by any white settlers, so as to be undisturbed.

General Canby, with his well-balanced and upright character, saw the point of view of the Modocs and tried to persuade the Indian agents to grant the tribe at least the equivalent of their request. Canby had so well tried to understand the redman that by many savages he was called the "Indian's Friend." But the agents could not agree to such compliance with Indian wishes. They insisted that the Modocs be conducted to the Klamath reservation. General Canby then tried to convince the authorities that they were doing the Modocs an injustice. But the agents, who did not have to fight, were impatient and desired to use force. Finally Canby was compelled to join the troops who were then in the lava beds, whither the Modocs had gone. The Modocs by this time were thoroughly and justly enraged at the duplicity of the government. On account of annoyances of being moved hither and yon, they had many times lost their crops and other subsistence. But it was a hard matter for the troops to round them up as long as they retreated from boulder to boulder and offered no target in the pedregal, where one place

looked like another.   After a time, but too late, the authorities
in Washington decided to have a cessation of hostilities.   Peace
commissioners were appointed, but the Indians, knowing the
caliber of the appointees, would not treat with them.   Finally
General Canby, Dr. Thomas, Mr. Meacham, and Mr. Dyer
seemed to be agreeable to both parties at issue.   An overture
from Bogus Charley, the Modocs' representative, suggested a   *March 10*
meeting of the commissioners with the chiefs, all unarmed, at   *1873*
a neutral spot.   After some hesitation, in which the commissioners sensed treachery, they repaired dutifully to the place
appointed.   When they were all seated, the chiefs drew revolvers
from under their clothing and killed every one of these excellent
men.

The mishandling of this whole matter by the Indian agents
now plunged both sides into real war; 2 companies of the Fourth
Artillery, 1 company of the Twelfth Infantry and 14 friendly   *April 26*
Indians, while making a reconnaissance, were entrapped in the   *1873*
lava beds.   The recruits who had just joined, ran disgracefully.
All of the officers, noncommissioned officers and most of the old
soldiers were either killed or wounded.

General Jefferson C. Davis, who had taken General Canby's
place now put bivouacs all over the lava beds and succeeded in
running the Modocs into the open country.   Captain Jack, the
Indian's Chief, was finally captured.   When met by his pursuers
he was sitting on a log.   All he said was, "My legs have given   *June 3*
out," and then he remained silent.   *1873*

Captain Jack, Schonchin, Boston Charley and Black Jim,
were finally hanged at Fort Klamath, Oregon.   Thus the Modocs   *Oct. 3*
were forced on the warpath, hunted down and largely extermi-   *1873*
nated.   General Canby, Dr. Thomas, Meacham and Dyer were
sacrificed on the altar of mismanagement and high-handedness.
It is small wonder that Dr. Thomas' son has since contended
that the government murdered his father, because it did not
heed General Canby's plainly sound advice in the first place.
But the tragic irony of the whole affair was that after all this
terrible loss had taken place, the general's counsel was found
best to follow.   The remaining Modocs were transported to a
reservation away from the Klamaths, all they had asked in the
beginning.

1873

In spite of its difficulties, the army showed a spirit of general progress. Lieutenant Ruffner, of the engineers, explored the Ute country, which was heretofore unknown, and made a complete map of the geological and topographical features of the whereabouts of the tribes located in that region. When, shortly afterward, some miners killed a few of the Ute warriors, that powerful and intelligent tribe rose to crush the whites. It was due largely to Ruffner's informative maps that the troops were able to punish the miners and bring the Utes to terms.

1873

About this time, too, the Springfield rifle, model '69, was adopted. It was a breechloader, but for single shots. Its caliber was reduced to 45 and its muzzle velocity was 1,350 feet per second. It was a dependable weapon, but the Henry and Remington repeaters were better, and officers and men provided themselves with the latter whenever they could afford to do so. Consequently the soldier had to buy for his own and the country's defense, a weapon that the nation should have furnished him.

1874

In the next year the army's work became more and more unappreciated. The enlisted strength of the companies which had had to be expanded was cut down to make a total of 25,000. The number of general officers was reduced in proportion. Altogether about a modern brigade was left to take care of our entire country. The army with all its high-mindedness and exertions was unseen, unknown and unpopular. It was difficult for the service to get even the most mediocre recruits. Emigrants and derelicts, many of whom could scarcely read and write, were put on lonely posts, to become the expert defenders and protectors of our country.

Here and there little fusses with the Indians put some soldiers in their graves. Here and there were long marches and excruciating suffering. Here and there the little remnants worked with might and main to acquit themselves nobly. And the country seldom looked beyond the Mississippi to hear the ominous sounds of massacre and depredation that the troops were trying vainly to suppress.

Aug. 30 1874

It is seldom one hears even now of the many minor engagements then prevalent throughout the west. Five companies of the Sixth Cavalry, for instance, drove off a superior force

of Comanches and Kiowas near the Red River. Captain A. R.
Chaffee was conspicuous in leading a charge that saved defeat.
Then Lieutenant Baldwin, with 3 men, while bearing dispatches
for reënforcements, held off 125 Indians for one whole day.
His little party dug pits, kept up their fire and, although one
man was seriously wounded, made their escape in the night.

In addition to the prevalent actions in the west, the army
was called upon to keep the peace in all manner of ways. Fearing trouble in the legislature in New Orleans, President Grant
sent General Sheridan to the scene of the difficulties. Troops
were stationed about the state house when the legislature assem- *Jan. 4*
bled. The attitude of the community was grave and ominous. *1875*
General Sheridan's account is graphic.

"One Wiltz jumped on the platform, seized the speaker's
chair and gavel, and declared himself speaker. On motions
from the floor, and without ballots, he in the same way declared
other gentlemen elected secretary and sergeant-at-arms, and
having directed the latter to appoint assistants, a hundred or
more men scattered about the hall, suddenly opened their coats,
displaying badges on which was inscribed 'assistant sergeant-at-
arms,' and the minority were in possession of the legislature.
The excitement was intense; knives and pistols were drawn;
several fisticuffs occurred; the shooting was so deafening that
little could be heard.

"In all this turmoil, in which bloodshed was imminent, the
military posse behaved with great discretion. When Mr. Wiltz,
the usurping speaker of the house, called for troops to prevent
bloodshed, they were given them. When the Governor of the
State called for a posse for the same purpose and to enforce the
law, it was furnished also. Had this not been done it is my
firm belief that scenes of bloodshed would have ensued."

As little groups of soldiers were allaying troubles in the
south, so were similar detachments attempting to quell the growing Indian uprisings. So small was the army by this time that *End of year*
the little posts with their utmost energy could not stem the ris- *1875*
ing tide of Indian consolidation. Since 1869 there had been
no less than 203 actions with the redmen. The Sioux especially,

having allied themselves with the Cheyennes, formed a strong
nation of intrepid warriors. Something determined had to be
done in order to rescue the central west from the grip of these
savages, who had left their reservations. It was decided that
3 columns under Generals Gibbon, Crook and Custer were to
strike the tribes who were in the vicinity of the Big Horn near
the sources of the Powder River. Crook was the first one to
make a start. General J. J. Reynolds, in the van of the column,
with 10 troops of the Second and Third Cavalry, surprised the
March 17 1876 village of Crazy Horse. The troops, under a severe fire, were
eagerly destroying the lodges of this tribe when Reynolds for
apparently no reason suddenly decided to retreat. So unexpected was his retirement that several wounded troopers were
left to the mercy of the Indians, who followed the cavalrymen
and recovered a herd of 700 horses. The loss to Reynolds' command was 4 men killed, 6 wounded and 66 badly frostbitten
(the temperature being about 30 below zero). Crook, coming
on the scene with the infantry, behaved toward Reynolds much
as Washington did with Lee at Monmouth.

After this defeat, it was necessary to reorganize the command at Fort Fetterman, Wyoming. The new force consisted
of 10 companies of the Third, and 5 of the Second Cavalry; and
3 companies of the Ninth and 2 of the Fourth Infantry—in all
May 28 1876 about 1,200 men. Crook personally took command. The expedition started toward the villages of Crazy Horse and Sitting
May 29 1876 Bull somewhere on the Rosebud River. The country in that
vicinity was little known and the whereabouts of these chiefs
less so. When Crook neared the Tongue River he received a defiant note from Crazy Horse warning him that there would be
June 9 1876 trouble if he crossed the stream. One evening shortly after the
command had passed over the river, the Indians opened fire on
the tents of the camp. But the soldiers were not occupying
their nomadic home at that moment. Crook immediately
attacked the redskins, who fled. There was little loss on either
side, and the action was indecisive.

Crook now saw that he must get rid of his wagon train and
move with dispatch if he was to overtake his prey. Not having
June 16 1876 sufficient horses he mounted the infantry on mules. The foot
soldiers had a few riding lessons on their long-eared steeds and

the command moved off again. About 250 Crow and Shoshone
scouts now accompanied the 1,150 mounted men. The soldier
had but one blanket and no tent.

Crook knew that his movements were known to the Sioux,
so that surprise was impossible. The second day of the march, *June 17*
at eight o'clock in the morning, some 6,000 Indians charged *1876*
down upon the little body of soldiers. The fighting was hot
and furious, the cavalry in 3 columns charging at once. Charge
and countercharge seemed only to cause the Indians to spring
from the ground at each fresh assault. So fierce was the contest
and so soon did Crook's command come to find that it was fighting for its life, that Mills, who had been sent on down the cañon
to destroy the villages, had to be recalled. Colonel Guy V.
Henry, with half of his face shot off, kept to his saddle and led
his men until he fell from weakness off his horse.

There were too many Indians and too few troops. General
Crook, although he drove off the savages, had to retire to his
wagons back at Goose Creek, because he lacked ammunition and
had many wounded.

While Crook was preparing for another offensive at his
camp, Terry's command, which now combined Gibbon's and
Custer's troops, was on the move. The whole force, consisting
of the Seventh Cavalry, 4 companies of the Second Cavalry, 6
companies of the Seventh Infantry, 6 of the Twentieth Infantry,
and a battery of 3 Gatling guns, encamped on the Yellowstone *June 21*
River. Not a soul of Terry's command had an inkling that *1876*
there was abroad a force of such size as Crook had just met and
had narrowly escaped. Even had they been aware of the
strength against them, the knowledge could have made little difference. This was all the force from the little United States
Army that could be spared and it had to act.

Custer with the Seventh Cavalry was ordered to advance
down the Rosebud until he struck the headwaters of the Tongue
River. Gibbon was to go directly to the mouth of the Big
Horn so as to shut off the Indians from that direction and to
reënforce Custer. The latter started down the Rosebud as *June 22*
ordered, but when he fell upon a fresh Indian trail he followed *1876*
it instead of keeping to the course directed. Several days later *June 25*
(Sunday) Indian signs showed him to be near the camp of the *1876*

hostiles. He must have known from the Indian footprints,
which crossed his trail, that his whereabouts were known to
them. At any rate, he then ordered Benteen to move along
the bluffs on the left and Reno to move straight up the valley on
Benteen's right. When Reno discovered the Indian village, he
reported the fact to Custer who ordered him to charge it. In
the meantime Custer himself struck out along the bluffs on the
right. Reno, who had no experience in Indian fighting, but
had had a splendid record in the Civil War, delivered a faint-
hearted charge and finally retired to the bluffs to the right of
the river, where he was hemmed in on all sides by hordes of
savages. Benteen, with his column, finding nothing in his path,
received an order from Custer to come on as quickly as possible
with the ammunition packs. Not knowing where Custer was,
Benteen charged down the valley only to find Reno's command
in desperate straits. Dividing his ammunition with Reno he
helped in holding the mass of warriors there in check. For
hours this little group was huddled together on the bluffs. The
unscathed and wounded alike were parched with thirst. Much
firing could be heard about two miles further on where Custer
evidently was. Then the shots grew fainter and finally stopped.
Reno's force was promptly attacked by a large force of warriors.
Night fell with Reno's command, after making a hazardous
counterattack, settling down to strengthen and defend its posi-

*June 26
1876
June 27
1876*

tions under conditions of utter discomfort and apprehension.
The next day the Indians renewed their attack, but a splendid
charge by Benteen, followed by Reno, drove them back. By
night the savages had packed up their tepees and left the valley.
The next day Terry and Gibbon came upon the scene to the
rescue. A detachment was sent to find Custer's command. On
a ridge about two miles away 212 bodies were discovered.
The clothing had been removed and most of the bodies were un-
speakably mutilated and scalped. The Seventh Cavalry lost in
this engagement 265 killed and 52 wounded. The Indians, too,
had doubtless suffered but they had made good their escape.
The disaster was complete with no good effect for the whites.
Whatever else may be said, a small band of soldiers was made
to operate on exterior lines, seek out a powerful and doughty
enemy and try to overwhelm him. Besides, the Seventh Cavalry

was armed with inferior carbines, whereas the Indians had splendid repeaters furnished by the government.[18] Again, there seemed to be no money to buy the best arms for the soldiers but somehow there was plenty with which to furnish excellent weapons to the Indians.

The Custer annihilation produced a tremendous sensation on the public mind. Every one implicated was blamed and many were investigated—except the government which by its reductions had caused the frightful carnage. The whole effective army would scarcely have been enough to have rounded up the Indians of this region. On the other hand, a sufficient force of trained men could have saved the great spilling of blood and Custer's command.

At any rate the army kept on at its task. Crook was reënforced with Merritt's Fifth Cavalry, which gave him in all about 2,000 men. He immediately moved out with each man carrying no change of clothing—only a blanket, 4 days' rations, a poncho and 100 rounds of ammunition. After several marches in the stifling heat, dust and finally rain, the suffering became keen. Finerty's diary says: *Aug. 4 1876*

"We had no tents, and had to sleep in puddles. The rain kept pouring down until the afternoon of the succeeding day, retarding our march and making every man of the command feel as if possessed of a devil. Officers and men slept in rain and dirt, drank coarse coffee and ate hardtack and raw bacon. *Aug. 11 1876*

"The rain and mud made the marching terrible, and some of Terry's young infantry (recruits)—they had met General Terry's command, and remained and marched with it for some days—lay down exhausted in the dirt. Many of them had to be placed on pack mules or carried on travois. . . . Every company of the Second, Third and Fifth Cavalry had to abandon or shoot used-up horses. . . . We made thirty miles over a most infernal country before halting. Chambers' 'astonishing infantry' made the full march—not a man fell out of ranks. The Roman legions or the army of Austerlitz never made better *Aug. 13 1876*

---

[18] It is interesting to note that while all this slaughter was taking place on account of our insufficiency of troops, Congress was reducing the Medical Corps (June, 1876).

time than the splendid detachments of the Fourth, Fourteenth, and Ninth Infantry. . . . There was very little wood. We had to sleep at night in pools of water, thankful to get a chance to lie down.

Aug. 15
1876
"The horses staggered in the columns by scores. Very frequently a played-out horse would fall as if shot. Dozens of dismounted cavalrymen toiled painfully along over steep, rugged hills in the rear of the column. . . . Our whole line of march was dotted with dead or abandoned horses. Some of the newly enlisted infantry grew desperate, their feet bleeding and their legs swollen from the continuous tramp. . . . Many of the young foot soldiers seemed injured for life.

"Gibbon's men marched like Romans, Chambers' men rivaled O'Leary and Weston (but these were all veterans)."

Sept. 7
1876
It came to the point where Crook realized that food and forage must be obtained at once or they would all die in the wilderness. Captain Anson Mills with 150 men, all that could still march, was to make his way to Deadwood City, Dakota, and get any kind of provisions he could find. The Indians had combed the country of game and the sun had killed the grass. The last hard tack had been eaten the day before. Wild onions and a little horse meat remained.

Sept. 8
1876

Sept. 9
1876
Mills started out without hesitation and without rations, his men and horses being mere shadows of their former selves. The next day, he came upon the fresh tracks of Indians. Lying in a ravine and locating the warriors' lodges by means of scouts, he moved out at dawn the next morning. This gasping force in 3 well-ordered columns attacked and surprised the savages, killed and captured a few, and drove the remainder to the hills. The Indian camp, which was full of supplies, now had to be held against a counterattack of the redskins. Disposing his men carefully, Mills sent word to Crook of his plight and of the provisions at hand. Crook immediately took the trail, arriving at eleven o'clock in the morning and finding that Mills still held sway. At the approach of these reënforcements the Indians, who were still firing from the bluffs, retired, but a small group that had taken refuge in a formidable cave refused to submit and kept up a heavy fire. Crook, realizing that there must be

a prominent Indian concealed there, besieged the little party and finally succeeded in inducing those who were not killed or wounded to come forth. American Horse, the chief of this tribe, was borne out by two young braves. He had been terribly wounded in the abdomen, and held a piece of wood between his teeth in order not to show his torture. Throwing his rifle on the ground, he submitted. He died that night.

In the meantime Crazy Horse, who had been a few miles away with 600 warriors, charged the troops. Crook's assembled command drove them off. The effect of this entire engagement was to capture American Horse and a few Indians and to save Crook's men from extinction. But nothing decisive against the savages was yet accomplished.

Crook, realizing the hopelessness of this kind of work, repaired to Fort Fetterman in order to organize a winter campaign. His force finally consisted of 2 companies of the Third, 6 of the Fourth and 2 of the Fifth Cavalry; 6 companies of the Ninth, 2 of the Fourteenth and 3 of the Twenty-third Infantry; and 4 batteries of the Fourth Artillery.

While Crook was thus preparing his column for an advance, General Miles with only 500 men of the Fifth Infantry was in the vicinity of the mouth of the Tongue River. In the way of comfort, clothing and supplies Miles' command was well provided against the cold. It was indeed fortunate for the men that they were well equipped with fur caps and mittens, because the mercury actually froze several times during the winter. Colonel Otis, with 4 companies of the Twenty-third Infantry, having pushed back a large force of Miniconjous, San Arcos, Brules and Unkpapas under the instigation of the medicine man, Sitting Bull, joined Miles' force. Since Otis had captured a wagon train of supplies, his reënforcement was *Oct. 18 1876* especially acceptable. The whole command now numbered about 850 and one gun. Miles then marched to meet Sitting Bull who *Oct. 21 1876* at a parley asked that the Indians solely occupy the west and that the whites vacate. The old medicine man was so obdurate that Miles, finally despairing of a peaceful settlement, gave him fifteen minutes to prepare for battle. The attack was bloody and doubtful for some time. Though the odds were 4 to 1 against them, the troops succeeded in driving the Indians forty miles up the valley from their village, in destroying it and in capturing most of their supplies. The result was that the large body of savages could not subsist. Several hundred broke into small parties and scattered, but 2,600 of them surrendered under promise of good treatment. Miles, who could not take them along with him on account of his slender stock of provisions, told them to report at the Spotted Tail or Red Cloud Agencies, which most of them ultimately did.

Oct. 24 1876

Meanwhile, Crook at Fetterman had managed to find out from a captured Cheyenne that the principal village of his tribe was located in a cañon through which ran the headwaters of Crazy Woman's Fork of the Powder River. Immediately Crook sent out Colonel Mackenzie with 10 companies of the Second, Fourth and Fifth Cavalry, and 350 Pawnee, Crow, Shoshone and friendly Cheyennes—1,100 men altogether. They reached the cañon which proved to be a gloomy, icebound gorge in the Big Horn Mountains, there about 3,000 feet high. Numerous icy creeks made the channel almost impossible to follow. The sufferings of the men as they plowed through this great fissure in the earth were, though different, just as intense as those Crook had borne earlier in the year. On the other hand it was a blessing for the troops that the Cheyennes believed their position to be impregnable. The Indians had put out little guard. Moving forward in the frigid, moonlit night, Mackenzie surrounded their position in the same noiseless way as Custer had done with another tribe several years before. At daybreak the camp was completely surprised. The Indians fled naked from their wigwams or cut slits in their tepees from which they fired. Many of their number were killed, their horses taken and their Chief Dull Knife lost. Although their bodies were entirely nude, they swarmed back to the village in the freezing weather. Then McKinney's company charged a rocky height and drove them back, but when he was returning a terrific countercharge resulted in his death and the wounding of a half dozen troopers. There was some confusion over this occurrence. Hand to hand fighting took place in which the whole force surged back and forth. Then the Indian scouts on the flanks saved the day by charging to the assistance of the troops. However, the fighting had to continue until dark in order to hold the savages back while

Nov. 24 1876

their village was being destroyed. Great quantities of supplies,
all that the Cheyennes had, fell into Mackenzie's hands. The
Cheyennes then began to draw off and to take up a strong position six miles further up the cañon from which Mackenzie
could not dislodge them. Eventually he had to return to his
camp. *Nov. 27 1876*

The sufferings inflicted upon the Indians were frightful.
They had no clothing or food in this awful weather. Many
babies and children froze to death in one night. One infant was
saved by the ghastly device of sticking him in the warm entrails
of a freshly butchered horse. Making their way to Crazy Horse
the Cheyennes asked him for succor, but that chief said he had
nothing to give and dismissed them. So angered were they at
this rebuff that they set out forthwith to the nearest reservations,
gave themselves up and went out against Crazy Horse with our
troops later.

The main mission now was to capture or destroy Crazy
Horse's band. Miles with 5 companies of the Fifth Infantry,
2 of the Twenty-second and 2 Napoleon guns started for the
camp of that chief in the valley of the Tongue River south of
the Yellowstone. At first there were a few skirmishes with the
advance parties of Indians, who kept moving toward the mountains. Finally there were captured a Cheyenne warrior and
woman who informed the officers of the exact location of Crazy
Horse's villages. Miles moved directly toward them. He found
the redskins occupying a height which could be easily seen. The
place was very difficult to attack. The troops would have to
ascend steep cliffs from where the Indians could pour in a con-
verging fire. Seeing that Crazy Horse was willing to accept
battle, Miles had his men out of range eat breakfast in full view
of the gesticulating savages. After the meal, the troops began
a very odd pitched battle in which there was neither surprise nor
ambush. Miles' men with great difficulty ascended the cliffs
under a galling fire. The artillery, which had been carried concealed in the wagons, suddenly unlimbered and dropped shells
upon the savages, who were greatly surprised at this proceeding.
The attack all along the line was scarcely a charge. With their
heavy ammunition and winter clothing, it was slow, toilsome
work for the soldiers to scale the icy, snowbound cliffs. But

Dec. 29 1876

Jan. 8 1877

Miles' men doggedly crawled to their goal. Then ensued some stubborn hand to hand fighting, some enfilading of the Indian position and Crazy Horse retreated. The last of the battle was fought in a blinding snow storm. In their fight the Indians left much baggage. So bereft were they of supplies and ammunition that the next spring Crazy Horse and his band came into the agency.

May 1877

Only one band under Lame Deer and Iron Star remained to be subdued. In the spring Miles pursued it, overtook it and captured its village. Lame Deer and Iron Star were killed, although Colonel Miles did his best to take them alive. It seems that after the engagement was over, an unfortunate accident occurred. The Indians misinterpreted the meaning of the movements of one of the soldiers. They thought the position of his rifle indicated treachery. The chiefs took point-blank aim at Colonel Miles and would have killed him, had they not been shot down in the nick of time.

Further west the Lower Nez Percés were driven to desperation by the unjust and inhuman actions of the Interior Department. This tribe for seventy years had been uninterruptedly the friends of the whites, had always stood out for peace and had to their credit a long list of benefits rendered to the settlers from the time of their befriending the Lewis and Clarke expedition. When low white characters killed some of their number, they did not retaliate; neither did our law punish the offenders. When the government decided to put them on a reservation, all these redmen asked for was a little strip of poor land in the Wallawa region. Of this they had already been defrauded: the agents, having promised it to them, had afterwards for no good reason reversed their decision. General Howard, the department commander, saw the point of view of these high-type Indians, and recommended that they be not confined to any reservation until they committed overt acts. Our avarice, however, decided differently. Howard with his troops was ordered to put them on the Lapwai reservation, whither they did not want to go. The movement would deprive them of their herds and other property. Already the insults the whites had heaped upon them were sufficient to cause any normal person to be enraged. But when they felt they could not subsist under the new order, they felt themselves to be at the end of amicable relations.

Even then Young Joseph, their chief, did not want to resist. Captain Whipple had to tell him that a higher authority than any army officer had decided he must go. Then Joseph was induced by his warriors to take up arms. After attempting to ward off the blow for some little time the Lower Nez Percés, about 300 warriors, were forced on the warpath. Regretfully the army and these Indians went into conflict.

Captain Perry, with 2 small companies of the First Cavalry, 90 men, all that could be spared for the duty, was sent to compel them to go on the reservation. He met the Indians at the head of White Bird Cañon. They had been watching his movements by scouts and even with field glasses. Besides outnumbering him over 3 to 1, the Nez Percés were superb physical specimens, well-educated and well-disciplined. They could march in column of fours, form twos and line from a gallop, build fortifications and maneuver well in action. It is not surprising, then, that Young Joseph skillfully ambushed Perry's command, drove *June 17 1877* them back and killed 1 officer and 33 men. It was with the utmost dexterity and bravery that Perry succeeded at all in extricating the surviving soldiers.

General Howard now had to collect more troops and hurry forward with them in person. He took 1 company of the Fourth *June 22 1877* Artillery, acting as infantry, 5 companies of the Twenty-first Infantry, 2 troops of the First Cavalry, 2 Gatling guns, and 1 howitzer, 227 men in all. Joseph had by this time about 400 braves. Howard came up with the Indians at the Clear- *July 11 1877* water. All day long Howard charged and the Indians countercharged. Finally the soldiers' lines had to be extended to two miles and a half in width. At night each side strengthened its breastworks. The next day Howard was reënforced by a fresh company of the First Cavalry, which attempted to turn the left *July 12 1877* of the Nez Percés line. Then the Indians fled and made good their escape with their supplies. Although Howard took their village, Joseph's band got out of the valley and over the Lolo trail faster than the troops could follow. The route covered is probably the most difficult one in the west, so that the Indians naturally outmarched General Howard's force.

General Gibbon at Helena, Montana, had in the meantime been warned by telegraph of the flight of the Nez Percés. He set out to meet them with a mixed force of 17 officers, 132 cavalrymen and 34 citizens, all he could collect. Learning of their whereabouts he waited until the night and at dawn attacked their village, completely surprising them. Though the Nez Percés were driven out, they returned and reoccupied their village and incidentally took Gibbon's howitzer. The soldiers, driven behind barricades and trenches, defended themselves as best they could. That night the redmen drew off, leaving Gibbon's command crippled and unable to follow. Gibbon himself was severely wounded. His force was so small that he, a general officer, had felt himself obliged to use a rifle and help in the fire as a private soldier. He suffered a loss of 29 killed and 40 wounded in the action.

Aug. 9
1877

The Nez Percés now crossed the Great Divide and camped on the Camas Prairie. But the telegraph was clicking its news to other troops in the path of this tribe. Colonel Sturgis proceeded from the Powder River country with 6 companies of the Seventh Cavalry and some Crow scouts, in all about 350 men. He overtook Joseph's force across the Yellowstone, pursued him, and took over 400 ponies. Nevertheless the Indians, fighting a rear-guard action, made their escape along the Mussel Shell River to Cow Island on the Missouri.

Sept. 3
1877
Sept. 14
1877
Sept.23
1877

In the meantime, Colonel Miles left Fort Keogh with 4 companies of the Seventh Cavalry, 4 companies of the Second Cavalry, a company and a half of the Fifth Infantry, 1 company of scouts, a breechloading Hotchkiss and a 12-pounder Napoleon gun. Meeting the Indians in their camp on Eagle Creek near the Bear Paw Mountains, Miles drove them to the ravines where he was unable to dislodge them. The fighting was severe and at close quarters. Joseph's position could be carried only with great loss and that chief could not escape because he felt he could not leave his wounded. Although the army howitzer did some damage, the siege was kept up for four days with intense suffering on both sides. At the end of that time, after having fought his way for justice through three territories, after never having scalped, outraged or mutilated the whites, after having bested and outwitted the few soldiers

Sept. 30
1877

sent against him, Young Joseph came out to Colonel Miles under protection of a white flag. Pointing to the heavens, this warrior, superb in face and stature, said simply, "From where the sun now stands I fight no more against the white man!"

Colonel Miles promised Joseph, according to the government's agreement, that he should be returned to the Lapwai reservation. But the government promptly stultified Miles by sending this tribe to an unhealthful region in the Indian territory where 50 per cent of their number died. Thus passed out the Lower Nez Percés and many a gallant soldier because General Howard's advice at the outset was not followed. Subsequently Colonel Miles, after efforts of years, had the remnants of the tribe transferred to the land of their nativity (1884).

The Nez Percés' uprising was not the only outbreak of this year. The Bannocks, the Mexicans across the border, the Indians of Alaska and the communists of our own country were bringing trouble in various parts of the land.

In Pittsburg and other cities, especially of Maryland and Pennsylvania, labor uprisings had so shaken the country that one city was burned and the National Guard of three states *July 1877* had to be called out. Even 30,000 militia could not quell the riot in Pittsburg. It took a small force of regulars to overawe the mob and restore tranquillity.

While all this was happening and the army was striving to save the nation from its enemies and errors, a great outcry arose against it in the interest of economy. There seemed to be no uneasiness over the inhuman loss of life of the soldiers due to their small numbers. This history cannot record the innumerable, unheralded affairs that kept sending soldiers into eternity, nor can it show in detail that hundreds of skirmishes and battles had never occurred if a sufficient army had existed. The Yellowstone expeditions of 1871, 1872 and 1873, the Indian Territory troubles of 1874, the Nevada disturbances of 1875 and the Ute and Snake uprisings of 1878, could not have been born, had there been on the scene of action a force sufficient to awe the Indian, and see that the proper provisions were given him. Similarly, the building of the great railways could have moved along rapidly and without hindrance or bloodshed, had there been troops enough to make the crafty Indian think twice before he struck. In a few places where the commands were comparatively large, the assembled soldiers would be paraded before the Indians, when it was suspected that the redmen were about to break out from their reservations. This show of strength usually calmed the savage breast.

An instance in point is the rising of the Bannocks at this time. They had lost their hunting lands, been forced on an inhospitable reservation, had to face continued encroachments of the whites and, to cap all, had to subsist on an appropriation that allowed them only two and one-half cents a day per capita. Naturally they grew arrogant and hostile. When a drunken Indian shot at and wounded two teamsters, he was arrested at the expense of the killing of an agency employee. Troops were called for as a result. The Bannocks later left their reservations mostly on account of insufficient food, and fled to the Camas Prairie where they killed several settlers. A vigorous campaign by General Howard resulted in the capture of 1,000 of them. At Clark's Fork a battle had to be fought in which 20 Bannock lodges were taken.

Aug.
1877

Sept. 5
1877

While the army was making its uphill fights and was losing its men more by its slenderness than any other cause, back east the legislators were doing much to increase the mortality.

The Fifty-fourth Congress, a most responsive body of politicians, while soldiers and officers were sacrificing themselves on the altar of patriotism, failed to pass an appropriation bill for their pay. Officers had to borrow funds at interest in order to live through the year. For this period the army's services were gratuitous.

Fiscal Year
1877–1878

1878

All through the winter and spring advocates on the floor of the House, without promptings of their constituents, attacked both the services [19] in the bitterest of terms—"for the sake of economy." It was pleasing to stone an institution that could not retaliate. As long as the soldier, in his remoteness, had no domicile in order to vote—did not influence the district at home —he was harmless to the congressman. It looked at one time as if the army would be reduced to 10,000 men. Seeing the great range of territory over which the soldier had to be con-

---

[19] Army and Navy.

stantly on the alert and fighting, it seems hardly possible that intelligent men could have taken this view.

However, the outcome was not as bad as might have been expected. After a year had passed, the appropriation bill came *June 1878* through with the pay. But legislation stopped all promotions above the grade of captain and reduced considerably the allowances of officers. For the heroism of the army, as outlined on these pages, Congress chastised, rebuked and derided but seldom rewarded.

Indians to the number of 375,000 had to be held in check on their reservations. In addition, Sitting Bull across the border in Canada was collecting a combined force of the tribes already there and of those who had taken refuge from the United States. The whole mass might strike at any moment. The Mexican outlaws, too, in large bodies were making regular incursions across the border in the south.

The army had grown so small that many of the troops of Alaska had to be withdrawn. Such action was an invitation for outbreaks in the far north. Many tribes in the United States were so ill-treated and starved by the Indian agents and the stinginess in Washington that they were ready to fight anybody. The Bannocks and Pi Utes left their reservation for this reason and went upon the warpath. Captain Evan Miles, with 75 picked men and as many Crow scouts, while on his way to the Yellowstone, heard of this tribe's withdrawal. He was soon reënforced by 7 companies of the Twenty-first Infantry, 2 foot batteries of the Fourth Artillery and 1 troop of the First Cavalry, all of which were on separate errands in that vicinity. With these troops he took up the pursuit at once. Making a record march of thirty-five miles in one day, he overtook the Indians near the Umatilla Agency, Oregon. Surprising them in the early morning, he took several hundred prisoners, killed *July 13 1878* 11, wounded many and captured 250 horses, with a loss to himself of several soldiers among whom was Captain A. S. Bennet, Fifth Infantry. The Bannocks were thus pushed back toward their reservation.

So uninviting, on account of pay and the arduous, thankless duty of the soldier, had the army become, that its effective strength was below 20,000. Desertion had played its part naturally and heavily. The recruits were largely desperadoes or those who couldn't read or write. In short it was all a high-minded officer could do to keep himself and the wheel going. But he was high-minded or the development of the United States would have rocked and tottered.

1879

The number of general officers was reduced to a mere hand-ful. Sherman was general of the army; Sheridan, lieutenant general; Hancock, Schofield, and McDowell, major generals; and Pope, Howard, Terry, Ord, Augur, and Crook, brigadier generals.[20] The few thousand mobile troops were spread over 3 divisions, 8 departments and 11 districts in trying to compass the territory of the United States.

While there was constant fighting for these inadequate num-bers, the service did not shirk its duty in improving itself. The effort to have a well-regulated method of target practice is an

Aug. 7
1879

example. The Laidley system was adopted. The Ordnance Department tried to equip the army with better targets. Each man was to have an allowance of 20 rounds of ammunition per month for this purpose and prizes and furloughs were to be given to the best shots.

The Sioux again were on the warpath. General Miles, with 9 companies of the Second Cavalry, 7 companies of the Fifth Infantry and some scouts, crossed the Missouri at Fort Peck and proceeded to the Milk River. There the troops encountered a number of Indians under the leadership of Sitting Bull. The

July 17
1879

force was too small to capture the tribes. After a severe engage-ment which was begun by a daring attack on the part of the few soldiers, the errant redmen fled across the 49th parallel and were safe.

It was not long after this that the Utes grew restless and quite antagonistic toward the Indian agent at the White River Agency, Colorado. Major Thornburg, accordingly, was ordered to move from Fort Steele. He collected 3 companies of the

Sept. 21
1879

Fifth Cavalry and 1 of the Fourth Infantry, about 200 men altogether, and marched toward the scene of the trouble. When he had been about a week on his way, he was attacked by about 300 well-armed warriors. Thornburg and 10 of his men

---

[20] West Point was a separate "Department."

were killed. Captain Payne gathered the remainder and re- Sept. 29
1879
treated to the wagons where he prepared to make a stout defense.
So outnumbered was this little band of regulars that all it
could do, trapped as it stood, was to keep itself from being
exterminated. A message finally found its way through to
General Crook, who ordered Colonel Wesley Merritt, with 530
men of the Fifth Cavalry, to hasten to the relief of Payne's
command. When Merritt reached the beleaguered soldiers, he
found that a company of the Ninth Cavalry had arrived the
day before. Generals Sheridan and Crook, by rushing reënforce- *Oct. 5*
ments to Merritt, swelled his command to the gigantic figure *1879*
of 1,000 effectives. Merritt then pushed on to the agency.
There he found the houses burned and the Indian agent and
10 of his employees murdered. The Utes had again taken their
vengeance. While Merritt's command was held in the vicinity
of the White River Agency until further developments, Lieutenant Weir and William Hammer, chief of scouts, while hunting deer, were attacked and killed by the Indians. Great alarm
was now felt throughout Colorado. Colonel Merritt's force was
raised to 1,500 men by robbing other parts of the country of
its protection. In addition, Colonel Mackenzie, with 6 companies of the Fourth Cavalry was brought from Fort Clark,
Texas. Colonel Hatch with 450 men of the Ninth Cavalry
came from New Mexico. The Utes at last being awed by this
army of troops, being pacified by the overtures of General
Charles Adams of Colorado (who incidentally succeeded in
having released 3 white women and 2 children held by the
Utes) and being convinced by the persuasive words of their
head chief, Ouray, fell into a state of quiescence. Up to this
time, 11 citizens, 2 officers and 12 soldiers had been killed *Nov. 1*
and 41 soldiers wounded by this outbreak. *1879*

Most of the troops of this expedition were shortly thereafter
returned to their posts. But 4 companies of the Fifth Cavalry
and parts of the Fourth, Seventh, Ninth and Fourteenth Infantry regiments remained near the ruined agency. They hutted
and sheltered themselves as best they could through a severe
winter and with great privation and suffering. In the summer *July 7*
of the next year they were relieved by 6 companies of the *1880*
Sixth Infantry.

As the army fought and bore the brunt on the one hand, so it prepared itself in its technic. A new *Cavalry Drill Regulations* was published at this time. It seemed to adapt the movements of the mounted service more thoroughly to the work on the plains. Provision was made very carefully for handling each contingency of march or action. Besides a dismounted drill in 2 ranks made the use of the Cavalry more extended. The captain's command was still called a company, the major's a battalion, and the lieutenant's a platoon.

Thus the army in this period after the Civil War plodded along, too dispersed most of the time to collect in even respectable detachments. It marched through parching heat and arctic cold only to find precarious battle or distasteful execution of bureaucratic injustice at the end. Through blood and hardship it tried to square the government for its criminal blunders. Hungry, thirsty, exhausted and wounded the soldier too often fought in actions which he did not believe justified. But his loyalty made him answer the command of his nation and he went forward.

And he carried on in the face of the deepest ingratitude of his people. His pay was cut, his comrades summarily discharged, his supplies and arms made inferior to those of his enemy and any hope of promotion blotted out. Surrounded by thousands of savages in a vast prairie, he could count at most a few hundred with him to help hold them in check. Why he went on, why he went through the agonies of hell for a nation that kicked him at every turn, is almost beyond human analysis.

And yet the awful marches and these heroic fights were the soldier's main dependence. He got away from the most provincial garrison life into which any government ever forced an army. Living in flimsy shacks, without the commonest conveniences found in the east, he froze in winter and stifled in summer. Tenderly reared women heroically went through these hardships with their husbands. Breakfast was often eaten when the water in the tumblers had a crust of ice upon them. Dinner at other times was served when swarms of insects would rob the appetite. Winter or summer, in or out of the fort, there was no escape from the rough life of the frontier. But through

these grim days there was time to find compassion and succor
for the suffering squaw or the white family driven in from
their settlements.   The post was the haven of all classes, and
in this comfort many a soldier's wife found an outlet from the
dread monotony.

With stables in the morning early, with breakfast next,
then parade, then drill and stables in the afternoon, the work
of the day, except the endless fatigue, was over.   There could
be no more than rudimentary exercises for from 38 to 50 men.
There could be no training.   When lieutenants and captains
expected to hold their same grade for 20 or 30 years and were
not afterwards disappointed in this, and when these very officers
had been generals over large commands in the Civil War, a
great wave of ambition and spirit could hardly grip their
energies.   With few books, an occasional mail, no golf courses,
no tennis courts, no activities to arouse the interest even of a
spectator, the soldier was really closed to the recreation of the
bottle and cards.   The sutler's store was the only club and its
rough boards and hot stove a place of rare comfort.   But with
all this desultory life, there was little trouble over gambling
and a surprisingly small amount of drunkenness.   In this age
of fulsome entertainment, one cannot visualize the barrenness
that then enclosed the soldier's life.

When the commanding officer had too great a proportion
of illiterates and desperadoes in his organization, when savagery,
rudeness and the outbreaks of the lawless loomed on every hand,
he had to have a hard discipline that looks severe in the New
York Library.   He had at times to resort to the ball and chain,
to close confinement and the harshest restrictions of his officers
and men.   He had to have the most rigid formality at the
mess table, to inculcate an unwavering respect for rank and to
notice the smallest details of official and social customs.   He
had to be a czar or he could not have lived peaceably in his
military oasis on a threatening desert.   He had to watch the
little things of his small province or soon they would be big
things.   The very life blood of his command depended upon
his supervision of what appear to us now to be the pettiest of
details.   He had to be "hard boiled" or he, his handful of
soldiers and the surrounding country could not have survived.

The nation forced him into this position, as it forced the demise of Thornburg, Canby and even Custer's command and the death of many another soldier, when it made beggarly detachments fight an overwhelming quantity of wily savages on their own soil. The government as usual scrupled on money for an army, but it did not seem to be anxious about the loss of life that resulted from parsimony. And so the army was thrown into dark ages of hopelessness. Though he grumbled, the soldier did more than his duty, sustained by an unfaltering honor that faced death for an ideal.

CHAPTER X

THE ARMY'S RENAISSANCE

FIRST PHASE

(1881–1898)

NOTWITHSTANDING the cudgelings of stress, neglect and hostility that beset the soldier, the army began to be restless for something better. The stir of honest ambition, that lies close to true American hearts, plainly started *1881* to transform itself into concrete movement. If the powers denied to the service a chance of handling the larger units in maneuver, then the military man would do the next best thing and move imaginary forces on paper and would read of the best technic and tactics from books. If the government prevented practice, at least the officer could voluntarily absorb more theory. He could thus have some advancement in the knowledge of the most intricate and extensive profession found in civilization.

When the general of the army[1] laid the foundation of the School of Application for Infantry and Cavalry at Fort Leaven- *May 7* worth, Kansas, he sowed the seed of advanced learning in the *1881* service. Although the course of instruction then prescribed for this institution was primitive and elementary, the very installation was the beginning of general and special service schools that were to spring up later and make our officers the peers in the art and science of war of any in the world. Thus the army began to wake itself, unaided, from the dark ages of provincial life into which the nation had thrown it.

---

[1] General Sherman.

The nucleus of progressives who built up a first- and a second-year course at Leavenworth little knew that the efforts of this institution were to be one of the great factors in the successes of two modern wars. Neither did they realize that their onward-looking efforts would step by step cause an officer to have a continuous education throughout his career. At first officers were detailed from their regiments to be students and those who were in command of troops at the school were in general to be instructors. The first year [2] was taken up with the rudiments of a general education and the second with certain books on the science and art of war. Papers by both students and instructors were to be read at various times.

1881

The beginning of any renaissance is too dim, as we know, to throw a full light upon conditions at once. The army went along in this year without much to alleviate the load of its irksome and humdrum duties. In fact, Congress let it rest dormant for the next seventeen years without doing a single vital thing toward its strength or monetary needs. But within the service there was a decided ripple of constructive unrest which tended toward practical and theoretical efficiency in spite of the unsympathetic aloofness of the government.

---

[2] FIRST CLASS:
    Mahan's Outposts.
    Myer's Signaling.
    Mahan's (Wheeler's) Field Fortifications.
    Woolsey's International Law and Laws of War.
    Ive's Military Law.
    Operations of War (Hamley).
    The Lessons of War as Taught by the Great Masters (Colonel France J. Soady).
    Lectures by professors and essays prepared by students from general reading.
Practical instruction in surveying and reconnoitering by itineraries and field notes, as prescribed for the use of the army.

FOR THE SECOND CLASS:
    Correct reading aloud, with care and precision, with proper accent and pauses, to be heard and understood.
    Writing, a plain hand easy to read, designed for the use of the party receiving, and not an exhibition of haste and negligence of the writer, especially the signature.
    Grammar (Bingham).
    Arithmetic (Hagar).
    Geometry (Chauvenet).
    Trigonometry (Chauvenet).
    General Sketch of History (Freeman).
    History of the United States (Seavey, Goodrich).

Emory Upton

A distinct evidence of this movement toward higher standards was the work of Brevet Major General Emory Upton.
He had been sent abroad to study the workings of the armies
of Europe and Asia. His report upon his return had led him
to make an exhaustive study of the organization and management of our armies in the past. The work was entitled *The
Military Policy of the United States*. His research and comments clearly demonstrated that our country had really had
no sound policy up to that time. Unfortunately he had finished
only the review of the use and abuse of our military forces
down to the middle of the Civil War, when he died. It was *March 15
1881*
many years later, as we shall see, that the fruits of his tireless
labors were brought to light by a fearless Secretary of War.
It was also a long time afterward, when we had successfully
miscarried, that the recommendations of his report upon his
tour abroad met with favor from the politician. But every one
of his precepts was followed to the letter and to the country's
betterment, even if it did take a long time to move our legislators to act toward that end. The 3-battalion organization for
infantry and cavalry, the interchangeability of line and staff
officers, the examination as a condition to promotion, the establishment of a general staff and the extension of military education were embodied among his conclusions; and they were all
afterwards put into effect, though most of them did not reach
fulfillment until we had had another war with its needless
death rate.

Fighting Indians went on with frequency in the west during
this year, but the actions though difficult and full of hazard,
were small. One matter of importance occurred in concluding
affairs in the Sioux country. Sitting Bull, with his followers,
had kept to the British possessions well out of reach of our
soldiers. But forays into the United States by some of his
warriors had been so severely met by detachments of the army,
that the savages had either been driven back with heavy loss or
had come into the reservations. His force had grown feebler,
too, by hunger and disease. His influence was gone and most
of his people had abandoned him. Worn out and unable to exist
longer in his cold habitat, he came into Fort Buford, Dakota, *July 20
1881*
and gave himself up. With him were 45 warriors, 67 women

and 73 children. This act marked the termination of the bitterest conflicts with the savages.

But the Indian fights were not over by any means. The Indian agents in Arizona had so harshly mishandled the Apaches, whom Crook had left in a peaceable state after years of the utmost toil, honesty and care, that the President felt obliged to reassign that officer (who was now a brigadier general) to the command of that department. When Crook arrived, he found that his labor during the seventies was absolutely undone. These tribes had been so defrauded and abused, in the interim, that they were all upon the warpath. From semi-civilized quiescence they had lapsed into barbarous strife in a space of half a dozen years. The agents had ejected them from their reservations because silver had been found in the ground that they occupied. These members of the "Indian Ring" had flung them into prison to languish for months without charges against them, had starved them, had taken away their crops, had given them little hearing in a court of justice and in general had treated them like cattle. As one reads of the outrages perpetrated on these savages, one can hardly believe them to be the work of white men.

Summer
1882

General Crook again went into this difficult and tremendous country of huge mountains, deep cañons, cactus, and sultry dust. He could have led his troops against these spurned savages with glory to himself and without criticism from any one. Being a man of character and training he set for himself the task of winning back the Apaches' confidence by peaceful means. With a small escort he visited these tribes and heard their grievances at great personal risk. He investigated their complaints and in almost every case found that the Apaches had been heinously treated. The old chieftains and squaws told him stories that would have wrung pity from a hardened criminal. The way in which they met him—a real friend and champion after all these years—was pathetic in its childlike appeal. The faces of the old men brightened and the squaws wept when they again saw his face and heard him in council.

The government wisely put the complete control of Indian affairs in that district in his hands. It was not long before he again restored order, confidence and peaceful conditions among the redmen without resort to a single battle. Old Pedro's outburst shows clearly that the army officer more than any other individual served his country by clinging to peace until every proper means of persuasion was exhausted:

"When you (General Crook) were here, whenever you said a thing we knew that it was true, and we kept it in our minds. When Colonel Green was here, our women and children were happy and our young people grew up contented. And I remember Brown, Randall, and the other officers who treated us kindly and were our friends. I used to be happy; now, I am all the time thinking and crying, and I say, 'Where is old Colonel John Green, and Randall, and those other good officers, and what has become of them? Where have they gone? Why don't they come back?' And the young men all say the same thing."

While Crook was using his power in this fruitful and pacific way, the "Indian Agent Ring" was sending out newspaper stories of murders and depredations committed by the Indians. Their purpose was to involve General Crook in a fight, so as to drive the Apaches away from land on which they wished to profiteer. The General investigated each case, found it to be a fiction and stopped the rumor. Thus he reached out with one hand and throttled sinister threatenings and with the other soothed the maltreated tribes of Arizona. He set the Indians to work and made them satisfied by his justice, kindness and lack of compromise.

But there was one tribe, the Chiricahua Apache, that had taken refuge in the Sierra Madres over the border in Mexico. With these redmen General Crook was unable to treat. It seems that their flight took place after an incident which was a culmination of many previous wrongs. A police officer in attempting to arrest a young Indian on a minor charge fired into a group of Apaches into which the young buck had fled. The result was that the policeman killed a squaw instead of his quarry. The Indians immediately retaliated by killing the officer and playing football with his head. Fearing vengeance they escaped into Mexico.

March
1883
Later, a band of this tribe under Chato conducted raids from their strongholds in the mountains on settlers and citizens in the United States. It was necessary now for General Crook *April 23*
1883 to take action. After having proceeded across the border and having conferred with the Mexican military leaders, who encouraged him, he set out from Willcox with 7 skeleton companies of the Third and Sixth Cavalry, all that he could assemble. Later on, Captain Crawford, Third Cavalry, joined *April 28*
1883 him with 100 more Apache scouts, making the whole command about 50 officers and soldiers, and not quite 200 friendly Indians. Was not this a pretty force for a rich, sizable nation to give a general officer for the purpose of whipping hundreds of Indians in one of the most natural strongholds God ever made? *May 1*
1883 The command pressed on across the boundary line and came into the high broken country of the Sierra Madres. The *May 15*
1883 scouts in advance came up with the Chiricahuas and succeeded in frightening them off and getting their camp. General Crook then let a young squaw and a boy, whom the scouts had captured, make their way back to the camp of Geronimo, their leader. When that chieftain heard that General Crook was in command and that all the Apaches of Arizona had come back as friends of the white man, he immediately sent out runners to notify all the tribe to come in. He then came in himself. Over 200 of the Chiricahuas finally gave themselves up and *July*
1883 Arizona was at peace again under a just administrator. In two years, General Crook had restored to tranquillity a territory that would have taken a decade to conquer. How much bloodshed might have been saved in the seventies, had men such as Canby, Howard, Miles and scores of others been given complete control, is inestimable. As it was, untrained civilians by their connivings for gain, became the agitators who fomented war.

While these activities were going on with the Indian, the *1883* army showed more signs of interior improvement. General P. St. George Cooke gave to the service a new *Cavalry Tactics* as the result of his experience and investigations. The manual is both interesting and instructive. He developed from previous recommendations the double column of fours so as to form mounted units into more compact bodies. He called the company organization a "troop," for the first time it had so been

termed in regulations. He assigned the troop officers to positions which are similar to the ones they now occupy and sized
the troopers from the tallest in the middle to the shortest on
either flank.

Through the efforts of the Ordnance Department, the rifle
was improved as far as it could be with the money allotted by
Congress. Though the Lee magazine rifle had been adopted
(1882) it could not be issued in large quantities because there
seemed to be no funds for that sort of product. So the Spring- *1884*
field model was improved as a single loader. It was fitted
with the Buffington rear sight, which for the first time equipped
our rifle with a device that allowed for the drift of the bullet.
It was a 45-caliber weapon and shot fairly accurately at 200
and 300 yards. To it could be attached 3 types of bayonet, the
triangular, the spade or trowel, and the cylindrical ramrod.[3] It
was as good a single-shot, black-powder weapon as then existed,
and the best the army could produce with the funds at hand.

The blue uniform with red facings for artillery, sky blue
for the infantry and yellow for the cavalry was not much *Aug. 14*
changed in cut over that of the Civil War. The fatigue cap *1884*
was somewhat lower in crown.

The noncommissioned officers wore above the elbow large
chevrons of cloth for the fatigue blouse and of gold for the
dress coat. On overcoats the chevron was worn below the elbow.
The fatigue coat had a low falling collar.

Improvements in seacoast fortification had been let run along
by the reluctance of Congress to such a degree that all sorts
of guns of obsolete type presented a picturesque but useless
array on our shores. Finally by suggestions of certain progressives in the army and House and Senate, an act was passed
which authorized a board of officers to draw up a scheme of *March 3*
modern fortifications for our seacoast defenses. As a result the *1885*
Endicott Board really enunciated the scheme of protection of
our shores which proved twenty years later to be most useful.
The recommendations contemplated the establishment of 2,362
guns and emplacements. Up to the war with Spain only 151
of these had been installed.

---

[3] This weapon was largely used in the war with Spain.

To return to Arizona, we find that for two years General Crook had succeeded in keeping the Apaches satisfied, peaceful and industrious. Such conditions were evidently too drab for the Indian agents who felt that they had been robbed of their control in that vicinity. On one occasion they refused to let the Indians have an irrigating ditch which had been staked out by certain army officers. At various times the agents tried to throw aspersions on Captain Crawford's character because he had taken the Indians' part. They also allowed the sale of liquor to the savages. As long as greed and avarice were at the bottom of the civilian agents' motives, there naturally followed argument with the military man. The result was that the Indian was led into uncertainty. While authorities of the Interior Department haggled and when one white man would give an order or permission only to have it countermanded by another, it was impossible for the savage to discriminate between the parties at issue or to understand the causes of his treatment. He did not know what to expect. As a result Geronimo and *May 17 1885* Nachez with 124 Chiricahuas left their reservation for the Sierra Madres. General Crook pursued the same tactics that had been so successful before. With Apache scouts, led by officers of the army and backed by the troops, he hunted down the warriors in their little groups. It was a taxing and endless job that occupied the summer and fall, but Geronimo, finally seeing the hopelessness of further struggle, sent word to General Crook that he desired a conference. It was not long before the general met him at a picturesque spot called "Cañon de los Embudos." For several days Geronimo argued his point and *March 27 1886* refused to accept the terms offered, but when "Chihuahua," a fine old chieftain, voluntarily surrendered, Geronimo followed suit. But Geronimo was not yet ensconced upon the reservation. On the way in, he must have changed his mind for he *April 1886* gave the troops the slip. It was at this time that General Crook was superseded by General Miles. With detachments, mostly of the Fourth Cavalry, the new commander followed up Crook's plan. But it was several months before the wily *July 1886* chieftain could be taken. Captain Lawton and Surgeon Leonard Wood rendered conspicuous service in finally capturing him. Although there were minor outbreaks of Apaches afterward, this episode marked the virtual end of the conflicts with these tribes.

While Crook and others were rounding out the salvation of the Apaches with little bloodshed, the army in other parts was called upon to do a different sort of national police. The Chinese laborers in the mines of Wyoming were having violent troubles with their employers. When part of the army was called out to suppress this uprising, it did its usual work of *Sept., Oct. 1885* restoring order with little bloodshed.

The schools in the army were by this time on a fair road *Nov.* to substantial advancement. It was little thought, when *1886* Lieutenant Arthur L. Wagner was sent to Leavenworth as instructor of military art, that he was going to be such a great factor in developing the curriculum of that school. For eleven years he was to influence its standards, he being there without intermission throughout that time. It was during this period that he wrote the *Campaign of Königgrätz* (1889), *The Service of Security and Information* (1893) and *Organization and Tactics* (1895). These works were particularly needed by the service. They suited the requirements of all branches and remained for years standard authorities on these important phases of military instruction. They were the result of wide research and able condensation and suited to the everyday use of troops. Ever since their issue the service at large has been influenced by them. It was through Wagner's efforts that the courses at Leavenworth were raised to a higher standard, especially in the field of military art. His fine personality and tireless energy made him truly the Sylvanus Thayer of the General Service schools.

From the impetus of the Leavenworth courses came a desire for more specific professional learning in the various branches of the service. Not only was it apparent that officers should be cognizant of strategy and tactics in general, but that they should also be experts in the technic and tactics of the various arms to which they belonged. After much persuasion, a "school of instruction" of drill and practice for cavalry and light artil- *Jan. 29* lery was authorized by Congress. Although the institution was *1887* not established until five years later, the authorization was at least certain for future possibilities. At length, such a school was placed at Fort Riley, Kansas (March 14, 1892).

While the army was improving its mind in order to be more efficient to fight, it was woefully deficient in materials for war. The large guns in the service seemed to be ill-supplied because of the usual lack of funds. Existing weapons and ammunition were obsolete. The 8-inch shell for instance had *March 21 1888* a cast-iron point and was unsuitable for armor-piercing purposes. Black powder was still in use at this late date in modern discovery. Tests were conducted by the Ordnance Department at Fort Hamilton, New York, with a pneumatic, dynamite, *April 24 1888* torpedo gun. The results as reported by the chief of that branch were fair, and he consequently recommended experiments with explosive gelatine or dynamite so as to increase the range and *June 14 1888* power of projectiles. But he later complained that Congress in its last two sessions had made no appropriations, so that experiments and the purchase of guns and ammunition for this purpose had to stop.

However, the next year the Congress did appropriate a sum for experimenting on the Pacific coast with 3 pneumatic, dyna- *June 1889* mite guns. But it so happened that the Watertown Arsenal had to suspend work on rifles of large caliber, because the plants of Watervliet and Watertown were too small to accommodate the manufacture of both cannon and small arms. Since the latter were in demand by the army, they had to take precedence to the exclusion of the larger weapons.

If lack of legislative attention deprived the army of many of its necessary tools, at least it could improve itself in its training and organization to the limit of its internal powers. The urge of progress in the service was growing rapidly and was manifesting itself in several ways. Where the work of the soldier was most tangled, where marching to and fro was incessant, where operating and guarding stage lines, quieting Indians, holding off desperadoes, allaying labor troubles and safeguarding the settlers was all in the work of the week, there was still time found for training. When it is realized that 1 company of the Second Infantry in a short campaign against *Spring 1889* the Bannocks marched over 1,300 miles, it is remarkable that the units of the service could thus find time for betterment toward no personal or selfish ends. An instance of such a thing is found in the field maneuvers of the Twenty-first Infantry Summer 1889 at Camp George Crook near Fort Robinson, Nebraska. Not only was the practice beneficial, but it was the first time the regiment had been assembled for twenty years.

Further, the service was anxious to better its standards and organization. The next year Congress was prevailed upon to June 16 1890 pass a law which required no outlay of money. Promotion below the grade of brigadier general was to be within each arm, corps or department of the army. Officers could now be transferred inside their branches without loss of rank entailed by the previous narrow limits of regimental promotion. The entire service by this move became more flexible in the interest of efficiency. To the same end this legislation provided for a rigid examination for promotion of all officers below the grade of major.

While this progress was being fostered in the service, some sorry Indian troubles again come into prominence. The great Sioux nation on its various reservations had become saturated with a new religion whose principal tenet was that an Indian Messiah was shortly to come, who would give the red race domination over the white. The belief provoked a fanaticism that entailed fasting, vapor baths and ghost dances, and drove many of these superstitious people to leave their reservations. A large force of savages had collected in the Bad Lands, 1,800 alone having stampeded to that place when General Brooke came to Pine Ridge with 5 companies of infantry and 3 of cavalry. Sitting Bull had been killed and a riot had ensued Dec. 15 1890 when the Indian police had tried to arrest the old medicine man. Sitting Bull's followers then made their escape to Big Foot's village, 40 miles to the northwest. It became a matter of moment then to keep Big Foot from slipping away into the Bad Lands, from which place incursions could be carried on at will. General Brooke ordered Colonel Forsyth to intercept Big Foot's band and to disarm the Indians peaceably if possible. With 2 battalions of the Seventh Cavalry and some Hotchkiss guns, Forsyth surrounded the camp at Wounded Knee Creek Dec. 29 1890 and invited the warriors to a council, whereupon 106 of them came out and sat on the ground in front of their tepees. The

Indians were then sent in groups of 20 to bring out their arms. The first group could discover only two weapons, whereupon Forsyth had to order soldiers to search the premises. They found fifty rifles. While this operation was going on, one of the seated Indians drew a rifle from under his blanket and fired upon the soldiers. In a second the whole camp was ablaze. The other warriors who had similarly concealed their weapons opened at once upon the troops. Though taken by surprise, the soldiers soon collected themselves. The battle raged from a little after eight in the morning until three in the afternoon. There were little tactics involved, but each soldier went about his business in an orderly way. When it was seen that there was no more danger, Colonel Forsyth ordered his men to desist, saying, "We did not come here to butcher them." It had been a bloody affair, 146 Indians having to be buried on the field and about half that number of officers and soldiers having been killed or wounded. Colonel Forsyth took the remainder of the redmen back to the reservation. Some troops of the Sixth, Seventh, Eighth and Ninth Cavalry and Second and Twenty-first Infantry then surrounded other errant bands. The work was taxing in this very cold winter and it was not what one might call holiday pleasure. While the soldiers on all sides were closing in, the Indians saw the hopelessness of further resistance and surrendered. To show the Indian the power of the white man, this large command, which finally included several regiments of infantry, was reviewed by General Miles in the presence of the redmen. The warriors were so highly impressed that no further outbursts of a grave nature have since occurred with these tribes.

Dec. 29 1890

Jan. 14 1891

Feb. 1891

Right upon the heels of this action came several internal improvements in the service. Congress passed a law which compelled the retirement of officers upon reaching the age of 64. By opening up an unlimited list for those who were over age, men who had outgrown their fitness for activities in the field could be properly cared for. More efficient work could thus be had by younger men at the head of troops.

Oct. 3 1891

This year also marks the first issue by the War Department of three separate sets of drill regulations for "Infantry, Cavalry and Artillery." They represented the work of the best minds of the service in contradistinction to the output of private publications. The infantry drill included "setting-up exercises" and a "bayonet exercise" by the count. Loading was executed quickly and without motions. The soldier half cocked his piece, opened the chamber at the breech, took out the empty shell, inserted a loaded one, closed the chamber and was ready to fire. For drill, such complicated movements as "fours right, left front into line faced to the rear" still persisted and showed traces of intricacy. But as a whole the marchings were comparatively simple. For the cavalry, the troop in single rank was divided into 2, 3, or 4 platoons, depending upon the number of fours. The squadron consisted of not more than 4 and not less than 2 troops. For the artillery, the battery consisted of 2 or 3 platoons and a platoon of 2 sections. A section was composed of a piece with its caisson. Each carriage was drawn by six horses. The battery officers consisted of 1 captain and 4 lieutenants. The gun detachment for field batteries was composed of 5 privates and 2 corporals; for heavier and sea-coast batteries, the service of the piece required more than that number.

It was in the latter part of this year that troubles along *1891* the Rio Grande sprang up, much as they did twenty-five years later. One Garza was a leader of a large band of outlaws who committed depredations, stole property and killed Americans. His retinue was composed of bandits on both sides of the boundary line, who were liable to appear at any point between Brownsville and the source of the river. The troops had to cover tremendous distances and be ready to fight at any moment. The Third Cavalry, under Colonel Anson Mills, was conspicuous later in helping to quell these disturbances, which lasted over two years.

It was at this period that the Ordnance Department made *1892* its great advance in small arms when it adopted a foreign rifle, the Krag-Jorgensen, and started this weapon's manufacture at the Springfield armory. Money for its production was so limited that it was all the department could do to supply the regular army. But the powder was at last smokeless and the weapon had a magazine which held 5 cartridges. Each cartridge was loaded with 40 grains of powder and a bullet .308 of an inch in diameter. The muzzle velocity was about 2,000 feet per second. This was the most marked advance in small arms since the application of the percussion cap, and of much greater value, as shall be seen in a war which is soon to come.

1893

The next year hard times struck the country like an avalanche. Labor uprisings began to take place. The panic spread through most of the United States. The militia either would or could not quell these gigantic outbreaks. Mobs of the worst classes burned and looted cars. The Governor of Illinois refused to call out the militia of his state for the suppression of lawlessness. President Cleveland acted at once for the pro-

1894

tection of national mails and the restoration of order. The federal troops were ordered to the scene of difficulty, wherever they were available, and in every instance brought quietude with little or no bloodshed. In this connection it should be noted that the soldiers were used between 1886 and 1895 in 328 different civil troubles extending through 49 states and territories.[4]

These hard times, driving men from a livelihood in civil life, caused a tremendous number to apply for enlistment in the service. It was possible to recruit the army up to strength and to select the best men from among the many who applied. The result was the recruitment of an army enlisted personnel of such a quality as has seldom, if ever, been known in our history. Although it is a travesty on any nation to produce an army from the ashes of a labor conflagration rather than by direct inducement, the effect of this slump in business was to give to the regulars for the war that was approaching, an efficiency that served the country well. What Congress failed to create, Providence provided.

While the army was taking on a more efficient complexion, rumors of Indian troubles again put some of its forces on the move. It seems that the Bannocks had been once more aroused. The difficulty arose when certain lawless civilians killed two Indians and one child while the latter were on a hunting expedition. The Governor of Wyoming and the Indian agent at Fort Hall, Idaho, asked for troops on account of the resulting

---

4 Troops did not relish such police duty.

threatening attitude of the Bannocks toward the settlers. A squadron of the Ninth Cavalry and a battalion of the Eighth Infantry under Major Adna Chaffee were sent by rail to Market Lake, Idaho, whence they marched to the scene of possible trouble, in order to prevent collision between the Indians and the settlers. General Coppinger accompanied the expedition. *July 31 1895* When this force arrived at Jackson's Hole, the excitement promptly subsided. The main body was shortly withdrawn, but 2 troops of the Ninth Cavalry remained at Jackson's Hole and Teton Pass in order to keep order until a judicial settlement of the affair could be made.

These were times of improvement not only in schools, but *1896* in small arms and in drill regulations, about the only features the army could perfect without money. The Krag was rebuilt so as to make it a steadier and more dependable weapon for expert shots at long ranges. The powder was more carefully manufactured so as to give it greater uniformity. A separate drill regulation for light artillery and a new one for the cavalry, expanded the former regulations to meet the requirements of the batteries and troops at full strength.

The service was affected by the discovery of gold in the Yukon valley of Alaska which caused a tremendous rush to *Fall 1896* that region. To the army fell the lot of policing and exploring this vast unbroken stretch of valuable territory. The Fourteenth Infantry, and parts of the Twenty-fifth, Fourth, Second, Eighteenth Infantry and of the Eighth and Ninth Cavalry, for the next two years, were constantly at work surveying routes and estimating the resources of this new country. Through snow and ice, over glaciers and rivers, by snowshoe and reindeer sledge, they gained minute information as to the mineral resources, topography, vegetation, timber, animals, birds and in fact everything of commercial value. This inestimable knowledge was achieved in addition to the labor of policing the country and making it safe.

In the United States proper the gradual conquering of the *1897* Indian and the growth of railroads helped the army to begin to concentrate in regimental units, so that it could train in the art of war. Of such preparation it had been heretofore deprived, because it had had to be scattered about in so many different posts. All through the latter part of the nineties decided effort was made to collect the small isolated units, so that practice marches and small problems could be undertaken. For instance, the Twelfth Infantry had been concentrated at Buffalo (July 26, 1887) for the first time it had been brought together since 1869. Several other regiments later were likewise gathered in from various places. So the Leavenworth and Riley graduates were slowly being accorded opportunity to test the results of their courses in tactical, strategic, and logistical studies, as well as in technical knowledge. The regular army, although still well spread out, was more highly developed and efficient than at any time in our previous history.

Beginning of 1898

However, there were less than 25,000 effective regulars [5] against a population of 73,000,000 people, the smallest proportional regular force existing at the beginning of any of our wars, except the Revolution. Congress for nearly thirty years had almost totally confined itself to ignoring or paring and cutting its land forces, while the territory of the country was expanding. Out of the 2,362 guns for seacoast defense recommended by the Endicott Board, whose plans had been adopted, barely 6 per cent were in position. There were no adequate staff departments and no general staff. Though the War with Spain had been foreseen for some time, nothing had been done toward changing our ludicrous, defensive weakness, let alone our offensive incapacity. Even the militia law was more than one hundred years old. The Spanish army on a peace footing numbered 128,183, and for all we knew was well trained. The

[5] AUTHORIZED STRENGTH OF THE ARMY

Departments	Officers	Men
Infantry, 25 regiments	877	13,125
Cavalry, 10 regiments	432	6,170
Artillery, 5 regiments	280	4,025
General and staff officers	362	
Ordnance department	56	605
Engineer department	109	500
Hospital corps	......	706
Miscellaneous	......	575
Total	2,116	25,706

militias of the various states as a whole had little understanding
and less practical knowledge of conduct in war, mainly because
of their negative treatment by legislators. The situation of the
United States would have been comic had it not turned out to
be tragic.

Even after the battleship *Maine* had been blown up in *Feb. 15 1898*
Havana Harbor and war was inevitable, Congress, instead of
building an army on broad and efficient lines, rejected the
excellent Hull Bill and contented itself with simply adding to *March 8 1898*
the regular forces 2 regiments of artillery.[6] This move brought
the regulars up to a paper strength of 28,747, almost 100,000
less than the Spanish forces.

When war was finally declared, the War Department ma- *April 25 1898*
chinery found itself clogged with thirty years' mold. The
management of small detachments, which already knew pretty
well how to take care of themselves, was as much as had been
necessary. The shrinkage and setbacks of the army during the
previous three decades were most apparent in the offices in
Washington. There the reflection of an overconfident and militarily careless people was clearly mirrored. Humdrum methods
and a tiny personnel brought little of value to an active, fighting
force. What would happen were the Farmer's Bank of Smithville suddenly compelled to take over the business of the Bank
of Commerce in New York City? Just what happened in our
war offices at the outbreak of the war—an attempt to transform
provincial methods into international facilities. And Congress
had just crushed a bill which offered to remedy these defects.
As a consequence, there were no accurate maps of the scene of
activities and no secret information of the new enemy's resources. The commissary, quartermaster and medical departments had, all told, only 258 officers fit to carry on duties in the
field. In addition, the ordnance department had no modern
guns and ammunition available, except for the little regular
army.

The regulars were still scattered over our wide country.
One regiment, the Fourteenth, had to be brought later clear
from Alaska to the front. Notwithstanding the news-stand size

---

[6] The Sixth and Seventh.

April 15
1898

of the War Department, it was not inert. Even before the declaration of war, being exasperated by the "masterful inactivity" of Congress, it had issued orders for the concentration of the infantry of the regular army at Tampa, Mobile and New Orleans.[7]

April 22
1898

While the regular soldiers were thus on the move, Congress decided as usual after we were committed to the conflict to make its own reorganization of the forces. All able-bodied male citizens between 18 and 45 were to be liable to military duty. The volunteer system of 1861 repeated itself with most of its mistakes. The enlistment was to be for two years or for the war, a term over which the recruit might gamble. For these temporary troops, the governors were to appoint officers in such a way that for any state or territory they would be in proportion to its population. Generals and higher staff officers

April 23
1898

April 24
1898

were to be selected in Washington. Following this enactment the President issued a call for 125,000 volunteers. The next day legislation more than doubled the size of the regular army

---

[7] The general officers of the regular army, just before the war, were Major Generals Miles (commanding the army), Merritt, and Brooke; Brigadier Generals Otis, Coppinger, Shafter, Graham, Wade and Merriam; and the heads of the staff bureaus: Brigadier Generals Greely (chief signal officer), Breckinridge (inspector general), Flagler (chief of ordnance), Sternberg (surgeon-general), Lieber (Judge-Advocate-General), Stanton (paymaster general), Wilson (chief of engineers), Ludington (quartermaster-general), Corbin (adjutant general), and Eagan (commissary general).
The following army corps were organized during the war:

CORPS ORGANIZED DURING WAR

Corps	Commander	Where organized	Strength, June 30
First	Major General Brooke	Camp Thomas	58,548
Third	Major General Wade		
Second	Major General Graham	Camp Alger	23,511
Fourth	Major General Coppinger	Mobile	20,816
Fifth	Major General Shafter	Tampa	15,736
Sixth	Major General Wilson		
Seventh	Major General Lee	Tampa (moved to Jacksonville)	19,156
Eighth	Major General Merritt	San Francisco and Manila	22,989

The Sixth Corps was never organized; General Wilson was assigned to command a division of the First Corps.

(62,597 men) by allowing the smaller units to recruit to larger strength and by adding a third battalion to a regiment in time of war. Another second lieutenant was given to each artillery battery. The war pay of the soldier, now that the volunteer appeared, was increased 20 per cent. But Congress was wary. It was careful to provide that as soon as hostilities were over the army should return to its former impotent size.

Such disjointed and impractical legislation could hardly give birth to anything other than hectic results. It was the same old story over again with the recruit, who preferred to go into the volunteers where he found comrades and an easier life. Neither could the regular army gain the numbers authorized by Congress before being launched into the scene of activities. Provision for adequate staff departments was still wanting, and volunteer office seekers overran Washington.

The plan for concentration camps at the southern ports had to be abandoned before being carried out, because these places were unsuitable for troops. Two other concentration points were designated—Camp Alger at Falls Church, Virginia; and Camp Thomas at Chickamauga, Tennessee. From these places troops could then be sent to Tampa, Jacksonville and Fernandina, Florida. The Seventeenth (regular) Infantry was the first to move from Columbus Barracks, Ohio, toward Chicka- *April 18* *1898* mauga. Indeed, the trained forces were naturally the only ones for some time to show signs of mobility, because they were the most ready.

The volunteers who flocked to respond to the first call of the President were generally in a sad state of uselessness. Although a few were well equipped with uniforms and equipment and under excellent control by their officers, the greater part lacked so much discipline, equipment and organization that they proved to be as much of a menace to friend as foe. On the other hand, the comparatively good volunteer regiments were so in spite of the neglect they had suffered.

Congress now began to reek with measures for a more ade- *May 11* *1898* quate force. Our highest legislative body at this juncture in war reminds one of the calf that had to have its ears pulled off to get it to the cow and its tail pulled off to get it away. A volunteer brigade of engineers was allowed, as was also an additional force of 10,000 enlisted men who should be immune to tropical diseases. The Medical Corps was increased by 15 assistant surgeons and as many contract surgeons as might be

required. A volunteer signal corps for service during the war and 2 additional assistant adjutant generals were also provided. This medley of acts was largely useless as later events proved. The country was again to learn that it is difficult to make up for lack of intelligent forehandedness.

Against General Miles' advice the President issued a second call for 75,000 men. The General thought that 50,000 highly trained soldiers would be better than a mass who could not be so easily disciplined and handled, and might simply be a burden to the country. We shall see the dire effects of ignoring General Miles' suggestion.

Then, Congress made provision for allowing regular officers to hold staff appointments in the volunteers without losing rank and grade in the army. This measure was good, as it had shown itself to be in the Civil War.

While all this legislation was taking place our potentiality was in chaos. Volunteers of every variety were rushing to

enlist, and then trying to struggle to the front. Dewey had won his battle of Manila and was waiting at Cavite for troops in order to take and occupy that city. Little expeditions with arms, ammunition and supplies had tried with more or less success to land at Cuban ports so as to give their cargoes to our allies in that country. Lieutenant Rowan had delivered his message to Garcia after a most racking and winding journey through tropical forests and over tortuous mountains. In a small fishing smack he had safely returned. But the army was not on the move. Supplies of all sorts were lacking, and Tampa had but a single-track railroad. For the troops that had assembled there, this was an irritating and protracted delay. One correspondent termed it the "rocking chair period." But the trained regulars were not idle. Drills and practice in making hasty intrenchments were the incessant work of troops under General Shafter. The movements and character of our soldiers, as they charged through the palmetto groves, rode their horses through the streams and worked with the precision of a fine machine, brought forth the highest comments from the foreign attachés. One war correspondent when admiring the physiques of these rugged, cheerful and canny men, remarked that it was only a pity there were not more of them.

But the supervision of the corps with its small and improvised staff could not overcome the difficulties that foresight alone should have prevented. The populace as usual was crying "On to Havana" as it had previously done with Boston, Canada, Mexico and Richmond. There was the customary shortage of rifles, ammunition, supplies, clothing and even food. Beside the regulars, there was a great lot of excellent youth—untrained. There were box cars on the sidings with provisions and clothing of many varieties, but the outside was unlabeled. An officer looking for beans would open a car to find patent-leather shoes. The volunteer soldiers were sometimes seen begging for food in the streets, while supplies in the cars lay rotting. There were no storage facilities. The docking space at Port Tampa was so limited that there was room for only eight vessels out of the thirty troop ships collected. Once, in docking, two vessels collided with serious injury to one boat.

But the administration in Washington grew so impatient to have the troops be off that urgent messages were sent to embark. General Miles was instructed to send 70,000 troops to Havana. *May 8 1898* When it was shown that there was not enough ammunition for such a command to fight one battle against 125,000 Spanish troops well armed with Mausers and protected by the strongest kind of fortifications, there was pause. General Shafter was then ordered to proceed to Mariel on the north coast of Cuba and establish himself there, but the navy could not furnish the requisite number of convoys. Orders were then issued to take *May 10 1898* 12,000 troops to Key West, but this plan had to be abandoned, because of the unsuitability of that place for soldiers, especially on account of the dearth of water. In the meantime the War Department was taxed to its utmost capacity, because the military forces were now bloated abnormally by the influx of thousands of volunteers.[8]

---

[8] During the war, camps were established for military purposes at Tampa, Fla.; Mobile, Ala.; Camp George H. Thomas, Ga.; Camp Alger, Va.; Camp Poland, Knoxville, Tenn.; Jacksonville, Fla.; Miami, Fla.; Fernandina, Fla.; Camp Wikoff, N. Y.; Camp Hamilton, near Lexington,

Finally General Miles left Washington for Tampa. There he found the disorder that always follows national apathy. Troops had to be camped so far from each other on account of sanitary and water facilities that there could be little cöoperation. It was impossible for receiving officers to supply the organizations quickly. The loading of transports was chaos. A battery would be placed on one vessel and its ammunition on another. Regiments were broken up and scattered among the troop ships. Medical stores were placed in the hold under all sorts of other freight. Lieutenant Colonel Roosevelt, in trying to get aboard the transport assigned to his Rough Riders, found it already occupied by 2 other regiments. General Miles wired Washington:

June 5 1898

"This expedition has been delayed through no fault of any one connected with it. It contains the principal part of the army which for intelligence and efficiency is not exceeded by any body of troops on earth. It contains fourteen of the best-conditioned regiments of volunteers, the last of which arrived this morning. Yet these have never been under fire. Between thirty and forty per cent are undrilled, and in one regiment over three hundred men had never fired a gun."

Then the President directed that the Fifth Corps sail at once with whatever force was ready. Nearly 16,000 men were crammed into the troop ships. The decks were so full that there was scarcely room to stir. Men who had brought blankets and overcoats lay down beside men in white and khaki trousers. There was every kind of hat from plain straw to sombrero. The

---

Ky.; Camp George G. Meade, Pa.; Camp Wheeler, Huntsville, Ala.; and Camp Shipp, Anniston, Ala.

VOLUNTEER ARMY, MAY 30 TO AUGUST 31, 1898

	Officers	Men	Total
Volunteer Army on May 30, 1898......	6,224	118,580	124,804
Volunteer Army on June 30............	7,169	153,355	160,524
Volunteer Army on July 31............	8,633	203,461	212,094
Volunteer Army on August 31.........	8,785	207,244	216,029

heat and odors made men temporarily ill. But after their tor-
ment they were off at last, and every one breathed satisfaction
and hope. But joy was short-lived. Some of the navy convoy
had sighted what were supposed to be Spanish war vessels, all
of which were then thought to be bottled up in Santiago Harbor.
The Fifth Corps at sea was turned back to Key West. There
it waited in anxiety, disappointment and discomfort. Finally,
came the verification that Cervera's fleet was just where it was
supposed to be—in Santiago Harbor. And the transports [9] *June 13, 1*
again set sail for the southeastern end of Cuba. *1898*

The voyage was not one of unadulterated pleasure. Those
who were putting to sea for the first time, never wanted to go
again. When the roughness of an inter-island passage is combined with crowding, poor food, little water, pine cots, the
neighing of horses and the noxious odors of congestion, the
traveler desires land and land only. The boats moved at the
rate of seven miles an hour, four miles an hour and often not at
all. Though disheartened, this body of men, most of whom
were fine specimens of manhood and well trained, were only
waiting to get a foothold on land so as to have this whacking
business over with in able style.

While they were still on their voyage, Congress was in
process of passing another military law. Though the act seems
out of harmony with the happenings of the day, it was nevertheless a good one. It authorized the summary court or trial of
enlisted men by a single officer. More speedy and simple *June 18*
justice could thus be rendered and much red tape and overhead *1898*
saved. There was not much that Congress could now do, but it
was trying hard to show interest after the country had let military training fall into dry rot.

By the time the troops reached Daiquiri, they were very
ready to go ashore. But the civilian captains of the transports, *June 20*
who apparently were not amenable to orders, thought otherwise. *1898*
They actually feared so much for the safety of their ships and
themselves, that they refused even in this critical moment to go
near the land. They stubbornly remained from two to twenty
miles from shore. And they were thus immovable in the face of

---

[9] Kent's First, Lawton's Second and Wheeler's Cavalry Divisions.

the fact that the Navy had so pounded the Cuban coast that what Spanish troops were there had fled inland. It took a great part of a day to locate one of the troop ships. In this state of affairs every boat and launch of the navy had to be utilized in the transfer. Since there were no lighters and flats, the animals had to be dropped into the water and made to swim ashore. Some fifty of them became confused, swam out to sea and were drowned. The movement of officers and men from vessel to vessel was so dangerous in the rough sea, that Colonel Van Horn received a mortal injury. Two men drowned in getting to shore because of the absence of landing facilities. Five days were thus occupied in getting the Fifth Corps from the water to the sands. Finally some 6,000 under Lawton found themselves at Daiquiri and the remainder at Siboney under Wheeler. No more than the supplies for daily consumption could be placed on shore until two weeks later.

June 25 1898

Shafter's plan was to have Lawton occupy a strong defensive position between Santiago and Siboney, and Bates secure some point between Siboney and Daiquiri. But General Wheeler, eager for the fray, sent General Young to attack the enemy in the vicinity of Las Guasimas, which lay in the direction of San Juan.

June 24 1898

Young advanced in 2 columns with the First and Tenth Cavalry on the left and the Rough Riders on the right.[10] He had only 2 guns and they were limited to 50 rounds of ammunition all told, although the Tenth had a Hotchkiss battery. The columns deployed in the thick jungle. To any one who has never seen a tropical forest, it is impossible to picture the density of these Cuban copses. Spanish bayonets that jag and arrest, matted vines that form layers of strong walls and undergrowth that ties the feet to the ground, make progress nigh impossible without a machete or large knife. Hampering the progress still more, the Spaniards poured in a hot fire. The troopers, advancing cautiously through these indescribable thickets and wire fences, could not see their targets and therefore could not reply to the fusillade. Colonel Wood's command

---

[10] All the cavalry acted as foot soldiers. There were few horses and it is doubtful if they could have been used in this campaign. The Rough Riders really became dogged walkers.

(then immediately led by Lieutenant Colonel Roosevelt) while
deploying late, was caught in column. Several of its members
fell, and Sergeant Hamilton Fish was killed. But the whole
line broke its way onward until the men could see the enemy,
when they opened fire. The regulars pressing in front and the
Rough Riders on the flank, caused the Spaniards behind their
strong intrenchments to leave in haste. The whole engagement
had occupied but an hour and a half. Considering the fact that
the Rough Riders had received their Krags only the day before
and were not familiar with them, great credit is due them in this
action. And of course, the regulars acted as troops of long
training should. The men were all so exhausted by the intense
heat and fatigue that they could not pursue.

During the delay of six days, while General Shafter, suffering with gout, remained on the transports, and General
Wheeler, the senior on shore, was straightening out his lines a
little beyond Las Guasimas, from where El Caney lay to his
right front and San Juan before him, another expedition was in
progress on the Pacific. After having captured Guam where
there was no resistance offered, General Anderson pushed on *June 20*
1898
toward Manila. He had 2,491 men: the First California, the
Second Oregon and 6 companies of the Fourteenth Infantry.
Two months after Dewey had won his fight against the Spanish *June 30*
squadron at Manila, the first troops of the United States reached *1898*
him. In the meantime, he had had to sit passively at Cavite,
because he had no landing forces. Once he felt he would have
to quit the island when he received rumors that a Spanish
fleet was leaving Spain.

On the very day that Anderson arrived at Manila, General
Shafter, who by now had alighted upon the Cuban shores,
decided to strike at once. In the meantime, General Duffield
with the Thirty-third and part of the Thirty-fourth Michigan *June 27*
volunteers had landed from Camp Alger. But this reënforce- *1898*
ment was more of an embarrassment than a help, principally
because of the lack of supplies. Shafter had not been able to
land his heavy guns and the diseases of the rainy season were
imminent. He himself said:

"These preparations were far from what I desired them to

be, but we were in a sickly climate; our supplies had to be brought forward by a narrow wagon road which the rains might at any time render impassable; fear was entertained that a storm might drive the vessels containing our stores to sea, thus separating us from our base of supplies; and, lastly, it was reported that General Pando, with 8,000 reënforcements for the enemy, was en route from Manzanillo, and might be expected in a few days."

Lawton's division, supported by Bates' brigade and Capron's battery, were to assault El Caney at daybreak the next day. The other 2 divisions were to march directly toward Santiago by the road through San Juan, with Kent on the left and Wheeler on the right. The Thirty-fourth Michigan back at Siboney was to be the reserve. General Duffield from that point was to threaten the Spanish detachment on the left at Fort Aguadores.

*July 1
1898*

General Lawton marched all night, and, due to General Chaffee's fine personal reconnaissance, was in position by daybreak. The attack upon El Caney was to be a slow affair. It does not portray the conditions to say that the country was thick, the enemy's blockhouses scattered and the Spaniard's resistance more fierce and heroic than at any other time during the war. Little by little in the maze, dimness and heat, the regiments closed in semicircular order upon the enemy. Since it was difficult to keep in touch, and the fire of the enemy was destructive, it took many hours to work slowly through the obstacles of man and nature. The Massachusetts regiment, the only volunteers with Lawton, had to be withdrawn because their old black-powder rifles were ineffective and simply threw up clouds of smoke which drew effective fire from the fortified enemy. It was three o'clock before the lines were in a position which averaged a distance of about a thousand yards from the enemy. Lawton's one little obsolete battery of artillery was ineffective. And so it turned out to be an infantry, bushwhacking fight.

In the meantime, Sumner and Kent had formed their divisions so as to pass through the dense country to one of the streams in their front, and thence through cultivated fields and over high ridges to their goal of San Juan. It took the 2 divisions more than six hours to advance through the woods to the first stream. The fighting thereafter reminds one of the individual methods of Resaca de la Palma. These troops suffered most of their losses while they were advancing through narrow and crowded trails and thick country and before they could reply to the fire of the Mauser bullets coming from an unknown direction. The soldiers generally displayed heroism, fortitude and dogged determination while all this was happening. The great exception was that of a well-known volunteer regiment whose officers skulked in large measure and whose men, therefore, except small detachments who joined the regulars, did likewise. While regular officers and soldiers were being killed and wounded, these untrained men hid along the trail. The regular cavalry and Colonel Leonard Wood's regiment could not keep such an orderly advance as Kent's infantry, principally because of the thicker country over which they had to operate. But they all plodded along heroically except the one volunteer regiment. The following is an extract from the report of the inspector general who was on the scene during this defection.[11]

"As stated, the Sixth and Sixteenth United States Infantry took the right-hand fork. General Kent indicated the left-hand route to Col. W. A. Downe's regiment, the Seventy-first New York Volunteers, an organization then having present for duty 44 officers and 855 men, 3 battalions, commanded as follows: First, Major W——; Second, Major W——; Third, Major K——. The First Battalion headed into the left-hand trail, but retreated or hunted cover in a panic occasioned by the explosion near by of a shrapnel and the loss of some of the Seventy-first's men.

"General Kent and every officer of his staff ineffectively tried by mandate, persuasion, and action to force the battalion into and along the pathway, but the men were thoroughly and,

---

[11] This inspector, afterwards a brigadier general in the regular army, before his death gave to the author the only copy of this report known to be in existence. The Secretary of War had ordered all the copies burned immediately after their printing, but the inspector saved one for himself.

all things considered, naturally demoralized. Confusion ensued, and the left-hand route to San Juan was congested by the First Battalion of the Seventy-first, some of the men of which prostrated themselves in the path. The majority of them crept into the bushes lining the route. The Third Battalion, Seventy-first New York Volunteers, Major K—— commanding Companies B, L, K, and E, was headed in by officers of General Kent's staff, encouraged by the division commander himself.

"This battalion passed somewhat farther into and along the left trail than the preceding one of the same regiment had done, but the tendency of the regiment was so obvious that it was apparent the Seventy-first as an organization, could not be gotten into its proper position, viz., on the left of the Sixth and Sixteenth United States regiments of infantry. The indecision of the occasion caused confusion, and the action of the Seventy-first New York Volunteers blocked the advance of the Third Brigade.

"Major Sharpe ran to order the Third Brigade to pass the position of the Seventy-first, panic stricken, as stated. He was aided in this duty by every officer of the division staff, including General Kent; and, without hesitation, the Ninth United States (Lieutenant Colonel Ewers), the Thirteenth (Lieutenant Colonel Liscum), 73 officers and 1,345 men, swung into the left path over and past the Seventy-first New York, and kept steadily on, exposed to a vicious fire from an, as yet to them, unseen foe."

Although this is a plain statement of facts, the Seventy-first New York should not be made to bear censure or ignominy. Suppose some of their officers did funk the fight. Suppose, too, that some of the men skulked in the bushes. What was the cause? A man ignorant of the habits of bugs and bees finds himself in an apiary. He is asked suddenly to open a hive and take out some honey. He hesitates, balks and finally refuses. He is keenly alive to the thousand darting stings that lurk within and swarm without. On the other hand, the keeper of the place walks boldly up to the hive and with a few deft movements takes out a toothsome comb. Could it be said that either of these men was more cowardly by nature than the other?

Their only difference in this instance lies in knowledge and training. Transform the stings of the bees into deadly bullets and the hives into blockhouses full of hostile, thinking, human beings, and we have the situation of the Seventy-first New York, as opposed to the troops of long training and discipline. It is the old story of the use and abuse of amateurs in war. These New York men had patriotically volunteered, had left their homes, business and pleasure, and had undergone great hardship. They were the victims of those superficial politicians who loudly contend that you can develop a clerk into a soldier overnight without murdering him or holding him up to shame in battle.

To go on with the story, the rest of the fight was mainly carried on by regular troops. Little clusters here and there climbed slowly the heights of San Juan. The men fired in groups, standing up in the long grass to take aim. Right along with the regulars went the Rough Riders. If they can be criticized at all, it is that their eagerness sometimes exceeded their technic, so that a colored regular regiment had to extricate them at one point. But they were picked men of no little experience in war or actions kindred to war. There was some artillery firing, when most of the troops were near the summit, and finally the garrison of the main blockhouse went flying, pursued by a murderous fire from the Tenth and Colonel Wood's cavalry. The cavalry that had taken Kettle Hill was also closing in, and before dark San Juan was in possession of the United States forces. Lawton over at El Caney had had a severe task in taking that position. In spite of orders to withdraw, he pressed on and reached his goal. At the end of the day San Juan and El Caney were both held by the American soldiers. Trained regular troops had again demonstrated their ability to go forward in spite of superhuman difficulties and sometimes superannuated leadership. The casualties for the day amounted to 593 of whom 94 had been killed.

For the next few days the time was spent in straightening out the lines before Santiago proper and in trying to adjust the difficulty of taking care of the sick and wounded.

Though every possible precaution had been taken to guard against the fevers of the rainy season, in this time when the men were abnormally fatigued, unacclimated and ignorant of the danger from mosquitoes, officers and soldiers in large percentage were prostrate with dengue, malarial and yellow fever and with dysentery. Due to the nation's previous lassitude during peace, there were no replacements at hand. Those who might come would be unready. Shafter was fearful that he would lose his only efficient troops right here when he was so close to his final objective. Surgeons, ambulances and medical supplies of all sorts were wanting, and the casualties from disease were beyond reason. This frightful condition calls to mind the splendid reduction of the Medical Department by the bright men of a previous Congress in the seventies. It is a fortunate thing that the Santiago forces were poorer in quality than our troops. For later, great boatloads of our stricken soldiers had to be transported to Montauk Point, Long Island. So just as the army was about to obtain its objective it dwindled to a fraction of its former self with no reënforcements in sight.

July 3 1898

While the lines were being intrenched for investment of Santiago, Sampson destroyed the Spanish fleet which had tried to make its escape. This victory saved the troops from a perilous position and put the Spaniard on the defensive. Al-

July 3 1898

though some 5,000 Spanish reënforcements had been allowed to slip through into Santiago by the Cubans, the enemy's added strength was not vital now. Our troops occupied their time in lengthening the entrenchments about the city. Although 4 field batteries and some field mortars were our only artillery, the lines were extended for the effective troops until they practically encircled Santiago.

July 8 1898

During this time negotiations for a surrender were opened by Shafter. Toral, the Spanish commander, made an offer of capitulation of the city with the reservation that his troops be allowed unmolested and without arms to go to Holguin. Although this audacious overture was acceptable to Shafter, it was not tolerated at Washington. Shafter then felt himself forced to try to take the city. Accordingly he warned the Span-

July 10 1898

ish authorities that he would open fire the next day. The bombardment was begun according to his threat, and lasted two days while being supported by our fleet. The loss of life was naturally small, but the destruction to buildings large.

During the latter part of this fire display, General Miles arrived from Washington. He brought with him the Sixth *July 11 1898* Massachusetts and part of the Sixth Illinois under command of Brigadier General Henry. During the preceding two days the First Illinois, the First District of Columbia and the Eighth Ohio Infantry, with 6 batteries of artillery under command of Brigadier General Randolph, had been landed.

Negotiations now took a more definite turn. Several conferences between the commanders ensued, but the Spaniards were sparring for time in order to get as good terms as possible. Finally it was settled that the surrender was to be unconditional and that the Spanish troops were to be conveyed at the expense of the United States back to Spain. The capitulation was then *July 15 1898* signed by all parties.

Thus ended the main action in the war with Spain. It was well it turned out so, for doubtless we should have lost 5,000 troops in taking the barricaded and barbed-wired city.

The formal surrender, when the United States troops *July 17 1898* marched in and hoisted the American flag, took place two days later.

The Santiago campaign was the most primitive in character. The science the army had taken so much pains to learn might, under such condition, be thought to be wasted. But since teamwork, discipline, decision and control are stressed particularly in theoretical tactics, maybe the work had not been in vain.

It remains now to follow two campaigns occurring simultaneously in a large island in the Pacific and a small one in the Atlantic.

While the battles of San Juan and El Caney were in prog- *July 1 1898* ress in the Western Hemisphere, Anderson, it will be remembered, had landed at Cavite in the Eastern. The troops under him could do little more than to reconnoiter and prepare a new camp—Camp Dewey—for Greene's brigade which was expected to arrive. When Brigadier General Greene made his *July 17 1898* appearance, he had with him a battalion each of the Eighteenth and Twenty-third Infantry, the First Colorado, the First Nebraska and the Tenth Pennsylvania Infantry, and 2 batteries of Utah Volunteer Artillery—about 3,586 men all told. General Greene then placed his troops in Camp Dewey

July 25
1898

and General Anderson remained at Cavite. Major General
Merritt, the commander, next arrived with his staff. Later

July 30
1898

Brigadier General MacArthur brought his brigade, consisting
of the Thirteenth Minnesota, the First North Dakota, the First
Idaho, the First Wyoming and 1 battalion each of the Eighteenth and Twenty-third Infantry. The Astor Battery, a gift
of John Jacob Astor, completed MacArthur's force, making a
total for his brigade of 4,847. General Merritt now had nearly
11,000 men, with the prospect of nearly 5,000 more, who were
on their way.

July 25
1898

The very day General Merritt arrived in Manila Bay, Gen-
eral Miles with the Sixth Massachusetts, the Sixth Illinois
Infantry, 275 recruits and 2 batteries each of the Third,
Fourth and Fifth Artillery, arrived at Guanica on the southern
coast of Porto Rico. He had left Cuba as promptly as he could.
One by one the little towns and garrisons of the province of
Santiago had surrendered when approached by army officers
bearing the news of the fall of the city. General Miles then
saw that there was nothing to interfere with his expedition to
Porto Rico. Taking with him only this small force that had
not been touched by disease, he sailed away, leaving eastern
Cuba in possession of the ailing Shafter and his stricken troops.
Arriving at Guanica, Miles took the town with no resistance.

July 26
1898

Next day General Garretson moved on Yauco four miles
toward San Juan (de Porto Rico) with 6 companies of the
Sixth Massachusetts and 1 of the Sixth Illinois. When near
the hacienda, Santa Desidera, the fire of a small Spanish force
spread confusion to 3 of the Massachusetts companies, who,
however, were soon rallied, and pressed forward, causing the

July 27
1898

Spaniards to retreat and leave the road open to Ponce. At that
seacoast town the next day Major General Ernst arrived with
the Second and Third Wisconsin and Sixteenth Pennsylvania
Infantry. The garrison at Ponce at once fled, leaving these

July 28
1898

troops a free landing, which they made the next day. Miles
now knowing that he had a firm foothold on the south of the
island, waited for the troops which he knew to be on the way.

July 31
1898

In three days, Brigadier General Schwan arrived from Tampa
with the Eleventh and Nineteenth Infantry, 1 troop of the Sec-

ond Cavalry and 2 batteries of the Seventh Artillery. Major General Brooke and Brigadier General Hains brought from Newport News the Third Illinois, the Fourth Ohio, the Fourth Pennsylvania, 1 company of the Eighth Infantry, 1 troop of the Sixth Cavalry, the Philadelphia City Troop, 2 troops of New York cavalry and Rodney's battalion of artillery. General Miles' plan was simple and well executed. Four columns were to march by different routes covering the entire island and to converge on San Juan, where the fleet was. When that stronghold would be taken the whole country would be in the hands of the United States. As he had saved the army from annihilation by frustrating the politicians' proposed attack on Havana instead of Santiago, so now he went into the back door of Porto Rico, while the front door was heavily guarded.

The columns must be taken up separately in order to understand what happened. General Schwan had the extreme western end of the island to cover with a small force of regulars (1,447 men), of the Eleventh Infantry, 1 troop of the Fifth Cavalry, 1 battery of Gatling guns, and 2 batteries of the Seventh Artillery. At Hormigueros he came upon over a thousand *Aug. 10* *1898* of the enemy posted on strong heights. Schwan's troops had to deploy in the fields, break through sugar cane and wire fences and pass over creeks under fire. As they came steadily on and approached the hills, the garrison fled. Next day he entered *Aug. 11* *1898* Mayaguez, a city of 22,000, with loss of 1 man killed and 6 wounded. Drenching rain and the fatigue of his men prevented pursuit of the enemy. The next day 6 companies of *Aug. 12* *1898* infantry, a platoon of cavalry and 2 guns pushed along with great difficulty into the mountains. Schwan followed with the remainder of his cavalry and directed his other forces to come after him as soon as possible. Toward Las Marias some 2,000 Spaniards had collected. The American regulars, though outnumbered, went forward as fast as they could to attack the Spaniards on the crest of a high ridge. After Schwan's men had poured in a heavy fire the Spaniards retreated, leaving a highly disorganized rear guard in their wake. Most of this latter force was captured, as was the Spaniard's commander, Colonel Soto. Schwan was about to complete his victory and attack Lares, when word reached him that the peace protocol between Spain

and the United States had been signed. This news ended the
fighting for him.

Aug. 8
1898
The next column toward the east was Henry's. After
he left Ponce, the going in the rough, hilly country was
slow. He had only oxcarts to haul his supplies. Aside from a
battalion of the Nineteenth Infantry and a troop of the Second
Cavalry, his command consisted of raw, unseasoned regiments
of volunteers. The discipline of the Massachusetts regiment on
the march and in camp had been bad in the vicinity of Ponce,
and in the subsequent advance. Their actions before Yauco
had been what you would expect of raw troops under political
guidance. After several of the officers resigned on the threat of
being placed before a board of inquiry, things in the regiment
went better. But there was a great deal of straggling on the
Aug. 8
1898
march. Only nine miles were covered the first day, and the
troops did not all reach Adjuntas (12 miles north of Ponce)
Aug. 10
1898
until two days later. When the news of the protocol came,
Henry was at Utuado with his regulars and 2 battalions of his
Massachusetts regiment, preparing to advance upon Arecibo.

General Wilson's third column, farther to the east, consisted
of Ernst's brigade of the Sixteenth Pennsylvania, the Second
and Third Wisconsin and 2 regular batteries of artillery. They
had just exchanged at Ponce their black-powder rifles for new
Krags with which they were unfamiliar. They first marched
east in order to take the central road direct to San Juan. General Wilson's service of information was so good that he knew
that a strong force of Spaniards were preparing to meet him
at Aibonita. On the way to that town a strong outpost of
Spaniards was discovered at Coamo. The Pennsylvania regi-
Aug. 9
1898
ment after bivouacking in the hills all night, marched twelve
miles over a difficult passage through the mountains and outflanked the Spaniards, who fled to Aibonita, leaving their dead
commander. The Pennsylvanians marched into Coamo with
201 prisoners. Pushing on, General Wilson sent his troop of
New York Cavalry ahead, which established an outpost five
miles in advance, where they came under the fire of the Spanish
Aug. 10, 11
1898
batteries. For two days General Wilson reconnoitered the
strong Aibonita position and brought up the remainder of his
forces. He decided on another flanking movement. Sending

General Ernst over a mountain trail to the left, he hoped to *Aug. 13*
1898 take the place from the rear. In the meantime he had engaged the Spaniard's attention by the use of his battery. The black powder of the artillery brought only a hot fire from the Spaniards, so that the battery had to be withdrawn. It lost in killed 1 officer, 1 man, and in wounded 6 men. General Wilson then, understanding that at any minute he might be ordered to suspend hostilities, delayed Ernst's flanking movement and called upon the Spaniards to surrender. It was not long after *Aug. 13* he received the refusal of the Spaniards that orders came from *1898* General Miles to suspend hostilities.

General Brooke's column on the extreme east had been delayed by the poor facilities for debarking his supplies at Arroyo. Two of his transports had run aground. Finally the *Aug. 5* infantry was ready to move. General Hains, with the Fourth *1898* Ohio and Third Illinois, brushed aside small detachments and took possession of Guayama. There was some minor fighting by reconnoitering parties beyond that town, but Brooke had now to wait until his cavalry and artillery could come ashore. After several days, he issued orders for an attack in front and *Aug. 12* flank by his entire force. He was about to take the enemy by *1898* surprise when the news of the protocol reached him. *Aug. 13*
1898

Thus the island of Porto Rico was in the clutch of the four fingers of General Miles' expedition when the cessation of hostilities came.

It is necessary to look into another hemisphere to see what the United States troops are doing there. Merritt was anxious to end the struggle at Manila by an immediate attack on that city. General Greene very tactfully arranged with Aguinaldo, leader of the insurgent forces, who was our virtual ally but seemed to be inimical to the United States, to clear the Calle Real, so that the American troops would have an open way for the *July 29* attack on the Spanish trenches. The American lines were then *1898* stretched out and intrenched within striking distance of Malate. *July 31* Just before midnight the Spaniards, attracted by the extensive *1898* dispositions, opened a very hot fire upon the Tenth Pennsylvania and the 4 guns of the Utah Artillery. A company of the Third Artillery and the California Infantry were hurried through a terrific tropical storm to reënforce the line. Although 10 men were killed and 43 wounded, the action was indecisive. Then Greene for many days extended his entrenchments to secure his right flank. The line was constructed with great hardship, because the men could not expose themselves without drawing the fire of the enemy. They had to lie down during incessant rains, shelter being impossible. Constant effort had to be spent in keeping the loose soil from slipping. Shoes were so uncomfortable that many men went barefoot, especially when the trenches were filled by as much as two feet of water. Few men could receive khaki before they left the United States, so that they sweltered in old blue woolen shirts and trousers. Nightly firing by the enemy with both small arms and artillery did not add to the rest of the men. As most of the rank and file were under fire for the first time, it was almost impossible, in the darkness and wet, to enforce fire discipline and control with so many green troops. In four nights 150,000 rounds of ammunition were uselessly expended.

Although General Merritt was anxious to bring this waiting period to a conclusion, the navy felt it was not prepared to deliver a heavy supporting fire. Meanwhile, negotiations were in progress between General Merritt and the Spanish officials. When surrender was demanded, the latter declined, but there was a tacit understanding that when the attack did occur, the Spaniards would make only a show of force, in order to save their honor.

Aug. 13
1898

The bombardment, begun by the navy, was followed by the army's artillery. For three quarters of an hour the shells flew while the Spaniards remained silent. When the magazine in the San Antonio fort exploded, General Greene sent the Colorado regiment forward. Then a few shots came from the enemy's lines. But our troops crossed the stream and entered the battered fortress unimpeded. After General MacArthur had fired his artillery at Blockhouse Fourteen, a squad of the Twenty-third Infantry scouted forward only to find the enemy's trenches empty. The forts, lines and blockhouses were then occupied by the entire force. Pushing forward into the streets of the suburbs, soldiers of the Minnesota regiment encountered unexpected resistance from a blockhouse there, where they were driven back in some disorder. MacArthur then brought up reënforcements, who had to march over a single road and through rice paddies and thick timber. Only a small proportion of his men could be put on the firing line. After a time the fire from the blockhouse diminished and the place was abandoned. The way to Paco and Manila was now open to MacArthur's men. Greene's brigade, less impeded than MacArthur's, made its way through Malate and Ermita with a few exchanges of shots. The whole force now moved on, and in the early afternoon found itself before the inner walled city where a white flag was flying. Generous terms were given the Spaniards, who were allowed to go home with all the honors of war; and Manila flew the American flag. The Americans had lost 20 killed and 105 wounded.

While peace negotiations were on foot, the regular forces were in a state of perplexity as to the future. The nation had now three islands on its hands, whether or not it wanted them. The only institution to which it could turn for control, police and civilization of the new soil, was the army. Any number of homeless refugees, insurrectos and untamed barbarians had to be brought into a setting of law and order. After victory, the usual clean-up would have to be made by the permanent troops.

The volunteers had a different outlook. Feeling that the war was now over they naturally clamored to be out of the service. Although a peace treaty had not yet been signed and their contracts with the government were not terminated, such *Aug. 18 1898* political pressure was brought to bear that 100,000 of them were ordered to be discharged. In Porto Rico and Cuba, the regulars were left high and dry with a big, distasteful work of reconstruction on their hands. In Manila, where the volunteers were greatly in preponderance, they could not be well let go while Aguinaldo was setting up an independent government. *Oct. 1898* Some 40,000 insurrectos were hovering around Manila. Congress was doing nothing to replace the volunteers who were going out.

Besides, the regular regiments were far below strength, because they had been unable to obtain their full quotas throughout the war. An average of 556 enlisted men per regiment in the regular forces fought at San Juan. Sickness had reduced some of these units later to as low as 300 men, whereas the authorized number amounted to 1,272. A paltry army was shrunken to a skeleton, in the face of conditions which required 100,000 trained men for the police and careful administration of these great islands, in great part sadly demoralized under Spanish rule.

Disease, too, was lessening the effectiveness of all the American forces. Though the volunteers were in a worse plight than the regulars, both had suffered extremely. The federal troops had been forced hurriedly into climatic conditions, with which no one was familiar. Although the regular officers took the greatest precautions, such new maladies as yellow and dengue fever were a puzzle to them at a time when the scientific knowledge of the deadly doses in mosquito bites were unknown. Most of the casualties among the regular troops were thus unpreventable at that period. On the other hand, although the volunteers lost 289 killed or mortally wounded in the war, they lost 3,848 from disease. And this figure is mostly made up of deaths occurring in the United States, where sickness could have been prevented by discipline and training. At the outset of the war, General Miles desired the volunteers to be placed in small camps in their own states where they could be instructed in their duties and responsibilities, given practice with proper arms and ammunition, have the advantage of learning tactics through tactical exercises, be efficient in guard duty, and acquire the thousand and one habits that are so vital to the life of a soldier and the success of an army. The General felt that, while the soldier was absorbing with little danger that discipline which is so essential to the safety of others, the larger camps could be the more carefully selected, especially for hygienic reasons. Then the smaller units could be formed into larger ones with some assurance of order, discipline and sanitation. But his advice was not to be taken. The answer was that there were not enough trained officers in the country to carry on such a program and the regulars could not be spared from the front. So the volunteers were hustled off without knowing the strenuous duty of a soldier to himself or his fellows. One war correspondent stated that "it always took one regular to offset the volunteer's mistakes, to help him cook his rations and to teach him to shelter

April 26
1898

himself and to keep himself clean." With poor equipment he was huddled in camps of meager facilities and extent. Camp Thomas had a capacity of 20,000 troops, yet 76,742 were sent there. Camp Alger was worse. Men died from typhoid fever by flies and like them. The War Commission stated:

"Large bodies of men who are not soldiers, under officers who have had little or no military training, cannot be brought together and held for many weeks in camp and remain healthy. If the water supply is not abundant or is not good; if the thoroughly well-established rules of sanitation are not observed; if the discipline of the camp puts little restriction on drunkenness and immorality; if the soldier does not know how to live and his officers do not watch him and teach him; if his food is poorly cared for and badly cooked, and he is permitted to eat and drink anything and everything he can find, sickness will certainly prevail. If, as at Camp Thomas, a regiment can go for ten days without digging sinks; if the sinks dug are not used or they quickly overflow and pollute the ground; if practically no protection is afforded against the liquor sellers and prostitutes of neighboring places; if commands are crowded together and tents seldom struck, or even never during the occupation of the camp; if no one is called to account for repeated violation of sanitary orders, it cannot be but that typhoid fever once introduced will spread, rapidly, widely.

"How much may be accomplished by intelligent and watchful supervision on the part of surgeons and regimental officers and the observance of the well-established rules of camp sanitation is shown by the record of the Eighth Massachusetts Volunteer Infantry at Camp Thomas. This regiment was for many weeks very healthy, while much sickness was occurring in regiments nearby, though the conditions of camp site, of water, and of drill were practically the same. . . .

"In conclusion it may be said that it is impossible to bring together a regiment of 1,300 men whose lives and habits have all been different and place them in camp, subject them to its discipline, diet and duties, without much complaint. They must become acclimated and accustomed to camp life before sickness can be prevented: and until the individual soldier appreciates the necessity of complying fully with the regulations and confines himself to the regular food—and this the soldier never does until experience teaches him the necessity—he will drink polluted water, eat noxious food that disturbs his digestive organs, and will not take care of himself, and no discipline or watching will prevent it. The imprudent acts of the soldiers are the first and greatest cause of sickness in camps."

The soldier must be disciplined, it is true, but the physician must be specially trained also. Camp hygiene is a distinct branch of the medical profession. One cannot expect an eye, ear, nose and throat specialist to understand camp sanitation thoroughly. Such work is the special province of the medical corps. Many good volunteer doctors from the home towns made a fizzle of sanitation at Alger and Thomas, simply because they had not been trained in that line. Others who knew what to do, were not backed up by the newly made line officers. At the beginning of the war the medical corps of the army, like the quartermaster corps, had a size proportional to the army total of 25,000 men. Yet this body had to take care of 223,235 volunteers at a moment's notice. Death and confusion logically resulted.

As the war with Spain was reaching its close, an even greater and longer conflict was coming to an end. The last of the Indian uprisings was taking place. It seems that the Pillager Chippewas near Leech Lake, Minnesota, felt themselves unjustly dealt with, when some of their number were arrested.

Sept. 30 1898

A detachment of 20 men of the Third Infantry was despatched from Fort Snelling to the scene of discontent, at the request of the Secretary of the Interior. Lieutenant Humphreys, commanding these few men, found the Indians to be so numerous and hostile, that he asked for reënforcements. Captain Wilkinson moved out shortly afterward with 80 men of the Third Infantry. At Sugar Point two Indians were arrested on the way, and, although the warriors' attitude was threatening, there

Oct. 5 1898

was no violence. Then an unfortunate accident occurred. A soldier inadvertently discharged his rifle. In a moment this latter detachment was fired upon from the underbrush. The troops could but defend themselves as well as possible. For two days they held out, at the end of which time they had beaten back the Chippewas. Captain Wilkinson and 6 men had been killed and 14 wounded, including some civil officers. After this affair, an additional force of 5 officers and 206 men from the Third Infantry arrived at the Leech Lake Agency. The Fourteenth Minnesota was also stationed along the Great Northern Railway. Soon afterward the Indians, for whom *Oct. 20, 21* warrants had been issued, were taken peaceably and order was *1898* restored in this tribe.

Thus ended the Indian wars. One newspaper man has estimated that it cost the government in these struggles over $1,000 for every redman who lived within our border. That is a tremendous figure. But it is safe to say that, with a small fraction of the total sum, a decent-sized army could have been trained and equipped in the beginning; the Indians could have been awed and controlled with little bloodshed by such a force; and two years of such treatment would have advanced railroads and commerce by a quarter of a century. Such an able management would also have prevented in large measure the unnecessary deaths that continuously blot over half of the history of our country.

Analogous to the dribbling loss that took place on the plains is the conduct of the war with Spain. To be sure, there was little that Congress could do after hostilities had overtaken us. Nothing could make up for our neglect in the previous thirty years. But when it rejected the Hull Bill, which called for a reorganization similar to the one before the World War, it threw its weight positively on the side of politics to the exclusion of efficiency and the saving of life and treasure.

Notwithstanding the great drawbacks of legislative deficiency, the trained forces, principally the regular army, showed that they could loyally and quickly go forward in carrying out their missions. The schooling and practice they had evolved from the pittance accorded by legislation proved to be invaluable. The scientific knowledge the regular had obtained had been gleaned by his own efforts and in spite of exterior hindrances. Although, such labor could not bring into the officer's pockets an extra dollar or promote him to a higher grade, he forged ahead with only his interest in his profession to stir him onward. The product of such unalloyed zeal told at San Juan and El Caney, the vital actions of the war. In addition to the fine character of the regular army, it must be remembered that regular officers to the number of 387 led volunteer units. It is acknowledged that the enemy was not as aggressive as might ordinarily have been expected. But the trained troops that beat their way over hot trails and through the jungle showered with a hail of Mauser bullets could not know that the Spaniard would retreat. At any rate, the battles were a great test of zeal and efficiency.

Dec. 10 1898
When the treaty of peace was signed, in the making of which General Merritt played a large part in Paris, the war had lasted exactly 109 days. Even so, we had paid a price far in excess of necessity—and would have paid more, had it not been for the exertions of the regular in the dark days when he began his own renaissance.

THE ARMY'S RENAISSANCE

Second Phase

(1899–1916)

I T is a fashion for the beginning of a renaissance to slip into history unnoticed. The second phase is filled with reactions that stand out more boldly. So it was not until after the Spanish-American War that the people found out that a highly efficient set of trained men had overcome hideous obstacles and had been the mainspring of success. The groups of onward-looking officers, in the eighties and nineties, who tugged and strained at the thongs of neglect and provincialism, with which circumstances had bound as high-minded a body of men as ever existed, were to witness soon some of the fruits of their sincere efforts.

Before the augmented army now lay a problem of a very delicate, trying and constructive nature, that of skillfully administering Porto Rico, Cuba, Hawaii, Guam and the Philip- *1899* pines. From Porto Rico the troops had been sent home. Hawaii was too new an acquisition to be dealt with, except politically. Guam was insignificant relatively. Accordingly, military attention had to fasten itself for the present on Cuba and the Philippines.

In Santiago, Cuba, then one of the filthiest cities on the Western Hemisphere, Colonel Leonard Wood had to deal with a situation that would have taxed the capacity of any administration. Refugees and half-starving natives who knew nothing of hygienic conditions and who spoke a Latin language had to be fed and controlled. They had to be taught by rigid discipline and rigorous measures that they could not pollute their premises. The city was divided into 5 sections, each under a medical inspector. Aiding these supervisors were subinspectors, also medical men, who specifically looked after the sewers, streets, houses, dispensaries and street cleaners. In the early stages of this renovation some 500 cubic yards of refuse were burned daily. Within a month the death rate dropped from an average of 70 to 20 a day. Only by imposing military discipline could Colonel Wood have effected his colossal task.

The situation in the Philippines was of a different character. Because the President had enunciated a policy of "benevolent assimilation" in order to pull the peace treaty through the Senate, General Otis in command at Manila was compelled to issue an order to the Filipinos which implied very mild dealings. In a few days, the mistake of such a policy was evident. The half-civilized natives, as they invariably act under such treatment, ascribed our overtures to cowardice and weakness. Their previous hostile attitude emphasized itself at once by defiance, accumulation of arms and open attack.

Jan. 4 1899

The army in the Philippines consisted of 20,870 men, 5,372 of whom were regulars. All of the volunteers and 1,650 of the regulars were entitled to their discharge. The volunteers were especially uneasy because similar organizations in the Western Hemisphere had been discharged. The ratification of the treaty of peace (April 11, 1899) was shortly to take place. Had these volunteers elected to go home they would have left General Otis with less than 4,000 men to operate in an unknown country infested with several hundred thousand native warriors. To the great credit of these volunteers they chose to remain and serve their country beyond the time required. This is the first case on record in the United States where volunteers acted so unanimously and patriotically. Even with this increment, there was left, after eliminating those who were acting as provost guard and civil administrators, only about 12,000 effective troops in the Philippines. Before this tremendous task of colonization by so few men, Congress still sat supinely awaiting developments.

Feb. 4 1899

But the development came inevitably in the shape of an attack on Manila by some 40,000 Tagalogs about 8:30 p.m. one evening. For three days the insurgents kept up a continuous fire, being very aggressive in the night time. But the Americans, though outnumbered, were able to throw back these

Feb. 4, 5, 6 1899

assaults after much hard fighting. The United States troops
lost some 250, whereas the insurgents lost about 3,000, in addition to the prisoners and 2 Krupp guns taken.

It took this outbreak to convince Congress that something
must be done to provide some sort of competent force to pacify
these islands. That body therefore passed an act "for increasing *March 2*
the efficiency" of the army of the United States. It was pro- *1899*
vided that the regular army consist of 3 major generals, 6
brigadier generals, 10 regiments of cavalry, 7 of artillery, 25
of infantry and the staff departments. Second lieutenants were
to be examined as to their proficiency before being taken into
the service and all grades above were to be filled by seniority,
except of course those of general officers. The Military Academy
was enlarged by giving to each congressional district, each territory and the District of Columbia the appointment of a cadet.
Twenty were allowed to be appointed by the President at large.
The President was authorized to keep the strength of the regular
army at a maximum of 65,000. Retired officers were allowed *March 2*
to be placed on active duty other than in command of troops. *1899*
Cooks were to have the same pay and allowance as sergeants
of infantry. In addition to the regular force thus outlined,
the President was authorized to raise 35,000 volunteers and to
organize them into 27 regiments of infantry, at the war strength
of the regular army, and 2 regiments of cavalry. Each regiment was allowed 1 surgeon with the rank of major and 2
assistant surgeons with rank of captain and first lieutenant
respectively. The discouraging part of this whole law was that
the force so created was but temporary. Except the regular
army as it existed after the war with Spain, all were to be
discharged not later than July 1, 1901. The main good feature
was that volunteer officers, instead of being appointed by the
states were to have federal commissions from the President.
The regular officers on duty with the volunteers, except the staff,
were to be continued. Some minor features, such as enlisted
men being allowed to make allotments of their pay for the
support of their families and relatives, were good things. But
in the main the law was a makeshift, as we shall see.

The character of the volunteers obtained under this act has
never been surpassed in our service. The field officers of the

regiments were selected from experienced officers in the regular army, and the company officers were taken principally from those who had served creditably in state organizations during the war with Spain. As a result, no less than 1,524 officers and 33,050 enlisted men were on their way to the Philippines six months after the law was signed by the President.

For the troops then around Manila, the new climate under the equatorial sun was immensely trying. The rainy season just closing was giving place to an intense heat which prostrated many of the men. In many places the terrain was so dense and the advance so difficult that it took the most determined grit to go ahead.

General MacArthur followed up the attack upon Manila with a sharp engagement which ended in the occupation of Caloocan, adjacent to the city. With the small force at General Otis' disposal this work was all that could be done. The purpose was to extend the lines and assure confidence in the city itself. Any wider operations were out of the question. There were hardly troops sufficient to garrison the towns taken, to occupy the country and protect the lines of communications. The army was now purely on the defensive, because it did not have enough troops to act otherwise.

*Feb. 11
1899*
*Feb. 26
1899*
*March 10
1899*
*March 17
1899*

However, the Island of Panay was occupied by General Miller and a battalion of the Twenty-third Infantry went into Cebu. General Smith seized the island of Negros and the city of Bacalod. Then General Wheaton captured Pasig and occupied Taguig.

At the latter place a counterattack upon Wheaton's forces embarrassed his troops for the moment, but finally he succeeded in driving the insurgents fifteen miles down the lake. Thus Wheaton was able to separate the Filipino forces of the north and south. General MacArthur then began an advance upon Malolos, the insurgent capital, which contained many stores for the insurrectos. Here the fighting was quite heavy, but

MacArthur was finally enabled to occupy the place and accomplish his mission.

General Otis was now in a position, because of the beginning of the dry season and the reënforcements of regulars, who had come in since March 10th, to carry on his operations in larger measure. It must be remembered that during this time the only additional forces available were the regulars throughout the United States and other island possessions. In other words, the home country, as usual, had to be stripped of its land defense in order to cover a relatively small territory in the Pacific. However, Lawton with a force of 1,409 troops crossed Laguna *April 10 1899* de Bay and captured Santa Cruz. The advance by General MacArthur was at a standstill especially beyond Malolos, because the insurgents now threatened his flanks and communications and there were not enough troops to guard a further extension. However, that doughty general as soon as possible re- *April 24 1899* sumed his advance, crossed the Angat River while 4,000 *May 5 1899* Filipinos were in his front, captured Calumpit and occupied San Fernando. In the meantime, General Lawton, with some *April 22 1899* 4,000 men, moved out through Norzagaray, Baliuag and San Miguel for the purpose of taking San Isidro, a very important insurgent stronghold. He captured the city, but was too late to take Aguinaldo, who had escaped north with his cabinet. By *May 17 1899* the combined operations of MacArthur and Lawton, in spite of the lack of reasonable forces, these men succeeded in gaining all the territory to the north of Manila.

Heat and amoebic dysentery had wrought such fearful havoc with General MacArthur's troops under the strain of continuous marching and fighting that his force was a matter of great concern to him. He reported that 4 of his regiments had an enlisted strength of 3,701 men altogether. Of those, 1,003 were sick and wounded so that he had an effective force of but 2,698 men, of whom, after all the details were made for special duty, 2,307 could be used on the firing line. Many of the latter were so weak that they could scarcely march five miles. Subtractions, too, had to be made from the troops around Manila. The Spaniards having withdrawn from the Mindanao and the Sulu Archipelago, it was necessary to send a force to occupy that part of the island group.

The situation was very critical for these few troops alone in the Far East. Washington was wiring to send the volunteer regiments home immediately. Although General Otis persuaded them to remain, by the end of May they had become very restless and desired to depart. The other troops were in large

measure sick and the time it would take to police this land looked
long. So weak were our forces that they could attempt to hold
only the principal city of Cebu. In the meantime the natives
in other parts were permitted to drift, grow in strength and
pursue the destructiveness of insurrectos. Since the only government that had existed had been sent away, there was no law
and order in most of the islands.

However, the Twenty-third Infantry proceeded to Cebu and
General Smith with 2 battalions of the First California Regiment went to Bacolod on the island of Negros. Seven hundred

*May 19
1899*

and fifty-five officers and men of the Twenty-third Infantry
occupied Jolo. In the vicinity of Manila General Lawton was
able to concentrate about 4,000 troops under Wheaton and
Ovenshine in order to disperse the enemy on his flanks. He

*June 10
1899*

attacked the Philippine entrenchments at Zapote River. In

*June 15
1899*

spite of stubborn resistance he carried these lines. He then received the surrender of Imus, of which place he took possession.

*June 16
1899*

The insurgents in the meantime attacked General MacArthur
at San Fernando where they were repulsed, Generals Funston

*July 1
1899*

and Hale figuring prominently in driving them back. A
similar attack was made later with the same results. The insurgents now having divided their forces and having retreated
to Dasmarinas and Malabon, General Wheaton pursued one of

*July 26
1899*

the columns and routed it. Then General Hale captured
Colomba on the southeastern part of Laguna de Bay.

The terrible consequences of piecemeal legislation now began
to manifest themselves. General Otis had to stop his operations in order to reorganize his forces. In the meantime the
insurgents were adding to their numbers, and organizing their
resources and strength for one of the most deadly guerrilla war-
fares in the nation's annals. Of the regulars, 60 per cent of
the enlisted men in the artillery and infantry regiments were
being discharged. By the end of July, 8,000 volunteers had
sailed for the United States. Of 32,200 men in Luzon and the
Visayas, only 20,000 were present for duty. Minor actions continued through this distressing dearth, notwithstanding the fact
that there had been a rainfall of forty-six inches in a single

*Aug. 31
1899*

month and many severe typhoons. In the meantime the new
organizations, filled with recruits, were beginning to arrive.

By the end of the summer the troops fit for duty outside of the city of Manila numbered about 13,500; 5,000 of these were required to hold the lines of communication. This decrepit and unstable condition of the army can be charged up to the months of blank legislation after the war with Spain. During that time, the forces in the Philippines had to march and fight against odds which increased their casualties beyond national necessity. We hear in the commercial world those apt phrases of "spending money in order to make it" and often about the "early bird." But when it came to war we somehow reasoned differently. We seemed to have the tiny shopkeeper's idea of that sort of business. By that view we lost billions, and incidentally strewed over the fields our dead brothers, husbands, sons and fathers prodigally.

Since the first fight of this year 19 officers and 342 enlisted *Feb.* men had been killed or mortally wounded: besides, 87 officers *1899* and 1,325 men had been wounded. The losses, therefore, for these few months' fighting totaled 107 officers and 1,667 enlisted men, or more than had been lost in the entire war with Spain. Few people realize under what handicaps the army was placed in these far-away islands of the orient, while a prosperous people in the home country were immersed in ethics, politics and business.

In Cavite and Morong, strong forces of insurrectos had attacked the Americans at various times and had been driven back. But in the plain of central Luzon, Aguinaldo still had his headquarters and had set up a dictatorship for his people. He was occupying Tarlac as his capital where he and his cabinet resided.

Generals MacArthur and Wheeler, as the dry season was *Sept. 28* again approaching, went forward and took Porac. Several *1899* weeks later three separate columns started out to make a vital stroke against Aguinaldo's territory. General Lawton with the *Oct. 12* principal force of 3,500 men, began the movement by proceeding *1899* to Arayat, where he drove the insurgents away. Later he *Oct. 18* occupied Cabiao and San Isidro. Before long he had in his *19, 1899* hands other towns such as Cabanatuan, Aliaga, and Talavera. *By Nov. 1* Young's cavalry having swept the flank west of the line of advance, Lawton's column then pushed on toward the north as far *1899*

Nov. 13
1899
as San Nicolas, which it occupied. Turning west it took Asingan
and Rosales. The results of this movement brought about the
establishment of a chain of outposts along the edges of the plain
of central Luzon. The force also coupled up with General
Wheaton, who had gone by water from Manila and had driven
1,200 insurgents out of the entrenchments at San Jacinto with
Nov. 5
1899
great loss. In the meantime General MacArthur, who had
started out from Angeles, had advanced up the line of the railway and had captured Magalan, Bamban, Capas, and Con-
cepcion. He then attacked and took Tarlac, Aguinaldo's
Nov. 12
1899
capital, but he was just too late to capture the insurgent leader,
who had fled with his forces. He then had to content himself
Nov. 17
1899
with the occupation of Gerona and Panique. Reaching
Nov. 20
1899
Dagupan, he coupled up with Wheaton, who had arrived there
the day before.

The outline of these actions stated in such brevity gives no
indication of what these troops overcame and suffered. Were
we to look back upon the tortures of the troops in the Everglades
of Florida, the Apache country of Arizona and Scott's column
in southern Mexico and were we to combine all those hardships,
we might have a picture of the intrepid work of these men.
General MacArthur says in his report:

"The division camped in extended order, occupied towns in
extended order, lived, marched, fought, and slept in extended
order, with a view to sudden attack or defense at any time during the day or night. That is to say, the entire command has in
effect, aside from the period of actual marching and fighting,
been on outpost duty, without reserve, respite or relief, for
nearly ninety days. . . . The sun, field rations, physical exertion, and the abnormal excitement arising from almost constant
exposure to fire action, have operated to bring about a general
enervation from which the men do not seem to readily recover."

The year of 1899, however, should not be closed without a
word for the work of General Young, who with a small force of
80 troopers of the Third Cavalry and some Macabebe scouts,
hotly pursued Aguinaldo in the hope of capturing him. With
Nov. 20
1899
only this small force he occupied San Fernando de Union after

a short fight and then reached Namacpacan. He then received Nov. 23
1899
reënforcements and proceeded to scour the northern provinces.
Going along the coast, he released American and Spanish
prisoners at various places and sent Major March eastward in
pursuit of the insurgent leader. At Tila Pass, high up in the
mountains, March encountered Aguinaldo's rear guard under
General Pilar. He attacked the Filipinos, captured Del Pilar
and killed 51 others, his own loss being only 2 killed and 9
wounded. In the meantime General Young took the enemy's
trench in the Tangandan mountains. But Aguinaldo eluded his
pursuers in fleeting and slippery fashion. However, the insurgents by the actions of this year could set up no claim to a
government in so much as the President of their Congress had
been captured, their capitals had been taken and Aguinaldo had
been driven into hiding.

Meanwhile, General Schwan, with 1,744 troops and 63
scouts, went out against the insurgents who were attacking our Oct. 7
1899
lines of communication in the south. Beyond Perez Dasmarinas
he killed 100 of them and destroyed their organization. Then
General Lawton was brought from the north for a similar
southern expedition. He started for San Mateo and Montalban
with 2 battalions of infantry, 9 troops of cavalry and 2 guns. Dec. 18
1899
His progress was impeded by the heavy rains which caused the
Mariquina to rise as only tropical rivers can do. It was while
superintending the crossing at San Mateo that he himself was
killed.

While some of the troops fell back with his body, Colonel
Lockett drove the enemy into the mountains. But after he had
drawn off, the insurgents again became aggressive and came
back as far as San Mateo. The insurrecto general, Santa Ana,
then attacked the American garrison at Subig. The offensive
was repulsed and a second advance by Lockett with some 2,500
troops caused a defeat at Montalban. Lockett routed the enemy, Dec. 29
1899
killed at least 80 and captured 24 together with much war material. His only loss was 1 drowned and 7 wounded.

Thus terminated the destructive year 1899 in the Philippines. The force now consisted all told, counting the sick, of
51,167 officers and men. Altogether 509 soldiers had been
killed, 2,223 had been wounded and about 1,000 had died of

disease. This enumeration includes the death of 1 general officer.

Though the Indian wars had ceased, another desperate conflict had taken their place. The regulars and volunteers in insufficient numbers and only half armed with Krags had to beat down in torrid weather another sort of barbarian. The days of Arizona repeated themselves under an equatorial sun. But the multitudes of Filipinos were even more perfidious and more prone to conduct small actions than the redmen. The trials of these unacclimated soldiers expressed themselves in dysentery, cholera, sleeplessness and wounds. Although the blue uniform was so stifling that it was slowly giving way to khaki, for days the soldier was wet, hungry and worn out by the endless vigil he had constantly to keep. Probably in the Philippine War more than in any other in our history did the military man shorten his life, if he survived at all.

*Jan. 4
1900*

Since it would take a volume to describe in detail these actions, the general operations can only be sketched. General Bates, succeeding General Lawton in command of the First Division of the Eighth Corps, set out to overcome the depredations of guerrilla warfare into which the Filipino troubles had settled. His force was better off than before. Since October, 1899, there had been received in the islands from the United States 25 fresh regiments. Wheaton delivered a series of attacks near Bacoor and Schwan moved along Laguna de Bay; and onward for 600 miles. These 2 columns had many small actions

*Feb. 8
1900*

in which intrenched positions and garrisoned towns were captured. The insurgent forces were either annihilated or dispersed, so that they never again raised their hands in this part of the country.

*Jan. 13
1900*

*Jan. 23
1900*

Meanwhile the Forty-third and Forty-seventh Volunteer Infantry and a battery of the Third Artillery under General Kobbé were sent to the islands of Samar, Leyte and Catanduanes. This officer overcame a decided resistance at Legaspi and captured the Chinese leader, Paua.

Generals Bates and Bell with about 2,300 men, having sailed from Manila, occupied the provinces of North and South Camarines and western Albay. General Bell was then appointed military governor of these districts and General Kobbé of Mindanao and the Jolo Archipelago. In General Bell's Department the insurgents who had been driven away from the north had taken refuge. His force defeated the insurrectos in a hot fight near the mouth of Bicol River, dispersing the Filipinos and capturing many supplies. *April 4 1900*

Another expedition of the Fortieth Volunteer Infantry, under General Bates, went to establish garrisons in Mindanao. *March 20 1900* Owing to General Bates' promptness and to the appearance of the gunboats, there was little resistance met at Surigao. The *March 27 1900* insurrecto chief, Garcia, surrendered with such cannon as he possessed. But a week later the insurgents returned from their mountain fastnesses and made a night attack on the American troops. There was much hand-to-hand fighting in the mix-up, but after a time the Filipinos were driven off, leaving 2 Americans killed and 11 wounded. *May 10, 16 1900*

One of the most daring expeditions was that conducted by Major March and Colonel Hare, who left Candon and Bangued *May 19 1900* in order to scour the northern province. March missed Aguinaldo by a close margin at Sagad, while Hare surprised and killed the chieftain Tinis near Malibcong. *May 15 1900*

General Arthur MacArthur succeeded General Otis in command of the Philippine troops and as governor-general. Under him were General Bates in Southern Luzon, General Hughes in *June 30 1900* the Visayas and General Kobbé in Mindanao and Jolo. His total forces numbered 63,284.

Congress, in the meantime, had done nothing for the creation of a permanent force large enough to police and hold our *Feb. 24 1900* island possessions and to be a safeguard at home. A procrasti- *April 4 1900* nating enactment continued in effect until June 30, 1901 the existing force of mixed regular and volunteers. Another caused the army to establish a military post at Des Moines, Iowa, and *May 25 1900* to proceed with the armament of our fortifications. Congress then revived the office of lieutenant general for the senior major *June 6 1900* general commanding the army. Two provisions which showed the belief in the school advancement of the army were the appropriation for a modern military hospital at the School at Leavenworth and the authorization for the establishment of an *May 26 1900* Army War College at Washington. The last law stated that the object of such a college was "the direction and coördination of the instruction in the various service schools." Thus was allowed a master school for all branches of the service and for higher work in military strategy and information. The college was established and improved in the next two years.

The war in the Philippines by the middle of the year had settled into guerrilla warfare and brigandage of the most subtle type. The inhabitants secreted their arms in their houses, in the jungle or buried them in the ground. They would give their word that they were friends and break faith. Giving the impression that they were going about the ordinary pursuits of a peaceful life, they would lead the soldiery to believe that they were loyal. But when an opportunity offered to attack a convoy or small parties on the march, they would suddenly rise, attack with vigor and quickly melt into the population, acting thereafter as if they had always been "amigos." Under such conditions, there could be no large actions, but the creese, bolo and spear, together with rifles, played havoc with lonely sentinels and small bands of Americans. In spite of such occurrences the army built over 400 posts in the Islands and many miles of road.

June 16 1900

While this difficult task was before the soldier in trying to civilize the Filipino with a Krag, trouble in the Far East brought a part of the forces into China. General Chaffee was to command the expedition which, in conjunction with the allied troops of the European powers, was to make the foreigners safe against the "Boxers." In Manila, General MacArthur received

July 6 1900

orders to dispatch a regiment to the scene of difficulty. The Ninth Infantry under Colonel Liscum, though delayed by a typhoon, acted with such promptness that it landed at Taku, China, nineteen days after it received its first instructions. The speed that this regiment showed is again an illustration of the celerity that is habitual with trained and ready leaders and troops. The province to which they were going made it impossible to receive supplies often, after they had landed. Since the small transport service for the Philippines could not be interrupted, and the port of Taku was closed in the winter season, it was necessary that the Ninth take with it all the rations, clothing and ammunition it might require for several months. Notwithstanding such handicap, this regiment found itself in China in record time. Five days later 2 battalions of the regiment arrived at Tientsin, about forty miles inland from Taku. With the British, French and Japanese this part of the Ninth helped in the attack of that strong, walled city. Having to go forward under very little cover, the Americans suffered extremely. For fifteen hours they were in the front line, exposed to a vicious fire. When the city was finally captured, 18 had been killed and 22 wounded. This total includes Colonel Liscum himself, who was among the dead. *July 13 1900*

A couple of weeks later the Fourteenth Infantry arrived, and finally General Chaffee. Shortly, thereafter, the movement against Peking, about seventy miles away, was begun. The American column, all told, consisted of the Ninth and Fourteenth Infantry, 2 troops of the Sixth Cavalry and 1 battery of the Fifth Artillery. In the early part of the march, the Chinese held up the progress along the Pei-Ho River. The Allies attacking on front and flank carried the position and took Pei-Ts'ang. The next day the column had a severe four-hour engagement at Yang Ts'un. Although the allies were successful, the Americans lost 7 killed and 65 wounded. After these actions the troops were granted a day of rest, so worn were they by the continuous fighting and intense heat. When the march was resumed, minor skirmishes took place all along the way until within about twelve miles of Peking. At that point, it was decided among the various commanders that the day would be spent in reconnaissance, but the Russians becoming ambitious (although they had been slow on the march) attacked the Tung Pien gate of the outer city. Although they forced an entrance, they were thrown into confusion after they were once inside. The other allies coming to their aid the next day, were able to blow up the gate by evening. When General Chaffee found the Fourteenth Infantry and the American guns there, he was able to effect an entrance and then to sweep the Tartar wall clear of the Chinese, so that the march to the British Compound could be resumed. South of the gate 2 companies of the Fourteenth had already scaled the walls, and placed the first flag of any foreign nation there. They then drove the Chinese southward to the Sha Huo gate. The relief of the legations could now be effected. The American forces had lost 177 officers *July 26, 29 1900* *Aug. 4 1900* *Aug. 5 1900* *Aug. 6 1900* *Aug. 13 1900* *Aug. 14 1900* and men in the entire campaign.   General Chaffee describes the conditions he found as follows:

"Upon entering the legations the appearance of the people and their surroundings, buildings, walls, streets, alleys, entrances, etc., showed every evidence of a confining siege.   Barricades were built everywhere and of every sort of material, native brick being largely used for their construction, topped with sand-bags made from every conceivable sort of cloth, from sheets and pillowcases to dress materials and brocaded curtains. Many of the legations were in ruins, and the English, Russian, and American, though standing and occupied, were filled with bullet holes from small arms, and often having larger apertures made by shell.

"The children presented a pitiable sight, white and wan for lack of proper food, but the adults, as a rule, seemed cheerful and little worse for their trying experience, except from anxiety and constant care.   They were living on short rations, a portion of which consisted of a very small piece of horse or mule meat daily.   The Christian Chinese were being fed upon whatever could be secured, and were often reduced to killing dogs for meat.

"All the surroundings indicated that the people had been closely besieged, confined to a small area without any comforts, no conveniences and barely existing from day to day in hope of succor."

Aug. 15
1900

When the Chinese opened fire from the Imperial City, Genereal Chaffee replied with four guns from the Ch'i Hua gate of the Tartar Wall.   Two of the outer gates of the Forbidden City were blown over by Riley's artillery, but Riley himself was killed.   A vigorous pursuit drove the Chinese from the four gates in succession, but any further offensive was blocked by a decision on the part of the Allied Council that they would not enter the Imperial City.   Upon the urgent request of the various ministers, the decision next day was reversed.   General Chaffee then reoccupied the line he had gained the day before.   But it was not until some days later the Allied troops entered the royal enclosure.

While this trouncing of the Boxer was going along, some *Aug. 28 29, 1900* 12,000 troops had been sent from America to reënforce the troops around Peking. They consisted of 7 regiments of infantry, 3 of cavalry and 2 of artillery. They had reached Nagasaki, Japan, where, because of the culmination of events just described, they were diverted to Manila to join the troops *Oct. 3 1900* there. General Chaffee then began the withdrawal of the American troops from China to Manila, except 1 regiment of infantry, 1 squadron of cavalry, and 1 light battery as a guard for the American Legation.

Late in the year General MacArthur, the Governor General *1900* of the Philippines, saw the profitlessness of treating the captured insurgents with consideration. They always responded with cruelty and treachery. Leniency seemed merely to cause more blood to be spilled. It had heretofore been the custom to disarm the captives and liberate them. These semicivilized natives, attributing such actions to fear, responded by further and greater depredations. General MacArthur, therefore, is- *Dec. 20 1900* sued a proclamation, which he had distributed everywhere in the islands. It stipulated that

"whenever action is necessary, the more drastic the application the better, provided only that unnecessary hardships and personal indignities shall not be imposed upon persons arrested and that the laws of war are not violated in any respect touching the treatment of prisoners."

Such a major operation on the insurrecto cut deep and saved the lives of many an American and native, although it did not please some American ethicists 6,000 miles away. From then on, all prisoners were to be held in custody and all who surrendered themselves were to be disarmed and released. In one month some 50 prominent Filipinos, insurgent officers, *Jan. 1901* agents, sympathizers and agitators were deported to the Island of Guam, with a consequent partial calm to the Philippines.

It was not until it was plain to every one that troubles abroad, even outside our possessions, were still persisting and that the time for the volunteers to be mustered out of the service was fast approaching, that Congress shouldered the detestable burden of revamping our common defense. It passed a law which caused the army to consist of 30 regiments of infantry, 15 regiments of cavalry [1] and 1 corps of artillery with the appropriate staff corps. The total strength was to be a maximum of 100,619 officers and men. The ranking general in command of the army was to be a lieutenant general. Of this hundred thousand, 12,000 were to be natives of Porto Rico and the Philippines who were not to serve outside those islands, and who were to have regular officers as their majors and captains. This move was the origin of the Philippine scouts and the Porto Rican regiment. In the artillery corps the strength of the units was fixed, but in the infantry it varied for a company from 65 to 146, and in the cavalry from 100 to 164 as the President might prescribe. Each regiment was to consist of 3 battalions of 4 companies each, an organization General Upton had twenty years previously shown to be sound. The general officers were to consist of 1 lieutenant general, 6 major generals and 15 brigadier generals. The most signal change was in the artillery corps: its various dissimilar units were to be combined under the control of a single "Chief," the ranking officer of the corps. Between the coast and the light artillery he could make such transfers as necessity demanded. The system of detail between the staff and line, another of Upton's recommendations, caused officers in the staff departments to have experience with troops and a consequent understanding of the needs of the fighting branches. An officer was to be on duty with the staff no longer than four years, when he had to be assigned again to troops. Not less than 20 per cent of the vacancies among officers made by the increase were to be filled before July first, and the same amount each succeeding year until the total would be attained. Men not over forty were eligible for the new appointments in the grades of first and second lieutenants only, providing they could pass the examinations before the examining boards. Enlisted men were eligible for second lieutenancies, if they had served one year and could pass the tests. The President was directed not only to main-

---

[1] This was the real beginning of the 26th, 27th, 28th, 29th and 30th Infantry and the 11th, 12th, 13th, 14th, 15th Cavalry regiments—mostly organized in 1902.

tain the army at its maximum strength until Congress should vote otherwise, but he was to be allowed to exceed the maximum allotted, when the army was recruiting men for service in the island possessions. Such a move allowed for casualties and discharges during the long journey. Two brigadier generals of volunteers were to be appointed in the regular army and retired as a reward for their services in the war with Spain, and 1 brigadier general from the retired list of the army, who had distinguished himself in command of a separate army, was to be appointed a major general retired. Looking to more extended training as a result of the awakening in the army, appropriation was made for four permanent camps of instruction for the regular army and National Guard. Retired officers could be detailed on duty with schools so as to be instructors in drill and tactics.

This legislation, though a step forward, came so late as to be embarrassing to General MacArthur. The new force could not be organized and transported in time to relieve the volunteers who were to go out in a few months. At the beginning of the year he had had about 70,000 troops. During the six months afterward he had to send home some 30,000. By the end of the year he had only some 43,000 left him. He *Dec. 1 1901* warned the War Department that after May 1 it would be safe to send away the volunteers, only if replaced by regulars. But there were no regulars to be had. On account of the great delay in legislation the Adjutant General was so distracted over the possible undoing of all the previous work in the Pacific that he had to ask Colonel Leonard Wood in Havana if the *Jan. 29 1901* Tenth Infantry could not be spared from the small force there. The United States proper did not have a regular infantry regiment within its borders.

Twenty-five regiments of United States Volunteers, trained and veteran troops, had to be mustered out according to the new law. They were all sprinkled well over the Philippine Islands. Their officers with detachments of these troops were governors of provinces, towns and districts, giving all sorts of civil and military administration in order to hold the great native population in check. Were they to be taken away, much of the country would be without restraint or the appearance of force which awed the insurrecto into respect and peace. Misery and bloodshed would have followed.

The army was fortunate, however, in the turn of events at this critical time when the regulars would otherwise have been left high and dry. The crafty chieftain, Aguinaldo, had so screened himself with mystery as to his whereabouts, that a very few of his own troops knew exactly the location of his headquarters. But by this time, through MacArthur's policies, it was beginning to sink into the insurrecto mind that to turn "Americanista" was the better part of valor. Two of Aguinaldo's messengers, bearing important dispatches in cipher, gave themselves up as friends of the United States at General Funston's headquarters. After a sleepless night during which the messages were being decoded, a very desperate plan formed itself in Funston's mind. Believing the words of these former insurrectos with reference to the position of Aguinaldo's hiding place, he conceived the idea of taking certain friendly Macabebe scouts, who spoke well the language of the district in which Aguinaldo was supposed to be, of dressing them up as insurrectos and of having them pose as a successful war party that had taken American prisoners. He and 4 other officers were to be the disarmed captives. After gaining General MacArthur's permission and holding the most minute rehearsals with 84 Macabebes, he and his party went aboard a naval vessel

March 14 1901

and were landed at night on the east coast of Luzon. It was one of those bold masquerades where any little slip in the play acting by any one of the number meant annihilation to the party. For one hundred and ten miles, through the thickest of trails, with next to no food, at times miraculously escaping

March 23 1901

discovery, they finally came to their goal, Palanan, and found Aguinaldo there. A rush by the Macabebes and the insurrecto leader and two of his cabinet were pinioned. The whole party with the prisoners were then brought back by a naval vessel to Manila.

July 4 1901

This occurrence was the start of the collapse of the Filipino resistance. Aguinaldo called on his countrymen to desist. Other insurgent leaders were taken prisoners and the insurrection was officially at an end, though many a soldier was killed thereafter. However, the army had made the Islands so safe

by its courageous feats, in spite of disease and treachery, that
it was now possible to install a civil governor of the Philippines—William H. Taft. General MacArthur, who was called *July 4*
back to the states, was succeeded by General Chaffee as military *1901*
governor. The army through this year had brought its total
of posts built and stations located up to 502. The Secretary
of War said:

"I cannot speak too highly of the work of the army in the
Philippines. The officers and men have been equal to the
best requirements, not only of military service, but of civil
administration with which they were charged in all its details
from the date of our occupancy in August, 1898."

Insurrection, however, continued in scattered places, especially in the provinces of Batangas and Samar. The troops
under General Bell and General Frederick D. Grant, after
many arduous pursuits, were able to take the two ringleaders, *April 16, 27*
Malvar and Lukban. But the main part of the activities was *1902*
over, with a total loss to the army of 330 officers and 6,746
enlisted men killed, dead or wounded. President Roosevelt
was at any rate enabled to announce the end of the insurrection *July 4*
and to grant complete "pardon and amnesty" to the natives. *1902*
The office of military governor was abolished with the thanks
of the President. However, the Mohammedan Moros were
still untamed in Sulu. Expeditions against them, notably
those of Colonel Frank Baldwin and Captain John J. Pershing,
were temporarily successful.

In Cuba, the forces under Brigadier General Leonard Wood
were withdrawn from the island after as great reconstruction *May 20*
work as had been known in history. Since Cuba had been *1902*
granted autonomy and had elected a President, Vice-President, *Feb. 24*
Senate and House of Representatives, the army's work was *1902*
over. But it had given the people a splendid example of how
to live in peace and health. While General Wood was using
his military forces to establish order, sanitation and discipline
and to supply the starving Cubans, Major W. C. Gorgas, of
the Medical Department, was conducting a ruthless war on
yellow fever, which for two hundred years had been the curse

of the West Indies. Even in our own country it is estimated there had been at least 500,000 cases of that disease in a century (1793–1900). Major Gorgas, with the backing of General Wood, had the cases at once reported, the suspect isolated and the habitation of the sick man thoroughly fumigated. A war of extermination was waged on the mosquito. Buildings and houses were screened and the natives taught personal hygiene. Such men as Major C. L. Furbush did their work with such despatch and consideration that Havana has since given many public expressions of its gratitude.

1902

In the same way the medical corps in the Philippines was confronted with the plague of Asiatic cholera. The devastations of the disease had reached the appalling number of 300,000 deaths. The skillful and determined measures taken by these hygienic experts practically eradicated this dread disease in two years, and soon brought it under control. Recognizing that water and food products are the only carriers of infection, most edibles and water were required to be boiled before eating. Quarantine was established on incoming shipping. The extermination of rats and other vermin was begun, and the Philippines were made livable. It must be remembered that the army was the pioneer in these matters.

Since the war with Spain, all of the regular infantry regiments had been required in the Philippines, with the exception of a few scattered companies. A large proportion of the regular cavalry, artillery and staff troops had been there most of the time.[2] In addition, 25 regiments of the United States Volunteers and 19 organizations of state troops had been necessary to augment the regulars, whose soldiers had seldom been in the United States since the war. To show the magnificent proportions of the Philippine contest, there had been 2,811 separate actions and battles in a little over three years. In most of these engagements the troops had been ambushed.

*Feb. 4
1899 to
July 4
1902*

Congress, seeing the results of trained and scientifically educated officers, was particularly liberal in its legislation covering army educational interests. It made an appropriation for enlarging the buildings at West Point and gave a generous

*June 28
1902*

---

[2] Volunteers about equaled the regulars in number.

allowance for the continuance of the Army War College, situ- *June 30*
ated at Washington Barracks on the outskirts of the capital. *1902*
Secretary Root realized that the military education of officers
was especially important after the effects of the law of 1901.
Out of 2,900 officers in the army, 1,818 had been appointed
since the beginning of the war with Spain and only 276 of the
latter were West Pointers. He realized that some systematic
and technical education would have to be imparted to these
men, who were possessed of practical experience with troops and
in a peculiar type of warfare, but had had little chance to lay
for themselves a military foundation. Accordingly, the "garrison school" made its appearance, and special service schools
were to follow. Demonstrations and maneuvers were also to
give practice to the soldier. This year joint maneuvers were *Sept.*
held on the New England coast with regular artillery and *1902*
militia against battle ships. Although this first trial was not
all that could be expected, it was a beginning of those exercises
in the field which were to give officers practice similar to that
of action; and inculcate in troops the necessary knowledge of
their duties and requirements.

A new cavalry drill regulation, which is essentially in ef- *1902*
fect to-day, appeared this year. The troop was formed in
single rank, with divisions for platoons and squads. The tallest
men were in the center and shortest on the flanks. The squadron, consisting of 4 troops, was drilled by the major.

After one hundred and eleven years of silence on the point,
the Congress considered again the militia. The "Dick Bill" *Jan. 21*
made for the first time federal mention of the National Guard, *1903*
which was the higher distinction among state troops known as
"organized militia." All other male citizens between the ages
of eighteen and forty-five, were to be known as the Reserve
Militia. The "organization, armament and discipline" of the
organized militia were in five years to be the same as those
features of the regular army. The organized militia was to
be paid during its activities and was required to participate
in practice marches, or go into a camp of instruction for five
consecutive days and to assemble for drill and instruction or
target practice at least twenty-four times during any year.
The act provided for the detail of regular army officers at

camps of instruction or for temporary duty with the militia. One bad feature of the law was that the service was entirely optional and that these able-bodied men were not subject to call. Neither were the governors of states bound to comply with the order of the President, when he requested the service of the National Guard. In fact the troops could disregard the call of the governor with impunity. The same old error was also committed—the militia could not be called out for more than nine months. No specific provisions were made for a volunteer reserve, which had been suggested.

Jan. 30
1903

Feb. 14
1903

Following an act allowing the higher officers of the Philippine Constabulary to be appointed from the regular army, came the signal legislation which created a general staff, whose main duty should be to prepare plans for national defense and for the mobilization of the forces in war against any nation. It was to consist of 1 chief, 2 general officers, 4 colonels, 6 lieutenant colonels, and 12 majors. Twenty captains were also to be selected from the captains and lieutenants in the army at large and to have the pay of a captain, mounted. The commanding general of the army was to become the chief of staff by virtue of his being the ranking officer in the service. Because the President was commander in chief under the constitution, the duties and title of this new office were more fitting for the work of actual administration. The chief of artillery,

March 3
1903

by a separate act, was made a brigadier general and was made an additional member of the General Staff.

The corner stone of the War College building was laid in Washington this year, at which exercises Secretary Root paid tribute to General Upton's memory, the man who had foreseen the necessity of such a thing as a general staff and a school of this kind thirty years before. It was this brilliant secretary who also had General Upton's *Military Policy of the United States* brought from its obscurity and published in book form.

The Moros in the Philippines still continued to give trouble to the army. Brave to the point of fanaticism and in many ways more cunning than the Indian, they became a continual menace for many years. Conspicuous among these actions was

April
1903

that of Captain John J. Pershing's detachment which destroyed a fort belonging to the Sultan of Baccalod. When, later, this same American force was fired upon by Taraca Moros during *May* *1903* an exploring tour of the American troops, several of the Moro forts were stormed and captured.

While these engagements in the Philippines were taking place, better lines were being followed in the War Department. Under the workings of the new general staff and at the sugges- *July 20* *1903* tion of Secretary Root, a joint Army and Navy Board of 4 officers from each of the services was created for the coördination of plans in case of war. General S. M. B. Young became *Aug. 15* *1903* the first chief of staff, who at once relieved the War College of the burden of projects falling to its lot and left it free to follow its immediate duties in reference to school work.

Along with better management went efforts at obtaining more skill. The first national rifle contest was held at Sea *Sept. 8, 9* *1903* Girt, New Jersey, in the fall of this year. Six prizes were awarded, the first being won by the team from the New York National Guard. The Army Rifle Team was fifth and the Marines sixth.

The American troops in the Philippines had been reduced to such an extent that toward the end of the year they num- *Oct. 15* *1903* bered only 843 officers and 14,667 men. This diminution left a tremendous task upon their hands. The Secretary of War, Root, was so gratified with their accomplishments that he said of the army:

"I do not think that any government ever had a body of public servants presenting a better standard of personal character, a higher average of competency, or a more completely controlling sense of public duty. A country is fortunate which has such officers to rely upon in time of need."

Although the Congress did not now raise the personnel, it did do something for material advancement. Realizing that *April 21* *1904* the new island possession ought to have permanent fortifications, after five years of thought on the matter it made substantial appropriation for defense. On another line, too, it showed *April 23* *1904* its appreciation of the veteran. Those officers below the grade of brigadier general who had been retired on account of wounds of after forty years' service, were to be advanced one grade, provided they had served in the Civil War.

Again the Moros in the Philippines continued to give trouble in Mindanao and Jolo. Datu Ali with some 3,000 followers defied all efforts to catch him for some time, his troops committing all sorts of depredations, especially at night. Pursuits by the American troops were almost constant. This old chieftain once agreed to surrender, but soon afterwards broke out in armed resistance, and so terrorized the country that we shall hear of him again.

March–Oct. 1904

In the states, combined maneuvers were carried on with enterprise and success. At American Lake, Washington, 1,687 regulars with 2,324 militia from Washington, Oregon and Idaho were placed in the field under command of General Funston; at Atascadero, California, 2,247 regulars with 2,181 National Guard of California were similarly placed under General MacArthur; and at Manassas, Virginia, 5,062 regulars and 21,234 eastern National Guard were under General Corbin. These troops had the actual practice in exercises and joint operations of those numerous details that actually confront troops on the ground. The eastern troops were assembled in Virginia upon the scene of action of the second battle of Bull Run of the Civil War. For two days they worked upon the situations that confronted Lee and Pope in 1862. The result was an exceptional benefit to the troops. It is a pity that such training could not be conducted during the next year, but Congress would not appropriate the funds.

July 1904
Aug. 1904
Sept. 1904

As to materials for war, this year marked the completion of about half of the recommendations of the Endicott Board submitted in 1885. It had been difficult to accomplish this small fraction of the contemplated task because of the shortage of enlisted men. They would not go into the service because of the small pay. Notwithstanding this condition, materials were purchased and many guns emplaced.

1904

It was in this year that the army was territorially divided into five grand divisions under major generals, each division being subdivided into departments under brigadier generals. The office of adjutant general ceased to exist and was replaced by that of a newly created military secretary, who was given the additional labor of the former record and pension office.

Another evidence of the renaissance in the army was the

establishment of the Army Staff College at Fort Leavenworth. *June 27 1904*
Its object was to instruct especially selected officers in the
duties of the General Staff of the army, to improve their qualifications as instructors and to prepare them for duty in the
Army War College. In addition to this direct purpose, they
were charged with the investigation of such military inventions,
discoveries and developments which would affect the various
arms of the service. The student personnel was limited at first
to from 9 to 15 officers of the artillery and engineers. Later,
selection was made from the upper half of the class of the
infantry and cavalry schools.

The army during this year dwindled to nearly half its
authorized size. At one time it numbered altogether 3,750 *Oct. 15 1904*
officers and 56,064 enlisted men. Because the pay was practically the same as it had been at the close of the Civil War,
privates could not be had and officers had a hard time to live
decently. Neither could the troops improve by practice in military work. Such maneuvers as had taken place in 1902, 1903,
1904, were out of the question, because of the lack of appropriation. Altogether it was a parsimonious time for the
service.

But as usual, improvements seemed to go along as far as it
could within the army. A very comprehensive set of infantry
drill regulations appeared. More reference was made to move- *1904*
ments in battle; the location and position of troops with reference to the ground was more carefully considered; and rapid
fire was prescribed at a distance of two hundred yards from
the enemy. The range for the rifle was classified as follows:

Up to   300 yards . . . . .short range.
           300 to 600 . . . . mid-range.
           600 to 1,000 . . . . .long-range.
       1,000 to 2,000 . . . . .extreme-range.

The company was divided into 2 platoons. The command
"fours right" became "squads right," and the normal attack
by battalion was given with great precision. Although it has
been found out since that there is nothing more detrimental
than a normal formation for attack, these drill regulations
showed a decided tendency toward battle movement rather than

pure drill. There was provision for instruction on varied ground against an imaginary enemy, when his position and force were merely assumed, against an outlined enemy when his position and force were indicated by only a few men, and against a represented enemy when the actual number of troops played the part of a hostile force.

In addition to other setbacks, shortage manifested itself in the officer personnel of the army. Through the detail of officers to the militia and to the staff, 25 per cent of the line officers and 11 per cent of the staff officers were absent from their posts on other highly necessary service. The Secretary of War felt that there should be a corresponding increase of officers in the various branches in order to fill this gap. President Roosevelt even made this suggestion the subject of a special message to Congress. But nothing was done. On the other hand, by the details of officers mentioned above, the regular had so well equipped the National Guard that Secretary Taft was able to report that, with few exceptions, the militia conformed to the organization of the regular army. However, the secretary pointed out that much remained to be accomplished in the line of supply, discipline and training before there would be anything like a high average of efficiency. Both the army and the National Guard had done all it could without the help of Congress.

Jan. 9
1905

Although he had failed with the legislators along other lines, President Roosevelt created a board to bring up to date the report of the Endicott Board. Headed by the secretary, Mr. Taft, this new commission contained the names of the best technical minds in the army and navy on fortification. These men were to have supervision of matters pertaining to our seacoast protection, to armament in general and to the disposition of torpedoes and mines.

Jan. 31
1905

A distinct loss to the service and the country occurred at this time in the death of Colonel Arthur L. Wagner, the foremost American strategist and military writer of his time. As a critical student of military history and tactics and the outstanding pioneer of the renaissance, he had left the impress of his knowledge and personality on the schools at Leavenworth to such a degree that in the high standard of that institution

July 17
1905

Arthur Lockwood Wagner

his labors are felt to-day. As soon as he came back from the Spanish-American War, in which he had served both in Cuba and the Philippines, he was made in succession Commandant of the Staff College at Fort Leavenworth, was appointed to the General Staff of the army and was given the directorship of the Army War College. He was chief umpire at the Manassas maneuvers in Virginia and was generally looked to as the final authority on military tactics and strategy. His personality was of such an engaging sort that he could readily place his fine technical and tactical knowledge in the hands of the student. One has said of him that his attitude was as courteous to the lowest ranking second lieutenant as to a general. What the service owes to him can scarcely be estimated. Much of the success of our troops in the World War was due to his incipient efforts in awakening the officer back in the nineties to the realization of the unique and endless study and practice required by his magnificent profession. The untimely tragedy of his death is all the more accentuated by the fact that at the very hour he was dying, his commission as a brigadier general in the regular army was lying on the President's desk for signature.

It is a singular coincidence that one of the effects of the thought induced by Wagner and others showed itself in a little over a month after his death. The Army Signal School was established at Fort Leavenworth for the purpose of preparing *Aug. 25 1905* officers of that corps for the active duties of that branch of the service. The work was largely laboratory in character and was conducted from a standpoint of experiment and research. It was there that some of the great inventions of Colonel Squier were later perfected, inventions which have been of benefit to the entire electrical world.

In the Philippines the depredations of Datu Ali had reached such a point that it was necessary to take drastic measures against all the outlaw bands. Although the utmost effort was made to have him surrender without resort to force, every attempt proved to be fruitless in dealing with this class of frenzied Mohammedans. Finally an expedition of 3 officers and 100 picked men from the Twenty-second Infantry and 1 officer and 10 Filipino Scouts under Captain Frank R. Mc-

Coy went against them. Seventy-seven men of this party, with cooked rations for one day and without baggage and other accouterments, set out from Digos. After many hardships they arrived at the Malalag River where they surprised and killed Datu Ali in his hiding place. The result of this success was the seizure and surrender of the hostile Moros and complete pacification of the Cotabato district. The character of the work performed by these troops was no less creditable and daring than that of Funston in the capture of Aguinaldo.

Oct. 16
1905

Oct. 22
1905

In the Philippines, the army had to be called into activity to quell disorders with which the constabulary and scouts were unable to cope. Notably, Colonel J. W. Duncan took a detachment of the Sixth Infantry against the stronghold of Bud-Dajo. The attack of the place was fraught with some of the most desperate fighting known in the army's many engagements in the islands. It looked for some time as if the place could not be carried. Finally Lieutenant Gordon Johnson, with a few men, made their way over the stockade and thus effected an entrance, so that the troops were able to disperse or kill the band of outlaw Moros.

March
1906

March 5–8
1906

On the west coast of the United States, the San Francisco fire had shocked the country and had spread lawlessness throughout the city. No organized body of men could be found to cope with the situation except the troops of the army. Hospitals and fire departments were buried in flames. So prompt was the action of the military man that in less than three hours after the catastrophe (5:14 to 8 o'clock) General Funston had taken charge of the city, and a heavy force of the Twenty-second Infantry, Sixth Cavalry, a detachment of the artillery corps under Colonel Morris, and 2 companies of the First Battalion of Engineers, occupied the principal streets. Fort Mason and the Presidio army posts afforded succor for thousands of homeless as in previous days on the plains. One report states of the soldiers that:

April 18
1906

"They were confronted by appalling conditions, which increased at an alarming rate, from hour to hour, until they threatened to swamp the puny human energies arrayed against them; courage, persistency and endurance won the day, but not until human nature was nearly exhausted. When Saturday morning came (there was no dawning in those days) it was apparent that the worst was over, as the fires had reached their limits, and all breathed more freely. But a new demand arose, or rather, one already existing had increased until it seemed almost impossible to meet its requirements—it was the question of how to feed and shelter hundreds of thousands of men, women and children whose homes had been destroyed, and occupation gone, many of them having lost all but what they were wearing. How this was done and what other assistance was rendered by the United States Army will be told by the extracts from the newspapers from April 18th to May 6th; and from other sources.

"It is proper here to note the first act by the Army, immediately succeeding the disaster, the promptness of which can not be too highly commended. The Department Commander, General Funston, sent a mounted messenger to Fort Mason and the Presidio, ordering all available forces to report promptly to the mayor to assist the police in guarding public property and preserving good order. To this act may be ascribed the perfect order and public safety at a time when lack of them would have resulted in anarchy and riot.

"Immediately after the earthquake General Henry G. Sharpe, Commissary General, ordered Colonel Davis to ship 400,000 rations from Portland, Oregon, to San Francisco; Major Geary was ordered to ship 300,000 rations from Seattle, Washington, and Captain Simonds was ordered to purchase 200,000 rations at Los Angeles and vicinity. The commissary storehouses at the Presidio, Fort Mason and Fort Miley were thrown open and rations issued to the hungry people. Bread in large quantities was baked and large kettles of coffee were made and distributed to the people. The following morning relief supplies began to pour in from neighboring cities and the Subsistence Department at once began to receive the supplies and arrange them for distribution."

The army was not satisfied with bringing San Francisco through from the first stages of its terrible shock, but performed all manner of services in putting the city on its feet again.

"So much general abuse and misappropriation of supplies existed openly on every hand, while the police force was so entirely inadequate, that the army was asked to assume the duty of distributing the relief stores. The troops had performed almost constant duty for nearly two weeks, and were utterly worn out. General Greely called for more troops, and while the number he called for could not be spared, two additional regiments, one of infantry and one of cavalry, were ordered to San Francisco for duty. Also, there were ordered by the Secretary of War, by telegraph, to report to General Greely for duty in conducting relief work, forty-five specially selected officers of experience and of proved administrative ability, all to proceed to San Francisco and report without delay. The orders were sent out from Washington late on April 30th, and received late that night, or on May 1st and on May 2nd the first arrivals reached San Francisco and reported at Division Headquarters, about sundown.

"Next morning the work of supplying over a quarter of a million people began in earnest. With scanty and broken-down transportation, telephone and telegraph lines down, with an insufficient force of troops to guard all points at which guards were needed the problem seemed staggering; yet it had to be solved, and that quickly."

And the army fully accomplished the work. It fed the starving populace, gave havens of comfort, killed looters, opened stores, supervised hospitals, got the fire under control, and many an officer and soldier did not sleep while the constant need for them existed.

In the West Indies the army was called into play on a very delicate mission. The Cuban government was beset with an insurrection of such alarming proportions that it requested assistance from the United States. At once the President dispatched 5 regiments of infantry, 2 of cavalry and several batteries of artillery. The ease with which they crept into the island and their dispatch of movement grandly attested to the existence of a general staff. After the arrival of so many well disciplined and well trained soldiers, the insurrection cooled and ceased. For over two years thereafter they kept order in Cuba by their very presence, and without resort to arms.

Congress now realizing that it had committed an error in not providing for joint maneuvers in 1905, appropriated *June 12 1906* $700,000 for the purpose. But the irony of this measure was not wholly realized until later. An inventory showed that there was so much of the army in Cuba, the Philippines, Hawaii, and Alaska that the United States proper had a mere shadow of troops. Since there were too few soldiers for the execution of exercises, there were none that year.

Congress also increased and reorganized the ordnance de- *June 25 1906* partment. That branch was to have 1 chief, with rank of brigadier general, 6 colonels, 9 lieutenant colonels, 19 majors, 25 captains and 25 first lieutenants. The temporary transfer of officers from the line of the army after examination was continued, as was also the advanced grade over the line commission for those temporarily detailed to the department. A powder factory, the first in the history of the army, was also *June 25 1906* provided for in the shape of Picatinny Arsenal at Dover, New Jersey. The service now could manufacture its own ammunition, and keep it uniform. The law also caused the erection of seacoast batteries on the island of Oahu, Hawaii, and allowed the building improvement at the Military Academy to proceed.

Echoes from other days faintly sounded in the west. Some 300 Ute Indians broke out from their Uintah reservation across Wyoming. The governor of the state had to call for United States troops, which were immediately furnished. The Utes were intercepted by the soldiers and led back to Fort Meade, South Dakota. It would appear from this episode that the previous statement in this history concerning the close of Indian Wars in 1898 was an error. But the flight of the Utes was more of an economic disturbance than a devastating outbreak, as the outcome clearly shows.

The encampments of this year were fraught with more marching and training in the field than at any previous time. Formal ceremonies were kept to the minimum; and spectacular exhibitions, such as sham battles having no military value, were eliminated; 49,717 troops, regulars and militia in about equal proportions, were assembled in seven camps over the country.

These maneuvers demonstrated the advantage of numbers in such practice. Accordingly, the Secretary of War, realizing that there was no longer necessity for the small posts of Indian times, recommended that the troops be combined into larger units so as to be organized on a tactical basis. Every officer then might gain actual experience in the work of administration, supply and movement incident to war. As it stood, officers had seldom had a chance to command more than a regiment and general officers were in the predicament of being forced to use the pen more than the stirrup. In some cases they were benefiting for the future welfare of the nation as much as engineers in jail. Besides, the Secretary's plan was a money-saving proposition. But politics which wanted the little post as a pie to its locality defeated the idea by ignoring it.

Feb. 1
1906

The report of the Coast Defense Board, or Taft Board, showed a rather depressing state of affairs on our shore line. It found, after its labors, that the coast defense we then had was able only to cause an enemy to land with mobile troops. It could keep off ships but not transports laden with soldiers. In other words, all the United States then possessed was a partial harbor defense. Chesapeake Bay was entirely open. The investigations proved that our lackadaisical legislative attempts in the past had but put us where we started—with a sole dependence upon the mobile army.

Jan. 25
1907

However, a signal and excellent change in the organization of the artillery corps came from Congress the next year. For a long time army officers had tried to show the law makers that field artillery, or artillery with the mobile army, did not bear much more resemblance to coast artillery in organization and duties than did cavalry to infantry. This contention caused the coast and field artillery to be separated into two distinct branches and to be incorporated into the line of the army. The chief of artillery was to become chief of coast artillery after a year. The field artillery was to consist of 6 regiments of 6 batteries each. The coast artillery was to consist of 700 officers and 19,147 men. As a consequence, the increase of officers in that branch was so great that promotion far exceeded that of any other arm for some time. Young

lieutenants became captains of artillery, whereas old lieutenants of infantry and cavalry still remained lieutenants.

A little over a month later the office of military secretary, *March 2 1907*
after a short life of two years, was converted back again into
that of adjutant general. The office of lieutenant general was
abolished.

It was at this time that representatives from the army began that great contribution to commerce and progress, the
Panama Canal. President Roosevelt realizing that civilians
could not finish this gigantic undertaking, turned to the army.
As Arthur Bullard says:

"Mr. Roosevelt, while President, came to the conclusion
that the canal could not be built by civilian engineers—men
trained in private enterprise. There was no way to make them
stick to the job. Successful construction men can always command high salaries. And men like Wallace and Stevens, who
are used to being their own masters, find the Government service, with its inevitable red tape, irksome. It is impossible to
established a permanent working force if the Boss is likely to
throw up the job any minute. Under such circumstances no
man feels sure of his position. For the spoils system, so much
decried in politics, is the ordinary practice in railroading and
construction work. What was needed was not only engineering genius, but executive stability. Mr. Roosevelt appointed
a Commission of army officers, men who would stay on the
job till they were ordered home."

Accordingly, after Mr. Stevens had resigned Colonel
George Goethals, corps of engineers, was appointed Chairman *April 1 1907*
and Chief Engineer of the Panama Canal Commission. At the
same time he was made Civil Governor of the Canal Zone.
The other members designated were Colonel H. F. Hodges,
Lieutenant Colonel D. D. Gaillard, Lieutenant Colonel Wil-
liam L. Sibert, corps of engineers; Civil Engineer H. H.
Rousseau, of the navy; Colonel W. C. Gorgas, medical corps;
Maurice H. Thatcher and Joseph B. Bishop (secretary).

What the project needed was a determined administrator

at the head and a staff of assistants who would loyally and punctually carry out their chief's wishes. Colonel Goethals was the soldier who let nothing interfere with his mission—to complete the canal. Colonel Gorgas, hand in hand with him, eliminated the yellow fever so that the dread of that disease did not continue to drive the laborers away. Colonel Goethals helped Gorgas in so doing, and the whole staff worked as a disciplined unit, irrespective of personal opinion. Colonel Goethals watched the calendar and his forces minutely. The loose ends were soon knotted. There was no graft. So much did army standards count, that President Roosevelt soon gave complete control of affairs to Goethals. And in the incredible space of six years, what the world had been trying to do for nearly half a century, was finished.

The army's activities in general at this time were very much scattered.[3] In the Philippines, the Pulojanes in Samar and Leyte were making it hard for the constabulary to control them. General Wood sent some detachments of infantry into the island. In a short time he was able to report the trouble at an end. The Army of Cuban Pacification too, under General Barry, was performing its work quietly. It kept the Cubans in leash without friction. A regiment also in the west

June 24 1907

[3] ARMY ACTIVITIES

Geographical distribution	Officers	Enlisted men	Total
In the United States............................	2,625	31,637	34,262
In Alaska.......................................	52	970	1,022
In the Philippines..............................	688	12,091	12,779
In Porto Rico..................................	3	6	9
In Cuba..	276	4,182	4,458
In Hawaii......................................	12	196	208
Troops *en route* and officers at other foreign stations.	94	1,108	1,202
In the Philippine Scouts........................	116	4,346	4,462
In the Porto Rico Regiment.....................	24	572	596
In the Hospital Corps, excluded by the Act of March 1, 1887 (24 Stat. L., 435), from being counted as part of the enlisted strength of the army........	.....	.....	3,400
Making a grand total of....................	3,890	55,108	62,398

conducted the Ute Indians on their long journey from Fort Meade, South Dakota, to the Cheyenne River Reservation.

But the members of the service were in a serious state of depletion, principally on account of the pay of the soldier. Men who could get from $1.75 to $2.50 a day as common laborers scarcely wished to be on a restraining post at $13 a month. Many a company during this time was reduced to as few as 8 privates. Since the skill required of an enlisted man was now much greater than ever before, the inducement to enter the service was still less attractive.

It was in this year that the War Department could not carry on maneuvers with the National Guard because the army was absent in many islands, in Alaska and at the Jamestown Exposition. However, some joint army and militia coast defense exercises took place along the Atlantic coast.

For the officers of the army the commander in chief raised the standards of physical fitness. Field officers, those officers of an age tending to corpulency, had to undergo test rides and other exercises in order to determine whether they could stand the strain of battle. This requirement caused a general movement within the service toward having all officers gain physical stamina far above that of the average civilian. Requirements for daily exercise and medical examinations were to keep the personnel active.

Congress opened the next year with the passage of an act to put the medical corps on a firmer basis and to increase its *April 23 1908* personnel. The corps was to consist of a medical corps proper, a reserve corps, a hospital corps, a nurse corps and dental surgeons. The medical corps proper was to consist of 1 surgeongeneral with rank of brigadier general, 14 colonels, 24 lieutenant colonels, 105 majors and 300 captains and first lieutenants. All officers in the corps were to have mounted pay. Young graduates of medical schools throughout the country could be appointed as first lieutenants of the reserve corps and were liable to service at the call of the President.

One of the greatest pieces of legislation for some years from the standpoint of morale and justice was the readjustment of *May 11 1908* pay both for officers and enlisted men. The new schedule, although not tending toward indulgence or extravagance, gave a living salary to the officer and a means of obtaining the proper quality and quantity of enlisted men.[4]

May 27
1908

A third law put the Porto Rico Provisional Regiment on a basis more nearly resembling the regular army. The name was changed to the "Porto Rico Regiment of Infantry of the United States Army." Its enlisted personnel was accepted for three years and its junior officers were given a status more nearly that of the regular army. In the same law, besides the allotment of $300,000 for the construction of gun and mortar batteries for our coast defenses, the sections took up seriously the improvement of the militia provisions. All able-bodied citizens between eighteen and forty-five were theoretically liable for service in the militia but there was no penalty in time of peace for disobedience to the terms of the act. The supply and organization was to be looked after on a more businesslike basis. The standard of the regular army was to be had within two years. The law

---

[4]
Lieutenant general	$11,000
Major general	8,000
Brigadier general	6,000
Colonel	4,000
Lieutenant colonel	3,500
Major	3,000
Captain	2,400
First lieutenant	2,000
Second lieutenant	1,700

RANK AND ARM OF SERVICE—BATTERY, TROOP, COMPANY	First enlistment
Sergeant, first class—signal corps	$45
First sergeant—artillery, cavalry, infantry, engineers	
Sergeant—engineers, ordnance, signal corps	36
Quartermaster sergeant—engineers	
Cook—artillery, cavalry, infantry, engineers, signal corps.	
Sergeant—artillery, cavalry, infantry	
Quartermaster sergeant—artillery, cavalry, infantry	30
Stable sergeant—field artillery	
Horseshoer—cavalry, field artillery	
Corporal—engineers, ordnance, signal corps	
Mechanic—coast artillery	24
Chief mechanic—field artillery	
Corporal—artillery, cavalry, infantry	
Artificer—infantry	21
Mechanic—field artillery	
Farrier, saddler, wagoner—cavalry	
Private, first class—engineers, ordnance, signal corps	18
Trumpeter—cavalry	
Musician—artillery, infantry, engineers	
Private—artillery, cavalry, infantry, signal corps	15
Private, second class—engineers, ordnance	

read well, in that it appeared to cause the militia to serve
wherever and whenever the President wished. But the governors could decline to send out a single man or to furnish
the proper type of officers, whenever those executives so decided.

Throughout the army there was particular zeal shown in
the improvement of its parts, in many ways. The pay bill had *1908*
increased the number of soldiers. There were now commands
large enough to allow the officer and soldier practice in the
field. Minor difficulties in the Philippines were suppressed
and the Army of Cuban Pacification was quietly delivering
peace. Eight camps of instruction and eleven artillery districts held joint exercises with the militia to the number of
75,000 men. This year also marked the complete issue of the
new United States magazine rifle, "model 1906," which for accuracy, speed and power far surpassed the Krag. The ammunition, the magazine and bolt action combined to secure greater
ease and speed in reloading. The effect of the establishment
of the Picatinny Arsenal was apparent; that plant was turning out about 500 pounds of uniform smokeless powder a
day. *1908*

It was this year that the Wright brothers made successful
flights with a biplane. Several army officers helped in these
progressive tests. One, indeed, lost his life so doing. Yet
the War Department was prevented from purchasing a single
plane because of the absence of funds allowed by Congress.
Although this was a new invention, whose efficiency had not
been fully shown, it was too bad that this apathy displayed
itself just nine years before we tackled the World War. Similarly there were absent, searchlights, submarine mines and
power plants for the coast defense. *June 13*
1908

In the summer the "Division of Militia Affairs" was created as a part of the general staff. All the militia records were
taken from the adjutant general's office and placed in the office
of the new bureau, which was to have the superintendence of
the organized and unorganized militia during peace so as to
coördinate the efforts of the National Guard with the work of
the regular army. Thus the state troops could be given more
recognition.

May 14
1908
The tests for physical fitness were put in force throughout the service with vigor. All field officers of the mobile army were to demonstrate to a medical officer that they could ride thirty miles a day for three consecutive days. For these older officers this distance had to be covered in periods of six hours for the first two days and in seven and a half hours for the other. Field officers of the coast artillery had to walk fifty miles in three days and in a total of twenty hours, the march on any day to be in consecutive hours. When any of these officers could not make the test, they were to be retired either for length of service or by a retiring board. All the junior officers below field grade were to have a physical examination each year.

1909
The activities of the army during the next year were wide and varied. In the Philippines the Moros, giving trouble to the civil authorities, had to be suppressed in many minor actions by the regulars. The Army of Cuban Pacification was
Jan.–April
1909
brought home, it having completed its usefulness without resort to force. Many defects were brought to light by the army in joint maneuvers with the National Guard of Massachusetts, Connecticut, New York, New Jersey and the District of Columbia. Means of supply and mobilization were particularly lacking, principally because the appropriations for vehicles had been inadequate.

March 3
1909
Congress passed a law which appointed a court of inquiry into the case of 3 companies of the Twenty-fifth Infantry. It seems that on one night three years before (August 13–14, 1906), certain colored soldiers of this regiment took their rifles from barracks and "shot up" the town of Brownsville, Texas, where the Twenty-fifth was then stationed. Investigation could not ascertain the culprits. Accordingly President Roosevelt summarily dismissed the 3 companies without honor. It subsequently developed that great provocation had been given these men by the Mexican element of Brownsville especially, and that there were many good old soldiers, not implicated in the riot, who had lost the value of all their service. Accordingly Congress at this time made provision for complete investigation of each case so as to return the innocent men to the colors and to give them back their lost time. Many were reinstated under this provision.

Effort within the army was made to have a modern type of equipment for infantry. A study by a board of 6 officers was begun at Rock Island Arsenal. The accouterments of the armies of the world were investigated. From the work of this board there was later evolved the modern infantry pack. April 28 1909

There was yet much to be desired if the efficiency of the service were to count in time of war. Secretary Dickinson, having investigated conditions from records and interviews, showed how nearly 40 per cent of the officers of the army were on detached duty, away from troop training. Such work as duty with National Guard, at schools, and at the Military Academy, left too much to be done by those who remained. He pointed out a need for more officers. He showed that there ought to be an appropriation of at least a half million for aeroplanes. He showed how West Point could not fill the vacancies and that the economy of turning out more cadets with about the same overhead at that plant was apparent. His remarks on the organized militia show what the service was trying to do, but that it could not make a truly efficient showing without Congressional help:

"Much remains to be done in the way of instruction. While the Constitution provides that discipline shall be the same as that of the Regular Army, it reserves to the States the authority of training the militia. It thus appears that while the War Department can fix standards it has no authority to take direct charge of the training and cause the organized militia thereby to attain such standards. The War Department may provide ways for training, make suggestions as to methods, and fix the standards that must be attained, but it cannot directly conduct the training. . . . As to the mobile state forces, it is specially desired to have them conform to the course at the Army School of the Line at Fort Leavenworth, Kans."

The efforts of the army tended toward practical as well as theoretical education. Field batteries of the Wisconsin, Minnesota, Michigan, Iowa, and Indiana National Guard participated in a school of instruction with a battalion of regular field artillery at Sparta, Wisconsin. Field schools for the instruction of medical officers were held at Sparta, Antietam and the San Francisco Presidio. One hundred and thirty-eight companies of militia coast artillery had been organized this year. In rifle practice 43 militia teams attended the national match at Camp Perry, Ohio. Seventy-eight civilian rifle clubs and 44 schoolboy rifle clubs had been built up.

But when it comes to real discipline and training, such exercises are but rudimentary. Something had to be done by Congress or our whole military organization would be useless in time of war. Secretary Dickinson showed, for instance, that the field artillery with its 48 batteries was far below proportion even for the small army we had. He showed that the posts of the army should be so arranged as to operate tactically instead of administratively and so as to coöperate with the National Guard. He pointed out that the small post was but an accidental result of Indian troubles, that it prevented training and should be abolished. He showed how much more money it took to run these many little plants than a comparatively few large ones. He conclusively proved that under his recommendations there would be vastly more economy, rapidity of mobilization and training of the militia. This logical suggestion was right on the line upon which the general staff had been working, and upon which Secretary Taft had expressed himself several years before. But Congress took no action on this matter.

April 12
1910
It did realize, however, the need of more graduates of the Military Academy and the economy of increase. Accordingly, it passed a law which allowed the Corps of Cadets to be increased by one-fourth its existing size. The enlargement was made by allowing to the Congressman an appointment every three years, instead of every four. This change did not affect the four-year course.

Aug. Sept.
1910
The activities of the army this year were various. A large proportion of regular troops was used in fighting the great forest fires in Montana, Idaho, Washington and Oregon. The soldiers performed excellent service, as would any well-disciplined body of men. But after all, this was scarcely the appropriate work for troops who needed technical and tactical prac-

tice. As well use engineers to dig ditches. By the withdrawal of so much of the army for this labor the plans for a camp of instruction for both regulars and National Guard at American Lake had to be relinquished. Either there was no other disciplined body of men for the job or the emergency was so great that the army was the only dependable resort. At any rate, the emergency could scarcely exist for two months, to the exclusion of more important activities.

During the summer, military tournaments of no tactical value were held at seven cities scattered over the United States. Competitions in drill, wall scaling, packing and bridge building caused certain troops to gain skill in elementary exercises, but the character of these events was more spectacular and athletic than fundamental.

The General Staff, meanwhile, had worked out a plan for combining the regulars and National Guard into 3 divisions composing a field army. Of course there was no money to try and test out this paper machine. But the scheme was meticulously drawn up and nicely tabulated. At least the army had marked everything out to the limit of its powers.

Other things had been suggested by the General Staff. In consonance with them, Secretary Dickinson showed Congress that there should be an elimination of inefficient and unprogressive officers, that there should be more officers, that we needed aircraft, guns and ammunition and, above all, that there should be a comprehensive law for the methodical mobilization of a volunteer army in time of war. He showed how no use had been made of the discharged soldier, who had had three years' good schooling and was qualified to enter a reserve army, and that there existed only 1 regular officer or soldier for every 10,000 inhabitants. He brought to light the fact that there was little reserve ammunition. The chief of staff, too, explained that at the current rate of appropriation, it would take fifty years to get an adequate reserve supply of field artillery material.

The Secretary summed up the whole matter when he said:

"In order to avoid the waste inseparable from going to war without full preparation, we must be ready with a complete system for passing from a peace to a war establishment. We should undertake without further delay the problem of simplifying and perfecting the administration and organization of the army to the end that the new army of regulars, organized militia, and volunteers may pass automatically from a peace to a war basis. We have vast military resources, and if we but organize them in time of peace it will not only have a tendency to prevent war, but should war come it will enable the nation to conduct its campaigns with a greater regard for economy and efficiency than has been hitherto possible. It is futile to attempt to place the military establishment of the country upon a proper basis, having due regard for economy and efficiency, by the passage of detached legislation."

Feb 27 1911

In the face of these sentiments, Congress voiced another "detached" law. It increased the corps of engineers by 5 colonels, 6 lieutenant colonels, 19 majors, 17 captains and 13 first lieutenants. The enlargement was to take place by lineal promotion and by the addition of second lieutenants in five annual increments. When the West Point quota of graduates was exhausted the remaining vacancies were to be filled by civilians who could pass a thorough examination.

March 1 1911

In these times of prosperity, the army, in general, was looked upon with disfavor. So common had it become for a certain class of our population to discriminate against soldiers, that Congress had to pass a law in order to give them the ordinary rights of citizens. Signs had been posted outside of places of amusement "No soldiers admitted." Insults and abuses had been heaped upon the man in uniform in various ways. It came to such a pass, that our lawmakers thought it wise to allow a fine of $500 to be imposed on any proprietor, manager or employee of a public place who caused such class distinction.

March 3 1911

Congress by this time saw the need of detailing officers to act as instructors of the National Guard. It accordingly passed a law which permitted the President to detach an officer for that purpose in the proportion of one for each regiment or separate battalion of infantry, and an equivalent number for other branches. Such detail was to create a vacancy for pro-

motion and allow corresponding appointments of second lieutenants.

At the same time, the injustice done to officers by regi- *March 3*
mental promotion before October 1, 1890, was overcome. Those *1911*
who had suffered by stagnation in a particular regiment and
had thus been topped by men of shorter length of service were
to be advanced to the grade they would have attained, had
promotion been always lineal in the particular branch of the
service. The ones who had been fortunately favored by regimental promotions were not to be affected.

By these acts Congress had added 12 engineer officers, 60
dental surgeons and some 200 line officers to meet the demands
of detached service. Although the vacancies were to be filled
in annual increments, West Point was still unable to fill the
quota of second lieutenants. Consequently many officers were
taken in from civil life, after rigid examination.

Similar care was taken with the recruitment of enlisted
men, 72 per cent of the applicants being rejected.

In the Philippines the Moros in the Sarangani peninsula of *1911*
Mindanao became so lawless that an expedition under Major Hei-
berg commanding some Philippine Scouts was sent against them.
After arduous labor by his and other columns, peace was restored.
At the same time detachments of the Regulars had their hands
full in preserving order in the Lake Lanao district, Mindanao.

One of the biggest demonstrations of the inefficacy of our
efficient regular army was the attempt to assemble in Texas a
division and some regiments of coast artillery. The border
along the Rio Grande was again so filled with unrest that it
was felt necessary to make a show of strength in Texas. Already 2 troops of cavalry had been dispatched to help the civil
authorities preserve the neutrality. But affairs became so
threatening that a larger force was necessary. Accordingly,
orders were issued for the concentration of a "maneuver divi- *March 6*
sion" at San Antonio. It was to be composed of 3 brigades of *1911*
infantry, 1 brigade of field artillery and 1 independent cavalry
brigade, with the necessary auxiliary troops, all under the command of Major General William H. Carter.[5] At the same time

---

[5] Author of many technical works especially a standard textbook on
"Hippology."

36 companies of coast artillery, equally divided into 3 regiments, were ordered to Galveston under Brigadier General Albert L. Mills. The officers of the staff and the troops were assembled from everywhere and had never had a chance to work together before. The division was never up to full strength during its entire stay and it was several months before the railroads could get the last regiments to their destination. General Wood, Chief of Staff, said of the division's work:

"The mobilization has emphasized the fact that our regiments in peace should be kept at greater strength, and it has also brought out very forcibly the necessity for a reserve with which to bring the regiments from their peace strength to full war strength. The experience in the mobilization in Texas has also emphasized the necessity for accumulating a sufficient quality of reserve supplies and the establishment of proper depots; in short, the necessity for proper military organization and preparedness for war."

The concentration took practically all of the various units of the United States Army within the continental limits and put them in a position to patrol the border from the mouth of the Rio Grande to San Diego, California. The maneuvers afforded the regulars an excellent object lesson of the workings of a regular division, something never demonstrated before in our history. It gave great practice to the staff and line in understanding our deficiencies with regard to supply and movement. Above all, it proved what the army had long known, that our land forces were deprived of making a showing against a stout enemy.

Although the elements of movement and strength were denied the service, the fruition of the renaissance was still manifesting itself. A School of Fire for Field Artillery was established at Fort Sill, Oklahoma. Its purpose was to give a thorough, practical and theoretical course of instruction in the principles and methods of field-artillery target practice. The service was doing the best it could to gain experience in military technic. But a school of this kind at that time looked pathetic and grotesque when it is realized that there was not

June 3
1911

enough field-artillery ammunition in the United States to last through a normal modern battle.

In other fields the army was also pushing ahead. The *1911* "Taylor system" of scientific management was put into effect at Watertown Arsenal. The bureaus and branches of the War Department were united with a resulting economy in overhead. Foreign service regiments were recruited up to full war strength before sending them abroad so as to save the expense of transporting separate recruits and to have a maximum number of soldiers in our possessions. Mounted troops were stationed where climate favored year-round training. A new *Infantry Drill Regulations* gave a more important place to combat than ever before prescribed in such a work. The mechanism of drill was subordinated to tactical principles which were laid down concretely, but with sufficient latitude for application.

It was this year more than any other that marked the decided change between the old army and the new. The forward- *1911* looking spirit had saturated the big percentage of the service. The officer became a practical progressive in his profession, or he was cast aside. Bad habits and laxity were treated with such harshness that the army was signally purged of the laggards. As for efficiency, it began to take on a business aspect. The soldier became primarily a worker. He was not limited to an eight-hour day. He had not only to keep fit but also to demonstrate his capacity for leadership and the proper execution of his tasks. In effect, a great milestone of the renaissance had been set up on the way toward larger fruition.

Actions were still going on in the Philippines, as is illustrated by the fact that the Moro outlaws were yet on the warpath. Captain E. G. Peyton with 2 troops of cavalry and 2 companies of Philippine scouts rounded up the worst of these outlaws in the island of Jolo and succeeded in reducing them. Twenty Moros were killed and 2 Americans wounded, 1 offi- *Jan. 14 1912* cer and 1 enlisted man.

So recurrent were the depredations of the Moros that a word might be here said about the peculiar nature of the activities of the soldier in grappling with these determined people.[6] In

---

[6] These facts were obtained, at the solicitation of the author, from an eyewitness.

the first place, the Moro was a Mohammedan. The Moro chief, or Datu, sometimes Maharajali Saakat, made his own laws for his particular gratification. Agriculture and trade were thus discouraged because the Datu took away the produce at his own pleasure. The main ambition of the Moro was, therefore, to get a rifle, which he could hide and keep. With every weapon he could purchase another wife or raise himself in rank and power. This power was mostly abused and a menace to our standards of civilization. Sleeping soldiers would be stabbed in the dead of night and their rifles seized. When Captain (now General) Pershing was Governor of the Moro province, he came to the conclusion that the key to progress for the Moro was to deprive him of his firearms. Accordingly, all that could be called in were taken and paid for. But Moro agitators harangued the people, contending that the Americans were taxing them, denying them slaves, limiting them to one wife and charging them for the privilege of being married. Open resistance by hundreds of Moros followed. They took refuge in the Bud Dajo crater in defiance of the orders of the governor. It would have been but a day's operation to have potted them where they were, but Captain Pershing understood that many ignorant and misguided men were among the contenders. It was then that Major Peyton, Philippine scouts, was ordered to conquer this band, but spare their lives if possible. He surrounded the pit and prepared to starve out the Moros. Double sentinel posts, one soldier with a rifle and another with a shotgun, were placed about the camp. These men did not sleep because they knew death in the shape of a creeping Moro would await them if they winked. Barbed wire besides was strung up near the main body. Sallies by the Moros night after night kept the soldiers engaged, when these half-civilized natives tried to cut their way out. Crazed or running Juaramentado, in religious frenzy, a single Moro with creese or bolo would charge a whole battalion of troops. Finally, all the Moros in the crater decided to come in, except 47, who disappeared in the jungle. But these latter ones were similarly forced to surrender later.

Jan. 1912

During the next year, a renegade Moro by the name of Dowd collected a band of outlaws in a very inaccessible place.

Major Peyton, with 5 companies of scouts, 1 company of infantry and 2 troops of cavalry, went against them. Dowd had committed all sorts of crimes, so that after being induced to come to a conference and having been told that nothing would be done to him if he surrendered, except to put him before a court, he departed with a defiant refusal. It was then that Major Peyton did a very unique thing. Finding the ordinary trails to Dowd's position well covered with fire, he resolved to cut new trails. The continual chopping in unseen places warned the Moros that the troops were coming on, but they could not see their targets and they did seem to be able to change their plan. A severe action followed, when most of the Moros were either killed or captured. Dowd escaped but was later killed in an effort to capture him.

Although all of the arms of the Moros were not yet taken, the troops for political reasons were withdrawn.[7] It was reported that quiet reigned. It did, with much robbery, murder, arson and peonage. When later, new troops, unacquainted with Moro customs, attempted to round up the increased number of recreant Mohammedans, their losses were unnecessary in many cases. One company, having to learn afresh the dangers that attended work with these savages, camped on the edge of a large lake where the surf was rolling high. In the night the noise of the waters kept the sentries from hearing sounds of lurking Moros. As a consequence, several stole into camp, cut off the captain's head and severely wounded a lieutenant.[8]

In the early part of the year the Maneuver Division and *1912* the First Separate Brigade were disbanded. But the border raids still continued. In fact, the withdrawal of the troops caused more depredations and seemed to be an open invitation to Orozco's rebel forces. The Ninth Cavalry was sent to Douglas, Arizona, and the Thirteenth to El Paso, Texas. These regiments were particularly successful in suppressing the attempt made in Texas by General Reyes to instigate an insurrection against Madero.

This command also enforced the embargo on arms and am-

---

[7] The Presidential elections were in sight.
[8] Thirty inf., 15 cav. and 6 F.A. regiments, 18 F.A. batteries, 6 sig. corps, 12 eng. and 24 C.A. companies in Philippines, 1899-1912.

munition for the Mexicans. It patrolled so carefully that it prevented raids on American ranches in Texas and Arizona. Before the end of the year there had to be upon the Mexican border 6 regiments of cavalry, 1½ regiments of infantry, 1 battalion of field artillery, 2 companies of coast artillery and 1 company of the signal corps: a total of 6,754 officers and men. During the summer 67,280 men of the organized militia participated with the regular troops in five joint maneuvers. The tactical work developed in these was very superior to anything in the past.

It was at this time that the floods along the Ohio and the Mississippi produced such tremendous trouble and loss that it was necessary to call out officers and troops of the regular *March, Apr* service to alleviate the suffering. So quietly, methodically and *1912* efficiently did the supply and the care of the refugees take place that there was little notice of the actions of the army by the public.

The mobile army in the United States was at this time scattered in some 49 posts throughout 24 different states. The average strength per garrison was less than 700 men. Effort was made by the General Staff to form these troops into a tactical organization of 3 infantry divisions composed of 2 or 3 brigades, with the proper attached troops. Of course this organization could be made only on paper as long as Congress persisted in scattering the army so widely and withholding from it the vital training necessary for large bodies of troops. A scheme of complete organization worked out by the War College Division of the General Staff tried to rectify the utter absence of technical and tactical organization throughout the country. A sound and definite policy was formulated. It estimated that at the outbreak of war with a first class power the United States should be capable of assembling at once an effective force of 460,000 mobile troops and 43,000 coast artillery. It gave this strength as a minimum for the first line neces- *July* sary. In addition it conservatively felt that plans should be *1912* made to raise 300,000 men. But these projects could not be carried out without legislative help.

Aug. 24 It was during this year that a very drastic "Manchu Law" *1912* was passed by Congress. It provided that officers who had **not** served two years of the previous six with a troop, battery or company should immediately be returned to troops and serve there the required time. Only certain officers of the Judge-Advocate-General's Department, the Ordnance Department and those on duty in the Panama Canal Zone were exempted. The law was sweeping in its effect and caused temporary demoralization in the service schools and some staff departments. However, the idea was sound in that it showed a desire to have an officer familiar with his duties of command as well as those of staff work.

At the same time, the quartermaster, subsistence and pay departments were combined and called a quartermaster corps under a chief with the rank of major general. Such consolidation made for better efficiency and economy. The control of these correlated branches now came under one man so that waste of material and motion could later be avoided.

It is interesting to note that there was a fair attempt this year to notice the air work of the army. An appropriation of $100,000 for the purchase, maintenance, operation and repair of airships and other aërial machines did not go very far, but it showed a tendency to note the existence of this new branch of the military service, however slightly.

One very important part of this law was the attempt by Congress to create a reserve for the regular army. When a man enlisted, he was to serve three years with the colors and four years with the reserves. The law as it stood was a good idea, but there was no provision in it for the payment of soldiers while in the reserve, except in case of war. Also, a man understanding the type of service upon which he was to enter hesitated about signing up for so long a time as seven years. In other words, certain compromises in the measure resulted in defeating its purpose. As a concrete example of what actually happened, the Secretary of War after two years was able to report that there existed the magnificent reserve in the United States of sixteen men.

A board of general officers presided over by Secretary Stimson met in Washington for the purpose of organizing as perfectly as possible the land forces of the United States for war, so that when an emergency came there would not be any great amount of turmoil or needless expense in passing from one stage to the other. Of course what the board could do was limited in view of the absence of legislation. However, the mobile army within the United States was given a tactical organization into divisions and brigades for the purpose of administering all military matters territorially. For this purpose, peace distribution was reorganized into six geographical departments: Eastern, Central, Western, Southern, Philippine and Hawaiian.

Feb. 6 1913

The Mexican frontier continued to be patrolled by 6,700 soldiers who tried to cover a territory of 1,600 miles in extent, from the Gulf of Mexico to thirty miles west of Nogales, Arizona. Huerta having succeeded Madero was opposed by Carranza, Villa and Zepata. Much firing took place on the territory adjacent to the boundary line, which was coveted by all the Mexican parties. Many refugees and wounded Mexicans came over the border. Often shots flew northward across the Rio Grande. A slight mistake on the part of the troops and international relations would have become very complicated. At length, the trouble became so acute that orders were issued for the concentration at Texas City and Galveston of the Second Division under Major General Wm. H. Carter. The 11,450 men making up these organizations were transported with great dispatch in comparison to the speed of the maneuver division of 1911. In a little over a week after the first orders were issued, all the troops had reached their destinations.

Feb. 21–24 1913

At war strength this division should have been 22,565. As it was, had the division been involved in hostilities, it would have been necessary to recruit it by 50 per cent in the face of the enemy, with the consequent disaster that has similarly overtaken such unreadiness in the past. Of the force assembled in Texas, the British and German military attachés stated that they had never seen a finer body of troops collected, nor had they seen better discipline, less intoxication or such perfect sanitary arrangements in camps. Although the country was drained of its trained forces, those who were ready were in perfect condition.

March 1913

In the valleys of the Ohio and the Mississippi, floods of a graver nature than the year before rendered many people homeless and caused much suffering. The army was again called upon to handle the situation. With energy, skill and dispatch supplies were distributed, refugees taken care of and the interruptions to business curtailed. In a similar way troops took care of the devastated regions of Omaha, Nebraska and Lower Peachtree, Alabama. Later the soldiers efficiently fought forest fires in California and in the Adirondacks.

A camp of instruction for regular cavalry was held at Winchester, Virginia. The Tenth, Eleventh and 2 squadrons of the Fifteenth Cavalry participated. Similarly camps of instruction for field artillery were held at Tobyhanna, Pennsylvania, Fort Riley, Kansas, and Fort Sill, Oklahoma. It was in this year that the army began really to spread its education to civilians other than the National Guard. Undergraduate students of seventeen years of age or over, who were physically qualified and recommended, were given the opportunity of taking a practical course of instruction. Two such camps were held at Gettysburg, Pennsylvania, and at the Presidio of Monterey, California, during six weeks of the summer. The object was to give training in maneuvers, tactics, care of troops, camp sanitation and rifle practice. The paramount idea was that of bringing to young men something which would render them more capable in sudden emergencies and make them, incidentally, more valuable citizens. There being no appropriation to cover all expenses, the students had to pay for their transportation as well as for their subsistence and clothing. Even with this voluntary drawback, at Gettysburg 159 young men from 63 universities and colleges, and at Monterey 85 from 27 educational institutions, received the course.

Another evidence of the renaissance was the establishment of the School of Musketry at Fort Sill, Oklahoma. Its purpose was especially that of giving instruction in small-arms firing. The founding of this school was the small beginning of the great Infantry School now at Fort Benning, Georgia, with its elaborate curriculum. Courses were given to both officers and enlisted men of the regular army and National Guard. Along this same line an aviation school at Augusta, Georgia, was transferred to Texas City, in order to participate in the operations of the Second Division. Although 15 aeroplanes consti-

July, Sept. 1913

July 18 to Sept. 30 1913

June 9 1913

tuted the entire equipment of the army aviation corps, two nonstop flights of 240 miles were made and sketches drawn by the reconnoitering officer. Of course we had no dirigible balloons of any sort.

Feb. 25
1914
March 19
1914

The appearance of new *Tables of Organization and Field Service Regulations* disclosed a tendency toward a more modern use of troops in the field. Improvements in administration and supply had been culled from the best of foreign methods. Officers and men were given more independence in the execution of their tasks. The idea of simply looking in the book to see what one had to do, was overcome by an emphasis upon principle rather than precept.

The troops in the Moro country of the Philippines were again on the move. Some trouble was experienced in getting the Moros to subside, after being some time without restraint. An action at Bud Tandu was decisive.

March 1
1914

April 25
1914

At last legislation conscientiously tried to put the volunteers on a sound basis for any emergency. The land forces of the United States were to consist of the "regular army, the organized land militia while in the service of the United States and such volunteer forces as Congress may authorize." The term of enlistment for volunteers was to be the same as that for regulars. No officer above the grade of colonel was to be appointed in the volunteers. The President could appoint regular officers to volunteer commissions in the proportion of 4 to each regiment of cavalry, field artillery or infantry, or to 12 companies of coast artillery; and not more than 1 to each volunteer battalion of engineers, signal corps or field artillery. The regular commissions were not to be vacated by the appointment of regulars to higher grades in the volunteers. By the removal of the regular officers for such purpose, temporary vacancies and promotion were created in the regular service. When war was imminent or upon us, all organizations of the land forces were to be recruited and maintained at their maximum strength. The measure showed the first inclination of Congress in our history to foresee the necessity for having an established status for the volunteer before the emergency occurred.

April 27
1914

Another act appropriated $250,000 for airships and other

aërial craft. It also authorized the Secretary of War to purchase a tract of land either near Tullahoma, Tennessee, or at Anniston, Alabama, for the purpose of establishing a permanent maneuver camp for the troops of the United States army and the National Guard.

The organization of aviation units was for the first time *July 18 1914* seriously given attention in legislation. An aviation section of the signal corps, to operate and supervise military aircraft, was to be composed of not more than 60 officers and 260 enlisted men. Officers were to be detailed to this work for four years and were to be classified either as junior military aviators or military aviators. The junior aviators were to have the rank, pay and allowances of a grade above that which they held in the line, provided they did not hold rank above that of first lieutenant. Only 15 military aviators were allowed. They were to have the rank, pay and allowance of a junior military aviator and also to receive an increase of 75 per cent of their pay. Both types of aviators could be given this higher rate of pay only when they were making regular and frequent flights. The hazard of the position of aviator was recognized when Congress allotted to the widow of an officer or enlisted man, killed as a result of an aviation accident, one year's full pay.

The task of patrolling the Mexican border, a duty most arduous and thankless, was performed by 250 officers and 8,260 enlisted men assigned from the Southern and Western Departments. Due to an unpleasantness which had arisen when Admiral Mayo was insulted by the Huerta Government at Vera Cruz it was thought necessary to bring the army into play in Mexico itself. Brigadier General Funston was ordered to go to Vera Cruz. He at once set out by way of Galveston with *April 23 1914* 4 regiments of infantry of the Fifth Brigade, Company E of the Second Battalion of Engineers and a field hospital. He *April 24 1914* was followed later by the Fourth Field Artillery from Texas City. General Funston reached Vera Cruz promptly and dis- *April 28 1914* embarked his troops. A little later he took command of the city. Under him were 225 officers, 3,832 enlisted men of the *April 30 1914* regular army and 113 officers and 3,333 men of the marines. He extended his line so as to include El Tejar, which controlled the water supply of the city.

Due to the change of government in Mexico there was little action that could be taken. However, the conduct and work of the troops were excellent in this trying situation. Officers and men had to deal very tactfully with the natives because they could neither go into Mexico nor go away from it. General Funston's predicament was all the more pitiable when it is considered that had he received an order to journey in the path that Winfield Scott had followed nearly seventy years before, he would have found that he could not budge. He had almost no transportation and a reduced peace strength which lowered his numbers to a pitiable figure. The Mexicans, too, were strong and armed with modern weapons. Thus a great nation of over 100,000,000 people for the third time in three years presented a spectacle to the world of being unable to assemble in their troubles even the semblance of a powerful force.

So successful had been the encampments, especially with the students, in the previous summer that effort was made to *July 6 to Aug. 7 1914* have two sets of two each this year. As a consequence 348 students were sent to Burlington, Vermont; 120 to Asheville, *June 26 to July 1 1914* North Carolina; 114 to Ludington, Michigan; and 85 to Monterey, California.

All through this year labor disturbances, especially in the coal regions, demanded the dispatch of regular troops to quell the disorder. Colorado, Montana and Arkansas were all visited by the Federal forces with the usual lulling effect. Such police work deprived the regular army of giving the instruction necessary in joint encampments with the National Guard. The consequence was that during this year there was almost a dearth of such field work. Even the camps for medical officers and schools of instruction for field artillery had to be canceled, with the exception of a field artillery encampment at Tobyhanna, Pennsylvania.

The legislation for the army during the second year of the World War was quite scattered. Several million dollars *March 3 1915* were spent on the armament of the Panama Canal. The enormous allotment of $15,000 for the purpose of having officers sent abroad to observe and study the war in Europe, did not show an excessive interest in the illuminating situation of a new type of warfare overseas. On this account officers of the highest merit could not be sent to the scene of the World War in order to learn the endless details of that mechanism which would have been so invaluable to us later. At this late date, Congress began to look at aviation a trifle more earnestly. Its extreme *March 4 1915* activity manifested itself in the appointment of 3 army officers who were to report on the "advisability of the acquisition by the government of land for an aviation school and training ground." The Porto Rico regiment of infantry was incorporated into the regular army, its officers being sprinkled about on the list with regular officers according to length of service. Modern discipline throughout the penitentiaries of the service had been put in vogue with success. Congress, therefore, changed the name of the military prisons at Fort Leavenworth, Kansas, to that of the United States Disciplinary Barracks. The thanks of Congress were extended to the members of the Isthmian Canal Commission. Colonel Goethals was raised to the grade of major general as was also Brigadier General William C. Gorgas. Colonel Hodges and Lieutenant Colonel Sibert were made brigadier generals of the line. A survey of the legislation effected this year, although no part of it was bad in itself, gives the impression of futility. The country was looking upon the World War in Europe as a spectator. That the mightiest conflict in history had embroiled half the civilized world caused little suspicion that somehow the fray might strike us, or a belief that we might be free from it with a little more intelligent strength.

Mr. Gardiner, Representative from Massachusetts, had offered excellent bills for appropriations for the aviation corps, for the making of a sufficient quantity of small-arms ammunition and for the production of field artillery material and ammunition. Although every one of these measures was decidedly necessary, even were we not going to be thrown into the World War two years later, the Congress overwhelmingly rejected them.

The state of the army at this time was deplorable in size and excellent in quality. It is sufficient to say that all the foot-loose mobile units we had within the borders of the United States consisted of 1 regiment and 1 squadron of cavalry and *April 30 1915*

1 regiment of field artillery.[9] There was not a single regiment of infantry in its quarters or permanent station. In other words, the army was doing war duty, especially on the Mexican border, with only the mounted force above shown free for emergency. Besides, 27 companies of coast artillery would soon have to be sent away in order to garrison forts in the Philippines, Hawaii and the Canal Zone. This is all the more striking when it is known that the army consisted at this time of 31 regiments of infantry, 15 regiments of cavalry, 6 regiments of field artillery, 170 companies of coast artillery, 8 companies of signal corps, 3 battalions and a detachment of engineers, 7 field hospitals, 8 ambulance companies, 1 evacuation hospital and the Philippine scouts.

Mr. Garrison, one of the ablest Secretaries of War this country has ever seen, and one who as much as any martyr sacrificed his personal interests for a principle, showed that, when the proper deductions of the naturally stationary troops were made, there remained but 24,602 men of the mobile forces in the entire regular army. This was a smaller actual strength than at any time since 1861, except in April, 1865, when we had so many trained veteran volunteers still in the service. Equal to the shortage in troops was that of the officers. Over 28 per cent of them were absent from their commands for the valid reasons of detached service and casualties. Only 200 line officers had been added to the service, when many times that number were needed. All manner of materials for war were absent. The United States had only 21 aëroplanes and no dirigibles, whereas France had 500 aeroplanes and 11 dirigibles and Great Britain 250 aeroplanes and 8 dirigibles at this time. The United States possessed all told not 700 3-inch field pieces, whereas France had 4,800 even prior to the beginning of the war in Europe. In the entire country, the ammunition for field artillery totaled only 5,800 rounds, or about all that would suffice for a two days' battle: as for

---

[9] Four troops of cavalry at Fort Sheridan, Ill.; 4 troops and 1 signal company at Fort Leavenworth; 2 troops at Fort Robinson, Nebraska; 1 regiment of field artillery at Fort Sill, Oklahoma; 4 troops of cavalry at Fort Meade, South Dakota; and 2 troops at Fort D. A. Russell, Wyoming.

rifle ammunition, there was enough on hand for only four days' fighting.

The organized militia of the entire United States amounted to only 127,410 men, including coast artillery and staff. Nothing of real value had been done to establish a "second line" on a firm basis, although efforts of the general staff had been incessant in its endeavor to gain a tactical organization of the combined regular army and militia. Outside of 1 New York and 1 Pennsylvania division, other National Guard units were woefully deficient in personnel, matériel and training.

The year ended with the carrying out of a very happy idea by General Wood, then in command of the Department of the East. He established a military instruction camp for business and professional men which was held at Plattsburg, New York. *Aug. 10– Sept. 6 1915* The way in which the attendants set aside their personal business and whole-heartedly entered into the spirit of rigorous discipline cannot be too highly complimented. The conduct and training of that month was something that was of the utmost value later in our participation in the war. Although the size of the assemblage made it only a drop in the bucket, it was the start of the training camp, which was to be a great factor later.

The affairs in Mexico, marked by the killing of defenseless Americans, grew to be of such grievous nature that the country clamored for retribution. For months the matter became more serious. Finally Pancho Villa with about 1,500 bandits rode *March 9 1916* across the border and attacked the defenseless town of Columbus, New Mexico. He looted the place with the usual brutality to women and children, killing 11 civilians, 9 soldiers, wounding many others and burning a number of buildings. Having cut the telegraph wires, he embarrassed the Thirteenth Cavalry in its communication with the town. Nevertheless, some 250 of the Thirteenth pursued the raiders, killing 40 of them and wounding many more. The regiment's loss was 1 killed.

It was found immediately necessary to send a force into Mexico, since the Carranza government had shown itself incapable of protecting Americans and American soil.

Brigadier General John J. Pershing was appointed to

command a punitive expedition for the purpose of rounding up Villa.[10] With great dispatch he began his crossing of the border from Columbus, having under him the Sixth and Sixteenth Infantry, the Eleventh and Thirteenth Cavalry, 1 battery of the Sixth Artillery, the First Aero Squadron, and some engineer, signal, ambulance and hospital troops. At the same time Colonel George A. Dodd with the Seventh and Tenth Cavalry and 1 battery of the Sixth Artillery crossed the border further west. The march south was exceedingly difficult both because Carranza refused the use of the railroads to the troops and because the villages, in most cases, could not be used. The available motor truck and pack train supply was far from adequate, almost disgraceful. As the troops proceeded farther and farther from their base, their hardships increased.

The expedition, too, had orders from Washington which embarrassed it. It was to proceed against Villa without occupying towns and without coming into conflict with Carranza forces. It was a difficult proposition thus to march in the waste places and to keep out of the way of the Mexicans who were actively hostile to the Americans.

Pershing had to be reënforced by more troops later. For instance, parts of the Twentieth and Twenty-fourth Infantry started from Columbus. Meanwhile some other regular regiments of the country were concentrated along the border, and an extra motor truck train was purchased.

The American troops reached a point two hundred miles south of the border in spite of these handicaps. Colonel Dodd

with about 400 men of his cavalry regiment surprised and attacked about 500 bandits under Villa at Guerrero. He scattered the force after a sharp fight and captured 2 machine guns and a large number of horses, saddles and arms. The Villa forces lost at least 30 killed, whereas the Americans had 4 men wounded, not seriously. This battle was the only one of the war which was directly concerned with Villa. The others were the results of the hostile attitude of the Carranza troops in apparent opposition to the first understanding between the two governments.

---

[10] His order organizing the expedition was dated March 14.

General Pershing's headquarters were transferred to Nami- *April 2*
quipa, about two hundred and twenty-five miles south of *1916*
Columbus. Supplies were more and more difficult to get, but
field bakeries and rolling kitchens began to count in relieving the
hunger of the troops.

Minor actions, on account of the opposition by Carranza, took
place at several Mexican towns. Colonel Brown, with 271
officers and men of the Tenth Cavalry, met Villistas at Agua *April 1*
Caliente. Captain Kendrick similarly with 96 officers and men *1916*
of the Seventh Cavalry had a brush with some Villistas at Agua *April 7*
Zarca. Major Howze with 264 officers and men of the Eleventh *1916*
Cavalry had a larger engagement at La Joya. All these actions *April 10*
were successful in driving back the enemy. *1916*

In scouting ahead of the column, Major Frank Tompkins
with 2 troops of the Thirteenth Cavalry came to the town of
Parral. General Lozano of the Carranzistas accompanied Major
Tompkins to his camp, but the Americans were followed by a
jeering mob of Mexicans who threw stones at them and fired in
their direction. Major Tompkins took up a defensive position
north of the railroad, and in superhuman self-control refrained,
under the orders of his government, to bring on a fight with
the Carranzistas. However, he was finally flanked out by a
superior force of Mexican troops, who did not seem to be controlled by their general. About 300 of them pursued the small *April 12*
force of American cavalry which had to withdraw under instruc- *1916*
tions that exasperated these brave but obedient men. The
scattering losses in this defensive retreat had been about 40
Mexicans against 2 American soldiers killed and 6 wounded. It
was not until fifteen miles of withdrawal had taken place that
the pursuing Mexicans ceased their fire. There the 2 troops
were reënforced by 1 squadron of the Tenth Cavalry and 4
machine guns.

This incident caused the general knowledge of what the
army was aware of long since, that the whole Mexican nation
was actively hostile to our troops. General Pershing was re- *April 18*
ënforced by 2,300 troops, including the Seventeenth Infantry, *1916*
the Fifth Cavalry and 1 battalion of the Fourth Field Artillery.

Small engagements scattered themselves about during the

April 20
1916

April 22
1916
remainder of the month. Colonel Brown with 45 men of the Seventh Cavalry drove back a small force of Villistas at Verde River. Colonel Dodd with 154 men of the Seventh Cavalry had a very successful battle with an equal number of Villistas at Tomachic.

A conference between the representatives of the two nations, Obregon and Trevino for Mexico and Generals Scott and Funston for the United States, was held at El Paso, Texas. While the deliberations, which seemed to reach a deadlock, were in progress, a raid was made by a party of Villa bandits, numbering about 50, on Glenn Springs, Texas. Nine men of the Fourteenth Cavalry, who were on picket duty there, were surrounded. Taking refuge in an adobe hut, they fought with great valor. But when the Mexicans set the roof afire, they had to flee: 3 were killed, 2 wounded and 2 badly burned. The Villistas also killed a boy in the village. Major Langhorne pursued the bandits, capturing 14 prisoners.

Early May
1916

May 5
1916

May 5
1916

At Ojos Azules in Mexico, Major Howze with a squadron of the Eleventh Cavalry routed with great success a force of the Villistas. These events caused the President to see that negotiations were futile, and that more strength would have to be applied to the wily work of the Carranzistas. Accordingly, he ordered the last of the regular mobile troops, who happened at that moment to be in the United States, to the border—the Third, Fourteenth, Twenty-first and Thirtieth Infantry, the Fifth Field Artillery and practically all of the remaining coast artillery. With the country so drained, he caused the governors of Arizona, New Mexico and Texas to send their National Guard to report to the regular army whose officers would federalize the militia organizations.

May 9
1916

May
1916

May 14, 25
1916
Minor actions continued through the month with Carranzistas in Mexico, the feeling growing more intense. Small detachments of the Sixth and Seventeenth Infantry, respectively, had sharp engagements at San Miguel de Rubio and Alamillo Cañon.

June 3
1916
It was while all this was happening that Congress, having a concrete example of the meagerness of our forces, passed a National Defense or Reorganization Act, which was one of the greatest advances over all previous military legislation. The

regular army was to consist of 65 regiments of infantry, 25 of cavalry and 21 of field artillery, an equivalent of 93 companies of coast artillery, 8 aero squadrons, 7 regiments of engineers, and the corresponding staff corps. This organization gave the country a peace force of 175,000 men as fighting units. The army of the United States was to include the regular army, the volunteer army, the officers' reserve corps, the enlisted reserve corps and the National Guard (while in the service of the United States). The mobile troops of the regular army were to be organized into divisions and brigades on a tactical basis. Four major-generals and 19 brigadiers were added to the line. The General Staff was to consist of the chief of staff, 2 general officers of the line, 10 colonels, 10 lieutenant colonels, 15 majors and 17 captains, to be detailed for four years at a time. The cavalry and infantry regiments had added to them a supply company, a headquarters company and a machine-gun company. A division had 3 brigades of 3 regiments each. The increase was to take place in five equal and annual installments. Promotion was equalized to a certain extent between branches by the addition of a small number of colonels to the infantry and cavalry. An officers' reserve corps was provided for by giving commissions to civilians proven to be qualified by examination. An enlisted reserve corps was to be built up by soldiers furloughed to the reserve, the enlistment for the regular soldier being three years with the colors and four years with the reserve. Men with character "excellent" could be transferred to the reserve after one year. Vocational training of the soldier was provided for, and federalizing about 425,000 National Guard could be had under the law. The medical corps was to consist of medical corps proper, medical reserve corps, dental corps, veterinary corps and nurse corps. A special provision authorized the Secretary of War to maintain training camps which gave opportunity for much more unified handling of state troops. The President, when authorized by Congress to use the land forces, could draft the National Guard and the National Guard Reserve into the service of the United States. The Corps of *May 4*
1916
Cadets by a previous act had been increased to a maximum of 1,334 cadets, by giving each Congressman two appointments.

Altogether legislation allowed the army a maximum war strength of 287,846 men.[11]

The training camp at Plattsburg was opened for business men in spite of the fact that there was scarcely any army in the country.

[11] OLD LAW

Organizations	Officers	Enlisted men	
		Min.	Max.
31 regiments infantry	1,531	25,035	56,315
15 regiments cavalry	750	12,240	18,540
6 regiments field artillery	246	5,010	7,116
3 batallions engineers	57	1,234	2,002
Coast artillery corps (170 companies)	701	.....	19,321
Total combatants	3,285	62,840	103,294
Signal corps	106	1,472	1,472
Medical department	504	4,012	4,012
Quartermaster corps	187	6,403	6,403
Other troops and staff departments	765	1,472	1,472
Philippine scouts	182	5,733	12,000
Total	5,029	81,932	128,653

NEW LAW

Organizations	Officers	Enlisted men	
		Min.	Max.
65 regiments infantry	3,314	85,865	126,230
25 regiments cavalry	1,300	24,350	36,250
21 regiments field artillery	876	17,752	26,361
7 regiments engineers	231	4,697	7,077
2 battalions mounted engineers	32	458	692
Band engineers	.....	.....	30
Coast artillery corps (263 companies)	1,201	.....	30,009
Total combatants	6,954	163,161	226,649
Signal corps	275	3,387	4,338
Medical department	1,750 to 2,365	10,500	14,100
Quartermaster corps	369	6.403	6,403
Other troops and staff departments	1,797	19,154	24,356
Philippine scouts	182	5,733	12,000
Total	11,327 to 11,942	208,338	287,846

On the Mexican border the number of American troops had materially increased, although the above law which could not be put in force for many months did not swell the total. The President had to resort to calling out more National Guard from the majority of the states in the Union. With great difficulty they were transported to camps along the border and in the United States, until by the end of the year some 75,000 were stretched along the Rio Grande. *June 18 1916*

In the meantime some 100 Mexicans attacked the Fourteenth Infantry camp at Laredo and killed 4 soldiers, and the next day a detachment of the Twenty-sixth Infantry was fired on at West Brownsville. *June 15 1916*

Within Mexico it was felt by General Pershing that a great force of Carranzistas were collecting at Laguna de Bay with malicious intent. Under Captains Charles D. Boyd and Lewis S. Morey 2 troops of the Tenth Cavalry were sent to scout toward the Mexicans and find out their strength. Having arrived within two miles of Carrizal, the troops halted and requested to pass through the town. The request was denied, but a conference between commanders took place outside the town. While this council was in progress a large force (about 400) of Mexican troops circled the camp, placing at advantageous points machine guns. When the Mexican commanders suddenly withdrew, the Carranza troops opened fire. The little force of 90 cavalrymen were in a distressing predicament, but gallantly formed and attacked. Captain Boyd and Lieutenant Adair were killed, besides 38 others killed or wounded. Captain Morey was severely wounded. The Americans finally made their way back in various ways except 24 who were captured. The Mexicans lost 40 killed and 39 wounded including General Gomez. *June 20 1916*

This marked the end of actual hostilities of a grave nature. The large force collected on the border alarmed Carranza to such a degree that he tamed his defiant attitude. Had such numbers been capable of action in the first place, doubtless the casualties of this expedition would have been foregone. A joint commission then tried to settle the difficulties, so that the troops were held in Mexico and in the United States, on both sides of the Rio Grande and in a very delicate and difficult situation.

They could move neither backward nor forward. Finally they were begun to be withdrawn because of a diplomatic protocol between the nations. Villa was still uncaptured.

General Pershing's task through this whole campaign was, to speak mildly, awkward. He had to advance with little transportation through the most trying part of a tensely hostile country. He was allowed to attack one party but not the other, while both were equally antagonistic. He was in the position of the man who had to walk into a hungry leopard's cage with orders to beat Mr. Leopard, but under no conditions resist Mrs. Leopard with her cubs. With such a mission, who could have done better?

The experiences of the army in this phase between the war with Spain and the World War had been cosmopolitan and diverse. It was all in the work of the year for an officer to be student, instructor, leader, governor, judge, jury, councilor, fighter, constructor, almsgiver, executive and peacemaker. It was in the work of the day for both officer and enlisted man to crawl through tormenting jungles or press forward over parching trails while deadly pestilence or Mauser bullet doggedly pursued. It has been impossible to record the many annihilations of whole companies and detachments as they were ambushed on the march as late as 1905. But more disheartening than any physical discomfort, disease or wounds, which the American soldier bears with fortitude and sportsmanship, was the criticism of his own people back home. After he had gone forward with only the good of his nation in his mind, it hurt him keenly to find the press construing his sincere struggles and daring achievements as acts of cruelty or selfishness.

Through all this gruelling can be traced the soldier's stubborn desire for the improvement of the service. His ambition and pride must psychologically point that way. He enters his profession without hope of wealth or gain, much as does the clergyman. He feels that he is about to engage in a noble undertaking, whose discipline is the very essence of high-mindedness. He finds himself cut off from private business enterprises both by regulations and his movements hither and yon. He does not change his job. He cannot be promoted a single grade through his own efforts, unless it be in that far-away time when he becomes a colonel. The outlet then for his energies is to be known to his superiors and inferiors as an efficient officer. When he finds, after study and practice, deficiencies that rob the army of its best results, he strives to have them remedied. When he sees lives and money expended uselessly by his nation, he is obsessed with the desire to prevent another such disaster. It is his invariable rule when confronted with any task, to think first of his duty to his nation. His superiors often change, but his employer—his country—always stays. There are no strings, no side issues. His duty runs straight between his master and himself. He feels his patriotism too deeply even to discuss the matter. He may not wave a flag, but he can grit his teeth.

CHAPTER XI

THE ARMY HUSTLED INTO WORLD WARS

(1917–1942)

WHEN April 6, 1917, tossed the American spectators onto the European gridiron, they had not even a high school squad to meet the professionals. The 1916 Defense Act had been merely the promise of a team for which only a few freshmen had reported. The army had no large tactical units in a modern sense, few weapons, a dearth of officers, no experience with trench warfare, little training and less strength. It had 9,750 officers of all grades and experience, while 180,000 of the utmost efficiency were immediately necessary.

On the other hand, it had received a signal blessing in disguise. Few have ever regarded Pancho Villa as a benefactor. But his crossing our border the previous year had given our President the excuse of training a large portion of the Regular Army and about 150,000 National Guardsmen on the Mexican border. The hardening, discipline and schooling in the field were the finest to date for the army and made possible later the ability of the American forces, especially the First, Second, Twenty-sixth and Forty-second Divisions, to turn the tide in March, 1918, in France. There has been much speculation since as to what might have happened had not Mr. Villa done us this temporary or ultimate ill-turn or favor.

The main antidote to our preparing after declaring came *May 18 1917* forty days and forty nights after our entry. The Congress executed a single piece of legislation to implement the entire American war effort. It consisted of two main advances: the first equitable draft legislation in our history, and adequate provision for training camps for officers. Major General Leonard Wood had been the army impulse behind the officers' training camps, and Major Douglas MacArthur had been the propulsion for the draft behind the newspapers.

The law caused the regular army to be brought up to full war

463

strength by providing immediately the five annual installments of the 1916 Act. It also authorized drafting into the military service any number of National Guard reserves, who were to be organized under proper officers at once. It allowed an additional force of 500,000 enlisted men to be raised and drafted for a national army, and gave the President authority to increase or decrease the size of the units of the regular army to suit the conditions to be met in Europe. It stipulated that all officers above the grade of colonel were to be appointed by the President with the advice and consent of the Senate. It caused machine-gun units to be created. This force of 1,000,000 men in round numbers could be called out, organized, and trained as soon as the President saw fit. He was further authorized to raise and maintain by voluntary enlistment not to exceed 4 infantry divisions. The enlisted men for the regular army, if possible, were to be gained by recruiting those who volunteered or by resorting to the selective draft. All other forces were to be raised and maintained by the selective draft exclusively. The whole contingent was to be placed uniformly under the regulations governing the regular army. The President was authorized to raise and maintain in addition any special and technical troops he might deem necessary. It was particularly provided that no bounty should be paid to any one as an inducement to enlist in the regular service. No person was allowed to furnish a substitute. All male persons between the ages of twenty-one and thirty, except those who were especially exempted by the law, were subject to registration and draft. The President was authorized to create all agencies of the national and state governments in order to carry out the draft. All officers and enlisted men of the forces raised were to be upon the same footing in regard to pay and allowances as the regular army. All enlisted men of the army of the United States, meaning all the forces obtained under this law, were to have their pay raised.[1]

---

[1] "All enlisted men of the Army of the United States in active service whose base pay does not exceed $21 per month shall receive an increase of $15 per month; those whose base pay is $24, an increase of $12 per month; those whose base pay is $31, $36, or $40, an increase of $8 per month; and those whose base pay is $45 or more, an increase of $6 per month: PROVIDED, That the increases of pay herein authorized shall not enter into the computation of the continuous-service pay."

The President was also authorized to make regulations concerning the prohibition of alcoholic liquors in or near military camps. He was also virtually required to prevent the setting up of houses of ill fame or brothels within such distances of any camp, station, fort, post, cantonment, training, or mobilization place as he might see fit.

Three days after the President signed this bill, 40,000 civilian candidates for commissions appeared at 16 large cantonments throughout the country—willing, green, and soft. To receive them at each camp were from 10 to 12 regular officers, scattered barracks, a few partially constructed shacks, and the open air. The average instructor had to teach, train, select, and recommend for commission about 150 men in less than three months. Second and third sets of training camps were later set up similarly.

Under such haste and pressure the products were named "90-day wonders." Although they humorously gave themselves this nickname, probably no nation ever saw any finer characters assembled. Their performances, despite the limited training their country allowed them, are brilliant pages in the records of the War Department, and their sacrifice because of their limited training lies underneath the crosses in France. But haste characterized the efforts to obtain enlisted men as well as officers.

For the immediate enforcement of the draft law, Major General E. H. Crowder was appointed provost marshal general. A registration day was at once fixed, and some 4,000 civilian *June 5 1917* registration boards over the country with a personnel of registrars and assistants to the number of 125,000 were appointed and organized. Registration day saw the enrollment of 10,000,000 names.

The manner of calling out these drafted men was the next problem. A great lottery was established in Washington which fixed the order of call for the whole. When this feature had been *July 20 1917* determined, the boards were required to call in the names according to the lists of numbers and have the recruits examined physically in order to complete the first national quota of 687,000 men. Shortly, the selective service system was ready to deliver to the national cantonments 180,000 men. In less than three months the nation had accepted and vigorously executed without any

serious friction that miraculous thing in a democracy—a compulsory service law.

To accommodate the organization of these inducted men into
divisions for overseas, camps had to be built at once for 41,000
men each. The difficulties presented to the army in construction
work were formidable. The enlargement that fell to the lot of
the Quartermaster Corps alone was colossal. The country had
no rendezvous such as our enemies had had long before the war,
because of the denial of such a thing in the previous decades.
While the old world had learned to take things pretty much as
they are, we were still counting on things as they ought to be.[2]

As we had no place for a large army here, so we had no
maneuver space, possible battlefields, or enough munitions. We
had to go beyond the seas for them. There was an insufficiency
of training schools and almost a total lack of artillery and airplanes. The government had to adopt the French auto-gun,
machine gun, 37-millimeter gun, the rifle grenade (V.B.), the
240-millimeter trench mortar and the Stokes mortar, which were
mostly supplied from abroad. Since nearly all of the regular
officers had been deprived of experience and of observation of the
World War I, the main instruction they could give the candidate
was found in pre-wartime regulations. So many blank forms
were necessary that some had to be dug up which dated back to
the 80's. The foremost necessity and possibility in the limited
time was to instill in young officers the element of discipline and
loyalty, if possible. It was impossible to teach young men from
all walks of life any deep military technic and art in these short
months and under such conditions. There were officers commissioned in the artillery who had never fired a gun, in the ordnance
who had never seen an arsenal, and in the infantry who had

---

[2] This principle is illuminated by an incident of an ordnance company
arriving in France in 1918. It was marched after reaching Brest to the
famous "Caserne de Pontanezan." Two of the enlisted men speedily found
their quarters and ambled through the historic barracks from which Rochambeau's men had started for America over 130 years before. Accustomed to
the hasty, wooden shacks of Camp Merritt, they were astonished at the
massive stone living quarters of the French Army. One of them remarked,
"Its queer how these French regard war as a permanent institution." It
was fortunate for America it was allowed this point of view, or was it?
(For this anecdote and comment the author is indebted to Dr. Randolph G.
Adams, Director of the William L. Clements Library, University of Michigan, who was the private.)

never been in command of men anywhere.   This condition was
the fault of no single person but rather the mass of the country
during the preceding five years.[3]

Scarcely had this Selective Service bill become a law, when
General Pershing in command of the American Expeditionary
Forces sailed with 53 officers and 146 enlisted men from the *May 28
1917*
United States.   The next contingent to arrive in France was the
division under Major General William L. Sibert consisting of *June 26
1917*
the Sixteenth, Eighteenth, Twenty-sixth and Twenty-eighth Infantry, together with the Fifth Marines.   Most of these units had
but a month before been guarding the Mexican border.   They
were practically all the trained troops in the country that could
be put at war strength and sent abroad.   It was not until much *Sept.
1917*
later that other divisions began to arrive.

At the beginning of the next year 1,325,000 men had been *Jan.
1918*
enrolled.   Forty-two divisions had been organized, 8 of which
were Regulars, 17 National Guard and 17 National Army.   Out
of these only 6 had been landed in France.   Only 4 on French
soil could be classified as fighting divisions by having completed
their training abroad.   They were the First and Second Divisions

---

[3] Much has had to be said on the previous pages of this history concerning what Congress has or has not done at various times.   If those facts have
amounted to criticism of that body, they are not to be so construed.   Our
nation has a representative form of government in which the legislator often
becomes the echo of his constituents.   According to our system he also has
to work under the lashes of the whips of his party, or stand alone as a sort
of Cataline and be discounted, even stultified.   So it would be manifestly
unjust to rail at Congress for its blunders, when the people are responsible
entirely for its systems and oftentimes its votes.   Albeit if the whole public
wanted a project intensely and vigorously enough, Congress would ordinarily
vote for it.   Unfortunately active minorities have too frequently overwhelmed negative majorities.   A constructive view was stated by a great
legislator and statesman to his constituents: "Certainly, gentlemen, it ought
to be the happiness and glory of a Representative to live in the strictest
union, the closest correspondence, and the most unreserved communication
with his constituents.   Their wishes ought to have great weight with him;
their opinion high respect; their business unremitted attention.   It is his
duty to sacrifice his repose, his pleasures, his satisfactions, to theirs; and
above all, ever and in all cases, to prefer their interest to his own.   But, his
unbiased opinion, his mature judgement, his enlightened conscience, he
ought not to sacrifice to you; to any man, or to any set of men living.
These he does not derive from your pleasure; no, nor from the Law and the
Constitution.   They are a trust from Providence, for the abuse of which he
is deeply answerable.   Your Representative owes you, not his industry only,
but his judgement; and he betrays instead of serving you, if he sacrifices it
to your opinion."   (Edmund Burke, Speech at his arrival at Bristol and at
the conclusion of the Poll, p. 14.   London, 1774, J. Wilkie, publisher.)

of Regulars and the Twenty-sixth and Forty-second Divisions of National Guard.

Since these units had exhausted the first quota of men called to the colors, General Crowder had to draft the remainder of the Class 1 men, while the War Department was setting in motion plans for other training camps. The effort on this side of the waters grew acceleratingly to fill General Pershing's requests for more and more supplies and men. But to get them over there was another story.

Throughout the war, transportation was an intricate problem with little tonnage on hand and with a sea infested with submarines. Both the general staff and the ports of embarkation were taxed to the extreme. It was not until the middle of the summer of our second year that facilities were brought into full swing toward bearing troops across the Atlantic.

Could an American army of any size be transported to France, properly staffed, organized, and made of any consequence in the fight? Such was the challenge to General Pershing. Many Allied generals and others were highly skeptical of such a possibility. Indeed, it appeared they were right when not a fraction of physical aid arrived on the Western Front until seven months after our declaration, and then but 1 regiment, the Eleventh Engineers at Passchendaele Ridge. Over nine months after we entered the war a division, the First, took over a quiet sector north of Toul. Similarly, a month later the Twenty-sixth Division appeared at Soissons and the Forty-second near Lunéville. The following month the Second went into line near Verdun, over eleven months after our entry—and, except for the excellent achievements of the small body of engineers, we had really not yet entered the fight. The French and British were disappointed and resentful. The American strength was a myth. In addition, General Pershing, following instructions with a steadfast backbone, was holding aloof in order to organize an American army instead of amalgamating in small groups with the British and French.

Whereas our late aid had been the fault of the American people in their habitual supineness before all our wars, General Pershing's reluctance to fight on any other conditions than as an American army was the wisest course in the long run because

1918

Nov. 6 1917

Jan. 19 1918

Mar. 18 1918

of the morale and genius of our people. To be known as part of a British or French unit was nausea to the American soldier. Yet both the tardiness of active entry and the aloofness until we were organized and trained as an army were plain betrayals in the eyes of our Allies. The American soldiers professed much but did little. Already there were a quarter of a million of them in France. And wasn't it nearly a year since they had been so noisy about the Yanks coming? *Mar. 15 1913*

General Pershing saw the serious consequences and compromised temporarily. When the German assaults made more reserves a question of victory or defeat, he placed his forces unhesitatingly at the disposal of Marshal Foch. The organization of a distinct American army languished, but the heroic actions of the First Division at Cantigny, the Second and Third Divisions at Château-Thierry and the Second Division at Belleau Woods, Bouresches and Vaux put an end to any question as to the effectiveness of American troops. *Mar. 21 1918* *May 28 and June 1 1918* *June 4- July 1 1918*

Although General Pershing promptly turned over his units to Marshal Foch, he tenaciously clung to the formation of a separate army whenever it could be safely achieved. He had by mid-summer taken pains to organize four army corps, the I, II, III and IV.⁴ In early summer he had gained permission from Mar- *July 1918*

---

⁴ General Pershing directed on Jan. 15, 1918 that Major General Hunter Liggett form the I Army Corps at Neufchâteau, giving him his staff (Lieutenant Colonel Malin Craig, chief of staff) and corps troops. General Pershing on Feb. 20, 1918, appointed Lieutenant Colonel George S. Simonds chief of staff of the II Corps, which was to comprise the American troops in the British area, and charged him with evolving the organization of corps headquarters and troops and the amalgamation of the units under American commanders; Major General George W. Read was its first commander, June 13, 1918. Similarly on March 30, 1918, Pershing designated Lieutenant Colonel Alfred W. Bjornstad as chief of staff of the III Corps with duties for our troops on the French front akin to Colonel Simonds' duties for the British; Major General William M. Wright assumed command June 17, 1918. On June 10, 1918, General Pershing designated Lieutenant Colonel Stuart Heintzelman as chief of staff of the IV Corps, to organize it and to relieve the I Corps at Neufchâteau June 21; he appointed Major General Joseph T. Dickman as corps commander, August 16, 1918. On July 7, 1918, General Pershing appointed Major General William M. Wright in command of the new V Corps and the next day Colonel Wilson B. Burtt as its chief of staff. The old III Corps became the new V Corps, except that the staff moved to the aid of the organization of the First American Army. On July 23, General Pershing appointed Major General Omar Bundy as temporary commander of the new VI Corps, and on July 30 he appointed Colonel Briant H. Wells as its chief of staff. On August 16, 1918, General Pershing designated Major General William M. Wright

June 6
1918

July 24
1918

Aug. 10
1918

Sept. 12
1918

shal Pétain to form an American army corps on the Château-Thierry front. Between then and midsummer he had worked vigorously on building the First American Army, which was completed in time for the next big offensive. The day after he took over his organized army headquarters, it was decided in a conference of Allied commanders-in-chief that the St. Mihiel salient should be reduced. General Pershing's First Army was assigned the principal task. The bitter contentions and recriminations of over a year were to be buried under the fruits of persistence and weight of American solidarity. The First Army was secretly concentrated on that front, Liggett's I Corps along the southern face or right side of the triangle, Dickman's IV Corps extending that side to the left, French divisions occupying the apex, and Cameron's V corps well up on the other side.[5] It was a steam-shovel movement with the French at the hinge.

In about twenty-four hours after the jump-off, the First and Twenty-sixth Divisions of the IV and V Corps respectively, met in the middle of the sector, and with the other divisions cut off the bulk of the Germans in the point of the salient, capturing

as temporary corps commander of the new VII Corps and appointed Major General George H. Cameron in command of the vacated V Corps. The VIII Corps was formed November 26, 1918, after the Armistice, with Major General Henry T. Allen as commander and Colonel George C. Marshall, Jr., as chief of staff. On November 16, 1918, General Pershing appointed Brigadier General William K. Naylor as chief of staff of the IX Corps and on November 18, Major General Adelbert Cronkhite as corps commander. The headquarters began to function on November 25 at Ligny-en-Barrois after the Armistice.

[5] This was the First Army of which General Pershing initially took command and which Lieutenant Colonel Hugh A. Drum, as its chief of staff, had started to organize July 4, 1918. General Pershing relinquished command on October 16 and turned it over to Major General Hunter Liggett, who became a Lieutenant General on November 1 and retained command until April 20, 1919. Colonel Drum became a brigadier general on October 14 and retained his position as chief of staff until April 16, 1919. The Second Army was started when General Pershing appointed Colonel Stuart Heintzelman to organize it as its chief of staff, September 9, 1918. Major General Robert L. Bullard became its first commander, October 12, 1918. He was promoted to lieutenant general November 1, 1918, and remained in command until April 15, 1919. Colonel Heintzelman was promoted to brigadier general October 13 and remained as chief of staff until April 15, 1919. The Third Army was ordered to be formed November 7, 1918, but was not begun until after the Armistice, on November 15, when Major General Joseph T. Dickman took command. He remained in that capacity until April 28, 1919, when Major General Edward F. McGlachlin, Jr., took command, relinquishing it to Lieutenant General Hunter Liggett, May 2, 1919, who retained it until July 2. The Third Army's chief of staff was Brigadier General Malin Craig from November 15, 1918, to July 2, 1919.

16,000 prisoners and much war material. The efficiency, celerity and success of the attack completely vindicated the formation and power of an American army.

Concurrently with the preparations for the St. Mihiel offensive went those for the Meuse-Argonne region. That theater had already been chosen by General Pershing for the fall offensive. Fifteen divisions were moved thence, including seven *Sept. 2* that had been in the St. Mihiel battle. *1918*

The three phases of the offensive are well described in vari- *Sept. 26-* ous histories of World War I—how the progress of the American *Oct. 3* *Oct. 4-31* soldiers went steadily forward in the face of mud, morass, cooties, *Nov. 1-11* machine-gun hornets, and every harrowing device and obstacle known to the cunning of the Germans—how in the last phase Pershing's armies threatened the German supply lines through Sedan—how intrepidity and desire scrambled certain units in *Nov. 11* their high endeavor to be the first to reach that city—and how *1918* the very threat was the deciding factor which produced the Armistice.

Similarly, there have been described actions of American forces on other fronts.

Major General William S. Graves' Siberian expedition, con- *Aug. 7* *1918—* sisting mainly of the Twenty-seventh and Thirty-first Infantry, *April 1* with its three-fold mission of guarding military stores, aiding the *1920* Czechs, and helping the Russians, while keeping free from Russian politics, presented cross-currents even more intricate than those of General Pershing in Mexico. With his expedition part of the time under Japanese command, furiously set upon by the Ogre of Chita, double-crossed by supposed Allies, the story of his help to the Czechs and extrication from his unhappy mission is one of the epics of defense against chameleon friend and foe in a far country.

Likewise to aid the Czechs, 143 officers and 4,344 enlisted *Aug. 27* *1918* men of the Eighty-fifth Division then arriving overseas, were sent under Lieutenant Colonel George E. Stewart [6] from Eng- land to Archangel, North Russia. The small force was stretched *Sept.* *1918* over 450 miles, in most dismal, lonely, arctic fighting. Its num- *to May* bers were more than decimated by casualties. Fighting under *1919*

---

[6] Later Colonel. See Dupuy's *Perish by the Sword*.

April 9 1919

Leaving June 3 1919

Sept. 29- Oct. 19 1918

Oct. 2- Oct. 10 1918

Oct. 30- Nov. 3 1918

July, 1918 to Armistice

British command its exploits have been obscured and its heroism little exploited. Later, Brigadier General Wilds P. Richardson [7] assumed command. The whole force was held in Russia over six months after the Armistice.

On other fronts, the American soldier likewise distinguished himself. The II Corps under Major General George W. Read advanced about 15 miles and pierced the Hindenburg Line near Le Cateau. The Second and Thirty-sixth Divisions in succession assaulted Mont Blanc between Rheims and the Argonne successfully and advanced nearly 14 miles to the Aisne River. Aiding the Sixth French Army in Belgium, the Thirty-seventh and Ninety-first Divisions with the artillery of the Twenty-eighth, by dauntless attacks, drove the enemy beyond the Escaut and to the Scheldt rivers.

Often forgotten is the work of the Three hundred and Thirty-second Infantry on the Italian front and its aid of the Italians against the Austrians, especially at the crossing of the Piave.

To commemorate the work of the Services of Supply would occupy a volume in itself. Its personnel of 644,540 at the time of the Armistice and its handling of eight million tons of munitions of every type from weapons to beans during the operations gives but a suggestion of the expanse of its task for more than two million men. The value, amount, and importance of its buying, handling, and transportation made it the world's largest single business undertaking up to that time.

Too many times shortages from the United States both in material and manpower hampered the A.E.F. in general and the S.O.S. in particular. The supply of trucks and ambulances was embarrassingly low for the need in midsummer of 1918. Hastily made transportation like the Camion and Caledon were frequently too simplified and undependable. The replacements necessary for building up units to efficient strength caused new

---

[7] Later Major General. A curious expedition of railway troops consisting of the One Hundred and Sixty-seventh Operation and One Hundred and Sixty-eighth Maintenance Companies under Major Edward E. MacMorland, Coast Artillery Corps, was put under General Richardson's administration for the purpose of operation and maintenance work on the Murmansk-Petrograd Railway. It arrived at Murmansk March 25, 1919. Operating some "broniviki," the expedition took part in minor engagements as the troops advanced to Lake Onega, about 600 miles. This contingent started for home July 28, 1919.

divisions arriving from the United States to be broken up for such purpose. Esprit and efficiency suffered appreciably for these and similar reasons.

Many of these defects were remedied by the time of the Armistice, when the United States was in a fair way to become militarily competent in its own right.

In retrospect, the war held much that should shame us now. The training of officers and soldiers had to be scant in too many instances. Inexperience and lack of knowledge incident to haste produced in themselves undue loss of life and munitions. Soldiers had to be placed on the line when many of them had not had time to know the use of the weapons they were handling. The assignment of officers and men to the multifarious duties of a modern army could not be made with sufficient appropriateness in the time allotted. Laundrymen in the ordnance department, engineers in the quartermaster corps, mechanics in the infantry, electricians in the provost marshal general's department and lawyers in the signal corps felt themselves to be square pegs in round holes. Had there been opportunity beforehand, had all organization not been compelled to be jammed together toward one, immediate, life-and-death end, men who were found inefficient in their assigned tasks would have been superior in their particular bent, as they sometimes were when accident or fortune allowed the transfer.

Promotion, too, had to be haphazard when there could exist no agencies for the proper classification of officers and men. As a rule, there were no coördinating offices that could thoroughly check up recommendations, because such an elaborate system had to give place in the rush to more important considerations. To the degree that a nation is late in its discipline and training, to that extent must the sufferings of the individual be increased.

So must the country's extravagances. Having thrust aside sufficient airplane manufacture and manipulation before the *May 12 June 15 1917* war, Congress hurriedly voted the sum of $44,250,000 after the outbreak of American hostilities. At that time we had altogether 55 serviceable aëroplanes, of which 51 were obsolete and 4 others nearly so. A joint army and navy board then made a program *July 1917* for obtaining 19,775 planes, at which Congress, believing money to be the panacea for all ills, voted $640,000,000. Time was re-

quired in selecting models and in having the machines built. In
the spring of the next year it was announced that we were short

1918

of aircraft. Where had the money gone? An investigation was
ordered, which came to nothing after 17,000 pages of testimony
had been taken down. As a matter of fact, the planes, irrespective of business methods, could not be had in so short a time, a

April
1918

fact which might have been obvious before the investigation.
One year after the declaration of war, we had in our service
abroad only 1 pursuit and 2 observation squadrons of French
planes flown by American pilots who had served in the French
Army before we came into the conflict. America with its own
craft could not before the Armistice have had superiority in the
air over the enemy. The story of those vital guns, the 3-inch
field pieces, is about the same in character as that of the aëroplanes. We could not get them in time and therefore were put
to the humiliating necessity of making inroads on the French
supply of 75-millimeter weapons. Vast sums appropriated for
materials had to be spent when values had risen to many times
the height they had stood before 1917 and when it was impossible to get delivery of the quantity to be purchased. As a result,
a large proportion of the money voted was poured later into
the bilge of post-bellum activities. Meanwhile General Pershing
lacked many weapons and machines for effective fighting. Although the quartermaster department executed a prodigious
task in constructing great cantonments over the country in the
few months allotted it, the buildings and surroundings were not
all that could have been expected of them, had our contractors
and builders had opportunity for such work a year before the
war. Cold and dampness were felt most keenly. Clothing, too,
as was the case with weapons and machines, could not be had in
sufficient quantities.

May
1918

But in addition to all these drawbacks of hurry, a greater
fact now stands out in bold relief. It took us over a year after
we had entered the war to get into any real offensive against the
enemy. And then, General Pershing could muster on the Western Front only 6 completely trained divisions in contrast to
the 160 that our Allies had placed there. During the first year
of our participation in the World War, we could bear no physical
aid in the fighting. Even considering the difficulties of trans-

portation overseas, it is conceded that we could have been a great factor in stemming the German tide sooner and could have saved thousands of lives and dollars lost during our delay for training purposes, had we as a nation been imbued with discipline and knowledge in the beginning.

To cap all, the selective draft revealed that almost half of the young manhood of our country was either defective or unfit for fighting.[8] Had a large percentage of our youth had the opportunity for the development best accorded in military camps, and had such exercises been carried on even for limited periods before the war, no one can doubt that this appalling figure would have been materially reduced. Meanwhile the boy would ordinarily have become more commercially efficient and a more self-reliant citizen.

Facing the problem of building an army on the rotten ruins of smug apathy looked many times hopeless and hapless to Pershing. But in spite of the brakes put on his efforts he did build a mighty fighting machine, which when it reached its peak had to be torn apart and taken down.

Three major tasks confronted the former A. E. F.: to occupy its part of Germany and hold it; to clean up in France, and to demobilize both in France and America.

The first task was put into execution with Pershing's customary celerity. Six days after the Armistice, the Third Army, commanded by Major General Joseph T. Dickman, began its march into Germany. The First, Second, Third, Fourth, Thirty-second, and Forty-second Divisions had had no time for rest from the recent battles before the long, wintry marches began into enemy territory. The army established a bridgehead at Coblenz with advance headquarters at Treves. Later the VII Corps under Major General William M. Wright, consisting of the Fifth, Eighty-ninth, and Ninetieth Divisions, was added to the army. The difficulties in occupied territory were many. The situation was novel for American troops, who acquitted themselves on the whole with dignity, decorum, and decency. The curious factor in this efficient effort was that the army had more trouble with its Allies than with its former enemies.

Nov. 17 1918

Nov. 22 1918

---

[8] Out of 2,750,000 young men examined 46.8 per cent could not pass the physical test for front-line soldiers.

July 2, 3
1919

In midsummer of the next year it was found expedient to dissolve the Third Army as an army and replace it next day with the name of the American Forces in Germany. Major General Henry T. Allen was designated its commander.[9] Decreasing

June 28
1919

necessity for such an army among former enemies in Europe became apparent after the Treaty of Versailles. Little by little troops were returned to the United States because control in occupied territory seemed less needed especially by a highly disciplined and weakened people. Five divisions left before fall.

Jan. 27
1923

Accordingly, General Allen withdrew the last of his American troops and turned the territorial command over to General Marty, commanding the French troops, four years after the Armistice.

The second problem in France, though little mentioned, was no light one. The Armistice suddenly reversed the whole process of the S.O.S. Men and supplies headed in had suddenly to be headed out. The current and slope of the stream had to be reversed. Construction had to give place to demolition. Over two million men were clamoring for discharge and home.

But there were chores in Europe still to do. Thousands of soldiers had to be repatriated, thousands had to be held against their will, surplus supplies had to be disposed of, myriads of claims had to be adjusted with a temperamental and exacting people, cemeteries had to be surveyed, improved, and reorganized, and a general overhaul and liquidation of the immense A.E.F. had to take place in an efficient and businesslike way. It was a delicate, unlovely, and critical task.

Aug. 22
1919

Many of these functions were begun and carried into execution by G.H.Q. of the A.E.F. However, it was dissolved and went home eight months after the Armistice. The natural successor to this work was the S.O.S., which had borne the brunt of many of these undertakings. Accordingly, its former chief of staff, Brigadier General W. D. Connor, was selected as chief of the American Forces in France, and all troops there were placed under his command. With dwindling forces and oft-times increasing difficulties, he carried on the work of leaving the American establishments with no bad trails or smells. It was not until

---

[9] The troops were the same except that the III Corps had been turned over to the S.O.S., July 1, 1919, for return to the United States.

well over a year after the Armistice that he and the last of the *Jan. 11*
1920 Americans in France could leave the country after having accomplished a clean-up of extraordinary self-respect.

The third problem confronted us here in our own country. The involved executive labor and burdens of demobilization which fell upon the shoulders of General Peyton C. March, the chief of staff of the army in the United States, are too often overlooked. The war, of course, in its character, as compared with previous wars, was unique. The immense size of modern armies entailed more complicated systems of supply and broader bases of industrial support at home. A war of position demanded a great outlay of ammunition and elaborate engineering. The advance in invention had caused complicated weapons to appear, whose use was little known at the beginning and whose attributes had to be learned by a multitude of new officers without any familiarity with that sort of thing before 1917.

After nineteen months of concentration of all national activities to one end, that of the production, upbuilding and maintenance of an effective war machine, it was necessary not only to tear down the structures in Siberia, Russia, and France, but to see that the consequent efflux did not interrupt activities in the United States. The welfare of the army and the country demanded that definite provision should be made for the wise distribution of men returned to civilian life. Economic and industrial conditions were absolutely dependent on the manner in which over two million soldiers were thrown back into employment or unemployment. Congestion of idle ex-soldiers in large cities had to be prevented. Positions had to be assured for discharged men. The disposal of surplus stocks of supply and material had to be judiciously watched.

In spite of the very delicate problems surrounding the dis- *Jan. 4*
1919 charge of these men, the Chief of Staff in this country had, within two months after the Armistice, demobilized 732,766 men. In a period of three months and four days afterward, he had *Feb. 15*
1919 methodically discharged 1,246,374 from the service—over twice as many as had been returned home during the same period after the Civil War. Not quite six months after the Armistice nearly two million men had been mustered out with little or no disturbance to business. The strength of the army of the United

States [10] on the day of the Armistice totaled 3,670,888 officers and men. By the middle of the next year 2,723,515 officers and men had been returned to civil life. The gigantic labor involved in this massive undertaking required a discernment and management that can scarcely be estimated.

June 28
1919

While on the one side these forces had to be disbanded skillfully, on the other they should not become civilians in such wholesale numbers as would leave the regular forces with no strength. Would the training of the country, as after all our other wars, be thrown into the discard? To add to the embarrassment, many officers and enlisted men of the permanent establishment had already become parts of organizations due for demobilization. Such a scheme had been found necessary in order to infiltrate an experienced personnel into those units which had had comparatively little training. To what were they to be transferred and what classes were to be absorbed? How many were to be retained and what were the inducements?

Certain factors helped to gain sympathetic and progressive answers to these questions. A vast proportion of the population of the country had actually been in the war or closely allied with it. The hardships and low rates of pay in comparison to the relative ease and high wages at home were generally recognized as unfair. Understanding the needs of soldiers was widespread.

A hint of the unprecedented recognition of the soldiers' plight after a war was exemplified in the ease with which Congress gave monetary succor. Because of the risen war prices of ordinary commodities, officers and soldiers with their pay stationary found living difficult. Accordingly, Congress passed a bill increasing the enlisted pay in general 20 per cent. Colonels and lieutenant colonels were to receive $600 a year extra pay,

May 18
1920

majors $840, captains $720, first lieutenants $600, and second lieutenants $420. The measure stated that the relief was but temporary and that the pay would be further adjusted when living conditions had become more normal. But the act showed the tendency of understanding and fairness.

But a more potent understanding came from those who had been discharged and had severed their connections with the

---

[10] Nov. 5, 1918, the national army, National Guard and regular army were known under the single name of the Army of the United States.

military service. There arose a universal cavil from them at the unnecessary hardships that had come to the soldier here and abroad. For the first time in our history there resulted from a conflict a true realization of the cause of thousands of unnecessary evils, hardships and deaths—our sloth and weakness before 1917. The veterans swore this thing should never happen again. They with other intelligent citizens brought their influence to bear upon the legislators. Many themselves were legislators and persons in high office. The sores were still fresh in their hearts, and people were listening to the soldier.

Accordingly there was enacted a National Defense Act which *June 4 1920* was the most comprehensive and suitable legislation ever made for the military service of the United States. The Army of the United States was to consist of the regular army, the National Guard when called into the service, the officers' reserve corps and the enlisted reserve corps. The combatant arms of the regular army were designated as the infantry, cavalry, field artillery, and coast artillery corps, the air service, the corps of engineers, and the signal corps. The noncombatant arms were the general staff corps, the adjutant general's department, inspector general's department, judge advocate-general's department, quartermaster corps, finance department, medical department, ordnance department, chemical warfare service, Officers of the Bureau of Insular Affairs, chaplains, cadets and professors of the Military Academy, Indian scouts, and detached and unassigned enlisted men. Except in time of war the total regular forces were not to exceed 280,000 officers and men. They were to be organized into divisions and such other units as were necessary for the immediate mobilization for national defense. To this end brigades, divisions, and army corps were authorized. For training and tactical control the country and its possessions were divided into corps areas with a major general in charge of each. The National Guard organizations within each area were to be part of that district and were to be given consideration in continuing their traditions and in developing their morale. The officers of the combatant arms of the regular army were to number 16,635 [11]

---

[11] These consisted of 21 major generals, 46 brigadier generals, 599 colonels, 674 lieutenant colonels, 2,245 majors, 4,490 captains, 4,266 first lieutenants, and 2,294 second lieutenants.

all told. The enlisted man's pay was placed on a more logical basis.[12]

The strength of the arms of the service was made more elastic. The President could increase, by transfer of officers and enlisted men, any branch by 15 per cent of its strength. All departments and branches were to have chiefs with the rank of major general, except the chemical warfare service with a brigadier general and the chaplains with a colonel. To fill the vacancies of this increase the new officers were to come from those who had served between April 6, 1917, and the passage of the Act. One of the greatest pieces of advancement of the new Act was the "single list." Officers were arranged for promotion entirely according to length of commissioned service and were to be advanced in grade eventually on the basis of that arrangement. By such means the disparity of promotions between the different arms of the service, which was due entirely to legislative increase of a particular branch, was eliminated. To keep the standard of the officer personnel up to a high grade, the elimination of unfit men was inaugurated. A board of officers was to place each year the entire officer personnel of the service in two classes, "A" and "B." If an officer was found to be in Class "B," he was a subject for elimination. All evidence in his case was to be passed upon before a court of inquiry. If he was then found to be a proper subject for elimination, he was discharged outright, provided his low classification was a result of his own misconduct. If otherwise, he was to receive retired pay at the rate of 2½ per cent a year for each year of commissioned service, unless he had served less than ten years, in which case he was discharged with one year's pay. An applicant for the rank and file could enlist for one or three years as he chose. Reserve officers could be commissioned by the President for a term of five years. However, if during those years an emergency arose, it was understood that they were to remain until six months after its termination. The President could establish

[12] The enlisted men were to be placed in seven grades with pay ranging from $74 for the first grade down to $30 for the seventh. They would receive 10 per cent increase for each five years of service until 40 per cent was reached. Those of the sixth and seventh grades in addition could be rated as specialists in six different classes. Their additional pay for the first class was $25, and for the sixth $3.

reserve officers' training corps in educational institutions in unlimited number. However, an institution undertaking to maintain such a corps was to have a regular officer detailed as a professor of military science and tactics. The school was to carry at least a two years' elective or compulsory military course, which should be a requisite with other studies for a student's graduation. The graduates of the advanced course of these reserve officers' training corps at colleges were to be eligible for a reserve officer's commission provided they passed through the training camps and accomplished such other work as the Secretary of War prescribed. Summer training camps were also provided for in unlimited quantity. For them the Secretary of War was to prescribe courses of about six weeks' duration. The National Guard officers could not be commissioned for federal use unless they had passed through the latter camps or had certain specific military experience and training.

This legislation was by all odds the greatest provision for the prolonging of peace and the efficient control of war ever enacted by the Congress. It took into account lessons of the recent struggle and suited itself to the genius of our people. The regular during the conflict had learned much from the civilian, and the civilian had in turn gained something substantial from the soldier. Although there had here and there been petty misunderstandings, due mostly to the conditions of our necessary hurry, never before were National Guard, reserves and regulars in such a healthy state of reciprocation and unity. The Army of the United States was by this Act to coalesce all these elements into a coöperative whole. Other influences helped to make this union possible. The American Legion contained all these heretofore separate classes and bound them together for broad patriotic usefulness. The professional soldier was no more isolated. He affiliated himself with civic clubs and tried as never before to fit himself into the life of the community. The law emphasized citizenship, and brought the National Guardsman, the Reservist, the college graduate and student into a camp of instruction under the guidance of regular officers and soldiers, newly indoctrinated under modern methods with the latest tactical teaching. The idea that a soldier was not a citizen or a citizen could not become an efficient soldier completely died out with the birth of this legislation. Better citizenship was to be gained by the professional soldier when he became more active in civilian problems and by the civilian when he grew to be a more scientific and disciplined soldier. For each regular there were five comrades in civil life who needed instruction from him.

It looked as though the United States at last had learned its lesson—that we were going to quit ourselves like men and be strong. The army took on new hope of sufficiency and progress. It also took on the labor and responsibility of modernization.

New services, such as air, chemical warfare, and tank, had to be placed on a firm basis. Other arms had to be revolutionized. New weapons had to be more thoroughly understood and properly assigned. The new army had to be welded into large tactical and administrative units which would not only take care of the United States proper and our island possessions but be a source of inspiration and knowledge in the home country.

The service was never before confronted with so vast an amount of knowledge to acquire and transmit. The 3 general service and 31 special service schools throughout the army had been either reconstructed or built afresh since the war. The officer had before him years of work as a student and months and years of duty as an instructor, while he sandwiched in the training of troops of the Army of the United States, if he were fortunate enough to receive such a detail.

By the middle of the next year it was found necessary to establish the army on a modern pay basis. The living conditions in most of the cantonments were rude, to say the least. It was very difficult to keep up a high state of morale, when every phase of life indicated penury. Congress found that the least it could do was to give officers and men a living wage, since the previous *June 10* temporary relief would soon expire. It therefore enacted a pay *1922* bill which gave in effect more pay to the upper grades and proportionally reduced that of the lower grades for both officers and enlisted men. The five-year fogy gave place to a more uniform increase for length of service, with little regard to rank. For officers, remuneration was composed of the base pay, the ration allowance, and the rental allowance. An officer with dependents received more than those without. In this way salaries more nearly conformed to the needs of the individual. In the enlisted

pay there were no allowances, but the monthly wage for the upper grade was increased. Finding that sometimes hardships
would be worked on the junior officers by having them receive
less than before, the legislators injected a saving clause which
stated that no officer then in the service would receive less than
under the 1908 schedule, the last before this one. Altogether the
Act gave the officer a chance to meet ordinary expenses, which
was all he could ask.

The outlook for the soldier was now hopeful. He had plenty
of constructive work before him, was taken care of, and was a
member of a well-constituted army. He could press forward in
saving the nation from future woes, and, above all, help in making it stalwart enough to ward off wars.

But alas, class upon class reverted to type. The worship of
ease grew with enjoyment, and physical sufficiency passed out
of the picture. It was the thing to expect a millennium. There
could be no more war for the United States. Did we not make
the world safe for democracy? Well-meaning idealists of a fatty
nation propagated rapidly within certain sects and schools.
Lobbies of Congress were filled with men and women who confused arms with war; who mistook preparation against war for
preparation for war; who had few experience tables to guide
them, having been taught in schools and colleges too much ill-
digested data and shavings of the whole truth of United States
history. In some quarters "mere" military history was ex-
punged entirely. The veteran of 1918 and the student of our
real archives were shouted down as hysterical jingoists, as were
Daniel and Savonarola of old. Many who had received rough
treatment during the war blamed it on soldiers and officers themselves. Societies sprang up which had the sure antidote for war.
Moving pictures, publications, and peace congresses emphasized
the horrors of war but offered no practical solution.

The Congress, without hindrance by the mass of the people, *June 30*
suddenly, after decided objection by the Secretary of War and *1922*
the Chief of Staff, reduced the army to 175,000 officers and men,
for a population of over 120,000,000 persons. Over 600 line
officers had to be cast out of the service and the enlisted force reduced by over 100,000. The medical, dental and veterinary
officers had a similar proportion ejected. All promotions were

to be stopped until January 1, 1923. Altogether, over 1,000 officers were to be eliminated before that time. Those discharged were to be given one year's pay, if they had less than ten years' service. If less than twenty years' service, they were to be accorded an annuity at the rate of 2½ per cent a year for each year of commissioned service. If more than twenty years' service, the rate was 3 per cent. In addition to the ejections, about 800 officers had to be demoted and recommissioned in their next lower grade. This legislation proved to be such a sweeping retrogression and so fraught with danger to the country that Congress later in the year made changes in the act. It gave back 50 colonels, 150 majors and 300 captains and limited the decrease of lieutenants to 500. Yet it provided that after the beginning of the next year, there should be no more than 12,000 officers on the

*Jan. 1
1923*

promotion list. Thus our country started in the right direction after a war but turned about in its tracks after a few strides and ran toward the opponents' goal.

The General Staff had to undo much of the work it had accomplished in 1921. After having carefully and energetically built up the service by a judicious selection of officers and a campaign of recruitment, it was compelled to oust many of the very men it had brought into the regular army. In addition to suffering the waste of building a structure in one year and of tearing it down in the next, the War Department could not carry out the National Defense Act of 1920. It could not make a tactical army, a fighting, ready force of minimum size.

*July 1
1922*

In protest against this pillaging of our safety, Secretary of War John W. Weeks and General Pershing raised their voices, but the majority neither heard nor heeded. Said Weeks in his report: "My conclusions are not entirely welcome at this time, when people have been hoping that nations had learned to avoid conflicts of force. My conclusions are, nevertheless, that we should continue to prepare for such conflicts. If it is unwelcome, it is no less true that Americans, like all other peoples, are subject to the law which punishes those nations who fail to prepare for defense, as well as those who fail to strive for peace." Said General Pershing: "It is my conviction that our Regular force is cut too much for safety." Both these men quoted advice of our sages:

GEORGE WASHINGTON: "There is a rank due to the United States among nations which will be withheld, if not absolutely lost, by the reputation of weakness. If we desire to avoid insult, we must be able to repel it; if we desire to secure peace, one of the most powerful instruments of our rising prosperity, it must be known that we are at all times ready for war."

THOMAS JEFFERSON: "None but an armed nation can dispense with a standing army; to keep our nation armed and disciplined is therefore at all times important."

PRESIDENT MONROE: "No Government will be disposed to violate our rights if it knows that we have the means and are prepared and resolved to defend them."

JOHN CALHOUN: "If our liberty should ever be endangered by the military power gaining the ascendency, it will be from the necessity of making those mighty and irregular efforts to retrieve our affairs, after a series of disasters, caused by a want of adequate military knowledge, just as in our physical system a state of the most dangerous excitement and paroxysm follows that of the greatest debility and prostration. To avoid these dangerous consequences and to prepare the country to meet a state of war, particularly at its commencement, with honor and safety, much must depend on the organization of our MILITARY PEACE establishment."

PRESIDENT ARTHUR: "If we heed to the teachings of history we shall not forget that in the life of every nation emergencies may arise when a resort to arms alone can save it from dishonor."

THEODORE ROOSEVELT: "Fatuous self-complacency or vanity, or shortsightedness in refusing to prepare for danger, is both foolish and wicked in such a Nation as ours; and past experience has shown that such fatuity in refusing to recognize or prepare for crises in advance is usually succeeded by a mad panic."

But these voices were squelched. The country had become prosperous. Rising stocks made falling strength. Presidents became obsessed with making a record of savings. Budgets and their directors became the masters, in the face of General Pershing's cry: "I repeat that this last force is not enough. It is my conviction that our Regular force is cut too much for safety."

Secretary Weeks courageously persisted:

"In the 10-year period from 1915 to 1924, while the total cost of national defense will have been doubled, the ratio of this cost to the total Federal Budget will have been decreased nearly one-half. . . . Our Federal Government maintains one soldier for each two and a half million dollars of national wealth, as its share of police protection against external criminal tendencies. . . . This figure of protection is the lowest, which we have maintained for 70 years. The nearest approaches to it were 1890 and 1910, when the ratio was roughly one soldier for each $2,000,000. One can not fail to appreciate that at both of these times we had been for years at peace and war was apparently not dreamed of as a future possibility. If we maintained an army on the basis of financial comparison with those periods in which our people recognized the ever-present possibility of conflict, we should now maintain over 300,000 enlisted men, instead of the 135,000 which we have.[13] Instead of maintaining a steady ratio, we have allowed our judgment to fluctuate with events."

He went on to show that Japan maintained one soldier for every $90,000 of national wealth or over 27 soldiers to our one. If we consider how much further a dollar goes in Japan, it is safe to say that that country was sacrificing approximately 100 times more than we for an army. Even Germany, forbidden to have an army after the Armistice, had a force one-fourth larger than that of the United States.

---

[13] He illustrated with the following table:

"National Wealth Ratio

1850, one soldier per $ 750,000; just after the Mexican War.
1860, one soldier per $1,250,000; war not probable.
1870, one soldier per $ 800,000; just after Civil War.
1880, one soldier per $1,500,000.
1890, one soldier per $2,200,000; no war in sight.
1900, one soldier per $1,000,000; just after Spanish American War.
1910, one soldier per $2,200,000; no war in sight.
1920, one soldier per $1,200,000; just after the World War.
1923, one soldier per $2,500,000; no war in sight.
Average ratio for periods—one soldier per $937,500; when no war was thought likely, $2,037,500."

Secretary Weeks also showed that "In one year we spent 6 times as much for soda and confectionery as we spent for military purposes; for tobacco nearly 4 times; for perfumery, jewelry, and other items of adornment, nearly 5 times; and for theaters, cabarets, and similar amusements, more than 3 times!"

Between 1921 and 1923, the total number of individuals under military training had decreased by 15,000. *July 1 1923*

Over and over between 1921 and 1926 this courageous Secretary kept pounding at the padlocked door of the office of the budget, despite frowns from the White House. In submitting his estimate in 1924, he admitted it did not express the military requirements *July 1 1924*

"in order to carry out the spirit and object of the National Defense Act. . . . Within the limiting figure allowed, it is not possible to meet the absolute requirements of the existing military organizations which are authorized by law. . . . The resulting figures have been submitted solely on the basis of allowing the material plant of the Army to run down temporarily, in the interests of immediate economy, with a full knowledge that this means a greater expense in future years to recover from accelerated deterioration. Working on such a basis, we have been accomplishing what we could, but difficulties rapidly increase. In the administration of our military affairs, as in all other things, there are limits to economy if efficiency is to be maintained."

The army under the yoke of parsimonious bondage had all of 12,000 officers and 118,750 enlisted men. Officers had to change stations so often in order to keep the units of the army going that the extra transportation ate up much of the savings of the budget.

Weapons and supplies were dwindling with no replacements or improvements in sight. In strong language Mr. Weeks pointed out the danger:

"Such a method of living must come to an end. We can not much longer subsist on the surpluses from the past or upon the essential reserve stored up against the future or with such intensive personnel efforts without impairing the efficiency of the establishment and its state of readiness for emergencies. Temporary economies should not be dragged out through repeated postponement of consideration for the future."

For those who are interested in why our air force and our mechanization and modernization of the army stood still, why we came up later to an emergency almost empty-handed, these words of Mr. Weeks may be pertinent:

July 1
1924

"It was 11 months after April 6, 1917, before an American-made airplane reached France, and the first ones—a squadron of 18 planes—flew over the front on August 2, 1918. Before November 11, only 628 American planes had been sent as far as the front. We can not improvise an Air Service, and yet it is indispensable that we be reasonably strong in aircraft at the very outset of a war. . . . A drastic reduction has been made each year since 1920 in the appropriations for experimental and research work:

Fiscal Year	Amount Appropriated
1921	$5,000,000
1922	4,300,000
1923	3,500,000
1924	3,000,000
1925	2,850,000

And so the appropriations proportionally dwindled through the next decade. There was insufficient money to make proper progress in improvement or numbers of weapons and machines. Likewise the army was incapable because of size and barriers to improvement to be ready for protection of the country in an emergency. In spite of the repetitions of Mr. Weeks that the strength of the regular army was insufficient to accomplish its mission of training and instruction of the civilian components as well as perfection of its own essential training, the army dwindled to 12,302 officers and 121,717 enlisted men. Deaf as the country was to warnings, these stout patriots persisted.

July 1
1925

The next year Mr. Dwight F. Davis, the new Secretary of War, took up the cudgels afresh. He brought out additionally the heightened national weakness, because of the lessening value of four million veterans of the World War. Age, physical disability, death, and other unfitness had depleted their ranks for active duty, so that the meager active forces became more ineffective relatively as a national insurance.

It was demonstrated to committees of Congress, it was noised in articles and speeches, it was made a nubbin in official reports that the size of our army was ridiculous and dangerous, that military art and technic were far more complex than in the war of 1917-1918; that tanks, artillery and other weapons had advanced and were advancing in other countries beyond us; that the air corps and aëroplanes were far below the strength contemplated by the Defense Act of 1920, and that every branch of the service had suffered reduction and strangling accordingly. And what happened? Nothing. There was a prevalent feeling throughout the country that other nations might fight, but never again would the United States, and certainly none of our boys would under any conditions be made to go overseas. Organizations went so far as to canvass young men to sign pledges not to fight for their country irrespective of the cause. Many people not only made the historic blunder of forgetting the possibility of internal war, but of predicating their stand on being able to foresee every possible cause.

The War Department became so coerced under this smugness and executive constriction that it even went to great lengths to express its gratification over the Commerce Act which expanded and aided civil aviation, without one lift in Congress to military flying. It had to make much of tid-bits. *1926*

The protests of Mr. Davis rise like final gasps of a valiant *July 1* hero: *1926*

"Every branch of the service could use to advantage more personnel, both commissioned and enlisted. Military art is far more complex than was the case prior to the World War. The Air Corps has been very considerably reduced below the strength contemplated by the National Defense Act of 1920, which same condition applies to even greater extent in practically every other branch of the service. . . . Prior annual reports have contained discussions of the requisites for actual fulfillment of the provisions of the National Defense Act. As yet the Act remains

an unaccomplished plan by reason of only a partial execution
of its provisions. We should not blindly delude ourselves into
the belief that a plan on paper is an accomplished thing. Congress has provided the plan. Its fulfillment depends on the de-
cisions of the citizens of the United States.''

The country was in these years flooded with pictures of the
horrors of war which showed all soldiers to be puppets of Mars
and bloody sadists. Societies persisted in confusing the military
man with militarism, and training with desire for war. Certain
groups of no mean numbers went so far as to strive to do away
with the R.O.T.C. in colleges. Such a move, had it been successful, would have robbed us of our main advancement in the
next war over previous wars and added to the huge unnecessary
slaughter to come.

So unpopular did military strength and training become
that government action on defense was pushed from the back
porch into the dog house. Many persons and organizations, who
after the World War had savagely demanded a protection for
our country, grew absorbed in other pursuits and were lulled by
general prosperity. In degree we resembled our decadence between the Revolution and 1812, with, of course, advanced intelligence.

Even the mouths of War Department spokesmen were
stopped with budgets. Military officials came to fear the executive knout for faithful expositions and requests. Open reports
of military insufficiency became tame, tepid and extinct. One
chief of staff was summarily recalled from the South by the
''authorities'' when he had the temerity to air to the public the
disgracefully squalid housing conditions into which the potential
defenders of the nation were squeezed and cooped.

1927
The army turned in on itself under the weight of suppression and opposition. Since our soldier, like Tommy Atkins, was
welcome in few pubs, he took refuge in places and activities
where he was appreciated. Reports of military authorities ceased
to herald deficiencies and dangers. Instead, they gloated over
their fronts on Rivers and Harbors, Inland Waterways, immi-
gration in the Philippines, Panama Canal, Flood Control and
organization, and planning for industrial mobilization.

One apparently bright spot was an act to expand the army *July 2 1926* air corps to 1,800 planes, 1,650 officers, and 15,000 enlisted men in five years. On the other hand, the fact that maneuvers for the entire Army were restricted to 1 division, a part of a cavalry brigade, and 201 aëroplanes near San Antonio, Texas, demon- *May 1927* strates without comment the pitiful state into which we had descended in our ideas of preparation. The next year there were *1928* no maneuvers and the budget dragon again reared its ugly head in allowing money for only a little over ten hours of flying during *Report* the year for the qualified pilots. In other words, legislation *of July 1 1928* gave with one hand a pittance of air power and with the other took away the means of training fliers.

The army attempted to brush up its little machine from within, if it could not expand it from without. Congress at the instigation of the General Staff passed a bill limiting General *May 21 1928* Staff eligibility. Except for those who were on the initial list, no officer would be added other than those graduated from the General Staff College, and none except such eligible list officers would be allowed on the War Department General Staff.

Pressure on Congress over the housing conditions of the army and lack of hangars, airdromes, and airfields for aviation became great enough to extract an appropriation of $13,268,284 *May 26 1928* mainly for flying facilities, but as for increased manpower, planes, or flying time, they remained as before.

Maneuvers of large units the next year dwindled to practice *1929* marches for troops and command post exercises for officers. There wasn't enough money. Congress failed to appropriate it. The five-year program for the air corps was lagging for the same reason. Out of the 1,800 planes authorized only 794 were available for tactical units. The manpower had to be taken from the rest of the army, robbing other branches of their effectiveness. Legislation had increased the air force at the expense of the army as a whole. Reading the army appropriation bill for that year reminds one of stuffing newspapers in broken windows.

In matters that required no funds Congress was responsive. The Chief of Staff was made a full four-star general. But the act was careful to state that he would receive the pay and *March 7, 1929* allowances of only a major general, two grades lower than general. It also put him on a par with the Chief of Naval Operations by giving him the same personal allowances for his position as the head of the navy had hitherto been receiving. This was but one indication of our military backwardness.

March and April 1929

Our nation could have seen the penny-wise foolishness of its general military policy, for on its doorstep were occurring disturbances of international import. American lives and property on the Mexican border were in jeopardy. Bad blood along the boundary had caused depredations. Troops were despatched to critical points, and it was only by judicious négotiations on the part of Brigadier General George Van Horn Moseley that affairs subsided. Brigadier General Frank S. Cocheu at Fort Huachuca, in addition to his troops, used air patrols along the border. It is significant that 18 United States planes constituted our air power for that disturbance. And at this very same time we had one soldier for every $2,800,000 worth of national wealth. Somebody went to great pains to show that it took several thousand dollars to kill one of the enemy in the World War, but nobody was particularly interested in how many of our own men we killed by spending less than two cents on the tax dollar.

Oct. 1929

Consciousness of the army became dimmer in the public mind after the financial crash. Our citizens were naturally absorbed in repairing accounts and binding up their debts. If military stability was necessary, this was no time to think about it. The government, all of us, must retrench.

1929

This spirit unfortunately pervaded our country when it was immensely important to get a head start on our future enemies. In the American Year Book appeared a statement which was a reflection of the thought of the War Department: [14]

"We are moving in a machine age, and in the interest of national defense, the Army must act accordingly. In the commercial world the machine has largely replaced manpower; so the Army must, to the fullest practicable degree, use machines in place of manpower in order that our manpower can occupy and hold ground without terrific losses incident to modern fire power. Our country, of all the world, is best able to take advantage of machines. Any great nation which fails to provide

---

[14] The article was written by the author among others at the instigation of the Secretary of War and after investigation of General Staff objectives.

for the utilization of mechanization to the utmost practicable degree must suffer the consequences of neglect in future wars. Furthermore, failure to prepare to meet an attack by a mechanized force may result in defeat by troops organized and equipped as of today. The Army must adopt, manufacture and use the various machines incident to mechanized force as of the best known models of today provided they are sufficiently better than existing equipment to warrant the expenditure of funds. In short, the Army must be a constantly functioning research laboratory. During the past year an exhaustive study of the matter has been made and a comprehensive report rendered which makes recommendations as to equipment required and costs. Any development of mechanization will demand funds.''

The next year experiments with mechanization and air went *1930* along on reduced appropriations. No progress on a large scale was possible, nor, with the funds available, was there a chance to make any appreciable strides with tanks, in spite of the inventions of civilians and progressive experiment within the army. There was no training for troops in large-scale maneuvers— only command post exercises for officers and certain inexpensive installations in the field. Appropriation-makers contented themselves with housing what had hitherto been left out in the rain. Over nineteen millions were appropriated for buildings for avia- *July 3 1930* tion, long needed to put previous acts into effect, and for other buildings to keep some of the army personnel under decent cover.

Throughout the first decade of this post-war period, in many quarters arose clamor against the huge expenditures for the army. During the year 1926, for example, army appropriations reached $350,463,848.06. But few realized that almost eighty millions of that sum went to purely civil activities such as Rivers and Harbors, Flood Control, Inland Waterways, Panama Canal and colonial possessions, and that a large part of the remainder provided assistance to 3,868 National Guard units in 1,400 cities and towns, the conduct of 50 separate C.M.T. camps, the supervision of 223 R.O.T.C. units, and competent instruction for 70,000 reserve officers. What was left went toward the training of personnel and progress of weapons of the slim regular army—less than a penny a day from the citizen, including the army. Not only was the complaint absurd, but the outlay was pathetically ludicrous in the light of after events.

With this shrinkage of means to carry out its main purpose under the National Defense Act, came a naturally resourceful attempt to make the army a constructive force in peacetime for peacetime pursuits. Such a course was popular and possible. As a war preventive and defense bastion, the army had sunk into the rôle of a fine planner rather than a definite builder. The materials and tools for practice could not be had. The army knew before it asked just what money it could and could not obtain from Congress, and in these times it definitely could not obtain enough to develop a reasonable protective force.

1926
to
1938

It was the smallest regular army in the world in relation to population, wealth or area. Its stocks of materials from the First World War had grown scant and poor without replacement. If they had been usable, they would have generally been obsolete. It would have been impossible to put in the field one modern, completely armed, regular division. In 1926 there were only 49,973 combatant troops of all branches in the United States proper. In that year also, for economy's sake, 1,500 non-commissioned officers, 1,496 privates first-class, and 1,380 specialists were discharged summarily. Those remaining in the service grew uncertain and apprehensive, with consequent loss of morale. It was almost impossible to keep spirits above par with increasing duties for a decreasing army.

Yet with all these blights the army performed many services for the public. The signal corps operated 37 radio and telegraph stations between Seattle and Alaska, turning over more than a quarter of a million dollars to the United States Treasury. Its work on high-frequency radio transmission and especially on the radio beacon were definite contributions both to communication and to transportation in general. It also operated the largest radio net in the world, giving its services free to 30 other departments of the government. The life saving the air corps performed in its work on the parachute can not be estimated. The improvements it fostered on the aërial camera and the bomb sight are unique in any army. Throughout this whole period, the work of our aviation units in bombing ice jams, photographing thousands of square miles for Geological and Geodetic

surveys, and scouting for incipient forest fires can be estimated
in hundreds of millions of dollars in savings. As the chemical
warfare service sought in its experiments to produce a knockout
gas for war, so it found means of ridding depots and warehouses
of vermin, rodents, moths, bats, and flour weevils. At a cost of
$106 in a western plant, over $75,000 worth of cloth goods was   *1926*
saved from moths by a single fumigation.

In floods, tornadoes, cyclones, typhoons, bursting dams, ice
jams, coal mine disasters, explosions, forest fires, blizzards, con-
flagrations and earthquakes, the army had during these post-war
years no peer in any organization for heroism, succor, promptness, and amount and kinds of supplies rendered. In the first
place, it was the only agency of the government that could be
first on the spot with sufficient blankets, cots, stoves, tents,
food, and medical supplies, and could furnish protection of life
and property. The blizzard in Omaha, Nebraska, the tornadoes
of Mississippi, Georgia and other states, the flood in Texarkana,
Arkansas, the hurricanes of Florida, Porto Rico and the New
England states, and the floods of the Ohio, Mississippi, Connecticut, and Susquehanna, are but a few of the disasters where the
army was first on the spot with essential needs. For example,
when the news of the Porto Rican hurricane arrived, it was a
matter of hours before nearly a million dollars' worth of every
conceivable aid, including two general hospitals, were planned
for or sent on their way by the army in army transports under
army personnel. Similar to these vast relief undertakings were
delegations from the army, who reconstructed the cemeteries of
our soldier dead abroad to the number of 30,792 graves. Also,
the Adjutant General produced gigantic results in caring for the
adjusted compensation for several million ex-soldiers.

All these public services provided an outlet for the soldier,
when he was stifled and prevented from performing his main
tasks enjoined by the Defense Act for our future safety. The
reason for this shunting is set forth in a statement to the Chief
Executive: "The means for making military policy effective are   *July 1*
provided for in the Budget. These are apportioned in accord-   *1930*
ance with the action of the Bureau of the Budget upon War
Department estimates, and after congressional approval or modification are made available to the War Department in annual

appropriation acts. The sufficiency of appropriations for military purposes has, of course, to be considered in connection with the general fiscal situation of the country and its needs for other governmental purposes. From what has already been stated elsewhere in this report, further discussion is unnecessary to support the general statement that the funds provided have been insufficient for even an approximate realization of the military system contemplated in the National Defense Act."

That was the parting shot of General Charles P. Summerall, as his tour of Chief of Staff of the army expired. He also showed that in 1913, 11 per cent of the national revenue was expended for military purposes, whereas in 1929, only 7.8 per cent was spent, and that the citizen out of every dollar of his taxes was delivering less than 2 cents for preparedness. The general went over the history of the army, outlining many of the defects of our military approach as it has been recorded in this volume. He showed how we had not learned, were unwilling to do so, and were growing weaker every day. He made a most significant statement in the light of after events: "A new element foreseen as a development in the armies of the future is the mechanized force." But on the powers this and his other observations were, as the soldier would say, "ricochets."

These post-depression years were as discouraging to outward-looking military men as any in our history. The public was as much interested in the army as in polar bears. The soldier was in the zoo or remote. He was doing well enough. We'll think about him sometime when we get in a jam.

Meanwhile, the military establishment was ill-housed, ill-paid, undermanned, obsoletely implemented, and fast declining into narrow routine. Scope, space, numbers, and training refused to keep pace with the growing population and power. The government appointed commissions to equalize the burdens and remove the profits of war; made gestures to abandon war as an instrument of national policy, when it had never been such a thing in our history, and uttered wholesale diatribes against war, as if it could be expelled by oratory, flirtation, or some secret exorcism. These were all very well, if they had been effective. But our future enemies grinned and built hungry guns—bigger and better guns and mechanisms. Unfortunately, the army was realistically inclined and not thinking in terms of a single depressive mood, of Utopia, of presidential reputation, or of political party maneuvering. It was charged with the safety of the people, while they insisted on flaunting their sugared wealth before foreign empty bellies.

When this military slough of despond had reached its low- *Nov. 1931* est and gloomiest level, General Douglas MacArthur was called to head the army as its Chief of Staff. It was almost as if the hand of Providence had plucked him by the shoulder, as it had done previously with Washington and Scott. Never did the service so need a champion of his caliber: young, vigorous, courageous, at once benignly gentle and properly severe, dynamic, attractive, and resourceful. Starting with an unparalleled record at West Point of being first in his class in scholarship, popularity, and military rank—all three of which qualities normally run counter to each other—he was catapulted into the service as a paragon, and should by all precedent have trickled into the oblivion of the number one man in Robert E. Lee's class. For the first ten years of his service it looked as though he was fast approaching that obscurity. But his was a personality for stout deeds. Piping routine did not interest him. His sensitive nostrils always scented danger. When Brigadier *Spring* General Frederick Funston went to Vera Cruz, MacArthur was *1914* among those present. Volunteering for a mission where he pierced the heart of Mexico and returned with valuable information after having risked his life continuously, he was recommended for the Medal of Honor, but the War Department could not see it that way. Just before our entry into World War I, *Summer* Secretary Baker made him head of the War Department Press *1916* Section. His innovations for truthful publicity and his aid to newspaper representatives combined to be the chief factors in educating the public and making it receptive to the coming Selective Service Law. When war was declared, he immediately asked for a commission as colonel of infantry in the national army and got it. His battle record as chief of staff of the Forty-second Division and brigade, and finally division commander, is an epic of heroism and the kind of leadership that makes men want to follow. His personal escapes from death remind one of the miraculous survivals of Washington and Scott. Picture him personally leading a patrol into no-man's land—all the 18 others killed, he the only one to return; cars demolished under him, he the only survivor; at the jump off of an attack personally mounting the parapet of a reluctant battalion and going forward himself before he heard the hesitant troops follow with a cheer; telling his aide who insisted on pulling him from under shell-fire, "Just get this straight, son. The best thing that could happen to the morale of the A.E.F. would be to have a general officer bumped off."

June
1919

Coming back from France and being selected as Superintendent of the Military Academy, he there showed his moral courage was not one whit lower than his physical. At once he spied those shiny wheels in any institution of a hundred and eighteen years' polish and tradition which appear as drivers but are simply brakes. He attacked outmoded régimes, razed the obsolete and effete summer camp, gave the sequestered cadets opportunity to touch the world, coördinated and broadened the scope of the curriculum, effected mass athletics, and neutralized the inbreeding. It was the first big going-over the Military Academy had had since Sylvanus Thayer put the best of educational Europe on the banks of the Hudson. The heroic fashion in which MacArthur always acted made the shock to the alumni world too much to bear. "He is destroying the Academy and the Corps," said the old graduate. MacArthur was relieved before his four-year tour was completed and he could more nearly complete his tidy reforms. Although some of his progressive moves were nullified after his departure, every one of them later came toddling back into the more abundant service of the Academy.

Nov.
1930

This was the man, fortunately for the United States, with mental, moral, and physical courage, who now took the helm of the army. And how the ship was floundering! The war machine had become a pretty loom, doing all sorts of fancy work for the nation. Those of its higher officers who would speak were morally muzzled. Rivers and Harbors, Flood Control, the Panama Canal, saving money, doing stunts for the public, outshone the obsolete guns, supplies, and strength for mobilization which characterized the land forces. At the end of the five-year air program there was a shortage of 183 planes and over 500

officers. Money for experiment with tanks and combat cars was
shrunken to impracticability. Stagnated promotions had lowered
esprit to the point where efficiency had to pull itself up by its
boot straps. Reserve corps and National Guard units held a
high percentage of officers who could not have field training each
year because of lack of funds. Although the R.O.T.C. in schools
and C.M.T. camps were growing in popularity, money was not
appropriated to cover 50 per cent of the applying personnel.

To the War Policies Commission, MacArthur showed the
possibilities of war, the mobilization plan as worked out by the
General Staff, the equalization of burdens in a Selective Service
system, the industrial planning and organization of industry
necessary, the results of a failure to prepare, the army procurement plans, and the necessity of adequate measures for an
army ready for emergency. He recommended to the commission
a public announcement of the policies to be undertaken:

"Those policies which will assure practical and efficient
peacetime preparation for the emergency of war, promulgated
and published in such a way as to have a serious, sobering effect
upon every man, woman, and child when he or she contemplates
the possibility of war.

"Those policies which will facilitate the successful conduct
of war and effect a just and equitable distribution of war's human and economic burdens when once it has been deliberately
undertaken.

"Those policies which will enable the nation to demobilize
after a war in a rational and orderly fashion."

While he was attempting to educate the public, he was also
striving to raise the spirits of the soldier. The same year the
various medals of our army were classified and appropriate ribbons and medals added, where before little reward had been
given for certain heroic actions. The Silver Star, Purple Heart,
and Distinguished Flying Cross were made separate and distinct
medals.

By the end of this same fiscal year the army had purchased
7 combat and 12 armored cars for experimental purposes at a
cost of $452,000. Since only two millions had been spent in the
previous twelve years for any such purpose, this was a signal

advance. The combat vehicles were ''Christie''[15] types for experiment at the cavalry center at Fort Knox in order to have the cavalry undergo mechanization. The others, also of modern design, were experimented with at the Infantry School, Fort Benning, Georgia, whither the Tank School and Tank Board were moved from Fort George G. Meade, Maryland, on account of better facilities for experimentation.

Seeing that Congress would not appropriate sufficient funds for such research and experiment, the General Staff bent its efforts on producing a pilot model that could be experimented with toward improvement. Every effort was made to restore to the attack its former power. Similarly, the cavalry was moved to switch its interest to armored cross-country cars. Working toward production in time of emergency as the next best solution to having tanks on hand, the offices of the Assistant Secretary of War and supply branches strove to gear industry toward tank, weapon, and aircraft production in quantity within twelve months after declaration of war. Modernization and advancement of anti-aircraft instruments were encouraged within the limited means available. Said General MacArthur to the public *July 1* in his report: ''Under the reduced appropriations of recent years *1932* the degree of preparedness that we have been able to attain does not approach in any particular that prescribed as necessary by Congress in 1920.'' Despite the unpopularity of his view in high quarters, he expostulated that the army was relatively lower than at any point in our history—119,888 enlisted men— ''below the point of safety.'' He was assailed by pacifistic reformers to do away with army transports and to amalgamate the War and Navy Departments so as to save money—a saving which could seriously abridge the usefulness and economy of these functions. These attacks he eminently resisted just as he decentralized the workings of the War Department toward greater efficiency.

July One of the most unpleasant tasks handed the army was the *1932* eviction of the Bonus Marchers from the city of Washington. In the wake of the depression came the foam of jobless unrest. Those who had risked their lives for the safety of the country in World War I felt that the country owed them a chance to

---

[15] Mr. Walter Christie, the progressive inventor of many types of tanks.

Douglas MacArthur

work. About 250 of these veterans started from Oregon and
California to march on Washington and peaceably to petition
Congress for the payment of a bonus legislated to be paid in
1945. Altogether, about 10,000 took up the line of march and
were at one time or other identified with the Marchers. The
farther they marched, the longer they stood in Washington, and
the more space, food, and shelter they asked for—700 hundred
hungry women and 300 children among them along the banks of
the Anacostia—the more they were feared and unwelcome. The
cry among the Marchers arose, "Cheered in 1917 and jeered in
1932." Relations between the Commissioners of Police of the
District of Columbia, Congress, the War Department, and the
representatives of the Marchers grew more and more strained.
The President decided to evict these veterans without any provision being made for their future existence. In a fracas with
police two Marchers were killed. Troops from Fort Myer bringing all the accoutrements of modern warfare did their job with
such discipline and force that no casualties resulted. General
MacArthur, who had been through the fires of the A.E.F. and
could have stayed in his office, personally led the way. It has
been inferred that he wanted to make certain no harm would
come to any American who had served his country bravely in
World War I.

The next year saw many changes which affected the army. *1933*
A new president on this side of the waters, Franklin D. Roosevelt, better disposed toward national defense, and a new head of
Germany, more disposed toward war, came into power. The
accessibility of the one and the possibility of the other were not
lost on MacArthur. Although he had fearlessly pounded the
desk of former presidential prelates, he had hitherto tempered
his words with the knowledge of the hopelessness of his truths.
A pea-shooter was as good for them as a 16-inch gun. Now
he could blaze away with everything and have some chance of
being heard.

Opportunity to show the army's efficiency and mettle came
suddenly with the swift reforms of the new President. The
Congress passed a bill to put a quarter of a million jobless men *March*
in reforestation work. The army disliked the task of taking *1933*
over a mass of men twice its size, of butting in on the Forest

Service, and of robbing the soldier oi his peacetime training. The army's representative so stated to the White House. The reply was: "You have given all the reasons in the world why the army should do this job. As a matter of fact, all the reasons you state show that nobody else can do it." The army got the job. The General Staff was wisely ready for that possibility. A month later, at the rate of 1,530 a day, 52,000 were enrolled, and 42 camps were established. Fifty-one days after that, 310,000 had been enrolled. The rate of reception and caring for this vast number was greater than that for both the army and navy during the World War. And this was peacetime, when the spirit, money, and coöperation of the people were not so great. And what did the soldiers have to do for these men? More than a preparatory boarding-school must do for its students. It had to examine them physically, classify them, clothe them, feed them, transport them, do all the work of paying them, put up their camps in the wilderness, and supervise their moral, mental, and spiritual welfare and conduct. Army training stopped. The soldier had to put every ounce of his energy into the task and spend many sleepless, working nights, if it were to be a go. The little available army, not one-eighth the size of those finally enrolled, had to press these raw men from every walk of life through their new work in a fair and orderly way.

The entering C.C.C. boys were of equal rank. There were no seniors, no foremen, no variations—just a crowd. They were not being received into any established organization. The whole structure had to be built from the ground up. The situation was as strange to the soldier as to the C.C.C. boy. The only recourse the army officer had for keeping contentment, orderliness, and efficiency were precept, example, and expulsion from camp. He was not allowed to use even minor forms of correction. He could not require the boy to stand up, look one in the eye, or say "Yes, sir" or "No, sir." This lack of means was a fearful handicap to the commander, when he was responsible for the safety, good order, and reputation of the lads in a strange community. But the records show surprisingly little discord for the vast numbers taken in. The records also show how proper sanitation, a balanced diet, daily medical attention, and patient supervision turned out. An inventory of 110 camps reveals that the boys gained from 5 to 27 pounds. Only 5 per cent left camp —a surprisingly small proportion when it is realized that their main qualification was lack of a job. Under skilful guidance they developed rapidly. The white anemic faces and flabby arms of early spring were changed into bronzed skins and bulging muscles in the late summer. And many a potential law-breaker was transformed into a citizen with a healthy mind and body. In the prevention of forest fires alone the C.C.C. paid for itself.

In the face of this superhuman social task for the country, and the fact that the $21-a-month trained soldier was making possible the encampments of the $30-a-month indigents, the ogre budgeteers came forth to do their deadly work on the army and army training. The sum appropriated for the army, a hangover *Mar. 4 1933* from the previous administration, cut the army sixty-five millions over the previous year, and then the Bureau of the Budget made an additional cut of eighty millions. And this just six years before the outbreak of the greatest war in history. General Mac-Arthur rushed into the breach and showed that such a slash would make of the army a federal constabulary. He specifically recounted what would happen to the military service while it was preoccupied with the C.C.C. movement: "The retirement of some 3,000 to 4,000 Regular officers; the discharge of about 12,000 to 15,000 enlisted men of the Regular Army; the elimination of field and armory drill training for the National Guard, of all active duty training for the Reserve Officers' Training Corps, of the Citizens' Military Training Camps, of field training for the Reserve Officers' Training Corps, and of field training for the Regular Army; the almost complete dismantling of the technical services of the Army, including the discharge of civilian technicians engaged in research, design, development and experiment; and the cessation of procurement of necessary equipment and nearly all supplies except clothing and food."

The result of this exposure was to have the appropriation for the military establishment cut by 33 per cent instead of 44 per cent. The effect was to cut down training for the three components of the army—the National Guard, reserves and regular army—to nothing effective. One hundred and sixty nine millions were immediately necessary for mechanization, motorization, anti-aircraft, modernization, and aircraft and were so

shown to be necessary even to a moron, but nothing came out of
the machine. Said MacArthur:

"Suspension of military training or further slashing into
the Army's existing organization would produce a tragic situation. . . . Efficiency would fall off rapidly. Future correction
would involve years of intensive work to make good months of
current neglect. In the event of an emergency human and material costs and risk of defeat would be multiplied. . . . Four
times during the nineteenth century the United States went to
war under conditions that forced us to incur needless sacrifices
by committing units to action under the leadership of hastily
and imperfectly trained commanders. In spite of these repeated
lessons, the same error was committed in 1917. In seeking evidence on this point we are not confined to testimony from the
leaders of our own Army. The writings of our Allies and of our
opponents in the late war are particularly revealing in their
comments upon American battle operations. Foch, Hindenburg,
Ludendorf, and many others have praised without stint the courage and dash of American units on the Western Front. But
even while those veterans of many battles were lost in admiration for the bravery of troops that could sustain appalling numbers of casualties and still keep on attacking, they were aghast
at the useless and costly sacrifices we made because of unskilled
leadership in the smaller units. Training—professional training—and the skill and knowledge and morale resulting therefrom
are the first indispensables to efficiency in combat."

And then he closed with this warning:

"In the obvious state of unrest now prevailing throughout
the world, evidences of which are plainly visible even in our own
country, an efficient and dependable military establishment, constantly responsive to the will of its Government, constitutes a
rock of stability and one of a nation's priceless possessions. . . .
It is my conviction that at this moment the Army's strength in
personnel and matériel and its readiness for employment are
below the danger line. I consider it of the most urgent importance to the United States that this condition be rectified
without delay."

But it was not rectified without delay, even though the new President was disposed toward sufficient strength. So the army did what it could to reorganize what it had. The forces within the United States were arranged into four armies, at least on paper; the air corps grew—despite its shrunken material and personnel—more efficient; the mobile arms sought greater effectiveness, and the army remained the seventeenth in strength of the great powers of the world, while it was mainly occupied in changing the linen of C.C.C. lads.

Other current economies did not help the spirits of the soldier. An economy bill had been passed just after the depression which made the service accept a payless furlough for 8⅓ per cent of its active duty. This year the deduction was changed to a straight 15 per cent pay cut. Every grade in the army was affected, but the private thus received the magnificent sum of $17.85 per month, while the C.C.C. lad for whom he was caring still received $30. The patient was receiving a salary while the doctor was given a pittance. *March 1933*

In fields outside the military ones appropriations flowed ripplingly. Two hundred and twenty million was allowed for Rivers and Harbors. The army engineers as usual did an excellent, economical job, putting 44,000 unemployed to work. Although the army did get ten millions for motorization (not mechanization) and seven and one-half millions for additional aircraft, it received no money for target practice or any adequate practical military training.

Besides, the air corps was saddled with carrying the air mail for the Post Office Department. For nearly four months army aviation carried 777,389 pounds of letters and packages for a distance of over one and one-half million miles without the loss of a single piece. Since the novel undertaking came upon the air corps in midwinter, there were casualties among planes and men during the period when mail administration, engineering, training, and routes had to be learned. But as a whole the work was performed heroically and efficiently by the only agency for the President at hand. *Feb. 19 to June 1 1934*

In spite of MacArthur's warnings, which since have sadly been realized as true prophecies, the regular army contained 118,750 enlisted men, over 3,000 less than the year preceding. *July 1 1934*

MacArthur showed that 165,000 was a minimum for efficiency and future possibilities; that the National Guard had only 175,000, whereas 210,000 were needed; that the reserve corps had only 89,000 officers, whereas 120,000 were needed; and that the enlisted reserve was zero, whereas 120,000 were needed. If all these increases had been made, the strength would not have been half that called for in the National Defense Act of 1920. And in addition, the army was called upon to look after the C.C.C., which would have entailed a still further increase over the provisions of 1920, if safety were to be considered. But safety and wanton loss of life and treasure in an emergency were not considered.

July 1
1934

The wee army, still the lowest of all the powers and lower than many not powers, was launched on civilian enterprises with all the more intensity and efficiency, from Rivers and Harbors to C.C.C. camps. Training for the army as an army or as a going defensive concern was still out. Even the progress of weapons and materials was stymied. The General Staff showed that our combat ''vehicles were hopelessly out of date.'' The army had altogether 80 Garand rifles. Of modern field pieces we had only models of better, speedier, and rangier ones. Of modern anti-tank and anti-aircraft guns and instruments there were the barest handfuls. The aircraft were about where they had been the year before.

Although appropriations for decent housing for army personnel had been enacted before the depression, afterward there was a standstill in release of funds. However, the President's public expenditures on his various social reforms benefited the army in two ways. Both the completion of the housing project and the filling of the tremendous deficiency of motor vehicles for the army came from the Public Works Administration.

Although there were some internal gains, the size of the army and military appropriations for munitions prevented the soldier from progressing or being a bulwark or even a nucleus in war. General MacArthur again rose to his full height and scorched the powers with intelligence on the full consequences that would ensue—consequences that were so tragically carried out later against him and his Philippine forces. Speaking for the pittance he had asked for the protection of the country—all he had any hope of obtaining, he said: ". . . Measured by any possible standard, full accomplishment of this program would still leave us far behind all other major powers in strength of organized land forces. Our relative standing would be no higher than 16th. Preparation on the scale proposed would, however, offer to our country a justified assurance in freedom from attack or, at the worst, from extreme consequences in the event of attack. . . . The proposals of the General Staff have been formulated with full regard for current governmental economy as well as in full realization of the fact that retrenchment that cripples national defense is extravagance past the point of folly. . . ."

In this report he took farewell of the army as its Chief of *July 1 1934* Staff, his four years expiring before the beginning of the next fiscal year. But he was destined not to go. Agreeing with his contentions and recognizing his merits in obtaining maximum strength under the current psychology of the country, the President held him on. By this time MacArthur should have been used to breaking precedents. But there was more to come.

Meanwhile some responsive tremors to his constant philippics were felt among military men to be a possible indication that Congress and the country were yielding to reason. The hump in the promotion lists, which had stopped the flow for those officers who had almost simultaneously come into the service at the time of World War I, was appreciably flattened. Congress passed a law which made the field grades 40 per cent of the *July 31 1935* officers of the army, so that younger officers could progress. It put, however, a length-of-service qualification for each grade.[16] But the act did serve to add a modicum of hope and spirit to the service.

Not only was the stagnation largely overcome, but the number of officers was slightly expanded. The law known as the Thomason Act allowed 1,000 young reserve officers, for a period *Aug. 30 1935* of ten years, to be trained annually with the regular army. Each year 50 of them were to be selected and placed in the permanent establishment. Although the act was a forward move

---

[16] Six per cent were to be colonels, 9 per cent lieutenant colonels, and 25 per cent majors. But one could not become a colonel unless he had completed 26 years' service; a lieutenant colonel, 20 years' service, and a major, 15 years' service.

and this fine type of officer was much needed, the influx of so many fairly green subalterns each year added to the burdens of the already depleted officer personnel. The first 52 were placed in the air corps and the remainder in the other arms in proportion to strength.

Under the final urgings of MacArthur, backed by Secretary George H. Dern, Congress finally in the annual appropriation act increased the enlisted strength of the army on paper to 165,000—still 115,000 below the 1920 Defense Act, but all that could be squeezed from the country. Although. 2,000 more officers were needed and asked for, they were not provided; however, the maximum number of cadets in the Military Academy was raised from 1,374 to 1,960, each Congressman and Senator receiving 3 appointments instead of 2, and the whole expansion to take place gradually until the first increased output would be noticeable in the Class of 1939—the year Hitler invaded Poland to set off World War II.

Fiscal Year Ending June 30 1936

June 7 1935

As these increases took place, more and more were army officers used for civil duties and taken away from training. Not only was it found necessary to use the soldier with the C.C.C., but with other agencies like the W.P.A., N.R.A., and P.W.A. The soldier, however faithfully he executed these urgent duties, felt deprived in not being able to undertake the task he had chosen. Naturally, there was a consequent let-down in his spirit.

In actual remuneration for services, the army was worse off than 30 years before. Expenses had gone up, but there had been only a slight advance in pay since 1908. This hardship was felt most keenly in the lower grades of officers and among enlisted men. MacArthur exposed this condition and begged for remedy. He also advocated a five-year aircraft procurement that would allow us in 1940 a complement of the very best and latest ships. Without petitioning Congress he could and did organize the army so as to include a general headquarters of the air force, which commanded all the combat elements of the air corps in the continental limits of the United States. The commanding general of the general headquarters was thereafter directly under the chief of staff in time of peace and under the commanding general of the field forces in time of war.

Among other progressive petitions of the Chief of Staff,

which if followed would have made 1942 less perilous to us, was a five-year progressive procurement program of munitions. Another was the five-year plan and pay for accumulating an enlisted reserve by allowing $12 a year for discharged men and $100 upon reënlistment.

These and other progressive plans were conceived and set in motion by General MacArthur. Heeded, they would have saved us much in life and treasure in 1941. But most of them were not heeded.

With what he got, MacArthur turned to the army and counseled it to husband and use to best advantage the driblets of military appropriations:

"It is thus evident that in many essential phases of military preparation Congress has recently authorized advances along lines urged by the War Department. In certain instances these authorizations follow in detail the recommendations submitted. The Army's task is to make the best possible use of the additional assets that have thus become available. This responsibility is a heavy one and it involves more than mere reenforcements of old formations or expansion of old conceptions. For 5 years the central theme of War Department recommendations to Congress has been the necessity for modernization of the Military Establishment. This purpose must influence the solution of every problem now facing us. Instant advantage must be taken of the present opportunity to mold our Army more distinctly into a unified, mobile, efficient and strictly modern machine. Clear vision must be supplemented by tireless energy, and no effort must be spared to derive the utmost in combat power from every dollar available for the Army."

In leaving his office MacArthur was the recipient of another broken precedent. The Secretary of War, Dern, issued a eulogy in his report to the President on a living Chief of Staff: "The great improvement that has recently been made in our Army is due in very large measure to the initiative, genius, energy, resourcefulness, and brilliant leadership of General MacArthur, who is completing a tour of duty as Chief of Staff. Long before he came to the War Department as the principal military adviser

July 1 1935

to the Secretary, General MacArthur had won exceptional honor and distinction by his courage on the battlefield, his devotion to duty and his attainments as a military leader. To the many and difficult problems encountered in the War Department, General MacArthur applied the same vision, intelligence, sound judgment and fairness that had won him renown throughout his service, and he has exhibited administrative ability of the highest order. On my recommendation you extended his tour of duty as Chief of Staff nearl˅ a year in order that he might be available to advise with the Congress on legislation of vital interest to the national defense. The President, the Secretary of War and the Congress have been extremely fortunate to have had his counsel and assistance at a time when our Army was being reorganized and modernized.''

Although General MacArthur left and Secretary Dern died, the military establishment benefited by their wisdom and persistence, despite public apathy and antagonism. In addition to the expansion of officers by additional cadets at the Military *June 16 1936* Academy and the Thomason Act, air corps reserve officers could be called to active duty for five years and receive $500 bonus at the end of three years, and the corps of engineers was increased *June 26 1936* by a brigadier general and 185 other officers. Although the expansions were not large in themselves, they displayed a tendency on the part of our lawmakers to be more farsighted.

Accordingly the general atmosphere of the soldier brightened. Better housing conditions, prospects of more fluid promotion, and the improved ratings of enlisted men for pay and advancement added to the hope of having an army some day.

On the other hand, the appropriations for sufficient equipment and modern weapons for even good training lagged. The legislative gentlemen seemed to be more interested in the High Commissioner of the Philippines and the $750,000 appropriated for his residence than in its safety. But the Philippine Government, aroused to its danger, did otherwise. Immediately, it made overtures for the services of our former Chief of Staff as soon as his tour had expired. Our President, upon the request of President-elect Quezon, detailed MacArthur as military ad-*Fall 1935* viser to the new commonwealth and chief of the Philippine commission of army officers.

The 165,000 enlisted men MacArthur had asked for our army actually amounted, when the smoke blew away, to only 146,826, because of fiscal limitations. On the other hand, motorization, mechanization and modernization of infantry, cavalry, field artillery, and anti-aircraft began to sprout. In the mechanized cavalry, brigade scout cars for 13 mechanized platoons were in process of procurement. A thousand different types of tactical and administrative vehicles had come on the scene and one battalion of field artillery was motorized to work with the mechanized cavalry brigade. More maintenance money was allowed for the aëroplanes we already had. On the other side, National Guard units had a bare skeleton of matériel for peacetime practice. Target practice and extensive maneuvers were not 10 per cent of necessary exercises, had a discerning glance been directed across the waters in either direction. *July 1 1936* *June 1936*

The succeeding Chief of Staff, General Malin Craig, did not pause in augmenting and abetting MacArthur's programs. He stated that the army was more efficient than at any time in its previous peacetime history, but was relatively weaker than the armies of other countries which were expanding. The army was below the 165,000 promised enlisted men by 6,374, and the officers still remained at 12,268. The enlisted strength at the rate it was increasing would not reach the already legislated number until 1939. *July 1 1937*

The army was much like the clergyman who had to earn his salary and beg it, too. Every now and then it would eke out a begrudged bit. And every now and then a wave of attention in another direction would completely eclipse it. Floods throughout the country and beach erosion on our waterfronts occupied the pity and energies of the public. The army was called in to make repairs. Although the work was necessary and done with a will, it further displaced the training of the army as an army. *1936*

On the other hand, some salutary measures were undertaken with and without the aid of the lawmakers. A Deficiency Act the year before had given an addition to the capacity of the Military Academy in the form of new barracks, academic buildings, armory, 50 sets of officers' quarters, and enlargement of the gymnasium to take care of the previous increase. A thousand new aëroplanes, by act of Congress, were on order and another *June 25 1936* thousand new ones on hand, the goal being 2,320 by June 30, 1940. There was no money in the country for more, it was felt. A new division, streamlined, of 3 regiments of infantry and 1 of reënforced artillery containing 13,500 men was contemplated as an improvement for certain tactical purposes over the square division of 4 regiments of infantry and 1 of artillery containing about 22,000 men. The new division in the vicinity of Fort Sam Houston, Texas, was tested and found to have promise in more flexibility, maneuverability, and ease of supply than the old division. Other maneuvers were held over the country, and the revival was a slight lift to training. Although the National Guard had come up to 192,000 and the reserves had 96,545 officers, they were both short of the minimum requirements. There were provided no anti-tank guns or equipment except a few models, and there was no money provided to buy more. Tanks in small quantities were still undergoing tests. An aëroplane cannon had not been obtained although desired by the army, and there were not enough modern 75's in good condition to go half way around the small army. The 105 howitzer had just been adopted. Motorization was not half complete, and small arm rifles were still woefully deficient. Yet as ever Congress was willing to legislate if not appropriate. It recognized the army by conceding an allowable celebration in its honor on the anniversary of the outbreak of World War I, April 6th of every year. The army was advised to assist civic bodies with appropriate celebrations.

*Mar. 16
1937*

*Jan. 28
1938*

The next year opened propitiously. The President with his usual foresight sent a message to Congress requesting nearly nine million dollars for anti-aircraft, $450,000 for pay of an enlisted reserve, six millions for manufacture of gages, dies and aids to manufacture of arms and munitions, and other increases for the army. Congress responded by giving what he asked and by raising the officer personnel of the regular army to 14,659, and by providing for enlisting discharged soldiers under 35 years old in the enlisted reserve at a salary of $24 a year. They could be recalled to active duty only in an emergency, when they would receive $3 per month for each month in the reserve up to $150. In order to cause rotation on the General Staff and to keep officers from stagnating on such duty, Congress made it

*April 13
1938*

*April 25
1938*

*April 22
1938*

obligatory for an officer to serve two years with troops out of
every six. The air corps was increased by 5,500 enlisted men, *June 11*
and in accordance with funds allotted ordered over fourteen mil- *1938*
lion dollars worth of fighting planes. Although legislation provided enough anti-aircraft to give a beginning of equipment to
15 regiments of the regular army and National Guard, the armament fire-control equipment and searchlights were insufficient to
make the armament effective. Anti-tank weapons were wanting.
One had been developed by the Ordnance Department, but there
were no funds for further development or supply. Finally,
money was appropriated for the last 2,000 or more aëroplanes
contemplated by the board on which Newton D. Baker was chairman, three years before. A flight of six of our bombers to the
inaugural ceremonies in Buenos Aires proved the superior efficiency of our planes and pilots. However, motorization still
lagged, and the number of 75-mm. guns and 105 howitzers for
the field artillery still fell far short of requirements. On the
other hand, Congress went four better by appropriating ten million dollars for educational orders for munitions of war, in order
to let commercial concerns familiarize themselves with the work
and manufacture of weapons and munitions. For this purpose,
two millions were set aside annually for the next five years. Notwithstanding the fact that in two of these years the orders were
going to be more emotional than educational, the office of the
Assistant Secretary of War under the able leadership of Louis
M. Johnson was able to induct business into aids that would prove
invaluable in 1941. However, there were many like Senator
Borah who uttered tirades against armament races and wanted *Dec. 3*
entry into war left up to a vote of the people. *1938*

These were the military happenings in our country while
Hitler was digesting Austria and masticating Sudetenland. The
general American apathy and lack of appreciation is typified in
the housing of the War Department in Washington. In the
State Building military activities were given less and less space.
Pushed hither and yon, the War Department was scattered
among 20 different buildings. The waste motion, embarrassment,
and inefficiency need not be elaborated beyond these facts. Over
and over the War Department asked for a single separate building, but nothing came of the matter.

Yet training for the soldier in the field looked promising. A valuable start was made in appropriations for large units in summer maneuvers. The Third Army conducted extensive maneuvers in the South for two weeks, and the Second Army contented itself with command post exercises at Fort Knox, Kentucky. There were also field tests in experimental infantry and cavalry divisions, GHQ air force and anti-aircraft maneuvers on the southern Atlantic coast, and joint army and navy exercises along the north Atlantic and in the caribbean.

Summer 1938

Two and one half years before the Japanese swooped down on Oahu, Wake Island, Guam, Midway, and Luzon, the enlisted strength of the army proper totaled 167,712. Although it had at last come up to the figure asked for by MacArthur, it was still over 112,000 below what was thought to be a safe minimum twenty years before. It lacked similarly 2,000 officers.

July 1 1939

Yet the country was becoming militarily air conscious. An act provided three hundred million dollars for a limit of 6,000 serviceable aëroplanes, an increase of 23,500 enlisted men for the air corps and a peacetime commissioned strength for the regular army of 16,719. But there was a catch to the last. The officer increase was to take place over a period of ten years and be completed by "June 30, 1949." In less than three years we were to be at war. In less than five months Hitler was to invade Poland and cause Europe to flame.

May 15 1939

In other branches of the service we were still sadly lacking in weapons and munitions of modern design. Said General Craig: "New devices of war are of critical importance. To be without them invites failure." Although funds were provided for partially equipping 400,000 men by the Congress, most of the weapons and transportation were on order and could not be furnished in any sizable quantities in the following two years, so that the maneuvers of the 4 armies, 1 each year since 1935, gave the soldiers and officers little or no practice with modern equipment or weapons. Neither was there sufficient ammunition to let the troops have experience in the manipulating and actual firing of their weapons on ranges.

On the other hand, the idea of field training was taking hold on the lawmakers, even if it was not going to catch up with the times. Armory drills for the National Guard and field training for 6 divisions of the regular army were intensified as much as appropriations would permit. The First Army in the East split into two maneuvers, one near Plattsburg, New York, and the other near Manassas, Virginia. Troops of the northern force consisted of the First Division and Eighteenth Brigade of the regular army and the Twenty-sixth, Twenty-seventh, Forty-third and Forty-fourth National Guard divisions. Troops of the southern force consisted of the Sixteenth Brigade of the regular army and the Twenty-eighth and Twenty-ninth National Guard divisions. The Fourth Army held a command post exercise at the Presidio of San Francisco for the training of approximately 700 officers. It was during these maneuvers that the President signed a bill allowing each of the four army commanders to be made a lieutenant general with the pay of a major general and the allowances of a vice admiral of the navy.[17] *Summer 1939* *Aug. 5 1939*

It was in this time when the army was faintly emerging from the doldrums of the twenties and early thirties, when many of the army personnel were still out on civilian duties, and military units were undermanned and in the lower ranks underofficered, that suddenly Germany attacked Poland, put on a blitzkrieg, and gobbled it in a matter of a little over two weeks. Despite the new design of tactics and amazing speed of synchronized air and mechanized avalanches, our country after the first shock settled down to the normal indifference that since our birth as a nation has nestled itself smugly between two mighty oceans. *Sept. 1 1939*

By the first of the next year, the United States had waked up to the fact that it might be inveigled into war, and dimly it recognized it had a puny army. Let's do something. The President called for increased armaments. But even with the convincing proof of German intentions and the unmistakable effectiveness of the blitzkrieg, the mass of the people were unable to see any dangers applicable to ourselves. Congress limited the number of replacement aëroplanes to 57 and cut out twelve million dollars for the defense of Alaska. *Jan. 4 1940*

---

[17] The next year, July 31, 1940, the law included commanders of Panama Canal and Hawaiian Departments. In our service Congress has been particularly reluctant in having pay go with the higher ranks. An officer can get beyond a major general in rank, responsibility and duties, but not in pay.

April 9
1940

May 10
1940

May 13
1940

May 17
1940

May 19
1940

May 16
1940

May 28
1940

May 31
1940

June 9
1940

June
13-15
1940

June 17
1940

June 20
1940

June 22
1940

During this awe-struck whisper period, while Congress and the people contemplated this idea, the Germans occupied Denmark and invaded Norway. They invaded the Netherlands, Belgium, and Luxembourg. They took Sedan and reached Rotterdam, cutting the Netherlands apart, and the Dutch ceased resistance. They penetrated 35 miles into France while pushing the British back in Belgium. They came within 80 miles of Paris.

By this time our country bestirred itself to such lengths that the President felt it possible to ask for 50,000 war planes and $1,182,000,000 appropriation for the army and navy.

While Congress considered and many of the population were aghast, Belgium surrendered, and the remnants of the thoroughly beaten British reached England from Dunkirk. The Germans bombed Paris and came within 35 miles of it. Italy openly linked herself with Germany, and the Nazis crossed the Seine and took Paris. They took Verdun, and France sued for peace.

The swift fall of our former ally, the cracking of the vaunted Maginot Line was our first real awakening.

Three days later a bill was introduced in Congress to provide for selective service for our manhood in war, commonly called the draft. And on the same day that France signed an armistice in reverse of the one in November, 1918, in the Compiègne Forest, our Congress passed a National Defense Tax Bill amounting to nearly a billion dollars a year and raised the national debt limit from forty-five to forty-nine billion dollars. It also acceded to the wishes of the Chief of Staff to speed up promotion. It provided for the promotion of officers on a length of service basis,[18] and for brigadier generals to be retired at the age of 62 and all other grades at 60. All officers below the grade of brigadier general and 60 years or over were to be retired by June 30, 1942. Major generals and above were not considered old until they were 64. The Secretary of War could hold out

---

[18] The captain, major and lieutenant colonel were to be promoted after 17, 23, and 28 years' commissioned service respectively in the regular army; the second and first lieutenant after 3 and 10 years respectively. The promotion list of colonels was limited to 705. Majors and lieutenant colonels could not be promoted unless they had held the lower grade for 6 and 5 years respectively.

5 per cent of the colonels and keep them on active duty until they
were 62. The bill gave opportunity and enthusiasm to younger
men but eliminated many older men with superior records and
high physical vigor whose experience and wisdom were difficult
to replace and in whom the government had an appreciable investment.

While the mass air raids were deluging the British Isles,
Italy was conquering British Somaliland, the Germans were entering Rumania, and Italy was invading Greece, the United
States again was the calf that had its ears pulled off to get it
to the cow and its tail pulled off to get it away. Money, the
cure-all, was shelled out from the pockets of Congress as fluidly
as it had been withheld frozenly before. A Supplemental Defense Appropriation Act was adopted for nearly two billions. *June 27 1940*
In a special message the President asked for nearly five billions more. Then Congress took action on a total defense bill of *July 1940*
over five billions. The country—quite scared now, except for
the destructive isolationists and idealistic pacifists—thought *Sept. 6 1940*
only in terms of billions. And billions more were to be flicked
off as thousands had been denied in the twenties. America as
usual was going to shoot the enemy with dollar bills. But time?

It was not of great moment. The Selective Service Bill
dragged on for 86 days, while France succumbed, Vichy became
a vassal state, mass raids intensified on Britain, and the Axis
forces roamed at will over successful roads in Europe, Asia, and
Africa, with tentacles in North and South America. The lawmakers were considering—considering their selfish interests and
personal views—while the man in the street knew better than to
sit naked in the open with hail storms flitting around the horizon. Great lobbies of well-intentioned homicides, with little
knowledge of our true history, brought forth arguments against
conscription as being undemocratic and favored the unequable,
wasteful volunteering. And so the Congress was made to dilly-
dally at the cost of delayed training and the lives and losses to
come on Oahu and the Bataan Peninsula. The bill was finally *Sept. 16 1940*
passed in early fall.[19]

Meanwhile, the army did what it could for itself, while the

---

[19] The first bill provided for ages between 21 and 36, later changed to
20 and 44. The act was modeled after the one of May, 1917.

lawmakers threw it crumbs and promises from the succession of political banquets. It did away with the normal courses at the

Feb. 1
1940

War, General Staff and Industrial colleges in order to use the plants and staffs for direct war purposes. Particularly did the office of the Assistant Secretary of War strike out on its own in the work of industrial mobilization. Swamped with sudden expansion many times the size of the year before, it placed orders with astounding rapidity. The ten-year program had to be compressed into two. Had it not been for its quiet foresight and exact plans made in the lean years with the aid of the Army Industrial College, the immense load for aëroplanes (six times the average annual purchase of the years preceding), semi-automatic rifle, anti-tank, anti-aircraft, seacoast weapons and equipment, all sorts of ammunition, fire-control matériel, tanks, combat vehicles, radios, telephones, searchlights, pontoon and other bridge equipment, medical supplies, gas masks, in fact all the tools of war could not have been shouldered. But the schedules that industrialists formerly had pleaded were out of the question suddenly, under the licking flames of Europe, were found reasonable and effective. Even with all the efficiency of the Assistant Secretary, Louis Johnson, these necessary supplies could not be immediately forthcoming. Time—with its six-year lead—could be gained on by only a few paces. The maneuvers of the First Army, commanded by Lieutenant General Hugh A.

August
1940

Drum in northern New York, disclosed a tragic rather than ludicrous want of weapons. In order to gain a similarity to actual usage in battle and a little practice, the Army Commander stimulated the construction by the various units of imitation weapons. Stove pipe, wood, sheet iron, and other materials were marked 60-mm. mortar and 50-cal. machine gun; certain motor trucks answered as tanks.

These maneuvers were part of the more extensive practice of large units during this year and an indication of the growing realization of our lack of training. In other parts of the country

Apr. 12
1940

large units likewise had practice. The First, Fifth and Sixth Divisions were concentrated in a corps at Fort Benning, Georgia, for two weeks of maneuver. The Second Division and First

Apr. 1
1940

Cavalry Division had maneuvers in east Texas, after which there were larger exercises between the Georgia and Texas corps on the Texas-Louisiana border. The Second Army, consisting of the Seventh Mechanized Cavalry Brigade of the regular army and the Thirty-second, Thirty-third, Thirty-seventh and Thirty- *June 1940* eighth National Guard Divisions under Lieutenant General Stanley H. Ford held two weeks of maneuver near Sparta, Wisconsin. The First Army consisted of the First Division of the regular army and the Twenty-sixth, Twenty-seventh, Twenty-eighth, Twenty-ninth, Forty-third and Forty-fourth National Guard Divisions. The Third Army under Lieutenant General Stanley D. Embick concentrated along the Sabine River in the Alexandria, Louisiana, area. It consisted of the Second Division and First Cavalry Division of regulars, and the Thirtieth, Thirty-first, Thirty-sixth and Forty-fifth Infantry Divisions and Twenty-third Cavalry Division of the National Guard. The Fourth Army under Lieutenant General John L. DeWitt concentrated at Fort Lewis, Washington, and Camp Ripley, Minnesota. It consisted of the Third and Sixth Divisions of the regular army and the Thirty-fourth, Thirty-fifth, Fortieth and Forty-first Divisions of the National Guard. In the early part of the year the Third Regular Division sailed 2,000 miles in 6 *Jan. 1940* transports off the California coast practicing landing technic and convoy regulation with the navy.

While the nation was registering 16,400,000 selectees, the *Oct. 16 1940* enlisted force of the regular army numbered approximately 250,000—still 30,000 less than the number called for in the National Defense Act of 1920.

Along with the lengthy discussion over the Selective Service went the similar protraction of just as vital legislation. If we were to get anywhere, we must call out and train through the next winter all components of our budding army. Clothing, shelter, camp sites, and all the appurtenances necessary for men training in cold weather were lacking. The War Department's original *May 1940* request for the federalization of the National Guard as of primary importance was forehandedly sent to Congress in the spring, so that construction could be ready and troops would not be exposed to disease and improper shelter when called out in the fall. There would have been ample time to engage sites and construct proper camps had Congress acted promptly. But the debates ran through the months, and the pleas of the Chief of

Staff of the army again remind one of Washington's supplications during the Revolution:

"Shelter is a serious problem at the present moment. We thought that Congress would settle the question of authority to order out the National Guard, and the matter of compulsory training by the first of August. On that basis, the Guard was to be brought into the Federal service during September and the first induction of men under the Selective Service Act during October. What has happened is that the weeks have been passing and we have no authority to enter into contracts to provide the additional shelter required. We have been trying to find some manner, some means for getting started. We want to proceed in an orderly and businesslike manner. We know exactly what we want to do and exactly where we want to do it, but we have neither the authority nor the funds and time is fleeting. So far as construction is concerned the winter is upon us, because it requires from 3 to 4 months to provide proper shelter. We had hopes at first to gain time by providing a progressive mobilization of the National Guard during the summer. We planned to put troops in tent camps, while better shelter was being prepared in the climates that demand special protection against the winter. However, weeks have come and have gone and we have been unable to make a start. The present uncertainties make a businesslike procedure almost impossible. We must make a start toward getting water lines laid; a start on the sewage-disposal systems; a start on the temporary roads and certainly the walks to keep our people out of the mud; and we must get under way the start of construction of temporary hospital facilities. These are fundamental necessities and take time to develop."

This plaint is so typical of the many that were made during this intense pre-war period and so explanatory of the principles which kept us on the defensive, with all its useless losses later, that it is given here in its entirety.

Aug. 27
1940
Sept. 9
1940
Sept. 24
1940
Authority calling the National Guard into federal service arrived in the fall, but the money for the camps did not come through until thirteen days later and for the Selective Service construction until nearly a month later. Had it not been that the

President in his forthright prevision put up twenty-nine and *Aug. 2*
one-half millions from his emergency fund for those necessary *1940*
and lengthy constructions such as hospitals and sewer systems,
so that the army could get going, disease, hardship, and waste
would have resulted. To add to the ''unbusinesslike'' procedure
the War Department was really forced to induct the National
Guard before it was ready for them, because it was warned that
a delay in induction might defeat passage of the Selective Service
Act. So at this ominous date the army was pummeled between
political caprices.

At the end of the year the War Department found itself *1940*
frantically attempting to expand an army of 172,000 into one
of one and one-half millions—over eight times its size, in a matter of months, with late funds and early winter. Specifically,
there were 1,400,000 men, of which 500,000 were to be in the
regular army, 270,000 in the National Guard, and 630,000 as
selectees.

Feverish military haste marked the last of 1940 and the beginning of 1941. An act provided for an Under Secretary of *Dec. 16*
War, an addition to the Assistant Secretary. The President *1940*
called upon Congress for increased armaments. Meanwhile, the *Jan. 4*
troops shivered, conducted schools, and such training without *1941*
sufficient weapons and target practice as cold hands and snow
camps would allow. Old units were drained of their experienced
men for training new units. The corner grocery store had to
produce a nation-wide chain by spring. About the time a commander would be whipping his units into some sort of shape,
his best instructors would be taken away. Both the parent store
and the home office had been too suddenly narrowed and cramped
to produce a finished and expensive business. But there was
surprisingly little hardship in proportion to the handicaps.

Meanwhile, constant attention had to be paid to the new *Oct. 28*
and successful methods in Europe, Asia, and Africa. Italy had *1940*
invaded Greece over the mountains of Albania. Germany had *Nov. 23*
overrun Rumania. Greece had turned the tables on Italy by *1940*
desperate mountain fighting and captured Porto Edda. The *Dec. 6*
British had put on some new desert fighting that captured Bardia *1940*
and trapped 25,000 Italians. But the Allies' successes were *Jan. 5*
short-lived. Nazi troops entered Bulgaria in the early spring, *1941*
Mar. 1
1941

captured the Balkan states and Greece, taking, killing, and putting to flight many British. Much was to be learned from this mountain and winter fighting, together with that in Finland. New methods of employement and new types of equipment were coming to light. The burden upon the small, trained army in acquiring trustworthy information and testing devices for their practical worth was almost beyond bearing or carrying to the proper spot.

However, despite blasts of weather, hurry of housing, hampering in labor, shortages of a multitude of supplies needed instantly, and the consequent speed of organization and erection, sufficient and acceptable shelter and facilities were through suffering gained for the troops by spring. Twenty-nine large reception centers throughout the country were completed where the huge quotas of volunteers and selectees could be received, classified, uniformed, given preliminary training, and sent on their way. Twenty-one replacement centers were established where each arm and service could get the thirteen weeks of basic training, after which the novitiate was passed on to his tactical command. In this way the progress of army units went along unimpeded by any interruption of having to train recruits on the side.

An indication of the increasing expansion of the army lay in a Congressional authorization to train 30,000 pilots and 100,000 mechanics annually for the air corps. Akin to that enlargement was the widened territory the army had to cover. New bases had to be organized in the Atlantic and occupied. Then came the most elaborate military training of large units ever to be conducted in this country. Every army in the continental United States was involved. Hitherto the larger headquarters had reckoned in divisions; they now did so in army

Jan.
1941

May 24-
June 30
1941
June 1-13
1941

June 2-28
1941
corps. The year started with joint army, navy and marine corps maneuvers near Puerto Rico, parts of the First Division of the regular army participating. In the spring the Fourth Army had extensive exercises at Fort Ord and Camp Hunter Liggett, California, as did the VIII Army Corps of the Third Army in the Brownwood, Texas, area. Simultaneously the VII Army Corps and the Second Army, with attached GHQ units, went nearly a month in the vicinity of Camp Forrest, Tennessee.

The Third Army had exercises for a fortnight near Camp Beauregard, Louisiana. The VII Army Corps and the Second Army with attached GHQ units held exercises near Camp Robinson, Arkansas. The V Army Corps contested against the VIII Army Corps near Camp Beauregard, Louisiana. The First Army consisting of the I, II and VI Army Corps held maneuvers in the Carolinas after which GHQ operated a maneuver between the First Army and the IV Corps of Third Army, with a mechanized corps attached to the IV Corps. The largest maneuvers were between the Second and Third Armies near Camp Beauregard, Louisiana. The main difference between these and prior exercises lay in the length of time each unit could practice continuously in the field. Instead of units being called for two weeks' training, which with preliminaries and postludes amounted on the average to little more than five days' actual practice for the larger units, warlike conditions were simulated in lengthier periods of knowledge and hardening and in the free type of exercise. Although there was still a lamentable lack of weapons and experience with them, the maneuvers were the most benefiting in the history of the country.

*June 16-2:
1941
Aug. 11-3(
1941*

*Aug. 16-3(
1941*

*Oct. 6-
Nov. 15
1941*

*Nov. 16-3(
1941*

*Sept. 1-30
1941*

Probably the largest advantage throughout this period over World War I conditions was the 100,000 officers in the officers' reserve corps, made up largely of R.O.T.C. graduates of our colleges, who had been faithfully keeping up with their military training theoretically and practically in the backward years, many having taken their fourteen days' field training every year that appropriations would permit. In addition to that substantial preparation the army established Officer Candidate schools for enlisted men who had given promise in their basic training of becoming excellent leaders. By a three-month course it was able to turn out about 10,000 officers a year when running to capacity.

1941

The President aided our military preparedness signally when he declared an "unlimited emergency."[20] The War Department had a freer hand and more supple reactions from the public. It set up a General Headquarters of the field forces at the War College to direct and supervise training, and trans-

*May 27
1941*

---

[20] He had declared a limited emergency September 8, 1939, after the attack on Poland.

ferred to it the War Plans Division of the War Department General Staff. So that the field forces could operate with fuller attention to field training, local administration and supply were transferred to the 9 corps areas in the United States, which ceased to function tactically. General Headquarters Air Force took over the command of the 4 air-defense areas of the United States and coördinated aviation, anti-aircraft, aircraft warning and balloon barrage defense in the various localities. Many new units had to be formed and old ones expanded—such as armored divisions, parachute troops, ski troops, anti-tank units, anti-aircraft units, mountain and desert troops, and motorized units. These expansions do not include the many new devices to be designed, improved and supplied especially in the Ordnance Department and Signal Corps.

An innovation in the assignment of officers to duty with troops came in with the emergency. Already the law for the older officers indicated the trend toward age as a criterion of efficiency and vigor. In the fall an order was issued from the War Department showing maximum ages for grades with troops. Those who were over the age were relieved, or would be when the particular age overtook them.[21] All above division commanders were exempt. If a promotion did not catch up with a second lieutenant before he was 31, he was unfit for troops; similarly with other grades. As it turned out, many of those relieved were more vigorous and efficient than the younger replacements. Commanders complained of having to begin much of their training all over again or be hampered by backward training because of sudden relief and inferior replacements. There was an appreciable loss of morale among many of the army's best and highest officers as they applied and suffered an iron-clad rule which made vigor an invariable function of age; as they saw officers who were accomplishing superior and extraordinary results with their men suddenly jerked away from their prospering commands; and as they unsuccessfully strove to gain a promotion for the subordinate so as to have him attain a higher age bracket and stay on. On the one side many felt a

Sept. 5 1941

---

[21] Major Generals (division commanders), 62; Brigadier Generals, 60; Colonels, 55; Lieutenant Colonels, 52; Majors, 47; Captains, 42; First Lieutenants, 35; Second Lieutenants, 31.

larger proportion of the relatively few capable military trainers in the United States could be more largely used as a matter of economy. On the other, many felt that the step toward youth and vigor was progressive in meeting the excessive drains of modern war with higher efficiency and stamina, and that the loss of morale was negligible and could not be avoided on account of our late preparations.

By summer the army was spread from Iceland and the *1941* Caribbean to Alaska and the Philippines. Port facilities of New York, Charleston, New Orleans, San Francisco, and Seattle had to be expanded immensely while troops were sneaked from the mainland without publicity. The strength of the forces was distributed thus: 456,000 to 29 divisions of 9 corps of 4 armies; *July 1 1941* 43,000 to 4 divisions of the armored force; 308,000 to 215 regiments of corps, army and GHQ troops; 167,000 to the air corps; 46,000 to harbor defenses; 120,000 to garrisons in the Pacific and Atlantic; 160,000 to corps areas which provided for the housekeeping and supply of 550 posts, stations, depots and ports; and about 150,000 selectees to replacement centers for training—making a grand total of 1,450,000.

A sad note was injected into this brisk war effort just when the army was beginning to feel that popular support of military strength at any cost had about crystallized. In early spring the War Department realized that legal limitations would by fall wreck the large armies which had been pieced together with so much pains and expense. The time of many National Guard units would expire after a year. Similarly the 75 to 90 per cent of reserve officers in various other units would be gone also, as would a large proportion of selectees. In other words, the vast force would evaporate with relatively few to carry on the training. In effect, the whole structure would have to be reared all over again from the first shovelful for the foundation, and most of the labor of a year would be lost to future training, if Congress did not under the "unlimited emergency" repeal the time limits, so that our land defense could be a going concern. The measure came before the Senate in midsummer and after heated debate was passed with an unimpressive majority. It caused arguments in the House which seemed to reveal more thought of the constituents than of the country as a whole. It was passed in the

August
1941
lower body by just one vote—just four months before the bombing of Pearl Harbor.

Even though there were sprags of politics in the wheels of the army's development, the United States for the first time in its history, though late, was preparing before declaring—was getting ready before war was thrust grimly on the country and the people. This unprecedented undertaking was bearing fruit, and it looked as if the advantage of time and preparation our potential enemies had gained over us in the past decades might after all be offset. It was too heartening to be true. This time our future Allies needed every munition we could make, in contrast to the last time when we needed almost every thing they
Mar. 11
1941
could make. The Lease-Lend bill became a law. We had to strip down and ship huge consignments over both oceans. As we were beginning to arm our comparatively meager force, we were suddenly disarmed and dismantled just before the extensive training periods of the year. Our unprecedented preparation, the foresight of a great President, the gruelling sweat and strain of the army had to be expended on our outposts of friendly nations. Naturally, certain elements of training at home had to lag.

Nevertheless, we had plenty of money if we did have little immediately to show for it. It was better than having no money and plenty of things to buy as in the twenties. The weaponless, large-scale maneuvers were immensely valuable for staffs and commanders to practice with large units, for hardening the troops, for finding out how badly large masses of transportation could be handled, for seeing how mechanization should not be used, and in general for gaining practical coöperation and
Dec. 1
1941
manipulation through trial and error. By the end of the exercises much of what not to do had been learned and the soldiers had been promised target practice with the weapons they had been toting and manipulating but had not had a chance to shoot. Again eleventh-hour preparation disappointed them. One
Dec. 7
1941
week after the last set of maneuvers Japan bombed Oahu, Wake, Midway, Guam, and the Philippine Islands in a Sunday morning surprise attack, and we were in the war lock, stock and barrel, with all our deficiencies on our backs.

We shelled out more money. Congress voted over ten billions for the armed forces, and the country rushed feverishly Dec. 15
1941 into production. Another bill went through in a few days to extend the draft for ages from 20 to 44. Politics, pacifism and isolation nearly disappeared in the catastrophe. Added to the thousands of casualties in Hawaii, and the vessels, planes and buildings destroyed, Wake Island after a gallant stand sur- Dec. 24
1941 rendered to the Japanese. The next day, Christmas, Hong Kong fell. Then the American and Filipino inhabitants of Manila, which had been declared an open city, were bombed by the Dec. 27
1941 Japanese.

Meanwhile, three columns from different landings bore down on the American and Philippine forces. In the first attack most of the aircraft and aviation facilities were destroyed, and there was a comparatively small handful of ground troops to oppose the landings of the Japanese.

The eyes of the world were focused on MacArthur. A year 1936 after he had taken charge of the military forces of the Islands he had been promoted to a Field Marshal by the Filipino Government while still an officer of the United States Army—another precedent broken. A year later he retired from active service of his country and devoted his attention to the upbuilding of Dec. 31
1937 the Islands. Four years later he was recalled to active duty by the President as Commander of the United States Forces in July 25
1941 the Far East. Successively he was made a lieutenant general and a general after being called from retirement—another precedent broken.

The United States especially and the world in general felt it was only a matter of weeks before Luzon would fall as all the rest of the key points between Japan and Australia had done. Slowly MacArthur was pushed back from front, rear and side. Daily the people of the United States awaited news of the capture and destruction of his small band. Daily he retired slowly, inflicting immense damage upon the enemy. Just when the trap was ready to spring and close upon his stubborn forces, he cleverly side-slipped them into the rugged, wooded Bataan Peninsula, where secretly he had prepared defensive positions.

In the United States training and production moved unobstructedly. By early spring Congress had appropriated during March 28
1942 the previous eight months over one hundred and sixty billions of dollars for the army and defense, whereas it had haggled over half that many millions a decade previously. It was possible to begin any number of projects hitherto denied. Orders for staggering numbers of weapons and munitions poured out upon manufacture. All sorts of specialized training were set on foot. Desert, air-borne, and mechanized forces were inaugurated and *March 27 1942* put in training. Major General Joseph W. Stilwell was promoted a lieutenant general and appointed Chief of Staff (after- *March 19 1942* wards Corps Commander) to Generalissimo Chiang Kai-shek, Commanding General of the Chinese forces in Burma, China and India. American divisions were in Ireland, Java, Australia, and islands other than Luzon in the Philippines.

The immense overhead in our national capital had grown unwieldy. The General Staff worked out a simplification of control and elimination of unnecessary offices at the direction of *March 9 1942* General George C. Marshall, Chief of Staff. The tripartite decentralization was approved by the President. The three subdivisions were designated Ground, Air, and Supply and commanded by lieutenant generals [22] who reported directly to the chief of staff. A number of offices were dispensed with, such as the chiefs of infantry, cavalry, field artillery and coast artillery, and large powers were entrusted to the three commanders.

Still MacArthur and his gallant band were holding out un- *March 25 1942* believably in the Bataan Mountains. For his brilliant heroism he was accorded the Congressional Medal of Honor. By this time people of the Allied nations were stirred with similar impulses. MacArthur must be saved. He must be held on for higher *Feb. 1942* command. Here was a possible savior. The President realizing the same need ordered him to repair to Australia, but MacArthur begged for a few weeks' delay. He wanted neither to depart from his command and his men nor to relinquish his fight in the Islands. But the administration was adamant in the end. MacArthur with his wife and son were spirited away in torpedo *Mar. 11 1942* boats, traveling four nights and waiting under cover for three days for the plane which finally arrived and carried them off to

---

[22] The first three were Lieutenant General Leslie J. McNair for the ground forces, Lieutenant General Henry H. Arnold, air forces, and Lieutenant General Brehon B. Somervell for supply.

Australia. There he was finally established as Commander-in-Chief of the General Headquarters of the Southwest Pacific Area, an officer of the United States Army becoming generalissimo over foreign forces—another precedent broken. *Apr. 21 1942*

But the sad remnants of the United States and Filipino divisions in Bataan were being worn down gradually. After MacArthur left, the mantle fell upon Major General Jonathan M. Wainwright, who had been mainly responsible for the execution of the remarkable retirement into the Peninsula. Although he was promoted a lieutenant general, he found himself in a sorry plight. Starvation, disease, exhaustion, and deprivation of the barest necessities of campaign had worn down his gallant units. The life line to the Philippines had been cut. The people of the United States who had in a previous decade objected to fortifying Guam or anything else, for fear of offending the Japanese, had seen to that. Two boat loads of supplies from America out of every three were sunk by Japanese explosives. Daily the men of Bataan looked to sea hopefully—then hopelessly. In the face of fresh Japanese numbers and mightier Japanese onslaughts Wainwright's force finally capitulated—worn down, worn out, killed, wounded or captured. He made his escape to Corregidor with all he could rescue, about 3,800,[23] while Major General Edward P. King, Jr., executed the formal surrender of the sad remnants of our countrymen. *April 9 1942*

So far the United States had only loss, humiliation, defeat, and anxiety in World War II.

"To maintain in peace a needlessly elaborate military establishment entails economic waste. But there can be no compromise with minimum requirements. In war there is no intermediate measure of success. Second best is to be defeated, and military defeat carries with it national disaster—political, economic, social and spiritual disaster."

Those were the words of MacArthur in 1935. Those were the ideas we were then too busy to notice. Those were the sores in the hearts of the surviving little band of Bataan.

---

[23] Approximately.

APPENDIX A

CONTAINING NAMES OF INCUMBENTS OF ALL PRINCIPAL OFFICES IN THE ARMY SINCE ITS CREATION

COMMANDERS IN CHIEF OF THE ARMY SINCE THE BEGINNING

Names	From	To
Washington, George	June 17, 1775	Dec. 23, 1783
Washington, George	April 30, 1789	Mar. 4, 1797
Adams, John	Mar. 4, 1797	Mar. 4, 1801
Jefferson, Thomas	Mar. 4, 1801	Mar. 4, 1809
Madison, James	Mar. 4, 1809	Mar. 4, 1817
Monroe, James	Mar. 4, 1817	Mar. 4, 1825
Adams, John Quincy	Mar. 4, 1825	Mar. 4, 1829
Jackson, Andrew	Mar. 4, 1829	Mar. 4, 1837
Van Buren, Martin	Mar. 4, 1837	Mar. 4, 1841
Harrison, William Henry	Mar. 4, 1841	April 4, 1841
Tyler, John	April 6, 1841	Mar. 4, 1845
Polk, James Knox	Mar. 4, 1845	Mar. 4, 1849
Taylor, Zachary	Mar. 4, 1849	July 9, 1850
Fillmore, Millard	July 9, 1850	Mar. 4, 1853
Pierce, Franklin	Mar. 4, 1853	Mar. 4, 1857
Buchanan, James	Mar. 4, 1857	Mar. 4, 1861
Lincoln, Abraham	Mar. 4, 1861	April 15, 1865
Johnson, Andrew	April 15, 1865	Mar. 4, 1869
Grant, Ulysses Simpson	Mar. 4, 1869	Mar. 4, 1877
Hayes, Rutherford Birchard	Mar. 4, 1877	Mar. 4, 1881
Garfield, James Abram	Mar. 4, 1881	Sept. 19, 1881
Arthur, Chester Allan	Sept. 20, 1881	Mar. 4, 1885
Cleveland, Grover	Mar. 4, 1885	Mar. 4, 1889
Harrison, Benjamin	Mar. 4, 1889	Mar. 4, 1893
Cleveland, Grover	Mar. 4, 1893	Mar. 4, 1897
McKinley, William	Mar. 4, 1897	Sept. 14, 1901
Roosevelt, Theodore	Sept. 14, 1901	Mar. 4, 1909
Taft, William H.	Mar. 4, 1909	Mar. 4, 1913
Wilson, Woodrow	Mar. 4, 1913	Mar. 4, 1921
Harding, Warren G.	Mar. 4, 1921	Aug. 2, 1923
Coolidge, Calvin	Aug. 3, 1923	Mar. 4, 1929
Hoover, Herbert	Mar. 4, 1929	Mar. 4, 1933
Roosevelt, Franklin Delano	Mar. 4, 1933	

SECRETARIES OF WAR SINCE THE BEGINNING

Names	From	To
Knox, Henry	Sept. 12, 1789	Dec. 31, 1794
Pickering, Timothy	Jan. 2, 1795	Dec. 10, 1795
McHenry, James	Jan. 27, 1796	May 13, 1800
Dexter, Samuel	May 13, 1800	Jan. 31, 1801
Dearborn, Henry	Mar. 5, 1801	Mar. 7, 1809

SECRETARIES OF WAR SINCE THE BEGINNING—*Continued*

Names	From	To
Eustis, William	Mar. 7, 1809	Jan. 13, 1813
Armstrong, John	Jan. 13, 1813	Sept. 27, 1814
Monroe, James	Sept. 27, 1814	Mar. 2, 1815
Crawford, William Harris	Aug. 1, 1815	Oct. 22, 1816
Calhoun, John Caldwell	Oct. 8, 1817	Mar. 7, 1825
Barbour, James	Mar. 7, 1825	May 23, 1828
Porter, Peter Buel	May 26, 1828	Mar. 9, 1829
Eaton, John Henry	Mar. 9, 1829	June 18, 1831
Cass, Lewis	Aug. 1, 1831	Oct. 5, 1836
Poinsett, Joel Roberts	Mar. 7, 1837	Mar. 5, 1841
Bell, John	Mar. 5, 1841	Sept. 13, 1841
Spencer, John Canfield	Oct. 12, 1841	Mar. 3, 1843
Porter, James Madison	Mar. 8, 1843	Jan. 30, 1844
Wilkins, William	Feb. 15, 1844	Mar. 4, 1845
Marcy, William Learned	Mar. 6, 1845	Mar. 4, 1849
Crawford, George Washington	Mar. 8, 1849	July 23, 1850
Conrad, Charles Magill	Aug. 15, 1850	Mar. 7, 1853
Davis, Jefferson	Mar. 7, 1853	Mar. 6, 1857
Floyd, John Buchanan	Mar. 6, 1857	Dec. 29, 1860
Holt, Joseph	Jan. 18, 1861	Mar. 5, 1861
Cameron, Simon	Mar. 5, 1861	Jan. 14, 1862
Stanton, Edwin McMasters	Jan. 15, 1862	May 28, 1869
Schofield, John McAllister	May 28, 1868	Mar. 11, 1869
Rawlins, John Aaron	Mar. 11, 1869	Sept. 6, 1869
Belknap, William Worth	Oct. 25, 1869	Mar. 2, 1876
Taft, Alphonso	Mar. 8, 1876	May 22, 1876
Cameron, James Donald	May 22, 1876	Mar. 3, 1877
McCrary, George Washington	Mar. 12, 1877	Dec. 10, 1879
Ramsey, Alexander	Dec. 10, 1879	Mar. 5, 1881
Lincoln, Robert Todd	Mar. 5, 1881	Mar. 5, 1885
Endicott, William Crowninshield	Mar. 5, 1885	Mar. 5, 1889
Proctor, Redfield	Mar. 5, 1889	Nov. 5, 1891
Elkins, Stephen Benton	Dec. 17, 1891	Mar. 5, 1893
Lamont, Daniel Scott	Mar. 5, 1893	Mar. 5, 1897
Alger, Russell Alexander	Mar. 5, 1897	Aug. 1, 1899
Root, Elihu	Aug. 1, 1899	Jan. 31, 1904
Taft, William H.	Feb. 1, 1904	June 30, 1908
Wright, Luke E.	July 1, 1908	Mar. 11, 1909
Dickinson, Jacob M.	Mar. 12, 1909	May 21, 1911
Stimson, Henry L.	May 22, 1911	Mar. 4, 1913
Garrison, Lindley M.	Mar. 5, 1913	Feb. 10, 1916
Scott, Hugh L., Sec. of War (*ad interim*)	Feb. 11, 1916	Mar. 8, 1916
Baker, Newton D.	Mar. 9, 1916	Mar. 4, 1921
Weeks, John W.	Mar. 5, 1921	Oct. 13, 1925
Davis, Dwight F.	Oct. 14, 1925	Mar. 5, 1929
Good, James W.	Mar. 6, 1929	Nov. 18, 1929
Hurley, Patrick J.	Dec. 9, 1929	Mar. 3, 1933
Dern, George H.	Mar. 4, 1933	Aug. 27, 1936
Woodring, Harry H.	Sept. 25, 1936	June 20, 1940
Stimson, Henry L.	July 10, 1940	

GENERALS IN CHIEF OF THE ARMY SINCE 1775

Names	From	To
Washington, George, Gen.	June 17, 1775	Dec. 23, 1783
Knox, Henry, Maj. Gen.	Dec. 23, 1783	June 20, 1784
Doughty, John, Capt. (Art.)	June 20, 1784	Aug. 12, 1784
Harmar, Josiah, Lieut. Col. (Inf.)	Aug. 12, 1784	Mar. 4, 1791
St. Clair, Arthur, Maj. Gen.	Mar. 4, 1791	Mar. 5, 1792
Wayne, Anthony, Maj. Gen.	April 13, 1792	Dec. 15, 1796
Wilkinson, James, Brig. Gen.	Dec. 15, 1796	July 13, 1798
Washington, George, Lieut. Gen.	July 13, 1798	Dec. 14, 1799
Hamilton, Alexander, Maj. Gen.	Dec. 14, 1799	June 15, 1800
Wilkinson, Jasper, Brig. Gen.	June 15, 1800	Jan. 27, 1812
Dearborn, Henry, Maj. Gen.	Jan. 27, 1812	June 15, 1815
Brown, Jacob, Maj. Gen.	June 15, 1815	Feb. 24, 1828
Macomb, Alexander, Maj. Gen.	May 29, 1828	June 25, 1841
Scott, Winfield, Maj. Gen.	July 5, 1841	Nov. 1, 1861
McClellan, G. B., Maj. Gen.	Nov. 1, 1861	Mar. 11, 1862
Halleck, H. W., Maj. Gen.	July 23, 1862	Mar. 9, 1864
Grant, U. S., Gen.	Mar. 9, 1864	Mar. 4, 1869
Sherman, W. T., Gen.	Mar. 8, 1869	Nov. 1, 1883
Sheridan, P. H., Gen.	Nov. 1, 1883	Aug. 5, 1888
Schofield, J. McA., Lieut. Gen.	Aug. 14, 1888	Sept. 29, 1895
Miles, N. A., Lieut. Gen.	Oct. 5, 1895	Aug. 8, 1903

CHIEFS OF STAFF SINCE GENERAL NELSON A. MILES, WHO WAS THE LAST GENERAL IN CHIEF OF THE ARMY

Names	From	To
Young, Samuel B. M., Lieut. Gen.	Aug. 15, 1903	Jan. 8, 1904
Chaffee, Adna R., Lieut. Gen.	Jan. 9, 1904	Jan. 14, 1906
Bates, John C., Maj. Gen.	Jan. 15, 1906	April 13, 1906
Bell, J. Franklin, Maj. Gen.	April 14, 1906	April 21, 1910
Wood, Leonard, Maj. Gen.	April 22, 1910	April 20, 1914
Wotherspoon, William W., Maj. Gen.	April 21, 1914	Nov. 15, 1914
Scott, Hugh L., Maj. Gen.	Nov. 16, 1914	Sept. 21, 1917
Bliss, Tasker H., Maj. Gen., Gen.	Sept. 22, 1917	May 18, 1918
March, Peyton C., Maj. Gen., Gen.	May 19, 1918	June 30, 1921
Pershing, John J, Gen.	July 1, 1921	Sept. 13, 1924
Hines, John L., Maj. Gen.	Sept. 14, 1924	Nov. 20, 1926
Summerall, Charles P., Gen.	Nov. 21, 1926	Nov. 20, 1930
MacArthur, Douglas, Gen.	Nov. 21, 1930	Oct. 1, 1935
Craig, Malin, Gen.	Oct. 2, 1935	Aug. 31, 1939
Marshall, George C., Gen.	Sept. 1, 1939	

QUARTERMASTER GENERALS SINCE FIRST INCUMBENT

From	To	Rank and Name	Title of Office
Aug. 14, 1775	Nov. 7, 1777	Maj. Gen. Thos. Mifflin	Qm. General
Mar. 2, 1778	Sept. 30, 1780	Maj. Gen. Nathaniel Greene	"
Aug. 5, 1780	July 25, 1785	Col. Timothy Pickering	"
Mar. 4, 1791	April 19, 1792	Samuel Hodgdon	Quartermaster
April 19, 1792	May 1, 1796	James O'Hara	"
June 1, 1796	June 1, 1802	John Wilkins	Qm. General
April 3, 1812	Mar. 2, 1813	Brig. Gen. Morgan Lewis	"
Mar. 21, 1813	June 5, 1816	Brig. Gen. Robert Swartwout	"
April 29, 1816	April 14, 1818	Col. James Mullany	Qm. General, North. Div.
April 29, 1816	April 14, 1818	Col. George Gibson	Qm. General, South. Div.

QUARTERMASTER GENERALS SINCE FIRST INCUMBENT—*Continued*

From	To	Rank and Name	Title of Office
May 8, 1818	June 10, 1860	Brig. Gen. T. S. Jesup	Qm. General
June 20, 1860	April 22, 1861	Brig. Gen. J. E. Johnston	"
May 15, 1861	Feb. 6, 1882	Brig. Gen. M. C. Meigs	"
Feb. 13, 1882	Feb. 23, 1882	Brig. Gen. D. H. Rucker	"
Feb. 23, 1882	July 1, 1883	Brig. Gen. Rufus Ingalls	"
July 1, 1883	June 16, 1890	Brig. Gen. S. B. Holabird	"
June 26, 1890	July 27, 1896	Brig. Gen. R. N. Batchelder	"
Aug. 19, 1896	Feb. 16, 1897	Brig. Gen. C. G. Sawtelle	"
Feb. 16, 1897	Feb. 3, 1898	Brig. Gen. G. H. Weeks	"
Feb. 3, 1898	April 12, 1903	Brig. Gen. M. I. Ludington	"
April 12, 1903	July 1, 1907	Brig. Gen. Charles F. Humphrey	"
July 1, 1907	Sept. 12, 1916	Maj. Gen. James B. Aleshire ...	"
Sept. 16, 1916	July 21, 1918	Maj. Gen. Henry G. Sharpe	"
July 22, 1918	Aug. 27, 1922	Maj. Gen. Harry L. Rogers * ...	"
Aug. 28, 1922	Jan. 2, 1926	Maj. Gen. William H. Hart †..	"
Jan. 3, 1926 ‡	Jan. 17, 1930	Maj. Gen. B. Frank Cheatham ..	"
Feb. 3, 1930	Feb. 3, 1934	Maj. Gen. John L. DeWitt	"
Feb. 3, 1934	Mar. 31, 1936	Maj. Gen. Louis H. Bash *....	"
April 1, 1936	Mar. 31, 1940	Maj. Gen. Henry Gibbins	"
April 1, 1940		Maj. Gen. Edmund B. Gregory ..	"

NOTE.—The act of March 3, 1799, provided that there shall be a quartermaster general with the rank, etc., of a major general. None was appointed to that grade.
* Retired.
† Died.
‡ Appointed Jan. 3, 1926; took office Jan. 18, 1926.

ADJUTANT GENERALS SINCE FIRST INCUMBENT

From	To	Rank and Name	Title of Office
June 17, 1775	June 5, 1776	Maj. Gen. Horatio Gates	Adj. General
June 5, 1776	Jan. 22, 1777	Col. Jos. Reed	"
Jan. 22, 1777	Feb. 20, 1777	Brig. Gen. Arthur St. Clair	Act. Adj. Gen.
Feb. 20, 1777	April 19, 1777	Brig. Gen. George Weedon	"
April 19, 1777	June 18, 1777	Col. Morgan Connor	Adj. General
June 18, 1777	Jan. 5, 1778	Col. Timothy Pickering	"
Jan. 5, 1778	Jan. 1, 1781	Col. Alexander Scammel	"
Jan. 8, 1781	Nov. 3, 1783	Brig. Gen. Edward Hand	"
Nov. 5, 1783	Oct. 28, 1787	Maj. William North	Adj. and Insp.
Oct. 28, 1787	Nov. 7, 1790	Lieut. Ebenezer Denny, Inf. Reg.	Act. Adjutant
Nov. 7, 1790	Sept. 4, 1791	Lieut. John Pratt, 1st Inf.	"
Sept. 4, 1791	Nov. 4, 1791	Lieut. Col. Winthrop Sargent, Mass. Militia	"
Nov. 4, 1791	Mar. 10, 1792	Lieut. Ebenezer Denny, 1st Inf. .	"
Mar. 10, 1792	Feb. 23, 1793	Lieut. Henry DeButts, 4th Inf. ..	"
Feb. 23, 1793	July 17, 1793	Maj. Michael Rudolph, Lt. Drag.	"
July 18, 1793	May 13, 1794	Capt. Edward Butler, 4th Sub-legion	"
May 13, 1794	Feb. 27, 1796	Maj. John Mills, 2d Sublegion ..	"
Feb. 27, 1796	Aug. 1, 1796	Maj. Jonathan Haskell, 4th Sub-legion	"
Aug. 1, 1796	Feb. 27, 1797	Capt. Edward Butler, 4th Sub-legion	"
Feb. 27, 1797	July 19, 1798	Maj. T. H. Cushing, 1st Inf.....	"
July 19, 1798	June 15, 1800	Brig. Gen. William North	Adj. General
June 15, 1800	April 2, 1807	Lieut. Col. T. H. Cushing, 2d Inf.	Adj. and Insp.
April 2, 1807	April 28, 1812	Maj. A. Y. Nicoll, Artillerists..	"
April 28, 1812	July 6, 1812	Lieut. Col. Alexander Macomb, Engr.	Act. Adj. Gen.
July 6, 1812	Mar. 12, 1813	Brig. Gen. T. H. Cushing	Adj. General
Mar. 12, 1813	April 27, 1813	Brig. Gen. Z. M. Pike	"
May 19, 1814	July 2, 1814	Brig. Gen. W. H. Winder	Adjutant and Insp. General
Nov. 22, 1814	June 1, 1821	Brig. Gen. Daniel Parker	"
Aug. 13, 1821	Mar. 22, 1822	Col. James Gadsden	Adj. General
May 8, 1822	Mar. 7, 1825	Capt. C. J. Nourse, 2d Art.	Act. Adj. Gen.
Mar. 7, 1825	July 15, 1852	Col. Roger Jones	Adj. General
July 15, 1852	Mar. 7, 1861	Col. Samuel Cooper	"
Mar. 7, 1861	Feb. 22, 1869	Brig. Gen. Lorenzo Thomas	"

Adjutant Generals Since First Incumbent—*Continued*

From	To	Rank and Name	Title of Office
Feb. 22, 1869	June 15, 1880	Brig. Gen. E. D. Townsend	"
June 15, 1880	May 28, 1889	Brig. Gen. R. C. Drum	"
June 7, 1889	June 24, 1892	Brig. Gen. J. C. Kelton	"
July 5, 1892	Nov. 5, 1893	Brig. Gen. Robert Williams	"
Nov. 6, 1893	Sept. 11, 1897	Brig. Gen. G. D. Ruggles	"
Sept. 11, 1897	Feb. 25, 1898	Brig. Gen. Samuel Breck	"
Feb. 25, 1898	April 14, 1906	Maj. Gen. Henry C. Corbin	"
April 23, 1904	Mar. 4, 1907	Maj. Gen. Fred C. Ainsworth ...	The Military Sec.
Mar. 5, 1907	Feb. 16, 1912	Maj. Gen. Fred C. Ainsworth ...	Adj. General
Feb. 17, 1912	June 11, 1912	Brig. Gen. William P. Hall	"
Aug. 5, 1912	Aug. 26, 1914	Brig. Gen. George Andrews	"
Aug. 27, 1914	Aug. 26, 1918	Maj. Gen. Henry P. McCain	"
Sept. 1, 1918	Aug. 31, 1922	Maj. Gen. Peter C. Harris	"
Sept. 1, 1922	July 1, 1927	Maj. Gen. Robert C. Davis	"
July 2, 1927	Dec. 30, 1928	Maj. Gen. Lutz Wahl	"
Dec. 31, 1928	Feb. 1, 1933	Maj. Gen. Charles H. Bridges ..	"
Feb. 2, 1933	Oct. 31, 1935	Maj. Gen. James F. McKinley ..	"
Nov. 1, 1935	April 30, 1938	Maj. Gen. Edgar T. Conley	"
May 1, 1938	April 30, 1942	Maj. Gen. Emory S. Adams	"
May 1, 1942		Maj. Gen. James A. Ulio	"

Inspector Generals Since First Incumbent

From	To	Rank and Name	Title of Office
July 8, 1777	Oct. 11, 1777	Col. Mottin de la Balme........	Insp. General of Cavalry
Aug. 11, 1777	Sept. 15, 1777	Maj. Gen. P. C. J. B. T. du Coudray	Insp. General of Ordnance and Military Stores
Dec. 13, 1777	April 28, 1778	Maj. Gen. Thomas Conway ...	Insp. General
May 5, 1778	April 15, 1784	Maj. Gen. F. W. A. Steuben (baron)	"
April 17, 1784	Oct. 28, 1787	Maj. William North	Inspector
Mar. 10, 1792	Feb. 23, 1793	Lieut. Henry DeButts, 4th Inf..	Acting Adj. and Insp.
Feb. 23, 1793	July 17, 1793	Maj. Michael Rudolph, Lt. Drag.	"
July 18, 1793	May 13, 1794	Capt. Edward Butler, 4th Sublegion	"
May 13, 1794	Feb. 27, 1796	Maj. John Mills, 2d Sublegion..	"
Feb. 27, 1796	Aug. 1, 1796	Maj. Jonathan Haskell, 4th Sublegion	"
Aug. 1, 1796	Feb. 27, 1797	Capt. Edward Butler, 4th Inf. .	"
Feb. 27, 1797	July 18, 1798	Maj. T. H. Cushing, 1st Inf. ...	"
July 18, 1798	June 15, 1800	Maj. Gen. Alexander Hamilton..	Insp. General
June 15, 1800	April 2, 1807	Maj. T. H. Cushing, 1st Inf...	Acting Adj. Gen. and Insp.
April 2, 1807	April 28, 1812	Maj. A. Y. Nicoll, Artillerists...	"
July 6, 1812	Mar. 3, 1813	Brig. Gen. Alexander Smythe ..	Insp. General
Mar. 12, 1813	April 27, 1813	Brig. Gen. Z. M. Pike	"
May 9, 1814	July 2, 1814	Brig. Gen. W. H. Winder	Adjutant and Insp. Gen.
Nov. 22, 1814	June 1, 1821	Brig. Gen. Daniel Parker	"
April 29, 1816	June 25, 1841	Col. J. E. Wood	Insp. General
May 3, 1816	Sept. 30, 1820	Col. A. P. Hayne	"
Oct. 1, 1820	Aug. 13, 1821	Col. James Gadsden	"
Nov. 10, 1821	Dec. 11, 1825	Col. S. B. Archer	"
Dec. 21, 1825	Jan. 8, 1849	Col. George Croghan	"
June 25, 1841	Sept. 25, 1861	Col. Sylvester Churchill	"
Aug. 9, 1861	Jan. 2, 1881	Brig. Gen. R. B. Marcy	"
Jan. 2, 1881	Mar. 8, 1885	Brig. Gen. D. B. Sacket ......;	"
Mar. 11, 1885	Sept. 20, 1885	Brig. Gen. N. H. Davis	"
Sept. 20, 1885	Aug. 20, 1888	Brig. Gen. Absalom Baird	"
Aug. 20, 1885	Sept. 26, 1889	Brig. Gen. Roger Jones	"
Jan. 30, 1889	April 11, 1903	Brig. Gen. J. C. Breckinridge..	"
April 11, 1903	April 12, 1903	Brig. Gen. P. D. Vroom	"
April 12, 1903	Sept. 30, 1906	Brig. Gen. George H. Burton..	"

INSPECTOR GENERALS SINCE FIRST INCUMBENT—*Continued*

From	To	Rank and Name	Title of Office
Oct. 1, 1906	Feb. 20, 1917	Brig. Gen. Ernest A. Garlington	Insp. General
Feb. 21, 1917	Nov. 6, 1921	Maj. Gen. John L. Chamberlain	"
Nov. 7, 1921	Sept. 27, 1927	Maj. Gen. Eli A. Helmick	"
Sept. 28, 1927	Jan. 11, 1930	Maj. Gen. W. C. Rivers	"
Jan. 29, 1930	Nov. 30, 1931	Maj. Gen. Hugh A. Drum	"
Dec. 1, 1931	Nov. 30, 1935	Maj. Gen. John F. Preston ...	"
Dec. 1, 1935	Dec. 23, 1939	Maj. Gen. Walter L. Reed	"
Dec. 24, 1939		Maj. Gen. Virgil L. Peterson ...	"

SURGEON GENERALS SINCE FIRST INCUMBENT

From	To	Rank and Name	Title of Office
July 27, 1775	Nov. 7, 1775	Benjamin Church	Director General and Chief Physician
Sept. 14, 1775	Jan. 9, 1777	Samuel Stringer	"
Oct. 17, 1775	Jan. 9, 1777	John Morgan	"
April 11, 1777	Jan. 3, 1781	William Shippen	Director General
Feb. 6, 1778	July 2, 1780	William Brown	"
May 22, 1780	Nov. 3, 1783	David Oliphant	"
Jan. 17, 1781	Nov. 3, 1783	John Cochran	"
April 11, 1777	Aug. —, 1777	Malachi Treat	Physician General, Northern Dept.
April 11, 1777	Mar. 9, 1778	A. R. Cutter	Physician General, Eastern Dept.
April 11, 1777	July 1, 1777	Walter Jones	Physician General, Middle Dept.
July 1, 1777	Jan. 30, 1778	Benjamin Rush	"
April 11, 1777	July 31, 1777	Francis Forgue	Surgeon-General, Northern Dept.
April 11, 1777	Oct. 6, 1778	Philip Turner	Surgeon-General, Eastern Dept.
April 11, 1777	July 1, 1777	Benjamin Rush	Surgeon-General, Middle Dept.
May 13, 1777	Feb. 6, 1778	William Brown	"
Feb. 21, 1778	Oct. 6, 1780	Charles McKnight	"
April 11, 1777	Jan. 1, 1781	John Bartlett	Physician and Surgeon-General, Northern Dept.
April 11, 1777	Oct. 6, 1780	William Burnet	Physician-General, and Surgeon-General, Eastern Dept.
April 11, 1777	Oct. 6, 1780	John Cochran	Physician-General, and Surgeon-General, Middle Dept.
Oct. 6, 1780	Jan. 17, 1781	John Cochran	Chief Physician and Surgeon
Mar. 3, 1781	Dec. 23, 1783	James Craik	"
Mar. 5, 1781	Nov. 3, 1783	William Burnet	"

Surgeon Generals Since First Incumbent—*Continued*

From	To	Rank and Name	Title of Office
July 15, 1776	Dec. 1, 1776	William Shippen	Chief Physician of the Flying Camp
May 15, 1781	Nov. 3, 1783	Peter Fayssoux	Chief Physician, Southern Dept.
Mar. 22, 1780	June —, 1782	James Brown	"
Oct. 6, 1780	Nov. 3, 1780	Malachi Treat	Chief Hosp. Physician
Oct. 6, 1780	Jan. 3, 1782	Charles McKnight	"
Oct. 6, 1780	Nov. 3, 1783	Thomas Bond	Purveyor
July 19, 1778	Nov. 3, 1783	Andrew Craigie	Apothecary
July 19, 1778	June 15, 1800	James Craik	Physician General
June 11, 1813	June 15, 1815	James Tilton	Physician and Surgeon-General
June 11, 1813	June 1, 1821	Francis LeBaron	Apothecary General
April 18, 1818	Oct. 17, 1836	Joseph Lowell	Surgeon-General
Nov. 30, 1836	May 15, 1861	Col. Thomas Lawson	"
May 15, 1861	April 14, 1862	Col. C. A. Finley	"
April 25, 1862	Aug. 18, 1864	Brig. Gen. W. A. Hammond ..	"
Aug. 22, 1864	June 30, 1882	Brig. Gen. J. K. Barnes	"
July 3, 1882	Oct. 10, 1883	Brig. Gen. C. H. Crane	"
Nov. 23, 1883	Aug. 6, 1886	Brig. Gen. Robert Murray ...	"
Nov. 18, 1886	Aug. 16, 1890	Brig. Gen. John Moore	"
Aug. 16, 1890	Dec. 4, 1890	Brig. Gen. J. H. Baxter	"
Dec. 23, 1890	May 29, 1893	Brig. Gen. Charles Sutherland..	"
May 30, 1893	June 8, 1902	Brig. Gen. G. M. Sternberg....	"
June 8, 1902	Sept. 7, 1902	Brig. Gen. W. H. Forwood ...	"
Sept. 7, 1902	Jan. 14, 1909	Brig. Gen. Robert M. O'Reilly..	"
Jan. 14, 1909	Dec. 27, 1913	Brig. Gen. George H. Torney..	"
Jan. 16, 1914	Oct. 3, 1918	Maj. Gen. William C. Gorgas ..	"
Oct. 4, 1918	May 31, 1931	Maj. Gen. Merritte W. Ireland.	"
June 1, 1931	May 31, 1935	Maj. Gen. Robert U. Patterson.	"
June 1, 1935	May 31, 1939	Maj. Gen. Charles R. Reynolds.	"
June 1, 1939		Maj. Gen. James C. Magee	"

Judge Advocate Generals Since First Incumbent

From	To	Rank and Name	Title of Office
July 29, 1775	April 9, 1777	Lieut. Col. William Tudor.....	Judge Advocate
April 10, 1777	June 3, 1782	Lieut. Col. John Laurence	"
July 9, 1782	Sept. 18, 1782	Lieut. Col. James Innis	"
Oct. 2, 1782	Nov. 3, 1783	First Lieut. Thomas Edwards, 9th Mass. Inf.	"
July 16, 1794	July 13, 1796	First Lieut. Campbell Smith, 4th Sublegion	"
June 2, 1797	June 1, 1802	Capt. Campbell Smith, 4th Inf...	"
Sept. 26, 1812	Dec. 16, 1814	Thomas Gales	"
Mar. 18, 1813	June 15, 1815	E. A. Bancker	"
May 7, 1813	June 15, 1815	J. S. Wills	"
July 19, 1813	April 14, 1818	J. T. Dent	"
Oct. 5, 1813	June 15, 1815	Stephen Lush, Jr.	"
July 9, 1814	June 15, 1815	W. H. Winder	"
Aug. 6, 1814	May 9, 1816	Henry Wheaton	"
Sept. 16, 1814	June 15, 1815	L. M. Parker	"
Dec. 19, 1814	June 15, 1815	Samuel Wilcocks	"
April 29, 1816	April 14, 1818	W. O. Winston	"
April 29, 1816	April 14, 1818	Thomas Hanson	"
May 3, 1816	July 23, 1818	Brig. Gen. W. H. Winder.....	"
July 9, 1816	June 1, 1821	S. A. Storrow	"
July 9, 1816	Jan. 15, 1817	J. L. Leib	"
Sept. 10, 1818	June 1, 1821	S. D. Hays	"
Mar. 2, 1849	Sept. 4, 1862	Bvt. Maj. J. E. Lee	"

JUDGE ADVOCATE GENERALS SINCE FIRST INCUMBENT—*Continued*

From	To	Rank and Name	Title of Office
Sept. 3, 1862	Dec. 1, 1875	Brig. Gen. Joseph Holt	Judge Advocate General
Dec. 1, 1875	Jan. 22, 1881	Brig. Gen. W. McK. Dunn	"
Feb. 18, 1881	Dec. 22, 1894	Brig. Gen. D. G. Swaim	"
Jan. 3, 1895	May 21, 1901	Brig. Gen. G. N. Lieber	"
May 21, 1901	May 22, 1901	Brig. Gen. T. F. Barr	"
May 22, 1901	May 24, 1901	Brig. Gen. J. W. Clous	"
May 24, 1901	Feb. 14, 1911	Brig. Gen. George B. Davis ..	"
Feb. 15, 1911	Feb. 14, 1923	Maj. Gen. Enoch H. Crowder..	"
Feb. 15, 1923	Nov. 15, 1924	Maj. Gen. Walter A. Bethel ...	"
Nov. 16, 1924	Nov. 15, 1928	Maj. Gen. J. A. Hull	"
Nov. 16, 1928	Feb. 28, 1931	Maj. Gen. Edward A. Kreger ..	"
Mar. 1, 1931	Nov. 30, 1933	Maj. Gen. Blanton Winship ...	"
Dec. 1, 1933	Nov. 30, 1937	Maj. Gen. Arthur W. Brown ..	"
Dec. 1, 1937	Nov. 30, 1941	Maj. Gen. Allen W. Gullion ...	"
Dec. 1, 1941		Maj. Gen. Myron C. Cramer ..	"

CHIEFS OF ENGINEERS SINCE FIRST INCUMBENT

From	To	Rank and Name	Title of Office
June 17, 1775	Aug. 5, 1776	Col. Richard Gridley	Chief Engineer
Aug. 5, 1776	Nov. 1, 1776	Col. Rufus Putnam	"
July 22, 1777	Oct. 10, 1783	Maj. Gen. L. L. Duportail	"
Feb. 26, 1795	May 7, 1798	Lieut. Col. Stephen Rochefontaine	Commandant Corps of Artillerists and Engineers
May 7, 1798	April 1, 1802	Lieut. Col. Henry Burbeck ...	"
July 3, 1802	June 20, 1803	Lieut. Col. Jonathan Williams .	Chief Engineer
April 19, 1805	July 31, 1812	Col. Jonathan Williams	"
July 31, 1812	Nov. 12, 1818	Col. J. G. Swift	"
Nov. 12, 1818	June 1, 1821	Col. W. K. Armistead	"
June 1, 1821	May 24, 1828	Col. Alexander Macomb	"
May 24, 1828	Dec. 6, 1838	Col. Charles Gratiot	"
Dec. 7, 1838	Mar. 3, 1863	Col. J. G. Totten	"
Mar. 3, 1863	April 22, 1864	Brig. Gen. J. G. Totten	"
April 22, 1864	Aug. 8, 1866	Brig. Gen. Richard Delafield ..	"
Aug. 8, 1866	June 30, 1879	Brig. Gen. A. A. Humphreys ..	"
June 30, 1879	Mar. 6, 1884	Brig. Gen. H. G. Wright	"
Mar. 6, 1884	Aug. 27, 1886	Brig. Gen. John Newton	"
Oct. 11, 1886	June 30, 1888	Brig. Gen. J. C. Duane	"
July 6, 1888	May 10, 1895	Brig. Gen. T. L. Casey	"
May 10, 1895	Feb. 1, 1897	Brig. Gen. W. P. Craighill ...	"
Feb. 1, 1897	April 30, 1901	Brig. Gen. J. M. Wilson	"
April 30, 1901	May 2, 1901	Brig. Gen. H. M. Robert	"
May 2, 1901	May 3, 1901	Brig. Gen. J. W. Barlow	"
May 3, 1901	Jan. 22, 1904	Brig. Gen. Geo. L. Gillespie ...	"
Jan. 23, 1904	May 25, 1908	Brig. Gen. Alexander Mackenzie	"
July 2, 1908	June 11, 1910	Brig. Gen. William L. Marshall	"
June 12, 1910	Aug. 11, 1913	Brig. Gen. William H. Bixby ..	"
Aug. 12, 1913	Oct. 11, 1913	Brig. Gen. William T. Rossell..	"
Oct. 12, 1913	Mar. 6, 1916	Brig. Gen. Dan C. Kingman ..	"
Mar. 7, 1916	Oct. 31, 1919	Maj. Gen. William M. Black ..	"
Jan. 9, 1920	June 19, 1924	Maj. Gen. Lansing H. Beach ..	"
June 19, 1924	June 27, 1926	Maj. Gen. Harry Taylor	"
June 27, 1926	Aug. 7, 1929	Maj. Gen. Edgar Jadwin	"
Aug. 7, 1929	Oct. 1, 1929	Brig. Gen. Herbert Deakyne *.	"
Oct. 1, 1929	Oct. 1, 1933	Maj. Gen. Lytle Brown	"
Oct. 1, 1933	Oct. 18, 1933	Maj. Gen. Lytle Brown *......	"
Oct. 18, 1933	Oct. 18, 1937	Maj. Gen. Edward M. Markham	"
Oct. 18, 1937	Sept. 5, 1941	Maj. Gen. Julian L. Schley ...	"
Sept. 5, 1941	Oct. 1, 1941	Maj. Gen. Eugene Reybold *...	"
Oct. 1, 1941		Maj. Gen. Eugene Reybold	"

* Acting.

CHIEFS OF ORDNANCE SINCE FIRST INCUMBENT

From	To	Rank and Name	Title of Office
Aug. 17, 1775	Dec. 1, 1775	Ezekiel Cheever	Commissary of Artillery Stores
July 16, 1776	Dec. 1, 1776	Col. Benjamin Flower	Commissary of Artillery Stores for Flying Camp
Jan. 18, 1777	April 30, 1778	Maj. Samuel French	Commissary of Artillery Stores
Feb. 1, 1777		Maj. George Peale	"
Feb. 1, 1777		Maj. Jonathan Gostelow	"
Feb. 5, 1777		Maj. Joseph Watkins	"
Mar. 8, 1777	Aug. 30, 1780	Maj. Charles Lukens	"
Sept. 17, 1782	Nov. 3, 1783	Maj. Richard Frothingham	"
Aug. 11, 1777	Sept. 15, 1777	Maj. Gen. P. C. J. B. T. du Coudray	Inspector General of Ordnance and Military Fortifications
July 16, 1776	April 28, 1781	Col. Benjamin Flower	Commissary General of Military Stores
July 12, 1781	June 20, 1784	Col. Samuel Hodgdon	"
July 2, 1812	Feb. 8, 1815	Col. Decius Wadsworth	Commissary General of Ordnance
Feb. 8, 1815	June 1, 1821	Col. Decius Wadsworth	Chief of Ordnance
May 30, 1832	Mar. 25, 1848	Col. George Bomford	"
Mar. 25, 1848	July 10, 1851	Col. George Talcott	"
July 10, 1851	April 23, 1861	Col. H. K. Craig	"
April 23, 1861	Sept. 15, 1863	Brig. Gen. J. W. Ripley	"
Sept. 15, 1863	Sept. 12, 1864	Brig. Gen. G. D. Ramsay	"
Sept. 12, 1864	May 20, 1874	Brig. Gen. A. B. Dyer	"
June 23, 1874	Jan. 22, 1891	Brig. Gen. S. V. Benét	"
Jan. 23, 1891	Mar. 29, 1899	Brig. Gen. D. W. Flagler	"
April 5, 1899	Nov. 22, 1901	Brig. Gen. A. R. Buffington...	"
Nov. 22, 1901	July 15, 1918	Maj. Gen. William Crozier ...	"
July 16, 1918	April 1, 1930	Maj. Gen. Clarence C. Williams	"
June 3, 1930 *	June 2, 1934	Maj. Gen. Samuel Hof	"
June 3, 1934	June 2, 1938	Maj. Gen. William H. Tschappat	"
June 6, 1938	May 31, 1942	Maj. Gen. Charles M. Wesson..	"
June 1, 1942		Maj. Gen. Levin Campbell	"

* Ranked from April 2, 1930.

CHIEF SIGNAL OFFICERS SINCE FIRST INCUMBENT

From	To	Rank and Name	Title of Office
June 27, 1860	Mar. 3, 1863	Maj. A. J. Myer	Signal Officer
Mar. 3, 1863	July 21, 1864	Col. A. J. Myer	Chief Signal Officer
Dec. 3, 1864	July 28, 1866	Col. Benj. F. Fisher	"
July 28, 1866	Aug. 24, 1880	Brig. Gen. A. J. Myer	"
Dec. 15, 1880	Jan. 16, 1887	Brig. Gen. W. B. Hazen	"
Mar. 3, 1887	Feb. 9, 1906	Brig. Gen. A. W. Greely	"
Feb. 10, 1906	Feb. 13, 1913	Brig. Gen. James Allen ....:..	"
Feb. 14, 1913	Feb. 13, 1917	Brig. Gen. George P. Scriven..	"
Feb. 14, 1917	Dec. 31, 1923	Maj. Gen. George O. Squier ...	Chief of Signal Corps
Jan. 1, 1924	Jan. 8, 1928	Maj. Gen. Charles McK. Saltzman	"
Jan. 9, 1928	June 30, 1931	Maj. Gen. George S. Gibbs	"
July 1, 1931	Dec. 31, 1934	Maj. Gen. Irving J. Carr	"
Jan. 1, 1935	Sept. 30, 1937	Maj. Gen. James B. Allison....	"
Oct. 1, 1937	Sept. 30, 1941	Maj. Gen. Joseph O. Mauborgne	"
Oct. 1, 1941		Maj. Gen. Dawson Olmstead ..	"

CHIEFS OF ARTILLERY SINCE FIRST INCUMBENT

From	To	Rank and Name	Title of Office
Feb. 27, 1903	Jan. 22, 1904	Brig. Gen. Wallace F. Randolph	Chief of Artillery
Jan. 22, 1904	June 19, 1905	Brig. Gen. John P. Story	"
June 20, 1905	Sept. 30, 1906	Brig. Gen. Samuel M. Mills ...	"
Oct. 1, 1906	June 30, 1908	Brig. Gen. Arthur Murray	"

CHIEFS OF COAST ARTILLERY SINCE FIRST INCUMBENT

From	To	Rank and Name	Title of Office
July 1, 1908	Mar. 14, 1911	Brig. Gen. Arthur Murray	Chief of Coast Artillery
Mar. 15, 1911	May 23, 1918	Maj. Gen. Erasmus M. Weaver.	"
May 24, 1918	Mar. 19, 1926	Maj. Gen. Frank W. Coe	"
Mar. 20, 1926	Mar. 21, 1930	Maj. Gen. Andrew Hero, Jr. ..	"
Mar. 22, 1930	Mar. 21, 1934	Maj. Gen. John W. Gulick	"
Mar. 26, 1934	Jan. 20, 1935	Maj. Gen. William F. Hase ...	"
Jan. 21, 1935	Mar. 31, 1936	Maj. Gen. Harry L. Steele	"
April 1, 1936	Mar. 31, 1940	Maj. Gen. Archibald H. Sunderland	"
April 1, 1940	Mar. 9, 1942	Maj. Gen. Joseph A. Green	"

NOTE.—Office discontinued, Executive Order, March 9, 1942.

CHIEFS OF FIELD ARTILLERY SINCE FIRST INCUMBENT

From	To	Rank and Name	Title of Office
July 1, 1920	Dec. 19, 1927	Maj. Gen. William J. Snow....	Chief of Field Artillery
Dec. 20, 1927	Feb. 15, 1930	Maj. Gen. Fred T. Austin	"
Mar. 10, 1930	Mar. 9, 1934	Maj. Gen. Harry G. Bishop ...	"
Mar. 26, 1934	Mar. 25, 1938	Maj. Gen. Upton Birnie, Jr....	"
Mar. 26, 1938	Mar. 9, 1942	Maj. Gen. Robert M. Danford..	"

NOTE.—Office discontinued, Executive Order, March 9, 1942.

CHIEFS OF CAVALRY SINCE FIRST INCUMBENT

From	To	Rank and Name	Title of Office
July 1, 1920	July 23, 1924	Maj. Gen. Willard A. Holbrook	Chief of Cavalry
July 24, 1924	Mar. 21, 1926	Maj. Gen. Malin Craig	"
Mar. 21, 1926	Mar. 20, 1930	Maj. Gen. Herbert B. Crosby..	"
Mar. 22, 1930	Mar. 21, 1934	Maj. Gen. Guy V. Henry	"
Mar. 26, 1934	Mar. 25, 1938	Maj. Gen. Leon B. Kromer ...	"
Mar. 26, 1938	Mar. 9, 1942	Maj. Gen. John K. Herr	"

NOTE.—Office discontinued, Executive Order, March 9, 1942.

CHIEFS OF INFANTRY SINCE FIRST INCUMBENT

From	To	Rank and Name	Title of Office
July 1, 1920	Mar. 27, 1925	Maj. Gen. Charles S. Farnsworth	Chief of Infantry
Mar. 28, 1925	Mar. 27, 1929	Maj. Gen. Robert H. Allen	"
Mar. 28, 1929	May 5, 1933	Maj. Gen. Stephen O. Fuqua ..	"
May 6, 1933	April 30, 1937	Maj. Gen. Edward Croft	"
May 24, 1937	April 30, 1941	Maj. Gen. George A. Lynch ...	"
May 31, 1941	Mar. 9, 1942	Maj. Gen. Courtney H. Hodges.	"

NOTE.—Office discontinued, Executive Order, March 9, 1942.

CHIEFS OF AIR SERVICE SINCE FIRST INCUMBENT

From	To	Rank and Name	Title of Office
July 1, 1920	Oct. 4, 1921	Maj. Gen. Charles T. Menoher..	Chief of Air Service
Oct. 5, 1921	Dec. 13, 1927	Maj. Gen. Mason M. Patrick...	Chief of Air Corps
Dec. 13, 1927	Dec. 20, 1931	Maj. Gen. J. E. Fechet	"
Dec. 20, 1931	Dec. 25, 1935	Maj. Gen. B. D. Foulois	"
Dec. 25, 1935	Sept. 29, 1938	Maj. Gen. Oscar Westover	"
Sept. 28, 1938	May 31, 1941	Maj. Gen. H. H. Arnold †	"
June 1, 1941		Maj. Gen. George H. Brett *...	"

* Now Lieutenant General on foreign duty. Maj. Gen. Walter R. Weaver is Acting Chief. † Now Lieut. Gen., Chief of Air Force.

CHIEF OF TANK CORPS SINCE FIRST INCUMBENT

From	To	Rank and Name	Remarks
Dec. 20, 1917		Brig. Gen. Samuel D. Rockenbach	Now a colonel of infantry. Tank corps is now attached to the infantry.

CHIEFS OF CHEMICAL WARFARE SERVICE SINCE FIRST INCUMBENT

From	To	Rank and Name	Title of Office
July 16, 1920	Mar. 4, 1921	Brig. Gen. Amos A. Fries	Chief of Chemical Warfare
Mar. 28, 1921	Feb. 23, 1925	Brig. Gen. Amos A. Fries	"
Feb. 24, 1925	Mar. 27, 1929	Maj. Gen. Amos A. Fries	"
Mar. 28, 1929	Mar. 27, 1933	Maj. Gen. Harry L. Gilchrist..	"
May 24, 1933	May 23, 1937	Maj. Gen. Claude E. Brigham..	"
May 24, 1937	April 30, 1941	Maj. Gen. Walter C. Baker ...	"
May 31, 1941		Maj. Gen. William N. Porter ..	"

SUPERINTENDENTS OF THE UNITED STATES MILITARY ACADEMY SINCE FIRST INCUMBENT

No.	Name	Army Rank When Appointed	From	To	Remarks
1	Williams, Jonathan	Major, Corps of Engineers	April 15, 1802	June 20, 1803 *	Resigned
2	Williams, Jonathan	Lieut. Colonel, Corps of Engineers	April 19, 1805 *	July 31, 1812	Resigned
3	Swift, Joseph G.	Colonel, Corps of Engineers	July 31, 1812	Mar. 24, 1814	Relieved
4	Partridge, Alden	Captain, Corps of Engineers	Jan. 3, 1815	July 28, 1817	Relieved
5	Thayer, Sylvanus	Captain, Corps of Engineers	July 28, 1817	July 1, 1833	Relieved
6	DeRussy, René	Major, Corps of Engineers	July 1, 1833	Sept. 1, 1838	Relieved
7	Delafield, Richard	Major, Corps of Engineers	Sept. 1, 1838	Aug. 15, 1845	Relieved
8	Brewerton, Henry	Captain, Corps of Engineers	Aug. 15, 1845	Sept. 1, 1852	Relieved
9	Lee, Robert E.	Captain, Corps of Engineers	Sept. 1, 1852	Mar. 31, 1855	Relieved
10	Barnard, John G.	Major, Corps of Engineers	Mar. 31, 1855	Sept. 8, 1856	Relieved
11	Delafield, Richard	Major, Corps of Engineers	Sept. 8, 1856	Jan. 23, 1861 †	Relieved
12	Beauregard, Peter G. T.	Captain, Corps of Engineers	Jan. 23, 1861 †	Jan. 28, 1861	Relieved
13	Delafield, Richard	Major, Corps of Engineers	Jan. 28, 1861	Mar. 1, 1861	Relieved
14	Bowman, Alexander H.	Major, Corps of Engineers	Mar. 1, 1861	July 8, 1864	Relieved
15	Tower, Zealous B.	Major, Corps of Engineers	July 8, 1864	Sept. 8, 1864	Relieved
16	Cullum, George W.	Lieut. Colonel, Corps of Engineers	Sept. 8, 1864	Aug. 28, 1866	Relieved
17	Pitcher, Thomas G.	Colonel, 44th Infantry	Aug. 28, 1866	Sept. 1, 1871	Relieved
18	Ruger, Thomas H.	Colonel, 18th Infantry	Sept. 1, 1871	Sept. 1, 1876	Relieved
19	Schofield, John M.	Major General, U. S. Army	Sept. 1, 1876	Jan. 21, 1881	Relieved
20	Howard, Oliver O.	Brigadier General, U. S. Army	Jan. 21, 1881	Sept. 1, 1882	Relieved
21	Merritt, Wesley	Colonel, 5th Cavalry	Sept. 1, 1882	July 1, 1887	Relieved
22	Parke, John G.	Colonel, Corps of Engineers	July 1, 1887	June 24, 1889	Relieved
23	Wilson, John M.	Lieut. Colonel, Corps of Engineers	Aug. 28, 1889	Mar. 31, 1893	Relieved
24	Ernst, Oswald H.	Major, Corps of Engineers	Mar. 31, 1893	Aug. 21, 1898	Relieved
25	Mills, Albert L.	1st Lieutenant, 1st Cavalry	Aug. 22, 1898	Aug. 31, 1906	Relieved
26	Scott, Hugh L.	Major, 14th Cavalry	Aug. 31, 1906	Aug. 31, 1910	Relieved
27	Barry, Thomas H.	Major General, U. S. Army	Aug. 31, 1910	Aug. 31, 1912	Relieved
28	Townsley, Clarence P.	Colonel, Coast Artillery Corps	Aug. 31, 1912	June 30, 1916	Relieved
29	Biddle, John	Colonel, Corps of Engineers	July 1, 1916	May 31, 1917	Relieved
30	Tillman, Samuel E.	Colonel, U. S. Army	June 11, 1917	June 11, 1919	Relieved
31	MacArthur, Douglas	Brigadier General, U. S. Army	June 12, 1919	June 30, 1922	Relieved
32	Sladen, Fred W.	Brigadier General, U. S. Army	July 1, 1922	Mar. 23, 1926	Relieved
33	Stewart, Merch B.	Brigadier General, U. S. Army	Mar. 24, 1926	Oct. 5, 1927	Retired
34	Winans, Edwin B.	Major General, U. S. Army	Oct. 23, 1927	Feb. 25, 1928	Relieved
35	Smith, William R.	Major General, U. S. Army	Feb. 26, 1928	April 30, 1932	Relieved
36	Connor, William D.	Major General, U. S. Army	May 1, 1932	Jan. 17, 1938	Retired
37	Benedict, Jay L.	Brigadier General, U. S. Army	Feb. 5, 1938	Nov. 17, 1940	Relieved
38	Eichelberger, Robert L.	Brigadier General, U. S. Army	Nov. 18, 1940	Jan. 11, 1942	Relieved
39	Wilby, Francis B.	Major General, U. S. Army	Jan. 13, 1942		Relieved

NOTE.—The selection of the Superintendents of the Military Academy was confined to the Corps of Engineers from the establishment of the Institution, March 16, 1802, till the passage of the law of July 13, 1866, which opened it to the entire Army. By the Act of June 12, 1858, the local rank of Colonel was conferred upon the Superintendent.

* Major Williams resigned June 20, 1803, on a point of command, and pending its settlement until April 19, 1805, when he again returned to serve as Chief Engineer, no permanent Superintendent of the Military Academy was appointed, the command devolving upon the senior officer of the Corps of Engineers present for duty.

† Bvt. Major P. G. T. Beauregard, Corps of Engineers, by order of John B. Floyd, Secretary of War, relieved Colonel Delafield, Jan. 23, 1861, from the superintendency of the Military Academy, but was himself displaced five days later, Jan. 28, 1861, by direction of the succeeding Secretary of War, Joseph Holt, the command again devolving upon Colonel Delafield.

APPENDIX B

COMMANDERS OF LARGER UNITS IN WORLD WAR I

I ARMY CORPS

Corps Commanders	Appointed
Maj Gen. Hunter Liggett	Jan. 20, 1918
Maj. Gen. Joseph T. Dickman	Oct. 12, 1918
Maj. Gen. William M. Wright	Nov. 13, 1918
Maj. Gen. Samuel D. Sturgis (ad interim)	Feb. 28, 1919
Maj. Gen. William M. Wright	Mar. 14, 1919 to Mar. 24

Chiefs of Staff	Appointed
Lt. Col. Malin Craig	Jan. 20, 1918
Col. Malin Craig	Mar. 27, 1918
Brig. Gen. Malin Craig	July 11, 1918
Col. Walter S. Grant	Nov. 12, 1918
Lt. Col. Royden E. Beebe (acting)	Dec. 31, 1918
Brig. Gen. William M. Fassett	Jan. 5, 1919 to Mar. 24

II ARMY CORPS

Corps Commanders	Appointed
No corps commander (Chief of Staff acts for Gen. Pershing)	Feb. 24, 1918
Maj. Gen. George W. Read	June 15, 1918 to Feb. 2, 1919

Chiefs of Staff	Appointed
Lt. Col. George S. Simonds	Feb. 24, 1918
Col. George S. Simonds	June 13, 1918
Brig. Gen. George S. Simonds	Oct. 13, 1918
Col. Fred E. Buchan	Feb. 1, 1919 to Feb. 2

III ARMY CORPS

Corps Commanders	Appointed
No corps commander (Chief of Staff acts for Gen. Pershing)	Mar. 30, 1918
Maj. Gen. William M. Wright	June 17, 1918
Maj. Gen. John E. McMahon (ad interim)	July 12, 1918
Maj. Gen. Robert L. Bullard	July 14, 1918
Maj. Gen. John L. Hines	Oct. 12, 1918
Maj. Gen. Edward F. McGlachlin, Jr. (ad interim)	Feb. 19, 1919
Maj Gen. John L. Hines	Mar. 5, 1919
Maj. Gen. Edward F. McGlachlin, Jr. (ad interim)	Apr. 29, 1919
Maj. Gen. John L. Hines	May 11, 1919 to July 1

Chiefs of Staff   *Appointed*
Lt. Col. Alfred W. Bjornstad.............Mar. 30, 1918
Col. Alfred W. Bjornstad ....May 8, 1918
Brig. Gen. Alfred W. Bjornstad ....July 12, 1918
Brig. Gen. Campbell King ....Oct. 23, 1918
Lt. Col. Martin C. Shallenberger (acting)..Mar. 25, 1919
Brig. Gen. Campbell King ....April 1, 1919 to July 1

IV ARMY CORPS

Corps Commanders   *Appointed*
No corps commander (Chief of Staff
    acts for Gen. Pershing) ....June 19, 1918
Maj. Gen. Joseph T. Dickman ....Aug. 18, 1918
Maj. Gen. Charles H. Muir ....Oct. 12, 1918
Maj. Gen. Robert L. Howze (ad interim) ..April 14, 1919
Maj. Gen. Charles P. Summerall ....May 2, 1918 to May 11

Chiefs of Staff   *Appointed*
Lt. Col. Stuart Heintzelman ....June 19, 1918
Col. Stuart Heintzelman ....July 31, 1918
Brig. Gen. Preston Brown ....Sept. 20, 1918
Brig. Gen. Briant H. Wells ....Oct. 17, 1918
Col. Walter Krueger (acting) ....May 11, 1919

V ARMY CORPS

Corps Commanders   *Appointed*
Maj. Gen. William M. Wright ....July 12, 1918
Maj. Gen. George H. Cameron ....Aug. 21, 1918
Maj. Gen. Charles P. Summerall..........Oct. 12, 1918 to Feb. 12, 1919

Chiefs of Staff   *Appointed*
Brig. Gen. Wilson B. Burtt ....July 12, 1918
Col. Thomas H. Emerson (acting) ....Dec. 12, 1918
Brig. Gen. Wilson B. Burtt ....Dec. 27, 1918
Col. Albert W. Forman ....Feb. 10, 1919 to Feb. 12

VI ARMY CORPS

Corps Commanders   *Appointed*
No Corps Commander ....Aug. 1, 1918
Maj. Gen. Omar Bundy ....Aug. 26, 1918
No Corps Commander (Chief of Staff acts) .Sept. 13, 1918
Maj. Gen. Charles C. Ballou ....Oct. 23, 1918
Maj. Gen. Charles T. Menoher ....Nov. 10, 1918
Maj. Gen. Charles H. Martin ....Dec. 17, 1918
Maj. Gen. George Bell, Jr. ....Dec. 20, 1918
Maj. Gen. Robert L. Bullard (ad interim) .Dec. 24, 1918
Maj. Gen. Adelbert Cronkhite ....Jan. 13, 1919
Maj. Gen. George Bell, Jr. (ad interim) ...Feb. 3, 1919
Maj. Gen. Adelbert Cronkhite ....Feb. 18, 1919
Maj. Gen. George Bell, Jr. (ad interim)..Mar. 25, 1919
Maj. Gen. Adelbert Cronkhite ....Mar. 27, 1919
Maj. Gen. George Bell, Jr. ....April 10, 1919 to April 11

Chiefs of Staff   *Appointed*
Col. Briant H. Wells ....July 30, 1918
Brig. Gen. Briant H. Wells ....Aug. 26, 1918
Col. George F. Baltzell (acting).........Oct. 17, 1918
Col. Edgar T. Collins ....Oct. 22, 1918 to April 11, 1919

VII ARMY CORPS

Corps Commanders   *Appointed*
Maj. Gen. William M. Wright ....Aug. 19, 1918
No corps commander (Chief of Staff
  acts for Gen. Pershing) ....Sept. 6, 1918
Maj. Gen. Omar Bundy ....Sept. 13, 1918
No corps commander (Chief of Staff
  acts as such) ....Oct. 25, 1918
Maj. Gen. William G. Haan ....Nov. 21, 1918
Maj. Gen. Charles H. Martin (ad interim)..April 23, 1919
Maj. Gen. Henry T. Allen ....May 8, 1919 to May 11

Chiefs of Staff   *Appointed*
Capt. Charles H. Gerhardt (acting) ......Aug. 20, 1918
Lt. Col. Gordon Johnston (acting) ....Aug. 24, 1918
Col. Campbell King ....Sept. 26, 1918
Brig. Gen. Campbell King ....Oct. 14, 1918
Col. Adna R. Chaffee (acting) ....Oct. 23, 1918
Col. Herbert J. Brees ....Oct. 27, 1918 to May 11, 1919

VIII ARMY CORPS

Corps Commanders   *Appointed*
Maj. Gen. Henry T. Allen ....Nov. 26, 1918
Maj. Gen. Walter H. Gordon ....April 15, 1919 to April 20

Chiefs of Staff   *Appointed*
Col. George C. Marshall, Jr. ....Nov. 26, 1918
Col. Hjalmer Erickson ....Jan. 15, 1919 to April 20

IX ARMY CORPS

Corps Commanders   *Appointed*
Maj. Gen. Adelbert Cronkhite ....Nov. 26, 1918
Lt. Gen. Robert L. Bullard (ad interim) ...Jan. 13, 1919
Maj. Gen. Joseph E. Kuhn (ad interim)..Jan. 18, 1919
Maj. Gen. William Weigel (ad interim)...Jan. 26, 1919
Maj. Gen. Joseph E. Kuhn (ad interim)..Jan. 31, 1919
Maj. Gen. Charles P. Summerall ....Feb. 28, 1919
Maj. Gen. Henry T. Allen ....Apr. 16, 1919
Maj. Gen. William Weigel (ad interim)..Apr. 21, 1919
Maj. Gen. Charles J. Bailey (ad interim) ..Apr. 25, 1919
Maj. Gen. Henry T. Allen ....Apr. 28, 1919 to May 5

Chiefs of Staff   *Appointed*
Brig. Gen. William K. Naylor............Nov. 26, 1918
Lt. Col. John B. Barnes (acting) ....Jan. 26, 1919
Brig. Gen. William K. Naylor...........Jan. 31, 1919 to May 5

DIVISION AND SERVICE COMMANDERS OF THE A. E. F.

Legend for the following tables:

*	ad interim
RA	Regular Army
NG	National Guard
NA	National Army

SERVICES OF SUPPLY

Names of Commanders	Dates
Colonel David S. Stanley *	July 5, 1917
Brig. Gen. Richard M. Blatchford	July 25, 1917
Maj. Gen. Richard M. Blatchford	Aug. 31, 1917
Brig. Gen. Mason M. Patrick *	Nov. 2, 1917
Maj. Gen. Francis J. Kernan	Nov. 28, 1917
Maj. Gen. James G. Harbord	July 29, 1918
Brig. Gen. William D. Connor	May 27—Aug. 31, 1919

Division	Designation Date	Troops From	Division Commanders, 1917-1918	
1 (RA)	May 24, 1917	(RA) Brownsville, Douglas, El Paso, San Benito, Forts Bliss, Ringgold, and Sam Houston, Washington Barracks, and Fort Oglethorpe	Brig. Gen. William L. Sibert	6/18/17
			Maj. Gen. William L. Sibert	6/27/17
			Maj. Gen. R. L. Bullard	12/14/17
			Brig. Gen. Beaumont B. Buck	4/5/18*
			Maj. Gen. R. L. Bullard	4/13/18
			Maj. Gen. C. P. Summerall	7/15/18
			Brig. Gen. F. E. Bamford	10/12/18*
			Brig. Gen. Frank Parker	10/18/18
			Maj. Gen. E. F. McGlachlin, Jr.	11/21/18
2 (RA)	Sept. 22, 1917	(RA) Chickamauga Park, El Paso, Gettysburg, Governors Island, Philadelphia, Syracuse, Forts Benjamin Harrison, Ethan Allen, Myer, Oglethorpe, Riley, Sam Houston, Camps Vail and Robinson; also, Marine Corps at Quantico or already in France	Brig. Gen. C. A. Doyen, USMC	10/26/17
			Maj. Gen. Omar Bundy	11/8/17
			Maj. Gen. J. G. Harbord	7/15/18
			Brig. Gen. J. A. Lejeune, USMC	7/26/18*
			Maj. Gen. J. G. Harbord	7/27/18
			Brig. Gen. J. A. Lejeune, USMC	7/28/18
			Maj. Gen. J. A. Lejeune, USMC	8/1/18
3 (RA)	Nov. 12, 1917	(RA) Camps Greene, Forrest, Shelby, Stuart, Stanley, and Travis, and Forts Bliss, Clark, Douglas, and Leavenworth, and Washington Barracks; also, drafts from Camps Devens, Dix, Lee, Meade, and Upton	Maj. Gen. J. T. Dickman	11/28/17
			Brig. Gen. J. A. Irons	2/11/18*
			Maj. Gen. J. T. Dickman	2/13/18
			Brig. Gen. J. A. Irons	2/27/18*
			Brig. Gen. Charles Crawford	3/8/18*
			Brig. Gen. J. A. Irons	3/10/18*
			Brig. Gen. Charles Crawford	3/19/18*
			Maj. Gen. J. T. Dickman	4/12/18
			Brig. Gen. F. W. Sladen	8/18/18*
			Maj. Gen. Beaumont B. Buck	8/27/18
			Brig. Gen. Preston Brown	10/18/18
			Maj. Gen. R. L. Howze	11/19/18
4 (RA)	Nov. 19, 1917	(RA) Camp Greene, Monterey, Vancouver Barracks; also, drafts from Camps Custer, Grant, Lewis, Pike, and Travis	Brig. Gen. G. H. Cameron	12/10/17
			Col. B. W. Atkinson	12/11/17*
			Brig. Gen. G. H. Cameron	12/13/17
			Maj. Gen. G. H. Cameron	12/20/17
			Brig. Gen. S. W. Miller	2/4/18*
			Maj. Gen. G. H. Cameron	2/6/18
			Brig. Gen. F. D. Webster	3/26/18*
			Maj. Gen. G. H. Cameron	3/27/18

Division	Designation Date	Troops From	Division Commanders 1917-1918	
			Brig. Gen. B. A. Poore	8/14/18*
			Maj. Gen. J. L. Hines	8/27/18
			Maj. Gen. G. H. Cameron	10/11/18
			Brig. Gen. B. A. Poore	10/22/18*
			Maj. Gen. Mark L. Hersey	10/31/18
			Maj. Gen. R. L. Howze	11/17/18
			Maj. Gen. Mark L. Hersey	11/19/18
5 (RA)	Nov. 17, 1917	(RA) Camps Forrest, Greene, Johnston, Logan, and Stanley, and Fort Leavenworth; also, recruits and drafts	Maj. Gen. C. H. Muir	12/11/17
			Col. William M. Morrow	12/13/17*
			Brig. Gen. J. E. McMahon	1/1/18
			Maj. Gen. J. E. McMahon	1/6/18
			Maj. Gen. Hanson E. Ely	10/18/18
6 (RA)	Nov. 17, 1917	(RA) Camps Forrest and Logan, Forts Leavenworth, Riley, and Sam Houston, Vancouver Barracks, etc.; also, drafts from Ga., Ind., Ky., Md., Minn., Ohio, Pa., S. C., Wis.	Col. Charles E. Tayman	11/26/17*
			Brig. Gen. James B. Erwin	12/29/17
			Maj. Gen. Walter H. Gordon	8/28/18
7 (RA)	Dec. 6, 1917	(RA) Chickamauga Park, Fort Bliss, Camp Logan, Wheeler, Vail, Greenleaf, Fort Sill, drafts from Ill., Iowa, Mo., Mich., and Pa.	Brig. Gen. C. H. Barth	1/1/18
			Brig. Gen. Tiemann N. Horn	2/17/18*
			Brig. Gen. C. H. Barth	2/25/18
			Brig. Gen. Tiemann N. Horn	6/7/18*
			Brig. Gen. C. H. Barth	6/21/18
			Brig. Gen. Lutz Wahl	10/24/18*
			Maj. Gen. Edmund Wittenmyer	10/28/18
8 (RA)	Dec. 17, 1917	(RA) Camps Fremont, Dodge, Johnston, Hawaiian Dept.	Col. Elmore F. Taggart	1/5/18*
			Col. G. W. VanDeusen	2/15/18*
			Brig. Gen. J. D. Leitch	2/25/18*
			Maj. Gen. J. F. Morrison	3/10/18
			Brig. Gen. J. D. Leitch	6/18/18*
			Maj. Gen. W. S. Graves	7/18/18
			Brig. Gen. J. D. Leitch	8/4/18*
			Maj. Gen. W. S. Graves	8/11/18
			Brig. Gen. J. D. Leitch	8/12/18*
			Maj. Gen. Eli A. Helmick	9/2/18
			Brig. Gen. J. J. Bradley	11/20/18*
			Maj. Gen. Eli A. Helmick	11/26/18
26 (NG)	July 18, 1917	(NG) Conn., Me., N. H., Mass., R. I., and Vt.; also, drafts from 76th Div.	Maj. Gen. C. R. Edwards	8/22/17
			Brig. Gen. P. E. Traub	10/12/17*
			Brig. Gen. C. H. Cole	10/22/17*
			Brig. Gen. P. E. Traub	10/31/17*
			Maj. Gen. C. R. Edwards	11/11/17
			Brig. Gen. P. E. Traub	11/25/17*
			Maj. Gen. C. R. Edwards	12/1/17
			Brig. Gen. Frank E. Bamford	10/25/18
			Maj. Gen. Harry C. Hale	11/19/18
27 (NG)	July 18, 1917	(NG) N. Y. (redesignates the 6th Div. NG. N. Y., as 27th Div., 7/18/17); also, drafts and recruits	Maj. Gen. J. F. O'Ryan	7/16/17
			Brig. Gen. C. L. Phillips	9/19/17*
			Maj. Gen. J. F. O'Ryan	12/6/17
			Brig. Gen. C. L. Phillips	12/23/17*
			Maj. Gen. J. F. O'Ryan	12/29/17
			Brig. Gen. C. L. Phillips	2/22/18*
			Maj. Gen. J. F. O'Ryan	3/1/18
			Brig. Gen. Palmer E. Pierce	6/16/18*
			Maj. Gen. J. F. O'Ryan	6/18/18
			Brig. Gen. Palmer E. Pierce	11/14/18*
			Maj. Gen. J. F. O'Ryan	11/23/18
28 (NG)	July 18, 1917	(NG) Pa. (redesignates 7th, Pa., as 28th); also, NA from Camps Lee, Meade, and Travis	Maj. Gen. C. M. Clement	7/17/17
			Brig. Gen. W. G. Price, Jr.	9/18/17*
			Brig. Gen. F. W. Stilwell	10/28/17*
			Maj. Gen. C. M. Clement	12/4/17

Division	Designation Date	Troops From	Division Commanders 1917-1918	
			Brig. Gen. F. W. Stilwell	12/11/17*
			Maj. Gen. C. H. Muir	12/15/17
			Brig. Gen. F. H. Albright	10/23/18*
			Maj. Gen. William H. Hay	10/25/18
29 (NG)	July 18, 1917	(NG) Del., Md., N. J., Va., and D. C.	Brig. Gen. Charles W. Barber	7/28/17
			Maj. Gen. Charles G. Morton	8/25/17
			Brig. Gen. William C. Rafferty	9/24/17*
			Maj. Gen. Charles G. Morton	12/6/17
			Brig. Gen. William C. Rafferty	12/11/17*
			Maj. Gen. Charles G. Morton	12/26/17
			Brig. Gen. William C. Rafferty	3/23/18*
			Maj. Gen. Charles G. Morton	3/26/18
30 (NG)	July 18, 1917	(NG) N. C., S. C., and Tenn.; also, draftees from Camps Gordon, Jackson, and Pike	Maj. Gen. J. F. Morrison	8/28/17
			Brig. Gen. William S. Scott	9/19/17*
			Maj. Gen. C. P. Townsley	10/14/17
			Brig. Gen. Samson L. Faison	12/1/17*
			Maj. Gen. C. P. Townsley	12/6/17
			Brig. Gen. Samson L. Faison	12/17/17*
			Brig. Gen. L. D. Tyson	12/22/17*
			Brig. Gen. G. G. Gatley	12/28/17*
			Brig. Gen. Samson L. Faison	1/1/18*
			Brig. Gen. L. D. Tyson	3/30/18*
			Brig. Gen. Samson L. Faison	4/7/18*
			Maj. Gen. G. W. Read	5/3/18
			Brig. Gen. R. H. Noble	6/12/18*
			Maj. Gen. G. W. Read	6/14/18
			Brig. Gen. Samson L. Faison	6/15/18*
			Maj. Gen. E. M. Lewis	7/18/18
			Brig. Gen. Samson L. Faison	12/23/18*
31 (NG)	July 18, 1917	(NG) Ala., Fla., and Ga.; also, drafts from these states as well as drafts from Mich. and Ill.	Maj. Gen. F. J. Kernan	8/25/17
			Brig. Gen. J. L. Hayden	9/18/17*
			Brig. Gen. W. A. Harris	11/21/17*
			Brig. Gen. J. L. Hayden	11/23/17*
			Brig. Gen. W. A. Harris	12/27/17*
			Brig. Gen. J. L. Hayden	1/1/18*
			Maj. Gen. F. H. French	3/15/18
			Brig. Gen. F. H. French	3/28/18
			Maj. Gen. L. S. Lyon	5/15/18
			Brig. Gen. J. L. Hayden	7/18/18*
			Maj. Gen. L. S. Lyon	7/19/18
			Brig. Gen. W. A. Harris	7/31/18*
			Maj. Gen. L. S. Lyon	8/1/18
			Brig. Gen. W. A. Harris	9/8/18*
			Maj. Gen. L. S. Lyon	9/14/18
			Brig. Gen. W. A. Harris	9/28/18
32 (NG)	July 18, 1917	(NG) Mich. and Wis.; also, draftees from Camps Custer and Grant	Maj. Gen. James Parker	8/26/17
			Brig. Gen. W. G. Haan	9/19/17*
			Maj. Gen. James Parker	12/7/17
			Brig. Gen. W. G. Haan	12/8/17
			Maj. Gen. W. G. Haan	2/7/18
			Maj. Gen. William Lassiter	11/20/18
33 (NG)	July 18, 1917	(NG) Ill.; also, NA from Camps Grant, Dodge, and Taylor	Maj. Gen. George Bell, Jr.	8/25/17
			Brig. Gen. H. D. Todd, Jr.	9/19/17*
			Maj. Gen. George Bell, Jr.	12/7/17
34 (NG)	July 18, 1917	(NG) Iowa, Minn., Neb., N. D., and S. D.; also, drafts from Camps Dodge and Funston, and replacements from Ariz., Colo., Kan., N. M., Okla., and Tex.	Brig. Gen. A. P. Blocksom	8/25/17
			Maj. Gen. A. P. Blocksom	8/29/17
			Brig. Gen. F. G. Mauldin	9/18/17*
			Maj. Gen. A. P. Blocksom	12/10/17
			Brig. Gen. Hubert A. Allen	12/24/17*
			Maj. Gen. A. P. Blocksom	12/27/17
			Brig. Gen. A. P. Blocksom	4/19/18*
			Brig. Gen. F. G. Mauldin	5/8/18*

Division	Designation Date	Troops From	Division Commanders 1917-1918	
			Brig. Gen. J. A. Johnston	7/4/18*
			Brig. Gen. Hubert A. Allen	8/24/18*
			Brig. Gen. J. A. Johnston	8/26/18*
			Maj. Gen. Beaumont B. Buck	10/22/18
			Brig. Gen. John A. Johnston	10/26/18*
35 (NG)	July 18, 1917	(NG) Kan., Mo.; also, draftees from Camps Funston, Travis, and Fort Leavenworth	Maj. Gen. William M. Wright	8/25/17
			Brig. Gen. L. G. Berry	9/18/17*
			Maj. Gen. William M. Wright	12/10/17
			Brig. Gen. L. G. Berry	12/24/17*
			Brig. Gen. C. H. Martin	12/26/17*
			Maj. Gen. William M. Wright	1/4/18
			Brig. Gen. Nathaniel F. McClure	6/15/18
			Maj. Gen. Peter E. Traub	7/20/18
			Brig. Gen. T. B. Dugan	11/1/18*
			Maj. Gen. Peter E. Traub	11/2/18
			Brig. Gen. T. B. Dugan	11/25/18*
			Maj. Gen. Peter E. Traub	12/7/18
			Brig. Gen. Thomas Dugan	12/27/18
36 (NG)	July 18, 1917	(NG) Okla. and Tex.; also, draftees to replace losses	Brig. Gen. E. St. J. Greble	8/23/17
			Maj. Gen. E. St. J. Greble	8/31/17
			Brig. Gen. George Blakely	9/18/17*
			Maj. Gen. E. St. J. Greble	12/6/17
			Brig. Gen. George Blakely	12/25/17*
			Maj. Gen. E. St. J. Greble	1/2/18
			Brig. Gen. E. St. J. Greble	3/15/18
			Brig. Gen. John A. Hulen	7/8/18*
			Maj. Gen. William R. Smith	7/13/18
37 (NG)	July 18, 1917	(NG) Ohio and W. Va.; also, draftees from Camp Sherman and replacements from losses to complete Division	Brig. Gen. William R. Smith	8/26/17
			Maj. Gen. C. G. Treat	9/3/17
			Brig. Gen. William R. Smith	9/18/17*
			Brig. Gen. William V. McMaken	11/13/17*
			Brig. Gen. William R. Smith	11/18/17*
			Maj. Gen. C. G. Treat	12/5/17
			Brig. Gen. William R. Smith	12/6/17
			Maj. Gen. C. G. Treat	12/9/17
			Brig. Gen. William R. Smith	3/29/18*
			Brig. Gen. Joseph A. Gaston	4/1/18*
			Maj. Gen. C. G. Treat	4/4/18
			Brig. Gen. Joseph A. Gaston	4/25/18*
			Maj. Gen. C. S. Farnsworth	5/8/18
			Brig. Gen. William M. Fassett	12/5/18*
			Maj. Gen. C. S. Farnsworth	12/10/18
38 (NG)	July 18, 1917	(NG) Ind. and Ky.—later amended to include troops of W. Va. (NG); also, drafts from 84th Div. as well as some from Ark., La., and Miss.	Maj. Gen. William H. Sage	8/25/17
			Brig. Gen. Edward M. Lewis	9/19/17*
			Brig. Gen. H. H. Whitney	11/8/17*
			Brig. Gen. Roger D. Williams	12/2/17*
			Brig. Gen. H. H. Whitney	12/5/17*
			Maj. Gen. William H. Sage	12/12/17
			Brig. Gen. William H. Sage	3/15/18*
			Brig. Gen. William V. Judson	4/15/18*
			Brig. Gen. F. M. Caldwell	7/10/18*
			Brig. Gen. Augustine McIntyre	7/12/18*
			Brig. Gen. F. M. Caldwell	7/18/18*
			Maj. Gen. Robert L. Howze	8/30/18
			Brig. Gen. F. M. Caldwell	10/18/18*
			Col. George T. Smith	10/24/18*
			Maj. Gen. Robert L. Howze	10/27/18
39 (NG)	July 18, 1917	(NG) Ark., La., and Miss. ORC officers from 84th Div. also, and drafts from 87th Div. (Ark., La., Miss.) as well as replacements and personnel from Camps Pike, Taylor, and Travis to complete Division	Maj. Gen. H. C. Hodges, Jr.	8/25/17
			Brig. Gen. Ira A. Haynes	9/18/17*
			Maj. Gen. H. C. Hodges, Jr.	10/1/17
			Brig. Gen. Ira A. Haynes	11/2/17*
			Maj. Gen. H. C. Hodges, Jr.	11/18/17
			Brig. Gen. Ira A. Haynes	11/27/17*
			Maj. Gen. H. C. Hodges, Jr.	2/26/18
			Brig. Gen. Ira A. Haynes	3/23/18*
			Maj. Gen. H. C. Hodges, Jr.	3/27/18

Division		Designation Date	Troops From	Division Commanders 1917-1918	
40	(NG)	July 18, 1917	(NG) Ariz., Calif., Colo., Nev., N. M., and Utah; also, officers from ORC and NA, drafts from Camps Lewis and Funston, and replacements from Lewis	Maj. Gen. F. S. Strong	8/25/17
				Brig. Gen. G. H. Cameron	9/18/17*
				Brig. Gen. L. S. Lyon	11/19/17*
				Brig. Gen. G. H. Cameron	11/23/17*
				Brig. Gen. L. S. Lyon	12/6/17*
				Maj. Gen. F. S. Strong	12/8/17
41	(NG)	July 18, 1917	(NG) Idaho, Mont., Ore., Wash., and Wyo.; also, parts of NG from D. C., N. D., S. D., and Colo., and some men from 91st Div. to complete the 41st	Maj. Gen. Hunter Liggett	9/18/17
				Brig. Gen. Henry Jervey	9/20/17*
				Brig. Gen. G. LeR. Irwin	12/12/17*
				Maj. Gen. Hunter Liggett	12/20/17
				Brig. Gen. G. LeR. Irwin	1/18/18*
				Brig. Gen. Richard Coulter, Jr.	1/23/18*
				Brig. Gen. Robert Alexander	2/14/18
				Brig. Gen. Edward Vollrath	2/28/18*
				Brig. Gen. Robert Alexander	3/11/18
				Brig. Gen. Edward Vollrath	4/14/18*
				Brig. Gen. Robert Alexander	4/24/18
				Brig. Gen. Edward Vollrath	8/3/18*
				Brig. Gen. W. S. Scott	8/19/18
				Maj. Gen. J. E. McMahon	10/21/18
				Brig. Gen. Edward Vollrath	10/24/18*
				Brig. Gen. Eli K. Cole, USMC	10/29/18
				Brig. Gen. Edward Vollrath	12/27/18*
				Maj. Gen. Peter E. Traub	12/29/18
42	(NG)	August 1, 1917	(NG) Ala., Calif., Colo., Ga., Ill., Ind., Iowa, Kan., La., Md., Mich., Minn., Mo., Neb., N. J., N. Y., N. C., Ohio, Okla., Ore., Pa., S. C., Tenn., Tex., Va., Wis., and D. C.	Maj. Gen. W. A. Mann	9/5/17
				Maj. Gen. Charles T. Menoher	12/19/17
				Brig. Gen. Douglas MacArthur	11/10/18
				Maj. Gen. C. A. F. Flagler	11/22/18
76	(NA)	August 5, 1917	(NA) Conn., Me. Mass., N. H., N. Y., R. I., and Vt.; also, officers and men from RA, and ORC and NA officers of first OTC	Maj. Gen. H. F. Hodges	8/5/17
				Brig. Gen. William Weigel	11/28/17*
				Maj. Gen. H. F. Hodges	2/13/18
				Brig. Gen. F. H. Albright	6/11/18*
				Maj. Gen. H. F. Hodges	6/13/18
				Lt. Col. Will D. Wills	11/22/18
				Lt. Col. William C. Danks	11/27/18
77	(NA)	August 5, 1917	(NA) New York City and adjoining counties. Officers and men from RA; ORC and NA officers of first OTC as well as drafts from Camp Devens and other places to complete Division	Maj. Gen. J. F. Bell	8/18/17
				Maj. Gen. G. W. Read	12/2/17*
				Brig. Gen. E. M. Johnson	12/4/17*
				Brig. Gen. Edmund Wittenmyer	3/8/18*
				Brig. Gen. E. M. Johnson	3/9/18*
				Maj. Gen. J. F. Bell	3/21/18
				Brig. Gen. E. M. Johnson	3/25/18*
				Maj. Gen. G. B. Duncan	5/8/18
				Brig. Gen. E. M. Johnson	7/20/18*
				Maj. Gen. G. B. Duncan	7/28/18
				Brig. Gen. E. M. Johnson	8/19/18*
				Maj. Gen. Robert Alexander	8/27/18
78	(NA)	August 5, 1917	(NA) Del., N. J., and N. Y.; also, officers and men of the RA, and ORC and NA officers of the first OTC, as well as transfers and drafts from New England, N. Y., N. J., and Ill. to complete Division	Maj. Gen. C. W. Kennedy	8/23/17
				Brig. Gen. J. S. Mallory	11/28/17*
				Brig. Gen. James T. Dean	12/28/17*
				Maj. Gen. Hugh L. Scott	1/2/18
				Brig. Gen. James T. Dean	2/21/18*
				Maj. Gen. Hugh L. Scott	2/24/18
				Brig. Gen. James T. Dean	3/16/18*
				Brig. Gen. J. H. McRae	4/20/18
				Maj. Gen. J. H. McRae	4/30/18
				Brig. Gen. James T. Dean	5/1/18*
				Maj. Gen. J. H. McRae	5/3/18

Division	Designation Date	Troops From	Division Commanders 1917-1918	
79 (NA)	August 5, 1917	(NA) Md., Pa., and D. C.; also, officers and men of the RA; ORC and NA officers of the first OTC, as well as drafts and transfers from N. Y., Ohio, R. I., and W. Va. to complete Division	Brig. Gen. Joseph E. Kuhn	8/25/17
			Maj. Gen. Joseph E. Kuhn	8/29/17
			Brig. Gen. W. J. Nicholson	11/26/17*
			Maj. Gen. Joseph E. Kuhn	2/17/18
			Brig. Gen. W. J. Nicholson	4/15/18*
			Maj. Gen. Joseph E. Kuhn	4/16/18
			Brig. Gen. W. J. Nicholson	5/22/18*
			Maj. Gen. Joseph E. Kuhn	6/8/18
			Brig. Gen. W. J. Nicholson	6/28/18*
			Maj. Gen. Joseph E. Kuhn	7/23/18
			Brig. Gen. E. M. Johnson	12/29/18*
			Maj. Gen. Joseph E. Kuhn	12/31/18
80 (NA)	August 5, 1917	(NA) Pa., Va., and W. Va.; also, officers and men of the RA; ORC and NA officers of the first OTC, as well as drafts and transfers to complete Division	Brig. Gen. Herman Hall	8/27/17*
			Maj. Gen. Adelbert Cronkhite	9/9/17
			Brig. Gen. L. M. Brett	11/26/17*
			Brig. Gen. C. S. Farnsworth	12/27/17*
			Brig. Gen. W. P. Richardson	12/28/17*
			Brig. Gen. G. G. Heiner	1/6/18*
			Brig. Gen. C. S. Farnsworth	1/7/18*
			Brig. Gen. W. P. Richardson	1/11/18*
			Brig. Gen. L. M. Brett	1/14/18*
			Maj. Gen. Adelbert Cronkhite	3/1/18
			Maj. Gen. S. D. Sturgis	11/22/18
81 (NA)	August 5, 1917	(NA) Fla., N. C., and S. C.; also, officers and men of the RA; ORC and NA officers of the first OTC, as well as drafts from Ala., Fla., Ga., N. C., S. C., and N. Y. to complete Division	Brig. Gen. Charles H. Barth	8/25/17
			Maj. Gen. Charles J. Bailey	10/8/17
			Brig. Gen. Charles H. Barth	11/24/17*
			Brig. Gen. G. W. McIver	12/28/17*
			Maj. Gen. Charles J. Bailey	3/11/18
			Brig. Gen. G. W. McIver	5/19/18*
			Brig. Gen. Munroe McFarland	5/24/18*
			Brig. Gen. G. W. McIver	5/29/18*
			Maj. Gen. Charles J. Bailey	5/30/18
			Brig. Gen. G. W. McIver	6/9/18*
			Maj. Gen. Charles J. Bailey	6/26/18
			Brig. Gen. G. W. McIver	6/30/18*
			Maj. Gen. Charles J. Bailey	7/3/18
82 (NA)	August 5, 1917	(NA) Ala., Ga., and Tenn.; also, officers and men of the RA; ORC and NA officers of the first OTC, as well replacements from New England and Middle Atlantic States, draftees from Camps Devens, Dodge, Gordon, Travis, and Upton, as well as fresh draftees from Ala., Ga., and Tenn.—all these to make up for the transfer almost en masse of NA men from Ala., Ga., and Tenn. to the 30th, 31st, and 81st Divisions.	Maj. Gen. Eben Swift	8/25/17
			Brig. Gen. James B. Erwin	11/24/17*
			Brig. Gen. W. P. Burnham	12/27/17*
			Brig. Gen. Marcus D. Cronin	3/23/18*
			Brig. Gen. W. P. Burnham	3/28/18
			Maj. Gen. W. P. Burnham	5/23/18
			Maj. Gen. George B. Duncan	10/4/18
83 (NA)	August 5, 1917	(NA) Ohio and Pa.; also, officers and men of the RA; ORC and NA officers of the first OTC, as well as drafts from Ky. and Ohio to complete Division	Brig. Gen. Edwin F. Glenn	8/25/17
			Maj. Gen. Edwin F. Glenn	9/7/17
			Brig. Gen. Frederick Perkins	1/13/18*
			Brig. Gen. Willard A. Holbrook	3/23/18*
			Maj. Gen. Edwin F. Glenn	4/3/18
84 (NA)	August 5, 1917	(NA) Ill., Ind., and Ky.; also, officers and men of the RA; ORC and NA officers of the first OTC as	Col. Wilber E. Wilder	8/25/17*
			Brig. Gen. Wilber E. Wilder	8/29/17*
			Maj. Gen. Harry C. Hale	10/6/17
			Brig. Gen. Wilber E. Wilder	11/26/17*

Division	Designation Date	Troops From	Division Commanders 1917-1918	
		well as second OTC. Drafts from N. D. and Mont. replace transfers to complete Division	Brig. Gen. Daniel B. Devore	12/13/17*
			Brig. Gen. Wilber E. Wilder	12/15/17*
			Maj. Gen. Harry C. Hale	3/1/18
			Brig. Gen. Wilber E. Wilder	6/1/18*
			Maj. Gen. Harry C. Hale	6/5/18
			Brig. Gen. Wilber E. Wilder	7/19/18*
			Maj. Gen. Harry C. Hale	7/21/18
			Brig. Gen. Wilber E. Wilder	10/18/18*
			Maj. Gen. Harry C. Hale	10/31/18
85 (NA)	August 5, 1917	(NA) Mich. and Wis.; also, officers and men of the RA; ORC and NA officers of the first OTC, as well as transfers (drafts) from Camps Grant and Taylor largely drawn from Ill., Ind., and Ky., to complete the Division	Maj. Gen. J. T. Dickman	8/25/17
			Brig. Gen. S. W. Miller	11/25/17*
			Maj. Gen. James Parker	12/13/17
			Brig. Gen. B. C. Morse	2/21/18*
			Maj. Gen. Chase W. Kennedy	2/27/18
			Brig. Gen. T. B. Dugan	8/3/18*
			Maj. Gen. Chase W. Kennedy	8/6/18
			Brig. Gen. T. B. Dugan	8/14/18*
			Maj. Gen. Chase W. Kennedy	8/16/18
			Col. B. W. Atkinson	10/26/18*
			Maj. Gen. Chase W. Kennedy	10/28/18
			Brig. Gen. G. D. Moore	12/23/18*
86 (NA)	August 5, 1917	(NA) Ill., Wis., as well as officers and men of the RA; ORC and NA officers of the first OTC; also, drafts and transfers—many from Minn. and Ill. made up the Division, part of which had been transferred to the 33d, 4th, and 85th Divisions	Maj. Gen. Thomas H. Barry	8/25/17
			Brig. Gen. Lyman W. V. Kennon	11/26/17*
			Maj. Gen. Thomas H. Barry	2/15/18
			Brig. Gen. Lyman W. V. Kennon	3/21/18*
			Brig. Gen. Charles H. Martin	4/18/18
			Maj. Gen. Charles H. Martin	4/30/18
			Brig. Gen. Lincoln C. Andrews	10/19/18*
			Col. Guy G. Palmer	10/24/18*
			Brig. Gen. Francis LeJ. Parker	11/8/18*
			Brig. Gen. Lincoln C. Andrews	11/9/18*
87 (NA)	August 5, 1917	(NA) Ala., Ark., La., and Miss.; also, officers and men of the RA; ORC and NA officers of the first OTC. To replace transfers to the 31st, 39th and 81st Divisions, draft detachments from Camps Custer, Dodge, Funston, Grant, Taylor, and Travis, as well as others from N. J., N. Y., and Pa. to complete Division	Brig. Gen. S. D. Sturgis	8/25/17
			Maj. Gen. S. D. Sturgis	8/28/17
			Brig. Gen. R. C. Van Vliet	11/13/17
			Maj. Gen. S. D. Sturgis	11/17/17
			Brig. Gen. R. C. Van Vliet	11/27/17*
			Maj. Gen. S. D. Sturgis	3/10/18
			Brig. Gen. W. F. Martin	10/2/18*
			Col. John O'Shea	10/6/18*
			Maj. Gen. S. D. Sturgis	10/23/18
			Brig. Gen. W. F. Martin	11/22/18
88 (NA)	August 5, 1917	(NA) Ill., Ia., Minn., and N. D.; also, officers and men of RA; ORC and NA officers of the first OTC. To make up for the transfers to the 30th, 33d, 34th, 82d, 87th, 35th, and 90th Divisions, replacements and fresh drafts from Mo., Neb., and S. D. complete Division	Maj. Gen. Edward H. Plummer	8/25/17
			Brig. Gen. Robert N. Getty	11/27/17*
			Maj. Gen. Edward H. Plummer	2/19/18
			Brig. Gen. Robert N. Getty	3/15/18*
			Brig. Gen. William D. Beach	5/24/18*
			Maj. Gen. William Weigel	9/10/18
89 (NA)	August 5, 1917	(NA) Ariz., Col., Kans., Mo., Neb., N. M., and S. D.; also, officers and men of RA; ORC and NA officers of the first OTC, as well as fresh drafts and transfers to complete the Division reduced by trans-	Maj. Gen. Leonard Wood	8/27/17
			Brig. Gen. Frank L. Winn	11/6/17*
			Maj. Gen. Leonard Wood	11/12/17
			Brig. Gen. Frank L. Winn	11/26/17*
			Brig. Gen. Thomas G. Hanson	12/24/17*
			Brig. Gen. Frank L. Winn	12/29/17*
			Col. James H. Reeves	1/7/18*
			Brig. Gen. Frank L. Winn	1/10/18*

Division	Designation Date	Troops From	Division Commanders 1917-1918	
		fers to the 3d, 4th, 35th, and other Divisions	Maj. Gen. Leonard Wood	4/12/18
			Brig. Gen. Frank L. Winn	6/1/18
			Maj. Gen. William M. Wright	9/6/18
			Maj. Gen. Frank L. Winn	11/12/18
90 (NA)	August 5, 1917	(NA) Okla. and Tex.; also, officers and men of RA; ORC and NA officers of the first OTC, as well as drafts from Ill., Minn., N. D., and S. D. to make up for transfers, complete the Division	Maj. Gen. Henry T. Allen	8/25/17
			Brig. Gen. Joseph A. Gaston	11/23/17*
			Brig. Gen. W. H. Johnston	12/27/17*
			Maj. Gen. Henry T. Allen	3/1/18
			Brig. Gen. Joseph P. O'Neil	11/24/18*
			Maj. Gen. Charles H. Martin	12/30/18
91 (NA)	August 5, 1917	(NA) Calif., Idaho, Mont., Nev., Ore., Wyo., Utah, and Wash.; also, officers and men of RA; ORC and NA officers of the first OTC.	Maj. Gen. Henry A. Greene	8/26/17
			Brig. Gen. James A. Irons	11/24/17*
			Brig. Gen. Frederick S. Foltz	12/25/17*
			Maj. Gen. Henry A. Greene	3/3/18
			Brig. Gen. Frederick S. Foltz	6/19/18*
			Maj. Gen. William H. Johnston	8/29/18
92 (NA)	Oct. 24, 1917	(NA) Colored—At Large. General, Field, and officers in technical branches and in field artillery above grade of first lieutenant are white.	Brig. Gen. Charles C. Ballou	10/29/17
			Brig. Gen. John E. McMahon	11/20/17*
			Brig. Gen. Malvern-Hill Barnum	11/29/17*
			Brig. Gen. John E. McMahon	12/1/17*
			Maj. Gen. Charles C. Ballou	12/3/17
			Maj. Gen. Charles H. Martin	11/19/18
			Brig. Gen. James B. Erwin	12/16/18
93 (Prov.)	Nov. 23, 1917	Colored — 185th, 186th Inf. Brigs. (former NG of N. Y. and Ill.) and NG units from Conn., D. C., Md., Mass., Ohio, and Tenn.; also, draftees from Fort Jackson. All officers are white.	Brig. Gen. Roy Hoffman	12/15/17

Grade	Pay Period	Annual Base Pay	Monthly Rates			
			Initial Monthly Pay	Over 3 Years' Service	Over 6 Years' Service	Over 9 Years' Service
General [1]		$8000	$666.67	$666.67	$666.67	$666.67
Lieutenant General [2]		8000	666.67	666.67	666.67	666.67
Major General		8000	666.67	666.67	666.67	666.67
Brigadier General		6000	500.00	500.00	500.00	500.00
Colonel	6	4000	333.33	350.00	366.67	383.33
Lieutenant Colonel [3]	5	3500	291.67	306.25	320.83	335.42
Major [4]	4	3000	250.00	262.50	275.00	287.50
Captain [5]	3	2400	200.00	210.00	220.00	230.00
First Lieutenant [6]	2	2000	166.67	175.00	183.33	191.67
Second Lieutenant [7]	1	1800	150.00	157.50	165.00	172.50
Masters, Army Mine Planter Service		2400	200.00	210.00	220.00	230.00
Chief Warrant Officers, First Mates, and Assistant		2100	175.00	183.75	192.50	201.25
Engineers, Army Mine Planter Service		1950	162.50	170.63	178.75	186.88
Warrant Officers (junior grade)		1800	150.00	157.50	165.00	172.50
Superintendents, Nurse Corps [8]		3580	298.33	313.33	328.33	343.33
Assistant Superintendents, Directors, and Assistant Directors [8]		2580	215.00	230.00	245.00	260.00
Chief Nurses [8]		1680	140.00	155.00	170.00	185.00
Nurses [8]		1080	90.00	105.00	120.00	135.00

[1] A full general or the Chief of Staff of the Army is entitled to the pay and allowances of a rear admiral of the Navy (upper half) and a personal money allowance of $2200 a year.

[2] A lieutenant general is entitled to the pay and allowances of a rear admiral of the Navy and a personal money allowance of $500 a year.

[3] A lieutenant colonel, after completing 30 years' service, is entitled to the pay of the 6th period or pay of a colonel as shown above.

[4] A major, after completing 23 years' service, is entitled to the pay of the 5th period or pay of a lieutenant colonel as shown above.

ARMY PAY SCALE

| | | | | | | | Rental and Subsistence Allowances (30-Day Month) | | | |
| | Monthly Rates | | | | | | With Dependents | | No Dependents | |
Over 12 Years' Service	Over 15 Years' Service	Over 18 Years' Service	Over 21 Years' Service	Over 24 Years' Service	Over 27 Years' Service	Over 30 Years' Service	Rental	Subsistence	Rental	Subsistence
$666.67	$666.67	$666.67	$666.67	$666.67	$666.67	$666.67	$120	$42	$105	$21
666.67	666.67	666.67	666.67	666.67	666.67	666.67	120	42	105	21
666.67	666.67	666.67	666.67	666.67	666.67	666.67	120	42	105	21
500.00	500.00	500.00	500.00	500.00	500.00	500.00	120	42	105	21
400.00	416.67	433.33	450.00	466.67	483.33	500.00	120	42	105	21
350.00	364.58	379.17	393.75	408.33	422.91	437.50	120	63	105	21
300.00	312.50	325.00	337.50	350.00	362.50	375.00	105	63	90	21
240.00	250.00	260.00	270.00	280.00	290.00	300.00	90	42	75	21
200.00	208.33	216.67	225.00	233.33	241.67	250.00	75	42	60	21
180.00	187.50	195.00	202.50	210.00	217.50	225.00	60	42	45	21
240.00	250.00	260.00	270.00	280.00	290.00	300.00	90	42	75	21
210.00	218.75	227.50	236.25	245.00	253.75	262.50	75	42	60	21
195.00	203.13	211.25	219.38	227.50	235.63	243.75	60	42	45	21
180.00	187.50	195.00	202.50	210.00	217.50	225.00	60	42	45	21
358.33	358.33	358.33	358.33	358.33	358.33	358.33	60	42	45	21
275.00	275.00	275.00	275.00	275.00	275.00	275.00	60	42	45	21
200.00	200.00	200.00	200.00	200.00	200.00	200.00	60	42	45	21
150.00	150.00	150.00	150.00	150.00	150.00	150.00	60	42	45	21

5 A captain, after completing 17 years' service, is entitled to the pay of the 4th period or pay of a major as shown above.

6 A first lieutenant, after completing 10 years' service, is entitled to the pay of the 3d period or pay of a captain as shown above.

7 A second lieutenant, after completing 5 years' service, is entitled to the pay of the 2d period or pay of a first lieutenant as shown above.

8 Nurses are all female under this provision.

Pay, Enlisted Personnel in Active Service, Monthly Rates

Pay Effective June 1, 1942

Within the United States

Grade	Base Pay	After 3 Years	After 6 Years	After 9 Years	After 12 Years	After 15 Years	After 18 Years	After 21 Years	After 24 Years	After 27 Years	After 30 Years
1. Master Sergeant	$138.00	$144.90	$151.80	$158.70	$165.60	$172.50	$179.40	$186.30	$193.20	$200.10	$207.00
2. First or Technical Sergeant	114.00	119.70	125.40	131.10	136.80	142.50	148.20	153.90	159.60	165.30	171.00
3. Staff Sergeant	96.00	100.80	105.60	110.40	115.20	120.00	124.80	129.60	134.40	139.20	144.00
4. Sergeant	78.00	81.90	85.80	89.70	93.60	97.50	101.40	105.30	109.20	113.10	117.00
5. Corporal	66.00	69.30	72.60	75.90	79.20	82.50	85.80	89.10	92.40	95.70	99.00
6. Private, first class	54.00	56.70	59.40	62.10	64.80	67.50	70.20	72.90	75.60	78.30	81.00
7. Private	50.00	52.50	55.00	57.50	60.00	62.50	65.00	67.50	70.00	72.50	75.00

Outside Continental Limits of the United States, Including Alaska (20% Increase in Base Pay Only)

20% Added — Longevity Computed on Base Pay without Addition of 20%

Grade	Base Pay	After 3 Years	After 6 Years	After 9 Years	After 12 Years	After 15 Years	After 18 Years	After 21 Years	After 24 Years	After 27 Years	After 30 Years
1. Master Sergeant	165.60	172.50	179.40	186.30	193.20	200.10	207.00	213.90	220.80	227.70	234.60
2. First or Technical Sergeant	136.80	142.50	148.20	153.90	159.60	165.30	171.00	176.70	182.40	188.10	193.80
3. Staff Sergeant	115.20	120.00	124.80	129.60	134.40	139.20	144.00	148.80	153.60	158.40	163.20
4. Sergeant	93.60	97.50	101.40	105.30	109.20	113.10	117.00	120.90	124.80	128.70	132.60
5. Corporal	79.20	82.50	85.80	89.10	92.40	95.70	99.00	102.30	105.60	108.90	112.20
6. Private, first class	64.80	67.50	70.20	72.90	75.60	78.30	81.00	83.70	86.40	89.10	91.80
7. Private	60.00	62.50	65.00	67.50	70.00	72.50	75.00	77.50	80.00	82.50	85.00

Note.—In addition to above monthly pay in currency, the enlisted man receives quarters, subsistence, and clothing in kind free. Should he be deprived on government duty of receiving any one or all of these items, he may receive money for same as follows: for personal quarters and subsistence, a commutation of $5.00 per day or less as the President may prescribe for the particular need; for enlisted men of the first three grades, an additional allowance for quarters of a dependent, when the dependent is prevented from dwelling with the soldier by reason of orders from competent authority; and for all soldiers, a commutation or money allowance for clothing not furnished the soldier in an amount prescribed by the President.

SELECTED BIBLIOGRAPHY

HISTORY

(General)

Beginnings of the American People.
CARL LOTUS BECKER.
Houghton Mifflin & Co., Boston, New York, 1915.

From Kingdom to Colony.
MARY DEVEREAUX.
Little, Brown & Co., Boston, 1899.

The History of the Rise, Progress and Establishment of the Independence of the United States of America.
WILLIAM GORDON.
Printed by Hodge, Allen & Campbell, New York, 1789.

Builders of the Nation, Vols. I, II, The Soldier.
GEORGE A. FORSYTH.
Imperial Publishing Co., New York, 1913.

History of the United States and Its People, 7 Vols.
E. M. AVERY.
Burrows Brothers, Cleveland, Ohio, 1909.

History of the United States from the Discovery of the American Continent, 10 Vols.
GEORGE BANCROFT.
Little, Brown & Co., Boston, 1852, 1874.

History of the United States, 1801–1807, 9 Vols.
HENRY ADAMS.
Charles Scribner's Sons, New York, 1921.

History of the United States, 1850–1877.
JAMES F. RHODES.
The Macmillan Co., New York, 1919.

The Critical Period of American History.
JOHN FISKE.
Houghton Mifflin & Co., Boston, New York, 1898.

History of the American People.
WOODROW WILSON.
Harper & Bros., New York, 1902.

History of the United States.
EDWARD CHANNING.
The Macmillan Co., New York, 1911.

Our Nation in the Building.
HELEN NICOLAY.
The Century Co., New York, 1918.

History of the United States from the Compromise of 1850.
JAMES FORD RHODES.
The Macmillan Co., New York, 1919.

A Short History of the United States Navy.
CLARK, STEVENS, ALDEN, KRAFFT.
J. B. Lippincott Co., Philadelphia, New York, 1911.

ACCOUNTS OF WARS, CAMPAIGNS AND BATTLES

The History of the American Revolution, Vols. I, II.
DAVID RAMSEY, M.P.
Printed for J. Stockdale, London, 1793.

The American Revolution, Vols. I, II.
JOHN FISKE.
Houghton Mifflin & Co., Boston, New York, 1892.

The Pictorial History of the American Revolution.
ROBERT SEARS.
R. Sears, New York; Redding & Co., Boston, 1847.

The American Revolution, Vols. I, II, III, IV.
SIR GEORGE OTTO TREVELYAN.
Longmans, Green & Co., London, New York, etc., 1921.

The Struggle for American Independence, Vols. I, II.
SIDNEY GEORGE FISHER.
J. B. Lippincott Co., Philadelphia, London, 1908.

The True History of the American Revolution.
SIDNEY GEORGE FISHER.
J. B. Lippincott & Co., Philadelphia, London, 1902.

History of the War of Independence of the United States of America, 3 Vols.
CHARLES BOTTA.
T. Brainard, New Haven, 1840.

The First American Civil War, 1775–1778, Vols. I, II.
HENRY BELCHER.
The Macmillan Co., Ltd., London, 1911.

Battles of the American Revolution.
H. B. CARRINGTON.
Barnes & Co., New York, Chicago, 1876.

Battles of America, Vols. I, II, III.
ROBERT TOMES.
Virtue & Co., New York, 1861.

Battles of Princeton and Trenton.
W. S. STRYKER.
Houghton Mifflin & Co., Boston, New York, 1898.

History of the American War, 1774–1781, Vols. I, II.
G. STEDMAN.
Printed by author, London, 1794.

France in the American Revolution.
JAMES BREEK PERKINS.
Houghton Mifflin & Co., Boston, New York, 1911.

Revolutionary Fights and Fighters.
CYRUS TOWNSEND BRADY.
McClure, Phillips & Co., New York, 1901.

The Yorktown Campaign, 1781.
H. P. JOHNSTON.
Harper & Bros., New York, 1881.

American Fights and Fighters, 1776–1815.
CYRUS TOWNSEND BRADY.
Doubleday, Page & Co., New York, 1913.

Arnold's Expedition to Quebec.
JOHN CODMAN, 2nd.
The Macmillan Co., New York, 1901.

History Regarding Phases of Revolutionary War.
Government Printing Office, Washington, D. C.

How Canada was Held for the Empire.
J. HANNAY.
Morang & Co., Toronto, Canada, 1902.

The War with the United States.
WILLIAM WOOD.
Brook & Company, Toronto, Glasgow, 1915.

Campaigns at Washington, 1814–1815.
"By author of *The Subaltern.*" (Anonymous.)
London, 1826.

Campaigns and Engineers of the War of 1812.
G. W. CULLUM.
James Miller, New York, 1879.

The Battle of New Orleans.
Z. F. SMITH.
J. P. Morton, Louisville, Ky., 1904.

History of the Late War, 1812.
H. M. BRACKENRIDGE.
J. Kay & Bro., Philadelphia, 1836.

1812: *The War and its Moral*, A Canadian Chronicle.
WILLIAM F. COFFIN.
John Lovell, Montreal, 1864.

History of the Late War, 1812–1815, Vols. I, II, III, IV.
C. J. INGERSOLL.
Lea & Blanchard, Philadelphia, 1845.

Military Occurrences of the Late War, 1812, Vols. I, II.
WILLIAM JAMES.
Printed by author, London, 1818.

History of Invasion and Capture of Washington.
JOHN S. WILLIAMS.
Harper & Bros., New York, 1857.

Principal Battles of the Late War, 1812.
Adjutant P. M. DAVIS.
Reprint by William Abbott, 1917.

The War with the United States.
WILLIAM WOOD.
Brook & Co., Toronto, Glasgow, 1915.

History of the War between the United States and Great Britain, 1812.
Anonymous.
John Low, New York, 1817.

Lossing's Pictorial Field Book of the War of 1812.
BENSON L. LOSSING.
Harper & Bros., New York, 1869.

"The Truth of the War of 1812 and the Necessity of our Knowing It."
GEORGE W. WINGATE.
President Public Schools' Athletic League.
North American Review, Vol. 189, June, 1909.

Historical Sketch of the Second War between the United States of America and Great Britain.
C. J. INGERSOLL.
Lea & Blanchard, Philadelphia, 1845–1849.

An Impartial and Correct History of the War between the United States of America and Great Britain, comprising particular detail of the Military and Naval Operations.
THOMAS O'CONNOR.
John Low, New York, 1817.

A Compendious Account of the Most Important Battles of the Late War (1812) to which is added curious adventures of Corporal Samuel Stubbs.
SAMUEL STUBBS.
H. Trumbull, Boston, 1815.

Battle of Bladensburg.
Lt. Colonel R. I. REES, Infantry.
The Infantry School Press, Fort Benning, Ga., 1921.

The Other Side; or Notes for the History of the War between Mexico and the United States.
RAMON ALCARAZ.
Translated from the Spanish by A. C. Ramsey.
J. Wiley, New York, 1850.

The Battle of Buena Vista.
JAMES HENRY CARLETON.
Harper & Bros., New York, 1848.

Our First War in Mexico.
FARNHAM BISHOP.
Stronger & Townsend, New York, 1853.

Campaign Sketches of the War with Mexico.
WILLIAM SEATON HENRY.
Harper & Bros., New York, 1847.

The Mexican War Diary of George B. McClellan.
GEORGE BRINTON MCCLELLAN.
Princeton University Press, Princeton, 1917.

The Mexican War.
EDWARD DEERING MANSFIELD.
A. S. Barnes & Co., New York; Derby, Bradley & Co., Cincinnati, 1848.

History of the War between Mexico and the United States.
BRANTZ MAYER.
Wiley & Putnam, New York, London, 1848.

The War with Mexico, Vols. I, II.
R. S. RIPLEY.
Harper & Bros., New York, 1849.

The United States and Mexico, 1821–1848.
GEORGE LOCKHART RIVES.
Charles Scribner's Sons, New York, 1913.

The War with Mexico, Vols. I, II.
JUSTIN HARVEY SMITH.
The Macmillan Co., New York, 1919.

History of the Mexican War.
CADMUS MARCELLUS WILCOX.
Church News Publishing Co., Washington, D. C., 1892.

The American Conflict.
HORACE GREELEY.
O. D. Case & Co., Hartford; C. & C. S. Sherwood, Chicago, 1873.

The Campaign of Chancellorsville, April 27 to May 5, 1863.
JAMES H. WILSON. (A critical review of Mayor John Bigelow's work on same subject.)
Chas. L. Story, Wilmington, Del., 1911.

The War of the Rebellion, Rebellion records covering seventy volumes.
U. S. War Department.
Government Printing Office, Washington, D. C., 1880–1901.

The Story of the Civil War, Vols. I, II.
JOHN CODMAN ROPES.
G. P. Putnam's Sons, New York, London, 1913.

From Fort Henry to Corinth.
MANNING FERGUSON FORCE.
Charles Scribner's Sons, New York, 1881.

The Photographic History of the Civil War, 9 Vols.
FRANCIS TREVELYAN MILLER, editor.
Review of Reviews Co., New York, 1911.

Battles and Leaders of the Civil War, Vols, I–IV.
ROBERT UNDERWOOD JOHNSON, editor.
The Century Co., New York, 1884–1887.

History of the Civil War of America, Vols. I–IV.
COMTE DE PARIS.
John C. Winston Co., Philadelphia, 1907.

U. S. History of the Civil War.
HENRY E. DAVIES.
D. Appleton & Co., New York, 1895.

U. S. History of the Civil War, Vols. I, II, III.
JOHN WILLIAM DRAPER.
Harper & Bros., New York, 1867.

U. S. History of the Civil War. Confederate Military History.
CLEMENT ANSELON EVANS.
Atlanta Confederate Publishing Co., Atlanta, Ga., 1899.

The Peninsula; McClellan's Campaign of 1862.
ALEXANDER S. WEBB.
Charles Scribner's Sons, New York, 1881.

The Union Indian Brigade in the Civil War.
WILEY BRITTON.
Franklin Hudson Publishing Co., Kansas City, 1922.

Campaigns of Stuart's Cavalry.
McCLELLAN, Private Print.

The Antietam and Fredericksburg.
FRANCIS WINTHROP PALFREY.
Charles Scribner's Sons, New York, 1882.

From Manassas to Appomattox.
JAMES LONGSTREET.
J. B. Lippincott Co., Philadelphia, 1896.

History of the Civil War in America, Vols. I–IV.
LOUIS PHILIPPE ALBERT D'ORLEANS, Paris.
J. H. Coates & Co., Philadelphia, 1875–1888.

History of the Civil War.
JAMES FORD RHODES.
The Macmillan Co., New York, 1917.

Stuart's Cavalry in the Gettysburg Campaign.
JOHN SINGLETON MOSBY.
Moffat, Yard & Co., New York, 1908.

Bibliography of State Participation in the Civil War, 1861–1866.
U. S. War Department.
Government Printing Office, Washington, D. C., 1913.

Military and Naval History of the Rebellion in the United States.
W. J. TENNEY, editor, *American Annual Cyclopaedia.*
D. Appleton & Co., New York, 1867.

The War of Secession.
GEORGE WILLIAM REDWAY.
S. Sonnenschein & Co., London, 1910.

The Army Under Pope.
JOHN CODMAN ROPES.
Charles Scribner's Sons, New York, 1881.

Grant's Campaign in Virginia.
GEORGE HENRY VAUGHN SAWYER.
The Macmillan Co., New York, 1908.

The Virginia Campaign of 1864 and 1865.
ANDREW ATKINSON HUMPHREYS.
Charles Scribner's Sons, New York, 1885.

Antietam and the Maryland and Virginia Campaigns of 1862 from the Government Records.
ISAAC WINTER HEYSINGER.
The Neale Publishing Co., New York, 1912.

The Mississippi Valley in the Civil War.
JOHN FISKE.
Houghton Mifflin & Co., New York, 1900.

Chancellorsville and Gettysburg.
ABNER DOUBLEDAY.
Charles Scribner's Sons, New York, 1882.

The March to the Sea.
JACOB DOLSON COX.
Charles Scribner's Sons, New York, 1885.

The Army of the Cumberland.
HENRY MARTYN CIST.
Charles Scribner's Sons, New York 1882.

The Mississippi.
FRANCIS VINTON GREENE.
Charles Scribner's Sons, New York, 1882.

American Civil War.
> JOHN H. ANDERSON.
> H. Rees, Ltd., London, 1910.

The Secret Service of the Confederate States in Europe.
> JAMES DUNWODY BULLOCH.
> G. P. Putnam's Sons, New York, 1884.

History of the Confederate States Navy from its Organization to the Surrender of its last Vessel.
> JOHN THOMAS SCHARF.
> Rogers & Sherwood, New York; A. L. Bancroft & Co., San Francisco, 1887.

Personal Recollections of a Cavalryman with Custer's Michigan Cavalry Brigade in Civil War.
> J. H. KIDD.
> Sentinel Printing Co., Iona, Mich., 1908.

History of the Corn Exchange Regiment.
> Pennsylvania Infantry.
> J. L. Smith, Philadelphia, 1888.

The History of the Confederate War, Vols. I, II.
> GEORGE CARY EGGLESTON.
> Sturgis and Walton Co., New York, 1910.

History of the Army of the Potomac.
> J. H. STINE.
> J. B. Rodgers Printing Co., Philadelphia, 1892

The American Army in the War of Secession.
> DE CHANAL.
> Geo. A. Spooner Publishing Co., Leavenworth, Kansas, 1894.

War of the Rebellion; Official Records of Union and Confederate Armies.
> U. S. War Department.
> Government Printing Office, Washington, D. C.

Grant's Campaigns of 1864 and 1865.
> CHARLES FRANCIS ATKINSON.
> H. Rees, Ltd., London, 1908.

Conduct of War Department in War with Spain, 6 Vols.
> Government Printing Office, 1900.

The War with Spain.
> HENRY CABOT LODGE.
> Harper & Bros., New York, 1899.

Child's History of the War with Spain.
> PERCIVAL G. MELBOURNE.
> F. T. Neely, New York, 1898.

Battles and Capitulation of Santiago de Cuba.
> JOSÉ MULLER Y TEJERRO.
> Translated from Spanish.
> Government Printing Office, Washington, D. C., 1898.

A History of the Spanish-American War.
> RICHARD H. TITHERINGTON.
> D. Appleton & Co., New York, 1900.

A Short History of the War with Spain.
> MARRION WILCOX.
> F. A. Stokes Co., New York, 1898.

The Campaign of Santiago de Cuba.
> HERBERT HOWLAND SERGEANT.
> A. C. McClung & Co., Chicago, 1907.

Lessons of the War with Spain.
> ALFRED T. MAHAN.
> Little, Brown & Co., Boston, 1899.

Cannon and Camera (War with Spain).
> W. I. LINCOLN ADAMS.
> D. Appleton & Co., New York, 1898.

Campaigning in Cuba.
> GEORGE KENNAN.
> The Century Co., New York, 1899.

The Rough Riders.
> THEODORE ROOSEVELT.
> Charles Scribner's Sons, New York, 1899.

The Cuban and Porto Rican Campaigns.
> RICHARD HARDING DAVIS.
> Charles Scribner's Sons, New York, 1898.

American Campaigns, Vols. I, II.
> MATTHEW FORNEY STEELE.
> B. S. Adams, Washington, 1909.

BIOGRAPHY

The Military Services and Public Life of Major General John Sullivan.
THOMAS COFFIN.
Wiggin & Lunt, Albany, N. Y.; J. Munsell, Boston, 1868.

The Life of Artemas Ward.
CHARLES MARTYN.
A. Ward, New York, 1921.

The Narrative of Lieutenant General Sir William Howe.
WILLIAM HOWE HOWE.
Printed by H. Baldwin, London, 1781.

Washington, the Soldier.
HENRY BEEBEE CARRINGTON.
Lamson, Wolffe & Co., Boston, New York, 1898.

Life of Peter Van Schoak.
HENRY VAN SCHOAK.
D. Appleton & Co., New York, 1842.

The Life of Major General Nathanael Greene.
G. W. GREEN.
G. P. Putnam's Sons, New York, 1867.

George Washington.
WASHINGTON IRVING.
Thomas Crowell Co., New York, 1916.

George Washington.
WOODROW WILSON.
Harper & Bros., New York, 1896.

Artemas Ward, first Commander in Chief of the American Revolution,
CHARLES MARTYN.
A. Ward, New York, 1921.

Abraham Lincoln; A History.
JOHN GEORGE NICOLAY.
The Century Co., New York, 1890.

Life of Andrew Jackson, Vols. I, II.
JOHN SPENCER BASSETT.
Doubleday, Page & Co., New York, 1911.

Life of Andrew Jackson.
JOHN S. JENKINS.
Porter & Coates, Philadelphia, 1880.

A Life of Major General George A. Custer.
FREDERICK WHITTAKER.
Sheldon & Co., New York, 1876.

Life of Major General William Henry Harrison.
ANONYMOUS.
Grigg & Elliot, and T. K. & P. G. Collins, Philadelphia.

Stonewall Jackson and the American Civil War.
GEORGE FRANCIS ROBERT HENDERSON.
Longmans, Green & Co., London, New York, 1911.

Life of General Zachary Taylor.
H. MONTGOMERY.
John C. Winston Co., Philadelphia, 1912.

Life of General Zachary Taylor.
JOSEPH REESE FRY.
Griggs, Elliott & Co., Philadelphia, 1847.

Sam Houston and the War of Independence in Texas.
ALFRED M. WILLIAMS.
Houghton Mifflin & Co., Boston, 1893.

How George Rogers Clark won the Northwest.
REUBEN GOLD THWAITES.
A. C. McClung & Co., Chicago, 1903.

The Life of Sam Houston.
C. E. Lester.
Davis, Porter & Coates, Philadelphia, 1866.

Personal Recollections of Distinguished Generals.
WILLIAM F. G. SHANKS.
Harper & Bros., New York, 1866.

The Life of General Scott.
An unsigned excerpt from an old magazine. Bound in pamphlet form.

Life and Public Services of General Andrew Jackson.
J. S. JENKINS.
H. H. Bancroft & Co., San Francisco, 1860.

The Life of Benedict Arnold.
I. ARNOLD.
Jansen, McClug, Chicago, 1880.

Political and Military Episodes in the Life of Rt. Honorable J. Burgoyne.
E. B. FONBLANGUE.
The Macmillan Co., London, 1876.

Nathan Hale, 1776.
H. P. JOHNSTON.
Yale University Press, 1914, New Haven.

The Life of John Marshall, Vols. I, II.
ALBERT J. BEVERIDGE.
Houghton Mifflin & Co., Boston, 1916.

George Washington.
HORACE E. SCUDDER.
Houghton Mifflin & Co., Boston, 1885.

George Washington.
WILLIAM ROSCOE THAYER.
Houghton Mifflin & Co., Boston, 1922.

Canadian Heroes Series. Isaac Brock.
WALTER R. NURSEY.
William Briggs, Toronto, 1908.

Sages and Heroes of the Revolution.
L. CARROLL HUDSON.
John Adams Lee Publishing Co., Boston, 1889.

Leading American Soldiers.
R. M. JOHNSTON.
Henry Holt & Co., New York, 1907.

Life and Campaigns of General McClellan.
G. S. HILLIARD.
J. B. Lippincott & Co., Philadelphia, 1864.

Men who are making America.
B. C. FORBES.
B. C. Forbes Publishing Co., New York, 1917.

Revolutionary Services and Civil Life of General William Hull.
MRS. MARIA (HULL) CAMPBELL.
D. Appleton & Co., New York, 1848.

Life and Correspondence of Joseph Reed, Vols. I, II.
WILLIAM BRADFORD REED.
Lindsey & Blakiston, Philadelphia, 1847.

AUTOBIOGRAPHY

Colonel Alexander K. McClure's Recollections of Half a Century.
ALEXANDER KELLY MCCLURE.
The Salem Press, Salem, Mass., 1902.

Autobiography of Lieutenant General Scott.
Sheldon & Co., New York, 1864.

Recollections of General Nelson A. Miles.
NELSON A. MILES.
The Werner Co., New York, Chicago, 1896.

Autobiography of Black Hawk.
Published by J. B. Patterson, Oquawoka, Ill., 1882.

Autobiography of an English Soldier.
GEORGE BALLENTINE.
Stronger & Townsend, New York, 1853.

DIARIES

My Diary North and South.
SIR WILLIAM HOWARD RUSSELL.
Bradbury & Sons, London, 1863.

A Soldier's Diary.
DAVID LANE.
Jackson (?), Mich., 1905.

*The Diary of a Young Officer Serving with the Armies of the United States
during the War of the Rebellion.*
JOSIAH MARSHALL FAVILL.
R. R. Donnelley & Sons, Chicago, 1909.

Diary of Gideon Welles, Vols. I, II, III, 1861–1869.
GIDEON WELLES.
Houghton Mifflin & Co., Boston, New York, 1909.

Diary of a Young Army Officer.
F. M. FAVILL.
R. R. Donnelley & Sons Co., Chicago, 1909.

Sketches of the Revolutionary War.
Old Manuscript of Diaries, etc.

LETTERS

Calendar of the Correspondence of George Washington, Commander-in-Chief of the Continental Army.
U. S. Library of Congress.

Letters of Richard Henry Lee, 1779–1794, Vols. I, II.
JAMES CURTIS BALLOGH.
The Macmillan Co., New York, 1914.

Army Letters, 1861–1865.
O. W. NORTON.
Privately Printed.
O. L. Deming, Chicago, 1903.

DESCRIPTIVE ACCOUNTS OF PERSONS, PLACES, AND INCIDENTS

Doctor Quintard, Chaplain C. S. A.
CHARLES TODD QUINTARD.
The University Press, Sewanee, Tenn., 1905.

Reminiscences of the Santiago Campaign.
JOHN BIGELOW.
Harper & Bros., New York, 1899.

Defense of General Hull.
Prepared from his manuscripts by his daughter.
Wells & Lilly, Boston, 1814.

History of Philip Kearny.
H. WATTS DE PEYSTER.
Old Print.

Ups and Downs of an Army Officer, 1866–1869, in Second and Tenth Cavalry.
G. A. ARMES.
Washington, D. C., 1900.

Under the Old Flag, Vols. I, II.
JAMES HARRISON WILSON.
D. Appleton & Co., New York, London, 1912.

A French Volunteer in the War of Independence.
ROBERT D. DOUGLAS.
Charles Carrington, Paris, 1898.

Recollections of the Early Days of the National Guard.
By an ex-orderly sergeant.
J. M. Bradstreet & Son, New York, 1868.

Military Miscellanies.
JAMES B. FRY.
Brentano's, New York, 1889.

History of West Point.
BOYNTON.
Old Print, 1871.

History of the War Department.
L. D. INGERSOLL.
Francis B. Mohun, Washington, D. C., 1879.

An Account of the Organization of the Army of the United States.
FAYETTE ROBINSON.
E. H. Butler & Co., Philadelphia, 1848.

History of the 20th United States Infantry, 1861–1902.
A. P. BURNHAM.
Published by Regimental Print.

History of the Army Service Schools, Fort Leavenworth, Kansas.
HENRY SHINDLER.
Staff College Press, Fort Leavenworth, Kas., 1908.

Building of the Pacific Railway.
EDWIN L. SABIN.
J. B. Lippincott & Co., Philadelphia, London, 1919.

The Winning of the West, Vols. I, II, III, IV.
THEODORE ROOSEVELT.
G. P. Putnam's Sons, New York, 1900.

The Centennial of the U. S. Military Academy, 1802–1902, Vols. I, II.
Government Printing Office, Washington, D. C., 1902.

The Private Soldier Under Washington.
CHARLES KNOWLES BOLTON.
Charles Scribner's Sons, New York, 1902.

Personal Recollections of the American Revolution.
MRS. LYDIA MINTURN POST.
Rudd & Carleton, New York, 1859.

Recollections of a Virginian in the Mexican, Indian, and Civil Wars.
DEBNEY HERNDON MAURY.
Charles Scribner's Sons, New York, 1894.

Military History Society of Massachusetts.
Printed by the Society.
J. R. Osgood & Co., Boston, 1881.

PERSONAL RECORDS AND CORRESPONDENCE

Military Reminiscences of the Civil War.
JACOB DOLSON COX.
Charles Scribner's Sons, New York, 1900.

Report of Major Philip Reade, I. G. U. S. V. in re War with Spain.
(Author has only copies known to be extant.)
Government Printing Office, Washington, D. C., 1899.

MEMOIRS

Recollections and Private Memoirs of Washington.
G. W. PARKE CUSTIS.
W. H. Moore, Washington, D. C., 1859.

Memoirs of a Volunteer in the War with Mexico.
JOHN R. KENLY.
J. B. Lippincott & Co., Philadelphia, 1873.

Personal Memoirs of P. H. Sheridan, Vols. I, II.
Charles L. Webster & Co., New York, 1888.

Memoirs of Robert E. Lee.
ARMISTEAD LINDSAY LONG.
J. M. Stoddart & Co., New York, Philadelphia, 1887.

Military Memoirs of Ulysses S. Grant, Vols. I, II, III.
ADAM BADEAU.
D. Appleton & Co., New York, 1868–1881.

Military Memoirs of a Confederate.
EDWARD PORTER ALEXANDER.
Charles Scribner's Sons, New York, 1907.

Personal Reminiscences of the War of 1861–1865.
WILLIAM HENRY MORGAN.
J. P. Bell Co., Lynchburg, Ga., 1911.

Memoirs of the American Revolution, Vol I.
MOULTRIE.
Publisher unknown.

Memories of Two Wars.   Cuban and Philippine Experiences.
FREDERICK FUNSTON, Brigadier General U. S. Army.
Charles Scribner's Sons, New York, 1914.

Memoirs of General W. T. Sherman.
By Himself.
D. Appleton & Co., New York, 1875.

REPORTS

American Archives, Fourth and Fifth Series, 9 Vols.
Government Printing Office, Washington, D. C., 1837.

Report on the Organization and Campaigns of the Army of the Potomac.
GEORGE BRINTON MCCLELLAN.
Sheldon & Co., New York, 1864.

Reports American Historical Association, 1901–1914.
Government Printing Office, Washington, D. C.

Report of Joint Committee on the Conduct of the War, 38th Congress.
Government Printing Office, Washington, D. C., 1865.

*Report of the Commission appointed by President to investigate conduct of
War Department in the War with Spain.*
Government Printing Office, Washington, D. C., 1900.

Adjutant Generals' Reports, 1880–1923.
Government Printing Office, Washington, D. C.,

Reports Secretary of War, 1866–1923.
Government Printing Office, Washington, D. C.

Reports of Chief of Staff, 1919–1920–1922.
Government Printing Office, Washington, D. C.

Miscellaneous Reports, 1776–1923.

*Special Report of the Secretary of War to the President on Conference on
Training for Citizenship and National Defense.*
Government Printing Office, Washington, D. C., 1923.

Report of General J. J. Pershing, Cabled to Secretary of War, Nov. 20,
1918.
War Department, Government Printing Office, Washington, D. C.,
Jan. 16, 1919.

Official Records of the Union and Confederate Navies in the War of Rebellion.
U. S. Navy Dept., Government Printing Office, Washington, D. C.

Report of the Engineer and Artillery Operations of the Army of the Potomac.
JOHN GROSS BARNARD.
D. Van Nostrand, New York, 1863.

Ordnance Reports, 1812–1922, Many volumes.
Government Printing Office, Washington, D. C.

Reports:

General Sumner, July 6, 1898.
General Hawkins.
General Shafter.
General Lawton.
General Bates.
General Kent.
Lieutenant J. H. Parker.
Company Commanders, 71st New York.
Sixteenth Infantry.
Sixth Infantry.
      On Battle San Juan, Cuba, 1898.

Reports of Explorations in the Territory of Alaska, War Department.
Government Printing Office, Washington, D. C., 1899.

War Department Reports, Many volumes.
Government Printing Office, Washington, D. C.

Record of the Organizations Engaged in the Campaign, Siege and Defense of Vicksburg.
U. S. Commission.
Government Printing Office, Washington, D. C., 1901.

STATISTICAL REPORTS AND RECORDS

Historical Register and Dictionary of the United States Army, Vols. **I, II.**
FRANCIS B. HEITMAN.
Government Printing Office, Washington, D. C., 1903.

Biographical Register of Officers and Graduates of United States Military Academy, at West Point, N. Y., Vols. I, II.
Bvt. Major General GEO. W. CULLUM.
D. Van Nostrand, New York, 1868–1879,

JOURNALS

A French Volunteer of the War of Independence.
DOUGLAS.
Paris, 1898.

Personal Recollections of the Revolution, a Private Journal.
SIDNEY BARCLAY.
Rudd & Racleton, New York, 1849.

Journal of Captain Pauseh, Burgoyne Campaign.
Translated by WILLIAM L. STONE.
Joel Munsell's Sons, Albany, 1886.

Journal of a Private: A Twelve Months Volunteer, 1846–1847.
GEORGE C. BURBER.
J. A. & U. P. James, Cincinnati, 1850.

Journal of William Feltman, 1781–1782.
Old Print.
U. S. M. A. Library, West Point, N. Y.

DOCUMENTS

Wayne's Orderly Book.
Original Manuscript.
Library, U. S. M. A., West Point, N. Y.

Mexican War Documents.
Wendell & Van Benthuysen, Washington, 1848.

Military Laws of the United States, 1776–1863.
Government Printing Office, Washington, D. C.

General Orders A.G.O., 1826–1842.
Published by Authority Secretary of War.

Extracts from General Orders, 1820.
Publisher unknown.

*Compilation of Official Documents, Organization of the Army of the United
States, 1789–1876.*
Government Printing Office, Washington, D. C.

Revolutionary Orders of General Washington.
WHITING.
Old Print.

General Orders of General Washington, 1782–1783.
  Old Print.

General Orders, The Volunteer Force.
  Government Printing Office, Washington, D. C.

Army Regulations, 1807.
  Printed by Government.

General Washington's Newburgh Orders, 1782.
  Old Manuscript.
  U. S. M. A. Library, West Point, N. Y.

Washington's Valley Forge Orders, 1778.
  Old Manuscript.

The Uniform of the Army of the United States.
  Compiled by direction of the Secretary of War, 1774–1889.
  Government Printing Office, Washington, D. C.

POLITICAL WORKS

Principles and Acts of the Revolution in America.
  HEZEKIAH NILES.
  A. S. Barnes & Co., New York, Chicago, New Orleans, 1876.

Rise and Fall of the Confederate Government.
  JEFFERSON DAVIS.
  D. Appleton & Co., New York, 1881.

The Relations of the United States and Spain.
  FRENCH ENSOR CHADWICK.
  Charles Scribner's Sons, New York, 1911.

Military Unpreparedness of the United States.
  FREDERIC LOUIS HINDEKOPER.
  The Macmillan Co., New York, 1915.

America's Duty as shown by our Military History.
  LEONARD WOOD.
  Reilly & Lee Co., Chicago, 1921.

The Outbreak of Rebellion.
  JOHN GEORGE NICOLAY.
  Charles Scribner's Sons, New York, 1881.

The End of an Era.
JOHN SERGEANT WISE.
Houghton Mifflin & Co., Boston, 1899.

The Frontier in American History.
FREDERICK JACKSON TURNER.
Henry Holt & Co., New York, 1920.

Panama, the Canal, The Country and the People.
ARTHUR BULLARD.
The Macmillan Co., New York, 1914.

Our Military History. Its Facts and Fallacies.
Major General LEONARD WOOD.
Reilly & Britton Co., Chicago, 1916.

TECHNICAL WORKS

Regulations for the Order and Discipline of the Troops of the United States, Von Steuben's Regulations.
Original Edition.
Published by Act of Congress, Philadelphia, March 29, 1779.

Administration of the American Revolutionary Army.
LOUIS CLINTON HATCH.
Longmans, Green Co., New York, London, 1904.

Elements of Military Art and Science.
HENRY WAGER HALLECK.
D. Appleton & Co., New York, London, 1863.

The Principles of Strategy as Illustrated by the Civil War.
WILLIAM KEITH NAYLOR.
Army Service Schools Press, Fort Leavenworth, Kas., 1917.

Army and Navy of America.
JACOB K. NEFF.
John S. Gable, Philadelphia, 1845.

The Colored Regulars, United States Army.
THEOPHILUS G. STEWARD.
A. M. E. Book Concern, Philadelphia, 1904.

General and Special Orders, U. S. Army, 1817–1923.

The Science of War.
GEORGE FRANCIS ROBERT HENDERSON.
Longmans, Green & Co., London. New York. 1905.

The Principles of Strategy.
JOHN BIGELOW.
G. P. Putnam's Sons, New York; T. Fisher Unwin, London, 1891.

The Gulf and Inland Waters.
ALFRED THAYER MAHAN.
Charles Scribner's Sons, New York, 1898.

Telegraphing in Battle.
JOHN EMMETT O'BRIEN.
The Raeder Press, Scranton, Pa., Wilkes-Barre, Pa., 1910.

Three Rivers, the James, the Potomac and the Hudson.
JOSEPH PEARSON FARLEY.
The Neale Publishing Co., New York, Washington, 1910.

Other Military Laws in separate Volumes since 1865.
Government Printing Office, Washington, D. C.

Instructions for Field Artillery, 1861.
Board of Officers.
J. B. Lippincott & Co., Philadelphia, 1861.

Infantry Tactics, 1861.
WINFIELD SCOTT.
Harper & Bros., New York, 1861.

Infantry Tactics, or Rules for the Exercises and Maneuvers of the United States Infantry, 1861, Vols. I, II, III.
Major General SCOTT.
Harper & Bros., New York, 1861.

Regulations and Instructions for the Field Service of the United States Cavalry in Time of War, 1861.
GEORGE B. McCLELLAN.
J. B. Lippincott & Co., Philadelphia, 1861.

United States Infantry Tactics, 1861.
"Graduate of the United States Military Academy and Retired Officers of the late Mexican War."
J. W. Fortune, New York, 1861.

Hardee's Infantry Tactics, Vols. I, II.
Major W. J. HARDEE, 1856.

Manual of Arms for Light Infantry, 1861.
> Colonel E. E. ELLSWORTH.
> P. T. Sherlock, 112 Dearborn St., Chicago, 1861.

Evolutions of Field Batteries of Artillery, 1860.
> Major ROBERT ANDERSON.
> D. Van Nostrand, New York, 1860.

Military Laws and Rules and Regulations for the Armies of the United States, 1813.
> Adjutant and Inspector General's Office, Washington, May 1, 1813.
>> Original Edition.
> Publisher unknown.

Drill Regulations for Light Artillery, 1896.
> Government Printing Office, Washington, D. C.

Cavalry Tactics, 1822.
> PIERCE DARROW.
> Oliver D. Cooke, Hartford, 1822.

Artillery Tactics, 1826.
> Original Edition.
> Published in Boston.

Treatise on the Military Art, 1798.
> E. HOYT.
> Benjamin Smead, Brattleboro, Vt.;   Russell & Ripley, Greenfield, Mass., 1798.

The Artillerist, 1821.
> Oliver D. Cooke, Hartford, Conn.; 1821.

A System of Exercises and Instruction of Field Artillery for Light or Horse Artillery, 1829.
> Department of War, Act of Congress of 2nd of March, 1829.
> Hilliard, Gray, Little & Wilkins, Boston.

Instruction for Field Artillery, 1839.
> Captain ROBERT ANDERSON.
> R. P. Desilver, Philadelphia, 1839.

Abridged Tactics, Book for the Militia, 1826.
> New York, 1826.

Abstract of a System of Exercise and Instruction of Field Artillery, 1834.
> JOHN L. WILSON, Captain U. S. Army.
>> A. E. Miller, Charleston, S. C.; 1834.

A System of Exercise and Instruction of Field Artillery, 1833.
Department of War.
Hilliard, Gray & Co., Boston, 1833.

Infantry Drill, for the Infantry of the United States, 1829.
F. Lucas, Jr., Baltimore, Md.

Military Tactics, 1838.
General RANSOM.
Concord, Mass., 1838.

Cavalry Tactics, 1841.
J. & G. S. Gideon, Printers, Washington, 1841.

Scott's Infantry Tactics, 1861, Vols. I, II.
Harper & Bros., New York, 1861.

A Hand Book for Infantry.
WILLIAM DUANE, 1814.
Printed in Philadelphia.

A Complete Treatise upon Artillery, 1819.
H. LALLEMAND.
G. S. Van Winkle, New York, 1829.

Instructions to be Observed for the Formations and Movements of the Cavalry.
WILLIAM RICHARDSON DAVIS, Esquire.
Abraham Lodge, Halifax, 1799.

The Administration of the American Revolutionary Army.
LOUIS CLINTON HATCH, Ph.D.
Longmans, Green & Co., New York, London & Bombay, 1904.

Instructions for Heavy Artillery.
Board of Officers.
Gideon & Co., Printers, Washington, 1851.

Instructions for Mountain Artillery.
Board of Officers.
Gideon & Co., Printers, Washington, 1851.

Infantry Tactics.
WINFIELD SCOTT.
Published in Boston, 1847.

Regulations for the Militia.
COOPER.
Published by Frank Desilver, 1837.

Cavalry Exercise Containing Instructions for the American Cavalry, 1801.
   E. A. JENKS.
   Printed, Portland, 1801.

Maneuvers of Horse Artillery.
   General KOSCIUSKO.
   Published by direction of the U. S. Military Philosophical Society,
   1808.

*Infantry Tactics for the Instruction of the Soldier, a Company Line of
   Skirmishers, Battalion, Brigade or Corps d'Armées.*
   Brigadier General SILAS CASEY, U. S. Army.
   D. Van Nostrand, New York, 1862.

Smith's Artillery, 1812.
   AMASA SMITH.
   Published by Isaiah Thomas, Jr., Boston, 1812.

Cavalry, Light Infantry and Rifle Tactics, 1834.
   Published Authority of War Department.   Original Edition.
   Publisher unknown.

Tactics and Regulations for the Militia, 1836.   Original Edition.
   Publisher Unknown.

The United States Army.
   FRANCIS V. GREENE.
   Scribner's Magazine, Sept., Oct., Nov., 1901.

Rifle and Infantry Tactics, 1863, Vols. I, II.
   Lieutenant General W. J. HARDEE, C. S. A.
   S. H. Goetzel, Mobile, 1863.

A New System of Infantry Tactics, 1869.
   Major-General EMORY UPTON.
   D. Appleton & Co., New York, 1869.

School of the Guides.
   Colonel EUGENE LE GAL.
   D. Van Nostrand, New York, 1862.

Instruction for Heavy Artillery, 1863.
   Board of Officers.
   Government Printing Office, Washington, D. C., 1863.

Infantry Tactics, Double and Single Rank, 1875.
   EMORY UPTON.
   D. Appleton & Co., New York, 1874.

Drill Regulations for Field Artillery United States Army, 1915.
War Department, Chief of Staff.
Government Printing Office, Washington, D. C.

United States Army Cavalry Tactics, 1880.
D. Appleton & Co., New York, 1886.

Drill Regulations for Cavalry, United States Army, 1863.
Original Volume.
Publisher unknown.

The Company Drill of Infantry of the Line, 1862.
J. MONROE.
D. Van Nostrand, New York, 1862.

Cavalry Tactics, 1883.
P. ST. GEORGE COOKE.
D. Van Nostrand, New York, 1883.

Infantry Drill Regulations United States Army, 1904.
Government Printing Office, Washington, D. C., 1904.

Infantry Drill Regulations United States Army, 1891.
Government Printing Office, Washington, D. C., 1891.

Artillery Drill Regulations United States Army, 1891.
Government Printing Office, Washington, D. C., 1891.

Instructions in Rifle and Carbine Firing for the United States Army, 1886.
STANHOPE E. BLUNT.
Charles Scribner's Sons, New York, 1886.

Field Artillery Tactics, 1863.
D. Van Nostrand, New York, 1863.

Field Artillery Tactics, 1864.
D. Van Nostrand, New York, 1864.

Drill Regulations for Light Artillery, United States Army, 1896.
Government Printing Office, Washington, D. C.

The Trooper's Manual, 1862.
J. LUCIUS DAVIS.
A. Morris, Richmond, Va., 1862.

Cavalry Drill Regulations, United States Army, 1891.
Government Printing Office, Washington, D. C., 1891.

Infantry Drill Regulations, 1911.
Government Printing Office, Washington. D. C., 1911.

The Army of the United States, 1789–1896.
    Edited by Brevet Brigadier-General THEO. F. RODENBOUGH and
        Major WILLIAM L. HASKIN.
    Private Print, 1896.

Drill Regulations for Cavalry, 1902.
    Government Printing Office, Washington, D. C.

Heavy Artillery, 1861.
    War Department.
    Government Printing Office, Washington, D. C.

Military Laws and Rules and Regulations for the Armies of the United States.
    Adjutant and Inspector General's Office, Washington, D. C., May 1,
        1813.

Artillery Tactics, 1826.
    Original Edition.
    Publisher unknown.

Abridged Tactics—School of the Soldier, 1833.
    Publisher unknown.

Instruction for Field Artillery, Horse and Foot, 1845.
    Original Edition.
    Publisher unknown.

Infantry Drill, 1828.
    Original Edition.
    Publisher unknown.

United States Infantry Drill Regulations, 1829.
    Original Edition.
    Publisher unknown.

Tactics and Regulations for the Militia, 1836.
    Original Edition, Boston, 1836.

Cavalry Tactics, 1841.
    Original Edition.
    Publisher unknown.

*System of Infantry Discipline for the United States Army, Plates with
    Explanation,* 1814.
    Publisher unknown.

Evolution of Field Batteries of Artillery, 1860.
    Major ROBERT ANDERSON.
    D. Van Nostrand, New York, 1860.

U. S. Infantry Drill Regulations, 1829.
   Original Edition.
   Publisher unknown.   Published by authority.

Infantry Drill, 1828.
   Original Edition.
   Publisher unknown.   Published by authority of Secretary of War.

Cooper's-Macomb's Tactics, 1855.
   Cooper, Macomb.
   Publisher unknown.   Published by authority.

Instructions for Heavy Artillery, 1845.
   Board of Officers.   Old Print.

The Recruit, 1845.
   Captain JOHN T. CAIRNS.
   Old Print.

Cavalry Exercises Containing Instructions for the American Cavalry.
   Printed for A. E. Jenks.   Sold at his bookstore, Portland, 1801.

Instructions for Mountain Artillery.
   Board of Officers.
   Government Printing Office, Washington, D. C., 1851.

Armies of To-day.
   By various authors.
   Harper & Bros., New York, 1893.

The American Military Library or Compendium of Modern Tactics.
   WILLIAM DUANE.
   Published by the Author, 1809.

The New International Encyclopedia.
   Dodd, Mead & Co., New York, 1914–1916.

Sanitation in Panama.
   WILLIAM CRAWFORD GORGAS.
   D. Appleton & Co., New York, London, 1918.

Percussion Locks, Bayonets with Clasps; To the Manual of Arms.
   Major-General WINFIELD SCOTT.
   Old Print, 1844.

Government of the Canal Zone.
   MAJOR GENERAL GEORGE W. GOETHALS.
   Princeton University Press, Princeton, N. J., 1915.

The American Rifle.
>TOWNSEND WHELEN.
>The Century Co., New York, 1918.

Our Rifles, Vols. I, II, III.
>CHARLES WINTHROP SAWYER.
>C. W. Sawyer, Boston, 1910.

A Complete Treatise Upon Artillery.
>H. LALLEMAND.
>Translated by DE RUSSY.
>C. S. Van Winkle, New York, 1819.

Military Policy of the United States.
>Bvt. Major General EMORY UPTON, U. S. Army.
>Government Printing Office, Washington, D. C, 1903.

STATE PAPERS

American State Papers, 1831–1861.
>Published by authority of Congress.
>Gales & Seaton, Washington.

Statistical Record of the Armies of the U. S.
>FREDERICK PHISTERER.
>Charles Scribner's Sons, New York, 1883.

The New International Year Book, 1916.
>Dodd, Mead & Co., New York, 1917.

NARRATIVES

Men and Things I saw in Civil War Days.
>JAMES FOWLER RUSTLING.
>Eaton & Maine, New York; Curts & Jennings, Cincinnati, 1899.

The Volunteer Soldier of America.
>JOHN ALEXANDER LOGAN.
>R. S. Peale & Co., Chicago, New York, 1887.

Narrative of Major-General Wool's Campaign in Mexico.
>FRANCIS BAYLIES.
>Little & Co., Albany, 1851.

Spirit of Old West Point, 1858–1862.
>MORRIS SCHAFF.
>Houghton Mifflin & Co., New York, 1907.

West Point.
ROBERT C. RICHARDSON.
G. P. Putnam's Sons, New York, 1917.

Army Life on the Pacific.
LAWRENCE KIP.
Redfield, New York, 1859.

Soldier and Pioneer.
E. L. ANDERSON.
G. P. Putnam's Sons, New York, 1879.

The Story of a Trooper.
F. COLBURN ADAMS.
Dick & Fitzgerald, New York, 1865.

Thrilling Days of Army Life.
GEORGE A. FORSYTH.
Harper & Bros., New York, 1900.

Three Months in the Southern States.
Sir A. J. L. FREMANTLE.
S. H. Goetzel, Mobile, 1864.

From Chattanooga to Petersburg.
WILLIAM FARRAR SMITH.
Houghton Mifflin & Co., New York, 1893.

In Cuba with Shafter.
JOHN D. MILEY.
Charles Scribner's Sons, New York, 1899.

The Romance of Conquest.
WILLIAM ELLIOT GRIFFIS.
W. A. Wilde & Co., Boston, Chicago, 1899.

Forty Years in the Army.
W. B. HAZEN.

Scenes and Adventures in the Army.
P. ST. GEORGE COOKE, 1859.

Army Sacrifices.
J. B. FRY, 1879.

From Everglade to Canyon with the Second Dragoons.
T. F. RODENBOUGH, 1875.

A Narrative of the Campaign in the Valley of the Shenandoah.
ROBERT PATTERSON.
J. Campbell, Philadelphia, 1865.

Camp Fires of the Confederacy.
BENJAMIN LA BREE.
Courier-Journal Job Printing Co., Louisville, Ky., 1898.

The Flying Gray-haired Yank.
MICHAEL EGAN.
Hubbard Brothers, Philadelphia, 1888.

The Lost Dispatch.
Personal Narratives.
Galesburg Printing & Publishing Co., Galesburg, Ill., 1889.

Reminiscences of the Santiago Campaign.
JOHN BIGELOW, Jr.
Harper & Bros., New York, London. 1899.

Bullet and Shell.
GEORGE FORRESTER WILLIAMS.
Fords, Howard & Hulbert, New York, 1883.

Reminiscences of a Mosby Guerrilla.
JOHN W. MUNSON.
Moffat, Yard & Co., New York, 1906.

A Private Chapter of the War.
GEORGE W. BAILEY.
G. I. Jones & Co., St. Louis, 1880.

Johnny Reb and Billy Yank.
ALEXANDER HUNTER.
The Neale Publishing Co., New York, Washington, 1905.

From Chattanooga to Petersburg under Generals Grant and Butler.
WILLIAM FARRAR SMITH.
Houghton Mifflin & Co., Boston, New York, 1893.

Reminiscences of a Private.
FRANK M. MIXSON.
The State Company, Columbia, S. C., 1910.

War Songs and Poems of the Southern Confederacy.
HENRY MARVIN WHARTON.
The John C. Winston Co., Philadelphia, Chicago, 1904.

Recollections of a Private.
WARREN LEE GOSS.
T. Y. Crowell & Co., New York, 1890.

The Iron Brigade; A Story of the Army of the Potomac.
CHARLES KING.
G. W. Dillingham Co., New York, 1902.

Hood's Texas Brigade.
JOSEPH BENJAMIN POLLEY.
The Neale Publishing Co., New York, Washington, 1910.

From Yorktown to Santiago with the Sixth U. S. Cavalry.
WILLIAM HARDING CARTER.
The Friedenwald Co., Baltimore, 1900.

The General's Double.
CHARLES KING.
J. B. Lippincott Co.. Philadelphia, 1898.

The Long Arm of Lee.
JENNINGS CROPPER WISE.
J. P. Bell Co., Lynchburg, Va., 1915.

Pennsylvania at Chickamauga and Chattanooga.
Pennsylvania Commission
W. A. Ray, State Printer, Harrisburg, Pa.

Three Years in the Sixth Corps.
GEORGE T. STEVENS.
S. R. Gray, Albany, N. Y., 1866.

The Story of a Cannoneer under Stonewall Jackson.
EDWARD A. MOORE.
J. P. Bell Co., Lynchburg, Va., 1910.

Serving the Republic.
NELSON A. MILES.
Harper & Bros., New York, 1911.

Series of Tales and Sketches.
By an American Soldier.
James Munroe & Co., Boston, 1845.

INDIANS AND INDIAN WARS

History of Philip Kearny.
H. Watts de Peyster

Handbook of American Indians North of Mexico, Vols. I, II.
  FREDERICK WEBB HODGE.
  Government Printing Office, Washington, D. C., 1907.

Memoirs and Travels among the Northern and Southern Indians.
  THOMAS L. M'KENNEY.
  Paine & Burgess, New York, 1846.

My Friend the Indian.
  JAMES McLAUGHLIN.
  Houghton Mifflin & Co., New York, 1910.

Thirty-three Years among Our Wild Indians.
  RICHARD IRVING DODGE.
  A. D. Worthington, Hartford, Conn., 1885.

The Story of the Indian.
  GEORGE BIRD GRINNELL.
  D. Appleton & Co., New York, 1923.

Indian Wars of the West.
  TIMOTHY FLINT.
  E. H. Flint, Cincinnati, 1833.

Indian Wars of the United States.
  WILLIAM V. MOORE.
  Jas. B. Smith & Co., Philadelphia, 1858.

Massacres of the Mountains.
  J. P. DUNN.
  Harper & Bros., New York, 1886.

On the Border with Crook.
  JOHN G. BOURKE.
  Charles Scribner's Sons, New York, 1891.

An Apache Campaign.
  JOHN G. BOURKE.
  Charles Scribner's Sons, New York, 1886.

Narratives of Indian Warfare in the West.
  SAMUEL L. METCALF.
  William G. Hunt, Lexington, Ky., 1821.

The Fighting Cheyennes.
  GEORGE BIRD GRINNELL.
  Charles Scribner's Sons, New York, 1915.

Indian Bibliography.
  Field.

The Plains of the Great West.
R. I. DODGE.

Nez Percé Joseph.
O. O. HOWARD.
Lothrop, Lee & Shepard Co., Boston, 1881.

The Indian Wars of the United States.
E. S. ELLIS.

Absaraka, Land of Massacre.
H. B. CARRINGTON.

Discovery of the Yosemite and the Indian War of 1851.
H. C. BUNNELL.
Chicago, Ill., 1880.

My Life on the Plains.
G. A. CUSTER, 1874.

Campaigns with Crook and Stories of Army Life.
Captain CHARLES KING.
Harper & Bros., New York, 1905.

Thirty Years of Army Life on the Border.
General R. B. MARCY.
Harper & Bros., New York, 1866.

Indian Fights and Fighters, 1876–1900.
CYRUS TOWNSEND BRADY, LL.D.
Doubleday, Page & Co., New York, 1916.

The Life of Sitting Bull and the History of the Indian War, 1890–1891.
W. FLETCHER JOHNSON.
Edgewood Publishing Company, Philadelphia, 1891.

Our Wild Indians.
R. I. DODGE.
A. D. Worthington & Co., Hartford, Conn., 1882; A. G. Nettleton, Chicago, 1882.

PERIODICALS

Volumes of the Military Service Institution from 1880–1917.
Published at Governor's Island, New York Harbor.

All Volumes of Army and Navy Journal, 1865–1923.
Published at Park Row, 20 Vesey St., and 354 4th Ave., New York City.

Additional Bibliography

A Guide to the Military History of the World War, 1914-1918.
    Thomas G. Frothingham.
    Little, Brown and Company, Boston, 1921.
A History of the Great War.
    John Buchan.
    Houghton Mifflin Company, Boston, 1922.
The World Crisis.
    Rt. Hon. Winston S. Churchill.
    Charles Scribner's Sons, New York, 1923-29.
Grandeur and Misery of Victory.
    Georges Clemenceau.
    Harcourt, Brace and Company, NewYork, 1930.
A History of the Great War, 1914-1918.
    C. R. M. F. Cruttwell.
    The Clarendon Press, Oxford, 1936.
The War in Outline, 1914-1918.
    Liddell Hart, Basil Henry.
    Random House, New York, 1936.
*History of the World War: An Authentic Narrative of the World's
    Greatest War.*
    Francis A. March, Ph.D., Richard J. Beamish.
    The United Publishers of the United States and Canada, Philadelphia
    and Chicago, 1919.
The Making of a State: Memories and Observations, 1914-1918.
    Dr. Thomas Garrigue Masaryk.
    G. Allen and Unwin Ltd., London, 1927.
Perish by the Sword.
    Major R. Ernest Dupuy.
    Military Service Publishing Company, Harrisburg, 1939.
Edmund Burke: Speech at His Arrival at Bristol.
    J. Wilkie, London, 1774.
BEF—The Whole Story of the Bonus Army.
    As told to William C. White by Walter W. Waters.
    John Day, New York, 1933.
Soldiers Unmasked.
    Lt. Col. William A. Ganoe.
    Military Service Publishing Company, Harrisburg, 1939.
Reports of Secretary of War to President, 1922-1941.
Reports of Chief of Staff and Assistant Secretaries, 1919-1940.
Order of Battle of the United States Land Forces in the World War,
    American Expeditionary Forces—Divisions, 1931.
Order of Battle of the United States Land Forces in the World War,
    American Expeditionary Forces—G.H.Q. Armies, Army Corps,
    Services of Supply and Separate Forces, 1936.

Acts of Congress, War Department Orders, Memoranda, Bulletins, 1919-1942.

The American Year Book, 1925-40.

Correspondence and data in Historical Section, Army War College. Old Files and Old Records Sections, Adjutant General's Office, Washington, D. C.

Original sources of World War, Historical Section, Army War College, Washington, D. C.

INDEX

Accouterments. *See* Equipment.
Adair, Lieutenant, 459
Adams, Charles, Brig. Gen., 351
Adams, Emory S., Maj. Gen., 534
Adams, John, President, 2, 28, 53, 85, 94, 531
Adams, John Quincy, President, 531
Adirondack Mountains, 447
Adjuntas, Porto Rico, 388
Adjusted Compensation, 495
Adjutant, position of, 33, 104, 118, 121, 146, 181, 200, 259, 261, 307 f.
Adjutant general, the, 72, 104, 148, 167, 196, 261, 308, 372, 374, 413, 420, 433, 534
Adjutant general's department, 153, 479, 495
Advance guards, tactical, 84
Aërial camera, 494
Aëro squadrons, 457
Aëroplanes, 433, 435, 437, 445, 447 ff., 452, 473 f., 488 f., 491 f., 500, 503, 506, 508, 511 ff., 527
Africa, 517, 521
Agents. *See* Civil, Indian, Military.
Agua Caliente, Mexico, 455
Agua Nueva, Mexico, 215, 218
Agua Zarca, Mexico, 455
Aguinaldo, Amilio, 389, 391, 401, 403 ff., 407, 414, 424
Ai, Palestine, 134
Aibonita, Porto Rico, 388 f.
Aide de camp, 52, 54, 67, 86, 137
Ainsworth, F. C., Maj. Gen., 534
Air corps, 489, 491, 494, 505, 508, 513 f., 522, 525, 541; chiefs of, 541
Air Corps Reserve, 510
Air defense areas, 524
Air force. *See* Air corps and service; GHQ, 508, 514, 524
Air forces, 528
Air mail flown, by air corps, 505
Air mechanics, 522
Air patrols, 492
Air pilots, 474, 513, 522. *See also* Aviators.
Air program, 491, 498
Air raids, 517

Air service, 445, 448, 451, 479, 482, 488; chiefs of, 541
Air squadron, 457, 488
Air-borne troops, 528
Aircraft, 433, 435, 437, 445, 447 ff., 452, 473 f., 488 f., 491 f., 500, 503, 506, 508, 511 ff.; 518, 527
Aircraft procurement, 508 f.
Aircraft warning, 524
Airdromes, 491
Airfields, 491
Airplanes. *See* Aëroplanes.
Aisne River, France, 472
Alabama, 178, 205, 248
Alabama claims, 302
Alamillo Cañon, Mexico, 456
Alaska, 317, 331, 347, 349, 369, 371, 427, 431, 515, 525
Albania, 521
Albright, F. H., Brig. Gen., 548
Aleshire, J. B., Maj. Gen., 534
Alexander, Robert, Maj. Gen., 550
Alexandria, La., 519
Alexandria, Va., 268
Alger, Russell Alexander, 532
Aliaga, P. I., 403
Allegheny arsenal, 190
Allegheny River, 65
Allen, Ethan, 38
Allen, Henry T., Maj. Gen., 470, 476, 545
Allen, Hubert A., Brig. Gen., 548
Allen, James, Brig. Gen., 539
Allen, Robert H., Maj. Gen., 540
Allen's revolver, 240
Alliance, French, 62
Allies, 468 f., 474, 476, 504, 521, 526, 528
Allison, J. B., Maj. Gen., 539
Allotments, pay, 260, 399
Allowances, rental, 555. *See also* Pay.
Allowances, subsistence, 555. *See also* Subsistence.
Ambulances, shortage of, 472
Ambulance companies, 452, 454
Amelia Island, Fla., 162
American Army (separate), 469-71